Shaping the Sierra

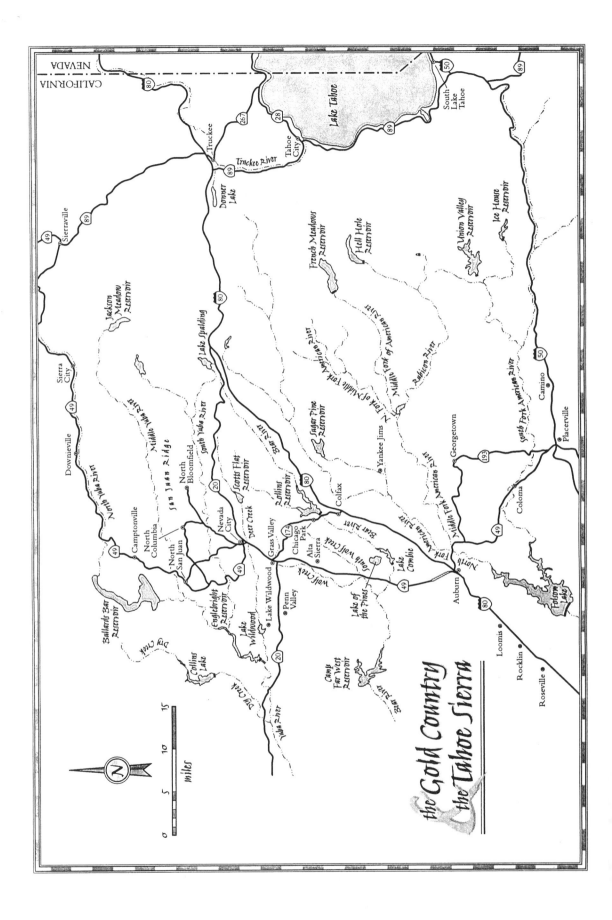

the Gold Country & the Tahoe Sierra

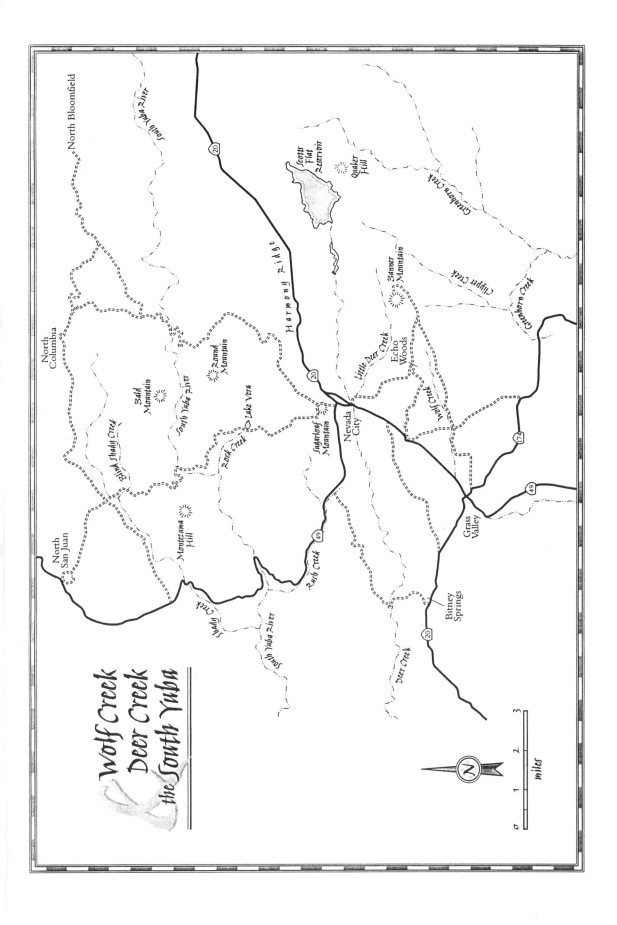

Wolf Creek
Deer Creek
& the South Yuba

The publisher gratefully acknowledges the generous contribution
to this book provided by The General Endowment Fund of the
Associates of the University of California Press.

Shaping the Sierra

Nature, Culture, and Conflict in the Changing West

Timothy P. Duane

UNIVERSITY OF CALIFORNIA PRESS
Berkeley   Los Angeles   London

Maps by Janice C. Fong
Figures by Laura Simonds Southworth
Photos ©1998 by Timothy P. Duane

University of California Press
Berkeley and Los Angeles, California

University of California Press, Ltd.
London, England

First paperback printing 2000

Library of Congress Cataloging-in-Publication Data

Duane, Timothy P., 1960–.
  Shaping the Sierra : nature, culture, and conflict in the changing west / Timothy P. Duane.
      p. cm.
  Includes bibliographic references and index
  ISBN 0-520-22676-3 (pbk. : alk. paper)
    1. Environmental policy—Sierra Nevada (Calif. and Nev.).   2. Environmental
policy—West (U.S.).   3. Sierra Nevada (Calif. and Nev.)—Environmental conditions.
4. Sierra Nevada (Calif. and Nev.)—Population.   5. West (U.S.)—Population.   6. Sustainable development—Sierra Nevada (Calif. and Nev.)   I. Title.
   GE185.S54D83   1999
   363.7′009794′4—dc 21   98-4212

Printed in the United States of America

08   07   06   05   04   03   02   01   00

    9   8   7   6   5   4   3   2   1

The paper used in this publication meets the
minimum requirements of ANSI/NISO Z39.48-1992 (R 1997)
(*Permanence of Paper*). ♾

For Teresa,
who has let me borrow her family's past
in the Sierra Nevada

and Cody,
who will inherit our family's future
in the Range of Light

CONTENTS

FIGURES, MAPS, AND TABLES

FIGURES

MAPS

TABLES

PREFACE

> To leave a place is to begin its story, and in stories, places endure.
>
> Christine S. Cozzers, 1996

The U.S. Census Bureau declared America's frontier closed in 1890 (Turner [1906] 1962), but it has taken more than a century for that reality to take hold in the arid and mountainous West. California's booming population growth has now brought the plastic palm trees and the In-N-Out Burger joints of Los Angeles to the Sierra Nevada and the rest of rural California.[1] The fax-modem and FedEx have diminished both time and space across the great expanse of otherwise uninhabitable lands west of the hundredth meridian, generating a dramatic set of changes in the social, cultural, economic, demographic, technological, and institutional context of the Sierra Nevada and the rest of the rural West (Riebsame and Robb 1997). The economic lifeline that now ties the region to its metropolitan centers and the rest of the nation is the combination of cellular phone and satellite uplink, allowing retirees and information workers to place their stock market orders via the Internet without ever leaving their homes.

Some of us can therefore now have our cake and eat it, too—as long as we have the skills and financial capital necessary to compete as footloose entrepreneurs in the emerging economy that is making yet another "New West."[2] Not surprisingly, blue-collar woods workers facing job loss and higher housing prices are not amused by all of this (B. Brown 1995). Plastic palm trees are no substitute for old-growth conifer forests if either your livelihood or your amenity preferences depend on Nature in its raw form. Plastic palms also make bad wildlife habitat. As a result we see intense clashes between differing sets of interests and of values today in the rural West. The Sierra Nevada is no exception, for here the transformation that accompanies rapid population growth has been occurring both longer and more intensely than in the rest of the rural West.

Human desires for both livelihood and amenities also conflict because public

land and resource management policies have generally failed to recognize and respect their interdependence. This is, at least in part, a result of the structure of our existing institutional arrangements for land and resource management. We find ourselves in conflict today along two dimensions in the Sierra Nevada and across the rural West: first, over the relationship between individual places as communities and the broader social, economic, and ecological systems that influence those places; and, second, over the specific interests and values within those increasingly heterogeneous places. These conflicts are heightened further by two related factors: the increased scarcity of resources and competition for those resources that now accompany the true closing of the frontier; and the increasing likelihood of any one party's actions affecting others (the result of increased average population densities associated with increased population). The context for resolving land and resource management conflicts has therefore changed radically over the past three decades.

All of this is occurring at a time of rapid and perhaps unprecedented changes at a national and global level that may parallel the Agricultural and Industrial Revolutions in its significance (Castells 1996; 1997). The latter gave rise to many of our existing land and resource management institutions, but those institutions are ill-equipped to reconcile emerging social conflicts and to mediate the relationship between Nature and Culture that the Information Revolution portends. If we are to develop a viable framework for land and resource management in the post-frontier world, we must explore the effects of these sweeping changes with an open mind about the permanence of those institutions. Institutions are not immutable. We can choose our own destiny as long as we are willing to embrace uncertainty for the sake of adaptability.

In this book I explore the possibilities for change and constructive adaptation to these enormous pressures. I do so through a study of the Sierra Nevada and some of the individuals, organizations, and social institutions struggling with these issues in the real world. More specifically, I have tried to answer five related questions about rapid growth in the Sierra Nevada:

1. What forces are driving population growth in the Sierra Nevada?
2. What are the likely consequences of that population growth?
3. What alternative patterns could mitigate the negative consequences of growth?
4. What factors are preventing those alternatives from being adopted or implemented?
5. What institutional innovations could overcome those impediments to change?

In short, I have sought to explain the phenomena that have buffeted the Sierra Nevada over the past three decades and to offer suggestions for mitigating their

negative effects through conscious policy and action. I have also sought to derive lessons from the Sierra Nevada that could be helpful to other small towns and rural areas experiencing similar changes. Many of those lessons should be broadly applicable beyond the Sierra Nevada, for the situation across the rural West today looks very much like it did in the Sierra Nevada just two to three decades ago. The extensive experience of Sierra Nevadan communities is unfortunately dominated by failures of both policy and vision, but it also offers some promising successes.

THE STRUCTURE OF THE BOOK

The book begins with an introduction to the Sierra Nevada and its capacity to inspire passion in so many people. My own narrative is central to this point, for I am writing as a participant in as well as an observer of the changes transforming the Sierra Nevada. My personal experience is bound to color my interpretation, but it is also my most important scholarly resource because of its depth and breadth. On this point Lewis Mumford's observations in his 1938 classic, *The Culture of Cities,* are also relevant to rural areas: "The most important original sources for the student of cities are not written or printed documents: they are the cities themselves, and the chief use of a literature, perhaps, is to provide clues and answers for the problems raised by a field study of the urban environment. There is no way of abbreviating this first-hand exploration of the environment and the first-hand experience that comes from living and working in cities: indeed it is partly for lack of it that so many sociological analyses of the city have been so far from satisfactory" (498).

There are many literatures with relevance to the problems confronted in this book, so I introduce key ideas from the literature on political economy of growth machines, land use planning, ecosystem management, sociology, political science, and law. This literature review includes a discussion of factors driving rapid population growth and the social, economic, and ecological consequences of that growth. By necessity this discussion of individual literatures is brief, for the focus of my effort here is on synthesis. The primary contribution of this book is an integrated analysis of the transformation of the Sierra Nevada as a result of rapid population growth and far-reaching social, economic, technological, and institutional change. It is part environmental history, part regional geography, and part applied policy analysis.

This book includes both original theory and original empirical research, however, so I have not limited myself to secondary sources. I introduce an expanded notion of economics, for example, that explicitly accounts for the amenity values of the environment in today's social context. This is a central theme that I will emphasize throughout the book: economic and ecological well-being are not nec-

essarily in conflict in the Sierra Nevada, even if they often appear in conflict under narrower traditional conceptions of economic rationality. The evidence for this will be documented below. I also provide an analysis of the economic structure of the rapidly growing communities of the Sierra Nevada that gives substance to the theory of amenity-based residential location choice. This analysis helps to frame the political conflicts over growth in the region.

The politics of property directly constrain institutional innovations for managing growth, however, so I discuss this tension—in both legal and political terms—before documenting the political history of land use planning in western Nevada County, California. This case study illustrates how the dynamics of conflict over exchange values and use values have altered the political terms of the debate in an increasingly diverse Sierra Nevada. The new social context is filled with conflict, but it also presents opportunities for reconciling the traditional interests of rural communities with the emerging social values that now dominate American society. Rural communities are increasingly being brought into the orbit of the metropolitan mainstream through both market expansion and cultural integration through migration. These expanding connections could undermine important social, economic, and ecological aspects of rural communities but also may hold the seeds for institutional and cultural innovation in those communities. The possibilities for sustainable development in the Sierra Nevada are therefore strong—although I make it clear that some fundamental changes will be necessary first.

I conclude the book by suggesting specific policy measures to develop viable land and resource management strategies and to ensure their successful implementation. These policy recommendations emphasize the relationship between local, state, and federal government agencies and the effect of private land development on biodiversity. A more sweeping set of institutional changes in public land and resource management is probably necessary to protect biodiversity, but I defer those recommendations to another book to be published by the University of California Press in the future. The latter book focuses on the relationship between values, ethics, and institutions in addressing social and ecological values in public land and resource management in the West (Duane, forthcoming). *Shaping the Sierra,* in contrast, focuses on how we should manage population growth and human settlement on private lands.

THE IMPORTANCE OF STORIES

It is not enough to discuss only the academic literature or to examine empirical data to determine the social, demographic, economic, and ecological trends of the region. Such a dry analysis would not begin to convey the influence of population growth on the people and places that constitute the exurban landscape. For this reason, I have chosen to tell a story about this place in order to make sense of the literature, the secondary data, and the real-world changes and conflicts experienced by real people in a real place. I rely on three very different but complementary approaches to tell that story: 1) a review of the relevant literature and discussions of the theoretical context of social, economic, and ecological phenomena; 2) empirical data analysis to evaluate the relationship between the case study and the literature and/or theory; and 3) a qualitative narrative that explores dimensions of the problem that are otherwise inaccessible through secondary data. Furthermore, the story I weave throughout this book offers an opportunity to interpret the meaning of these phenomena and their implications in a new way.

My narrative does not pretend to be either objective or neutral; it is my story, and this book is my attempt to make sense of a world that is changing rapidly and that has profound implications for both me and the place I call *home*. My values are intricately bound up with the narrative. As William Cronon has noted, "If our goal is to tell tales that make the past meaningful, then we cannot escape struggling over the values that define what meaning is" (1992, 1370). He adds that "to try to escape the value judgments that accompany storytelling is to miss the point of history itself, for the stories we tell, like the questions we ask, are all finally about value" (ibid., 1376). In many ways, then, this book is an environmental history of one subregion of the Sierra Nevada from the mid-1960s through the mid-1990s—as seen through my eyes and the values produced by the selective filters I carry. Only time will tell if it becomes the story of the rest of the Sierra Nevada or the story of other communities and regions throughout the West. If the lessons of this story are in fact learned, those other communities may be able to avoid the degree of social conflict and environmental degradation that has accompanied the recent wave of Sierra Nevada settlement.

This is not the only story possible, but the story I now believe to be true.

UNDERLYING THEORIES AND THEMES

Even when the theory is not explicit, every story is built on theory. This story is no exception. My choice of events, sequence, and emphasis all reflect an underlying view of the world and the relationships that drive social, economic, and ecological phenomena in the rapidly changing rural West. While I have used an inductive approach to weave my narrative, I also draw on specific literature to construct the framework within which I tell the story. Though the book itself is the ultimate statement of my underlying theory, let me briefly describe several particularly important strands of the literature. They constitute a useful set of filters that have helped me interpret the setting and events of the Sierra Nevada over the past three decades.

The first theme is of coevolution and the relationship between Culture and Nature. The two are inseparable, for the landscapes of the modern world have all been touched by human hands. The perceptive capacities of humans and the effects of those human hands on those landscapes are in turn influenced by the landscapes, for Culture is heavily influenced by context. This is a central theme in cultural geography and environmental history, but it is also a theme in the history of planning. I have chosen to focus on this relationship between Culture and Nature.

My dictionary defines *culture* as "the concepts, habits, skills, art, instruments, institutions, etc. of a given people in a given period." This is a gross simplification, of course, but I use the term here to mean those dimensions of all these things listed above (including "etc.") that relate "a given people in a given period" to a given place. My capitalized Culture is therefore that aspect of culture that reflects people's relationship to Nature. The term *nature* is an extremely complex, contested, and changing concept, of course, and its meaning fills an entire page of my dictionary. One definition—"the sum total of all things in time and space; the entire physical universe"—is clearly too broad, but others—such as "natural scenery, including the plants and animals that are part of it"—are too narrow. Neil Evernden's 1984 account, *The Social Creation of Nature*, highlights how the term has developed over time and under the influence of changes in culture, and he distinguishes *nature* (the actual physical form and processes that operate in the world or the universe) from *Nature* (our social conceptions of that form and those processes). I use the latter term in reference to my use of the term *Culture:* it is how the nonhuman natural world functions for a given people in a given period in a given place. Nature is not purely a social construct, however, for it manifests itself in physical ways that affect Culture.

Arid environments generate specific social responses through innovation and organization that may give rise to irrigation-dependent agriculture, for example, which may in turn generate what Donald Worster has called "hydraulic societies" (1985b). Those social structures may, as Worster has argued, be built on inequities of knowledge and power that unfairly concentrate wealth and well-being in the hands of a few at the expense of the many. Alternatively, rich soils and abundant rainfall may combine with moderate temperatures to create dense stands of forests, voluminous flows of water, and nutrient-rich ecological systems to support what Richard White has called an "organic machine" in the Pacific Northwest (1996). White documents how the relationship between salmon spawning patterns and the energy loss associated with their upstream migration influenced patterns of Native American resource use along the Columbia River. Moreover, modern industrial society has organized itself there in very specific ways in order primarily to extract hydroelectric power, irrigation water, and timber harvests from the ecological systems of the region. Richard Norgaard has made the point of coevolution more generally in his work on ecological economics (1994), as have many anthropologists (Durham 1979), geographers (Parsons 1985), and environmental historians (Cronon 1991; Merchant 1992; White 1991; Worster 1985b). I continue in this tradition. I therefore emphasize how changes in the ecological landscape have altered social and economic relationships to that landscape and how changes in those social and economic relationships have profound consequences for the ecological conditions of the landscape.

The second tradition I draw on is that of the adolescent field of environmental planning. Born in the late 1960s as an attempt to integrate natural and social science disciplines in land use planning, environmental planning (sometimes called ecological planning) is explicitly concerned with how ecological factors are incorporated into decision-making. More specifically, the field has strong roots in physical planning and landscape architecture and has traditionally focused primarily on the spatial dimension of human activity (Steiner et al. 1988). I have a joint appointment on the faculty at the University of California at Berkeley in the Department of Landscape Architecture and Environmental Planning and the Department of City and Regional Planning. Along with the Department of Architecture, both of my academic departments are part of the College of Environmental Design.[3] All three departments trace their roots to a common concern for physical planning and the spatial dimensions and implications of human activity in the landscape.

Frederick Steiner, Gerald Young, and Ervin Zube state that

> ecological planning, like most fields, owes a large debt to a small handful of visionary thinkers. Three giants who span the late nineteenth and early twentieth centuries deserve special mention: George Perkins Marsh [who published the influential book *Man and Nature; or, Physical Geography as Modified by Human Action* in 1864], John Wesley Powell [whose *Report on the Lands of the Arid Region of the United States* in 1879 helped lay the groundwork for both the U.S. Geological Survey and the U.S. Bureau of Reclamation], and Patrick Geddes [a botanist and land planner whose emphasis on regional planning based on ecological conditions laid the foundation for the Regional Planning Association of America (RPAA) and the pioneering and influential work of Benton MacKaye and Lewis Mumford]. (Ibid., 31–32)

The RPAA—and, in particular, the ideas of MacKaye and Mumford within the RPAA—played an especially important role in advocating an approach to planning based in part on social institutions that would recognize the "ecological region" as the primary planning unit. As Mark Luccarelli describes their approach in his 1995 book *Lewis Mumford and the Ecological Region: The Politics of Planning,* regionalism is about much more than jurisdictional boundaries: "Regionalism concerns the imaginative recovery of place. This implied both a sense of place informed by the scientific and imaginative exploration of the environment and an idea of culture as linked to the geographic associations of place."[4]

Other important influences on environmental planning include Jens Jenson, Henry Cowles, Warren Manning, Ebenezer Howard, and Ian McHarg. McHarg's influence has been the most pervasive as a result of his 1969 book *Design with Nature,* but recent scholarship in the field has embraced a wide range of natural-science influences. The environmental planning profession brings together engineers, geologists, hydrologists, soil scientists, botanists, wildlife biologists, biogeographers, landscape ecologists, anthropologists, and planners (Ortolano 1997). Computerized decision-support systems have also become more important in recent decades, and a great deal of professional practice now depends heavily on the use of Geographic Information Systems to assemble, analyze, and integrate scientific information.[5]

Social and economic influences have had relatively less influence on environmental planning scholarship and practice than the natural sciences, however, for the profession still views its role primarily as that of scientific expert and information integrator who brings the knowledge of natural science to decision-making (Canter 1996). Humans are recognized as important to that final step, but the field still clings to a notion of science as objective fact that fails to incorporate important perspectives from critical theory (Fainter 1996). Moreover, the behavior of humans and their resulting settlement patterns and economic activity are largely treated as exogenous variables in standard environmental planning practice. I explicitly reject this perspective, however, and seek here to extend the domain of environmental planning by drawing on the theory, methods, and findings of social science. In this vein I follow in the footsteps of Mumford. Luccarelli argues that Mumford's focus was on "the alienation of culture from nature." This remains the central concern of environmental planning today, although it is usually couched in technical rather than cultural terms. "Mumford's imaginative resolution," says Luccarelli, "rests on the reconciliation of the natural region with the social world. For his sense of the organic was not a call for nature as wilderness but a plea 'for joining the elements of Nature and Culture.'"[6]

My approach to "joining the elements of Nature and Culture" relies heavily on the tools of economic and institutional analysis to evaluate their coevolving relationship. In this sense, I also focus on the social world of the changing region. Specifically, I emphasize an ecological economics perspective that goes beyond the narrower neoclassical formulation of environmental economics. My economic perspective, and the point that our interpretation of economic relationships is in turn embedded within complex social, cultural, and institutional contexts, is at the heart of my argument. The story I tell here is one of changing social and economic relations that have altered the relationship between Nature and Culture in the Sierra Nevada. Those changes are occurring at multiple spatial and temporal scales, but they are most pronounced in rural communities experiencing rapid population growth. Our institutional arrangements for interpreting those changes and for adopting policies to respond to them are, however, ill-equipped to address the new context. More specifically, these institutions are actually designed in such a way that they are bound to misinterpret key information about the evolving relationship and are highly likely to adopt and implement policies that will undermine environmental quality in a way that will degrade social, economic, and ecological conditions.

In this regard I am echoing claims made by Thomas Michael Power in his 1996 book *Lost Landscapes and Failed Economies: The Search for a Value of Place.* I am doing so in a very specific context, however, one that highlights the relationship between rapid population growth, the factors driving that population growth, and the political economy of population growth in rural communities. My story is primarily about the impacts of growth on the quality of life in these regions, while Power focused on the effects of commodity extraction activities on local economic well-being. I am therefore attempting to confront directly some of what Ed Marston has called "the warts on the West's service economy" (1996c). I agree with Power that population growth and economic development in the rural West are now driven primarily by amenity rather than commodity values, but I also agree with Marston that the ongoing transformation of the region has imposed significant social and environmental costs.[7] I offer specific policy responses to mitigate those impacts while recognizing the opportunities associated with this transformation.

What is driving population growth in the rural West? Here I draw on a rich literature on the phenomenon, produced by researchers who have been studying it at a variety of scales over the past quarter century, to place the experience of the Sierra Nevada in its broader context. Most of these sources have relied on secondary data aggregated at the county level, however, which does not allow one to discern the influences on and of rapid population growth at the bioregion, watershed, or community level. Moreover, the literature has very few detailed longitudinal case studies that show how specific communities respond to growth pressures over a long period of time, and how growth—and social responses to growth—affects social, economic, and ecological conditions.[8] This book offers such a study, showing that there is enormous variation over both space and time in such communities.

I am particularly interested in how Nature and Culture have coevolved (and are still coevolving) in the face of these pressures, so I have used an inductive approach in this book. My methods and the structure of the book are designed to gain a rich, "thick" description of a specific case in order to generate hypotheses and test the relevance of the literature. This approach has been widely used in history, anthropology, and some branches of sociology to generate contextualized knowledge. It contrasts with the deductive approach, which tests a falsifiable hypothesis through quantitative analysis alone and is more common in economics, demography, and much of sociology (King et al. 1994). The true test of its validity will be whether it resonates with those who are actually experiencing these changes. Scholarly critiques are also important, of course, but this book will be worthless if it does not have meaning for the nonacademics trying to make sense of the changing West and to manage its land and resources sustainably.

ACKNOWLEDGMENTS

This book would not have been possible without the help and support of many friends and colleagues. Howard Boyer, Rowan Rowntree, Michael Barbour, Anna Steding, Katie Laddish, Fran Violich, and an anonymous reviewer provided extremely helpful comments on an earlier draft. Howard Boyer has been an excellent editor and advocate within UC Press, while Janice Fong and Laura Southworth produced fabulous maps and illustrations under a tight deadline. Bonita Hurd tackled the copyediting with a fine eye for detail that has improved the book considerably. Erika Büky, Mimi Kusch, Jan Johnson, Reed Malcolm, and Sarah Dry shepherded the book through the production process. I look forward to working with all of them on my second book with UC Press.

Don Erman has been supportive both through the Sierra Nevada Ecosystem Project (SNEP) and as Director of the Centers for Water and Wildland Resources at the University of California at Davis. Greg Greenwood has been an inspiration and a critical observer of theses issues, while fellow SNEP Science Team members Rowan Rowntree, Bill Stewart, Jonathan Kusel, Larry Ruth, Dennis Machida, Doug Leisz, Frank Davis, and Connie Millar provided important feedback during my SNEP work from 1993 to 1996. Jeff Romm, Louise Fortmann, and Ted Bradshaw also provided helpful reviews of my SNEP reports. I received excellent research assistance on this book and the SNEP work from Phil Griffiths, Dan Barry, Chris Thomas, Jennifer Knauer, Ian Moore, Will Caldicott, Karl Goldstein, and Anna Steding. Chico Muller, Bob Thompson, Wicaksono Sarosa, Jumbi Edulbehrum, Cecilia Collados, and Michael Fainter all helped direct me to literature that has influenced this work. All of my students have challenged me both in the classroom and one-on-one. Larry Zulch, Richard Zulch, and Walt Hays helped me print the massive manuscript by lending me their printers and toner cartridges at Dantz Development.

Dozens of people with a love of the Sierra Nevada also helped along the way, including Laurel Ames, Debbie Austin, Eric Beckwitt, Steve Beckwitt, David Beesley, Brian Bisnett, Lucy Blake, Linda Blum, Louis Blumberg, Nina Boehlin, Sharon Boivin, Bruce Boyd, Len Brackett, Bill Bramlette, Patti Brissenden, John Buckley, John Casey, Bill Center, Dale Creighton, Rebecca Coffman, Lyn Daniels, Sam Dardick, Jim Doolittle, Richard Drace, Elizabeth Eddins, David Edelson, Glenda Edwards, Daniel Emmett, Bob Erickson, Priscila Franco, Barbara Getz, Bette Goodrich, the late Harley Greiman, Tracy Grubbs, Don Harkin, Bob Hawkins, Frannie Hoover, Jim Hurley, Bob Johnson, Mark Johnson, Ailleen Jorgensen, Paul Jorgensen, Tom Knudson, Tony Lashbrook, Andrea Lawrence, Rick Luskin, the late Dean Malley, Elizabeth Martin, Sally Miller, Rochelle Nason, Erin Noel, Kathy Noland, Tom Noland, Pat Norman, Laurie Oberholtzer, Phil Pister, Misha Renclair, Pierre Rivas, Mary Scoonover, Gary Snyder, Jan Stevens, Deane Swickard, Peter Van Zant, the late Frank Wells, Doug Wheeler, Jim Wilson, and Kimery Wiltshire. My apologies to the many more I have failed to mention.

Although I am no longer in contact with many of them, several of my former teachers have had a profound effect on me and this book. I would like to thank Bill Anderson, Richard Soule, Gary Musick, and Nancy Wasley at Nevada Union High School, and Gil Masters, Bruce MacGregor, Leonard Ortolano, Lyna Wiggins, Jim Sweeney, and the late Bill Rivers at Stanford University. They all encouraged me, challenged me, and nurtured my writing and research skills at critical times in my life. I hope that I can have a similar influence on my students.

I received financial support for this work from the Beatrix Farrand Fund of the Department of Landscape Architecture and Environmental Planning, the Committee on Research of the Faculty Senate, and the Townsend Center for the Humanities (all at the University of California at Berkeley). Additional funding for related research was provided by the White Mountain Research Station of the University of California; the U.S. Forest Service, through the Sierra Nevada Ecosystem Project and the Inyo National Forest; the California Region of the Nature Conservancy; and Environment Now. Of course, none of them are responsible for any errors, and they have not endorsed any part of the book itself.

Bill and Christney McGlashan generously provided a room with a view of Donner Lake in Truckee for reading, writing, and editing in the summer of 1996 and for periodic visits since. Their support has been invaluable ever since my son, Cody, was born in September 1995. They are both wonderful grandparents and great in-laws, and this book would not have been possible without the support they have given to our entire family. My parents, Ken and Judy Duane, also nurtured my love of the mountains and my relationship with Nature. My brother, Dan, and my sister, Terrie, were fellow explorers in my formative years who shared many of my most important experiences. They have all been influential.

My greatest thanks go to my son, Cody, and to my wife, Teresa. Teresa's support has been more important than anything else. This book simply would not have been finished without her.

ABBREVIATIONS

ACEC   Area of Critical Environmental Concern

BCDC   San Francisco Bay Conservation and Development Commission

BCSD   Business Council on Sustainable Development

BLM   Bureau of Land Management, U.S. Department of the Interior

BMA   biodiversity management area

CABPRO   California Association of Business, Property and Resource Owners

CASPO   California Spotted Owl Technical Committee Report

CCD   County Census Division

CCSCE   Center for the Continuing Study of the California Economy

CDF   California Department of Forestry and Fire Protection

CEQA   California Environmental Quality Act of 1970

CFA   California Forestry Association

CPR   common-pool resource

CRMP   Coordinated Resource Management Plan

DOF   Department of Finance, State of California

DWR   Department of Water Resources, State of California

EDAW   Eckbo, Dean, Austin, and Williams

EDD   Employment Development Department, State of California

EIA   Environmental Impact Assessment

EIR   Environmental Impact Report

EIS   Environmental Impact Statement

EPA	U.S. Environmental Protection Agency
ESA	Endangered Species Act
GAO	General Accounting Office, U.S. Congress
GAP	Gap Analysis Program, U.S. Fish and Wildlife Service
GIS	Geographic Information System
HCP	Habitat Conservation Plan under the ESA
IPES	Individual parcel evaluation system, Tahoe Regional Planning Agency
LAPI	Locally Adjusted Personal Income
LCDC	Land Conservation and Development Commission, State of Oregon
LCP	Local Coastal Plan under the California Coastal Act
LDC	less developed country
NBS	National Biological Survey or Service, U.S. Department of the Interior
NCCP	Natural Communities Conservation Planning
NCCRG	Nevada County Citizens for Responsible Growth
NEPA	National Environmental Policy Act of 1969
NID	Nevada Irrigation District
OPR	Office of Planning and Research, State of California
PEARL	Protect Environment, Agriculture, and Rural Landscape, Livingston County
PG&E	Pacific Gas and Electric Company
RPAA	Regional Planning Association of America
RQC	Rural Quality Coalition of Nevada County
SACOG	Sacramento Area Council of Governments
SBC	Sierra Business Council
SNA	Sierra Nevada Alliance
SNEP	Sierra Nevada Ecosystem Project
TDC	Transferable Development Credit
TDR	Transferable Development Right
TOT	transient occupancy tax
TPZ	Timber Production Zone
TRPA	Tahoe Regional Planning Agency
UC	University of California
UGB	Urban Growth Boundary
USFS	United States Forest Service, U.S. Department of Agriculture
WHR	Wildlife-Habitat Relationships model
YWI	Yuba Watershed Institute

/\\/\\/\\

CHAPTER ONE

The Range of Light

> The superficial inducement, the exotic, the picturesque has an effect only on the foreigner. To portray a city, a native must have other, deeper motives — motives of one who travels into the past instead of into the distance. A native's book about his city will always be related to memoirs; the writer has not spent his childhood there in vain.
>
> Walter Benjamin, 1990

Little Deer Creek slips off the northwest slope of 3,899-foot Banner Mountain, gathering a trickle of light snow and rain on its journey to the sea. Dipping down through a transition zone forest, its waters are cooled in the shade of ponderosa pine, Douglas fir, incense cedar, black oak, madrone, manzanita, and ceanothus. Spring brings the glorious bloom of the dogwood, only to see the white petals beaten to the ground with a late April rain. Deep in the shadows where the sun rarely shines, the snow lingers longer to water an occasional big-leafed maple. A brilliant explosion of color comes with the fall. Black oaks turn orange and yellow against the mixed greens of the conifers, while the bark of the madrone and manzanita glow a deep reddish brown against the red clay of the earth. The maple leaves stand out with the burnt red of a New England autumn, conjuring up visions of Henry David Thoreau and Walden Pond deep in the Sierra woods. The white-leaf manzanita leaves hold their gray-green reflectance through the winter as the leaves of *Quercus kellogii* (black oak) turn brown and drop to the ground.

Dropping down toward Nevada City, at around 2,900 feet the small but perennial creek is crossed by a flume for an irrigation ditch. A small diversion in Little Deer Creek occasionally picks up a high flow and sends it into the Cascade Ditch, but the ditch is overgrown with blackberries and filled with oak leaves. The creek drops down another fifty feet and crosses a dirt four-wheel-drive road called Banner Mountain Trail, where a swarm of butterflies gathers every spring to drink the waters. The road will be dry and dusty by August, sending a milky batch of soil into the clear waters of the creek with every Jeep that crosses. There is very little development in this part of the watershed, though, so it doesn't appear to be a major problem at this point. This road is mainly used by mountain bikers and joggers living in the town below or in one of the many houses tucked away in the woods above. For now, the region is still largely open space.[1]

Soon the creek is crossed by another irrigation ditch, although this one is much larger. Like the Cascade Ditch, the D-S Canal flows with water diverted by the Nevada Irrigation District from Deer Creek. The irrigation district was organized as a special agency of the state in 1921 to bring water to farmers in the foothills, but much of its new demand comes from residential and commercial development. It is governed by an elected board of directors, with voting power proportional to both population and the land area within the district's boundaries (Miller 1996). Many of its waterworks in the high Sierra were originally developed to support the local mining industry and to generate hydroelectric power. The plumbing system near the source is among the most complex ever designed or built. Water is diverted from one watershed to another and then back to the first via a maze of dams, canals, ditches, and hydroelectric generators. The water that flows through the D-S Canal and the Cascade Ditch may have originated in the upper watersheds of the Middle Yuba River, South Yuba River, or Bear River. Some of it then leaks out of the wooden flumes and flows back via Little Deer Creek into Deer Creek, which runs through the gold rush town of Nevada City. Along the way Little Deer Creek will pass through Pioneer Park, where I played Little League games and families gather on the Fourth of July to celebrate the birth of the nation. Watermelons chill in the cool creek beneath the shade of pines and oaks. Little Deer Creek makes its final run past left field and the tennis courts in a concrete-lined channel, however, devoid of shade or cover for fish along its artificial banks.

From Nevada City, Deer Creek flows downstream past the sewage treatment plant to the dam at Lake Wildwood, which blocks salmon and steelhead migrations. The reservoir was constructed in 1970 as the centerpiece of a thirty-six-hundred-home gated subdivision (*Grass Valley–Nevada City Union* 1970e). The lake gathers pesticide and effluent runoff from the golf course and septic tanks, then spills downstream into Deer Creek before it joins the main stem of the Yuba River just below Englebright Reservoir.[2] Here the river nourishes one of the most important native anadromous fisheries in Northern California before snaking through the flood levees and hydraulic mining debris of the valley to merge with the Feather River at Marysville and Yuba City. The Feather in turn joins the Sacramento in the valley for the long, circuitous journey through the Sacramento–San Joaquin Delta. Each drop of Banner Mountain runoff then ends up either going south in the massive aqueducts of the California State Water Project or the Central Valley Project, or back to the Pacific Ocean via the Golden Gate. In either case, the water of Little Deer Creek touches the lives of nearly every resident of the burgeoning state of California.[3]

I grew up near the headwaters of Little Deer Creek in a place called Echo Woods, and I have hiked or biked for hours across the rolling contours of its watershed. Technically, my home was on the other side of the watershed divide, near the headwaters of Wolf Creek. One reached our home on Echo Drive with a short trip on Cascade Way, however, whose path paralleled its namesake watercourse. The Cascade Ditch offered an uninterrupted journey of wilderness adventure for six miles upstream from the junction of Gracie Road to Red Dog Road. The waters of the Wolf Creek drainage gathered in the town of Grass Valley before joining another branch of Wolf Creek draining the Chicago Park area to the southeast. Together, they traveled onward to the Bear River and Camp Far West reservoir before joining the Feather River near Rio Oso. Like a small Continental Divide, our home straddling the ridge leading to Banner Mountain linked us to both Nevada City to the north and Grass Valley to the south. As if to recognize the significance of our spot on the watershed boundary, we had a Nevada City address and a Grass Valley phone number. Together these two towns constituted one community bound by a shared history of mining (Bean 1867; Thompson and West 1880; Mann 1982).

I imprinted on this landscape. Like a newborn discovering the subtle lines of his mother's smile, I learned the contours and colors of the middle-elevation forests of the Banner Mountain divide and came to call them home after moving here as an eleven-year-old. I can't get the place out of my system; it keeps calling me back, and it will probably always be home to me. I hiked continuously for the first month of my first summer back home after going away for college, covering about two hundred miles in and around the Little Deer Creek watershed with my trusty dog, Dusty. It was as if a life force had been drained from me after nine months in the Bay Area; I needed to reacquaint myself with my home range to recharge. Only then did I have the energy and the peace of mind to work full-time to pay for college. I found a job doing construction and installation of solar energy systems, allowing me to breathe the air and smell the breeze every day in the hot summer sun of the foothills. I sometimes worked down among the oaks and grasses of the rolling foothills of Penn Valley, where my grandparents were living when we first discovered Nevada City. It was near here that I once explored the falls of Squirrel Creek one summer day with a friend in high school. We were both in Dick Soule's biology class, so we took the time to watch for wildlife and identify the live oaks, blue oaks, and black oaks growing among the rocks. I still remember our startling discovery of a single newt in the hot sun, seeking cover beside a small pool of water in the nearly desiccated pools of Squirrel Creek. Only a trickle of water tumbled down over the face of the precipice. The drought of 1976–77 had just begun. I doubt the newt survived the difficult conditions of the next two summers, but it stood there for me in 1976 as a poignant reminder of how precious and fragile our place on the planet is.

Years later, I came upon another newt in the waters of Rush Creek above the South Yuba River. Rotating his legs around their strangely jointed sockets, he moved out cautiously into the fast-flowing water. It was the peak of the spring runoff along a steep gradient down into the canyon. The water was a powerful force against his small and fragile body. His sticky toes clung to the rocky bed of the small stream as he worked his way like a rock climber up a slippery face. One leg moved while the other three held him in place, then another reached out to move him farther upstream. Inch by inch he worked his way out into the current and toward a small rock island midstream. I watched for fifteen or twenty minutes as he advanced a mere three feet. Suddenly, a stronger wave of water swept him from his foothold, to a calmer place eighteen or twenty inches downstream. He regathered his equilibrium, turned upstream again, and began the slow process of rotating his arms and legs forward in movement. And so it has been with my own insufficient understanding of this place and the many complex forces affecting its prospects.

What was it about this place? Was it the people, the landscape, or the pattern of daily living that I desired? Perhaps most important, what was the relationship among these three elements? Certain aspects of metropolitan life continued to appeal to me, but I still found myself longing for more intimate and daily contact with the natural world.

Now I am back again, still struggling with the questions that first inspired me to study environmental planning: What is our relationship to the natural environment? How can we accommodate the forces of population growth and the legitimate need for economic development and affordable housing without destroying the natural environment? What does that growth and our relationship to the natural environment mean for our relationships to each other and our communities? Fundamentally, can we construct a sustainable way of living in the Sierra Nevada and throughout the rural, small-town, and exurban West that will maintain the well-being of both human communities and the natural environment? If we can, what will be the relationship between the Sierra Nevada and the many people who depend on it or care about it but don't live here? These are perennial questions that apply to almost any community or place. They are especially apt questions for rural communities in the rapidly changing, resource-dependent western United States. Unless we can answer them in the places we know best, however, I don't know how we can pretend to know the answers to these questions for any other community or place. As Wendell Berry has stated so well, our global problems are really just an aggregated set of local problems (1989).

I am in search of a place called Harmony Ridge. It appears on my local map as the ridge extending due east from Sugar Loaf Mountain, which is just north of town. Highway 20 climbs east up the dry, chaparral-covered southern flank of Harmony

Ridge above Deer Creek, offering fine views of Banner Mountain and the Little Deer Creek drainage to the south. Parting the waters at the top of the ridge, the northern slopes descend to the South Yuba River clothed in the denser vegetation found in the upper reaches of Little Deer Creek. This physical place is not the real Harmony Ridge, however, despite its claim to that name on the U.S. Geological Survey map. Harmony Ridge is a concept, an idea, a vision, an ideal; it is everywhere in possibility yet nowhere in reality. There has been much talk of "sustainable development" over the past few years, but we have not yet established patterns of sustainability in rural resource-dependent communities in the industrialized countries. Harmony Ridge is my name for that place where sustainable development is both the vision *and* the practice in the Sierra Nevada. I believe we can find the nascent bedrock foundations of Harmony Ridge throughout the Sierra Nevada if we take the time to listen and understand what is driving development in the region. This is my challenge in this book, and I believe it is the challenge of the twenty-first century for all of humanity. Only time will tell if we will ever find or create a true Harmony Ridge. Many utopic visions have failed in the past, and we may be no more successful in our rehabilitation of the Sierra Nevada.

Today I am living on a spur ridge connected to the northern flank of Montezuma Hill, which sits atop the southwestern edge of the San Juan Ridge north of Nevada City. I look westward out my window across the rolling and jagged terrain of the ridge toward the confluence of the South Yuba River and the Middle Yuba River, with the tule fog of the Sacramento Valley beyond. The 2,117-foot Sutter Buttes, the smallest mountain range in the world, poke their ancient and weathered volcanic heads up out of the fog to catch the warm rays of the winter sun. One hundred miles away from me sits a portion of the Coast Ranges of Northern California. It has been cold lately, and the top of this part of the Coast Ranges is marked by a layer of white. We sit about twenty-five hundred feet above sea level here and, as of the first of the year, have not yet had snow. It has tried to snow many times, however, and the trees have been blanketed in the silent colors of winter just about five miles east of here and five hundred feet above us in elevation. Winter will soon come down the mountain and cover our porch with her blanket.

Although I have moved north of Harmony Ridge and Nevada City into the South Yuba watershed, I am still within my home range. Like the mountain lion, I have a home range and intimate knowledge of a landscape that covers around one hundred square miles. My extended habitat is an order of magnitude larger, however, covering the 978 square miles of Nevada County or a comparable area along Highway 49 in the western Sierra Nevada foothills. Nevada City is about ten miles from here as the robin flies, and we are seventeen miles from town by road. Banner Mountain is clearly visible from Montezuma Hill to the south, maintaining my connection to Echo Woods and Little Deer Creek. I appreciate glimpses of its familiar shape as I hike or bike around the area. Standing guard over the gaslit streets of Nevada City, it is a symbol for me that I am still in my home range. It seems as if there has forever been a forest fire lookout on the top of Banner Mountain, and you can see Mount Diablo from it, more than 150 miles away on a clear day. Banner Mountain now flashes red at night with an ungainly communications tower, and owners of new homes seeking wider views have scarred the mountain's face by removing too many trees. It nevertheless triggers a deep feeling of comfort when I see it in the distance.

Other cues also have their power: the crunch of the deeply lobed leaves of the black oak as I walk across the ground, the smell of ponderosa pine and incense cedar, the soft touch of a Douglas fir branch. Winter brings the smell of wood smoke and the sweat of wood chopping, summer the smells of the Pacific Ocean and the Central Valley rising up the western slope past the house. Fall offers the brilliant palette, spring the green buds of life returning as the snow line melts its way up the slope. The sound of a blue jay or a flock of robins marks summer or fall in my mind. And always the sunsets linger on in an ever-changing dance of light, clouds, night, and sky.

On this spot in the Yuba watershed of the Sierra Nevada mountain range, the complexities of our relationship to the natural environment are overwhelming. Yet as Aldo Leopold has written, "Only the mountain has lived long enough to listen objectively to the howl of a wolf" ([1949] 1970, 137). Only the mountains themselves can be objective about Nature; our interpretations are too heavily influenced by Culture. And as we move from the cities and suburbs into the rural West, both Nature and Culture are changing in response to our new relationship to the landscape. Those changes, we will see, hold profound implications for how we manage the Sierra Nevada.

IN THE SHADOWS OF THE RANGE OF LIGHT

The Sierra Nevada is a remarkable mountain range. Stretching approximately 430 miles from north to south and nearly 70 miles in width at times, it covers almost 28,000 square miles (18 million acres) (Sierra Nevada Ecosystem Project 1994; Palmer 1988). The Sierra Nevada is the largest continuous mountain range in the United States outside Alaska and is larger than the area covered by the Swiss, French, and Italian Alps combined (Whitney 1979). It is larger than ten of the fifty states and nearly as large as two others (for comparison, the state of Maine is about 31,000 square miles). Approximately three-fifths (10.7 million acres) of its land area is federally owned, dominated by portions of nine national forests (Lassen, Plumas, Tahoe, Eldorado, Stanislaus, Sierra, Sequoia, Inyo, and Toiyabe) and three national parks (Yosemite, Sequoia, and Kings Canyon).[4] The national forests total 8.1 million acres, the national parks (including Devil's Postpile

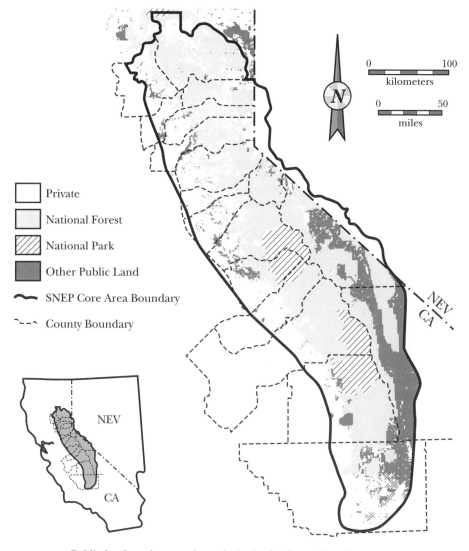

MAP 1.1. Public lands and county boundaries in the Sierra Nevada.

National Monument) total 1.6 million acres.[5] The U.S. Department of the Interior Bureau of Land Management administers another million acres of federal land in the Sierra Nevada. Approximately 3.3 million acres (31 percent) of the federally owned land have been designated as wilderness by Congress since passage of the Wilderness Act of 1964.[6] Today it is the only place in the "lower forty-eight" where you can still draw a straight line on a map and not cross a road for more than 150 miles (Foreman and Wolke 1992).

The Sierra Nevada's natural environment has played an important role in the development of land and resource management policy in the United States. It was the focus of the first major environmental lawsuit in California in 1884, which pitted the state's growing agricultural industry against its historically dominant mining industry (Kelley 1959). The Sierra Nevada was also the setting for the classic battle from 1908 to 1913 between preservationist visionary John Muir and utilitarian forester Gifford Pinchot over the damming of the Hetch Hetchy Valley in Yosemite National Park to provide water and power to the city of San Francisco.[7] Both the national park and national forest systems had early origins in the Sierra Nevada, with the establishment of Yosemite National Park in 1890 and the Sequoia Forest Reserve in 1891 (Beesley 1994a; Hirt 1994, xvii–xviii; Hays 1959; Wilkinson 1992a). (Yosemite had previously been reserved for protection as early as 1864 [Raymond 1948], preceding the establishment of Yellowstone National Park by eight years and the Wilderness Act by a full century.) One of the most important environmental organizations in the world, the Sierra Club, was organized in 1892 "to preserve and protect" the Sierra Nevada from exploitation. The club's first president was John Muir (Fox 1981).

Muir is the single figure most responsible for bringing the wonders of the Sierra Nevada to a wider consciousness. His many articles for *Century* magazine in the late nineteenth century exposed a national audience to the grandeur of Yosemite, the giant sequoias, and the remarkable peaks and canyons of the Sierra back country. His later books advanced an ecocentric philosophy drawing on the transcendentalism of Emerson and Thoreau (ibid.; Greene 1991), while painting a rich and detailed portrait of the Sierra landscape. He was a brilliant writer. Mark Twain, Jack London, Bret Harte, Mary Austin, and John Burroughs also set pen to paper to describe the Sierra, but Muir captured the spirit and grandeur of his home range like no other. His love of the Sierra Nevada began the first day he saw it in 1868:

> Looking eastward from the summit of the Pacheco Pass one shining morning, a landscape was displayed that after all my wanderings still appears as the most beautiful I have ever beheld. At my feet lay the Great Central Valley of California, level and flowery, like a lake of pure sunshine, forty or fifty miles wide, five hundred miles long, one rich furred garden of yellow *Compositae*. And from the eastern boundary of this vast golden flower-bed rose the mighty Sierra, miles in height, and so gloriously colored and so radiant, it seemed not clothed with light, but wholly composed of it, like the wall of some celestial city. Along the top and extending a good way down, was a rich pearl-gray belt of snow; below it a belt of blue and dark purple, marking the extension of the forests; and stretching along the base of the range a broad belt of rose-purple; all these colors, from the blue sky to the yellow valley smoothly blending as they do in a rainbow, making a wall of light ineffably fine. Then it seemed to me that the Sierra should be called, not the Nevada or Snowy Range, but the Range of Light. And after ten years of wandering and wondering in the heart of it, rejoicing in its glorious floods of light, the white beams of the morning streaming through the passes, the noonday radiance on the crystal rocks, the flush of the alpenglow, and the irised spray of countless waterfalls, it still seems above all others the Range of Light, the most divinely beautiful of all the mountain-chains I have seen.[8]

The Sierra is a land of superlatives. Within its vast area, it has more than five hundred peaks over 12,000 feet in elevation. Among them is the highest peak in the contiguous United States, Mount Whitney (14, 498 feet), and at least a dozen more peaks more than 14,000 feet. Lake Tahoe is the second-largest alpine lake in the world and the largest in North America. If drained, its cobalt blue and aquamarine waters would cover the entire state of California to a depth of fourteen inches—and natural runoff would take roughly seven hundred years to refill the lake. The Sierra also holds what some consider to be the deepest canyon in North America, Kings Canyon, which drops 8,240 feet from its mountain-edged rim to the river below (for comparison, it is only a 5,800-foot drop from Grand Canyon's North Rim at Bright Angel Point down to the Colorado River below) (Palmer 1988).

The Sierra Nevada marks the boundary between the complex Mediterranean flora and fauna of the California ecoregion, the cold, dry, isolated ecoregion of the Great Basin, and the hot, dry southwestern deserts, making it a rich and complex place ecologically (Schoenherr 1992; Sierra Nevada Ecosystem Project 1996). Its sharp eastern escarpment is a zone of steep ecological gradients, while the gentler western slope acts as a smooth escalator for Pacific storms moving east. The vertical climb from the Owens Valley to the highest peaks in the eastern Sierra Nevada exceeds 10,000 feet in less than ten miles. The significant latitudinal variation across the range also creates a gradient of ecological conditions and species. For any given latitude and elevation, local conditions of soils, slope, and aspect combine to create even greater variety. Unlike the more homogenous forested areas of the Pacific Northwest, the Sierra Nevada is a rich mosaic of vegetation and wildlife habitat types. It is heterogeneous and patchy, creating natural variability in assemblages of its ecosystems.

The boundaries of the Sierra Nevada bioregion are therefore difficult to fix precisely. Geologically, it is bound on the north by the waters of Lake Almanor, beneath which the granite batholith of the Sierra meets the active volcanic structure of the Cascade Range, while the southern boundary is marked by Tehachapi Pass and the Transverse Range. The western slope rolls gently across the foothills to meet the flat alluvial plain of the Central Valley; the eastern slope drops precipitously to the Basin and Range country of the Owens Valley, Mono Lake, and the Walker, Carson, and Truckee Rivers. The biogeographic boundary of the Sierra Nevada can be marked by topography, using an elevation or slope steepness as the criterion; it can also be marked by climate, geology, hydrology, vegetation, or wildlife. No single criterion offers a clear, precise, and consistent boundary around the Sierra Nevada. Instead, the combination of these factors characterizes the Range of Light. As a result of its adjacency to so many different types of ecoregions, different parts of the Sierra may hold quite different assemblages of species. This makes it one of the richest mountain ranges in the world in terms of biodiversity (Sierra Nevada Ecosystem Project 1996). There are more native plant species in the Sierra than in the entire United States east of the Mississippi River (Shevock 1996).

The single constant reality of natural processes is change. Any appearance of stability is the result of a temporary equilibrium between opposing forces, with that balance destined to shift in response to natural and anthropocentric disturbances. Ecological systems are in a dynamic equilibrium, and the state of the ecosystem can change dynamically within the framework of a stable system (Holling 1995). While earlier models of ecological succession were probably wrong in their emphasis on the achievement of a stable climax state, they do offer the important insight that the processes of ecological change are conditional. *If* a given condition exists, *then* other conditions may exist. Movement from one state to another may appear *chaotic,* but it is not *random.* The challenge, of course, is that we do not understand those conditionalities very well or the boundaries of dynamic equilibrium for most ecological systems.

The Sierra Nevada is no exception. As the forces of geology push up its eastern face, the forces of hydrology erode away its surface. The topography and ecology of the Sierra Nevada today reflect the cycles of climate and geologic action that have preceded us. It is therefore necessary to understand the range's geologic past to explore its ecological present. As Stephen Whitney puts it, "The Sierra Nevada is essentially an enormous piece of the earth's crust that rose thousands of feet along a series of faults, or fractures, on its eastern side, tilting westward in the process to form an asymmetrical mountain range with a broad, gently sloping western flank and narrow, precipitous eastern escarpment. Ranges formed in this way are known as tilted fault-blocks and include, in addition to the Sierra, the Basin ranges of northern Nevada" (1979, 18). Because of the Sierra's position as the largest and most westerly range of this type, however, it serves as an effective barrier for moisture-laden Pacific storms and casts a rain shadow across the Nevada landscape. The range is therefore a vital determinant of climatic conditions in Nevada as well as California. To the west, it captures the water that serves as the lifeblood of California; to the east, it ensures desert conditions in Nevada and limits access to the moderating influence of maritime conditions. Winters are harsh on the east side and mild on the western slope.

The average annual precipitation in the Yosemite area at an elevation of around 5,500 feet is seventy-five inches, while it decreases to only twenty inches at the same elevation on the eastern slope (Schoenherr 1992). The high-desert town of Bishop, in the nearby Owens Valley east of the Sierra Nevada at around 4,000 feet, receives only six inches each year (Vorster 1992). More than half of the annual precipitation in the Sierra Nevada falls during January, February, and March. In contrast with the Rockies and other mountain ranges that receive frequent summer thunderstorms, only 3 percent of the annual precipitation falls in the summer

(Schoenherr 1992). As a result, the annual summer drought cycle of California's Mediterranean climate creates a gap between the primary growing season and the primary period of precipitation. The snowpack of the Sierra Nevada is much more important to California hydrology than the rainfall, for the annual melt cycle in April through June can be captured for summer irrigation. The snowpack is also the key factor determining the availability of soil moisture to support the magnificent mixed-conifer forests of the Sierra Nevada in the prime summer growing season. They receive too little precipitation in the summer to survive without groundwater sources, usually stored in the soil from the late-melting snowpack.

The lower snow line is generally around 3,000 feet (ibid.), although occasionally snow falls as low as 1,000 to 1,500 feet. Because of the significant latitudinal range of the Sierra Nevada, the snow line is somewhat lower in the north and higher in the south. Adiabatic cooling of Pacific storms on the Sierra escalator also results in higher precipitation at higher elevations, increasing from around ten inches in the great Central Valley in the west to ninety inches at around 8,000 feet (ibid.). Precipitation above 8,000 feet is not recorded by any official weather station, but it is generally believed to decline above 9,000 feet (ibid.). Up to 90 percent of annual precipitation may fall as snow in the highest elevation; it reached up to eighty-six feet deep at Donner Pass (elevation 7,088 feet) in the winter of 1982–83.[9] Because storms are wetter and warmer when they first reach the Sierra, snow is generally heavier and more moist in the Sierra than in the Rockies. Skiers call it Sierra cement. It is hard work to plow fresh tracks through the snow the morning after a big dump.

The two key factors determining the distribution of tree species in the Sierra Nevada are precipitation and temperature (McBride 1993). Precipitation is usually a limiting factor in the lower elevations, where adiabatic cooling is insufficient to generate the minimum precipitation necessary to support larger forms of vegetation. Temperature is usually the limiting factor in the upper elevations, where many tree species cannot survive extreme winter conditions. Vegetation patterns reflect these differences in precipitation and temperature from north to south and from west to east. The ponderosa pine belt may extend down to 1,000–1,500 feet in the north, for example, but may not be found below 4,000–5,000 feet in the southern Sierra, where conditions are warmer and more arid. Similarly, the ponderosa pine zone will give way to the mixed conifer zone between 4,000 and 6,000 feet, where winter snows and subfreezing temperatures linger for months on end. Moreover, many tree species widely distributed on the western slope may be found on the drier east side only along riparian corridors. The temperature and precipitation gradients are much steeper on the eastern slope, resulting in more dramatic variation in conditions in relatively short distances. Hot desert temperatures in the summer or extreme lows in the winter are also more likely to be limiting factors at the lower elevations in the eastern Sierra Nevada.

FIGURE 1.1.   Yosemite Valley with El Capitan, Half Dome, and Bridalveil Falls.

Despite the gentleness of the western slope, however, it too has many steep environmental gradients, primarily determined by the many canyons that cut across the range and drain waterways. As Allan Schoenherr notes, "The major force responsible for the appearance of the Sierra today is glaciation" (Schoenherr 1992, 85). From north to south, the Sierra Nevada is canyon after ridge after canyon after ridge. (I gained a new appreciation for this when I hiked two hundred miles one summer on the John Muir Trail from Tuolumne Meadows to Mount Whitney.) The most famous example of glacial evidence is Yosemite Valley, with its classic U-shaped valley, its hanging waterfalls, and a floor more than 3,000 feet below the rim. There are few sights (if any) more spectacular anywhere in the world. Standing at the edge of Glacier Point, you can feel the glaciers streaming past either side of Half Dome and flowing together down past El Capitan and Sentinel Dome. The distant pinnacles of the Cathedral Range tower above Tuolumne Meadows, peeking their heads above the ice to view the transformation of the Sierra Nevada. To the south lies a series of pinnacles known as the Minarets, with Mount Ritter and Banner Peak standing beside them, where once a glacier sixty miles in length dropped below what is now the headwaters of the San Joaquin River. Today one can get a feel for these powerful flows of ice and rock in the Wrangell Mountains of Alaska, where the racetrack stripes of multiple glaciers still

FIGURE 1.2.   Converging glaciers in Wrangell–St. Elias National Park, Alaska.

merge beneath the tumbling icefalls on the face of Mount Blackburn. The waters beneath them still run chalky with their finely ground glacial silts, as those in the Sierra once did.

Today the streams of the High Sierra run clear. There are still some glaciers in the northern and eastern shadows of the Range of Light, but they have been retreating since the end of the Little Ice Age in the late nineteenth century. The southernmost glacier in the United States is Palisade Glacier, tucked in the shadows of the Palisade Peaks in the eastern Sierra above Big Pine, which stand more than 14,000 feet high. Many Sierra canyons now have a more V-shaped profile, reflecting aggressive down-cutting activity by water. The work of tearing down mountains is never done. Here, the hydrologic cycle drops water molecules nearly three miles above sea level and more than one hundred miles from the San Francisco Bay and the Golden Gate. Tumbling back down to the source, the water converts the potential energy of its elevation into the forceful action of erosion. Its energy is dissipated with every grain of sand moved, every leaf washed from the bank and into the current. Dancing across the rocks, water takes free flight over a precipice to a pool of spray below. Soon it washes the bodies of returning salmon and steelhead trout, who have struggled upstream to compose and decompose in one final act. Finally, it mingles with the salty still water of the Sacramento–San

Joaquin Delta, and is eventually flushed out to the Pacific Ocean. Along the way, it has dropped the soils of the Sierra Nevada to replenish the fertile agricultural lands of the great Central Valley (Johnson et al. 1993).

At least that is how the system operated before the mid-nineteenth century. Since that time humans have been an ever-present force in the Sierra, and we now may have as great an influence on the hydrology and erosional forces of the range as natural processes do. We have dammed the great rivers and captured the tumbling waterfalls with reservoirs and hydroelectric power plants, sending the energy of the waters to cities and farms throughout California. In the process we have halted the cycles of flooding and drought that once spread the soils of the Sierra Nevada over the great Central Valley. Those same dams have blocked the salmon and steelhead in their upstream migration; the fish now stop at the hatcheries below the foaming water, where reproduction will proceed artificially. Their dying carcasses no longer feed a pyramid of other life forms, as the decaying salmon in the Chilkit Valley of southeastern Alaska feed hundreds of bald eagles every winter today. Downstream in the delta, the water is just as likely to be sucked into the powerful pumps of the California State Water Project or the Central Valley Project as it is to be flushed through the Carquinez Straits, San Pablo Bay, San Francisco Bay, and the Golden Gate. Taken into one of the water projects, it will travel south to feed farms, families, commerce, and the seemingly endless forces of growth (Hundley 1992).

If it ends up on the west side of the San Joaquin Valley in the Westlands Water District, it may percolate down through the soil to meet an impermeable clay barrier that leaches the heavy metal selenium. It will then travel through the soil and into a drainage system that will take it north to the Kesterson Wildlife Refuge, where toxic selenium will accumulate in the terminal pool of water collecting the drainage wastes. There it will kill migrating waterfowl and contribute to deformed and dead newborn chicks. Birthed with promise in the high Sierra, the dancing waters will die a slow death without ever reaching the Pacific (Harris 1991).

COMMODIFYING NATURE
AND SETTLING THE FRONTIER

In addition to topography and climate, the geology of the Sierra Nevada has determined the soils of both the mountain range and the fertile Central Valley. These soils have in turn combined with topography and climate to determine the productive potential for biomass in the Sierra, which has then influenced the distribution of Sierran wildlife species. Moreover, the geologic history of the Sierra is the dominant factor in both the determination of the types of, and the distribution of, activities pursued by humans in the range. From gold mining to water resources diversions, the geology and topography of the Sierra are fundamental to California's existence as a modern state. Today these factors influence the availability of groundwater and the capacity of soils to handle septic system effluent for residential development in the area. The natural resources of the Sierra Nevada are therefore still the primary determinant of human settlement and economic activity in California. California, in turn, is the tail that often wags the dog known as the West (Quillen 1993).

Not surprisingly, all of these natural riches have drawn human interest. For centuries before Euro-American settlement in California, Native Americans moved up- and downslope with the seasons to harvest the bounty of Sierra oaks and wildlife. They were primarily hunter-gatherers but appeared to practice elements of agriculture and managed the landscape (mainly through fire) to promote conditions for desirable flora and fauna (Blackburn and Anderson 1993; Walton 1992). Spanish, Russian, and Mexican settlers arrived at the Pacific Coast and generally stayed near it; "una gran Sierra Nevada" (the large, rocky, snow-covered range) to the inland east was of little interest (Farquhar 1965; Whitney 1979). The Sierra Nevada was seen chiefly as a difficult barrier both to eastward and westward migration (Beesley 1994a; 1996; Rose 1987). Spanish cartographers first placed the Sierra Nevada on a map in 1776, the same year the Presidio was established in San Francisco. The first verified crossing of the Sierra by Euro-Americans was not made until a half century later, however, by the American trapper and explorer Jedidiah Smith, in 1827. For the next two decades, the Sierra remained largely a troublesome barrier not worth settling. The great Central Valley of California and the Sacramento–San Joaquin Delta offered abundant wildlife, rich soils, level land, and a mild climate for agricultural production (Johnson et al. 1994). There was little reason to venture into the harsher climate and more difficult terrain of the Sierra Nevada. The ill-fated crossing of the Donner Party in the harsh winter of 1846–1847 reinforced the perception of the range as a dangerous and foreboding place, discouraging potential travelers from the East (McGlashan 1986; Stewart 1960).

That view of the Sierra Nevada changed dramatically one winter day in 1848, when James Marshall discovered gold at Sutter's Mill near the South Fork of the American River in Coloma (Paul 1947). Only 4 ships dropped anchor in San Francisco Bay in 1848, but word of Marshall's discovery kindled gold fever throughout the country and the world. A flood of new migrants poured through the Golden Gate on 695 ships in 1849 (*Grass Valley–Nevada City Union* 1994a). Thousands more crossed by land over the difficult deserts and mountains of the unsettled West. In one fell swoop, California was settled at the same time that the "Great West" between Chicago and the Rocky Mountains still held old-growth forests rather than mills and factories (Cronon 1991). It is easy to forget what an important role Marshall's discovery played in the westward expansion of the

American nation. Mining in the Rockies generally occurred later, since settlers passed right through the intermountain West in their quest for California (Worster 1985b). Marshall's discovery at Coloma brought large-scale American civilization to the Pacific Coast and the pressures of industrialization onto the slopes of the Sierra Nevada.

The Range of Light has been the subject of intense development pressure ever since. The ensuing gold rush brought hordes of fortune-seekers to the Mother Lode of the foothills; they left few stones unturned or waterways undiverted in their search for instant riches. The Native Americans were quickly displaced through disease and, in some cases, forced removal.[10] The new migrants also needed wood for fuel and timber, placing pressures on forest resources whose effects can still be seen today. Discovery of silver in the nearby Comstock Lode of Nevada in 1859 created additional pressure, eventually leading to the nearly complete deforestation of the Lake Tahoe Basin. Sheep and cattle were introduced to the Sierra meadows to provide meat and hides for the miners, and crops and orchards were planted to provide food. In short, most of the Sierra Nevada was directly affected by the discovery of gold and silver on either side of the range (Beesley 1994a; Verner et al. 1992; Weeks et al. 1943).

Within only two more decades, the Central Pacific Railroad crossed the Sierra Nevada at Donner Pass to link California to the rest of the nation in the earliest days of Reconstruction. As part of a set of policy incentives to encourage construction of the railroad, the company received alternating sections (one square mile each) along the railroad right-of-way.[11] This pattern of checkerboard private and public land ownership remains with us today, and it has made land and resource management policy more complex and difficult in the Sierra Nevada. The human overlay of ownership, plotted with an eye toward efficient disposal of land rather than toward the hydrologic and ecological boundaries of the landscape (Stegner 1954; Wilkinson 1992a), today jars against the biophysical realities of Sierra Nevada ecosystems. Decisions made in one era to promote one set of goals still have dramatic consequences more than 130 years later.

The nineteenth-century network of water resource developments has also left a legacy with lasting effects. Modern subdivisions are still served by artificial waterways once built for hydraulic mining operations, which also led to the development of modern technologies such as hydroelectric generation and long-distance telephone service. Both hardrock quartz mining and hydraulic mining required large investments of capital and complex organizational structures, and the value of Sierra Nevada gold made it worthwhile to invest in new technologies. The Pelton wheel was invented near Camptonville in the Yuba watershed of the northern Sierra Nevada, and it remains the core technology of hydroelectric generation. Pacific Gas and Electric Company, the largest investor-owned utility in the United States, got its start when a group of small electric companies combined resources

FIGURE 1.3.   Hydraulic mining damage at Malakoff Diggins State Historic Park.

following a meeting in the gold rush town of nearby Nevada City.[12] Facing the
daunting task of managing dams and reservoirs in the high Sierra in order to
divert water to the ancient riverbeds of the San Juan Ridge for hydraulic mining,
mining company engineers developed the first long-distance telephone line in
order to maintain communication along the downstream canal.[13] This, too, took
place in the Yuba watershed north of Nevada City. By 1880, there were more than
two thousand miles of ditches, canals, and flumes in Nevada County (Thompson
and West 1880).

Expansion of that system for mining ended with the Sawyer decision of 1884,
which required hydraulic mining operations to capture the debris they washed
from the hills before it flowed down to the valley, where it filled the riverbeds and
flooded farmers' fields (Kelley 1959). Agriculture was on the ascendance in
California and diversion of the Sierra's bountiful water for agricultural uses would
soon make the Central Valley and Southern California the fruit and vegetable bas-
ket of the world. A series of small, locally supported irrigation projects received a
boost with passage of the Newlands Act of 1902, which established the U.S.
Reclamation Service (Stegner 1954). The federal government soon developed
the topographic and hydrologic information necessary for large-scale water
resources development. The New Deal expanded federal investments in the
1930s, leading to the development of the Central Valley Project, with Shasta Dam

on the upper Sacramento River in 1945, Friant Dam on the San Joaquin River in 1948, and Folsom Dam on the American River in 1955. With the rivers impounded behind dams, and streams channelized in the Central Valley by the Army Corps of Engineers, the hydrologic regime of California was radically altered. Seasonal flooding of the valley was eliminated completely or at least moderated by retaining the annual snowmelt behind dams in the Sierra Nevada foothills. That water was then used to generate hydroelectric power and was diverted for irrigation use by California's agricultural industry. The desert was made to bloom with the melted snows of the Sierra Nevada.

California's population also exploded in the twentieth century, and has increased more than tenfold since 1920. Like the Spanish, Russian, and Mexican immigrants before them, Americans settled primarily near the coastal regions. Even the larger inland settlements, such as Sacramento, were accessible by water through San Francisco Bay and the Sacramento–San Joaquin Delta. At first these small cities could meet their needs through local resources. Growing populations called for expanding sources of water, however, and the Coast Ranges did not provide a reliable year-round supply.[14] Recognizing that an inadequate supply of water could stop expansion of their metropolitan regions, boosters and visionaries in the urban centers of the state looked to the Sierra Nevada for long-term supplies in the first three decades of the twentieth century. The city of Los Angeles's Department of Water and Power reached nearly three hundred miles north to capture the surface runoff and groundwater resources of the Owens Valley in 1913 and eventually the Mono Basin in 1941 (Kahrl 1982; Walton 1992; Hundley 1992). The East Bay Municipal Utility District dammed and diverted the Mokelumne River drainage in 1929, and San Francisco tapped the Tuolumne River watershed in Yosemite National Park's Hetch Hetchy Valley in 1934. The Colorado River was also diverted for irrigation use in the Imperial and Coachella Valleys and by the Metropolitan Water District of Southern California in 1941 (Hundley 1992). The Sierra Nevada accounts for only 28 percent of California's average annual surface water runoff,[15] but approximately 60 percent of all the water consumed in California originates there.[16] The Sierra Nevada is literally the source of life for California.

This has not come without its costs, of course. Downstream of the dams and diversions, entire reaches of once-vibrant rivers and streams have been dewatered. Following an ethical and legal framework that valued water only when it was utilized for economic production, very few obligations have been imposed on water diverters to protect downstream ecological values.[17] The stunning salmon migrations of the past are gone, replaced by a waning stock of hatchery-raised fish that sometimes migrate in the wrong direction in response to the pull of the massive pumps lifting water out of the delta for its southern journey by concrete canal.[18] The California plumbing system is a remarkable study in engineering and eco-

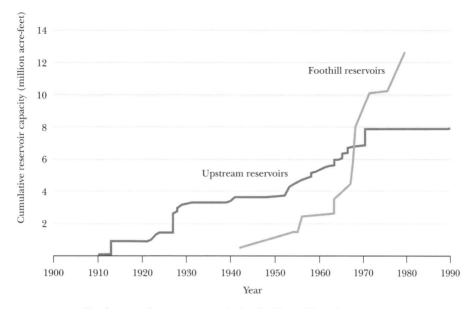

FIGURE 1.4.   Total reservoir storage capacity in the Sierra Nevada, 1900–90.

nomic efficiency: it is an extremely cost-effective way to move water through space and time from a "wasted" state to a "useful" state. It has also proven to be a highly efficient system, however, for destroying the ecological structure and function of entire ecohydrologic systems. The result is a depauperate remnant of what once was rich beyond our modern imagination. The social objective and definition of "the greatest good of the greatest number in the long run" did not include seven generations of wildlife and fish (Wilkinson 1992a, 128). Equally important, the social objective did not include consideration of future human beings who might see those wildlife and fish as beneficial to human well-being even when not "utilized." Any water that could be economically captured was taken away from Nature. Utilitarianism dominated the logic of our Culture and its relationship to Nature.

EMERGING CONFLICTS
OVER LAND AND RESOURCE MANAGEMENT

It has now been 150 years since that fateful day when a shiny piece of soft metal caught James Marshall's eye in the Lotus Valley (Center et al. 1989), and the enthusiasm that greeted Marshall's discovery has been replaced by a social conflict over the future of the Range of Light. The Native Americans displaced and murdered as a result of the gold rush undoubtedly did not share the enthusiasm of the new settlers, but there was widespread agreement within the Euro-American cultures of the mid-nineteenth century that the precious metal should be removed from the landscape in order to improve human well-being. There was also a general expectation that the "settlers" would quickly move on to other fields of dreams once the riches of the Mother Lode were exhausted. With the exception of a few romantic and transcendentalist thinkers like Emerson and Thoreau, the dominant American ideology of progress through material acquisition and consumption was the norm. Few questioned the central American ideal of "progress." Manifest Destiny also called for American expansion and an empire from the Atlantic to the Pacific, and the frontier and wilderness needed to be conquered. This was not simply a case of pursuing what was in any individual's or the nation's self-interest: it was ordained to constitute divine destiny, the fulfillment of God's wishes for the young nation.[19] Impediments to achievement of that goal—whether natural conditions, aesthetic concerns, indigenous people, women, or even contrary ideas and values—were to be eliminated or controlled through force (Merchant 1980). The ends justified the means, and there was no question about whether a greater good would be achieved through an alternative path of history. Indeed, history itself was seen as having a single, focused, and predetermined path.

This social consensus—if, indeed, it ever truly existed beyond those who controlled political and economic power, intellectual discourse, and the documentation of history—has since broken down. Cracks in the facade of homogeneous *interests* appeared with the Sawyer decision of 1884, where the environmental effects of hydraulic mining were deemed to be too damaging to the economic interests of downstream farmers (Kelley 1959). Cracks in the facade of homogeneous *values* emerged in the conflict between Muir and Pinchot over Hetch Hetchy, where two different visions of Nature and the appropriate human relationship to the natural world were offered. Pinchot's still represented the dominant view, but a growing minority joined Muir and the young Sierra Club to challenge that view (Fox 1981). The cracks widened in the 1930s with Aldo Leopold's conservation ethic and the establishment of the Wilderness Society, which lobbied for formal recognition of Muir's values in management of the public domain. An alternative value system was then more widely articulated by Leopold in 1948 in "The Land Ethic," an essay published posthumously in 1949 in the small book *A Sand County Almanac* (1949; Meine 1988). Thirteen years later, in her book *Silent Spring*, Rachel Carson challenged the implicit logic of an industrial society built on a network of toxic chemicals (1962). A broader set of social changes also challenged mainstream American values and the dominant power structures in the 1960s through the Civil Rights movement and protests against the Vietnam War. By the time Neil Armstrong pressed the first human footprint into the Sea of Tranquillity on July 20, 1969, the image sent back from Apollo 11 of a fragile planet Earth was already deep in the American consciousness. The National Environmental Policy Act was signed into law on the first day of 1970, and the first Earth Day was held just a few months later. The 1970s began with a new set of values dominating American ideas about the environment (Dunlap 1991a; Kempton et al. 1995). Thoreau, Muir, Leopold, and Carson were now popular in paperback and Pinchot's works were out of print.

The implications of this shift are still being felt, and they have not yet been fully recognized by the dominant Culture, with its institutional incentives guiding most land and resource management agencies. Within the U.S. Forest Service, for example, a letter written by Pinchot in 1909 is still considered a sacred text (Wilkinson 1993). Outside the Forest Service, the American public is likely to embrace elements of both Pinchot and Muir. In 1989–90, roughly three-quarters of Americans considered themselves to be "environmentalists" (Dunlap 1991a, 309; Kempton et al. 1995). This self-identification has remained high since the late 1960s through a wide range of economic circumstances, although the relative importance of environmental issues in the public mind has waxed and waned. A strong attempt by the Reagan administration in the early 1980s to turn back environmentalist gains had the opposite effect, for example, mobilizing environmentalists and swelling the memberships of the large environmental groups (Dunlap 1987). Interior Secretary James Watt finally had to leave his post before Reagan's reelection campaign.[20] Another surge in memberships and donations occurred in the late 1980s and early 1990s around Earth Day 1990. More recently, the so-called Wise Use movement has mobilized a counterattack that has had some success with a public wary of big government (Jacobs 1995; Sneed 1994a; 1994b). Together with the economic recession in the early 1990s, it has had a negative effective on environmental-group memberships. That reactionary movement is, in fact, tapping into public concerns about the *means* of environmental policy, rather than the *ends*. There is now a deep-rooted acceptance of environmentalist values. The new Republican majority in Congress discovered this when it tried to dismantle a quarter century of modern environmental legislation and regulation in 1995–96. The attempt generated a backlash that cut across age, income, gender, and ethnic and regional identities (Cushman 1996; *New York Times* 1996).

Yet those values are still far from being universally accepted. Moreover, any shift in policies and institutions to embrace these emerging social values will require a new distribution of costs and benefits. This clearly challenges many powerful interests who benefit from the distributive structure of the current system.[21] There is consequently significant social conflict over the future of land and resource management and environmental policy, especially in the western United States, where the federal government owns 48 percent of all land in the states of Montana, Idaho, Wyoming, Colorado, Utah, New Mexico, Arizona, California, Nevada, Oregon, and Washington and 68 percent of Alaska (totaling about one-third of the entire United States) (Horner 1996). Much of this public land is located in

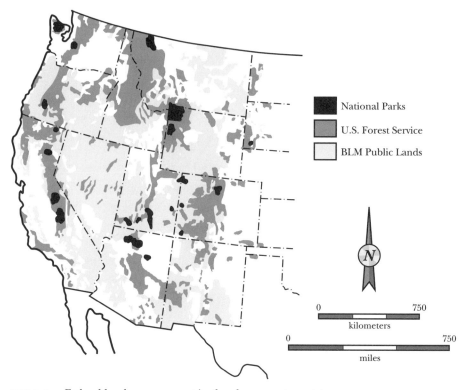

National Parks

U.S. Forest Service

BLM Public Lands

0   750
kilometers

0   750
miles

MAP 1.2.   Federal land management in the eleven western states.

mountainous regions, which were not settled as early or as extensively as more agriculturally productive valleys and river bottoms.

The Sierra Nevada is an example of such a region. The Sierra Nevada is also unusually close to the largest concentration of humans in the western United States, however, forcing it to face many of the pressures of the changing West a bit earlier than some of its counterpart regions in the Pacific Northwest, the desert Southwest, the Great Basin, and the Rocky Mountains. California's exploding population demands much from the Sierra Nevada, and Nevada is the fastest-growing state in the nation, with another 1 million residents. California alone exceeds the combined populations of the ten other western states, which have only 25 million people between them (U.S. Bureau of Census 1996). From urban settlement to intensive recreational use, from water quality to endangered species concerns, the Sierra Nevada has faced environmental challenges and social conflicts that other parts of the West have only recently encountered (Barringer 1993; *New York Times* 1993; Brooke 1995; 1996a; 1996b; Egan 1996; Johnson 1996). The wave of migrants from California's urban areas has been breaking against the Sierra since the late 1960s, and it finally crashed onto the shores of the rest of the West in the late 1980s (*High Country News* 1994b). The Sierra Nevada therefore offers an interesting laboratory for exploring these conflicts and policy challenges for lessons and insights. What can be learned from this region may then have relevance throughout the West (Schrag 1998).

THE SIERRA IN PERIL:
POLITICAL MOBILIZATION IN THE 1990S

The debate on the future of the Sierra Nevada took a significant turn in June 1991, when the *Sacramento Bee* published a five-part series of articles by writer Tom Knudson, "Majesty and Tragedy: The Sierra in Peril." In one bold stroke, the series changed the terms of the debate about environmental quality and land and resource management issues in the Range of Light. Before the series, the health of Sierra Nevada ecosystems had been debated within the context and confines of issue-specific state and federal policy debates. Federal forest policy and state air pollution regulations, for example, were being decided with their relationship to each other—and to the Sierra Nevada specifically—as only marginal elements of the policy debate. The "Sierra in Peril" series changed that forever. The new debate was about the health of the Sierra Nevada per se, with a new emphasis on the interwoven relationships between seemingly disparate factors affecting the area and policies then under consideration to mitigate those effects. This interdisciplinary view raised questions about the relationships between population growth, air quality, and forest health—which established a new context within which to view federal forest policy. A similar shift occurred in a number of other areas covered by the *Bee* articles.

Knudson painted a gloomy picture of devastation and environmental degradation, arguing that the government had failed to prevent abuses even on public lands. His articles had immediate influence. Environmentalists called for state and federal action to address what they saw as a crisis in the Sierra Nevada, while commodity-production interests called the series sensationalist and unfounded. "Save a tree, cancel the *Bee*" said one bumper sticker that started appearing on offroad vehicles and logging trucks in the Sierra Nevada.[22] "Yellow journalism" cried some, invoking the image of a press dominated by elite urban liberals who cared little for the fate of poor, resource-dependent rural communities and working people. The Pulitzer Prize committee disagreed, awarding Knudson and the *Bee* journalism's highest honor for the series.[23]

The time was ripe for a galvanizing force, and the "Sierra in Peril" series helped generate a new focus on the Sierra Nevada as a unit. The Sierra Club was formed a century earlier with a similar perspective, and Francis Farquhar had taken a rangewide view in his book *History of the Sierra Nevada* in 1965. More recently, Tim Palmer had explored the many pressures on the range and the social conflict surrounding land and resource management policies in his 1988 book, *The Sierra Nevada: A Mountain Journey*.[24] But neither Farquhar's book nor Palmer's had the influence of Knudson's series.

In September 1991, California Resources Secretary Douglas Wheeler announced a Sierra Summit to be held in November 1991. "Getting on the invitation list is like getting tickets to the Governor's Ball," said one senior organizer, who was barraged with calls and letters (Erman 1991). The Sierra Summit was attended by approximately 150 representatives of state and federal agencies, environmental groups, local industries, and local government. Tom Knudson was the only journalist invited to cover the event, but a group of timber workers from United Forest Families gained access by protesting outside the meeting place at Fallen Leaf Lake in the snow. Complaints about limited access then led to a series of regional public workshops during the spring of 1992. These workshops were intended to solicit public input on the process and the policy issues confronting the Sierra Nevada region, but they proved to be controversial. The Quincy workshop was highly structured and seemed to bring people together in search of solutions to the problems of the community,[25] which was timber-dependent and had been facing economic stagnation. In contrast, a follow-up workshop in Placerville was packed with representatives from the United Forest Families group, many of whom had driven from other parts of the Sierra with their logging equipment. It was a hostile audience, one that protested what some described as a secretive attempt by big government to create a new layer of regional government. Many of them verbally attacked the state representatives and Sierra Summit steering committee members, and their rhetoric was encouraged by the representative of a conservative state assemblyman representing much of the region. It was an intimidating experience for many.[26] Other workshops were held in Mariposa, Visalia (near the southern Sierra Nevada in the Central Valley), and Bishop. An estimated total of fifteen hundred people participated in the five workshops (California Resources Agency 1992b).

The hostile response by some parts of the public can be traced directly to two types of fears: fear of loss of local control, with the potential for state and federal agencies to institute some new kind of regional government structure that might overrule local land use planning prerogatives; and fear of greater environmental restrictions on commodity production activities, particularly timber harvesting. Both of these fears were linked to the establishment in September 1991 of the innovative California Executive Council on Biodiversity, which brought state and federal land and resource management agencies together to coordinate their efforts. Ten agency directors signed a memorandum of understanding that called for managing biodiversity issues along "bioregional" lines; an accompanying map delineated the ten major "Bioregions of California" (California Resources Agency 1991). Each of the agency directors promised to reorganize his or her agency to

MAP 1.3.   The ten major bioregions of California.

address the decline of biological diversity in California by shifting the institutional approach to problems: from single-agency, single-issue to multiagency, multi-issue, bioregional solutions. The biodiversity memorandum of understanding also called for the ultimate establishment of a "bioregional council" for each of the bioregions and "watershed or landscape associations" within each bioregion to promote coordinated problem-solving at the local level. None of this was mandatory, however; the memorandum of understanding simply pledged commitment to coordinated problem-solving.

Local governments were not originally represented among the signatories, however, and many of their representatives feared that the agreement could lead to regional entities modeled on the California Coastal Commission or the Tahoe Regional Planning Agency. Several unrelated bills that called for greater regional government powers in order to coordinate land use, air quality, and transportation planning in metropolitan areas were, coincidentally, before the state legislature in

1991. A statewide Growth Management Task Force was also studying institutional alternatives that included an expansion of land use powers for regional authorities (Governor's Interagency Council on Growth Management 1993). Secretary Wheeler tried to clarify "that the new agreement on biodiversity confers no new authority, no new layers of government, no new restrictions on land use. It does reflect a firm belief that government agencies should talk to each other and to local communities before making decisions which affect their neighbors" (Wheeler 1992). The Sierra Summit was announced by Wheeler's office around the same time as the biodiversity memorandum of understanding, however, and the former was seen by many Sierra Nevada residents and their local representatives as a first step toward implementing the latter. Subsequent amendments to the agreement have added representation for local governments through regional associations, but Wheeler recognizes that it was a political oversight that still hampers relations between his agency and local governments (1994).

The Sierra Summit process identified three subjects "as crucial to the future of the mountain range ecosystem": 1) information ("Improving the quality and accessibility of information and data on the natural resources, the economy, and the communities of the Sierra"); 2) coordination ("Fostering communication and coordination among state and federal agencies, local governments, and private citizens and groups in managing natural resources"); and 3) economic development ("Developing strategies to encourage sustainable economic development and diversification, taking into account effects on communities and natural resources") (California Resources Agency 1992a). The July 1992 report of the Sierra Summit Steering Committee proposed seventeen specific actions to address these three areas (ibid.). A year-long Sierra Nevada Research Planning effort was then funded by the Resources Agency in 1993–94, which attempted to establish priorities for research and assessment (Sierra Nevada Ecosystem Project 1994). A related statewide effort to establish the California Environmental Resources and Evaluation System as an on-line database of geographic and other resource information attempts to meet both the information and coordination needs identified in the report.[27] Finally, the California Biodiversity Council meets on a quarterly basis and is trying to improve coordination and eliminate conflicting policies among its signatory members. Significant progress has not yet been made in the area of economic development for the region, however.

The "official" Sierra Summit was followed by other regional conferences. Environmental groups organized the Sierra Now conference in August 1992, which was attended by more than four hundred people.[28] That conference spawned the Sierra Nevada Alliance (SNA) in 1993, a coalition of local and national environmental groups interested in the Sierra Nevada. The Alliance is modeled on the successful Greater Yellowstone Coalition, and a majority of its board members live in the Sierra Nevada. Then, in June 1993, nearly two hundred people attended the Sierra Economic Summit, which was organized by representatives of the Wise Use movement as a response to the Sierra Now conference (Nevada County Business Association and California Forestry Association 1993). Organizers of this conference formed the Sierra Communities Council as a counter to the Sierra Nevada Alliance (Landowski 1994–96; Lauer 1994g). Finally, a group called the Sierra Business Council formed in 1994 to represent businesses in the region that support environmental protection as an essential foundation of economic development (Blake 1993–97). The Business Council bridges the constituencies of both the SNA and the Sierra Communities Council, making it clear that many people view environmental and economic goals as being mutually compatible rather than in direct conflict. It has clearly been the region's most successful organization to date, producing the influential *Sierra Wealth Index* in 1996 (Marois 1996b) and the *Planning for Prosperity* report in 1997 (Martin 1997; Griffith 1997).

A wide range of voices now claims to represent the interests of Sierra Nevada residents. This reflects the heterogeneity of the population and communities in the region, and the dramatic changes the region has undergone over the past few decades. The Sierra Nevada has been experiencing growth even more rapid than that of the rest of California. While the bulk of the state's new residents have settled near the existing urban regions of Southern California and the Bay Area, some rural areas are growing at a faster rate. This "rural renaissance" is occurring in areas now taking on the characteristics of both rural and urban areas, but which are not on the immediate fringes of metropolitan areas (suburban areas). These exurban areas are seeing significant growth throughout the country (Nelson 1992). Like many other areas in the rural and small-town western United States, much of the Sierra Nevada population is becoming exurban.

The Sierra Nevada region grew by more than 65 percent in the 1970s, 39 percent in the 1980s, and a total of 130 percent from 1970 to 1990. This compares with overall growth of 49 percent for all of California and 22 percent for the entire United States in the same period.[29] This rapid population growth boosted the population of the Sierra Region from slightly under 273,000 in 1970 to around 619,000 in 1990. The absolute increase in population has been steady at slightly over 175,000 per decade, even if the rate of growth appears to have dropped from the 1970s to the 1980s (the result of a larger base population in 1980 than in 1970). More people moved into the Sierra Nevada during 1970 to 1990 than migrated into the area during the entire gold rush through the 1850s. The result has been a dramatic change in social, demographic, and economic characteristics of Sierra Nevada residents.[30] This in turn has altered the economic and social relationships between residents and Sierra ecosystems. It is this changing relationship between Nature and Culture that explains current social conflict yet also presents opportunities for moving the region toward a sustainable future.

In particular, the amenity values of natural resources increasingly dominate commodity values for local residents (Duane 1993a). Many communities still rely primarily on timber or mineral extraction for their economic livelihood, but they are geographically concentrated in a few subregions of the Sierra Nevada. Other areas have developed strong economic dependence on tourism and recreation, which have significant seasonal variations in local employment and income. Finally, some areas have diversified their economic base and now depend on a wide range of economic activities: logging, mining, recreation, and tourism have been supplemented by retirees and commuters to metropolitan regions. Many members of the latter two groups have located in the Sierra Nevada primarily for "quality of life" reasons, which often reflect the amenity values of natural resources and the environment (J. Moore Methods 1992). Moreover, construction associated with rapid population growth and services associated with these latter two groups (who generate their income and wealth from activities outside the region) have become important sources of employment for local residents. Finally, a small but potentially significant group of telecommuters and technologically advanced industries are also locating in the Sierra Nevada in response to quality of life considerations.

Taking place in this complex setting is the public debate on the status of the region's ecosystems, the trends affecting those ecosystems, and the social, economic, and institutional implications of various policy alternatives for the management of those ecosystems. That debate about the Sierra Nevada is not isolated in space or time, however, but is occurring within the broader context of social conflict over land and resource management policies in the western United States. The "Sierra in Peril" series changed the terms of the public debate to consider the entire Sierra Nevada as a complex and interdependent entity against the backdrop of this broader social conflict. In its broadest sense, this debate is about the shift from a primary (but by no means exclusive) emphasis on commodity production to a more central role for environmental protection in the rural West. Because there is significant social conflict on these broader issues, the public debate about and future policy direction for the Sierra Nevada have became a test case for the exploration of a complex set of ideas regarding ecosystem health, social needs, institutional structures, and environmental values. This background has shaped the debate and made it of national rather than regional importance. For both environmentalists and the Wise Use movement, the Sierra Nevada is a battlefield on which the terms of a larger war for the future of the West may be determined.[31] Not surprisingly, this has distorted and colored some of the debate.

Old-growth forest policy was the most controversial and widely debated issue affecting interpretations of the "Sierra in Peril" series in June 1991. Two major ballot initiatives related to state forest policy had narrowly failed at the polls only seven months earlier, and the environmental community was threatening litigation against the Forest Service if it did not modify timber management practices to protect the habitat needs of the California spotted owl (*Strix occidentalis occidentalis*).[32] Similar litigation over the northern spotted owl (*Strix occidentalis caurina*) had resulted in dramatic reductions in timber harvests on federal lands in the Pacific Northwest over the previous few years, and the Bush administration was promoting the view that society faced an either/or choice: "owls versus jobs" became the rallying cry (Yaffee 1994; Forest Ecosystem Management and Assessment Team 1993; Shannon and Johnson 1994; Johnson et al. 1995). "Save a logger—eat an owl," proclaimed one T-shirt worn in rural areas of the Pacific Northwest.[33] This rhetorical tone had spread to the Sierra Nevada by 1991.

Governor Pete Wilson and his resources secretary, Doug Wheeler, took office in January 1991 with all parties calling for new policies to avoid either ecological or economic catastrophe in the Sierra Nevada. Much of the most visible controversy over forest policy remained focused on the redwood and Douglas fir forests of California's northern coast (Harris 1995), but the future of those areas would largely be decided by litigation over the northern spotted owl and actions taken to protect it under the federal Endangered Species Act (ESA). The U.S. Fish and Wildlife Service had listed the northern spotted owl as threatened under the ESA in June 1990 following years of debate, and the ESA had much stricter requirements for protection than either the National Forest Management Act or the National Environmental Policy Act (NEPA). But because the California spotted owl was not yet listed under the ESA, there was more flexibility for state and federal policy in the forests of the Sierra Nevada. Proactive policy in 1991 could conceivably avoid the more restrictive constraints that could be imposed following listing under the ESA. Both the state and federal governments therefore sought to develop a forest management strategy for the California spotted owl that would avoid its being listed.

In the Pacific Northwest the Forest Service selected the northern spotted owl as a "management indicator species" in the 1980s to represent a range of species' needs in forest planning and management (Yaffee 1994). Similarly, in the Sierra Nevada the Forest Service designated the California spotted owl as a "sensitive" species that warranted special consideration. Both regions relied on designation of spotted owl habitat areas to protect a limited area around identified nesting, roosting, and foraging owls (Wildlands Resource Center 1994; Yaffee 1994; USDA Forest Service 1993). Subsequent research leading to the listing of the northern spotted owl under the ESA suggested that such a strategy was inadequate to protect the long-term viability of either owl subspecies. The regional office of the Forest Service therefore instituted a new policy in California to conduct a cumulative effects analysis to determine the effects of forest management actions on the owls (Wildlands Resource Center 1994; Yaffee 1994). In early 1991, however, environmental groups challenged this approach, filing administrative appeals to prevent Forest Service timber sales in the Sierra Nevada (Wildlands Resource Center 1994; Natural Resources Defense Council 1991).

State and federal land and resource managers responded to the legal vulnerability of the existing strategy in June 1991 by forming the California Spotted Owl Assessment and Planning Team (CASPO). This team was cochaired by Doug Wheeler and Ron Stewart, who was then the regional forester responsible for all national forests in California.[34] Other agencies, environmentalists, and industry groups were also represented on the CASPO team. A technical team was delegated the responsibility of assessing the status of the California spotted owl and developing alternative approaches to ensuring California spotted owl viability. A separate policy implementation planning team was established to evaluate the social, economic, and institutional implications of alternative policies proposed by the technical team (Wildlands Resource Center 1994). The technical team issued its draft report in May 1992, and the policy implementation planning team issued its final report in May 1994 (Verner et al. 1992; Wildlands Resource Center 1994). An interim CASPO policy was adopted by the Forest Service in January 1993 to implement the technical team's recommendations until a long-term policy could be developed. That interim policy followed the CASPO technical team guidelines, restricting harvests on federal lands so that no tree larger than thirty inches in diameter at breast height could be harvested. Additional requirements resulted in a significant drop in federal timber harvests to less than half of the amount harvested during the 1982 recession (Stewart 1996; U.S. Forest Service 1996).

While much of the political attention has focused on old-growth and ancient-forest issues, other policy developments in California and the West have also been important. In general, these revolve around both the difficult problem of protecting biological diversity and the apparent failure of existing approaches to maintain native biological diversity (Grumbine 1992; Jensen et al. 1993). Institutional innovation in the early 1990s at the federal, state, and local levels moved agencies away from the single-species "emergency room" strategy of the ESA to a set of more proactive, multiple-species planning strategies that may be able to protect biological diversity without resorting to the extreme restrictions generally imposed under the ESA. This theme lay at the heart of both the initiative by California Resources Secretary Doug Wheeler to establish the Executive Council on Biological Diversity and a similar effort by Bruce Babbitt, the Clinton administration's secretary of the interior, to create the National Biological Survey in 1993. The former established formal mechanisms for improved information sharing and policy coordination among federal, state, and local land and resource planning and management agencies. The latter attempted to begin the systematic collection, coordination, and dissemination of ecological information necessary for improved decision-making. Together they promised to make consideration of ecological information an earlier step in the planning and decision-making process than had been mandated by either NEPA or the California Environmental Quality Act (CEQA), its state counterpart. They also sought to *avoid* application of the federal or state Endangered Species Act whenever possible, but biodiversity protection continues to occur primarily as a result of the existence of a strong ESA. The possibility of ESA application has therefore, paradoxically, both brought groups to the negotiating table and promoted less reliance on the ESA. It is doubtful that such cooperation would exist without a strong ESA, however.

Once the U.S. Fish and Wildlife Service has declared a species as threatened or endangered under the ESA, it is illegal under section 9 to "take" the species indirectly through elimination or damage of that species' habitat (Beatley 1994, 17–18). This provision—which was interpreted broadly by the Ninth Circuit Court of Appeals, then confirmed by the U.S. Supreme Court in the *Sweet Home* decision in 1995—places severe limitations on any development that may take any habitat of any listed species and therefore result in harm to that species as defined by the Act.[35] There need not be a finding of specific harm against specific individual members of that species to limit development.[36] In the Pacific Northwest, the northern spotted owl listing imposed restrictions on forest management activities because of their effect on habitat. Ironically, these restrictions made the owl economically the most important species in Oregon or Washington: timber production throughout the region hinged on the fate of the owl.

In California, the potential listing of the coastal California gnatcatcher (*Polioptila californica californica*), a songbird that relies primarily on the coastal sage scrub of Southern California for habitat, carried the greatest potential economic consequences. Wheeler and his deputy, Michael Mantell, argued against a listing by the Fish and Wildlife Service in late 1991 with a promise to develop a comprehensive plan that would ensure the viability of the gnatcatcher. The framework for their approach was embodied in the new Natural Communities Conservation Planning (NCCP) program, which had just been adopted by the state legislature and signed into California law by Governor Wilson (Mueller 1994). The NCCP called for systematic planning, establishment of a reserve system to protect critical habitat, and agreements to allow the continued conversion of some remaining habitat through development that was incorporated into the NCCP plan (Mann and Plummer 1995; Stevens 1996; 1997a). This was quite important in 1991, when the boom of the last California growth spurt had not yet busted with defense spending cutbacks, significant domestic emigration out of Southern California, and the collapse of the Southern California real estate market (Teitz 1990). Billions of dollars of California real estate could be tied up in 1991 if the gnatcatcher were listed under the ESA, yet it was not clear that all of the potential gnatcatcher habitat was either necessary or sufficient to ensure gnatcatcher viability.[37] Avoiding an ESA listing and allowing development to go forward was therefore the primary goal of the original NCCP proposal for coastal sage scrub. The Irvine

Company, one of the largest landowners and real estate developers in Southern California, was one of Wilson's strongest supporters and helped develop the legislation. Moreover, Wilson was a former mayor of San Diego, where he enjoyed strong support from the development community.

The NCCP also represented an important new approach to the conservation of biological diversity, however, that has ultimately cut across partisan lines and presidential administrations. Under section 10, the existing ESA already allowed issuance of an "incidental take" permit following the development of a habitat conservation plan (HCP) to establish protections for listed species. The HCP and incidental take provisions allow some development activity to proceed while theoretically ensuring protection of the listed species. This section was introduced in the 1982 amendments to the ESA but by the early 1990s had been applied in only a handful of cases (Beatley 1994b). By 1996 that number had exploded, with more than three hundred HCPs under development (Sax 1996b). The principles underlying the HCP concept are solid: development should not continue to harm habitat unless a plan is in place to ensure protection of the listed species. Moreover, the HCP concept recognizes that allowing some development to occur on marginal habitat may help pay for the protection of more important habitat; indeed, if the land is economically valuable enough, it may pay for even greater protection of the species through acquisition of a greater area of habitat in another area. Habitat conservation plans have generally therefore been developed through a negotiation process between developers, environmentalists, and regulators (Beatley 1994b). In theory, each HCP both protects the listed species and wards off the specter of the ESA "shutting down all development." In fact, a study of implementation of the ESA from 1987 to 1991 shows that only a minuscule fraction of federal projects have been stopped as a result of the ESA. Of the 73,808 projects reviewed, only 19 were blocked through the consultation process required under section 7 of the ESA (Wilderness Society 1992, 18). More typically they have been modified to mitigate the effects on the listed species.

In a twist that almost ensures inadequate information and reduced flexibility, however, an HCP is typically prepared *after* a species has already been listed.[38] The prospect of applying the full force of the ESA to stop further development activity has always been the hammer that has brought developers to the table and made them willing to give up some development potential in order to move forward. The NCCP approach calls for conducting multiple-species planning *before* any species relying on the habitat in the area under study is listed under the ESA. In theory, this should reduce the likelihood of future listings. Moreover, it can be incorporated into other planning processes at the state and local level to influence land use plans and infrastructure project designs by public agencies. This is exactly what is necessary to reduce the risk of what Bruce Babbitt has called "national train wrecks" under the ESA when policy is not made until there are apparently irreconcilable conflicts between the economy and the environment. The Clinton administration endorsed use of the NCCP system in March 1993 by giving the gnatcatcher a special listing as a threatened rather than an endangered species (California Department of Fish and Game 1993). Without the NCCP, the more stringent standards of the ESA would have applied to thousands of acres of prime Southern California real estate. The state and federal governments—one led by a Republican, the other by a Democrat—joined together to try an experiment in the gnatcatcher's case in the belief that the economy and the environment were not necessarily in conflict. While the effort was made rather late in the gnatcatcher's case, it followed the adage that "an ounce of prevention is worth a pound of cure," nonetheless. This elevates the importance of good planning at the outset.

Good planning requires good information, however. Lacking good information, we invariably make decisions without understanding the consequences of our actions. The essence of decision-making is the evaluation of information; therefore, decisions tend to rely on whatever information is available. Many of our current environmental problems can be traced to a lack of critical information at the time of decision. In other cases, of course, decisions were and are still made with full knowledge of the negative environmental consequences. One of the foundational principles of the environmental impact assessment (EIA) provisions of both NEPA and CEQA is that information will improve decision-making. Neither NEPA nor CEQA is brought to bear until a specific project has been defined, however, and by that stage in the process a public agency is usually facing a "build or don't build" or an "approve or don't approve" decision. This then creates a stark choice for decision makers, where protecting environmental quality often appears to require significant sacrifices or economic costs. The only options appear to be either to degrade environmental quality, impose costly mitigation measures, or force the abandonment of a project. As Bob Twiss notes, there is a "cone of diminishing flexibility" as one moves through time in the planning process: the earlier that information is considered in the process, the more flexibility there is to respond to it by modifying the project to reduce or mitigate the negative environmental effects (1991). Unfortunately, since application of NEPA and CEQA generally occurs late in that process, by the time a project is undergoing an EIA the economic costs of changing the project are great and the flexibility to modify it is relatively small.

Part of the problem is that the EIA process has become the primary means of generating information for both project review and general planning purposes (Landis et al. 1995). Rather than systematically collect information that can then inform project design early in the planning process, we more typically design the project and *then* collect information about its possible effects. Not surprisingly, there are often negative environmental results and significant social conflicts over development projects. Information about most environmental resources is spotty, with the most detailed information available only where a full-scale EIA has been completed. Moreover, even long-range planning efforts by local and state governments sometimes depend on current development for funding. Not surprisingly, this has created an inherent conflict of interest between objective evaluation of the environmental consequences of development and the need to keep the planning department operating. Planning and EIA consultants also face a conflict, for their livelihood also depends on continued development (and the required EIA). This has resulted in some notable cases of "biostitution" (derived from the word *prostitution*), where some consultants willingly violate professional standards and scientific criteria when paid enough.[39] Apparently they believe they will lose their business or job if they tell the truth.[40]

In some cases, however, this lack of information for planning and evaluation is not the result of funding limitations or an inability to find qualified professional consultants. It may simply be that politically powerful individuals do not want public agency staff to generate information that could later be used to reduce the potential for windfall profits at public or environmental expense. In these cases, planners are sometimes explicitly told *not* to "look under the rock." We all may suspect that something important is under the rock, and we all may have a pretty good idea of what will come crawling out if we lift it up to look. But to do so would end the free ride that politically powerful individuals may now enjoy, creating a strong disincentive to generating information about what is under the rock. "It is an adage of California planning law," a rural county planner once said to me, "that your General Plan is adequate until somebody sues you and a court finds it inadequate."[41] We therefore often pretend to be "planning" without fully understanding the consequences of our decisions, as long as nobody is willing to challenge the General Plan and force local planners to "look under the rock."

The absence of good, reliable, consistently accepted information about the state of the Sierra Nevada reflects a combination of these factors. The resulting deficiency of information has also clearly been an impediment to policy analysis and decision-making, for there is little agreement on some basic questions: How much old-growth forest is left in the Sierra? How many people are employed in the timber industry in the Sierra? How many people rely on recreation and tourism? How frequently did fire occur in different areas of the Sierra before active fire suppression? How did Native Americans manage fire to promote acorn production? What effect will another doubling of the Sierra population likely have on water quality? Tom Knudson laid out one interpretation of some of these questions in the "Sierra in Peril," and the Sierra Now conference took the position that the Range of Light did indeed face a crisis (Environment Now 1993). The organizers of the Sierra Economic Summit and the Sierra Communities Council disagreed, however, arguing that the Sierra Nevada had never been healthier and that the real threat to ecosystem health was stricter environmental regulations that reduced commodity production (Nevada County Business Association and California

Forestry Association 1993; Sierra Communities Council 1993). In testimony to Congress, the Forest Service, Wilderness Society, and Sierran Biodiversity Institute offered widely diverging estimates of the extent and characteristics of remaining old-growth forests (F. Davis 1996). Who was right? More important, how could Congress, the Forest Service, the state, or local governments make decisions in the absence of generally agreed upon scientific information?

This problem is not unique to the Sierra Nevada. Researchers with the Fish and Wildlife Service confronted it in the late 1980s, when they frequently faced the nearly impossible challenge of trying to save threatened and endangered species after all of the species' critical habitat was either in private hands or had been irreparably damaged by public management decisions. Nobody had ever systematically determined what types of habitat were in public versus private ownership, or whether the habitat within public ownership was protected from intensive and extensive development activities. Beginning in Idaho, the Fish and Wildlife Service initiated the "Gap Analysis Program" (GAP) in the late 1980s to identify gaps in public ownership of critical habitats (Scott et al. 1991). The program also sought to determine which public lands had the highest value for protection of native biological diversity. Those lands that could protect a wide range of potentially threatened or endangered species, for example, presumably had higher value than those that might protect only a single species in the same total land area. The total costs of maintaining biodiversity could be minimized by identifying these high-priority areas and encouraging responsible public agencies (though usually not the Fish and Wildlife Service) to manage them for protection. The Idaho pilot project was then expanded in the early 1990s with an intention to include the entire country (eventually) through the new National Biological Survey (NBS).

Simply creating an inventory like this should improve the likelihood that public lands would be managed to play a prominent role in the protection of biodiversity. This in turn should reduce the need to restrict activities on private lands. Ironically, the Wise Use movement opposed establishment of the NBS on the grounds that it threatened private property rights. If anything, a systematic inventory of all public and private lands should *reduce* the negative economic and social consequences of applying the ESA late in Twiss's "cone of diminishing flexibility." This parallels the establishment of the United States Geological Survey in 1879, which developed information fundamental to the settlement of the country and development of its resources (Stegner 1954). The NBS was modeled in many ways on the U.S. Geological Survey, another agency within Bruce Babbitt's Department of the Interior. Unfortunately, the Republican-controlled Congress elected in 1994 enacted drastic reductions in both the scale and the scope of activities by both of these information-generating agencies. These budget cutbacks for science in all federal land and resource management agencies have delayed the completion of the GAP, and the new GOP Congress allocated funds for NBS efforts with the limitation that no funds "be used to conduct new surveys on private property unless specifically authorized in writing by the property owner."[42] This has restricted data-gathering and analysis. The NBS has subsequently been eliminated as a separate agency and it now resides within the U.S. Geological Survey as the Biological Resources Division. Babbitt's vision of a comprehensive survey has been downsized dramatically.

While valuable, the GAP analysis remains a broad-scale inventory that does not offer detailed enough information to answer some of the policy questions facing decision makers in the Sierra Nevada. Moreover, an inventory and simple identification of gaps in public coverage of key habitats does not include an evaluation of the present, historical, or likely future conditions or causes for those conditions in the ecosystems of the Sierra Nevada. In late 1992, Congress therefore called for a scientific study of old-growth forests in the Sierra Nevada and appropriated $150,000 for it.[43] Another bill, which was read into the record but not passed by either house, called for a much more comprehensive study of the entire Sierra Nevada.[44] The embattled chief of the federal Forest Service, Dale Robertson, then committed another $7 million of Forest Service research funds over a three-year period to establish the Sierra Nevada Ecosystem Project (SNEP) (Sierra Nevada Ecosystem Project 1994; Aune 1995). This commitment represented a major step by the Forest Service toward generating the information base necessary to implement ecosystem management.[45] There are other significant impediments to implementing the concept, of course, but SNEP was a response to the Sierra Summit's identified need for better information about the Sierra Nevada. It represents an investment in intellectual capital.

The final SNEP report was issued in June 1996 in a four-volume set totaling more than three thousand pages. It represents the most comprehensive and systematic assessment of the Sierra Nevada to date, and the SNEP work serves as the foundation for much of the analytic and substantive content of my own work.[46] Most important, the establishment of an *independent* science team allowed SNEP to "look under the rock" without political constraints.

This now permits the policy debate on the Sierra Nevada to proceed from a common base of knowledge—although interpretations of that knowledge still vary. Those interpretations depend on a theoretical framework that influences how we filter information, but the framework is usually not explicitly delineated. The next chapter will outline the key theoretical ideas that I will use to interpret both SNEP's findings and the complex social dynamics that have led to and responded to SNEP. My focus will be on the relevance of social and ecological theories to the problem of managing rapid population growth in the Sierra Nevada while protecting social, ecological, and economic values.

/\/\\/\

CHAPTER TWO

Theoretical Foundations

What is the shift in resource-management paradigms? Simply put, we are now called upon to manage complex and still poorly understood systems in the light of an unknown future in ways that do not reduce the ability of future generations to do the same thing. Biodiversity may be used as a measure of the options open to future generations.

Gregory B. Greenwood, 1995

Over the many years that I have worked on this book, I at first presumed that better information would lead to better decisions.[1] I implicitly defined *better* to mean leading to outcomes that did not degrade the things I valued, so my values are an important part of the equation. More specifically, I thought that our failure to mitigate the negative effects of growth was the result of an inability to understand the negative consequences of our actions. My experience since then has revealed political power as a critical determinant of whether, how, and when information is used in decision-making.

In this regard I have relied on a theory developed by John R. Logan and Harvey L. Molotch in their 1987 book, *Urban Fortunes: The Political Economy of Place*, which builds on Molotch's 1976 theory of "growth machines." Logan and Molotch focus on the social dynamics of urban environments as they undergo growth and change, but their framework also applies to rapidly growing rural communities facing urbanization pressures. They argue that the fundamental conflict in urban sociology is one between "use" and "exchange" values, where the market values associated with land as a commodity (exchange values) contrast with the broader role of specific places as socially situated contexts for a variety of other life functions (use values).[2] They also argue that land is "a special sort of commodity: a place to be bought and sold, rented and leased, as well as used for making a life" and that "locational conflicts" are traceable to "commodification" of "the communal living space." As they emphasize, "markets are social phenomena," and "the fundamental attributes of all commodities, but particularly of land and buildings, are the social contexts through which they are used and exchanged" (1–3). I follow in this tradition of focusing on the social context of growth.

Logan and Molotch argue that the Chicago school of human ecology, which posits "an interest-driven social construction of cities," is inadequate to explain urban sociology because theoretical approaches claiming that *interests* organize markets "ignore that markets themselves are the result of cultures." Marxian approaches are also inadequate, however, for they emphasize class interests to the point that "the only actors who matter . . . are the corporate capitalists." Instead, Logan and Molotch offer a model of locational conflict predicated on the existence of growth machines that represent coalitions of interests who use government as a vehicle for advancing an ideological context for policy debate as well as specific policies to create benefits through growth. "Although growth is often portrayed as beneficial to all residents of all places," they note, "in reality the advantages and disadvantages of growth are unevenly distributed." These distributional consequences are at the heart of land use conflicts. Logan and Molotch then highlight how various actors in the growth debate attempt to influence that distribution (4, 9, 11, 13).

Real estate markets have three unique features that encourage specific types of actions:

> "place is indispensable; all human activity must occur somewhere" (17);
> "the stakes involved in the relationship to place can be high," because "place is . . . not a discrete element" due to its relationship to how other commodities will be used—including other places (18);
> "land markets are inherently monopolistic" because "the quantity is fixed by place" when "every parcel of land is unique in the idiosyncratic access it provides to other parcels and uses" (23).

The result is that exchange values are determined primarily by the *spatial structure* of the city, which in turn is subject to manipulation and influence by government action: "Property prices go down as well as up, but less because of what entrepreneurs do with their own holdings than because of the changing relations among properties. This dynamic accounts for much of the energy of the urban system as . . . entrepreneurs strive to increase their rent by revamping the spatial organization of the city" (ibid.).

Logan and Molotch acknowledge that "property owners can and do alter the content of their holdings" through development, but they argue that "new construction has less bearing on market dynamics than such reasoning would imply" (24–25). This is the result of both the unique features of real estate cited above and the low fraction of all land that is on the market at any one time. In fact, they demonstrate that increased rates of housing construction generally translate into *higher* housing costs (establishing a new, higher equilibrium price in the exchange market) even after accounting for demand factors. Growth therefore increases prices generally while differentially increasing the values of some properties in relationship to the others.

"Government activity," argue Logan and Molotch, "distributes and redistributes rents among owners" through infrastructure investments and regulatory decisions. "Such institutional involvement in the use and exchange of place is endemic to human settlement" and "can be traced at least as far back as the English enclosure laws, which ushered in the Industrial Revolution, the modern state, and the property commodity" (28). Growth machines in the American context "are historical, dating from frontier America, but take different forms and have different impacts depending upon time and context" (13). My work seeks to explore the dynamics of growth machines and their interaction with the broader community—including those who organize in resistance to the growth machine—in the context of rapidly growing rural communities over the past three decades. Although it is only one region and one time, my case study leads me to expand on Logan and Molotch's framework to reflect the conditions encountered in that case.

Logan and Molotch identify three types of entrepreneurs who benefit from growth: 1) "Serendipitous Entrepreneurs" (who are not really entrepreneurs at all, but inherit their land or otherwise inadvertently gain value from growth); 2) "Active Entrepreneurs" (who "seek out the right place to be in the future" and depend on their good forecasting skill in order to acquire lands at low prices and realize speculative gains; and 3) "Structural Speculators" (who "seek to alter the conditions that structure the market. Their strategy is to *create* differential rents by influencing the larger arena of decision making that will determine locational advantage") (29–30). Logan and Molotch go on to say, "Among the entrepreneurial types, the structural speculators are the most important; their behaviors reverberate through every aspect of the urban scene. People out to structure markets tend not to work in isolation; they work together in organized groups" (31–32).

The structural speculators work together with other pro-growth interests and governmental representatives to become what Logan and Molotch call a growth machine. The members of the growth machine share important values as well as interests regarding land use regulation: "They unite behind the doctrine of value-free development—the notion that free markets alone should determine land use. In the entrepreneur's view, land-use regulation endangers both society at large and the specific localities favored as production sites" (ibid.). Not all members of the community benefit from growth, however, and this generates conflict. The economic dimension of how these benefits and costs are distributed is discussed below, but our immediate concern in the Sierra Nevada is with the political consequence: growth machines sometimes generate a counterforce of citizen organizations focused on use values. The case study of Nevada County's planning process shows how just this sort of counterorganization has emerged in the Sierra Nevada to emphasize use values. I argue here that the broader approach to economic analysis below shows that these use values are still economic, however, even if they do not always translate into exchange values. This distinction must be recognized in order to develop institutional responses to growth conflicts that are "win-win" rather than "zero sum."

Logan and Molotch critique the neoclassical argument that people can simply move if they no longer "prefer" the resulting environment,[3] arguing that there are significant constraints on individual mobility as a result of the fact that "ordinary people's resources are too small to easily carry them through the uncertainty of migration, and their residential use values, important for survival, are tied to a particular setting" (40). The result is that people stay and fight change rather than move from one community "product" to another, as consumers might in a commodity market for other goods or services. Places therefore "achieve their reality through social organization in the pursuit of use and exchange values," and "there is nothing necessarily optimizing in the purposive and conflictual strategies by which this process goes on" (43). This helps to explain the intense emotion found in most land use conflicts over growth.

Like Logan and Molotch, Thomas K. Rudel finds ecological theories of urban development (which argue that political activities have little influence, because patterns and processes of development are driven by location and technology) deficient because of their failure to account for political-economic factors. Among the prevailing political-economic theories of urban development, however, he finds both Manuel Castells's "arenas for collective consumption" model (where conflict can be explained as between consumptive classes) and neo-Marxian models (which describe a capitalist development faction in conflict with an urban proletariat, which is defending the neighborhoods) to be deficient in their treatment of developers. The neo-Marxian models also fail to explain the behavior of elite homeowners (as opponents of growth) and the variable degrees and types of interactions that occur in locational conflicts. Rudel finds potential insight in the many case studies of the historical development process that exist, but their contribution is limited by their emphasis on context-specific factors and lack of variation in their underlying communities (they are generally of large cities). Finally, he suggests that emerging theories of collective action (discussed more below) highlight the importance of the *sequence* of actions in any relationship as a critical determinant of individual behavior toward others. He therefore develops a research design to remedy these deficiencies.

He does so by taking Molotch's original framework an important step further by asking the next question: what type of social conflict emerges between growth machines and local residents in different contexts, and what factors explain differences in those relationships? His 1989 book, *Situations and Strategies in American*

Land-Use Planning, develops a successional model of social control, where cities use one of the following methods depending on their context as a function of their relationship to the metropolitan economy and their internal social dynamics:

> *Bilateral relational controls:* for slow-growing rural areas, where spillover effects are minor as a result of low densities and the fact that most landowners have an interest in retaining flexibility to change their own land uses in the future.
>
> *Rules:* for rapidly growing rural areas, where spillover effects are increasingly likely as a result of higher densities, but where many landowners still have an interest in retaining flexibility to change their own land uses in the future. The rules are not necessarily enforced unless there are complaints, which in turn usually come from new residential landowners primarily interested in land use stability.
>
> *Trilateral controls:* in slow-growing urban places, where there is less undeveloped land and existing uses are more stable. The increased likelihood of spillover effects from changed land uses combines with increased political power for parties that will not benefit from change, leading to irreconcilable conflicts that must be resolved by a third party, such as the judicial system.

Social control through bilateral relational systems depends on individual-to-individual interactions, where landowners may complain to each other if a changed use is likely to lead to spillover effects. Each actor in the bilateral exchange will in turn consider the dispute in the context of a broad range of other relationships, where the complainee may want to gain the favor of the complainer at some point in the future. Resolution of these disputes, if the parties expect to have an ongoing relationship, will therefore be characterized by both accommodation and tolerance. It is typified by the "live and let live" attitude described by Robert Ellickson in his 1991 book, *Order without Law: How Neighbors Settle Disputes,* a study of how rural residents in Shasta County, California, handled cattle trespass under two different legal regimes.[4] Ellickson quotes Donald Black as saying that "law varies inversely with other social control" (Black 1976, 176), and Ellickson's case study shows that Shasta County residents use a variety of nonlegal forms of social control to influence the behavior of anyone generating spillover effects from their activities. In fact, their reliance on these other forms often depends on the existence of unwritten rules that establish social norms and expectations. I will discuss rule-based systems of social control in more detail below, but for now let us continue with Rudel's typology of communities.

Rudel argues that rapidly growing rural communities rely increasingly on rules over bilateral relations, since the likelihood of conflict increases with greater density and an increasing share of landowners who prefer stability to change in their property expectations. These rules do not necessarily require legal codification, although one would expect that at a more advanced stage of this process. They may also not be enforced consistently or to the letter of the law except in circumstances where there is a complaint about a spillover effect. Rule-based systems can therefore take a variety of forms and coexist with bilateral relational controls. As Ellickson found in Shasta County, informal rules may be more important than law. This is also consistent with the evolution of land use planning in the Nevada County case.

Growth invariably increases social conflict, however, as density and the likelihood of spillover effects for any proposed land use change also increase. Moreover, the land likely to be affected by any land use change is probably inhabited by residents who prefer stability in their land use expectations. Those who want flexibility for future land use conversion become a small minority. Unlike the sparsely populated rural community, the landowners have fewer ongoing relational ties to each other and so are less likely to consider a specific conflict over land use change in the context of a broader set of conflicts, debts, opportunities, and interdependencies. It is also nearly impossible to write rules adequate to address the full range of potential conflicts without relying on third parties for interpretation. As a result, conflicts in this social context are difficult to resolve through either bilateral relational controls or rules, and trilateral controls are required: a third party must resolve the conflict by interpreting the rules in light of the situation-specific factors at issue. This often translates into legal institutions and formal conflict resolution by the courts, although it can also take the form of decision-making by government agencies. (Depending on the scale of the community and influence of the stakeholders on the decision makers, however, the local planning commission or city council may base its decisions on a wide range of factors beyond the formalized rules ostensibly guiding decision-making. In smaller communities, for example, personal relationships between those involved in a conflict and the formal decision makers may be quite important. This is certainly true in Nevada County.)

Under these conditions the institutional context for third-party decision-making may be as critical as the internal dynamics of the community. Courts, for example, base decisions primarily on legal rules tied to statute and precedent rather than local political power. City councils, however, may be under the control of and part of the growth machine and therefore more likely to favor exchange over use values. The specific institutional context of the trilateral decision-making authority is therefore a critical determinant of both power relations within the community and the desirability of trilateral control. Some parties (e.g., wealthy residents concerned about use values) may prefer outside venues because of their effect on power dynamics, while others (e.g., poorer residents concerned about use values) may be disadvantaged by the economic, technical, or legal resources necessary for participation in them.

TABLE 2.1   Relationship between Density, Growth Rate,
Conflict, and Social Control

Location and land market	Slow-growing rural areas	Fast-growing urban-rural fringe	Slow-growing if declining areas in the metropolitan core
Average density	Low		High
Land use	Less specialized		More specialized and intense
Conflict over land use	Low incidence over land use change		High incidence over land use change
Land use controls	Bilateral relational	Rule-based	Trilateral relational

SOURCE: Rudel 1989, p. 30. Used with permission.

Rudel offers "richer" and "poorer" variations on each of these three themes, leading to nine major classes of communities as a function of wealth, location, and land market characteristics. He then characterizes a series of variables (extent of developed land, land users, developers, landscape, conflict, and land-use control) along a continuum to describe the social and physical conditions of these communities. This framework allows him to establish hypotheses about these patterns and then to select communities within which to test those hypotheses in the dimensions he has selected. He notes in his opening pages that the existing literature on growth machines and forms of social control is limited by the lack of case studies along the full range of variables. He therefore used the variables to select four case-study communities in Connecticut for further study. These dimensions are summarized in Table 2.1.

The case studies led Rudel to add two additional variables to his original specification: 1) the timing of development in relationship to development in other places (because rule-based systems and trilateral controls may be diffused from urban areas to rural areas earlier than otherwise expected); and 2) the organization of local government (in terms of how the proportion of affected landowners for any given spillover effect is a function of both jurisdictional scale and the heterogeneity of interests represented, which he hypothesized were positively correlated with each other). The most rural areas, in other words, are less likely to rely primarily on bilateral relational controls if they developed late in comparison to other areas, which would export their rule-based and trilateral control systems to the latecomers. Larger cities, however, are more likely to diminish the influence of antigrowth groups as a result of the smaller representation of those groups within the community and the decreased likelihood that their concerns are widely shared by others (because the spillover effects are localized within the larger community). Both of these additions are relevant to my study of growth and change in the Sierra Nevada.

Rudel relied on a cross-sectional sample to test his hypotheses, while my case study of the Sierra Nevada represents a longitudinal study of a region that includes communities representing all three stages over time (in Nevada County), as well as all three stages at one time (over space across the entire Sierra Nevada). For this reason it offers an opportunity to understand the dynamics of the transition from one form of social control to another. My study also shows that the dynamics of growth in rural communities are consistent with Logan and Molotch's growth machine model, but future projections of social dynamics must be modified to account for both emerging theories of collective action and institutional innovation and the specific forces driving the reverse migration and the growth of exurbia. Let us therefore examine the latter in order to better understand how the social context of the Sierra Nevada is changing.

REVERSE MIGRATION AND THE GROWTH OF EXURBIA

The influx of new exurban residents to the Sierra Nevada, together with the transformation of rural economies, has resulted in more diversified economic and social systems that are part rural and part urban, or exurban. These exurban communities are characterized by economic activity usually associated with urban settings but also by social relations typically associated with rural areas. This new condition has implications for both the physical and cultural landscapes of previously rural areas. These changes can also transform the economic and political power relationships within rural communities and between those communities and extraregional, state, national, or global systems of power (Nelson 1992; Zukin 1991; Duane 1992b). Arthur C. Nelson offers a comprehensive discussion of exurban regions in his 1992 article "Characterizing Exurbia." The term first appeared in a 1955 book called *The Exurbanites,* which described a group of people living farther out in the metropolitan orbit than existing rail lines (Spectorsky 1955). *Webster's New World Dictionary* first offered a definition of the exurbs in 1972: "a region, generally semi-rural, beyond the suburbs of a city, inhabited by persons in the upper income group . . . commuting to the city as . . . business or professional person[s]" (Nelson 1992). That definition appeared just as rapid growth pressure accelerated in the Sierra Nevada foothills of California. Most writers emphasize exurbanites' economic dependence on nearby metropolitan areas accessible via daily automobile commute (ibid.; Joseph and Smit 1981). This theme is repeated in Nelson's 1994 paper coauthored with Thomas Sanchez, in which they suggest that exurbanization may simply be an expansion and extension of suburbanization (Sanchez and Nelson 1994). Resolving this issue is of central importance to our understanding of the factors driving rapid nonmetropolitan population growth, for it influences our interpretation of the relative importance of different types of economic values to local economic well-being. Relevant data have generally been too aggregated to allow a definitive conclusion, however, since counties (especially in the West) are generally large. Many different types of communities and economic activities may therefore be dispersed throughout a county, making it a heterogeneous unit. My analysis below will show that counties are a poor basis for understanding either the Sierra Nevada or exurban growth processes and patterns.

Emphasis on the need to commute to metropolitan employment on some regular basis reflects to some degree the metropolitan orientation of academic departments of city and regional or urban planning.[5] This interpretation is also predicated in part on an industrial model of economic activity, but it may not be an accurate characterization in a postindustrial information economy. It also reflects some strong evidence that the boom in nonmetropolitan population growth has been most pronounced near existing metropolitan areas, however, so we should not discount the importance of proximity to metropolitan regions as a critical driving force in the growth of exurbia. The west-central Sierra Nevada counties of Nevada, Placer, and El Dorado accounted for 40 percent of population growth in the Sierra Region from 1970 to 1990, and those counties each have a significant population of commuters to the greater Sacramento metropolitan area. Expansion of that metropolitan area will tend over time to include portions of those counties, just as suburban regions in the past were once small towns or rural areas. In fact, increases in population density in these three counties are highly correlated with increases in population density in Sacramento County. Population growth in Sacramento County, in turn, is highly correlated with population growth trends in the greater San Francisco Bay Area. This reflects the phenomenal growth in California's population in the twentieth century. On average it doubled roughly every twenty years through 1970, and the state added 10 million more people (a 50 percent increase) from 1970 to 1990 (Teitz 1990; Bradshaw and Muller 1994). With such growth rates, metropolitan influences were bound to reach into the Sierra Nevada.

But exurban growth is not limited to areas within commuting distance of metropolitan areas. The total land area affected by exurban growth is also not necessarily dominated by commuters. Moreover, as I describe below, a series of trends begun in the 1970s and 1980s has now converged to reduce the need for *physical* proximity while retaining the need for some type of *economic* integration with metropolitan areas. The "space of flows" (economic, social, cultural, and informational) becomes central to the cultural and economic geography of a region: its ties to other regions (and even its own sense of place) are no longer constrained by physical geography (Castells 1989; 1996). Exurban regions can therefore have economic and cultural links to metropolitan centers and the global economy even when well beyond commuting distance. Nonspatial "communities" of interest and identity may then become more important determinants of economic and social relationships than one's physical location. The Internet and cyberspace could replace the car and the town square or boardroom for some people and some functions. This has the potential to promote further growth in exurban areas without physical proximity to metropolitan areas. At the same time, of course, limited access to new technologies could further isolate some rural areas from the economic mainstream.

Nelson has estimated that approximately one-fourth of all American residents lived in exurban counties in 1985, and that those exurban counties accounted for nearly 30 percent of all population growth between 1965 and 1985. He also estimated that the land area of those counties covered nearly a third of the United States. This shift toward an exurban growth pattern appears to have accelerated since 1985. As Nelson notes, however, this assessment at the county level was limited by the structure of census data available at the time of his analysis. Many counties include subareas that are urban, suburban, exurban, and rural, making it difficult to associate the gross land area of the county categories cited above with the net land area that may reflect an exurban pattern of settlement. This is particularly true in the western United States, where counties are generally much larger in area than those found in other parts of the country. Placer County, for example, is classified as metropolitan by the Census Bureau because it has one city (Roseville) with a population greater than fifty thousand persons. Roseville is outside of the Sierra Nevada proper, however, and it is doubtful that the presence of Roseville within the jurisdictional boundaries of Placer County makes Squaw Valley near northern Lake Tahoe part of the Sacramento metropolitan region. Portions of El Dorado County are much closer to Sacramento in terms of commuting times, yet the entire county was classified as nonmetropolitan in the 1990 census. Further spatial analysis of the census data is necessary to determine actual patterns of density and sprawl and the relationship between growth in urban, rural, and exurban areas. Differentiation between different types of exurban growth patterns is also necessary.[6] My disaggregation of county-level data (described below) allows assessment of the phenomenon of exurban development in the Sierra Nevada with less interference from spillover data from metropolitan centers within or adjacent to Sierra Nevada counties. It can also help resolve the debate over whether a true reverse migration is occurring that is not simply suburban development in formerly nonmetropolitan counties.

Whether or not the historical pattern of rural-to-urban migration in the United States has been reversed in *aggregate* for the country, *net* statistics for migration between rural and urban or metropolitan and nonmetropolitan regions do not reveal the uneven distribution of population growth within and among rural areas. As suggested by the commuter-oriented perspective on exurban growth, many of the nonmetropolitan counties showing rapid growth in the 1970 to 1990 period were contiguous to suburban counties that were part of an adjacent metropolitan region. Many of the other nonmetropolitan regions that grew rapidly during this period were quite distant from metropolitan regions and were adjacent to large areas of contiguous public lands. These are areas generally judged to have scenic amenities, clean air, and ready access to recreational opportunities. Many other rural areas—in particular, those with one-dimensional economies that depend on agriculture, forestry, or mineral extraction—are continuing to experience the historical pattern of *decline*, masking the emergence of an exodus from urban areas to exurban regions offering amenities. The exodus to exurbia therefore appears to be associated with both a classic process of suburbanization *and* an ongoing transformation of rural economies from a commodities-oriented, natural resource-extractive industrial base to a services-oriented, amenity-driven base. Even as aggregate national statistics show a slowdown of urban-to-rural growth, growth continues rapidly in many desirable small towns and nonmetropolitan areas not adjacent to metropolitan areas.

Moreover, as Kenneth Johnson notes, it is important to distinguish between natural increase and migration as a source of changes in the total population of a region. Many agriculture-dependent regions had significantly greater gross emigration than the net migration figures show. The migration patterns were masked by relatively high natural increases, which have historically been greater in rural than urban areas (1993).

The broad reverse migration from urban to rural areas was first identified by demographer Calvin Beale in 1975 and confirmed by the 1980 census. The 1980 census showed that, for the first time in American history, nonmetropolitan areas had grown faster than metropolitan areas during the previous decade. This so-called rural renaissance brought great hope to residents and planners in many rural areas that had experienced consistent decline throughout the previous century. A general sense of opportunity in rural areas came from this macro-level reading of the census data: rural areas might have more economic opportunities in the 1980s. The 1990 census, however, showed that urban areas had again grown faster than rural areas, and the serious economic difficulties of many agriculture-dependent regions highlighted how short-lived and illusory the rural renaissance had been for many areas.[7] Many planners concluded that the population redistribution in the 1970s was just an aberration. Others argued that the apparent reverse migration was merely a statistical anomaly resulting from either reclassification of counties from rural to urban between the 1970 and 1980 censuses or spillover growth from metropolitan regions to adjacent nonmetropolitan counties. This interpretation argued that the historical rural-to-urban migration pattern still held, but that there had been a shift *within* metropolitan regions to the outlying urban edge. The evidence also showed, however, that the counterurbanization pattern held even when "adjacency" was controlled: rural counties not adjacent to metropolitan areas also experienced net in-migration. This debate and the difficulty of differentiating rural from urban counties led to a number of recommendations for reformation of the Census Bureau's definitions of rural and urban areas to avoid the problem of "moving targets" every ten years (Lang 1986; Nelson 1992). Nelson argued in 1992 that the Census Bureau should go even further and categorize counties as either urban, rural, or exurban.

Not all exurban areas are alike, however, and it is important to distinguish characteristics among nonmetropolitan regions. Nelson's suggestion is important in order to break out of the urban/rural dichotomy, but it runs the risk of lumping all exurban regions together. As I suggested earlier, the rural renaissance has continued unabated for most amenity-oriented regions—while it may never have really existed for regions that continued to rely on agriculture or extractive industries for economic development. This distinction among rural areas may be much more important to rural development than the gross statistical shift from urban to rural areas identified in the 1970s. Just as movements within metropolitan regions have dramatically changed the planning challenge for urban America, differential rural development patterns call for different strategies in different rural areas. The problem is that both the census data and researchers have often lumped together all rural or exurban areas, making it difficult to identify the source of rapid growth in some areas. Judith Davis and her colleagues make an important contribution to our understanding of exurbia with their distinction between rural, small town, and exurban land use patterns and residents in their study near Portland, but their analysis addresses only the social, demographic, economic, and commuting characteristics of these "types" (Davis et al. 1994). I go further here by also exploring the range of land use patterns emerging in the exurban landscape, their potential implications for social, economic, and ecological well-being, and policy mechanisms for managing exurban growth.

FACTORS DRIVING THE EXODUS TO EXURBIA

Dominant theories of economic development in rural regions generally predict that rapid growth will occur primarily as a result of expansion of resource extraction in those areas (Power 1996a). I use the term *dominant* to refer to the social role of these theories within the context of rural communities and the social construction of economic development that dominates discourse within those communities. (Economic development specialists in academia may have long since rejected these theories, but they still dominate local discourse.) This reflects a "base" view of the economy where exports of primary commodities are believed to be the foundation for all local economic activity. Indeed, this appears to be what drove population growth in most rural and exurban regions before the 1970s. Some economic expansion of extractive industries did occur for subperiods of the 1970s and 1980s (e.g., the western slope Rocky Mountain energy boom of the late 1970s and early 1980s; the increase in timber harvesting in the Pacific Northwest during the mid- to late 1980s), but these industries generally *decreased* their employment over the 1970–90 period. Some of this decrease was associated with improved labor productivity and consolidation of operations, while some was driven by contraction of production (caused by either market forces or environmental restrictions). In either case, however, those communities that grew the fastest generally grew despite the *decline* of employment and total wages or income in the extractive sectors. An extraction boom was therefore generally *not* driving population growth. Timber-dependent communities were the slowest-growing areas in the Sierra Nevada, for example, while rapidly growing areas decreased timber-sector employment. Something else was driving the exodus to exurbia.

If not the extractive industry, what was the economic foundation for this growth? What allowed people to move to these areas, and why did they choose to move there in the 1970s and 1980s? Unlike the traditional resource-extractive base of these rural areas, the subtle yet profound transformation of the 1970s and 1980s was based on increasing recognition of the *amenity* value of natural resources (Moss 1987; Price et al. 1997). In some situations this has made resources more valuable in situ than they would be if extracted and exported as commodities for sale in the urban marketplace. This new valuation reflects a broad social change in the environmental values of Americans that has simultaneously challenged traditional approaches to land and resource management over the past three decades. The new values are nevertheless not yet reflected in many of the public land and resource management policies of federal, state, or local agencies. As a result, traditional approaches to land and resource management often conflict with emerging local values as the transformation continues through amenity-driven migration and economic diversification of the exurban landscape.

The following factors have converged recently to fuel the exodus to exurbia:

Quality of life preferences: Americans have always indicated a preference for small towns and rural lifestyles in surveys but have generally settled in urban areas because of the greater range of economic opportunities. As Nelson notes, "The latent desire of Americans for the Jeffersonian rural life-style drives exurban development" (1992, 352; Carlino 1985; Elazar 1987). As a result of the factors outlined below, "the latent preference can now be expressed" (Nelson 1992, 352; Blackwood and Carpenter 1978). Against this background—of American *preferences* for rural regions and small-town living—exurbia has boomed.[8] Many Americans clearly prefer metropolitan life, but they remain a minority of the population except in the case of young, single individuals. Most would prefer to live in a small town or rural area if they could find meaningful work there that provided an adequate income to maintain their lifestyle. Indeed, these same preferences have driven the suburbanization of the American landscape within metropolitan regions (Jackson 1985).

Deconcentration of metropolitan employment: The shape and extent of the American metropolis have changed dramatically since World War II and the initial investments in the interstate highway system a decade later, and these changes have clearly affected the desirability and feasibility of exurban development. In part the exurban growth of the 1970s and 1980s simply reflected the expansion of the American population and economy during the 1950s and 1960s, which created new opportunities to live in the country while working in the city. More important, however, deconcentration of employment within metropolitan regions shifted commercial development to the periphery during the 1970s and 1980s. This put many exurban locations within commuting distance of new employment opportunities (Garreau 1991; Cervero 1986; 1991; 1993). Completion of the interstate highway system had a profound effect on the expansion of the metropolitan sphere, because development in distant "greenfield" landscapes was heavily subsidized by the federal government. Doubling the radius of potential commute range *quadruples* the total area that can be settled within that range, opening up the exurban landscape to settlement as a result of the accessibility of fringe metropolitan economic activity.

Information technologies: The microchip and personal computer have diminished the need for traditional forms of organizational structure and eliminated the need to have a large critical mass of resources in order to take advantage of economies of scale in information management. What could once be done only by a large corporation with a specialized data processing department can now be accomplished by an individual with a thousand-dollar personal computer. This has opened up the structure of business, creating new opportunities for smaller groups. Independent employment opportunities also have been reinforced by corporate and governmental downsizing and increasing reliance on outsourcing work to off-payroll contractors in the 1990s—thereby eliminating the costs of benefits and overhead from the primary company's production costs. In some cases these small groups and individuals—no longer dependent on employment in the downtown headquarters of a major corporation—have then chosen to relocate based on other criteria.

Telecommunications technologies: The computer modem, facsimile machine, cellular phone, and cable or satellite television have made it possible to sever many of the historical relationships between economic activity and location. Just as the personal computer allowed individuals to analyze data without relying on the corporate bureaucracy, these technologies allow the analysis to be completed anywhere within communications range. The establishment of Federal Express has made small towns in rural areas just as "close" to markets as urban areas. Moreover, access to cultural material that was historically available only in urban areas—such as timely news, opera or symphony, and major league sporting events—is now possible with satellite dish or cable television. One no longer need live in an urban area to gain many of its amenities and access to its wide choices and specialized consumer markets.[9]

Globalization of the economy: The expansion of global markets and the relative decline of American dominance of the domestic market have combined to create new opportunities for business outside the United States. This means that an increasing share of business is done with customers far from domestic urban centers—making it less necessary to be in those urban centers than it was when the customer base was primarily located in the nearby region. One may need to be based in New York if all of one's customers are there, but if one's customers are spread from New York to London to Tokyo, one can just as well be in a small town in the Sierra Nevada. Access to an airport for occasional business trips is all that is necessary.

Shift from manufacturing to services: Just as globalization has reduced the relative importance of an urban location, the shift in the relative importance of services and value-added manufacturing (with relatively low material intensity, such as computer software) makes proximity to markets and/or raw materials less important than before. There are now a number of economic activities that have no significant transportation costs associated with them. This shift is of course made possible partly by the other social, demographic, technological, and economic trends described here. Growth in the service sector also reflects a general trend in maturing, so-called postindustrial economies, where manufacturing often provides a smaller share of total economic value.[10] Moreover, the economic value of manufactured products per pound of material has increased, reducing the relative transportation cost disadvantages of exurban manufacturing locations for high-value-added products (e.g., computer software, electronics).

Aging of the population: The elderly over sixty-five are now the fastest-growing age group in American society (Thurow 1996; Seelye 1997). The aging of the U.S. population, together with the increasing wealth of urban retirees (a result of both equity gains and stronger retirement savings), has created a new pool of empty nesters able to live wherever they want. This group can live off the so-called mailbox economy, bringing outside income into the local economy and generating a multiplier effect as well as a demand for specialized services (e.g., health care and financial advising). Exurban areas experiencing rapid growth tend to have a disproportionate share of retirees, and this generally reflects in-migration rather than a natural increase for that age group.[11]

Equity gains of urbanites: Rapid population growth in urban areas during the 1970s and 1980s—particularly in California—created strong consumer demand for housing. Many of the existing homeowners were therefore able to sell their metropolitan homes for significant capital gains based on the difference between their investment and appreciation. These "equity refugees" were able to move from urban areas with high housing costs to rural areas with relatively low housing costs—in some cases buying new houses mortgage-free. In many cases the desire to avoid capital gains taxes compels investment in a new home of comparable or greater value, however, driving up the cost of housing in the exurban area facing growth.[12]

Lower cost of living: Housing values (and the overall cost of living) are generally lower in nonmetropolitan areas. This differential creates incentives to move from urban to rural regions that are consistent with strictly economic models of human behavior. Among nonmetropolitan areas, however, housing values (and therefore costs) are generally *highest* in those amenity-oriented regions experiencing rapid growth. While they are certainly an important factor, lower housing values alone are unable to explain the migration to exurban areas. Moreover, wages are also generally lower in exurbia than in metropolitan areas.

Decline of metropolitan schools: Declining quality in and public support for public schools in metropolitan areas has led many urban families to send their school-age children to private schools. (This has particularly been true in California since the passage of Proposition 13 in 1978.) The increased costs of private education exacerbate the gap between the costs of housing and other services in urban areas and their costs in rural areas. In such cases, moving to exurban areas becomes more cost-effective than when metropolitan public schools are considered good, and some families are able to get by with significantly less household income in rural areas. Private schools in metropolitan areas can cost from $5,000 to $10,000 per student per year. Avoiding those costs alone can translate into savings for a mortgage of approximately $80,000–$170,000 for a family with two children. This was the range of median housing values in the Sierra Nevada in 1990.[13] Some public school districts in the area have also been leaders in the state's charter school movement, allowing students a choice of schools within the public system (Garcia 1996; Lauer 1997).

Increase in metropolitan violence: Significant increases in metropolitan violence occurred throughout the 1980s in the United States, despite a more than doubling of the incarceration rate. This violence has decreased the perception of security and well-being that many metropolitan-area residents still maintained throughout the 1960s and 1970s, when suburban communities were generally deemed free of the crime found in the central city. The increasing concern about safety has led some urban and suburban residents to flee to rural areas, which are generally viewed as safer. In some cases even these are not considered safe enough, and many wealthy exurbanites have moved into gated communities that offer at least the perception of even greater residential safety. Some of these communities emphasize safety and security in their real estate marketing campaigns.[14]

Ethnic and racial homogeneity: Racism in American society may also explain some of the exodus to exurbia (Walsh 1991; Blakely and Snyder 1997; Niedorf 1996e). Metropolitan regions in America are increasingly multiethnic, multiracial, and multicultural. At the same time that white populations have reached minority status in many of California's metropolitan areas, the ethnic composition of the exurban areas experiencing rapid growth is overwhelmingly white. It is difficult to determine how important racism is as a determinant of migration, but the exodus to exurbia parallels the migration to suburbia of the 1950s and 1960s. Statistically valid survey data on the role of racism as a factor determining location choice by exurban migrants to the Sierra Nevada are not available.

Recreation and tourism: One of the fastest-growing industries in the 1970s and 1980s was recreation and tourism, and Americans primarily traveled domestically. Recreation and tourism is now a $35 billion industry in California alone; Disney World in Florida receives more visitors annually than the nation of France. Increasing interest in outdoor recreation has placed greater and greater pressure on national parks and other public lands. By the year 2000, recreation is expected to account for $97.8 billion worth of activity in the national forests, while fish and wildlife will generate another $12.9 billion through hunting and fishing license fees, equipment purchases, and associated recreation and travel. (This contrasts with only $10.1 billion generated by mineral extraction, $3.5 billion by timber, and $1 billion by grazing [Christensen 1996b].) Increasing tourism in those areas has in turn exposed many people to nearby communities, which have then become targets for residential relocation.[15]

All of these factors have converged over the past three decades to facilitate rapid population growth in many communities in the rural West (*Marin Independent Journal* 1997). That growth has in turn been the focus of social conflict between exchange and use values and between newcomers and old-timers (Ringholz 1992; 1996). These communities are struggling over how to address their collective future, even though they often regard the interests of each faction in the conflict as in conflict with each other. To understand why requires a look at theories of collective action and the development of social capital, for social capital is a necessary ingredient for resolution of many conflicts over growth.

COLLECTIVE ACTION AND SOCIAL CAPITAL

Theories of collective action have developed in the political science, sociology, and economics literatures to explain an apparent puzzle: why do people cooperate in situations in which maximizing their own welfare would appear to favor noncooperative behavior? A related question is: how can we design institutions to encourage cooperative behavior if total social welfare can be maximized only through cooperation? These questions are central to the problems of resource management and environmental quality, which often exhibit "public good" characteristics or involve spillover effects that negatively influence others' welfare (called "externalities" in economics). The economic theory underlying these questions is discussed in detail below; here I will sketch the key findings from the literature on collective action in the face of such conditions.

The simplest problem of collective action involves just two individuals; it has been captured in game theory by what is known as the "prisoner's dilemma," in which two prisoners face incentives that would yield to the individual the highest expected value benefits if they don't cooperate with each other, but would yield higher expected value benefits to them as a group if they do cooperate with each other. Assuming that the two have no ability to communicate with each other except through their actions and the resulting consequences, game theory suggests that the individuals will generally not cooperate if they face this situation only once. Robert Axelrod demonstrated in his 1984 book, *The Evolution of Cooperation,* that a *series* of games between two people led to a different outcome, however: a given player could maximize both his individual expected value benefits and the group's total expected value benefits by risking cooperation and then responding tit-for-tat by echoing the other participant's last move in subsequent games (Axelrod 1984; Ellickson 1991; Putnam 1993). This simplified simulation helps to explain why cooperative structures appear and evolve and suggests that both *reciprocal cooperation* and *repeated interactions* are necessary for stable cooperative arrangements. Indeed, this model may accurately (although in a simplified form) capture the key social conditions that support Rudel's hypothesized reliance on bilateral relational social controls in slow-growing rural areas.

The prisoner's dilemma formulation, however, has many limiting assumptions that restrict its usefulness when considering situations with more "players," broader opportunities for interaction and communication, uncertainty, and transaction costs associated with monitoring both conditions and compliance. The latter conditions typify what Garrett Hardin called the "tragedy of the commons" in a 1968 article in *Science,* but more accurately describe a broader class of circumstances involving common-pool resources (CPRs). A common-pool resource is one "sufficiently large as to make it costly (but not impossible) to exclude potential beneficiaries from gaining benefits from its use" (Ostrom 1990, 30). Managers of CPRs therefore face classic public-good problems of "free riders" guilty of shirking responsibilities for managing the CPR, as well as aspects that act as incentives for overconsumption of the resource to everyone else's detriment. There may be a variety of institutional arrangements for managing CPRs, however, and Hardin's analysis and conclusions are predicated on a particular social regime characterizing an open access CPR (Ostrom 1990). Other social arrangements are possible (and many of those alternatives exist in the real world) that do not necessarily lead to the "tragedy" outlined by Hardin. What can explain the persistence of these arrangements, which appear to have been organized by the participants in the management regime rather than by outside parties? What can be learned from them?

Elinor Ostrom explores these questions in depth in her 1990 book, *Governing the Commons: The Evolution of Institutions for Collective Action* (2–8). She emphasizes the need to move beyond metaphors like the prisoner's dilemma, the "tragedy of the commons," and "the logic of collective action," and expands the theory of the new institutionalism by empirically assessing real-world examples of successful collective action and identifying their common features. Moreover, she examines cases of unsuccessful cooperation to determine if they either lack those features or share additional features. She notes that successful cases rarely manifest in either of the extreme forms widely advocated by policy analysts: neither centralized control by the state nor complete privatization appears necessary to achieve stable equilibrium arrangements for sustainable resource use. "Institutions are rarely either public or private—the 'market' or the 'state,'" says Ostrom. "Many successful CPR institutions are rich mixtures of 'private-like' and 'public-like' institutions defying classification in a sterile dichotomy" (14). She then offers two basic hypotheses about why some groups are successful and others are not, saying that success is the result of factors internal to a given group, such as their ability to communicate, or externally imposed restrictions on the group or its relationship to external sources of power (21). Both prove important in the case studies from the Sierra Nevada I explore here, for the external relationships (e.g., whether or not state or federal law protects biodiversity) often influence internal group dynamics (e.g., the willingness of some parties to negotiate and reach agreement with others).

Ostrom's case studies involve from fifty to fifteen thousand people, involve institutional arrangements that have persisted for at least a century to as long as millennia, and include mountain meadows and forests, irrigation systems, ground-water management, and fisheries in Switzerland, Japan, Spain, the Philippines, Turkey, Sri Lanka, Nova Scotia, and California. She notes that "there are limits on the types of CPRs studied here: (1) renewable rather than nonrenewable resources, (2) situations where substantial scarcity exists, rather than abundance, and (3) situations in which the users can substantially harm one another, but not situations in which participants can produce major external harm for others. Thus, all asymmetrical pollution problems are excluded, as is any situation in which a group can form a cartel and control a sufficient part of the market to affect market price" (26). Some of these restrictions will prove to be significant in the context of the Sierra Nevada, but Ostrom's results are nevertheless a useful starting point for exploring the conditions of successful collective action.

She ultimately outlines eight "design principles" for long-enduring CPR institutions, each of which is "an essential element or condition that helps to account for the success of these institutions in sustaining the CPRs and gaining the compliance of generation after generation of appropriators to the rules of use" (90). Her cases of successful institutions generally had all of the elements, while the fragile or unsuccessful CPR management regimes were usually missing several of them: 1) clearly defined boundaries, 2) congruence between appropriation and provision rules and local conditions, 3) collective-choice arrangements, 4) monitoring systems accountable to the appropriators, 5) graduated sanctions for noncompliance, 6) conflict resolution mechanisms, 7) minimal recognition of the rights of appropriators to organize their own institutions, and, for CPRs that were part of larger systems, 8) organization in multiple layers of nested enterprises (ibid.).

Two general themes emerge from this list, which reflect Ostrom's original hypotheses: internal group dynamics and the opportunity to participate in system design, monitoring, and conflict resolution are important; and the relationship between the management regime and external institutional arrangements matters. Both of these themes recur in my case study of the Sierra Nevada, where land and resource management regimes both function at a variety of levels (e.g., federal, state, local) and with a complex set of relationships to each other.

The internal dynamics of collective action take on particular importance in the Sierra Nevada case, however, for land use planning institutions are focused at the community level through cities and counties. The relationship between those institutions and external factors is important and will be discussed later, but let me pursue the issue of internal relationships further at this point. In particular, I want to address the concept of social capital.

As Robert D. Putnam and his colleagues note in their 1993 book, *Making Democracy Work: Civic Traditions in Modern Italy,* "Success in overcoming dilemmas of collective action and the self-defeating opportunism that they spawn depends on the broader social context within which any particular game is played. Voluntary cooperation is easier in a community that has inherited a substantial stock of social capital, in the form of norms of reciprocity and networks of civic engagement. Social capital here refers to features of social organization, such as trust, norms, and networks, that can improve the efficiency of society by facilitating coordinated actions" (167). Unlike Axelrod's game theory–based analysis of cooperative behavior between two strangers, however, Putnam and his colleagues emphasize the social context within which social capital can be developed. Trust among community members is seen as critical, and "social trust in complex modern settings can arise from two related sources—norms of reciprocity and networks of civic engagement" (171). Moreover, they suggest that people's willingness to reciprocate "is likely to be associated with dense networks of social exchange" (172). This formulation highlights the importance of civil society as the context for establishing those networks. People are more likely to work together if they deal with each other in a wide variety of contexts, and if they see each other as having comparable power.

This framework also highlights the "embeddedness" of all relationships within a social and institutional context that goes beyond yet influences a wide range of seemingly bilateral transactions. It therefore helps to frame our understanding of Rudel's typology of social control, as well as Logan and Molotch's typology of entrepreneurs and their relationship to other actors in any given situation in which the growth machine faces conflicts over use and exchange values. "Trust is generated and malfeasance discouraged when agreements are 'embedded' within a larger structure of personal relations and social networks," note Putnam and his colleagues.[16] "The embeddedness approach predicts that the mix of order and disorder, of cooperation and opportunism, in a society will depend on the pre-existing social networks" (1993, 173). The structure of civic engagement is therefore *historically contingent* and develops over long periods of time.

This is perhaps the most profound finding of *Making Democracy Work:* in their study of twenty regional governments established in Italy in the early 1970s, the single variable that best explained variation in the performance of those otherwise common institutional structures—after controlling for economic characteristics, social characteristics, size, ethnicity, and many other variables—was a history and tradition of civic engagement. This suggests that Ostrom's design principles, while *necessary* conditions, may not be *sufficient* conditions for the establishment of successful institutions for collective action. "The civic community has deep historical roots," observe Putnam and his colleagues, and "this is a depressing observation for those who view institutional design as a strategy for political change" (183). It is not enough to design the right institutional form; there must also be fertile soil in which to plant those institutional arrangements. In a sobering conclusion, they go so far as to suggest that there are "two social equilibria" toward which the twenty regional case studies tended (177). One was built on cooperation and generated success, while the other, similar to the prisoner's dilemma condition, avoided cooperation and mired the community in dysfunctionality and squalor. Convergence of all cases toward one of these two outcomes reflects the positive feedback loop implicit in the model of social capital generation: trust and cooperation generate further trust and cooperation, while mistrust and defection generate further mistrust and defection. Social capital accounts therefore tend to move in either a positive or a negative direction with momentum.

How then can we generate social capital by design, if our ability to do so is constrained or enhanced by our existing stock of social capital? More specifically, what form must social networks take for a successful outcome? Finally, how will rapid population growth in a community affect those networks and the viability of social-capital-generation processes? The answers to these questions determine whether the Sierra Nevada and similarly situated rural communities facing rapid population growth will be able to overcome their collective need to establish institutional innovations that will provide for successful collective action. The historical roots of social conflict in a region affect our attempts at conflict resolution across issues and levels of social aggregation. Some approaches have enhanced our ability to generate "norms of reciprocity and networks of civic engagement," while others have undermined and depleted social capital.[17]

The balance of power among competing interests is critical to the outcome. Putnam and his colleagues emphasize that only horizontal networks, where people have equivalent status and power, are likely to enhance social capital. Vertical networks, with their resulting asymmetric relations of hierarchy and dependence, do not enhance social capital (173). Moreover, "the denser such [horizontal] networks in a community, the more likely that its citizens will be able to cooperate for mutual benefit" (ibid.). These denser networks of civic engagement increase the potential costs of defecting from social cooperation by allowing the rapid transmission of information about behavior among members of the community, whether regarding positive models of behavior or reputations of shirking (173–74).

These conclusions have important implications for both the design of social institutions and the likelihood of success in our efforts to solve the dilemmas of collective action now facing the Sierra Nevada and the communities of the rural West. They suggest that formal institutions are not enough; we must also engage civil society to transcend formal *governments* in our efforts at *governance*. This is occurring at a time of dramatic change and is consistent with other trends toward what Manuel Castells calls "the rise of the network society" (1996; 1997). The critical challenge is to design and implement institutional contexts in which the proper relationship between horizontal and vertical networks can enhance our capacity for collective action. Annalee Saxenian has demonstrated similar success for horizontal networks in her 1994 book, *Regional Advantage: Culture and Competition in Silicon Valley and Route 128*. One of the key factors constraining innovation in the high-technology sector in the Route 128 region (outside Boston) was the brittleness of vertical networks and the paucity of horizontal networks across firms and industries. Silicon Valley, in contrast, has a regional economy built on horizontal networks. Similarly, the effectiveness of social control by the rural residents of Shasta County depended on the establishment of horizontal networks, not the vertical networks associated with the law.[18] Those residents also had embedded relationships that built on a long history of social capital formation. Rapid population growth in rural communities threatens that history.

This has important implications for land and resource management in exurban communities as they become increasingly heterogeneous and less likely to maintain highly connected horizontal networks that span the community. Nevada County's history over the past three decades demonstrates this: increasing population has brought increasing anonymity and decreasing horizontal linkages, thereby decreasing the shared sense of destiny and interest that previously held (at least within social classes). Civil society and bilateral relationships still play an important role in conflict resolution, but reliance on the formal institutions of government for conflict resolution is increasing: trilateral relational controls are displacing bilateral controls. The viability of formal institutional structures and their relationship to civil society are therefore important factors influencing the likelihood of achieving viable land and resource management regimes. In view of this, I want to look next at the relationship between institutional structures and their viability in the context of rapid change and the potential destruction of long-held relationships and beliefs.

COMMUNITY PARTICIPATION IN PLANNING

Community participation is not a luxury in planning. The form of community participation matters, too, so we should not rush blindly to embrace *any* form of community participation without regard to whether it will lead to effective planning. An effective planning regime can identify social values, translate them into social goals and management objectives, then implement programs on the ground that will achieve those objectives. An effective regime will therefore be able to resolve the highly polarized conflict that now surrounds land and resource management issues. Community participation schemes may or may not be able to accomplish this, depending on both their design and the character of the various types of conflicts that may exist between community members. The lessons of Putnam, Ostrom, and Ellickson are relevant here.

But what do I mean when I use the term *community*? There are at least three types of communities that should be considered in land and resource management, and they sometimes overlap and/or conflict: 1) communities of *place,* which are tied to a physical space through geography; 2) communities of *identity,* which are tied to each other through social characteristics but may transcend place; and 3) communities of *interest,* which may have commonalities in how they relate to a particular ecosystem or resource as beneficiaries of that place or contributors to its condition. The cases I will discuss here are focused on communities of place, but a privileged position for communities of place may conflict with existing arrangements that may favor particular communities of interest. There is consequently a need to reconcile communities of interest with communities of place in order to address the full range of human concerns. This is especially true when the communities of interest are the owners of the public domain. It is also true when the policy issues or the effects of an action in question—such as the protection of biodiversity—affect many nonlocal interests.

Community "participation" in planning often takes the form of mere "tokenism" (Canter 1996), however, through the formalized procedural mandates of state and federal law. This led Paul Davidoff to promote an "advocacy planning" approach to the planners' role in a seminal article published in 1965. The problem of tokenism persists three decades later as many agencies continue to pursue the classic "decide, announce, defend" strategy of project planning and policy development. At the other extreme, community participation could conceivably take the form of complete delegation of analysis and decision-making authority to the community for management of public lands or true town meeting–style democratic action on all public policy decisions (Canter 1996). In this model the communities may practice tokenism in relationship to the agencies and the nonlocal interests they represent, however, turning the traditional model on its head. Both of these extremes have occurred in the Sierra Nevada in ecosystem management efforts involving the U.S. Forest Service (Duane 1997). Local planning agencies often practice tokenism when community participation results in policy preferences inconsistent with the political interests of the growth machine. This is what happened in the Nevada County General Plan update process described below.

An alternative model for community participation has recently emerged in planning practice and the social science literature based on the principles of collaborative planning. The new approach is described by Judith Innes as "planning through consensus building," and it has the potential to redefine planning practice to produce shared meanings that build social capital:

> Consensus building has emerged parallel to the idea of "communicative rationality," drawn largely from Habermas [1984], developed by Dryzek [1990] for policy making (he also calls it "discursive democracy"), and applied to planning by Forester [1989], Sager [1994], and Innes [1995], among others. A decision is "communicatively rational" to the degree that it is reached consensually through deliberations

involving all stakeholders, where all are equally empowered and fully informed, and where the conditions of ideal speech are met (statements are comprehensible, scientifically true, and offered by those who can legitimately speak and who speak sincerely). Communicatively rational decisions, then, are those that come about because there are good reasons for them rather than because of the political or economic power of particular stakeholders. For these processes to be truly communicatively rational, they must also reflect "emancipatory knowledge," or knowledge of the deeper reality hidden behind popular myths, scientific theories, and the arguments and rationalizations in common use. Such knowledge can come through dialectic, self-reflection, praxis—the broad and deep experience of those who know how to do things in the world—and from discourse that challenges prevailing assumptions. (1996a, 461)

Innes argues that consensus-based approaches offer a method for discerning the public interest without unduly biasing it to reflect asymmetrical power relationships (1996a). It is important to maintain parity in the power relationships among these stakeholders, however, for asymmetry will otherwise give some parties a "best alternative to a negotiated agreement" that will encourage defection from participation in the consensus-based process (Fisher and Ury 1982). This makes the institutional context of trilateral relational controls critical. As one participant in a complicated collaborative planning process put it, "Consensus works best when fear is equitably distributed" (Bobker 1997). This helps to explain why 81 percent of the 105 "cooperative ecosystem management" case studies recently reviewed by Stephen Yaffee and his students involved a species listed under the federal Endangered Species Act (Yaffee et al. 1996). The ESA listing generated considerable uncertainty for powerful stakeholders, giving them a strong incentive to participate in cooperative ecosystem management. A very different outcome would have been likely in the absence of the ESA hammer held over the heads of some of the parties. Equitable power relationships are therefore a necessary prerequisite to successful application of Yaffee's principles for success: 1) "involve all stakeholders early," 2) "use an open, clear, and collaborative process," 3) "secure adequate resources and agency support," 4) "use broad, flexible, science-based land management approaches," and 5) "ensure [that] communities and agencies understand each other's concerns" (35–38).

These principles—together with the critical point regarding power and its role in generating the conditions that can support communicative rationality—are worth bearing in mind as we evaluate both the case study discussed below and other proposals for community participation in land and resource management. It is also useful to distinguish between the four different types (or causes) of social conflict delineated by Creighton[19] and summarized by Canter:

1. *Cognitive conflict*—Cognitive conflict occurs when people have different understandings or judgements as to the facts of a case.
2. *Values conflict*—Values conflict is a dispute over goals—for example, whether

an action or outcome is desirable (or undesirable) or should (or should not) occur.

3. *Interest conflict*—Since the costs and benefits resulting from an action are rarely distributed equally, some people will have a greater interest in an action than others. Some may have an interest in assuring it does not occur. As a result, it is possible to have agreement on facts, and on values, and still have conflict based on interests.

4. *Relationship conflict*—There are several psychologically oriented bases for conflict. Every time people communicate, they communicate both content (information, facts) and relationship (how much someone is valued, accepted, etc.). Decision-making processes can also communicate relationships—decision-making processes may, for example, favor those groups which are well enough financed and organized to present scientific supporting data over those which primarily argue from a values base. The result is that there are a number of emotional motivations that may lead to conflict on grounds other than facts, values or interests. (1996, 610)

These conflicts are not unique to land and resource management, but they emerge as central to the task of implementing successful land and resource management and planning efforts on the ground in real places with real communities. These different sources of conflict also help to explain why reasonable people can disagree about the desirability of implementing specific policy, planning, or management actions. We must go beyond tokenism in public participation.[20] Tokenism may meet the letter of the law but it is generally not adequate from the perspective of the community. Agencies or other groups that practice tokenism are unlikely to be successful in implementing their proposals, for disempowered communities can often still block policy and project implementation through litigation and other means.

Unless the communities of place have goals, values, and interests consistent with those of the communities of interest, communities of interest will continue to resist the decentralization of power to consensus-based decision-making at the local level. Moreover, unless there is some homogeneity of goals, values, and interests within the local communities of place, there will continue to be a lack of consensus within the community. The key to successful community participation in land and resource management is complete involvement of all stakeholders with equivalent status and power.

Any devolution of authority to local communities of place must therefore be coupled with a strong responsibility to meet the long-term goals of the broader society. This caveat regarding responsibility is critical, for actions of local groups must still be consistent with interests of the broader state and federal citizenry.[21] Despite some dramatic changes in the social, demographic, and economic characteristics of western communities, the local politics of most are still generally dominated by commodity extraction interests (Marston 1989). Calls for greater local control are more often issued by the Wise Use movement than the environmental community, for the latter finds its strength in the political and economic resources of urban and eastern constituencies. The history of wilderness and national park designation in the United States is generally one of national interests overriding local economic interests.[22] Local control is not necessarily consistent with the principles of the emerging paradigm of ecosystem management, which purports to offer a framework for integrated management across jurisdictions to maintain ecological systems (Grumbine 1994; 1997; U.S. Department of the Interior, Interagency Ecosystem Management Task Force 1995; Ecological Stewardship Workshop 1995; N. Christensen 1996). Local control will therefore not necessarily result in reduced conflict and management practices that will resolve conflicting needs. Neither will so-called consensus efforts that violate the principles of communicative rationality.[23] The distribution of *power* is critical to all such efforts.

ECOLOGICAL THEORY AND INSTITUTIONAL DYNAMICS

Population growth is the most important change confronting rural communities of the mountainous West, but it is not occurring in isolation from other dramatic changes in the regional environment. In general terms, it is taking place against a backdrop of vast public lands whose future is highly contested: development versus preservation, commodity versus ecological values, and national versus local control over management. Moreover, that conflict has intensified as both the scarcity of some ecological systems and the competing demands for their use have increased dramatically. We have now reached the edge of the continent and are fighting over the final scraps of the American frontier. As the former U.S. Forest Service Chief Jack Ward Thomas has put it, "We didn't run into the Spotted Owl—we ran into the Pacific Ocean" (1995). In 1890, the entire population of the United States was less than twice what California's population is today, and the Golden State alone is expected to have as many residents in 2040 as the entire nation held in 1890 (California Department of Finance 1993). The United States is projected to have nearly 400 million people by 2050, which means that we will add more than twice the 1890 population of the nation over the next five decades.[24] Already those population pressures, combined with intensive patterns of resource consumption and extensive patterns of human settlement, have placed many ecological systems on the brink of collapse.

This phenomenon is not confined to the rural West, and there is an important literature that explores the emerging crisis in ecological management. This literature is discussed in more detail elsewhere,[25] but let me introduce here an important set of theoretical ideas from a 1995 book by Lance Gunderson, C. S. Holling, and Stephen Light, *Barriers and Bridges to the Renewal of Ecosystems and Institutions.* Their theoretical framework, which was developed primarily by Holling, offers a useful perspective from which to view the processes of population growth and social change as they affect both the ecosystems and institutions in the Sierra Nevada. It also serves as the foundation, together with the theoretical frameworks outlined above, for many of my recommendations for institutional innovations to deal with these conflicts.

Holling hypothesized a four-stage model for ecological processes that extends the traditional climax model of succession associated with F. E. Clements (1916). The Clementsian model, which dominated ecological science for a half century, was a two-stage model that included an "exploitation" stage of rapid colonization followed by a "conservation" stage of climax vegetation (Holling 1995, 19). New theories of change, however, "rationalize the paradoxes of stability and instability, of order and disorder, and of stasis and evolutionary change" by adding two stages to the model: release (creative destruction) and reorganization (ibid., 20). These revisions began to be developed in the 1960s and were widely adopted in ecological science by the late 1980s (Walker 1981; Botkin 1990), following Thomas Kuhn's classic description of a paradigm shift (1962).

Let us look briefly at the four-stage model to clarify how it may help us explore the coevolution of Nature and Culture—and the prospects for future coevolution—in the Sierra Nevada (see fig. 2.1). Note that Holling plots the four stages in three ways: as discrete steps in a sequence, as interconnected flows without a beginning or end, and as functions of two variables: "connectedness" (on the x-axis) and "stored capital" (on the y-axis). This formulation is intended to characterize an ecological system, but it parallels the language of social capital and networks.

Holling has taken the emerging (and converging) ecological theory one step further and attempted to apply it to managed ecological systems. Specifically, he studied twenty-three cases of resource management where increased success in managing one output invariably led to the collapse of the ecological system through a loss of resilience. He found in those cases that narrow problem definition by the human institutions responsible for the management regime constrained their ability to perceive changes in spatial homogeneity at a landscape scale. This meant that the collapse of these systems was not anticipated, because the agencies had shifted their research and monitoring efforts from the original focus on system outputs to improving the efficiency of the agency itself. Monitoring efforts were therefore focused on performance indicators rather than the health of the system. Success in narrowing the variability of the target outputs also tended to increase social dependence on those outputs, generating significant conflict over resource management when the resiliency of the system finally collapsed. This pat-

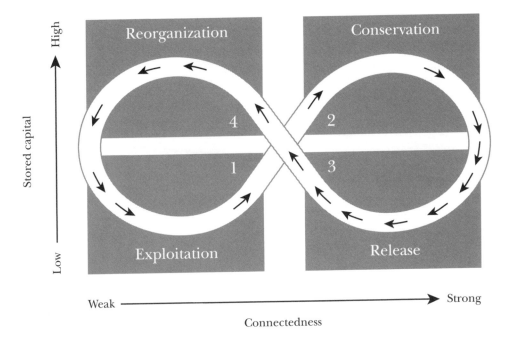

FIGURE 2.1.   Four-stage model of ecological systems as a function of connectedness and stored capital. Adapted from *Barriers and Bridges to the Renewal of Ecosystems and Institutions*, Lance H. Gunderson, C. S. Holling, and Stephen S. Light, eds. Copyright © 1995, Columbia University Press. Reprinted with permission of the publisher.

tern of coevolution in both ecological and institutional systems suggested to Holling that the four-stage model could be applied to the entire system.

Holling's summary of the new ecological theory seems suitable for application to the land and resource management and planning institutions that dominate the rural West. Its key features are these: 1) patterns and processes occur at a variety of spatial and temporal scales; 2) there are asymmetric interactions among different levels, with larger and slower levels maintaining constraints within which the smaller and faster systems operate; and 3) the higher-level systems are especially vulnerable to disruption from small disturbances at critical times in their operating cycle (Holling 1995, 22–24). This helps to explain how seemingly small changes in seemingly insignificant variables can result in dramatic changes in larger systems. The state of a system may then suddenly jump to a new state through punctuated equilibrium.

Holling's framework addresses the relationship between different spatial and temporal scales in a way that can also be useful for linking different institutional levels of analysis. Some phenomena occur across large spatial scales and have long temporal cycles, while others occur at different scales in space and time. Holling's model suggests that some of these scales may be more or less important to the vul-

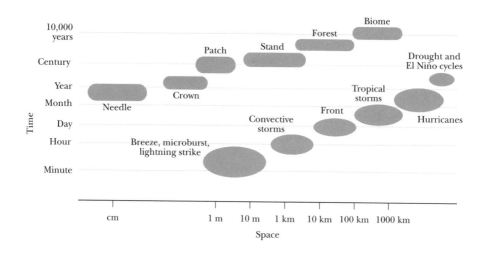

FIGURE 2.2.   Typical temporal and spatial scales of ecological phenomena. Source: See figure 2.1.

nerability of a system at different stages. Annual variations in insect infestations may be constrained by slower, longer-term cycles such as forest structure, but those smaller variations may become critical at specific stages of forest development. Differentiating the ecological process by spatial and temporal scales is critical.

System vulnerability is particularly high under two conditions: 1) "when the system becomes overconnected and brittle as it slowly moves toward maturity" (which "is also the phase where, in human organizations, the rebellion of aggressive interest groups can precipitate an inexorable demand for change"), and 2) "at the stage of reorganization," when "the system is underconnected, with weak organization and weak regulation. . . . At this stage, instability comes because of loss of regulation rather than from the brittleness of reduced resilience. It is this phase in a system—ecological or human—where the individual or small groups of individuals can make the greatest structural change for the future." Just as ecological systems go through phases of "birth, growth, death and renewal," therefore, so must ecological *management* regimes (24–25). Unlike the horizontal networks that characterize the generation of social capital, however, the system becomes "overconnected" when it is dominated by strong hierarchical networks. These vertical structures typify most of the land and resource management institutions we have today, and they may help to explain why conflicts in the Sierra Nevada are dominated by "crisis, conflict, and gridlock." "The pathology is broken," claims Holling, "when the issue is seen as a strategic one of adaptive policy management, of science at the appropriate scales, and of understanding human behavior, not a procedural one of institutional control" (9).

The problems we face in ecological management, Holling notes, "are not purely ecological, economic, or social. They are a combination of all three and require understanding of the interrelations between nature and people in different settings, performing different roles" (4). Holling says that there is a tremendous mismatch between ecological, economic, and social systems, and he suggests that aligning them would lead to constructive solutions. This is the challenge of institutional design. "When issues are polarized," however, "it is a time of deep frustration. Conflicts are extreme, mutual suspicions dominate, and cooperation seems the road to personal defeat" (3). This describes the current situation in the rural West, which sounds a great deal like the stable but unhappy equilibrium noted by Putnam and his colleagues in their study of Italy and collective choice. It also represents the uncooperative outcomes of the prisoner's dilemma.

The Holling framework has implications for managing population growth and land use conflict, land and resource management in general, and institutional innovation designed to respond to the conflict and crises that continue to beset the entire region. It is also critical at a variety of levels, because "theories determine the questions we ask, the problems we perceive, the data we collect and analyze, and the policies and actions we initiate. Theories that do not match the problem can be at best delusions and at worst dangerous" (19). A central theoretical tenet that emerges from Holling's work is that "evolving managed ecosystems and the societies with which they are linked involve unknowability and unpredictability," requiring "flexibility for adapting to surprises" (14).

This finding is still lost in the dominant paradigm of resource-management-by-experts. Stanley Fish's work on the importance of "interpretive communities" highlights how the Culture of an agency or an interest group reproduces itself by reinforcing those aspects of interpretation that best support the worldview that the social group holds in common (1980; 1989). James Throgmorton has also demonstrated how the rhetoric of planning itself is ultimately a means of exerting power to frame the questions, to choose the tools by which we interpret data, and to determine the meanings we ascribe to the answers that emerge from the planning process (1994; 1996). I will not discuss the work of Fish and Throgmorton in detail here, but I do want to acknowledge explicitly that this book reflects my membership in and contribution to an interpretive community engaging at several levels in a discourse about the future of the Sierra Nevada. The planning process itself is in this sense a text that reflects a wide range of power relationships and differential advantages associated with information and knowledge. I have tried my best to be fair to competing stories, but make no mistake about it: my focus on the theoretical frameworks of Logan and Molotch, Rudel, Ostrom, Ellickson, Putnam, and Holling reflects an underlying view of the world that is not necessarily "objective." It is nevertheless true in that the story I tell here is consistent with my understanding of the world.[26]

Other stories have made more sense at different times in the Sierra Nevada, and we must keep their rationale in mind if we are to understand the historical basis for the current conflicts. I have therefore turned to the history of human settlement in the region to gain such insight. That history helps to explain why many of our current institutions and approaches to land and resource management are encountering serious challenges in the face of emerging social and economic values.

NATURE, CULTURE, AND HISTORY

My wife Teresa's great-great-great-grandfather John Keiser was twenty-two years old when the Mexican-American War broke out in the spring of 1846. By fall he had volunteered for duty, had left his home in Pennsylvania, and was fighting on the American side somewhere in the desert Southwest. He returned to Pennsylvania at the end of the war to rejoin his family, but he caught forty-niner fever the next year. John and his three brothers then went west to California to make their fortunes. They arrived in Hangtown (now Placerville) and prospected for a short time, then explored the diggings around Yankee Jim's and crossed the South Fork of the American River to Georgetown. His three brothers eventually returned to the Midwest and East Coast, but John settled on the Georgetown Divide in El Dorado County and helped discover the Mameluke Hill strike. In June 1853 he went back for his wife, Elizabeth, and first child, Ella, who traveled to California via the Isthmus of Panama. Their second child, Lenora (Nona) Gertrude Keiser, was born after the return to California, near Georgetown, on February 18, 1854. She grew up in the foothills of the Sierra Nevada until 1866, when the family moved up and over the mountains to Coburn's Station, "a mere stage-stop on the Dutch Flat Wagon Road" (McGlashan 1977). Three years later the Central Pacific railroad made Coburn's Station one of its primary depots as the first transcontinental trains prepared for their ascent up the steep eastern slope of the Sierra Nevada. The Keisers became one of the first families of what the Central Pacific subsequently named Truckee, on the eastern side of Nevada County. There John Keiser became town constable, a hotel proprietor, and the father-in-law of one of Truckee's most famous citizens, Charles Fayette (C. F.) McGlashan, who moved to Truckee in 1872.

John Keiser died in a horse accident in Truckee Plaza on May 27, 1886, but C. F. lived long enough to know his grandson—who was Teresa's grandfather, Robert McGlashan. Bob died the day before his eightieth birthday in 1995, but through him we can trace a direct link to C. F.'s and Keiser's lives in the nineteenth century.[27] John Keiser was the first generation of his family to make a home in the Sierra Nevada, but his great-great-great-great-grandson Cody Duane-McGlashan is now the seventh generation to do so. Cody therefore directly links me to John Keiser in a way that makes "seven generations" much more than a mere abstraction. Cody is also the first link through a chain of seven more generations that connect me to the year 2170. That sounds like a long, long time from now, but it represents the time frame necessary to create old-growth forest conditions again in the Range of Light. Cody arrived on the planet Earth in 1995 at the midpoint in the links between 1820 and 2170—a 350-year period that roughly approximates the total time to date of Euro-American settlement of the North American continent.[28]

Truckee and its surroundings were in a strategic transportation location at the eastern foot of the Sierra Nevada when McGlashan arrived, but the Truckee River route was still haunted by the ghosts of the Donner Party. The Donner Party had become trapped by early winter snows while attempting to cross the Sierra Nevada in October 1846. Of the eighty-nine members of the party who took the "left hand turn" at Fort Bridger that took them off the main route to California, only forty-five made it through the journey into the spring (Stewart 1960; Lamar 1997). Many of those survivors had to resort to cannibalism, leaving a legacy that stalked them until their deaths. In 1996 their descendants gathered solemnly at Donner Lake to commemorate the sesquicentennial of that horrible "ordeal by hunger" (Stewart 1960). The harsh reality of the power of Nature in the Sierra Nevada— and the Sierra Nevada's enduring symbolic identity as a barrier to be overcome, rather than a place of value where one might linger purposefully—was cemented by the story of the Donner Party.

This dominant image of the Sierra as a barrier to travel even limited its exploration for extractive resources. Following John Marshall's gold discovery in January 1848, however, the cultural value of humans dominating Nature was reinforced by the gold rush. The new settlers crossed into the mountains and immediately set out to relieve the hills of their riches. Digging invasively into the earth, they believed the jewels of value were meant to be removed for human use and benefit. The resources of the Sierra Nevada had no value in situ. There was no market for Nature's aesthetics or recreation in an early industrial economy with limited leisure time.[29]

C. F. McGlashan was conceived on the Wisconsin frontier soon after the Donner Party began to struggle with the early snows of 1846–1847. He was born August 12, 1847, at Beaver Dam, north of Janesville, Wisconsin. Wisconsin was then at the edge of the "Great West," a largely unpopulated region that was just falling to the ax and plow (Cronon 1991; Fox 1981; Naden and Blue 1992). By 1851 his family had also begun the westward migration to California. The journey took more than three years, as they waited out the winters first in Missouri and then at the Great Salt Lake. Finally they arrived in Placerville in 1854, where an uncle "had struck gold and invested in a boarding house for steady income" (McGlashan 1977, 22). Opportunities were limited for latecomers, however, for at least a quarter of a million immigrants had already rushed into California during the first five years of the gold rush; gold production had peaked in 1852 (Lamar 1997). Consolidation and increased centralization were occurring as the industry shifted from the easily reached placer deposits to the harder to reach hardrock quartz and tertiary gravel deposits. Getting the gold out in these cases required intensive and extensive capital investment. After a short time in the Mother Lode near Cook's Bar along the Cosumnes River, the McGlashan family moved on across the Central Valley to the Sonoma County town of Healdsburg, where they had heard that cheap land was still available.

C. F. returned to El Dorado County in 1865 after completing high school and teaching for a year in Sonoma County. He came to teach at the Cold Spring school near Placerville. His sister Ann had moved there earlier, and he needed to save money before going east to school in June 1868. Then, after graduating, he returned to the Sierra Nevada as the principal of Placerville High School, in the spring of 1871. By December he was married to Jenny Mumson, whose family moved to Truckee early the next year. C. F. and Jenny soon followed them, and C. F. became the superintendent and principal of the Truckee area schools. They arrived in Truckee at the three-year-old railroad depot on July 12, 1872. Truckee was a rugged town in those days. It was also full of hope and optimism about the future. "This was the railroad age," wrote C. F.'s granddaughter, Nona McGlashan, a full century later, "and Truckee was a railroad town. It was still the Comstock's hour and Truckee fed timber to insatiable Washoe mines" (McGlashan 1977). C. F. took full advantage of the opportunities presented just three years after the opening of the railroad. He studied law with books borrowed from the Boca library, wrote articles for newspapers in the local area and Sacramento, and finally left the field of education in 1874 to start his law practice in January 1875. Together with Will Edwards, a coeditor of the *Truckee Republican,* he announced in April 1875 that a "Guidebook to the Sierra" would be published soon. Tourism had significant potential in the Sierra Nevada, and C. F. ultimately did all he could to promote it in Truckee.

He also chimed in on a pollution controversy regarding sawdust in the Truckee River, however, reflecting the dominant views of his time. "With his contemporaries of the 1870s," writes Nona McGlashan, "he had little patience with those who counseled caution in the interests of ecology, with this difference: He believed such problems as pollutants should be met and overcome by, as he termed it, 'the genius of man's inventive brain.' He did not believe the responsible industry should be curtailed. With his generation he used terms like 'illimitable' forests— and believed, in truth, they were. Not until the Big Bonanza ended and the long logging flumes decayed, would they note uneasily the bald, stump-dotted hills where no tree would ever grow back."[30]

C. F. McGlashan lived long enough to see these changes in the Sierra Nevada landscape. He became publisher of the *Truckee Republican* in 1878 and was elected to the state legislature to represent the region in 1884. In that capacity he served on the Assembly Mining Committee to deal with the aftermath of the landmark Sawyer decision.[31] While he left the area briefly to become editor and publisher of the *Santa Barbara Press,* from 1880 to 1883, he spent most of his remaining life in Truckee, and died there on January 6, 1931. He had a rich and productive life. It was also a life that reflected his times and the contemporary values of society. He was a firm believer in the dominant ideal that Nature was to be harnessed for human benefit, and his personal experience as an inventor reinforced his belief that technology could overcome all problems. After all, the establishment of the Central Pacific railroad had already transformed the nation in his first quarter century. The town of Truckee was full of optimism when C. F. McGlashan arrived in 1872. Much of the West was still waiting to be settled, and the railroad was going to help the American people settle it.

Congress reinforced this vision of settling the West by passing the Hardrock Mining Act that year, which encouraged further development of the nation's mineral resources (Wilkinson 1992a). After agriculture, extractive commodity production was seen as the foundation of economic well-being. Ironically, in the same session Congress also established the nation's first national park, at Yellowstone (Sunset Magazine 1970; Clark and Minta 1994). These two acts—one designed to ensure complete exploitation and utilization of natural resources on the remaining public lands, the other designed to preserve a relic of the natural wonders of North America—captured the "either/or" mentality of the time. Except for the remnants preserved as museum pieces, Nature's bounty was to be pulled from the ground and shipped to urban markets where it had value. Recreation, tourism, aesthetics, and scientific study of ecological processes were reserved only for limited areas. This legacy of dualism and an "either/or" perspective on land and resource management persisted for the next century in the structure and mission of the primary federal land and resource management agencies. The National Park Service had a mandate to protect resources and promote access to those resources for the public's aesthetic and recreational enjoyment (Winks 1996), while the Forest Service and Bureau of Land Management were charged primarily with exploiting those resources and ensuring commodity production from federal lands.[32]

The world changed a lot in the century between C. F.'s arrival in Nevada County in July 1872 and my own arrival in July 1971. The story of our respective experiences in the Sierra Nevada is the story of a massive ecological and economic transformation—or what I call the "ecotransformation"—of both the physical and cultural landscapes of the Sierra Nevada and the rural West. I have collapsed these two processes of change into a single term to highlight their interdependency and coevolutionary relationship. The construction of social reality reflects an underlying physical reality, while our social conceptions of that reality result in behavior and actions affecting the physical world. Ecology and economics, Nature and Culture, therefore interact with each other in complex ways. C. F. McGlashan's arrival in Nevada County reflected a Culture and a set of social values and ideas about Nature that were vastly different from those that dominated American society when my family moved to the mountains. Understanding those differences— and how we continue to apply nineteenth-century solutions to twenty-first-century problems, despite the coevolutionary development of a new relationship between Nature and Culture in the rural and exurban West—is essential to resolution of the land and resource management conflicts in the Range of Light.

CHAPTER THREE

Λ.V.V.Λ

The Exodus to Exurbia

Suburbia kept alive the ideal of a balance between man and nature in a society that seemed dedicated to destroying it. That is its legacy.

Robert Fishman, 1987

My family first came to Nevada County in 1970 during a visit to my grandparents, who had just moved to the area. My grandfather, who managed the Base Exchanges at Beale, Mather, and McClellan Air Force Bases in the Sacramento area, made Beale Air Force Base his headquarters, located just across the county line in Yuba County. They settled on five acres of land in the peaceful agricultural community of Penn Valley. Their land was a mix of pastureland and oaks, with rolling terrain surrounding the flat plain of the valley.

One day we drove up Highway 20 to visit Grass Valley and Nevada City. "You'll just love it," my grandmother told my mother. We had been living in the San Joaquin Valley for three years and my mother longed to live in the mountains. My father often joked that she wished she had married a park ranger rather than an Air Force officer. They met at South Lake Tahoe in 1956 while she was working for the summer at a college friend's family's lodge. All our family vacations involved camping trips to state and national parks and forests. My father had just retired from the Air Force and our family now had some new flexibility in terms of where we might settle next. A small town in the Sierra Nevada seemed a likely candidate.

The drive up Highway 20 was winding and scenic. We followed the path of Squirrel Creek, which dropped down from pines to oaks before joining Deer Creek in Penn Valley. The climb up the hill reminded me of our many drives to Yosemite on Highway 140 up the Merced River canyon. The vegetation was familiar; the smell of the air brought back fond memories. I knew we were going someplace special. The flat and arid landscape of the valley had always seemed foreign and hostile to me, while the tree-covered topography of the mountains felt much more familiar.

We wandered about Grass Valley and then headed up the new freeway, which had just opened on New Year's Day, to Nevada City. We turned off at the first exit in the Deer Creek watershed and rambled up into the hills, looking for a park for a picnic, although we didn't really need one. We could stop almost anywhere and it would feel like we were in a state park on one of our camping trips. We chose a road named Pinewoods, looking out over the Deer Creek watershed down to Nevada City. The sky was a brilliant blue and the air smelled of pines. The sweet sound of whistling birds filled the air, and a slight wind ruffled the leaves and needles of the trees. It was much more comfortable here than in the hot valley down below.

Within six months my parents returned and bought a house on an acre only two miles above our picnic spot. We moved to Nevada County the first week of July 1971.

SOCIAL AND DEMOGRAPHIC CHANGE
IN THE SIERRA NEVADA

There is no political jurisdiction with boundaries that coincide with the ecosystem or bioregional boundaries of the Sierra Nevada mountain range, but California's biodiversity memorandum of understanding delineates rough boundaries for the Sierra Nevada bioregion consistent with those used later by the Sierra Nevada Ecosystem Project and others (Duane 1993c). Understanding the social, demographic, and economic characteristics of the Sierra Nevada population and the ecotransformation occurring within the region requires a bioregional analysis. The Sierra Nevada region lies within portions of eighteen California counties and three Nevada counties, but only nine of the California counties are completely within the Sierra Nevada bioregion. I have therefore analyzed census data by using only those County Census Divisions (CCDs) largely within the Sierra Nevada bioregion, creating a composite of CCDs that is approximately coterminous with the boundaries of the Sierra Nevada bioregion.[1] With the exception of the population within the Lake Tahoe Basin, residents of the three counties in Nevada live outside the Sierra Nevada proper.[2]

My analysis determined that only 26 percent of the population in the eighteen Sierra Region counties in California actually resided within the Sierra Region of those counties. The Sierra Region population also differed from both the overall population of Sierra Region counties and California's statewide population in social, demographic, and economic characteristics (Duane 1993a; Griffiths 1993). This has important implications for land and resource management and planning, for the primary locus of political power within the eighteen-county region lies outside the Sierra Nevada. Moreover, the Sierra Nevada was home to only about 2

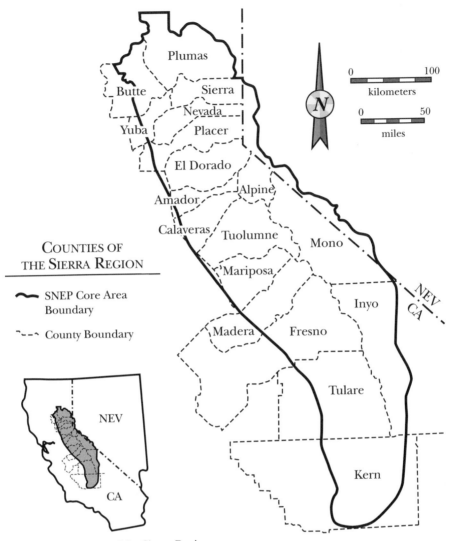

MAP 3.1.   Counties of the Sierra Region.

percent of California's population in 1990 (while covering 18 percent of its land area). Remarkably, neither the state nor other analysts seemed to recognize the importance of this distinction (i.e., the distinction between the Sierra Region found within the eighteen counties, and the entire area covered by the eighteen counties) in the Sierra Summit process in 1991–92. Political and administrative institutions do not generally collect data along bioregional lines, so it is difficult to analyze trends for any ecological unit that does not happen to coincide with existing political jurisdictions. This has hampered all policy discussions about the Sierra Nevada, from the Sierra Summit process in 1991 through the SNEP analysis and report in 1996.

The most significant element of social and economic change in the Sierra Nevada from 1970 to 1990 was the unprecedented population growth. Growing at more than two and a half times the 49 percent population growth for the entire state of California, the Sierra Region's 130 percent growth during that period was also much greater than the 77 percent growth experienced by the aggregated eighteen-county total. Growth within the Sierra Region itself was nearly exactly the same in absolute terms in the 1970s (175,472 people) and the 1980s (174,101 people). In contrast, the eighteen-county region grew faster in the 1980s than the 1970s (597,935 vs. 452,241). This occurred in the context of much greater growth in California in the 1980s than the 1970s (6,092,000 vs. 3,697,000). As a result of the larger base population in 1980 than 1970, of course, the percentage growth rate in the Sierra Region was lower in the 1980s than in the 1970s.

Nearly 13 percent of those who were California residents in 1990 did not live in California in 1985, but only 7 percent of the 1990 Sierra Region residents lived outside the state in 1985. State-level population growth has been dominated by three sources: natural increase, foreign immigration (both legal and illegal), and net domestic migration from other states (Teitz 1990). Since the 1990 census, the state has experienced relatively high natural increases and continues to accommodate about one-fourth to one-third of the legal foreign immigration to the United States (California Department of Finance 1993). Illegal immigrants are much more difficult to account for, but California clearly has a disproportionate share of the nation's illegal immigration. Domestic migration literally reversed itself, however, in the early 1990s: whereas the state grew by 339,000 people per year from 1980 through 1990 through net domestic migration from other states, there was net domestic emigration from 1991 to 1997 (Bonfante 1993; California Department of Finance 1996). An estimated 818,000 Californians moved from California to the interior West between 1985 and 1991 (Bonfante 1993), with net emigration peaking in 1992–93 at 83,000. Since then, net migration rates have fallen (to only 16,000 in 1996) and domestic immigrants are expected to exceed emigrants again by 1998 (California Department of Finance 1997, 9). Unlike the rest of California (especially metropolitan areas and the Central Valley), the Sierra Region experienced low natural increases, low foreign immigration, and low domestic migration from other states from 1970 to 1990. Most of the population growth in the Sierra Region during this period was instead the result of migration from other parts of California. More than one-fourth (27 percent) of the 1990 Sierra Region residents lived in a different county within California in 1985. Given that the population of the entire Sierra Region grew by 39 percent in the 1980s, we would expect that at least 20 percent of the 1990 Sierra Region population was nonresident in 1985 (half the newcomers in the 1980s). Combined with the 7 percent of 1990 Sierra Region residents who were out of state in 1985, however, this means that more than one-third of 1990 Sierra Region residents were not resident in the same county only five years earlier. Some Sierra Region residents may have moved across county lines and remained within the Sierra Region, but this suggests that the turnover rate among migrants is much greater than the net changes in population would suggest. Fully 40 percent of residents of the Lake Tahoe Basin and Truckee areas in 1990 did not live in the same county in 1985.[3] Pat Jobes has estimated that four out of five migrants to the interior West's fast-growing small towns "don't stick," according to Ed Marston (1996c, 15), but there are no good data for the Sierra Nevada that would allow such an estimate. (Note that any short-term residents who moved into the Sierra Region between decennial census enumerations would not appear in the census data, so the rates reported above represent a low estimate of turnover rates.)

The high turnover rates are also partially explained by the demographic characteristics of the Sierra Region population and its new migrants. The population of the Sierra Nevada in 1990 was considerably older than the population of California. The percentage of people over 55 in the Sierra Region (27 percent) was 50 percent greater than the percentage for the state (18 percent). The proportion of people aged 15 to 24 was also lower in the Sierra Region (25 percent) than in California (34 percent). The percentages of people under 15 and from ages 35 to 54 were similar for the Sierra Region and the state. A coarse regional analysis of age-cohort changes from 1980 to 1990 suggests there has been a net emigration of young adults from ages 15 to 34 and net immigration of adults aged 35 to 54 and over 55 years of age. Despite the perception by some that only retirees are moving into the Sierra Region, the source of population growth appears to be both retirees and working-age adults. The 35-to-54 age cohort grew by nearly 7 percent in the Sierra Region from 1980 to 1990, while the over-55 age cohort remained relatively stable. This contrasts with an increase of slightly under 7 percent in the 35-to-54 cohort and a 1.5 percent decline in the over-55 age group for the state as a whole. Despite the larger proportion of older residents, then, much of the immigration by additional retirees during the 1980s merely replaced those in the same cohort who had moved out of the region or passed away. Because the Sierra Region has a disproportionately larger share of persons over 55 and a disproportionately smaller share of persons under 5, natural increase accounts for a very small fraction of annual population increases.[4]

A more detailed cohort-survival analysis of data for Nevada County shows that working-age adults are also bringing with them (or moving because of) young elementary-school-age children. Indeed, it appears that having a member of the household reach the age of kindergarten may be a critical factor driving migration to the Sierra Region. The model projects that fewer children will migrate to Nevada County when either under 5 years of age or between 15 and 19 than if in

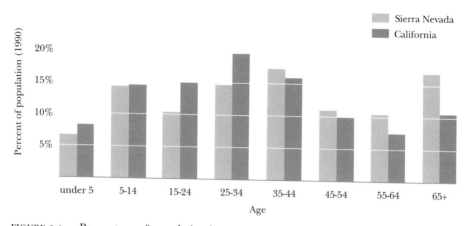

FIGURE 3.1.   Percentage of population by age in the Sierra Nevada and California, 1990.

the 5-to-9- and 10-to-14-year age groups. Following graduation from high school, young adults appear to emigrate either for school, employment, or the excitement of urban life; they are replaced not by immigrants in the same age cohort, but by families in their thirties with young children who have reached school age. Similar numbers of migrants in the 30-to-34-, 35-to-39-, 40-to-44-, and 45-to-49-year age cohorts are projected to migrate to Nevada County in the 1990s. Finally, a much larger cohort of retirees over age 50 are projected to move into the area, based on the 1980–90 trends.

The projected migration patterns for Nevada County and the state are quite different. The state projection shows emigration for all age classes from 60 to 84, while immigration is strong in the 20-to-29-year age class (which includes emigration for Nevada County). It is important, however, to note another factor, in addition to migration characteristics: Nevada County's general fertility rate was only sixty-two per thousand females, compared to an average of seventy-three per thousand females for all of California. Migration is therefore a more significant factor in population growth in the Sierra Region than for the state.[5] California's growth, in contrast, is now increasingly fueled by natural increases.[6]

The characteristic that most distinguishes the Sierra Region from the rest of California, however, is not its age structure or the degree of domestic migration from other parts of California driving population growth but the fact that the population of the Sierra Region is overwhelmingly white. This ethnic homogeneity of the region's population has been cited by some as the primary reason for in-migration (Walsh 1991). While the state is becoming increasingly heterogeneous in cultural and ethnic terms, approximately 92 percent of the Sierra Region was white in 1990. Nevada County was more than 97 percent white in 1990, making it the most ethnically homogeneous county in the state. The comparative figure for the state was 69 percent. Three of the Sierra Region counties (Amador, Tuolumne,

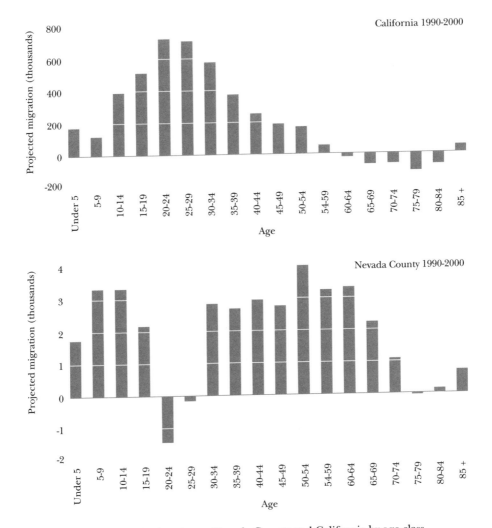

FIGURE 3.2.   Projected migration to Nevada County and California by age class, 1990–2000.

and Kern) also have state correctional facilities that account for a significant fraction of each county's population (approximately 10 percent of Amador County's total population). The inmates at these state prisons are much more ethnically heterogeneous, with only 7,296 of the 24,177 inmates (30 percent) being white. The nonincarcerated population of the Sierra Region is therefore 94 percent white; nonwhites are five times as common in the California population as in the Sierra Region population.[7]

The 1990 census is likely to have undercounted some nonwhite ethnic groups, however, and there appears to have been a significant increase in nonwhite residents of the Sierra Region in the 1990s. The undercounting is likely to have been most significant for Hispanics, or Latinos, which is also the group that appears to

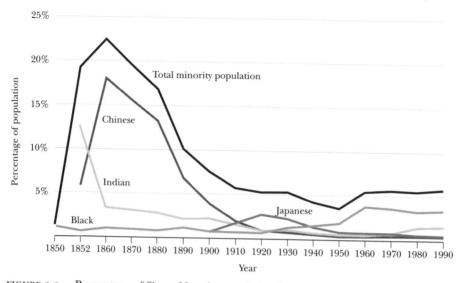

FIGURE 3.3.   Percentage of Sierra Nevada population by minority ethnicity, 1850–1990.

have increased the most (as a fraction of the total population) since 1990. South
Lake Tahoe resort casinos are increasingly employing Latinos or Filipinos instead
of young, seasonal white workers in low-wage kitchen and maintenance jobs. This
is a phenomenon most evident in the dominance of Spanish behind the kitchen
door or among the maids cleaning rooms at any high-rise casino (Ames 1992–95;
Jones 1996b). An informal economy has also appeared in some areas where many
Latinos gather at a regular spot each day for day wage labor. It is unclear whether
undocumented aliens are a significant part of this underground labor pool. Most
appear to be legitimate residents, either with citizenship or a green card allowing
work on a permanent resident visa.[8] This is certainly true for the more formal
employment sector in the tourism industry, but the Immigration and Natural-
ization Service has recently made several high-profile busts in western resort towns
that have highlighted the role of immigrant labor in the regional economy (Jones
1996b).

    The dominant ethnicity of the nonwhite population of the Sierra Region also
varies by subregion. Portions of the eastern Sierra Nevada have significant Native
American populations, for example, as a percentage of the relatively small total
subregional population. The greatest ethnic heterogeneity appears in the southern Sierra Nevada subregion, with its strong ties to the agricultural communities
of the southern Central Valley. There is a higher percentage of Hispanics in this
portion of the Sierra Region and a lower percentage of whites than in any other
subregion. In the next section, I will discuss these regional differences in relation
to the ecological resources of the Sierra Nevada.

THE SIX SUBREGIONS OF THE SIERRA NEVADA

Just as the Sierra Region looks different from either the eighteen-county region or the rest of California, there are significant differences in social, demographic, and economic characteristics between its subregions, counties, and communities. To understand the relationship between Nature and Culture in the exurban West and the rapidly changing Range of Light, it is therefore necessary to look more closely at these subregions, counties, and communities. The Sierra Nevada—like the rest of the exurban West—is complex both socially and ecologically. Although this represents somewhat of a simplification, I have disaggregated the Sierra Region's census data by county into the following geographic subregions (these include only the portion of each county within the Sierra Region defined above):

Gold Country: west slope of Nevada, Placer, and El Dorado Counties[9]
Mother Lode: Amador, Calaveras, Tuolumne, Mariposa, and Madera Counties[10]
Lake Tahoe: east slope of Nevada, Placer, and El Dorado Counties[11]
Northern Sierra: Butte, Plumas, Sierra, and Yuba Counties[12]
Eastern Sierra: Alpine, Mono, and Inyo Counties[13]
Southern Sierra: Fresno, Kern, and Tulare Counties[14]

These subregional aggregations are defined socially and institutionally, following the jurisdictional boundaries of counties. This is primarily to allow use of the many data sources collected at or aggregated to the county level. (I nevertheless limited my analysis to areas included within the CCDs in the Sierra Region of those counties.) Social and demographic analyses completed for SNEP defined a slightly different set of subregions, placing Alpine County in the greater Lake Tahoe subregion and including portions of Lassen County in the Northern Sierra subregion. The general conclusions that I reach here about the character of the subregions are nevertheless supported by the results of SNEP's analyses (Stewart 1996; Doak and Kusel 1996; Duane 1996a).

More than two-fifths (44 percent) of the Sierra Region population in 1990 lived in only three counties: Nevada, Placer, and El Dorado. If the county of Amador is included, 49 percent live within counties whose foothill regions are within commuting distance of the greater Sacramento metropolitan area, while 18 percent of these (8 percent of the entire Sierra Region) live within the Lake Tahoe–Truckee area. When the Lake Tahoe–Truckee subregion is combined with the Eastern Sierra subregion counties, more than 12 percent of the Sierra Region population lives east of the Sierra Nevada crest (although part of Alpine County is west of the crest, it is included here because of its subalpine location and economic dependence on recreation). These regional differences have important implications for the pattern of future urbanization and economic development.

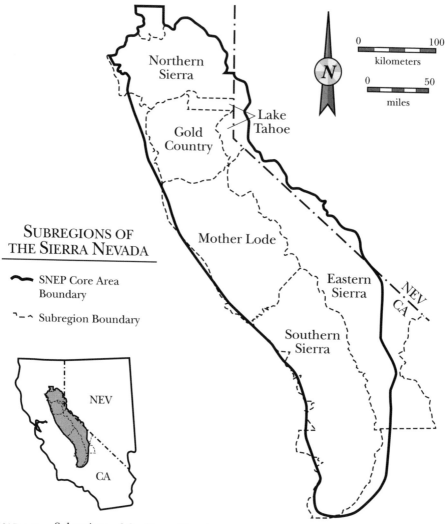

MAP 3.2.   Subregions of the Sierra Nevada.

Development of land and resource management strategies for the entire Sierra Region must therefore reflect these differences.

These subregional differences are particularly important in terms of economic development and the relative importance of different types of natural resources management strategies. Each region has a distinctive relationship to the Sierra Nevada environment. For this reason, a one-size-fits-all strategy for land and resource management or economic development is unlikely to be effective, since the different subregions and communities have such different underlying ecological, economic, and social characteristics. The relationship between Nature and Culture varies by subregion. Moreover, a community-by-community breakdown

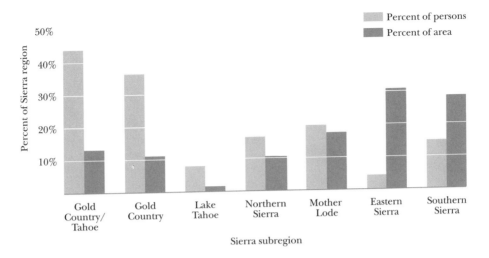

FIGURE 3.4.   Subregional shares of Sierra Nevada population and area, 1990.

shows significant variation in that relationship even within these subregions. Finally, there are additional important differences *within* Sierra Nevada communities that make them heterogeneous social units for analysis. These may reflect class, gender, tenure, or length of residence in the area. Differences within each of these groups may also reflect different environmental values. Migrants of the 1970s may differ significantly from migrants of the 1980s in terms of their primary motivations for moving to the Sierra Nevada. These different motivations may in turn translate into different behavioral patterns of land and resource management.

This latter point—that the differences between the resident population of the Sierra Region and the rest of the state of California may be less important than differences among residents of the Sierra—is critical. Early studies indicate that recent migrants to exurban areas tend to have more education, wealth, and income than earlier residents (Bradshaw and Blakely 1981). Equally significant, they often have different attitudes toward the Sierra Nevada environment and the local community (J. Moore Methods, 1992; Sierra Business Council 1997). This suggests a significant social transformation in the Sierra since the beginning of the rural renaissance nearly thirty years ago. Given the recent influx of new residents, at least 56 percent of current residents have been in the region less than twenty years and 28 percent less than ten. I will explore some of the ecological implications of these differences between "newcomers" and "old-timers" below in a detailed discussion of Nevada County.

With these caveats in mind, here is a general description of each subregion. (I have developed population forecasts for each subregion based on 1993 forecasts for the 1990–2040 period prepared at the county level by the Demographic

Research Unit of the California Department of Finance [DOF]. The subregional forecasts represent my projections, not the DOF's. My forecasting method for allocating the DOF forecasts is described in detail below).

The Gold Country

This is the focal point of Sierra Region population growth, and it is driven primarily by an influx of retirees, a desire for good quality of life, and expansion of the Sacramento metropolitan area. The area has experienced service-sector job growth, but offers lower wages than do urban areas. It has increasing commuter ties to the Sacramento metropolitan region (including electronics industry employment in the western Placer County cities of Roseville and Rocklin and the eastern Sacramento County city of Folsom). It also features a diversified economic base with some localized dependence on extractive industry, significant recreation and tourism, and high levels of income through transfer payments in the form of dividends and interest via the mailbox economy—which in turn creates service-sector employment in financial services and health care. This subregion has experienced the greatest change over the past three decades. It is home to 36 percent of Sierra Region residents, but 40 percent of the 1970–90 population increase. Some communities in this area are taking on suburban characteristics, including traffic congestion and increasing crime rates normally associated with metropolitan regions. Several gated communities market social and ethnic homogeneity and safety. Increasing housing costs have generated a reverse commute of service workers coming up to the region from the Sacramento metropolitan area. Between 30 and 50 percent of all employed workers living within this region commute to the Sacramento metropolitan area. Many others are employed in the electronics industry centered in Grass Valley and Nevada City, which exports high-technology products for worldwide use. Congestion and safety concerns along the Highway 49 transportation corridor constrain further development of manufacturing capacity, which is currently limited to the Interstate 80 and U.S. Highway 50 corridors, the only four-lane freeways in the Sierra Region. Extractive-industry dependence is primarily in the timber sector, with significant private timberlands under the ownership of Sierra Pacific Industries. There are mills operating in Camino (El Dorado County) and Folsom (just west of the El Dorado County line), but Nevada County's mills have closed. The gold rush towns of Nevada City, Grass Valley, Auburn, Georgetown, and Placerville draw tourists to festivals, sporting events, parades, and other events, with their quaint Victorian-era architecture and gaslights on the main streets. Historic state parks at the Coloma Gold Discovery Site, the Empire Mine, and Malakoff Diggins are also popular.

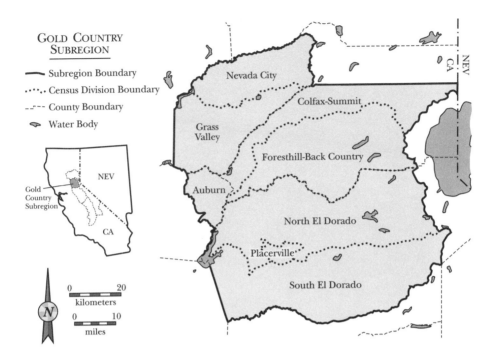

GOLD COUNTRY
SUBREGION

▬ Subregion Boundary
····· Census Division Boundary
‒·‒‒ County Boundary
◅ Water Body

Gold
Country
Subregion

NEV

CA

Nevada City

Colfax-Summit

Grass
Valley

Foresthill-Back Country

Auburn

North El Dorado

Placerville

South El Dorado

CA | NEV

0   20
kilometers
0   10
miles

N

MAP 3.3.   Gold Country subregion.

The Gold Country is the most populated and the fastest-growing part of the
Sierra Region. Parts of it more closely resemble suburban areas of the state than
the rural image of the Sierra Nevada. The 36 percent of the Sierra Region population that lives in this subregion inhabits only 11 percent of the entire Sierra
Region land area. The Gold Country is also the wealthiest subregion, with median
household income levels approaching (and in the South El Dorado CCD even
exceeding) the state median household income. Only in the Gold Country subregion did the growth in median housing value (109 percent) exceed the subregion's growth in median household income (101 percent) during the 1980s.
Median household income nevertheless grew at a higher rate here than in the
Sierra Region as a whole (89 percent) or in California (97 percent). These statistics suggest that the defining characteristic of the Gold Country is its increasing
integration into an urban and metropolitan economy. The potential environmental effects of increasing suburbanization present a significant challenge for the
subregion (Griffiths 1993, 35). This is the central issue facing the area and the
focus of my work here.

Gold Country communities comprise a prototypical exurban region in transition: there is a complex mix of economic activities, with resource dependency pri-

FIGURE 3.5.   Traffic congestion in the Gold Country subregion of the
Sierra Nevada.

marily tied to the landscape's amenities. Commodity extraction and recreation
and tourism are also important, but the primary value of the natural landscape is
as an attractant for residents. Based on the April 1993 DOF forecast, the population of the Gold Country CCDs is projected to grow 179 percent, from 222,837
in 1990 to 621,842 by the year 2040. As a result of regulatory constraints imposed
within the Lake Tahoe Basin since the 1970–80 period, however, this probably

understates the level of growth in this subregion: the balance of growth that we have forecast for the Lake Tahoe subregion would probably take place in the Gold Country subregion of Nevada, Placer, and El Dorado Counties instead. Based on the original forecast, however, the Gold Country subregion's growth rate is relatively low compared to both the Mother Lode and Southern Sierra subregions. The Gold Country subregion's share of overall Sierra Region population will therefore decrease from 36 percent in 1990 to only 30 percent by the year 2040.

The Mother Lode

This subregion is characterized by slower population growth and smaller absolute population than in the Gold Country, but similar factors drive its development (the Mother Lode's 1990 population density equals the Gold Country's 1970 density). It may have stronger ties to extractive industries (especially mining) than the Gold Country, and it presents a limited commute to Central Valley towns along the Highway 99 corridor. It features gateways to Yosemite and depends significantly on management, housing, and transportation decisions regarding park employees and visitors. The most rapid urbanization (and economic diversification) in the subregion is taking place in Tuolumne County near Sonora, at a critical transportation node connecting the valley, Highway 49, and access to Yosemite. Areas near Jackson are also within commuting distance of Sacramento, but that route is limited by the capacity of two-lane Highway 16. State prison facilities in Ione are an important source of local employment and hold about one-tenth of Amador County's total resident population. The proposed doubling of the state's prison population by the year 2000 under the so-called Three Strikes and You're Out initiative (Proposition 184, passed by California voters in 1994) could lead to further prison expansions. There are several gated communities in the region, but their housing values and average incomes are lower than those in the Gold Country. Agriculture and traditional commodity extraction activities are still more important to the local economy here than in the Gold Country—not unlike the Gold Country's characteristics twenty years ago. Sierra Pacific Industries recently purchased the lumber mill in Martell (from Georgia-Pacific) and the lumber mill west of Sonora near China Camp (from Fibreboard), and the Martell mill is expected to close (Foothill Conservancy 1997). In 1994, the Jamestown mine in Tuolumne County also shut down. Closure of the lumber mill in North Fork (Madera County) has led to a comprehensive effort to revitalize the community through economic diversification and new investments in infrastructure.[15] The nearby Yosemite gateway community of Oakhurst, in contrast, suffers from rapid, unplanned growth unleashed to meet the needs of ever-increasing tourists who cannot find accommodations in the national park itself. Major new subdivisions

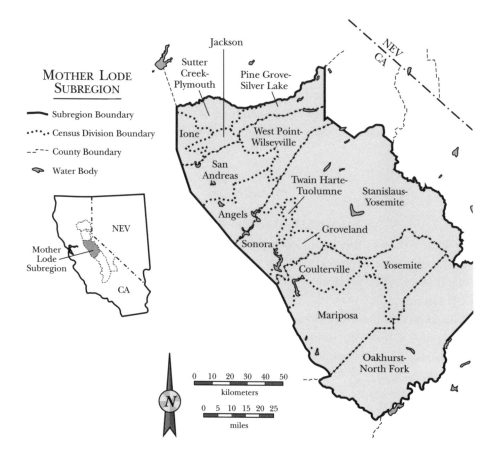

MAP 3.4.   Mother Lode subregion.

have also been proposed west of Sonora for Modesto-bound valley commuters (Malley 1992–93; Buckley 1993–97; Edwards 1992–93; 1996).

The Mother Lode population's age structure and pattern of personal income sources (i.e., a high percentage of persons over fifty-five, a low percentage of persons under fifteen, and a high proportion of unearned income) resemble those of the economically depressed Northern Sierra. Per capita values for this subregion are biased, however, by the presence of two state prisons. The subregion also has a high rate of population growth, high level of income growth, lower incidence of poverty, and high level of immigration from other parts of the state, however, suggesting that the Mother Lode is undergoing a type of economic transformation very different from that in the Northern Sierra subregion. The Mother Lode had

FIGURE 3.6.   Undeveloped land in the Mother Lode subregion of the Sierra Nevada.

the highest percentage of 1990 residents who lived in other California counties in 1985, and Amador and Calaveras Counties experienced some of the highest growth in the entire Sierra Region during the 1980s. The median value of owner-occupied housing in the Mother Lode was nevertheless only 60 percent of the state level in 1990, reflecting fewer price pressures here than in the Gold Country. The Mother Lode is in some ways the most representative of the popular image of growth in the Sierra Region: older persons and retirees moving into uncrowded rural communities, many of whom are probably equity refugees still taking advantage of lower rural housing prices. This is similar to the Gold Country in 1970, when average population densities were comparable. Growth patterns over the next twenty years may resemble those of the Gold Country from 1970 to 1990 if the population continues to grow at such a high rate, and if the subregion becomes increasingly integrated economically with the booming Central Valley. Planners and community leaders may therefore be able to learn significant lessons from the recent growth experiences in the neighboring counties to the north in the Gold Country subregion (Griffiths 1993, 37). Residents of the Mother Lode need only drive north on Highway 49 to see the future, if their own area's development patterns continue according to business as usual.

As in the Gold Country, Mother Lode communities illustrate the prototypical exurban region in transition: they hold a complex mix of economic activities, with resource dependency primarily tied to the landscape's amenities. The Mother Lode is at an earlier stage in the transformation process, however, and its greater distance from the Sacramento metropolitan area is likely to reduce the relative importance of suburban commuters. Based on the April 1993 DOF forecast, the population of the Mother Lode CCDs is projected to grow 236 percent, from 124,795 in 1990 to 418,900 by the year 2040. Despite this rapid growth, the subregion's share of overall Sierra Region population is expected to increase only slightly, from 20 percent in 1990 to 21 percent by the year 2040.

Lake Tahoe

Heavily dependent on tourism and recreation, including downhill skiing and gaming in Nevada casinos, this subregion has strong economic ties to the Bay Area. Some of its residents are retirees and others commute to Nevada jobs, but the influx of weekend and summer visitors drives the economy. The Lake Tahoe subregion has a much higher fraction of renters and seasonally vacant housing units than the rest of the Sierra (except the town of Mammoth Lakes in Mono County, in the Eastern Sierra subregion, which has a similar profile). All-weather access via Interstate 80 and U.S. Highway 50 has made the Lake Tahoe region the scene of weekly traffic jams as Bay Area and Sacramento-area residents flock to the mountains on Friday evening and return on Sunday. Lake Tahoe also remains an internationally recognized travel destination; Reno and South Lake Tahoe draw visitors interested in cabaret entertainment and gaming. The establishment of the Tahoe Regional Planning Agency in 1969 has resulted in development restrictions within the Lake Tahoe Basin, however, and spillover growth is now concentrated near the town of Truckee and along the Truckee River corridor near Highway 89.[16] Historic timber-cutting practices, together with the recent drought, have created forest conditions that threaten the amenity value of and heighten fire risk for the subregion's forests (Elliott-Fisk et al. 1996; Machida 1995).

Increased development of expensive exurban homes now makes forest health a paramount economic issue, but management prescriptions are limited by the presence of the very same homes. Internet access and other technologies are increasing the viability of two-home residents in the subregion, who live part-time in the Bay Area and part-time in the Lake Tahoe area. (Truckee is only three hours from San Francisco—close enough for a commuter to reach the Bay Area in time for an afternoon meeting and, after perhaps a second day of meetings, to make it home that same day.) As a result, many "second homes" are beginning to see year-round occupation. The communities in this region are isolated from the county seats of their respective counties, however, which are "over the hill" in Nevada City, Auburn, and Placerville. This isolation from local government deci-

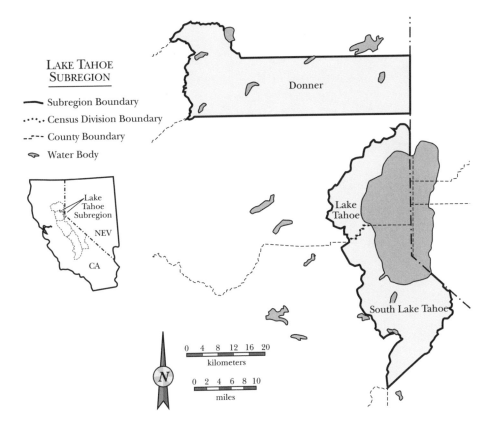

MAP 3.5.   Lake Tahoe subregion.

sion makers finally led to the incorporation of Truckee in 1993. A similar situation on the Nevada side of Lake Tahoe has led to secession attempts by the Incline Village portion of Washoe County.

The average population density of more than one person per 8.5 acres in the Lake Tahoe subregion is higher than in any other subregion of the Sierra Region. Moreover, because a large part of the Donner CCD in Nevada County is quite far from Lake Tahoe itself, the population density is actually significantly higher immediately around the lake. Development of the Tahoe Basin proper generally preceded the development of the rest of the Sierra Region, and the high rate of population growth in the 1970s decreased dramatically in the 1980s as stricter planning regulations took effect. Despite the fact that a high percentage of housing in the Tahoe Basin is for seasonal use (more than 30 percent of it), the most surprising trend distinguishing the Lake Tahoe subregion from the rest of the Sierra Region is the comparative stagnation of owner-occupied housing values

FIGURE 3.7.   Traffic and gaming casinos in the Lake Tahoe subregion of the Sierra
Nevada.

during the 1980s. The median value of owner-occupied housing in the subregion
increased by only 30 percent over the decade, compared to 130 percent growth
for the state median housing value. The median value of owner-occupied housing
in all of the CCDs in the Lake Tahoe subregion actually exceeded the median
value for California in 1980, but after the slow growth in those values during the
1980s the median values ranged from only 61 to 78 percent of the state level in
1990. Income from wages and salaries forms a high percentage of personal
income, and the population of the Lake Tahoe subregion is much younger than
that of the rest of the Sierra Region. The subregion also has the lowest percentage
of longtime residents, and a higher percentage of its 1990 population lived outside the state in 1985 than did that of either the Sierra Region or California
(Griffiths 1993, 36).

   The communities in this region are prototypically resource-dependent on
recreation and tourism, with very limited ties (except historical) to commodity
extraction. Many of the issues confronting the exurban Gold Country are also relevant here, for these communities are in the same counties as the Gold Country.
Based on the April 1993 DOF forecast, the population of the Lake Tahoe CCDs is
projected to grow 147 percent, from 48,329 in 1990 to 119,453 by the year 2040.
As a result of regulatory constraints that have been imposed within the Lake Tahoe
Basin since the 1970–80 period, however, this probably overstates the level of

growth in this subregion. Instead, the balance of growth will probably take place in the Gold Country subregion of Nevada, Placer, and El Dorado Counties or in the "bathtub ring" outside Tahoe Regional Planning Agency controls (including Squaw Valley and Truckee).[17] If the Lake Tahoe subregion continues to grow according to this forecast, its share of overall Sierra Region population will remain steady at 8 percent through the year 2040.

The Eastern Sierra

This subregion, too, is heavily dependent on tourism and recreation, including downhill skiing. It is also a gateway to national parks and wilderness areas. While no one commutes to or maintains strong economic ties to the Central Valley, there are strong social and cultural ties between this subregion and both Los Angeles and Nevada. A significant amount of water is exported to Los Angeles; hydroelectric power is generated here for Southern California Edison and the Los Angeles Department of Water and Power. Public ownership of local lands by the Los Angeles Department of Water and Power, Forest Service, and Bureau of Land Management dominates the area. National Park Service management of Yosemite, Sequoia–Kings Canyon, and the Devil's Postpile directly affects the local economy. This area is isolated geographically from Northern and Central California throughout the winter months, yet it is closely tied to Southern California through both a long history of conflict over water resources development and continuing economic dependence on Southern Californian tourists. Population growth has been limited primarily by the availability of private land and water supplies, although the downturn in the Southern California economy (together with the state's long drought) negatively affected the Mammoth Mountain ski area in the late 1980s and early 1990s. Non-skiing recreation continues to grow, and seasonal shifts in visitation have dampened extreme swings in economic activity and employment. The annual summer opening of the Tioga Pass Road is still a critical event in the economic lifeblood of the region, however, for it increases access for Northern and Central California visitors. The communities of Mammoth Lakes and Bishop are more prosperous and more closely tied to the recreation and tourism trade, while communities in southern Inyo County and northern Mono County do not benefit as directly economically. There are also significant differences in income levels and poverty by ethnicity; the Native American population does not appear to benefit from local economic activity generated by the recreation and tourism sectors.

The Eastern Sierra subregion is distinguished by three characteristics: physical isolation, sparse population, and a recreation and tourism industry that has engendered a large variation in the relative level of local economic development and wealth. The region's population did experience some growth during the rural

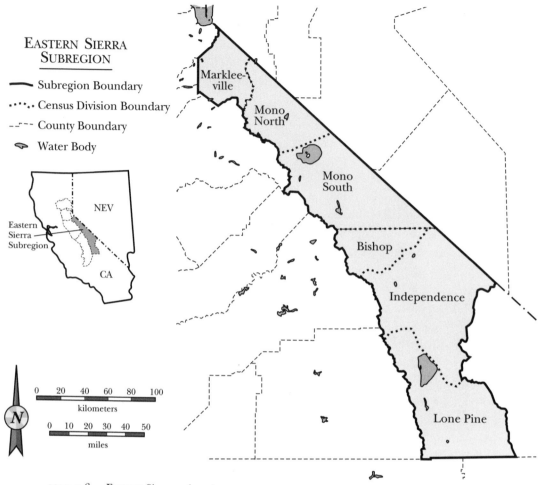

MAP 3.6.   Eastern Sierra subregion.

renaissance of the 1970s, but overall population growth from 1970 to 1990 was far lower than for the rest of the Sierra Nevada. The Eastern Sierra was the least populated and slowest growing part of the Sierra Region in 1990. The importance of the recreation and tourism industry in the Eastern Sierra is indicated by the differences between the Mono South CCD (and to a lesser degree the Bishop and Markleeville CCDs) and the rest of the subregion in nearly every social and economic characteristic. The similarity of the Mono South CCD to the Lake Tahoe subregion suggests that the developed recreation opportunities around the town of Mammoth Lakes have a dominating effect on the socioeconomic statistics for the subregion. Most of the Eastern Sierra is relatively poor, however, with a high incidence of poverty and low levels of household income growth. The Mono South CCD, in contrast, had a median household income level in 1990 that was 30 percent higher than in any other CCD in the subregion (Griffiths 1993, 37, 39).

FIGURE 3.8.   Remnants of ranching in the Eastern Sierra subregion of the Sierra Nevada.

The communities in this region are prototypically resource-dependent on recreation and tourism, although historical ties to grazing still dominate the cultural landscape. Even local cattle ranchers are now marketing the Old West to tourists.[18] Based on the April 1993 DOF forecast, the population of the Eastern Sierra CCDs is projected to grow 136 percent, from 28,509 in 1990 to 67,418 by the year 2040. This relatively slow growth rate means that the subregion's share of overall Sierra Region population will decrease from 5 percent in 1990 to only 3 percent by the year 2040.

The Northern Sierra

The timber industry and tourism dominate this area. Retirees are concentrated in a part of Butte County, and there are few commuters. Water export and power generation represent significant watershed value. The Northern Sierra stands out among the various subregions with its greater unemployment and poverty, and its lower levels of education, economic diversification, and population turnover, as well as its heavier dependence on government. Butte County was brought to the verge of bankruptcy in the late 1980s as it struggled with its declining economy in

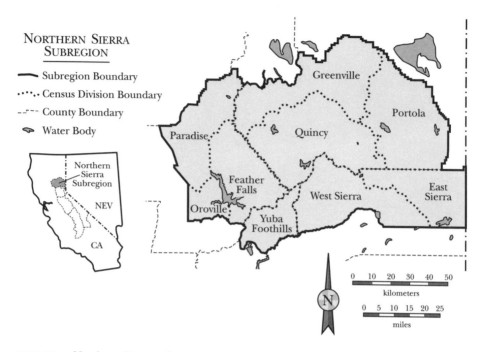

MAP 3.7.   Northern Sierra subregion.

the post–Proposition 13 era and a growing social services burden (Thurlow 1989). Plumas and Sierra Counties are the most timber-dependent in the state, according to two criteria: the percentage of the workforce employed in the timber sector, and the percentage of local government revenues that depend on timber harvests. Cutbacks in federal timber harvests in the 1990s have therefore had a disproportionate influence on local government revenues and local timber-sector employment than in other subregions. Extensive hydroelectric and water resources development in the Feather River watershed generate natural resource exports valued at more than $1 billion per year,[19] but very little of that value is returned to the local economy at present. The Plumas Corporation (a nonprofit economic development agency) has worked with PG&E to reduce the effects of upstream sediment loss on hydroelectric production, but upstream investments by downstream beneficiaries of Feather River water resources have been very limited. Recent proposals to reform federal timber harvests include provisions to complete labor-intensive landscape restoration activity through funding tied to a water user fee (Duane 1995; 1997b). Economic diversification along the lines of the Gold Country, Lake Tahoe, or Mother Lode subregions is limited by the geographic isolation of the Northern Sierra communities from metropolitan areas

Aggregate statistics representing the Northern Sierra are weighted toward the densely populated CCDs in the foothills of Butte County, which contain 77 per-

FIGURE 3.9.   Logs at a lumber mill in the Northern Sierra subregion of the Sierra Nevada.

cent of the subregion's population. At higher elevations, in Plumas and Sierra Counties, the Northern Sierra is relatively unpopulated, with densities of less than one person per 85 acres. This is only one-tenth the average density of the Lake Tahoe subregion. Population growth from 1970 to 1990 was well below the rate for the Sierra Nevada as a whole, and it fell off dramatically in the 1980s. The Northern Sierra has the highest percentage of longtime residents, the highest percentage of population over the age of fifty-five, the lowest income levels, and the lowest percentage of seasonal housing in the Sierra Region. During the 1980s, the percentage of older residents increased and the household incomes decreased relative to the rest of the Sierra Region and the state. Although the circulation of unearned income injected into the Northern Sierra by the growing elderly population offers some potential for diversification, the lack of communication and transportation links to the rest of California and the recent decline of the timber industry suggest that economic development considerations will be a fundamental concern in the Northern Sierra in the future (Griffiths 1993, 34–35).

The communities in this region are prototypically resource-dependent on commodity extraction, although there are opportunities for recreation and tourism. There are also interesting opportunities to link resource exports to landscape restoration and investments in watershed health. Based on the April 1993 DOF forecast, the population of the Northern Sierra CCDs is projected to grow 149 percent, from 102,110 in 1990 to 254,563 by the year 2040. This relatively slow cent, from 102,110 in 1990 to 254,563 by the year 2040. This relatively slow growth rate means that the subregion's share of overall Sierra Region population will decrease slightly from 16 percent in 1990 to 13 percent by the year 2040.

The Southern Sierra

This area has strong ties to the agriculture-dominated Central Valley counties; only a small minority of the population of each of its counties lives in the Sierra Region. More of its residents work in agriculture than in the rest of the Sierra Nevada. The area also has the highest fraction of nonwhite residents, primarily of Hispanic descent. This subregion functions as the gateway to tourism and recreation in Sequoia and Kings Canyon National Parks, as well as to wilderness areas important for backcountry recreation and to developed recreation sites at hydroelectric reservoirs. The Southern Sierra has experienced lower absolute population growth and has a smaller population than northern counties, but it has seen rapid growth in relative terms, comparable to that in the Gold Country. Visitation to Sequoia and Kings Canyon National Parks is becoming increasingly important to the local economy. There is also a sovereign Native American tribe that is managing its resources for a multitude of objectives at the Tule River Indian Reservation (Baker and Stewart 1996). The Central Valley Project and Friant Dam provide significant water resources from the San Joaquin River to Central Valley irrigators; the Kern County Water Agency has tapped the Kern River watershed. Changes in federal and state water policy (e.g., the Central Valley Project Improvement Act of 1992) could have important influences on future management of these resources. As in the case of the Feather River, very little of the economic value of these resources is returned to local communities within the Sierra Region. The expanding metropolitan centers of Fresno and Bakersfield increasingly dominate the entire region's economy, with much of the recent growth in the Southern Sierra subregion apparently the result of commuters working in the Central Valley (Graber 1994–97; Baxter 1992–96; Cloer 1992–93). Gang-related violence in both cities is one factor driving migration within Fresno and Kern Counties from the larger urban centers up to the foothills of the Sierra Region. Political control for local government remains within the Central Valley, however, for the Sierra Region accounts for only a small fraction of the population of these counties. The Central Valley is in turn dominated by agriculture and oil and gas production interests.[20] Forty percent of Fresno County lies in the Sierra Region, but only 4 percent of its residents live there. Sierra Region residents therefore represent only one-fifth of one county supervisor's constituency, while valley issues dominate county government.

Absolute population growth for the Southern Sierra subregion from 1970 to 1990 was slightly less than in the Mother Lode subregion, but the percentage

MAP 3.8.   Southern Sierra subregion.

growth was higher because of the lower base population in 1970. From 1970 to 1990, the Sierra Region portions of Kern and Madera Counties had the highest population growth rates of any of the eighteen core Sierra Region counties in California. The Southern Sierra has the lowest percentage of population that is white, although the subregion as a whole is still above the average for the state. Parts of the Southern Sierra nevertheless reflect an ethnic composition more similar to that of California as a whole. Climatic and geological factors that allow agricultural activity at higher elevations here than in other parts of the Sierra Region, together with the historical ties of many nonwhite ethnic groups to Central Valley agriculture, may partially explain this subregional characteristic (Griffiths 1993, 39–40).

It is difficult to isolate statistics for the Sierra Region of Fresno, Tulare, and Kern Counties, since the overwhelming majority of all social and economic activity occurs in the non-Sierran portions of those counties. This also makes the

FIGURE 3.10.   Giant sequoia and young fir in the Southern Sierra subregion of the Sierra Nevada.

growth allocation model least reliable for this part of the Sierra Region. Based on the April 1993 DOF forecast, however, the population of the Southern Sierra CCDs is projected to grow a remarkable 384 percent, from 92,366 in 1990 to 447,479 by the year 2040. This rapid growth rate means that the subregion's share of overall Sierra Region population will increase dramatically, from 15 percent in 1990 to 25 percent by the year 2040. The southern Sierra Nevada foothills are steeper than those in the Gold Country and Mother Lode, however, and severe air quality problems in the southern San Joaquin Valley could result in development restrictions (or altered patterns of metropolitan development in the valley itself) that would constrain development in the area. These projections are therefore the most uncertain in the entire Sierra Region as a result of the fact that the Southern Sierra subregion represents only a fraction of the overall population of the Sierra counties in the subregion.

INCOME AND EMPLOYMENT IN THE SIERRA NEVADA

Based on the 1990 census data at the CCD level, the weighted average of median household incomes of the entire Sierra Region ($29,595) was only five-sixths the median household income for California as a whole ($35,798).[21] This reflected a slower median income growth of only 89 percent in the Sierra Region versus 96 percent growth in the state from 1980 to 1990. The Sierra Region median income therefore dropped from 86 percent of the state median income in 1980 to 83 percent of the state median income in 1990. As shown above, however, median incomes in some subregions and communities of the Sierra Region exceed the state median income level. This makes generalizations about the entire Sierra Region somewhat unreliable.

The 1990 census data appear to understate significant sources of income, however, when compared with the Locally Adjusted Personal Income (LAPI) data prepared at the county level based on *actual* 1989 income tax returns. Wage and salary income is accurately reported in the 1990 census data, but census respondents significantly underreported (by a factor of two to three) the transfer payments they receive (Stewart 1996). These transfer payments constitute a significant part of total personal and household income in the Sierra Region. Transfer payments include interest, dividends, rent, retirement, Social Security, and public assistance payments. Many retirees and working white-collar migrants to the Sierra Region (many of whom commute to the Central Valley) have significant wealth and have moved to the Sierra Region with equity gains from the sale of homes in a highly appreciated metropolitan real estate market. These residents are likely to have high interest, dividend, rent, and retirement income. Many lower-income residents of the Sierra Region are also likely to receive a significant fraction of their total income through transfer payments in the form of Social Security and public assistance. Underestimating transfer payments by this magnitude in the 1990 census is therefore likely to understate average and median incomes and overstate the percentage of the population below the poverty line.

Despite this bias, however, the Sierra Region had a lower poverty rate (10 percent) than the state of California (13 percent) in the 1990 census.[22] It is also clear—even with the underreported transfer payments—that wage and salary income is a less important source of personal income in the Sierra Region than in California as a whole. Sierra Region residents derived only 62 percent of their total personal income from wages and salaries in 1989 (the income year that is the basis for responses to the 1990 census questions), compared with 74 percent for Californians overall. An additional 11 percent was derived from nonfarm self-employment, which is significantly greater than the corresponding state figure of 8 percent. This is consistent with several of the factors cited above as sources of rapid nonmetropolitan population growth. While I did not live in the Sierra Nevada in either 1989 or 1990, my own income from 1985 to 1991 was completely based on nonfarm self-employment as an independent consultant. This included significant income that I brought into the Sierra Region in 1986–88 while living in Nevada County and working on my Ph.D. dissertation at Stanford

University. My self-employment was made possible through innovations in telecommunications and computing technologies. The availability of Federal Express also allowed me to communicate inexpensively with consulting clients and my dissertation committee in the San Francisco Bay Area, while corporate restructuring created new opportunities to work with large organizations outside the Sierra Region. Neither my job nor my income showed up in the statistics of the Employment Development Department (EDD), however, which records only wage and salary income for employment within each county. To the EDD, nonfarm self-employment (the source of my locally generated income) does not count as a job.

The EDD's county-level time-series data on tax revenues and employment differ from the census data in that they record *employment* within a given county and its monthly, seasonal, and annual variation. In contrast, the census data reflect the characteristics of the *residents* of a given county or CCD, and are recorded only once per decade. Residents who commute outside the county and/or the Sierra Region are therefore captured in the census data, while employees commuting into a county from another county are captured in the EDD data. Self-employed or retired individuals are also excluded from the EDD data.[23]

Residents of the Sierra Region who commute to the Sacramento metropolitan area, other Central Valley towns, or Reno are also left out of the EDD data for the Sierra Region. Their incomes still benefit the local Sierra Nevada economy, but their jobs and their wages and salaries are recorded by the EDD in Sacramento or other counties. (It is likely that commuters spend much of their income near their places of work, however, so their incomes do not get spent entirely within the local Sierra Region economy.) Relying on the EDD data to understand the Sierra Region economy is therefore likely to lead to erroneous conclusions that miss the importance of both nonfarm self-employment and income-generating residents of the Sierra Region who commute to work outside the county. This in turn has important implications for our understanding of the relationship between humans and the ecological resources of the Range of Light. It is therefore important to assess *all* sources of total personal income to understand the Sierra Region economy.

Transfer payments accounted for 25 percent of the Sierra Region income reported in the 1990 census, more than half again as large a fraction as the California average of 16 percent. As noted above, a comparison of the county-level LAPI data for 1989 and the county-level census data for 1990 shows that transfer payments were underreported by a factor of two to three in the 1990 census. Unfortunately, the LAPI adjustments are for county-level data and cannot be applied directly to the subcounty data at the census CCD level to generate a corrected table of income for the Sierra Region. Assuming that transfer payments are also underreported by a factor of two to three for the Sierra Region portion of the eighteen-county area, however, we can make a rough adjustment to the Sierra Region data. If transfer payments are underestimated by a factor of two (i.e., only

50 percent are reported), the percentage of total personal income derived from transfer payments in the Sierra Region increases from 25 to 40 percent. The fraction of total personal income derived from transfer payments jumps to 50 percent of total personal income if one assumes a threefold underreporting (i.e., only one-third of transfer payments were reported) in the 1990 census. This makes transfer payments a critical element of any economic analysis of the Sierra Nevada bioregion. They are likely to be of importance equal to wage and salary sources of total personal income, and they generate local jobs that multiply their effect.[24]

How important is wage and salary income from employment of Sierra Region residents in jobs within the Sierra Region? The wage and salary personal income figures from the 1990 census (either in their original form or after the LAPI adjustments) include income from commuters actually working outside the Sierra Region. Approximately 30 percent of employed residents of Nevada County and nearly 50 percent of employed residents in El Dorado County are employed outside the county and the Sierra Region (Nevada County Planning Department 1994; El Dorado County Community Development Department 1994). A smaller fraction of the employed residents of Placer County work outside the county, but a significant fraction of Sierra Region residents of Placer County who also work within Placer County do so outside the Sierra Nevada in the Sacramento metropolitan area employment centers of Roseville and Rocklin. (In 1990 over three-fifths of Placer County's population was in the non–Sierra Region portion of the county.) We can probably assume that at least 40 percent of employed residents of Placer County who live in the Sierra Region work outside the Sierra Region (the average of Nevada and El Dorado Counties). The western slope of these three counties accounted for 36 percent of the entire Sierra Region population in 1990. The median household income for every single CCD in this subregion was higher than both the state median household income and the weighted average median income for the Sierra Region in 1990, with the weighted average for this subregion ($34,613) being 17 percent higher than the weighted average for the Sierra Region ($29,595). The fraction of total personal income from wage and salary sources in this subregion is nevertheless similar to the Sierra Region's overall average (both 62 percent).

Based on EDD data for wage and salary levels for employment by county, it is likely that wage and salary incomes of those who commute from this subregion of the Sierra Region to the Sacramento metropolitan area account for a disproportionate share of total wage and salary income for the Sierra Region. Given that 30 to 50 percent of the wage and salary earners living in this part of the Sierra Region commute outside the Sierra Region for employment, close to half the wage and salary income in this subregion is therefore probably generated through employment outside the Sierra Region. Assuming that the 17 percent higher weighted average median household income for the subregion is a reasonable proxy for the subregion's share of total personal income (i.e., that mean household incomes are also 17 percent higher for this subregion than for the Sierra Region as a whole), this subregion would account for 42 percent of total Sierra Region household income. If half of the wage and salary income from the subregion is the result of employment outside the Sierra Region, then at least 21 percent of the wage and salary income for the Sierra Region is not related directly to employment within the region. This very conservative figure ignores all other commuting by Sierra Region residents in the other fifteen counties in the Sierra Region. Some of these clearly have significant commuter populations working in the Central Valley employment centers of Sacramento, Stockton, Modesto, Merced, Fresno, and Bakersfield. Others have commuters working in Nevada. A reasonable estimate is that around 10 percent of all other employed residents of the Sierra Region are employed outside the Sierra Region. This 10 percent figure would apply to the remaining 58 percent of wage and salary income not addressed above (assuming that the Sacramento metropolitan area commute-shed of western Nevada, Placer, and El Dorado Counties accounts for 42 percent of total personal income for the Sierra Region). A rough estimate of nearly 27 percent of all wage and salary income would therefore come from employment by Sierra Region residents in jobs located outside the Sierra Region.[25]

Accounting for the LAPI adjustments, this means that between 14 and 16 percent of total personal income for the Sierra Region is derived from outside employment. Combined with the 40 to 50 percent of total personal income resulting from transfer payments, between 56 and 64 percent of total personal income is generated outside the Sierra Region.[26] Only 36 to 44 percent of total personal income in the Sierra Region is therefore the result of wage and salary income or nonfarm self-employment income generated within the region. We can safely say that roughly $3 out of every $5 of total personal income in the Sierra Region is not generated by Sierra Region employment. This conclusion is based on a relatively conservative set of assumptions about the share of total personal income brought in by commuters.[27] As we shall see, much of that income is brought into the Sierra Region economy indirectly through the location decisions of firms and residents seeking the amenities of exurbia. Regional economic dependence on the ecological resources of the Sierra Nevada is therefore closely tied to the amenity services provided by the region, not only the extractive commodities that have traditionally been assumed to be the economic base of resource-dependent economies in the rural West. This has important implications for land and resource management in the Range of Light.

One element of the Sierra Region's economic amenities from 1970 to 1990 was the area's relatively low housing costs. The weighted average median value of owner-occupied houses in the Sierra Region was $128,678 in 1990, only two-thirds the median value of $195,500 for California. Despite significant growth pressures, that value increased only 80 percent from 1980 to 1990, while the median value for the state went up by 131 percent. The median value of a Sierra Region owner-occupied home therefore dropped from 84 percent of the state median to 68 percent from 1980 to 1990. In addition to these relatively low housing costs, a much higher fraction of Sierra Region homes are seasonal units—nearly 17 percent versus less than 2 percent for the state of California as a whole. As a result, the housing market in the Sierra Region is quite different from that of the rest of California. As of 1990 it was also much more affordable, since Sierra Region median incomes were 83 percent of the state median while median housing costs in the area were only 68 percent of the state median.

The 1990 census data is the most comprehensive data source we have for the Sierra Nevada population, but it is already outdated in many respects. The lag in housing-value growth between the metropolitan areas of California and the Sierra Nevada led to a surge of price pressures and real estate speculation in the late 1980s and early 1990s. This resulted in significant increases in prices during 1990 and 1991 that are not reflected in the median values reported by the 1990 census data. Many urbanites cashed out on this significant appreciation in urban markets and built trophy homes in the Sierra Nevada. The real estate development industry also built many new homes on speculation that the price feeding frenzy in urban markets would continue to support demand for high-end custom homes in the Sierra Nevada. This phenomenon was greatest in the counties within commuting distance of the Sacramento metropolitan area, but it also occurred in more remote areas such as the Lake Almanor peninsula in the Northern Sierra subregion. These equity refugees were not constrained by the need to maintain a job and wage or salary income. Unbelievable appreciation in their metropolitan houses gave them after-mortgage equity gains that often exceeded the total cost of buying a house in the lower-cost real estate market of the Sierra Nevada; without a monthly mortgage, these exurbanites could get by with considerably less monthly income. The wealth of these exurban equity refugees is therefore considerably more than their income might suggest. This has created a new crisis in affordable housing in the Sierra Nevada. There is now a countercommute of service workers going up Highways 50, 80, and 49 from the Sacramento metropolitan area every morning to work in the communities of the Sierra Nevada foothills. In the words of former El Dorado County Supervisor Bill Center, "The BMWs are going down the hill while the Pontiacs are going up the hill every morning"; then they reverse direction and pass each other again each evening. Median housing values are now lower in the Sacramento metropolitan area than in the foothill communities within the commute-shed.

Time-series analysis of housing markets demonstrates how rapid increases immediately after the 1990 census created the new affordability gap. Prices dropped again slightly and average listing times on the market increased as the rest of the state dropped into recession, but they did not drop as significantly as housing prices in the hyperinflated metropolitan markets (Marois 1995a). The flood of equity refugees has subsided a bit, however, demonstrating how dependent Sierra Region migration pressures are on the economic conditions in the metropolitan regions of California. Southern California lost an estimated half million jobs in the aerospace and defense sector from 1990 to 1994.[28] Many of these jobs were held by highly paid homeowners whose demand for housing helped to drive up housing prices in metropolitan areas. That demand created the equity gains that then allowed other metropolitan residents to exit to exurbia. Loss of those jobs has helped dry up equity gains (from 1991 to 1996).

Increases in Sierra Nevada housing prices have generally held at levels comparable to 1989–90, however, and this suggests that low-cost housing may no longer be a significant draw for new migrants in the 1990s and beyond. Median home prices jumped in Nevada County from around $120,000 in 1986 to a high of nearly $200,000 in 1990, but by 1995 they were back at levels comparable to those in 1989 (around $160,000) (Marois 1995a). Moreover, significant equity gains in metropolitan California real estate markets may be dampened by the hyperinflated values that existed in the late 1980s and their subsequent collapse in the early 1990s.[29] The combination of reduced metropolitan housing costs and increased Sierra Nevada housing costs means that equity refugees have less of an incentive to move based simply on the economic advantages associated with housing costs. As a result, future exurbanites may depend even more on employment income than recent migrants have had to, in order to make the move to exurbia. This raises important questions about future commute patterns; the traffic congestion of emerging patterns of exurban development, and this congestion's effect on air quality; and the economic and social mix of the emerging communities of exurbia. All these factors will affect population growth in the Sierra Region, for quality of life appears to be the primary impetus in population growth.[30]

FUTURE GROWTH PROJECTIONS
FOR THE SIERRA NEVADA

The Demographic Research Unit of the California Department of Finance produced its most recent county-level population projections in April 1993 for the period 1990–2040 (California Department of Finance 1993). The Center for the Continuing Study of the California Economy (CCSCE), an independent research institution in Palo Alto, California, has also produced a set of county-level population projections for the year 2005 (Center for the Continuing Study of the California Economy 1995). The CCSCE projections are consistent with the DOF projections, but the DOF projections extend much further into the future. I will therefore focus here on the DOF projections and their implications for the Sierra Nevada. The CCSCE forecast for the eighteen counties in the Sierra Region for the year 2005 is 3,671,300. This is slightly lower than the average of the DOF forecasts for 2000 (3,421,600) and 2010 (4,356,800), which is equal to 3,889,200 (approximately 6 percent higher than the CCSCE forecast). This is within the range of two alternative forecasts that I developed for the Sierra Region based on DOF forecasts. Because the DOF forecasts are available only for the county level, I had to estimate which portion of future growth in each county would occur within the Sierra Region of each county. As noted above, detailed data for population growth are available for the CCD level for only the 1970–90 period. Those data show that the Sierra Region gained approximately 175,000 residents each decade between 1970 and 1980 and between 1980 and 1990. Continuing that absolute level of growth from 1990 to 2040 would lead to a Sierra Region population of approximately 1.5 million.

I developed a simple model for allocating shares of county-level DOF population growth forecasts to each of the Sierra Region CCDs based on one of three simple ratios: the fraction of county-level growth in each CCD from 1970 to 1980; the fraction of county-level growth in each CCD from 1980 to 1990; or the fraction of county-level growth in each CCD from 1970 to 1990. Individual CCDs in the Sierra Region varied, with some CCDs having a greater share of county-level growth in one decade than the other. For the entire Sierra Region, however, the 1970–80 share of aggregate county-level growth for the eighteen-county region was around 8 percent greater than the 1980–90 share. The estimates I presented above are based on the highest estimate (from 1970–80 shares). These population forecasts could therefore be as much as 14 percent greater than the CCSCE forecasts and up to a third greater than the level reached if absolute population growth of 175,000 per decade continued in the Sierra Region from 1990 to 2040.[31] The effects on specific areas will vary widely by CCD.

Those DOF projections are quite daunting, but they appear to be plausible at least in the short term: California's population had already grown from slightly under 30 million in 1990 to 32.6 million at the beginning of 1997 (California Department of Finance 1997). The 1993 DOF forecast for the year 2000 projects a statewide population of more than 36 million (California Department of Finance 1993). Maintaining the current level of absolute growth would bring the population to only 34 million by 2000, but increasing legal international immigration and natural increases could result in meeting the DOF forecast. The next two largest states, Florida and Texas, had populations of about 18 million each in 1994. California could therefore equal the population of those two states' combined 1990 population (which was also equal to the combined population of the twenty-four smallest states in 1990) by the year 2000.

Based on the 1993 DOF forecast, I estimate that the Sierra Region population will more than *triple* from slightly over 600,000 in 1990 to nearly 2 million people (1,964,200) by the year 2040.[32] The lower CCSCE estimation function (14 percent below the "high" DOF forecast) would yield a Sierra Region population of 1,722,138 by the year 2040. This total would be comparable to the entire San Francisco Bay Area's population in 1940 (1,734,308).[33] The overall growth rate for the Sierra Nevada from 1990 to 2040 (226 percent) would also be comparable to the growth rate experienced by the Bay Area from 1940 to 1990 (247 percent). The projections are therefore within the range of recent experience in Northern California, albeit that of a metropolitan region. The combined population of Sacramento and San Joaquin Counties (which include two of the primary commuter destinations for residents of the western Sierra Nevada foothills) grew by 400 percent from 1940 to 1990. Individual counties in the Bay Area experienced a wide range of growth rates during that same period. The highest-density county and employment center of the region, San Francisco, grew by only 14 percent. This primarily reflected the severe physical constraints on growth in the small, forty-nine-square-mile city. Alameda County grew ten times as fast, at 149 percent, Napa County grew by 289 percent, and Marin County's population expanded by 335 percent. Most of Marin County's growth occurred from 1940 to 1970, when the population jumped from 52,907 to 208,652. It grew only an additional 10 percent, to 230,069, in 1970–90. This was the result of adoption of a complex set of growth management tools and a strict general plan in the early 1970s (Hart 1992; Teitz 1990). The experience of Marin County may have relevance to other counties in the Sierra Region, such as Nevada and El Dorado Counties, which are now facing rapid growth pressures and have recently updated their general plans.

With the exception of Marin County (and, to some degree, San Mateo County on the San Francisco Peninsula) (Teitz 1990), the Bay Area's suburban counties accommodated most of the growth in the region over the past fifty years and grew at rates comparable to those forecast for some Sierra Region counties over the next fifty years. Sonoma County grew by 462 percent, San Mateo County by 481 percent, Solano County by 593 percent, and Contra Costa County by a remarkable 700 percent as the 1940 population of 100,450 mushroomed to 803,732 by 1990. Sacramento County grew by 511 percent during the same period, from 170,333 in 1940 to 1,041,219 by 1990. San Joaquin County, however, to the south of Sacramento County and containing the port city of Stockton on the San Joaquin River, grew at a much slower 258 percent during this period. San Joaquin County's population of 134,207 was 79 percent of Sacramento County's population in 1940, but it grew to only 480,628 by 1990 (46 percent of Sacramento County's population). This differential growth rate between Sacramento and San Joaquin Counties can be attributed both to the rapid growth in state government during this period (when California's population grew from 6.9 million to 30 million), the substitution of capital and energy for labor in the agricultural sector, and the construction of Interstate 80 through the Sacramento area. The latter effectively integrated Sacramento with the Bay Area, while Stockton and San Joaquin County remained more isolated economically from the Bay Area. Sacramento emerged as both the center of state government and as an economic extension of the Bay Area, while Stockton continued to function only as a regional center for the northern San Joaquin Valley and the delta region.[34]

This latter point is a critical one, for it helps to explain the subregional concentration of growth within the Sierra Region. Access to the Bay Area along Interstate 80 allowed firms based in the Bay Area to locate manufacturing facilities in the greater Sacramento metropolitan area in the 1970s and 1980s, where land costs were considerably lower than in the rapidly urbanizing Bay Area. These business location decisions reflected both the economics of site development (i.e., each company's own facilities) and the economics of residential location choice (i.e., each company's employees' own residences). The former could have led to facility location decisions that shifted manufacturing activities out of the Bay Area (in particular, the Santa Clara Valley for high-technology companies) to a wide range of locations with good transportation access. The latter, however, which includes both the cost of living and the amenity value of residential location, resulted in the location of manufacturing activities between Sacramento and the Sierra Nevada foothills. This location is actually *less* convenient than other relatively low-cost locations along Interstate 80 between Sacramento and the Bay Area, because it requires additional travel time and additional risks of delays while crossing the Sacramento metropolitan area. It is *more* convenient for *employees*, however, who want to live in the Sierra Nevada foothills or at least in that part of the Sacramento metropolitan area that will provide easy recreational access to the Sierra Nevada and the American River.[35] Access to the residential amenities of the Sierra Nevada appears to have been a primary factor in the location choices of Bay Area firms relocating manufacturing facilities outside the Bay Area. The original decision to relocate those facilities was, in turn, the result of rapid growth in the Bay Area that both increased the cost of land and housing and decreased the quality of life for many employees through increased traffic delays and decreased open space. The transformation of the Bay Area landscape therefore had a direct bearing on the forces that have begun to transform the Sierra Nevada landscape over the past quarter century. The fate of the Sierra Nevada is inextricably tied to the fate of California's metropolitan centers.

Examples of these new employment centers can be found along Interstate 80 northeast of Sacramento in Placer County and along U.S. Highway 50 on the eastern edge of Sacramento County. The former includes facilities for Hewlett-Packard and NEC, both located in Roseville and fueling nearby residential development in Rocklin and Loomis. Perhaps the most extreme example of this relocation phenomenon exists in the eastern Sacramento County town of Folsom, where Intel has developed a large complex of buildings that employed nearly 2,750 people in 1994 and that are home to Intel's six major product divisions as well as Intel's North and South American Sales and Marketing Operation. It is also world headquarters for the company's Information Technology organization. The corporate headquarters remains in Silicon Valley, but new technologies now allow worldwide corporate activities to be coordinated from a satellite facility located 150 miles away. That satellite facility sits on a bluff above the American River just a few miles from El Dorado County and a less-than-thirty-minute drive from either the gold rush town of Placerville or the state capital. The 236-acre facility had a gross payroll of about $100 million in 1994. Construction of a new 320,000-square-foot building in 1994–95 cost $52 million, and it employs an additional 1,750 workers. The total employment at the Intel Folsom site is now 4,500 employees, with a payroll of between $150 and $200 million per year (Intel 1994). This employment base, together with the multiplier effect of the site through subcontractors and employee expenditures in the community, is likely to fuel much of the nearby Sierra Region's population growth.[36]

A significant fraction of the overall population growth into the Sierra Region from 1970 to 1990 appears to be suburban rather than exurban in character, replicating the classic processes of suburbanization observed within metropolitan regions elsewhere. The literature on suburbia is therefore relevant to our understanding of both historical growth patterns and the DOF population forecasts. This literature includes a wide range of population growth models based on a "gravity" concept of a nested hierarchy of "urban fields" (Hart 1991). In Northern California, this model indirectly links the west-central Sierra Nevada foothills to the Bay Area through the Sacramento metropolitan area. San Francisco is the central city core of the Bay Area; an urban field of lower-density employment centers exists throughout the Bay Area. Both those peripheral centers and the Sacramento metropolitan areas are effectively linked to and dependent on the well-being of that central city core through transportation networks and economic flows. The need to be physically proximate to the central city is now being challenged through the emergence of what Manuel Castells (1989) has called "the informational city," however, allowing a more dispersed and far-flung economic sphere less closely linked to the central city. As Robert Cervero (1993) has also demonstrated, employment generation on the periphery of the Bay Area metropolitan region is now greater than that in the central cities of San Francisco, Oakland, and San Jose. This deconcentration creates further opportunities for more dispersed residential locations still within commuting distance of employment. A similar phenomenon in the Sacramento metropolitan area has in turn made some sections of the Sierra foothills part of what Kenneth T. Jackson called the "crabgrass frontier" in his definitive 1985 book on the suburbanization of the United States.

In that respect we have much to learn from Jackson's history of suburbanization. In particular, he shows that the rapid rates of growth forecast for the Sierra Nevada are not unusual historically and have also been experienced by other rural regions outside the San Francisco Bay Area and Sacramento. These rapid rates of growth on the suburban and exurban frontier often accompany a slowing of growth as a result of density saturation in the metropolitan central city. Brooklyn, New York, was a sleepy rural village of only 7,125 people in 1820 (while nearby New York City, isolated across the East River, already had 123,706 residents). "In the next four decades," writes Jackson, "however, the town of Brooklyn was transformed" after regular ferries began in 1814 to connect residents with New York City (25). Brooklyn more than doubled in population during each of the next few decades, jumping to 266,661 by 1860. "Whether it was easy access, pleasant surroundings, cheap land, or low taxes," notes Jackson, "the suburb was growing faster than the city by 1800" (29). By 1890 the population of Brooklyn was 806,343, while New York City exceeded 2.5 million people. Brooklyn itself had grown from merely 6 percent of New York City's population to 32 percent in seventy years (27). "One wag noted that Brooklyn 'sold nature wholesale' to real-estate developers," says Jackson, "for sale to homeowners at retail" (29). This sounds quite a bit like today's Sierra Nevada real estate market. Many of the same factors that drew people to Brooklyn in 1830 are now drawing Sacramento commuters to the Gold Country.

These attractions have historically been accessible only to residents of a particular class, however, leading Robert Fishman (1987) to call the American suburbs a "bourgeois utopia." In his book by that name he refers to the middle-class suburb of privilege, a residential community beyond the core of a large city. The development that he describes is more restrictive than the broader patterns and processes driving today's exurban growth, but it has many of the same roots. More important, it accurately describes the subset of exurban Sierra Nevada development most like the classic middle-class commuter suburb. Much of what we are now seeing in the Sierra Nevada is similar in motivation (if not urban form) to that which first constituted a suburb in 1750 in London—having a house "in the country." The need for the exclusion of others from the suburb is important now, as it was two hundred years ago, in part to ensure the preservation of this idyllic setting. Establishment of successful gated communities with relatively high suburban densities is therefore not surprising in the context of this historic pattern of suburbanization. Fishman outlines three primary factors driving suburban development: the desire for life in a picturesque space; protection of the family; and avoidance of urban problems. All three appear to be important considerations in the residential location decisions of recent migrants to the Sierra Nevada and other exurban areas throughout the rural West. Historical processes of suburbanization are therefore relevant to our understanding of the processes driving exurban growth in the Sierra Nevada.

Like the "crabgrass frontier" of Brooklyn from 1820 to 1890, the west-central Sierra Nevada foothills of the Gold Country could gain a similar share of the greater Sacramento metropolitan region's population from 1970 to 2040. And like the "bourgeois utopias" of historical London, the values of many migrants to the Sierra Nevada may reflect basic truisms about human nature and the search for the ideal as much as new technologies and lower housing costs. Suburban development certainly reflects transportation commute times, economic conditions, and land markets, but it also reflects the values, dreams, and lives of the migrants in the places they left for suburbia. Ironically, many of the exurban migrants of the past few decades have come from suburbia. This raises a fundamental question confronting planners and citizens in the Sierra Nevada today: how can we avoid a development process that will destroy the very features that make the region a desirable place to live? The historical record is not encouraging, with the recent exodus to exurbia serving as strong evidence that the suburban ideal has not maintained itself in the face of a wide range of forces that have transformed metropolitan areas throughout the country. Meeting that challenge in the face of significant continuing population growth will not be easy in the Sierra Nevada.

Based on the DOF forecasts, many other subregions of the Sierra Nevada are likely to experience similar increases in commuting and suburbanization as the metropolitan centers of Stockton, Modesto, Fresno, and Bakersfield continue to grow.[37] Fresno and Bakersfield, the southernmost population centers in the San Joaquin Valley, are emerging as significant metropolitan areas in their own right. Fresno had a population of more than 350,000 in 1990, with nearly 800,000 in the Fresno metropolitan area (equal to the city of San Jose). Fresno County nevertheless still produces more agricultural value than any other county in the United States (a distinction held by Los Angeles County fifty years earlier) (Mike Davis 1990). Bakersfield, the capital of Kern County, had a population of about 175,000 in 1990, and its metropolitan area was more than 300,000. Kern County remains a commodity-oriented economy, however, producing more oil than any other county in the United States. Agriculture is also very important here, and oil pumps are often working away alongside farm equipment in the fields. Neither Fresno nor Bakersfield is closely tied to the Bay Area through commuting patterns.

The more northerly communities of Stockton and Modesto have become increasingly linked to the Bay Area economy through the development and expansion of Interstates 5, 580, and 205, and Highway 120. These highways now link residents in Stockton, Modesto, and the nearby towns of Tracy and Manteca to jobs across Altamont Pass in the Livermore Valley area near the intersection of Interstates 580 and 680. From there commuters can go north to San Ramon and

Walnut Creek, or south to Fremont, San Jose, and the greater Silicon Valley, or they can continue west to the East Bay Area employment centers of Oakland and Berkeley. These commutes sometimes total two hours each way, but people are apparently willing to make them in order to have an affordable (or larger) home. They sometimes ride in vanpools, where they can sleep or read each way, but they more typically ride in single-occupant automobiles that get stuck in traffic jams on Altamont Pass.[38]

These bedroom communities, which until recently were sleepy agricultural towns, are now sprouting commercial centers to provide services to the commuters when they are actually at home. Times have changed since George Lucas grew up in Modesto, where the images in his film *American Graffiti* originated as young Lucas cruised McHenry Avenue. A large sign at the entrance to town still says "Water, Wealth, Contentment, Health" (Johnson et al. 1993, frontispiece), but it is getting harder and harder to find the community's core. Freeway interchanges along state Route 99 now bustle with neon and traffic jams. Gang violence has also appeared, just as it has in Stockton, Fresno, and Bakersfield. These valley towns are becoming suburban centers. A large mall in Modesto, a boat lot in Stockton with growing sales, and the emergence of dining establishments to feed the commute-weary commuters have all sprung up. These in turn create new employment opportunities both for other residents in the Central Valley and for those willing to commute from the nearby Sierra Nevada foothills. Relatively few probably commute from the foothills to these lower-paid service jobs, but the potential is there for new, higher-paid employment.[39] In this way the expansion of the Bay Area directly affects the suburbanization of the Sierra Nevada.

Increasing population densities in Sacramento and San Joaquin Counties have been closely tied to increasing densities in the Bay Area.[40] A similar relationship appears to hold between Sacramento County and the Gold Country counties of Nevada, Placer, and El Dorado.[41]

The average population densities in the Gold Country counties are still considerably lower than the average densities in the metropolitan counties. This is not surprising, but it is exaggerated by the fact that the Gold Country counties have large areas of public land and private industrial timber land, where there is no potential for residences. Because of its relatively small land area, the average density for Sacramento County is also comparable to the average density for the Bay Area (it was lower in 1940 and 1950, almost exactly the same in 1960 and 1970, and higher in 1970 and 1980). San Joaquin County's average density is midway between that of Sacramento and the Gold Country. Average densities in the Gold Country counties in 1990 (one person per five to nine acres) were comparable to average densities in Marin County in 1940, Sonoma County from 1950 to 1970, Solano County until 1950, and Napa County until 1980. The growth patterns and experience in those Bay Area counties from 1940 to 1990 are therefore relevant to the future growth patterns and experience likely for the Sierra Region. Even Amador and Calaveras Counties, which are within commuting distance of Sacramento and San Joaquin Counties, had average densities in 1990 (one person per thirteen to twenty-one acres) that were comparable to those of Napa from 1940 to 1950 and Solano and Sonoma in 1940.

Individual counties and CCDs in the Sierra Region will have widely varying rates of growth under the April 1993 DOF forecast. The Sierra Region of three of the most remote counties (Plumas, Sierra, and Inyo) will accumulate less than twice their 1990 population by the year 2040, while eight counties will gain double to triple their 1990 population by 2040. Seven counties are expected to see their Sierra Region population actually more than triple. Based on the simple growth allocation model described above, two CCDs are projected to increase by more than tenfold. These estimates reflect unusual circumstances in their 1970–80 growth patterns, however, that are unlikely to continue for an extended period of time. Only the Yosemite CCD of Mariposa County, which lost population from 1970 to 1980 as a result of the relocation of housing for National Park Service employees, is projected to have a smaller population in 2040 than in 1990.

The DOF population forecasts are highly uncertain, of course, for population forecasting is a risky business. The early 1990s saw significant domestic emigration from California, for example, taking some growth pressure off the state and the Sierra Nevada. The forecasts may therefore overstate growth in the Sierra Region as the greater rural and exurban West absorbs an increasing fraction of the exodus from California's metropolitan areas. Conversely, the forecasts may overstate the capacity of metropolitan areas to absorb additional growth in the state. If the overall state-level growth forecasts are accurate (they seem to be reasonable for at least the decade of the 1990s), then this would suggest that nonmetropolitan population forecasts (such as for the Sierra Region counties) are understated. Much of the Sierra Region growth is also projected to occur in counties within commuting distance of the secondary metropolitan centers of the Central Valley. Those metropolitan centers may actually carry a greater fraction of their respective counties' overall population growth. Expansion of those metropolitan centers will, however, also create new employment and service opportunities for the Sierra Nevada foothills. The bottom line is that population growth forecasts are highly uncertain over even short periods of time. Significant population growth is nonetheless highly likely for most of the Sierra Nevada, even if the precise levels of such growth are difficult to predict.

Only time will tell if the April 1993 DOF forecasts will accurately predict Sierra Region growth for the next fifty years. The DOF made similar fifty-year forecasts in 1971 for Alpine, Amador, Butte, Calaveras, El Dorado, Nevada, Placer, Plumas, Sierra, and Yuba Counties, which projected a total increase from 334,500 in 1970 to 465,200 in 1990 and 695,500 in 2020.[42] This projected doubling of the total population for these ten counties over fifty years was much faster than previous rates of growth for the region, and many observers probably doubted that the region would reach a population of 695,500 by the year 2020. The fifty-year DOF forecast turned out to be *low,* however, for the 1990 census showed that those ten counties had *already* reached a population of 703,856 in only twenty years.[43] The population of those counties by the year 2020 will therefore undoubtedly be much higher than the 1971 DOF projection. Continued growth at that absolute rate for those ten counties (i.e., 184,678 persons per decade) would result in a population of 1,257,890 by the year 2020. This would be 81 percent greater than the predicted population.

The DOF forecast for a tripling of the Sierra Region population from 1990 to 2040 is therefore plausible, and a doubling is certainly probable. Even if population growth in the Sierra Region stayed steady at 175,000 per decade (the same absolute level as 1970 to 1990), the total Sierra Region population would increase by 140 percent. The range of likely population estimates for the Sierra Region is therefore from approximately 1.5 to approximately 2 million people by the year 2040. The aggregate total of the highest growth forecast for each individual CCD would result in a total Sierra Region population of 2.4 million, but that is much less likely without significant expansion of the transportation infrastructure between the valley and the foothills.

NATURE AND CULTURE IN THE NEW WEST

Penn Valley has kept some of its traditional culture and customs alive through an annual rodeo and barbecue. We walked to the rodeo grounds from my grandparents' place our first year in Nevada County, while many of the local kids rode their horses to the show with pride. An open-pit barbecue featured a side of beef accompanied by free-flowing beer; cowboy hats and scuffed boots dominated the scene. Snap-button shirts with yokes fit right in with the sound of eight-track tapes spilling country music out of the large American-made four-wheel-drive pickup trucks. The rodeo grounds were simple. A few bleachers held most of the imported fans, while others gathered around the outer edge of the paddock to watch their neighbors and friends get tossed through the air and onto the dusty ground. I stood on the edge of the fence with my brother, braving the snorting of the dust-kicking, heavy-horned bulls forced into this spectacle of man versus beast. The image was simple: humans could triumph over Nature if enough skill and perseverance were applied. The bronco riders were technically competing against each other, but Nature was the real adversary. The Great Western Rodeo was a celebration of Man the Conqueror.

Today the rodeo ground stands behind the fire station across the street from a collection of parking lots, little shops, and large trophy homes. Down the old highway much of the former pastureland is covered with self-storage facilities and asphalt. I drove down the old Penn Valley highway recently with Teresa to show her my grandparents' old house, and it seemed downright crowded among a group of chopped-up parcels on either side. A large, modern hay storage facility had been constructed near the long driveway to their set-back house. It seemed like an industrial encroachment on a pastoral scene, but at least it represented a link to the landscape and its agricultural past. Today it serves to provide feed for the many equestrians who own horses but don't have enough land to support them with on-site pasture. Local self-sufficiency has diminished, while market linkages have strengthened.

The Nevada County Fair has also decided to drop the rodeo from its program this year. Formerly a two-night affair in a four-day fair run, the rodeo was reduced to a one-night run as the county's demographics changed. It will now be replaced with "Fast Fridays," a series of motorcycle and automobile races designed to appeal to a less nostalgic crowd. The county fair was always a place to meet and visit with the rest of the community after a long summer, for the fair was held the week before school started. I remember how that always followed our first week of intensive twice-a-day high school football workouts, and our reward was the opportunity to wear our football jerseys to the fair at the end of the week. We strutted around the most beautiful fairgrounds in California with the blue-and-gold jerseys of the Nevada Union High School Miners. Performers were largely local, and I once played my guitar and sang on the Pine Tree Stage sandwiched into the schedule between Nelda Honey's Dance Troupe and Mumzy the Clown. People came to the fair to see their community, not big-time entertainment from out of town.

The Loggers Olympics were also a regular feature on Saturday afternoons, celebrating the skill and tenacity of an important part of the local workforce. As a twelve-year-old I watched awe-struck while the local loggers raced up a telephone pole and back down with their spiked boots and loose belts. Double-buck sawing teams competed using traditional, century-old technology that could still slice through a three-foot-diameter pine tree log in just minutes. The saws sang to the rhythm of the experienced teams as sawdust sprayed their faces and covered their arms. This was not just for show or the entertainment of spectators; it was also a community validation of the importance of this kind of work. We didn't know all of the loggers, of course, for many of them came from other parts of the Sierra Nevada to compete. There were always at least a few local favorites, though, whose faces were familiar. Working in the woods or in a local sawmill was still an attractive option for high school graduates in the early 1970s.

The community has changed dramatically since then, however, and the county fair has increasingly shifted its attention to providing entertainment that can compete with the metropolitan venues of Sacramento and the Bay Area. The Oak

Ridge Boys and Glen Campbell are scheduled to perform in the grandstand arena this year. My friends in the local band Harmony Ridge will probably open for Glen Campbell. The date for the fair also switched a few years ago to a weekend in early August and expanded to five days—which eliminated direct competition in late August with the California State Fair at Cal Expo in Sacramento, which offered similar types of big-name entertainment attractions. The fair has now entered the world of mass-market entertainment and competition for market share, and its product is now available in metropolitan areas. Many locals still attend to see the 4-H kids and the Future Farmers of America exhibits, of course, but they are becoming a smaller and smaller fraction of the gate. The Oak Ridge Boys or Kathy Matthea now draw a bigger market of paying customers than the Loggers Olympics. Fewer and fewer local residents have ties to logging, farming, or ranching or have children participating in 4-H or Future Farmers of America.[44] More and more have come here from metropolitan areas and want to see metropolitan entertainment.

We were proud to be the Miners when I was cocaptain of the varsity football team twenty years ago at Nevada Union. It linked us to our heritage, the landscape, and the community. We competed in the Sierra Foothill League back then, which included some Sacramento Valley schools in Roseville and the Marysville–Yuba City area. We used to laugh about the irrelevance and meaninglessness of our opponents' mascots: the Vikings, the Tigers, and other creatures who had never inhabited the area and constituted mere icons for combat. These were purely symbolic images, with no connection to place, landscape, or community. In contrast, I led a fund-raising effort my senior year that acquired a statue of a gold miner for the entrance to the high school: this image was also iconographic and symbolic, but it was tied to a real history and a real place. Yes, gold mining was basically dead in Nevada County during the years I played football representing the mighty Miners. But many of my teammates' fathers had worked in the hardrock mines that permeated the earth beneath the town of Grass Valley. The mines had just closed in 1956, only fifteen years before I moved to the area. The links between mining and the community still dominated both the social and personal histories of the people in that place as recently as twenty-five years ago. The Vikings and the Tigers could make no such claim for their mascots.

Selection of the mascot name *Miners* was also meant to convey other attributes: we were hard-working, blue-collar, nonelitist, team players who could endure hardship. There's no reason to think that this was truer of my teammates than players at other schools, of course, but it was an important source of team identity and cohesion. Our mostly suburban competitors were viewed among my teammates as coming from pampered, elitist, white-collar families that didn't know the true value of either work or hardship. Moreover, we had earned the title Miners after a difficult struggle at the lower levels of the athletic hierarchy. The junior varsity team was known as the Nuggets, while the freshman players were called the Loggers. Mining was represented as having higher status than logging, although a nod was still given to that heritage in the community. Logging was more danger-ous, less stable, and lower-paying than mining, however, so it is not surprising that one advanced from being a Logger to being a Miner. This in turn reflected the economic and political power structure of the community and the power with which extractive industry had come to forge the community's identity. More peo-ple were employed by the Grass Valley Group in the electronics industry than min-ing and logging combined by the time I played football at Nevada Union, but the community identity was still tied to extractive industry as the source of economic well-being. We drank a dreadful mix of electrolytes and bad lemonade after each football practice that we called "Miner's Sweat." It might have just as well been "Circuit Board Cleanser," but that symbol would not have tied us to our landscape. We were Miners and Loggers because we lived in a landscape of enormous wealth and power. As Richard White has emphasized in his book *The Organic Machine,* the Culture of our community knew Nature primarily through work (1996).

The football field, like the county fair, was a place where the community came together. Our high school was fed by nearly a dozen elementary schools that cov-ered the entire county west of the Sierra Nevada crest. Whether you had attended a one-room schoolhouse or the larger junior high schools in Grass Valley and Nevada City, all were equal among the striped intervals marking the practice field turf. The sons of doctors, lawyers, farmers, and loggers all competed equally: there was no segregation based on economic class, as there is in most metropolitan areas through the economics of housing location choices. Private schools were also not an option locally: if you lived in the area, your children attended Nevada Union.[45] This helped to create a community of interest that transcended class. Geographical isolation from other communities—our arch-rivals were located twenty-five miles away, across the Bear River at Placer High School in Auburn— also helped to forge a single community identity. The school district boundaries were not based on arbitrary lines separating two municipalities that looked the same on either side of the line. Booster club support was tremendous whenever the team traveled "down the hill" to face competitors from the valley. The entire community was on the football field.

Today the booster support is stronger than ever. The Nevada Union football team has been enormously successful, winning championships in eight of the past nine years. A second high school, Bear River, opened in 1985 in the southern part of Nevada County to accommodate rapid growth in the area (Garcia 1996). It also won the league and section titles this year. Something fundamental has changed, however, in the relationship between these football teams and the Sacramento metropolitan area. Nevada Union is now part of the Capital Athletic League, so its rivals are now the largest schools in the Sacramento area. Despite being located some sixty miles from Sacramento, the Miners played for the city championship this fall and defeated their new arch-rival, the Grant High School Pacers. *City* champions? My teammates and I would have spit out the phrase, offended by the juxtaposition of the word *city* with our identity as a community and as a team. Through the changes of the past three decades, however, the communities of western Nevada County have become increasingly integrated into the social and economic life of the Sacramento metropolitan area. High school athletic league realignment simply reflects these changes by bringing Nevada Union into the metropolitan sphere.

Establishment of a second high school has also contributed to fragmentation of the community's identity. The players on the Bear River team now call themselves the Bruins, which is a nice reference to the school's namesake and a local star among the historical fauna. The Bear River marks Nevada County's southern boundary with Placer County, however, and it draws one's gaze from the historic towns of Grass Valley and Nevada City in the north toward Auburn and the valley below. There is now a four-lane highway most of the way between Bear River High School and Interstate 80 in Auburn. The gated community of Lake of the Pines is across Combie Road from the new high school, and most of its residents receive mail with an Auburn address. The intersection of Combie Road and Highway 49 is jammed with Sacramento-bound commuters as the school buses and high school kids arrive for their morning classes. "Miners"? "Loggers"? How quaint. These people live on quarter-acre lots with a golf course, twenty-four-hour security, neighbors right over the back fence, and a long list of covenants, codes, and restrictions on their title deeds. It is difficult to differentiate their social and economic characteristics from those in any affluent California suburb. They live in a highly regulated and predictable environment, not the rural landscape of Little Deer Creek and Banner Mountain.

The ten-foot-high statue of a gold miner that has guarded the entrance to Nevada Union High School since I graduated in 1978 seems irrelevant today. He now looks down on two stumps at the end of his upturned arms, since both hands were broken off by vandals and not replaced. Without hands, he has symbolically lost his capacity to work the land. He must now rely on his mind—both to manipulate the symbols of the postindustrial information age, and to recall the community's commodity-extraction past through the echoed memories of a smaller and smaller fraction of the community. It has been a full generation since the mines closed in 1956, and no more than one out of five members of the area's population still remembers the sound of the whistle, the crash of the stamp mill, or the smell of the sunlit air after a long shift deep in the shaft of the Idaho-Maryland, the Empire, or the Northstar. Day by day, the old miners' names appear in the obituary pages of the *Grass Valley–Nevada City Union*. Today their sons and daughters work in construction, retail trade, and tourism, or in the flatlands down

FIGURE 3.11.   Statue of gold miner at the entrance to Nevada Union High School, Grass Valley.

below. They have been replaced in the local economy by well-educated knowledge workers and the transfer payments of equity refugees who earned their wealth in the metropolitan areas. "Primary" economic activity is secondary or tertiary to them.

There is no "working landscape" or "middle landscape" in the vision, culture, and lives of these creatures of modern metropolitan America (Hiss 1990). In some ways, they still hold the perceptions of the Congress that sat in Washington, D.C., when Teresa's great-great-grandfather C. F. McGlashan first moved to Nevada County in 1872. That vision was one with two simple alternatives: there existed unique and special landscapes of Nature (to be preserved for their aesthetic, cultural, and ecological values as museum pieces representing the West before Euro-American settlement); and there was the rest of the natural world (available and intended for human exploitation through commodity extraction for export to urban industrial markets). This is what Congress said when it passed both the Yellowstone legislation and the Hardrock Mining Law in 1872. More than a century later, this simplification of the relationship between humans and the natural world still appears to dominate our conceptions of Nature. And despite the dramatic ecotransformation that has occurred in the past three decades, the assumptions and values that dominated cultural constructions of the Sierra Nevada landscape in 1872 still dominate much of the discourse today. Ironically, these implicit assumptions—and our false reliance on a model of landscape economics that is no longer valid—have the potential to undermine the social, economic, and ecological well-being of existing and emerging communities in the exurban West. We are approaching the future as if through a rearview mirror, with a view of land and resource economics that focuses our attention on cash flow and ignores the fundamental assets that constitute real economic wealth.

We must therefore examine how the ecotransformation of the past three decades requires us to apply a more comprehensive framework to our analysis of landscape economics. Economics is about much more than money: the quality-of-life considerations driving the exodus to exurbia represent real economic assets. In fact, their value dwarfs the value of commodity extraction in the Range of Light.

CHAPTER FOUR

/\\.\\/\\.\\/\\.\\

Economics and the Environment

A Natural State: True luxury is living in your own private forest. The essence of The Cedars is the serenity of nature and knowing that it will always remain that way. An elegant, gate guarded community of stately homes and estate acreage.

Real estate ad published in the *Grass Valley–Nevada City Union,* 1995

I am looking out my window at the first day of spring. The California black oak trees are now leafing out with a touch of light green, following the lead of the California buckeyes. The buckeyes beat everyone to the punch when they sprang open six weeks ago. They also dropped their leaves six weeks before the oaks, however, which gave them roughly an equal period of winter dormancy. Each relies on different thresholds of light, warmth, and precipitation. The oaks out my western window are more ambitious than those on the north slope, for they receive a stronger dose of sun whenever the clouds break. The landscape is filled with multiple hues of green, gray, tan, yellow, and brown: the manzanita leaves, the digger or foothill pines, the ponderosa pines, and the thick clumps of mistletoe hanging in the oak trees have created a patchwork feast for my anxious eye. It has been a long, dark, and wet winter here in the Sierra Nevada foothills this year. The seasonal cycle of the spring equinox reminds me that life is always being reborn.

Despite the season, there was a touch of fresh snow on the ground when we awoke this morning. Surprisingly, this has happened only once all year. Most of the storms that blasted California this winter came from the southwest somewhere between Hawaii and Mexico. This "Pineapple Express" brought storm after storm into the state laden with heavy tropical moisture. In contrast, this storm followed the more typical pattern that I've come to know here over the past quarter century: cold and frosty, it dropped down out of the Gulf of Alaska and let us know that winter is not merely a state of increased precipitation. It also means freezing temperatures, frosts that kill crops in their most vulnerable stage, and a general period when the Northern Hemisphere is tilted away from the sun. We passed the

FIGURE 4.1.   South Yuba River near Nevada City and the San Juan Ridge, Nevada County.

midpoint on our journey around the sun today, but it will still be several months before the earth and the atmosphere heat up enough to call it summer. March and April always bring more rain, even if it is mitigated by the brilliant wildflowers and fresh green of the budding leaves.

Yesterday we heard the river's roar from near the top of the ridge. We were walking down the slope away from the river when I thought I heard a car behind us on the gravel road. I looked back and waited, but the car never appeared. We continued walking. A moment later I stopped again, thinking the car was just about to appear on the crest of the hill. Then it became apparent that the sound was a natural one: the roaring river, some twelve hundred feet below and two miles away by dirt road, was calling out to us from the canyon. Echoing off the far wall, the sound of rushing water bounced across the ridgeline and brought us back to our place in the watershed. This is not a place where the sound of rubber tires on gravel dominates or continues endlessly with such abandon. This is a place where the sounds of Nature dominate the sounds of Culture. And it is within this context that we live our daily lives. Nature is not "out there" or in a special park reserved for museum-like preservation; it is around us and within us. The water that falls on my hair is the same water that comprises my body; the water that roars down the canyon is the same water that made the glorious explosion of spring leaves on the oak trees possible. Our pond overflows and runs down a small ravine, soaking into the ground there only to be pumped out later to fill our sink. It will then slip back down the drain, through the septic system, and out into a leach field for percolation back into the groundwater. We are living within a set of closed systems.

This experience has enormous value to me, and I would gladly give up many things to experience it on a daily basis. The deer in the yard, the squirrel on the rock, the robin with the worm, and the first pink blossoms on the manzanita are all important to me in a narrow, anthropocentric, utilitarian way. I also believe they have their own intrinsic value, and the relationships among and between them have a value reflecting a whole that cannot be equaled by the sum of its parts. But where do these things show up in the so-called economic analyses that I have read about the South Yuba River, Nevada County, the Sierra Nevada, or the rest of the exurban West? If these things are the primary reason that I and many other people live here, why are they not counted when we talk about land and resource economics? Clearly, these things have a narrow economic value within the context of a real estate market that emphasizes the natural environment as an amenity. They therefore have economic value even within the narrow context of marketable commodities. But is economics really only about things you can buy and sell?

Anil Gupta, who is part of the Indian Institute of Management, tells a story that helps to place this question in context. It seems there was once a beloved prince in India who came to a village often to meet with the people. He liked to challenge them with paradoxes. One day he drew a line on a piece of paper and asked them to make it shorter *without touching the line itself on the piece of paper.* All the wise men and women of the village pondered this puzzle for many days, even completing complex mathematical calculations to determine ingenious ways to solve the problem. They considered heating the paper to shrink it and the line itself, and they analyzed the properties of the ink from the prince's pen. Finally, a child came up to the piece of paper and drew a *longer* line next to the original line. The riddle had been solved. The first line was now "shorter." *Context determines content* (Gupta 1994).

This principle is well recognized in the field of semiotics, which, according to Ferdinand de Saussure (1959), the founder of semiotics, "analyzes the process of meaning and signification, of how meaning is derived from signs and symbols." Michael Fainter notes that "the principal assumption underlying semiotics is that signs/symbols acquire meaning only within a system, for it is the relationship among the signs/symbols that grant each sign/symbol its meaning" (1996, 16). While this framework has primarily been applied to linguistics, critical theorists have also applied it to other "texts" such as planning discourses. Here I will argue that it is equally important for how we interpret the relationship between economics and the environment, Culture and Nature, People and Place, in the Sierra Nevada. In particular, the changing context within which the decisions about land and resource management must take place in rural communities has changed the meaning (content) of what is economic.[1]

Land and resource management policy have been struggling with a set of problems throughout the West, using analytic tools and techniques of implementation predicated on a set of assumptions that determine the context of the problem. That context includes an institutional setting that relies on an accounting system that measures only a subset of the economic values of the landscape. As a result of that context, other values are not now recognized as economic content. Solutions to the problems we face are therefore seriously limited by the context within which the content of the problems is defined. For this reason, we must look carefully at the changing context of land and resource economics in the exurban West to determine if the content may be different from what we have assumed. That changed context may then lead to new interpretations of both the limitations on action and the opportunities for land and resource management. Amenity values will then be seen as critically important to landscape economics.

NONPRICE VALUES
AND BENEFIT-COST ANALYSIS

The economics of environmental quality is central to the Sierra Nevada, but scholars, local business people, local government officials, and local planners have given it only limited attention. This reflects a basic misunderstanding about economics. For most people, economics is exclusively about money. It is not. Economics is about allocating scarce resources where tradeoffs exist among competing objectives; money just happens to be the primary means by which our society mediates those tradeoffs (Power 1996a). Economics therefore requires social choices to achieve goals and objectives that satisfy social preferences consistent with a broad range of social values (Daly 1977; 1996). Money and the things it can buy can satisfy only a subset of those preferences, and some of our social values may conflict with the consequences of satisfying particular preferences. It is therefore necessary to think about economics in its broadest sense to address the social conflict that has erupted over land and resource management in the exurban West. Economics includes both exchange values and use values, in Logan and Molotch's lexicon (1987). I will lay out a framework here that can help to explain the social conflict in economic terms, then in later chapters I will develop particular aspects of that framework and apply it to particular issues facing the Sierra Nevada and exurban West. But first I want to discuss a theoretical framework for landscape economics and amenity values.

Because money is such a familiar and uniform metric, planners and policy analysts have attempted to use monetization to estimate the value of nonprice factors through a method called benefit-cost analysis. This technique was first widely applied in the context of water resources planning in the 1930s (Grant et al. 1976; Howe 1979). Federal investments in large dams, either for flood control, irrigation, or hydroelectric generation, were often not justified by the direct economic benefits that could be derived from them through revenue-generating activities. Irrigation water and electricity could be sold, for example, but the benefits of flood control were difficult to market. Congress therefore adopted language in the Flood Control Act of 1936 that said, "The Federal Government should improve or participate in the improvement of navigable waters or their tributaries, including watersheds thereof, for flood-control purposes if the benefits *to whomsoever they may accrue are in excess of the estimated costs,* and if the lives and social security of people are otherwise adversely affected" (emphasis added).[2]

This created a system in which planners could count economic benefits not normally measured by markets in the familiar metric of money changing hands. Unlike private enterprise, the public sector was taking on projects that would otherwise not be developed, for the sake of public-good characteristics of their benefits. Public goods are those that have two distinguishing characteristics: they are nonexclusive, meaning it is difficult to exclude people from getting the benefits of the project;[3] and they are nonrivalrous, so that allowing any individual to get the benefits of the project does not diminish the capacity of others to gain the project's benefits.[4] These two characteristics result in what is called a "market failure" in neoclassical economics: the private market "fails" to provide public goods and services to the level demanded based on the level of benefits that would accrue to their beneficiaries (Sichel and Eckstein 1977; Stokey and Zeckhauser 1978). In other words, the benefits of providing a public good exceed the costs— but, because of the nonexclusivity and nonrivalry characteristics of the public good, private enterprise does not step forward and provide the good through a traditional market. The private enterprise would not be able to recover its costs and would go out of business quickly. In contrast, the public sector could provide the good or service and collect revenues through taxation (an indirect, nonmarket transaction) to cover the costs. This has traditionally provided a rationale for government intervention to provide the good or service, because the benefits of doing so exceed the costs of providing it. In theory, this improves overall economic efficiency and the operation of the private market.[5] This theory is most often relied on to justify provision of public infrastructure systems and defense spending (ibid.). It has also been extended to environmental "goods and services," such as clean air (Baumol and Oates 1979).

But a benefit-cost analysis can be manipulated in at least four ways to make a project look better than it really is: 1) expand the "benefits" to include some that are not really a result of the project, 2) ignore some "costs" that will occur as a result of the project, 3) manipulate the discount rate to maximize the present value of benefits and minimize the present value of costs, 4) manipulate where the benefits and costs are placed in the final equation used to determine the benefit-cost ratio, in order to increase the ratio and the project's apparent cost-effectiveness. All four of these techniques, combined with a variety of more specific tricks for achieving each of the individual results, have been thoroughly tested and developed over the years by analysts and agencies intent on building infrastructure projects of questionable value.

Perhaps the greatest challenge is calculating the costs and benefits of a project or policy. The critical problem with cost estimation is that it usually focuses on changes in cash flow and income rather than changes in assets and wealth. Costs are rather narrowly defined as private financial costs (i.e., money that the entity developing the project must spend). Indirect costs are rarely included. Direct costs are easily identifiable and difficult to hide; indirect costs are not easily identifiable and are difficult to trace to specific projects. They are usually diffuse and may accrue over the life of the project—or, in the case of some of the most dangerous costs, such as nuclear waste, well after the life of the project. They are, in other words, somebody else's problem.[6] Often these costs accrue to the environment or to social groups (e.g., indigenous people) who have little economic or political power in society. They are borne by neither the producer nor the consumer of the goods or services that are counted as the benefits of the proposed project, so they constitute externalities to the market transaction linking producers and consumers. These externalities represent another market failure and serve as a rationale for public-sector market intervention.

Valuing externalities, like public goods, is a difficult problem in economics. By definition, externalities accrue outside the market and therefore can not be valued directly through prices. Both positive and negative externalities can exist, although negative externalities are the usual focus.[7] These include environmental damages, social dislocation, and congestion costs associated with rivalrous access to what may have been public goods in an uncongested condition. Water pollution from urban runoff, air pollution from a coal-fired power plant, the flooding of a town to build a new reservoir, and the frustrations of delayed commuters all constitute potentially significant economic costs. They generally do not involve the direct expenditure of financial resources as costs borne by the proposed project. Even the valuation of a home in the town site designated for flooding requires some difficult value judgments and the implicit assignment of property rights.

Amory Lovins of the Rocky Mountain Institute best described this dilemma in a story he calls "And How Much for Your Grandmother?" (1990). The British highway authorities were getting set to extend a motorway through a village and needed to condemn some homes by means of eminent domain. They checked local real estate prices, estimated the value of those homes on the real estate market, and notified the owners that the British government was condemning their homes and would compensate them with fair market value. To the surprise of the British economists, the homeowners—some of whose families had lived in these houses for multiple generations—furiously responded that they would not sell at *any* price. The economists tried to explain to the homeowners that they were acting irrationally—according to economic theory. The homeowners repeated their "infinite" valuation of their own properties. The economists concluded that the homeowners, recognizing that the government's motorway project depended on their cooperation, were simply holding out for a higher price than the homes were truly worth. They thought this was a case of strategic bidding, that it merely represented gaming behavior, not the homeowners' true valuation of their property. They could not accept that the homeowners truly did value their homes more than any amount of money, and that this could be a rational position.

This conclusion failed to recognize a critical weakness in the agency's underlying economic theory: it presumed that the *government* held the right to take the homes, not that the *homeowners* held the right to keep them. This is a critical difference. If the government holds the right, the homeowners are constrained by their income and wealth in their ability to pay the government to avoid having their property taken away from them. The amount one "bids" under these circumstances is known as one's willingness to pay. In contrast, the homeowners would not be constrained by their income or wealth if the government had to pay the homeowners to give up their homes and the homeowners could refuse. The price at which they would be willing to accept compensation for the lost value of their present homes is known as one's willingness to accept or willingness to be compensated.

Economic theory suggests, for a variety of complex reasons, that willingness to pay should equal willingness to accept or willingness to be compensated (Hanemann 1994). This argument is based in part on a famous article published in 1960 by Ronald H. Coase that articulated what is today known as Coase's Theorem. Coase demonstrated that the efficient allocation of resources does not depend on the initial distribution of property rights *if* a specific set of conditions exist. Unfortunately, those conditions rarely exist in reality.

Coase's Theorem has been treated as gospel by the economics profession, but in many cases it has been misapplied where Coase's presumed conditions are violated. Consequently there are serious problems with application of Coase's Theorem to nonmarket values, for there are no markets in which consumers' demand preferences can be equilibrated with producers' supply capacities. Not surprisingly, real-life humans in the British motorway case did not follow the model set out by economic theory. Their willingness to pay was constrained by income and wealth, so it was lower than their willingness to accept. Some things are actually so valuable to people that they will not trade them for anything. "And How Much for Your Grandmother?" may ask a question reasonable to an economist, but it is an absurd question for anyone familiar with the basic elements of human behavior. Grandma is *not* for sale—at *any* price. Despite economic theory, this is a *rational* response for valuing a nonmarket "good" that has no substitute. The British motorway example shows that many people feel the same way about "home" and "place" if they have a long-standing relationship to it.

This result is consistent with the personal experience of most of us, but it makes the economic valuation of externalities extremely difficult. It also highlights the importance of social values regarding the distribution of property rights in determining the results of economic analysis. All too often these value choices are implicit rather than explicit. When they do come out into the open, many people find the implicit value choices abhorrent. This is what the former World Bank economist Lawrence Summers learned when a memo he wrote in December 1991 was leaked, which asked the rhetorical question: "Just between you and me, shouldn't the World Bank be encouraging more migration of dirty industries to the LDCs [less developed countries]?" (Weisskopf 1992). The uproar over that document and concern about Summers's ability to support environmental policies ultimately scuttled his chance to become chair of the Council of Economic Advisors the next year following the election of President Clinton.[8] It also helped make visible an important issue, however, that would resurface in the Republican Congress's attempt to adopt new risk-analysis requirements for regulation in 1995–96. The controversy over risk analysis focuses on the valuation of human health and the monetization of human life.

Benefit-cost analysis attempts to monetize the value of human health and human life. This then allows risk analysis to serve as the basis for decision-making that explicitly considers the tradeoffs between the allocation of scarce economic resources and investments to improve (or at least avoid degrading) human health. In theory, this information allows society to make the most informed choices possible and to make those investments that best enhance human health. Its economic resources would therefore be allocated "efficiently."

Unfortunately, the problem of valuation through monetization collapses important information into a single metric. This then limits our ability to understand the full implications of our choices, for the things we really care about—human health and human lives—have been transmuted into monetary values through assumptions and analytic techniques of questionable moral value. In particular, the primary means of determining the value of reductions in human health or of the loss of human life is to rely on the earning potential of the individuals affected. A twenty-two-year-old male college graduate with a high lifetime earning potential has a high present value in economic terms, while an unemployed woman in her sixties has a low present value of lifetime earning potential. The potential death of the unemployed woman from air pollution will therefore be treated as being much less significant in a benefit-cost analysis than the death of the young college graduate. Policies that favor the protection of the young college graduate's life will therefore seem more efficient and desirable in a benefit-cost analysis than those that protect the unemployed woman's life. Taking this model to its logical outcome, Summers described the result in language that was rational but cold and dehumanizing in its tone. It was not well received.

Environmental damages are also problematic, for they too require "market proxies" to determine the economic value of the damages. This may work for some environmental damages, such as the loss in future timber potential as a result of air pollution. Most environmental goods and services do not have market proxies, however, and their true value may go far beyond the utilitarian goods and services they provide to humans. Indeed, many human activities would simply be impossible without a healthy environment. Either the cost of providing those environmental systems through artificial means is prohibitive or it is impossible to replicate them. (Gretchen Daily and her colleagues recently estimated the global value of these environmental services at more than $3 *trillion.*)[9] In most cases we do not understand the complex structure and function of natural systems and would not be able to replicate them. Even in those cases where we *think* we know how they work, we are likely to fail to capture important attributes that could be critical to the long-term viability of the system.[10] Finally, many of the values that humans place on ecological systems are spiritual or nonutilitarian. Like our grandmothers, they may seem priceless to us. The assumptions we make about the distribution of property rights are therefore critical to valuation. What price can we put on the extinction of a species? Who has the right to determine this value? These are deeply philosophical questions that require explicit value choices (Wilson 1988; Kellert 1995; Pryne 1995).

One of those value choices is the relationship between present and future generations' rights to good health, a clean environment, and economic and social well-being. Benefit-cost analysis "discounts" the future benefits and costs that occur beyond the short-term time horizon in such a way that they typically have very little influence on even a very long-lived investment. Short-term economic consequences therefore dominate the conclusions of benefit-cost analysis approaches. A higher discount rate will amplify this effect, while a lower discount rate increases the relative importance of more distant future values in the present value calculation. The rationale for this approach is that short-term "investments" can yield long-term returns on capital.

This result makes sense in the case of private investments focusing only on direct economic benefits and costs that have markets and are denominated in financial terms. It is a bit problematic, however, when discounting is applied to indirect benefits and costs not marketed or easily monetized. These include human health, human lives, and irreversible environmental damages. Even if they can be valued adequately and accurately for purposes of analysis, the process of discounting future values implies a very specific distribution of rights and responsibilities across generations. We are saying that our children's *lives* are less valuable than our own, and that our grandchildren's health is even less valuable. In fact, in a benefit-cost analysis the discounted value of our grandchildren's lives is unlikely to have any significant effect on decisions we will make today that could profoundly affect their future. Once again, difficult and profound value choices are hidden behind the mask of economic analysis. Discounting is not a value-neutral technical exercise.

Irreversible environmental costs are another class of future benefits and costs that do not fit the assumptions underlying the rationale of discounting. Discounting assumes that the present value of assets is greater than the future value of assets because those assets will be able to generate additional benefits during the intervening period. But what if the future stream of benefits will be truncated by the elimination of the natural capital that makes such benefits possible? Most important, how do we account for the *irreversibility* of some environmental effects? The methods of discounting assume that the world will continue to function as it has in the past and that the uncertainty and risk associated with future benefits and costs are distributed normally around some mean estimates of those future values. Neither those assumptions nor those methods are well-suited for asymmetrical risks (Duane 1989).

These problems have led some analysts to argue for a "social discount rate" of 0 percent in order to increase the relative importance of long-term costs and benefits in benefit-cost analysis. This approach is intuitively appealing, but it may only be appropriate for those values not captured in markets and therefore subject to quantifiable returns on investment that would improve the well-being of future generations. Others have argued for a more complex distribution of rights to future generations in our analysis of projects affecting future generations

(Howarth and Norgaard 1992; 1995). This approach has more promise, although it still suffers from the inherent uncertainty associated with trying to forecast what future generations' preferences will be. We already regret some of the decisions of our recent ancestors, and many of their choices were justified through benefit-cost analysis. Humility may be the most important ingredient missing from our current analytic approach.

SOCIAL EQUITY AND ECONOMIC EFFICIENCY

In addition to these problems in calculating benefit-cost ratios, there are a number of important issues swept under the rug as a result of selecting benefit-cost analysis as the basis for public policy. Benefit-cost analysis has always emphasized economic *efficiency* (at least in theory) and relied on simplifying assumptions to reduce the world to a single, monetized metric. In particular, *equity* issues were explicitly ignored in the writing of the Flood Control Act of 1936. Social conflict over land and resource management, however, is often the result of the *distributive* consequences of public policies. The beneficiaries of a project are often not the ones bearing its costs. It is therefore important to consider who gains and who loses as well as the total level of benefits and costs that will accrue to society at large under the proposed project. This requires some understanding of the initial or existing state of the world in social terms: who has assets affected by the project, who doesn't, and what is the relationship between them? Who will bear the costs of a project, and who will benefit from the project? Will one group be subsidizing another? Will a few individuals benefit at a cost to many and the community as a whole? Finding the answers to these questions requires us to peel away the veneer of social harmony and equality that clothes benefit-cost analysis and to recognize some of the gross inequities that exist in American society (Goldsmith and Blakely 1992).

The assumptions of social harmony, common interests, and economic equity implicit in benefit-cost analysis are not limited to the public policy debate about infrastructure investments. These same flawed assumptions underlie most public discourse about economics and the environment and represent fundamental tenets of utilitarianism, the philosophical perspective that dominates land and resource management in most state and federal agencies. In the words of Gifford Pinchot, father of the U.S. Forest Service, the federal forests were to be managed for "the greatest good of the greatest number in the long run" (Wilkinson 1992a, 128). Local governments also sometimes act as if the distributive consequences of public policies are unimportant, although they are at the heart of social conflict and politics. Those distributive aspects simply do not surface in the more technical language of "objective" economic analysis, which focuses on efficiency.

Efficiency in the allocation of resources is simply assumed by many to be independent of equity considerations. This is clearly not true, however, for different *initial* distributions of resources lead to different "efficient" allocations of resources. Economic theory therefore recognizes some of the important links between efficiency and equity. The reason is that preferences for goods and services are in part a function of the economic state of the individual expressing the preference. The marginal utility of most additional goods and services declines as the demand for those goods and services is saturated for a given individual. A proffered car has limited value to me, for example, if I already have a car. It has much greater value to me—and, therefore, an efficient allocation of resources would result in my higher demand for cars—if I don't already have a car. Alternative distribution of resources will therefore change the relative positions of individuals along the marginal utility functions, thereby altering the demand for goods and services. Scarce resources would then be allocated most efficiently in a manner different from that which would have occurred under an alternative distribution of resources. There are conditions where the efficient allocations may converge across alternative distributions, but there is no general allocation that is efficient across the full range of alternative distributions. For this reason, any system of evaluation that ignores the distribution of costs and benefits is likely to benefit those with the greatest wealth and power while reducing the relative wealth of those with the least wealth and power. Not surprisingly, this is what we generally rely on today to evaluate public policies that have enormous distributive consequences. There is also a widening gap between the richest and poorest segments of American society, with the top fifth receiving more than 48 percent of the nation's income in 1993—while the bottom fifth received less than 4 percent. This was a new record for unequal distribution of income.[11]

This conservative assumption about the desirability of maintaining the existing distribution of resources is made more explicit in the definition of *Pareto optimality,* which is usually the basis for determining whether or not an alternative policy is efficient. A Pareto optimal choice is one that results in the maximum gain in total societal welfare (summed across all members of society affected by the choice) without reducing any individual's welfare. *Any* reduction in the welfare of any individual as a result of one alternative eliminates that alternative from consideration under the Pareto criterion, even if the alternative would increase total welfare much more than those that meet the Pareto criterion. This criterion protects individual rights from the tyranny of the majority, where an individual's well-being might be sacrificed to improve the well-being of the rest of society.[12] It also protects an entire *class* of individuals, however, from policies that could improve overall social well-being but which would result in some reduction in their wealth. It assumes that the existing distribution of wealth is somehow just or sacrosanct. It is truly conservative in its view of private property, and it confers explicit rights associated with that private property that are placed above other rights that may have validity in and of themselves. Hiding behind the allegedly technical, objective, and neutral language of economics is therefore a fundamental social choice about the distribution of rights in our society. There is no *theoretical* reason why Pareto optimality *should* be the criterion for evaluation of alternatives; it was simply chosen to reflect a particular set of social *values*.

Thus, values are at the heart of economics; we simply rarely recognize this as true. Specialization in our society, together with the abstract and highly technical language of both public policy and economics, have removed this basic truth from the understanding of most citizens. Efforts to turn economics into a science have also clothed it in a false armor of language purporting to offer value-neutral, objective tools for technical application to society's problems by a group of isolated experts. Economics is instead fundamentally about social choices: how will we allocate our resources to satisfy our needs? Our approach to economics must therefore address how we will determine our needs as a society, including the public goods and environmental services that are not and generally can not be provided by private markets.

ENVIRONMENTALLY SUSTAINABLE DEVELOPMENT

Utility theory in economics is predicated on the concept of consumer preferences. According to this model, we each have our own set of preferences that reflects how we value different goods and services. The marginal utility of additional "normal" goods declines as we satisfy our preferences for those goods, leading to greater substitution for other goods as we saturate our demand. All economic agents (either individuals or institutions) are then assumed to make economic choices (i.e., decisions to allocate scarce resources) in order to maximize utility or welfare. This utility-maximizing behavior is what is deemed to be rational choice. Any apparent deviation from "rational" economic behavior can be explained theoretically as a result of either incomplete information on the part of the decision maker or a failure to capture preferences adequately in the economic model (Keeney and Raiffa 1993).

By reducing the world of economic choice and individual behavior to utility-maximizing preferences, however, utility theory denies the possibility for rational decisions by either individuals or institutions that reflect nonutilitarian values. One might choose to do something because of a sense of moral obligation, for example, or in response to a social taboo that constrains behavior by defining what is ethically acceptable behavior. Economists often clash with philosophers, cultural anthropologists, and sociologists when this occurs. Neoclassical economists would argue that these choices still reflect economic preferences, while many philosophers, cultural anthropologists, and sociologists would generally argue that these socially defined protocols and ethical constraints constitute the framework *within* which utility-maximizing behavior may occur. They do not then constitute preferences, but are the skeletal basis on which preferences are determined and choices made. They are the foundation of the social process we call economics, not merely an incidental element among an infinite number of goods and services and utility-maximizing preference functions. They are the *context* that determines the *content* of economics.

I side with the philosophers, cultural anthropologists, and sociologists on this point. It is consistent with my personal experience and with a vast amount of empirical evidence of human behavior and decision making. It is not the dominant view within our society, however, for worship at the altar of economics increasingly dominates our Culture. Nearly every college student takes Econ 1, but far fewer plumb the complex depths of philosophy, cultural anthropology, and sociology to understand the cultural context within which economics has taken on such near-religious significance in our Culture. Our society has placed the pursuit of the almighty dollar above and ahead of nearly all other activities. This has resulted in nearly unquestioning acceptance of analytic techniques and economic rationales like those discussed above in benefit-cost analysis and risk analysis. The deeper value choices implicit in such analytic approaches are not generally understood by either the producers or the consumers of these analyses. We therefore continue to make public policy decisions as a society while looking through the highly selective filter called *economics*. That filter explicitly attempts to remove all nonmonetary aspects of economics that are nonutilitarian.

This approach has generated its own set of problems, however, that over the past few decades has led to both social and academic critiques of its implicit assumptions. One strain of critique emerged in the so-called development literature, questioning whether the dominant model of "development" truly improved the lives of those undergoing the "development." That dominant model, which sought to replicate the path of industrialization of the West through capital-intensive investments in the so-called developing countries, or less developed countries (LDCs), also appeared to decrease self-sufficiency while increasing inequities and poverty within the countries targeted for "development." Most of the benefits of this approach have accrued to urban elites within the LDCs and in the West, where control of capital resided. Local control has shifted to global institutions and multinational corporations, most of which are located in the West and controlled by the elites of the West, who are also their primary beneficiaries. Local agricultural production in the LDCs has shifted from local produce to export commodities, which has then increased local economic dependence on global markets. The volatility of commodities prices has crashed LDC economies that had accrued significant debt to pay for investments in industrial infrastructure and export-oriented agricultural production. Global economic institutions like the International Monetary Fund then imposed austerity measures on the LDC to ensure debt repayment. These austerity measures hit the least-advantaged groups within LDC society the hardest. Rural-to-urban migration has increased to the megacities of the LDCs, but unemployment and poverty have also swelled in the growing urban areas. Moreover, the growing hardships of the LDC underclass have been accompanied by increasing pollution in urban areas as a result of industrialization and the growing use of motor vehicles and congestion. Those remaining in the rural areas of the LDCs have also faced pollution problems and health threats associated with pesticide applications and intensified land use.

Environmental concerns emerged concurrent with these problems of development and the growing critique of the dominant paradigm of economics in the 1960s, 1970s, and 1980s. Economists demonstrated how public goods and externalities could lead to market failures that then led to excessive levels of pollution and its deleterious effects. Defined largely within the framework of neoclassical economic theory, environmental economics emerged in the late 1960s and 1970s as a field that sought resolution of these market failures through economic means. Theoretically, internalizing the costs of pollution should lead to improved efficiency and reduced pollution, for example, as consumers would consume less of a good if its full costs were recognized. This in turn would create incentives for producers to reduce pollution in order to reduce their costs of production. Environmental economists had relatively little influence on the initial formation of pollution control policy in the United States, however, as technology-forcing, command-and-control regulatory approaches were selected as the primary means of reducing pollution (Baumol and Oates 1979; Fisher 1981; Krutilla 1967).

This social choice reflected the technological optimism and the deep political mistrust of large corporations and state governments in the late 1960s and early 1970s. The technological optimism was a result of the successful Apollo moon landing program, while the intense social conflict over the Vietnam War fueled mistrust of large corporations and government. Centralization of regulatory control in the federal government (rather than the states) reflected the expansion of its role in national life through the Civil Rights movement. Together, these nonenvironmental and noneconomic social forces helped forge an environmental policy that sought to conquer pollution through technological innovation. The primary burden for stopping pollution was also placed on producers rather than consumers. The theoretical arguments of the neoclassical environmental economists therefore remained academic under this technology-forcing, command-and-control system (Duane 1992a).

By the 1980s, a new generation of activists was seriously challenging the basic premises of development economics and environmental policy. Like the social activists of the late 1960s, they began to ask whether a more fundamental change in the underlying framework would be necessary to achieve a socially just world. Their own conception of such a world was predicated on a set of assumptions different from the dominant economic model. Their own activism was not utility-maximizing behavior, so it seemed self-evident to them that the model itself did not reflect reality. Their reality was one based on utility-maximizing behavior within the constraints of social taboos and ethical principles. Economics, in other words, was a process by which social choices were to be made to allocate scarce resources subject to a set of nonmarket values. Identifying those social constraints required an explicit consideration of the values implicit in the utility-maximizing economic model of preferences and its associated analytic tools and institutions. The model, the tools, and the institutions were all challenged on the grounds that they reflected the class interests of elite industrialists in the West and urban elites within the LDCs. The interests and values of the rest of the planet were therefore not well represented in either the framework or the dominant social choices.

The dominant approach to development—advocated by the World Bank through its lending policies and by other international aid organizations through their focus on industrialization of the developing economies—was and remains predicated on a model that accepts increasing inequality in the early stages of development in exchange for faster rates of improvement in average conditions. Average incomes are, in other words, expected to go up faster if higher levels of economic inequity are tolerated. In theory this condition represents only a transition phase that will be followed by faster gains for those at the bottom income bracket. This "trickle down" theory was challenged briefly in the late 1970s and early 1980s by Paul Streeten and his colleagues at the World Bank, and it continues to be challenged by development activists in the nongovernmental organization sector. Streeten's approach is summarized in *First Things First: Meeting Basic Human Needs in the Developing Countries,* which included extensive examples of countries that had managed to improve social well-being without necessarily raising incomes or inequality through industrialization (Streeten et al. 1981). These nations' policies emphasized social spending over tax cuts, however, and that message fell on deaf ears as the Reagan administration came to power the same year. Aid policies moved away from the basic-needs approach in the 1980s toward a fiscal austerity model that emphasized free markets and structural adjustment to reduce debt as well as regulatory controls. The result was increasing investments in development projects that threatened the social, economic, and ecological sustainability of human activity in the less developed countries.

This conflict gave rise to a new call for "sustainable development." Research on the general problem of sustainable development predates the term, which first appeared in public policy discourse in the book *Building a Sustainable Society* by Lester Brown and the Worldwatch Institute in 1981. A comprehensive report on *Sustainable Development of the Biosphere* by the International Institute for Applied

Systems Analysis was edited by William C. Clark and R. E. Munn in 1986. The term has, however, seen its most significant attention and expansion since the 1987 publication of the report *Our Common Future* by the World Commission on Environment and Development, also called the Brundtland Commission (after its chair, the former prime minister of Norway). The report laid the foundation for the United Nations Conference on Environment and Development in Rio de Janeiro in June 1992. Unlike the original U.N. Conference on the Environment in Stockholm in June 1972, the Rio conference explicitly linked environmental issues to questions of development. Indian Prime Minister Indira Gandhi had challenged the delegates at the Stockholm meeting with the claim that poverty is the greatest polluter. She argued that environmental concerns were a luxury of the rich countries, while most of the world's population had to struggle each day simply to survive. The globalization of many environmental issues in the 1980s (e.g., stratospheric ozone depletion, global climate change, and loss of biodiversity) made it increasingly apparent that the fate of the industrialized nations and the LDCs were inextricably linked. Action was not likely to occur on those global environmental issues unless the development issues facing the LDCs were also resolved. This led to the Brundtland Commission report and the more integrated conference theme at the Rio conference.

Sustainable development was the theme of the so-called Earth Summit, and it resulted in the largest gathering of heads of state for any purpose in history. The "Rio Declaration" and "Agenda 21" documents emerging from that conference called for changes in both environmental and development policy to support a "sustainable development" path. Specific interpretation of those terms remained ambiguous but has generally followed the language of the Brundtland Commission. This paralleled important changes in policies by both national governments and multilateral institutions, such as the establishment of the Global Environment Facility by the World Bank (1992). Other agencies strengthened their environmental programs, and businesses joined the debate through the Business Council on Sustainable Development and the establishment of environmental audit programs. In his 1993 book, *The Ecology of Commerce*, Paul Hawken laid down the challenge for business and highlighted business's critical role in achieving sustainable development. The term *sustainable development* is now used widely in policy debates, activist newsletters, and academic discourse. It still appears to mean widely differing things to different people, however, which is one of the reasons the term has gained such widespread use.

According to the Brundtland Commission, "Humanity has the ability to make development sustainable—to ensure that it meets the needs of the present without compromising the ability of future generations to meet their own needs" (World Commission on Environment and Development 1987, 8). This is the most widely cited definition of sustainable development, but it leaves a number of specific terms ambiguous. Moreover, its focus on human needs does not encompass the broader perspective of maintaining ecological structure and function even though there may not be utilitarian values associated with such ecological integrity (Nash 1989; Merchant 1992; Callicott 1987a; 1989; Des Jardins 1997). The literature on sustainable development generally recognizes three dimensions of sustainability: ecological, economic, and social. Herman Daly's book *Steady-State Economics* outlined a framework for sustainability in economics (1991 [1977]), laying the foundation for the establishment of the International Society for Ecological Economics and the journal *Ecological Economics* in 1987 (*Ecological Economics* 1987–present). The Rio conference and the concurrent Global Forum (attended by more than a thousand representatives of nongovernmental organizations) drew greater attention to the social dimension of sustainability. Subsequent literature has also emphasized this dimension, as well as issues of political legitimacy and political stability. Despite this wide-ranging debate, however, there remain significant gaps in current research on and understanding of sustainable development.

First, the sustainable-development debate has largely focused on the so-called developing countries, without adequately addressing problems of either development or the environment within the existing pattern of industrial economic activity in the so-called developed countries. There is an implicit assumption in the policy debate that existing patterns of economic activity in the developed nations are sustainable, and that the only question is how to ensure that currently undeveloped countries can move to a developed state sustainably. This means that the model of a desired future condition may go unchallenged and be perpetuated through adoption of that model by the LDCs. Consequently, there is a need to address issues of sustainability in the industrialized countries. Recent literature has drawn connections between consumption levels and sustainability (Durning 1992; Menzel 1994), but there has been relatively little systematic analysis of the sustainability of industrial systems. The President's Council on Sustainable Development made an effort to link sustainability to the American situation, but its composition precluded discussion of many of the most fundamental issues. The council therefore largely accepted the Brundtland Commission's "grow-your-way-to-sustainability" approach.

Second, the sustainable-development debate has generally been at an abstract level (e.g., how to incorporate degradation of natural capital into national income accounts) or focused on specific technologies (e.g., the relative advantages of solar photovoltaics versus nuclear power). Exploration of the intermediate level of metropolitan and regional planning—and the spatial dimension of development at that scale—has been primarily limited to physical form (e.g., neotraditional suburbs, transit-oriented developments) imbedded within the larger context of a spatial and economic system that is not necessarily sustainable. Mathis Wackernagel and William Rees have highlighted this issue in their book *Our Ecological Footprint*, which traces the offsite land requirements associated with maintaining production and consumption in urban nodes (1996). They found that residents in the Vancouver metropolitan area required 4.3 hectares (10.6 acres) per person to meet their needs, or about nineteen times the land area that was actually settled (14–15). The average resident of the Netherlands needed only fifteen times the settled land area, but this is still far beyond the carrying capacity of Holland (15; Buitenkamp et al. 1992; Friends of the Earth Netherlands 1994). There is clearly an urgent need to link the abstract macro and technology-specific micro scales through a systematic assessment of metropolitan and regional patterns. This could draw on emerging models of industrial ecology as well as the flow models of energy and resources in metropolitan areas developed in the 1970s and early 1980s (Tibbs 1993). New computing technologies and software interfaces allow more accessible simulation models (Hannon and Ruth 1994). These in turn can be used to explore the multiple dimensions of the sustainability debate. The multiple scales at which I am assessing the Sierra Nevada bioregion—regional, subregional, county or watershed, and community—must *all* be addressed for sustainability.[13]

Finally, much of the sustainable-development debate has focused on resource issues in the tropics. While deforestation and other phenomena associated with development in the tropics are certainly important, these have tended to displace the attention of the public in the temperate zones from the effects of temperate zone development. This gap is particularly evident in regard to biodiversity and habitat, which is closely related to metropolitan and regional patterns. The ecosystems found in the Sierra Nevada are also notably rich in species, though, and those species represent elements of biodiversity that would be lost even if tropical conservation efforts are successful (Shevock 1996). We must address these issues of sustainability for the temperate regions. It is difficult to imagine effective reductions in biodiversity losses in the tropical nations of Latin America, Asia, and Africa unless we simultaneously stem the loss of biodiversity in our own backyard. "Do as I say, not as I do" is a weak basis for gaining international cooperation on global environmental issues.

Meeting and reconciling all the objectives of sustainable development will therefore be difficult. In some cases, direct trade-offs may exist among and between competing goals. In some cases it will be possible to promote policies that support all three dimensions of sustainable development; in other cases, promoting one dimension might shift attention away from (and thereby reduce the viability of) achieving sustainable development in another dimension. Scott Campbell has noted that these three dimensions parallel the traditional planning concerns of economic efficiency, environmental impacts, and social equity (1996). Others have highlighted the fact that sustainable development is really a dialectic process of discovery and modification of both goals and the processes we might pursue to achieve them, for there is no end-state that constitutes sustainable development. Both of these insights place the planning profession at the center of the academic and professional debate over sustainable development.

There has been considerable confusion, however, between the term *sustainable development* and terms that sound similar but have quite different meanings. The most egregious of these is the inadvertent substitution of the word *sustained* for *sustainable* and the word *growth* for *development.* This puts the wolf of sustained growth in the sheep's clothing of sustainable development. They are not the same thing; in fact, the term *sustainable development* is largely a reaction to decades of obsessive attention to sustained growth as a substitute for development and without regard for the negative consequences of such an obsession. The word *sustainability* has two critical elements: *sustain,* meaning to maintain in perpetuity, and *ability,* meaning the capacity to sustain. The word *development* is also not the same thing as *growth:* the former implies either a *qualitative* change through an evolutionary process of maturation *or* a *quantitative* change in scale, while *growth* addresses only the *quantitative* dimension of economic output. Growth may be one element of development, but it is not a comprehensive substitute for a more qualitative evolutionary process (Daly 1991; Costanza 1990; Norgaard 1994).

In fairness to the pro-growth perspective, I should add here that economic growth is necessary just to maintain current standards of living as long as population growth continues. Moreover, inflation can eat away at the real value of people's assets and income, decreasing the real purchasing power and economic well-being in material terms if not compensated for by economic growth that represents real improvements in productivity. In the absence of either population growth or inflation, moreover, economic growth represents a more efficient allocation of resources so as to produce greater material throughput (i.e., flow of produced goods that are then consumed). This means that people are better off materially than they would be in the absence of such growth—but that may be at the cost of depleting the natural capital that provides important environmental goods and services (Collados 1997). Much of the current "need" for economic growth is the result of rapid population growth, however, which forces us to run faster and faster just to stay in place, to avoid losing ground materially. Economic growth that does not exceed population growth is therefore merely expansion of the economy without improvement in economic well-being, and that expansion often entails significant costs that reduce both social and environmental well-being in the process.

We must also sustain the planet's ability to maintain economic, ecological, and social well-being for a much longer time horizon than the typical life cycle of most benefit-cost analyses. The decisions we make will in large part be determined by the time frame within which we consider the consequences. As noted above, the present system of economic analysis through benefit-cost analysis and discounted net present values emphasizes the short-term period facing the present generation. Even our children's health and the consequences of our actions in our children's lifetimes are heavily discounted under this approach. This may lead to a path that will turn out to be sustainable, but it would merely be a coincidence if that were true. If sustainability is our goal, we must explicitly state over what time frame we want to sustain our ability. The lifetime of the existing generation is clearly too short, but an infinite time horizon is too abstract a concept for our minds to grasp fully. Maintaining systems in perpetuity is a laudable goal, but claiming such a goal moves the implications of our decisions from the particular to the abstract.

I suggest that we instead select an intermediate time frame that is tangible in relation to human lives and experience: the "seven generations" criterion of some Native American cultures. It is a long time into the future, but not so long that we cannot identify with seven generations into our past. It will give us a benchmark to evaluate the consequences of land and resource management policies in the Sierra Nevada and throughout the exurban West: how will these policies affect the economic, ecological, and social conditions and their sustainability for the seventh generation from now? Let us therefore evaluate the consequences of our actions at least seven generations into the future: late in the twenty-second century, around the year 2170. My grandchildren's grandchildren's grandchildren will first enter the world around that year. And my great-grandchildren, whom I may know in the last decades of my own life, may know their great-grandchildren in the last decades of their lives. I am therefore directly linked to the seventh generation forward through real people I will know in my lifetime.

COMPREHENSIVE ECONOMIC ANALYSIS

The goal of land and resource management policy in the Sierra Nevada and the exurban West should be to achieve sustainable development that encompasses all three of the dimensions identified above: economic, ecological, and social sustainability. We should also evaluate the consequences of our actions for sustainability in those dimensions over at least the next seven generations. The specific determination of what should be achieved in each of these dimensions, however, must be developed in the context of the people and the place: the economic, ecological, and social context will determine what constitutes sustainable development in the Range of Light. What is appropriate in one place may not be appropriate in another. There are certain commonalities, however, between the issues facing the Sierra Nevada and at least the rest of the rural and exurban West. One of these is that environmental quality is the fundamental economic asset of the region. We cannot have a healthy Sierra Nevada economy in the long run without a healthy Sierra Nevada environment. Over the time span of seven generations, this principle is also probably true more generally for the rest of the planet. It is nevertheless a reality we generally ignore.

Current approaches to economic analysis for public policy decisions involving land and resource management generally focus only on the cash flow or expense statement of those decisions. Traditional analytic approaches therefore fail to address the effects of our decisions on the value of the underlying economic asset of environmental quality. In the language of ecological economics, we are ignoring the value of natural capital (Jansson et al. 1994). We therefore need to introduce a balance-sheet perspective to land and resource management policy through a framework for economic analysis that recognizes environmental quality and other amenity values. A number of ecological economists have been developing such a framework over the past few years through the International Society for Ecological Economics, led by the early work of Herman Daly (and the more recent work of Robert Costanza and economists at the London School of Economics) (Pearce and Turner 1990). The principles of ecological economics are summarized in the books *Ecological Economics: The Science and Management of Sustainability* and *Investing in Natural Capital: The Ecological Economics Approach to Sustainability*, products of the first two biennial conferences on ecological economics (Costanza 1991; Jansson et al. 1994). Subsequent conferences have focused on applications of the concepts and empirical case studies of ecological economics.

My own work in this area has focused on the problem of amenity valuation and how the emerging framework of ecological economics can be applied to land and resource management issues in the exurban West. This has been the subject of several interesting publications by Jeff Olson, Ray Rasker, and Mark Shaffer of the Wilderness Society that address the changing economic characteristics of the Greater Yellowstone Ecoregion (Rasker et al. 1992), the Pacific Northwest (Anderson and Olson 1991), and communities in the Rocky Mountains (Rasker 1993; 1994; Rasker and Glick 1994; Rasker et al. 1992). Michael Kinsley of the Rocky Mountain Institute has also been dealing with these issues in rural communities throughout the West. In academic circles, both Edward Whitelaw of the University of Oregon and Thomas Power (1996a) of the University of Montana have applied these concepts to their respective regions. While they are not economists, law professors Charles Wilkinson of the University of Colorado (1992a) and Joseph Sax at the University of California at Berkeley (1991) have also raised the issues of economic and social transformation in their work on land and resource management policy. There is a nucleus of exciting work emerging in this field that could radically change rural economic development analysis in the future.[14]

The framework I lay out here draws on work by all of these researchers and more. What we need when making social choices about the allocation of scarce resources is a method for comprehensive economic analysis that addresses *all* of the economic values that must be considered to achieve a sustainable future. Only a subset of those economic values is normally measured in monetary terms and accounted for in conventional economic analysis. In some cases, the conclusions one might reach based on that partial information can lead to decisions that degrade natural capital and reduce sustainability. It is therefore necessary to incorporate the full range of values into a comprehensive analysis. Only then will we fully understand the economic implications of our decisions; we otherwise run the risk of temporarily (and unsustainably) increasing our cash flow while simultaneously eroding benefit-generating asset values.

We must consider the following ten key elements in a comprehensive economic analysis for rural and exurban communities in order to evaluate how land and resource management policies affect local economic development and economic, ecological, and social sustainability.

Base Economic Activity and Exports

This is the foundation of local and regional economic analysis. It calculates the total value of goods and services exported from the local economy as the source of economic inputs into the local economy. In theory, the income derived from exports is the base of local economic activity. Local economic analysis often misapplies the theory, however, through a limited focus only on the direct export of goods and services associated with local employment.[15] As demonstrated above, though, the majority of total income in the Sierra Nevada is now associated with transfer payments, commuter incomes earned outside the region, and self-employment income, none of which is recorded in EDD data. Both the numerator and the denominator in traditional base analysis are therefore likely to be wrong as a result of failing to include these additional sources of income. The fraction of the local economic activity attributable to base export activities will also generally be overstated. Moreover, exports themselves are actually only required to equal imports in order to maintain a trade balance (Power 1996a). Trade within the local economy can sustain economic activity as long as the full range of specialized goods and services desired by local consumers is produced locally. Increasing diversification and complexity in exurban economies therefore reduces the relative importance of base export activities compared to isolated, single-industry, resource extraction-dependent rural economies. Base economic analysis is an important tool, but the ongoing transformation of the exurban West requires careful application of the tool within the new context of diverse and complex local economies. *Incomes,* rather than employment, are what now drive local economic activity. Counting jobs and ignoring transfer payments, commuter income, or self-employment will lead to incorrect conclusions from traditional application of base analysis techniques. The results will tend to overstate the importance of traditional resource extraction employment.

Multipliers and Local Economic Structure

For base jobs created within the local economy, every dollar of income earned by that employee gets spent either locally or outside the area. The degree of diversification and complexity of the local economy is one factor determining how many times that dollar gets turned over through spending and respending within the local economy. Other important factors influencing this multiplier effect are the relative competitiveness of local goods and services versus alternatives outside the area and the access local customers have to outside alternatives (Leontieff 1986). High prices at the local automobile dealer, for example, may lead local consumers in the Gold Country to drive down to Roseville, Folsom, or Sacramento when purchasing a new car. This is probably even more likely if those consumers are already commuting to employment in those areas, for they can then shop outside their own communities without the additional time and expense of making the long trip. Groceries, dinners out, and haircuts are purchases likely to be made locally, however, for the relative advantages of lower prices in the Sacramento metropolitan area are small. Moreover, higher land values in metropolitan areas may even make those items more expensive there than in the local economy.

The income earned by local residents can therefore either "multiply" through the local economy or "leak" outside the area and fail to generate additional jobs and income locally. This phenomenon is true at a variety of scales: the local economy, the regional economy, the state economy, and the national economy all have different multipliers. In general, multipliers tend to be higher as the scale of the economic unit is greater. This reflects the greater diversification and complexity associated with the higher levels of specialization possible through economies of scale. Even if the dollar "leaks" outside the Gold Country, then, it is likely to multiply its effect for some time in the Northern California economy. Depending on the mix of imports versus domestic products in the Northern California economy, it may then either leak overseas or multiply throughout the country. The specific income and employment effects of purchases within a local economy therefore reverberate throughout the larger-scale economy as a function of the complexity of that economy in providing a range of goods and services and the specific preferences of consumers. Depending on the source goods and services, the purchase of a Toyota in Auburn may affect employment and incomes either near a Toyota plant in Japan or near the New United Motors Manufacturing plant in Fremont, California. Workers from the latter plant may then reinject some of their income into the Gold Country economy en route to Lake Tahoe for a vacation of skiing or boating.

Like base analysis, multipliers are a familiar element of traditional economic analysis. Multipliers are frequently misapplied to rural and exurban economies, however, through two common mistakes. The first is use of a multiplier derived at a larger level of economic and/or geographic aggregation. These multipliers will tend to overstate the effect of export revenues, because they are based on analysis of economic activity within a structure generally more diversified and complex. The second mistake is use of outdated multipliers that reflect structural relationships within the local and regional economies that are no longer accurate. This is a significant problem in the rural and exurban West, where the changes of the past three decades have radically altered local economic structure. This mistake will tend to overstate the relative importance of those economic activities that dominated the local economy at the time of the original input-output analysis that generated the multiplier. Increased diversification and complexity in local rural and exurban economies should generally increase the multiplier effect for many expenditures, but increased leakage is also likely to be associated with an expanded commuter population. Expansion of diversity and complexity in the nearby greater metropolitan area (together with its physical expansion, which reduces the time and expense associated with taking advantage of consumer opportunities outside the local economy) will also tend to increase leakage from exurban to metropolitan economies and decrease local multipliers.

Employment Characteristics of Activities

The employment implications of a given level of income or spending are not always the same for either base economic activity or multiplier effects. Some jobs created by such spending are high-paying and stable, and offer benefits that reduce other social costs associated with the provision of services such as health care. Those same jobs may be available only to employees with advanced education, however, and those skills may not match the capabilities of the unemployed or underemployed local labor pool. New employees may have to be brought in from outside the area. This isn't necessarily a bad thing, for those new residents will usually bring a wide range of skills and resources to the local economy. Some of those skills and resources will translate into additional local economic benefits if and when those new residents break out on their own and establish entrepreneurial ventures that then employ more local residents. Other skills and resources build community capacity and improve social well-being through active involvement in community groups (Kusel 1996). It is nevertheless important to recognize the specific employment characteristics of different types of local economic activity. All too often, local economic analysis and economic development efforts focus on counting jobs without critically analyzing the employment characteristics of those jobs. Many jobs in resource extraction industries are highly paid on an hourly basis, but they suffer from high levels of occupational safety risk and high levels of instability resulting from seasonal and business-cycle fluctuations (Power 1996a). The long-term potential for maintaining those jobs in a community may also be threatened by strong incentives for corporate investors and managers to substitute labor-saving technology for workers (Stewart 1993; Power 1996a). Some jobs with lower hourly wages may therefore be even more desirable than these resource extraction jobs *if* they offer greater stability of employment. The same is true for many seasonal jobs in the recreation and tourism industries, which are often filled by temporary residents who do not put down roots or contribute to community capacity. The latter jobs tend to pay much lower hourly wages, however, than jobs in the resource extraction sector. In the words of Ed Marston, this is one of "the warts on the West's service economy" (1996c).

Despite these generalizations, some seasonal or part-time employment may be more desirable for some employees than full-time, year-round employment. Many residents (e.g., students, parents with young children, semiretired residents) may prefer the flexibility associated with seasonal or part-time employment. They would be locked out of the workforce if all jobs required full-time, year-round commitment. Matching the employment characteristics of local jobs with the employment needs and desires of local residents requires a wide range of employment opportunities in the local economy. Narrow, limited options will tend to meet the needs of only a few. Seasonal, part-time, or low-skill jobs are therefore not necessarily bad for the local economy if they improve the well-being of some local residents.

Nonmarket Assets and Amenity Values

This is where economic analysis gets complicated. As discussed above in the section on benefit-cost analysis, assigning a dollar amount to these nonmarket assets and amenity values is extremely difficult. They are nevertheless quite important to local economic activity. This is demonstrated by the quote from the real estate advertisement at the beginning of this chapter. A comprehensive economic analysis must therefore address them explicitly. Nonmonetary assessment of these values is a necessary component of any public discourse on land and resource management policy and local economic development. We must be able to state our values explicitly and through a wide range of methods and terms. The language of dollars is not the only language appropriate for discussing values. In fact, many philosophers have argued that it is a completely inappropriate language (Sagoff 1988).

Economists have attempted to estimate the monetary value of amenities primarily through two common techniques: hedonic pricing and contingent valuation. Hedonic pricing techniques compare the market value of similar goods and services that differ only in a single nonmarket characteristic (Wilman 1984). Two comparable houses in the Berkeley hills, for example, might be compared to determine the economic value of having a view of San Francisco. Assuming they are the same in all other relevant ways (e.g., same number of bedrooms and bathrooms, same total floor area, same access to parking and shopping, etc.), any difference in their market values can be attributed to the view. Local real estate agents recently estimated that an excellent view was worth around $25,000 in the market (Ratcliffe and Ratcliffe 1996). This kind of analysis is useful for those amenities that have indirect market values—even if there is no market in the "unbundled" commodity of interest, a value for that nonmarket good or service can be estimated based on market information. It is very difficult to apply, however, when a "bundle" of amenity values differentiate the two otherwise-comparable market goods or services. The ad for "The Cedars," for example, emphasizes both the natural environment and the security of a "gate guarded community." If there *is* a premium paid for building lots at the Cedars (and there appears to be one), which amenities are being valued? How much of the premium results from the natural environment, and how much is for the increased security? Is it Nature or Culture that increases the value? Hedonic pricing techniques leave a great deal of room for interpretation because of the indirect and multi-attribute nature of the amenities information.

Contingent valuation is a more direct means of estimating how prospective consumers value amenities, but it has a number of difficulties associated with it (Hanemann 1994). In particular, it does not rely on actual market information of consumers' "revealed preferences." The term *contingent valuation* reflects the idea that a monetary valuation can be estimated *contingent upon* the existence of a market for the good or service: *if* a market existed for the good or service, in other words, how much *would* one be willing to pay for the good or service? The contingent nature of the inquiry also makes it a bit abstract and unfamiliar to most people, however, which makes valuation estimates subject to considerable error. There is also the potential for strategic bidding by respondents. As discussed above, this approach requires an implicit assignment of property rights that may affect the values estimated. Because it is not based on empirically verifiable market information, many economists reject contingent valuation as an unreliable technique.[16] Valuing amenities is nevertheless critical to any comprehensive economic analysis framework, and hedonic pricing is a crude and ineffective measure for many nonmarket values. Failing to value these amenities is tantamount to assigning an implicit value of zero to them—hardly a more *accurate* estimation of value than could be achieved through these techniques. Contingent valuation studies can offer useful information on the *potential* economic value of nonmarketed goods and services. The results of those studies should then be considered in the context of other information.

Nonlocal Valuation of Nonmarket Assets

It is clear that nonmarket assets and amenity values are important to local economic development in the Sierra Nevada and throughout the rural and exurban West. These values are primarily associated with the residential and industrial location choices of the local community. They also affect recreation and tourism, which in turn affect local income and employment. Nonmarket assets accrue many other economic benefits outside the local economy, however, such as environmental quality. These include the environmental goods and services that support some resource extraction and commodity exports, such as timber or water. Maintaining the productive capacity of forest soils is essential to support timber production, for example, while erosion of those soils would negatively affect water quality, hydroelectric production, and reservoir capacity for downstream water resources users. There is no market in soil erosion, but these values have significant economic consequences. Other nonlocal communities of interest highly value ecological resources because of their amenity value. These ecological resources and amenity values may serve as the foundation for recreation and tourism within the local economy, for example, but the economic value placed on those activities by nonlocal users may not be reflected in the market value of local economic activity. Many types of recreation and tourism have public-good characteristics, so there may be a large consumer surplus associated with those activities. They will tend as a result to be overconsumed. The *monetary* value of recreation and tourism would therefore significantly understate the true *economic* value of those activities.

Finally, nonlocal communities of interest may value ecological resources for nonutilitarian or amenity reasons. They may recognize an option value associated with some future decision to use the resources, a bequest value associated with giving future generations the option of use (Fisher 1981; Krutilla 1967), or some intrinsic or inherent values that do not reflect usefulness to humans (Sagoff 1988; Norton 1991; Nash 1989). These latter values are the most difficult to quantify, for they challenge a central tenet of economics: that social decisions to allocate scarce resources should reflect only the preferences of *humans* and the value of those resources to *humans*. This is a topic of raging debate among both economists and philosophers, yet the fact is that some humans (myself among them) believe that such values exist. Yes, those abstract concepts of intrinsic and inherent value are ultimately translated into human actions within a social context of human choices and human values. Yes, those concepts will be subject to daunting intellectual challenge within the logical framework of modern economics and philosophy. Many spiritual and philosophical values incorporated into widely respected religious traditions face the same challenges, yet they persist in our modern world. Denying them intellectual legitimacy through the theoretical limits of neoclassical economics does not eliminate their existence. These are important personal and social values, and they help to explain much of the institutional context of land and resource management policy in the West. The same can be said for social values associated with images of the independent cowboy or the importance of irrigation as a foundation of democracy (Starrs 1989; Stegner 1954; Wilkinson 1992b; Worster 1985b). These are deeply held cultural ideas, yet they are not recognized by most economic analyses.

Influences on Value of Nonmarket Assets

Recognizing that these nonmarket assets have value both to the local economy and nonlocal communities of interest is a critical step in any economic analysis. It is not enough, however, simply to acknowledge their existence and importance. It is also necessary to evaluate how proposed strategies for local economic development will affect the underlying value of those assets. This is where economic analysis and ecological assessment begin to merge. It is impossible to understand how the value of those nonmarket assets will change unless there is baseline information on their current condition. We must also have a model of how local economic activities interact with and affect that condition and a monitoring program in place to determine whether our model is correct. Our understanding of the nature of the ecological system must also include attention to the natural range of variation in the system, the successional path(s) followed by that system, the critical thresholds in system properties that could lead to nonlinear changes in system characteristics, and the carrying capacity of the system for particular types of activities. This is an enormous amount of ecological information.

Not surprisingly, it is presently collected systematically for only that narrow part of the ecological system that provides commodity outputs having market value.[17] As a result, we generally fail to recognize or evaluate the consequences of our economic activities on the underlying value of nonmarket assets. Limited assessment of the ecological consequences of major economic activities does occur today through the EIR requirements of NEPA and CEQA. Those assessments are triggered only for major projects, however, and the cumulative effects of many smaller economic decisions are rarely addressed adequately. Moreover, the EIR is assembled late in the process of program and project planning and design, making the project difficult to change in more than marginal ways as a result of the advanced stage of project development by the time environmental information is incorporated.

A more systematic assessment of nonmarket asset values would reduce this problem. It would also link environmental assessment to the broader question of economic development—with direct feedback relationships between economic development efforts and the economic value of nonmarket assets. Environmental assessment, mitigation requirements, and subsequent monitoring programs would then all be part of an integrated economic development strategy rather than a cost burden seen as threatening economic development. Understanding the ecological systems that provide these nonmarket values is not a luxury; it is an essential step toward the design of local economic development strategies that are truly sustainable.

Our current system counts the depletion of natural capital as income while failing to recognize that the underlying asset value has simultaneously been *reduced*. Businesses practice what is called accrual accounting to avoid this very error: if they relied on cash-flow accounting only, General Motors managers would mistakenly view the dismantling and sale of the GM production line as good for business because it generated cash. Bit by bit, GM could sell off pieces of the factory and show nice quarterly "profits." This action would also gradually eliminate GM's capacity to produce vehicles, however, thereby eliminating their future capacity to produce income and employment. This would truly be an inappropriate accounting system, for *wealth* is at least as important as *income* to GM's shareholders. Yet that is exactly the kind of accounting system our current approach to economic analysis applies to the valuation of nonmarket assets (Repetto 1992). We therefore often mistake the conversion of natural capital through consumption as income.

Institutional Setting for Asset Management

It should be apparent by now that the monetary dimension of economics is heavily influenced by the institutional setting within which economic decisions are made. Depending on the accounting system, a particular decision may appear to be economic or not. Much of what we call economics is therefore distorted by the accounting system in use. It is therefore critical that the institutional setting for land and resource management be clearly understood when conducting a comprehensive economic analysis.[18] Many of the incentives for particular types of local economic development strategies originate in the institutional structure and accounting systems recognized as legitimate by those institutions. Local governments receive different types and levels of revenues from private versus public timber harvests within their jurisdiction, for example, creating incentives for local governments to favor greater timber harvests on public lands. Federal land managers may only get to keep the receipts from their timber sales for particular types of activities, however, while revenues from other types of activities on federal lands may go straight back into the federal Treasury. This creates incentives for particular types of activities. The economics of those activities depend on the institutionally determined incentive structure imbedded within the accounting framework of the activities. Many of these institutional systems date from the nineteenth century, while many of the more recent changes to those systems reflect an agency or professional Culture that does not necessarily embrace the changing social values of the past three decades (Wilkinson 1992a; O'Toole 1988; Duane forthcoming). Rarely is the recent transformation of the rural and exurban West recognized in the incentive structures of the dominant land and resource management institutions. Not surprisingly, these systems rarely create incentives to protect nonmarket asset values for long-term economic, ecological, and social sustainability. The result is a set of incentives for local economic development and land and resource management that may directly undermine sustainability.

This does not have to be the case. Institutions, accounting systems, and incentive structures are human creations. As such, they can be modified or replaced if they fail to meet evolving human needs. There are strong disincentives to enact radical change, of course, and many interests continue to benefit handsomely under the existing institutional system. The existing system should nevertheless not be viewed as immutable. Many strategies for local economic development are likely to succeed only if there are significant changes in that system. Institutional innovation at the international, federal, state, and local levels can be a strategy for local economic development.

Degree of Local and Public Control over Assets

This is a critical element of the institutional structure that creates the accounting framework and incentives structure within which local economic development and land and resource management are conducted. While a continuum is a more appropriate model, one can grossly simplify the degree of local and public control into the four general cases shown in Table 4.1 (examples in each cell are illustrative only).

TABLE 4.1   Degree of Local and Public Control over Land Use

	Public	Private
Local	County park	Local developer
Distant	Federal forest	Industrial forest

Each of these different categories of ownership operates within a different institutional context. Each therefore uses a different accounting system and faces a different incentive structure. As a result, the social pressures for, and opportunities to influence, land and resource management policy are different for each category. Not surprisingly, land and resource management policies differ across these categories, and have the potential to play very different roles in local economic development.

There may be equally important differences within each of these categories, of course. A local landowner with a house on one acre may behave differently than a local developer with several parcels of several thousand acres each.[19] Industrial forestry companies can also have different capital structures, creating different internal incentives for land and resource management. Some may focus on short-term liquidation of timber in order to pay off highly leveraged companies, while others may focus on long-term values.[20] The county department of transportation manages its land differently than the county parks department does, for they have different mandates and criteria for determining appropriate use. Different agencies within the federal government can also behave quite differently: the Park Service emphasizes visitor use and resource preservation (Winks 1996), while the Forest Service tends to emphasize commodity production (Wilkinson 1992a; O'Toole 1988; Hirt 1994). A more complex, n-dimensional matrix is therefore appropriate for analysis of the degree of local and public ownership of economic assets.

Ownership is often different from control, however, so it is important to link this analysis to the institutional analysis described above. Particular interest groups may have more influence than others with some agencies, for example, while some private landowners may be constrained in their land and resource management practices by local, state, or federal regulatory restrictions. The effects of alternative land and resource management policies on local economic development therefore depend on the interaction between these variables. Changing either the state of one of the variables or the relationship between them can affect local economic development.

Distribution of Economic Benefits and Costs

Despite the utilitarian focus of benefit-cost analysis on efficiency rather than equity, the distribution of economic benefits and costs does indeed matter. For this reason, explicit determination of the distribution of benefits and costs is necessary to resolve many social conflicts. Such an explicit disclosure also has political costs, however, for the few that sometimes benefit by riding on the backs of the many will no longer be able to claim the public good as the rationale for public subsidies that benefit their interests. Such claims dominate the history of land and resource management and local economic development. They are generally made by economic and political elites, and those elites continue to have clear interests in maintaining the status quo. This aspect of comprehensive economic analysis is, as a result, difficult to implement within the existing institutional context. That context reflects power relationships within our society that have proven extremely difficult to alter. The tangible costs of such institutional change would be borne directly by those few who now benefit from the existing system, while the abstract and intangible benefits of change would generally accrue diffusely to a much broader base of society. Under the existing system, that broad group faces relatively small direct costs individually. Those costs are also hidden behind and buried within a complex labyrinth of public budgets, tax codes, archaic and impenetrable environmental documents, and stonewalling bureaucracies. Not surprisingly, it has proven difficult to mobilize adequate political momentum for significant reform of land and resource management policies. It will be even more difficult to mobilize widespread public involvement in the intricacies of comprehensive economic analysis. Systematic assessment nevertheless requires explicit evaluation of the distribution of benefits and costs of both land and resource management and local economic development strategies. It is not enough just to count up the benefits and demonstrate that they exceed the costs. One must also determine: *whose* benefits? *whose* costs?

Neither economists nor scientists are comfortable with these questions. Many land and resource managers have also been trained in the positivist tradition of the natural sciences (Hirt 1994). Steeped in the utilitarianism of Gifford Pinchot, they rarely question the implicit value assumptions of either their agencies' mandates or their analytic tools. Social choices involve tradeoffs among individuals and groups, however, and agency managers have clearly experienced conflict over such tradeoffs over the past few decades. Most land and resource management agency managers therefore already recognize that their policy choices have distributional consequences. The time has come now to address those tradeoffs and distributional consequences explicitly in their analytic methods. It is too easy to blame politics for policy outcomes while hiding behind the utilitarian shield of objectivity and technical neutrality.

Future Trends in Population and Asset Values

All of our decisions are ultimately about the future. None of our actions can change the past; they, too, will manifest their effects and consequences in the future. Comprehensive economic analysis must therefore be forward-looking in its perspective. It cannot rely on the rearview mirror perspective of the world that brought us to accept a wide range of implicit assumptions about Nature and Culture. Nature and Culture are dynamic, and their relationship has been co-evolving for all of human existence. The ongoing transformation of the Sierra Nevada and the rest of the rural and exurban West is just one example of this coevolution. It highlights how both our perspective on Nature and our influence on it are continually changing (Worster 1985a; Cronon 1991; Merchant 1980).

What is deemed good for the land in one era is seen as the worst possible practice in another; we realize that the more we learn, the less we really know. Future generations will hold values different from ours. And as population continues to grow, it is clear that both market and nonmarket asset values will be affected. Historical trends are a useful aid in the modeling effort, but we must consider a wide range of future scenarios. Any projection of social, demographic, economic, technological, institutional, or ecological conditions must explicitly recognize enormous uncertainty. Managing risk must therefore be an essential element of land and resource management policies, as well as any local economic development strategy. Uncertainty is the only certainty we have about the future and our forecasts.

Risk analysis and decision analysis tools can help inform our understanding of uncertainty (Keeney and Raiffa 1993). Those tools are not adequate substitutes for good judgment, however, and they call for a certain degree of humility in their application. As discussed in the benefit-cost analysis section, using them also calls for important value judgments about future generations. Discounting may be an appropriate tool for analyzing the time value of and economic returns associated with marketable goods and services, but it is inappropriate to discount future health damages, human lives, and irreversible ecological damages. We must address questions of intergenerational equity directly (Howarth and Norgaard 1992; 1995). We will otherwise apply only our own values to decisions to develop land and resource management policies and local economic development strategies that may ultimately jeopardize the economic well-being of future generations. Such an approach is both unfair and unsustainable.

The ten elements described above are largely absent from traditional approaches to local economic development in the rural and exurban West, which focus on expansion of the economic base activities through increased resource extraction and commodity exports. Such expansion may not generate significant local benefits, however, if there are low local multipliers and the employment characteristics of the activities result in limited additional employment. The activities may also diminish the value of nonmarket economic assets highly valued both by local residents (whose residential location choice decisions may be dominated by nonmarket amenity values) and by nonlocal communities of interest. Depending on the institutional setting for land and resource management, it may be possible to capture some of those nonmarket values for greater local economic benefits. This will in part be a function of the degree of local control over those economic assets. The ultimate distribution of benefits and costs is also significant, for expansion of resource extraction activities (or amenity-oriented activities) may benefit a few members of the community (or nonlocal owners of capital invested in the local area) while the costs of the expansion are borne by the community as a whole and nonlocal communities of interest. Future trends in both local and nonlocal population characteristics may also increase the value of local nonmarket assets, and degradation of those values for short-term resource extraction may reduce the well-being of future generations. All of these implications must be addressed to determine what constitutes a viable land and resource management path to sustainable development.

DEPLETING THE REGION'S NATURAL CAPITAL

I was driving south on Highway 395 when I passed the first truck. It was fully loaded with large Jeffrey pine logs on a chilly winter day. The air was crisp and the road was empty here on the east side, for the tourists come over only on the weekends outside the summer months. I love this drive from Truckee down to Mammoth: across the Martis Valley, up and over Brockway Summit on 267, down to King's Beach at Lake Tahoe, around Crystal Bay and past Sand Harbor below the Flume Trail, up to Spooner Summit, then down to 395. It is getting more and more suburban south of Carson City through Gardnerville and Minden, but it still feels like old California once you get clear of the tract homes. Antelope Valley paints a classic picture with its alfalfa fields and leaning barns, and the climb up the Walker River is unbeatable. This is the real West.

The trucks kept passing me as I continued into Bridgeport. There to the right were Matterhorn Peak and the Hoover Wilderness, where my family hiked into Peeler Lake when I was sixteen. Our feeble tube tents were nearly washed away by rain the first night at Barney Lake, but we were treated to a spectacular sunset over the crest of Yosemite our second evening out. I looked westward then at the forested slopes of the upper Tuolumne River country and imagined future backpacking trips across that great roadless area. Two decades have passed since then, but the Tahoe-Yosemite Trail will someday bring me back to that unwalked territory.

By the time I reached Mono Lake I had counted a dozen fully laden trucks. Where could they be going? I drove into Lee Vining and saw one parked at a cafe, the driver sipping coffee by the window. His truck had Oregon license plates. We were a long way from the nearest mill and he had a winding and tiring drive ahead. Another truck roared past and on through town, and the number was now up to fourteen. Large-diameter, mature pines lay across the trailer as the truck went by in a blur. I could almost smell the sweet vanilla of the Jeffrey's bark; I imagined them upright by the side of a grassy meadow. I love to stick my nose deep into the bark for their smell when I'm out backpacking or on a hike.

Three more trucks passed me before I reached the turnoff to Mammoth Lakes. I don't know how many loads they took out that day, but I had passed seventeen on my drive between Highway 88 and Mammoth Lakes. I had come to Mammoth that day to give a talk about economics and the environment to the local collaborative group, the Coalition for Unified Recreation in the Eastern Sierra. The log-ging trucks presented a perfect opportunity to relate the abstract concepts of my talk to the specific choices facing communities and managers. Where were the eco-nomic and ecological assets of the area going, I asked, and what value was being returned to the local community in exchange? Large Jeffrey pine stands are increasingly rare in the eastern Sierra Nevada, making them increasingly valuable for both lumber consumption and recreational use. The logs on the trucks might inject some short-term cash into the local economy, but it would be a long time before their replacements would begin to provide comparable recreational and ecological values.

It turned out that the logs were going over the hill to Folsom, a former mining town that still had a functioning mill after the shakeouts of the 1982 recession and the timber cutbacks of the early 1990s. The town is also on the outskirts of Sacramento, however, and it is now the site of that large Intel manufacturing cam-pus that employs nearly forty-five hundred people. It would therefore be very difficult to argue that timber harvests on the Inyo National Forest were necessary to ensure community stability in the "mill town" of Folsom, where the yen-dollar exchange rate and new chip designs by Intel's competitors have a bigger influence on the community than employment at the mill. Some of the loggers on the job may have been local residents in Mono or Inyo County, but the log truck drivers were probably from the Sacramento Valley or southern Oregon. They would all surely gain income from the sale, as would the mill owners and those down the line employed in manufacturing wood products or in using them to build new houses and other buildings. These people weren't going to spend much money in Mammoth Lakes, though, and it was difficult to see how the local community would benefit at all from shipping its economic assets out of town.

In fact, the sale was probably going to hurt the area's economy. The Mammoth Lakes economy has become increasingly diversified over the past decade as winter visitation has accounted for a smaller and smaller share of overall tourism. Mammoth Mountain Ski Area has therefore become less and less important to the town's economy while fishing, backpacking, camping, tennis, horseback riding, golf, mountain biking, and other summer sports draw more and more visitors (Duane 1996b). Even designation of Death Valley National Park is likely to help the area, for tourists often travel a standard route now that connects Los Angeles, Las Vegas, Death Valley, Yosemite, and San Francisco. Bishop and Mammoth benefit from these travelers by selling them accommodations, meals, movies, trin-kets, and fun. Old-growth yellow pines represent an asset that could be a draw for some tourists—a picnic spot, a nature trail, or even wildlife photography could all depend on healthy east side pine forests.

All of those things are difficult to count, though, and they don't show up in the Forest Service's so-called optimization models for forest planning. What does show up are board feet, and it is a simple task then to assign an assumed number of jobs to every tree logged. The next step is to link those total job numbers to community stability, then stability to social well-being. Every step is flawed, of course, but completely justifiable given the underlying model.

Those Jeffrey pines are gone now, and Mammoth Lakes has very little to show for them.

CHAPTER FIVE

$\Lambda\Lambda\Lambda$

Ecotransformation
and Amenity Values

People care where they live and, given the choice, gravitate toward more desirable residential areas. Economic activity tends to follow them. Thus it cannot be said that environmental quality is only an aesthetic concern to be pursued if a community feels prosperous enough to afford it. Environmental quality has become a central element of local economic bases and a central determinant of local economic vitality. A community won't show much vitality, economic or social, if no one wants to live there.

Thomas Michael Power, 1996

John Casey is an experienced businessman who has spent his entire life in the wood products industry. He grew up in Oregon and then moved to the tiny town of Camptonville, California, after he married Claire South. John's father owned Sierra Mountain Mills, and they lived there when their oldest daughter, Kathleen, was just a baby. Within a decade they had a nice house on the lower part of Banner Mountain with a view of Nevada City and a swimming pool. John commuted to the mill every day over winding Highway 49, and every night a couple of Sierra Mountain Mills trucks followed him back to Nevada City, parking outside of Grass Valley, ready to take their loads of chips to the valley for processing. John was elected president of the Western Wood Products Association in the mid-1970s, and everything was looking up.

But that was before the crash. The recession of 1982 hit the industry hard just as it was having to adapt to new environmental regulations and increasing capitalization and automation. John struggled to keep the mills going, but ultimately lost them to more efficient competitors. The mill shut down and today it is vacant. I still find it eerie, whenever I climb the grade after the Middle Fork Yuba River crossing, seeing the empty mill site down the slope from the road. It has been only fifteen years, but already the mill is starting to look like a relic from the area's hydraulic mining past. Those operations stopped nearly a century earlier, yet their ghosts still haunt this landscape too.

John is no longer running a mill, but he is still in the wood products industry. He is also probably more successful now than he ever was with Sierra Mountain Mills. His new company, Caseywood, provides premium wood products to contractors and homeowners in the burgeoning development economy of the Gold Country. They do a lot of business in Truckee and Lake Tahoe, too, where custom designs call for the value-added wood products that Caseywood provides. Kathleen's brothers Kevin and Mark help run the business today, with their brother-in-law Brent, and John is clearly pleased that it will stay in the family when he retires in a few years. He is also on the board of directors of both the Sierra Nevada Memorial Hospital and Nevada County's Citizens Bank, and he'd like to devote more time to those pursuits and his family in the coming years. The house on Banner Mountain is now periodically filled with the sounds of grandchildren.

Although the John and I differ politically on many issues of land and resource management, he doesn't blame environmentalists for the demise of his mills. "I was in some mills on the north coast recently," he said, at the time the Forest Service was circulating its draft EIS for protecting the California spotted owl, "and I could see right there what put me out of business. You can literally see the writing on the wall: everything is computerized and automated. You have to be ready to make some major investments if you're going to stay competitive as a mill today" (Casey 1995). Technology and the market are driving the industry to be leaner, more efficient, and more concentrated in the hands of the largest companies. Sierra Mountain Mills was simply too small a player to survive in such an environment.

That trend toward consolidation and increased efficiency has been part of the timber industry at least since Gifford Pinchot, who advocated an industrial approach to forestry and silviculture that would maximize efficiency while minimizing costs. The timber industry and timber-dependent communities have no reason to believe that they are going to escape the notice of industrious capitalists interested in maximizing their profits. The industry is consolidating, and mills are going to close as a result. There are also going to be fewer jobs in the mills that remain for every log that flows past the saw. John Casey learned that the hard way, but it is a lesson that applies to every mill town in the Sierra Nevada.

John Casey managed to make a transition, as the community also did, and now he finds himself involved in three of the most promising areas of economic growth in the area: construction, finance, and health care. John Casey's story, we shall see, is also the story of the Gold Country's economic and ecological transformation and coming-of-age. In that story lies both the source of recent conflict over land and resource management and the potential resources—social, economic, ecological, and institutional—for its resolution in the Range of Light.

ECOTRANSFORMATION OF THE SIERRA NEVADA

I coined the term "ecotransformation" in 1993 to describe the parallel transformation of economic and ecological conditions in the Sierra Nevada that has been occurring with rapid population growth since the late 1960s. The term reflects my belief that Nature coevolves with Culture, and that both Nature and Culture are being radically transformed today in the rural and exurban regions of the American West. In particular, the *ecological* transformation of the region is being paralleled and driven by an *economic* transformation—hence the term "*eco*transformation." Moreover, the economic transformation has the potential to provide for an economic relationship between Nature and Culture that will support and restore natural ecological processes.

The West has a remarkable set of resident observers who have been watching the same phenomena from their own perspectives. Talented writers like Wallace Stegner, Edward Abbey, Charles Wilkinson, Barry Lopez, Gretel Ehrlich, Terry Tempest Williams, Gary Snyder, and Annie Dillard have all contributed to my understanding of the changing West. Ed and Betsy Marston and the staff at *High Country News* ("A Paper for People who Care about the West") in Paonia, Colorado, have kept their fingers on the pulse of the changing West with a fresh dose of news from the field every other week. Most of these writers focus on the Pacific Northwest, the Great Basin, the Rocky Mountains, or the Desert Southwest. Wallace Stegner wrote eloquently of the Sierra Nevada and Grass Valley in his Pulitzer Prize–winning 1972 novel, *Angle of Repose,* but the Range of Light has generally been left on the shelf as a difficult anomaly.

The Sierra Nevada has one foot in the intermountain West and one foot in metropolitan California, representing a wall that helped to protect the rest of the West from an onslaught of ex-California migrants through the 1970s and early 1980s. The wave crashed over the crest in the late 1980s, however, and the rest of the West now finds California to be the primary source of exurban migrants. The migration patterns that I first observed in the Sierra Nevada in the 1970s are now affecting land and resource management conflicts throughout the rest of the West (Ringholz 1996, Egan 1996). It is therefore appropriate to explore the ecotransformation of the Sierra Nevada within the broader context of the ecotransformation of the West in general.

I had not yet seen it when I first developed these ideas, but many of the principles underlying my idea of an ecotransformation of the Sierra Nevada and the exurban West are also discussed by Thomas Power in his 1996 book, *Lost Landscapes and Failed Economies: The Search for a Value of Place.*[1] I had the good fortune of reviewing a draft of Power's manuscript for Island Press in January 1995, so I have drawn on some of those ideas here. His work supplements and complements my own, for Power demonstrates that the traditional commodity-extraction view of rural economic development falsely pits economics against the environment in the rural West.

Power addresses five prevailing myths about land and resource economics and local economic development in his book: 1) that strict environmental policies and improved environmental quality are associated with decreased economic development, so there is necessarily a conflict between environmental quality and the economy; 2) that primary commodities production through extraction and agriculture is the foundation of economic development in rural areas, and that secondary or tertiary economic activities are only made possible through expansion of the base primary activities; 3) that expanded resource extraction from public lands and environmental degradation are necessary to support the primary economic activities that are the base of the economy; 4) that these primary activities provide higher-paying jobs, while secondary and tertiary service-sector jobs are lower paying or less stable; and 5) that local economic stability and local community well-being are negatively affected by decreasing commodity extraction and increasing service-sector employment.

These myths of what Power calls "folk economics" still dominate public debate about local economic development, land use planning, and land and resource management throughout the rural and exurban West. They are not supported by the evidence, however, and they reflect, in Power's words, a "rear-view mirror" view of the local economy (1996a, 9). Each of the myths of folk economics has some basis in a historical reality, but each has become less relevant to the emerging reality of the so-called New West as a result of a wide range of social, economic, technological, ecological, and institutional changes. We now find ourselves applying nineteenth-century ideas and institutional solutions to what will soon be a twenty-first-century economy. Not surprisingly, then, many of our land and resource management policies are ill-suited to address the emerging reality. Instead, they conflict directly with that reality because of their invalid assumptions and inappropriate emphasis on commodity extraction.

Some of these myths can be debunked by looking at answers to the simple question that Power asks of those who live in the rural and exurban West: "Just why are you living here[,] anyway?" (1994, 3–1). According to the folk-economics model, residential location decisions are based primarily on opportunities for employment. Those opportunities for employment, in turn, are based on base activity in the primary sectors. The free flow of labor and capital then follows the jobs, which follow the land and resource management policies that promote the expansion of resource extraction activity. Only then are new jobs created for local employment in the secondary and tertiary sectors, which then attracts new migrants to fill those jobs. The whole system is supposedly based on keeping mineral, timber, and agricultural production going in an area.

But why are people moving to the Sierra Nevada and the rest of the exurban West? Despite declines in employment in resource extraction, the exurban West continues to grow. Despite the claim that resource extraction brings economic prosperity, both the states and the communities that depend most on resource extraction have the highest unemployment rates, the greatest volatility in their

economies, the highest levels of poverty and many of its associated social problems, and the lowest levels of local control over their economic, ecological, and
social destinies (Meyer 1992; 1993). The emerging economy of the exurban West
is clearly based on something other than primary resource extraction. People are
not migrating to exurbia for the jobs; the jobs are migrating to exurbia for the
people. When jobs do not exist, people are still willing to give up significant monetary values in order to gain the amenity benefits of an exurban lifestyle. These
amenity benefits have true economic value. The true base activities in the exurban
West are therefore increasingly reliant on the economic value of natural resources
and environmental quality as *amenities,* rather than *commodities.* Economic development policies that emphasize expanded resource extraction at the cost of environmental degradation and reduced amenity values have the entire system upside
down and backwards.

Let's take a look at each of the myths that dominate the folk economics of land
and resource management in the West and how Power debunks them.

Rural Economic Development and Environmental Quality Are in Direct Conflict,
Meaning That Environmental Protection Costs Jobs

This is the familiar "owls versus jobs" argument, which became the rallying cry of
the Wise Use movement during the Bush administration (Yaffee 1994). The claim
is that environmental protection constrains economic development by increasing
the costs of economic activity, thereby reducing both demand and supply for those
economic goods and services whose production is constrained by environmental
protection. The increased costs of production associated with environmental protection can be either direct (e.g., installing pollution control equipment) or indirect (e.g., potentially harvested old-growth trees are protected in a national park,
reducing the supply of easily harvested timber and thereby forcing timber companies to cut more expensively harvested timber). This argument essentially treats
all nonmarket values as noneconomic. It also focuses on specific industries and
taps into the intuitively apparent conflict between jobs and the environment.

Empirical evidence does not support this intuitively "obvious" conclusion. In
fact, this argument appears to be false even when the analysis is limited to marketed values only. Stephen Meyer of the Massachusetts Institute of Technology has
conducted the most rigorous and systematic analysis of what he calls the "environmental impact hypothesis," using state-level data (1992). Under this hypothesis, there should be some correlation between economic performance and the
degree of environmental protection if there is indeed a conflict between jobs and
the environment. Because states have had wide discretion in implementation of
environmental regulations, Meyer pooled state-level economic and environmental
data for the 1970s and 1980s. He then grouped the states into three clusters for

each of the variables: high, medium, and low economic performance (as measured by a variety of standard market indicators) as well as high, medium, and low environmental protection (based on independent classification criteria and state rankings). Under the "owls versus jobs" argument, these two variables should be *negatively* correlated.

To Meyer's surprise, they were *positively* correlated (ibid.). Those states with the best economic performance, in other words, also had the strongest environmental protection. Conversely, those with the weakest environmental protection had the worst economic performance. Correlation is not causation, of course, and one could interpret this in two distinctly different ways: only when economic performance is strong can states afford strong environmental protection; or strong environmental protection is one of the conditions that supports strong economic performance. Meyer sought a more definitive explanation. He explored a variety of confounding variables that could explain the differences, including the relative size of different states' economies and their degree of manufacturing or other measures of economic diversification. The only variable that proved to be statistically significant was *the degree of dependence on primary resource extraction*. Those states with the highest dependence on these sectors had both the weakest environmental protection *and* the poorest economic performance. After controlling for this factor, the relationship between economic performance and environmental protection was no longer statistically significant (1993). The "environmental impact hypothesis" that environmental protection limits economic activity was nevertheless rejected.

Meyer's state-level analysis does not directly address whether or not *rural* or *exurban* economic development is in direct conflict with environmental protection, however, and that is the focus of my interest here. Rural areas are generally presumed to be the geographic subareas of states that most depend on resource extraction, however, so the significant negative relationship between dependence on resource extraction and overall economic performance at the state level should at least raise questions about the supposed conflict between rural or exurban economic development and environmental protection.

Rural Economic Development Is Based on Primary Resource Extraction Activity;
All Other Economic Activities Depend on It

The claim here is that only resource extraction activities are primary in the economy: only they function as the base of all other economic activity within a region. Primary-sector activities involve the extraction of raw materials (e.g., minerals, timber, water) and agricultural production. Secondary activities are those that convert the raw materials into finished goods through manufacturing production. Tertiary activities are those that fall primarily in the service sector and do not involve the physical manipulation of raw materials through either their extraction or their conversion to finished goods. This language of economics is "an approach as old as economics" (Power 1988, 109), but it also reflects the social and cultural values of a time when industrialization was just emerging in what had previously been an economic system dominated by agriculture and so-called primary activity. This view also reflects the economic and political power of resource extraction interests, with a rearview mirror perspective on rural economies.

It is, however, becoming less and less relevant as a postindustrial information-age economy transforms the mature industrial economy of the western United States. The implicit hierarchy of importance conveyed by the terms *primary* and *base* conflict with the economic evidence. As discussed above, an increasing fraction of total income in the Sierra Nevada and throughout the exurban West derives from transfer payments or income earned outside the region by commuters. Self-employment also accounts for a higher fraction of the remaining employment in these areas than it does in the rest of California. Moreover, primary-sector employment accounts for only a small fraction of even that slice of the economic pie that is recorded by the EDD. Marginal changes in that sector do not appear to have a significant effect on overall economic activity for most counties or communities. Complex trade patterns and specialization across an increasingly global economic system have also decreased any region's dependency on local primary production for a self-sufficient supply of the raw materials necessary for secondary or tertiary economic activities. The continuing migration of exurbanites to rural regions throughout the West—while employment in primary activities continues to decline—demonstrates that such primary economic activity is not the driver of local economic well-being.

This reflects a broader change in the American economy in the twentieth century. Both the absolute level of and the relative importance of primary-sector employment have been declining for the past two hundred years (Power 1996b). This has been the direct result of continuing capital substitution for labor and a shift in economic activity toward, at first, manufacturing and then services as the economy has matured. Labor productivity increased 5–10 percent per year in mining in the 1970s and 1980s, which cut labor needs in half in merely one decade for the same level of mineral output (Power 1996a, 106). It has more than doubled in the California timber industry from 1982 to 1997, dropping workforce requirements from six to only three workers per million board feet.[2] Coupled with expanded employment in other sectors, these improvements in labor productivity in the primary sector have decreased the relative importance of primary-sector employment. This is an expected development in the maturation process of an industrial economy. Increasing specialization and increasing complexity call for higher value-added utilization of labor in a market that now finds itself competing with low-wage labor throughout the world in the unstable

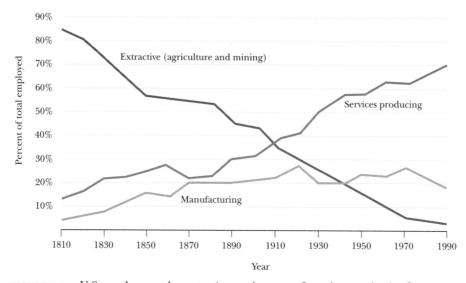

FIGURE 5.1.   U.S. employment by sector (extractive, manufacturing, services), 1810–1990. Adapted from *Lost Landscapes and Failed Economies: The Search for a Value of Place*, copyright © 1996 Thomas Michael Power. Published by Island Press, Washington, D.C., and Covelo, Calif. For more information, contact Island Press directly at 1-800-828-1302, info@island-press.org (E-mail), or www.islandpress.org (Website). Used with permission.

global commodities markets that dominate primary production. Not surprisingly, American labor is increasingly valued more highly for secondary and tertiary employment.

Once again, however, these broad trends may understate the importance of resource extraction in the rural and exurban portions of the West. The combination of increasing labor productivity, increasing exurban populations, increasing transfer payments, and stable or declining resource extraction levels have nevertheless combined to reduce the relative importance of primary employment in rural and exurban local economic development. It is still an important piece of the local economic pie, but it is no longer the base. Secondary or tertiary activities may now be the "primary" drivers.

Expansion in Resource Extraction Activity and Increased Environmental Degradation Are Necessary for Rural Economic Development

This myth is derived from the two myths described above. It depends on the false presumption that resource extraction is the foundation of rural economic development and that environmental protection is incompatible with economic activity. It is therefore also false, but many people appear to accept this myth without explicit consideration of its premises. It warrants some consideration as its own myth because of the political implications of its usual inference: that we should sacrifice environmental protection and accept environmental degradation in order to promote rural economic development. This is the point at which the general concepts outlined in the two myths above translate into policy implications with enormous distributional consequences. Specific interests would benefit by these policies, while the broader public would suffer the consequences of environmental degradation. This is particularly true for public lands, which in theory are held in trust and managed by state and federal land and resource management agencies for a broad set of public interests that go beyond the short-term financial well-being of resource extraction elites. Those same agencies sometimes invoke this derived myth to justify policies that conflict with those public trust responsibilities. While such policies are allegedly necessary to protect local economic well-being in rural resource-dependent communities, many of the benefits actually accrue only to elites controlling local resources (although the elites themselves are often not local). The economic and environmental costs, in contrast, often accrue to the general public and the nonelite majority of the members of resource-dependent communities.

Because the foundational assumptions are false, however, it is possible to draw the conclusion opposite this derived myth: that any expansion in resource extraction activity that results in increased environmental degradation may limit or even undermine rural economic development. Such an argument is difficult to make in the charged political atmosphere of the Sierra Nevada or other regions of the rural and the exurban West, however, for the benefits of commodity extraction are assumed to accrue to the working-class members of resource-dependent communities. This assumption is predicated on the next two myths, which Power also shows to be false.

Primary-Sector Resource Extraction Jobs Are More Stable and Higher Paying
Than Secondary and Tertiary Service-Sector Jobs

This myth argues against turning well-paid timber workers into "hamburger flippers" working for minimum wage. It is based on two assumptions: primary-sector resource extraction jobs are stable and well paid; and secondary- and tertiary-sector jobs (especially dreaded "service" jobs) are part-time and poorly paid. Each appears to be only partially true, however, so the overall statement is true only if one reports the facts selectively by narrowing one's focus to only a segment of each sector's jobs. One can not reach this conclusion by looking at each sector as a whole. Many resource extraction-sector jobs are in fact poorly paid, seasonal, and highly dangerous, while many service-sector jobs are highly paid and stable. After controlling for gender, in fact, the wage differential between primary and tertiary jobs for the overall economy is statistically insignificant (Power 1996a). Ethnicity is also a significant variable, for wages *within* the agricultural sector are notoriously low for immigrant farmworkers. The lower wages in service jobs probably have more to do with historical wage discrimination against women and minorities than inherent differences in the value of compensation for employment in services versus primary resource extraction. This thesis is supported by the fact that wages in the remanufacturing sector of the timber industry have declined in California as many of those jobs have relocated to urban areas with many minority workers (Stewart 1993).

The political problem, then, relates to the fact that the jobs most likely to be affected in primary resource extraction through either capital substitution or constraints on production as a result of environmental restrictions are held by white males without any college education. Those jobs are highly paid compared to the other jobs for which employees with this level of education and training are qualified. This is especially true within the more isolated and less complex (or diversified) local economies of many resource-dependent communities in the rural and exurban West (e.g., in the Northern Sierra subregion). It is therefore true that primary-sector resource extraction jobs held by this group are higher-paying than most of the other service-sector employment opportunities available to this group in rural communities.

For those areas experiencing rapid population growth, however, new opportunities in the construction sector have allowed those workers to be absorbed by the growing and diversifying economy without significant dislocation. This is true both for resource extraction workers who have lost their jobs and local residents who graduate from high school and then do not want to leave the area for employment. Historically, these relatively unskilled high school graduates would have gone to work in the resource extraction industries. Opportunities in that sector have declined over the past quarter century, however, which probably would have led to either significant emigration to metropolitan areas or significant local unemployment in the absence of exurban population growth. The expansion of the construction industry created new opportunities for these workers, allowing them to get local employment and to stay in the area. This did not occur in rural areas not experiencing rapid exurban population growth. Those communities have therefore found themselves with higher unemployment rates and a continuation of the historical problem of young people leaving for the bright lights and better educational and employment opportunities of metropolitan areas.

It is important to note, however, that neither resource extraction nor construction industry jobs are necessarily stable sources of employment for the relatively unskilled workers who stay behind after high school graduation. Like employment in the recreation and tourism sectors, both are highly seasonal. A significant period of seasonal unemployment or underemployment is typical because of weather fluctuations. Both resource extraction and construction also experience larger cycles of boom and bust that are primarily driven by factors outside the local area. Interest rates, the demand for housing, and migration patterns all affect the demand for timber, minerals, and local construction. Both industries are therefore subject to the same forces and have the same seasonal and cyclical characteristics. Low interest rates and good weather mean work, while high interest rates and bad weather mean unemployment. The emerging exurban economy has therefore not lessened the instability of employment and income for this group of workers.

It has reduced exposure to workplace injuries, however, for the resource-extraction sector has the worst record of occupational health and safety in the American economy. Timber-sector workers experience injuries at two to three times the average rate of all private-sector workers, while construction workers overall have an injury rate nearly twice the national average.[3] Mining workers have an injury rate only slightly higher than the national average. The higher wages prevalent in the resource extraction industries therefore represent in part compensation for the increased risk of worker injuries on the job. Resource extraction industries are therefore not significantly higher-paying than other industries after adjusting for both this occupational risk and the seasonality of employment.

Decreasing the Relative Role of Resource Extraction and Increasing Service-Sector Jobs Are Bad for Rural Economic Development

This is really just a restatement of the last two myths described above, which in turn depend partially on the first two myths. As Power makes clear, this shift in the relative importance of resource-extraction and service-sector jobs is a natural part of the maturation of industrial economies. There is no reason to believe that such maturation, which is generally believed to have improved the economic well-being of the nation as a whole, will not also benefit rural resource-dependent economies by increasing their complexity. Multipliers should be higher with this increased complexity, further reducing the relative importance of so-called base economic activity. This should result in improved local economic stability, an expanded range of opportunities for both customers and employees, and decreased neo-colonial dependence on external factors in the global economy. Rather than being bad for rural economic development, this would appear to meet the very definition of good economic development. It simply does it in a different way than the traditional path of resource-extraction-based economic expansion. But as Power has shown, that traditional path is based on mythical assumptions.

These myths converge to inform a view of the world that paints a stark picture of conflict between environmental policies and the economic well-being of rural resource-dependent communities. This montage of powerful icons is based on a very effective strategy by the Wise Use movement to make the unemployed timber worker the symbolic victim of urban elitists and government regulation run amok.

The strategy combines general claims about the relationship between resource extraction, environmental protection, and economic development with more specific claims about the influence of those public policies for environmental protection on the working-class members of rural resource-dependent communities. It deflects attention from the effects of decisions by absentee corporate mill owners to substitute new technology for expensive, unskilled labor or to shift production from the West Coast to the southeastern United States or eastern Siberia. It ignores the importance of education, training, occupational safety, and gender in determining wage rates. It fails to recognize the seasonal and business-cycle instabilities of both incomes and employment in resource extraction and construction, and it places all of the blame for such instabilities on land and resource management policies. In short, it makes the "owls versus jobs" argument more potent politically by clothing it in the image of a poor, hard-working, white male who has been shut out of work by elite urban environmentalists who "put owls above people." Not surprisingly, land and resource management decisions take on ideological fervor when such a stark outcome and polarized positions are presumed.

Surprisingly, these myths are held not only by lay people who are unfamiliar with the principles of economics or do not have access to the data and information that will dispel them. They also dominate discourse among economic development "experts" and community leaders throughout the rural and exurban West. Power argues that this reflects the political and economic power of local elites who benefit from the perpetuation of these myths. Local economic development policy of city councils and county boards of supervisors and commissioners in the rural and exurban West is dominated by recommendations from the Chamber of Commerce and consensus within a "good old boy" network deeply rooted in the historical economic traditions of the region. (This network also has many women, however, so it is inappropriate to call it simply the good old boy network. Perhaps "good old persons" is more appropriate, for it is often coincident with the local GOP Central Committee.) The primary providers of nonbusiness, expert information on economic development are university extension agents and rural economic development experts supported by grants from state and federal commodity-production programs. Not surprisingly, the U.S. Department of Agriculture and its agents bring an agriculture-oriented view to economic development. The BLM (sometimes known by environmentalists as the "Bureau of Livestock and Mining"), which has viewed its primary role in land and resource management policy historically in terms of utilitarian commodity production, also has strong alliances with the grazing and mining industries (Wilkinson 1992a). The Forest Service, still responsible to the secretary of agriculture rather than the secretary of the interior, continues to define its primary mission in terms of Gifford Pinchot's utilitarian views—where trees are seen as a crop to be harvested rather than a component of complex ecosystems that provide both ecolog-

FIGURE 5.2.   Oregon logger's son's pledge to an endangered heritage, in
the early 1990s. Courtesy of and copyright © 1990 Oregon Logging
Conference. Used with permission.

ical and amenity values. Alliances with timber interests satisfy the demands of western legislators, whose own political values and economic support bases still derive largely from commodity interests (Wilkinson 1992a; Hirt 1994; Yaffee 1944; Langston 1995).

A wide range of powerful elites therefore has a vested interest in perpetuating the myths that dominate the folk economics view of economic development in the rural and exurban West. They will lose very specific and tangible benefits if the system is challenged to reflect the emerging realities of exurbia. In contrast, those

interests who might benefit from such a challenge to the dominant myths are diffused and will benefit only abstractly. Social change is difficult to achieve when its
benefits are spread so thinly and they so directly confront highly concentrated
costs that will fall on a powerful few.

These biases cannot be explained, however, with only an interest-based model
of political and economic behavior and public choice. There is something deeper,
and it goes to the heart of the Culture of both rural western communities and the
disciplinary training of rural economic development professionals. The corporate
Culture of these professionals' agencies or universities reflects their origins in the
land-grant colleges and commodity-oriented agencies of the late nineteenth century and early twentieth century. They still mirror the times that made them: a
time of open frontier, untamed Nature, idealized self-sufficient yeoman farmers
("rugged individualists"), and a set of values that called for unlimited exploitation
of minerals and timber in the sparsely settled West. These underlying assumptions
about the state of Nature and humanity's responsibilities toward Nature still have
an important effect on land and resource management policy. Those assumptions
have been challenged over the past three decades throughout American society,
but change has come slowly to the underlying values of the professions and agencies charged with land and resource management in the West.

Those values and implicit assumptions must be critically evaluated in order to
determine what changes are necessary to bring those professions and agencies
into the next century. Today they continue to ask the questions that were relevant
in *yesterday's* western economy, for they operate under the shadow of the myths and
laws that Charles Wilkinson (1992a) calls the "Lords of Yesterday." The answers
they get will continue to be irrelevant unless and until they ask the questions that
will matter in the twenty-first century. The framework I outlined above for comprehensive economic analysis may help them ask the right questions in the future.
Even if the agencies and official bodies fail to do so, community members and the
interested public can raise these issues in the public discourse about economic
development. That process may then begin to move land and resource management policies into a better alignment with the new economic realities of the rural
and exurban West.

The ecotransformation of the rural and exurban West presents an opportunity
to reform land and resource management policies in ways that will then encourage land and resource managers to promote the long-term economic *and* ecological health of the region. Continuing traditional policies is likely to directly
undermine the long-term economic viability of some exurban regions by depleting the amenity resource base supporting the region. Reduced amenity values, in
the face of increased capital substitution for labor in the primary resource extraction industries, will then reduce the potential for the development of complex
local economies that can support a broad range of activities. The narrower

economies of those communities heavily dependent on export-oriented resource extraction activity will then also continue to export much of the revenue that comes into the local economy through the base activity of resource extraction. The multiplier effect, in other words, will be small relative to that of amenity-oriented economies that can support a broader range of economic activities. It is clear that higher multipliers depend on the scale of the local economy, of course, and that small amenity-oriented economies will continue to have relatively low multipliers. They will also maintain the capacity of their natural resources and the environment to continue to provide goods and services, however, whereas the commodity-extraction-oriented communities will deplete their natural capital and generally destroy their amenity base. Only one of these models can meet our criteria for sustainable development.

POLICY IMPLICATIONS OF THE ECOTRANSFORMATION

This brief sketch of the shifting basis for economic activity in the Sierra Nevada raises four critical points about the relationship between environmental quality, economic development, and the forces driving population growth in the Sierra Nevada. These points also apply to much of the resource-dependent rural and exurban West, now undergoing a similar ecotransformation:

Environmental quality is now becoming a more important economic asset for community development than the market commodity value of extracting natural resources.

Traditional resource extraction industries often cause environmental effects that directly conflict with the needs of those economic activities dependent on environmental quality.

Rapid growth is leading to demands for maintaining the quality of life and slower growth in the region, which reflect a new set of values held by the amenity migrants and equity refugees that are becoming the new residents.

Rapid growth itself can also threaten the quality of life in the region, potentially depleting the social and natural capital that is the foundation of economic and social well-being.

The result, not surprisingly, is a conflict within these communities over both those economic activities that were once the traditional economic base for the community and the population growth that could reduce the communities' dependence on those activities. Moreover, the people who most depend on that traditional economic base are usually the long-term residents of the community—while those who emphasize environmental quality are often recent exurban migrants. There are also conflicts of interest and class within each of these groups, of course, for they are far from homogeneous. Some of the newer residents have migrated to the exurban Sierra Nevada primarily because they were attracted *to* something about the social and ecological characteristics of the community and region. Others have migrated here primarily because they were running *from* something in metropolitan areas that threatened them. Often it is a combination of these two factors, but I believe the latter motivation began to dominate migration patterns in the late 1980s. These newer migrants are often less concerned with environmental quality than they are interested in social homogeneity and personal security. Sometimes they are also most comfortable behind the gated walls of a homogeneous suburban community that replicates the physical spaces they left behind. In contrast, many of the earlier migrants were seeking a "back to the land" connection with the natural environment through daily contact with Nature in a rural setting. These migrants sought low-density development patterns that maximized open space, wildlife habitat, recreational opportunities, and views of an undeveloped landscape. There is also a romantic idealism in this image of Nature, of course,[4] but it has very different implications for land and resource management than the gated community model.

As in the economic and political transition that accompanied what Robert Kelley (1959) called the "gold versus grain" controversy of the Sawyer decision in 1884, we are now in the midst of a major social, economic, and ecological transformation in the rural West. Any such transformation invariably involves conflict between different interests and different ways of viewing the changes. And, as in the battle over hydraulic mining, there are important distributive effects that will come with any new policies that may reflect the new realities of the ecotransformation. Agriculture was eclipsing mining in the California economy by the 1880s, and the Sawyer decision was necessary to adjust California land and resource management policy to reflect the new social, economic, and political reality. Today the commodity extraction value of California's natural resources is being eclipsed by their value as amenities for a wide range of information-age economic activities. Reforms on the order of the Sawyer decision may therefore be necessary to allow those new values to be reflected in public policies that best promote the emerging interests of society. Unlike the Sawyer decision, however, those reforms need not take the form of a judicial fiat that offers only an either-or choice between commodity extraction and amenity values. It is possible to find a third way toward a middle landscape that embraces both values. But in order to find that balance, we must recognize the reality of the ecotransformation. The myths we hold in folk economics will not be adequate as we debate our common future.

I firmly believe that such a win-win alternative can only be found in the real-world experiences of real-world people in real-world places. Solutions that will endure must be crafted over coffee and breakfast at the local level, not only in the halls of Sacramento or Washington. State and federal policies are still important, of course, and we will see that many state and federal policies are presently limiting the capacity of local communities in the Sierra Nevada to solve their conflicts over land and resource management policy. But the debates in the state legislature and Congress must be grounded in knowledge about how people interact with the Sierra Nevada environment at the community level. Our identities as residents of the Sierra Nevada are colored by the local particulars of the relationship between Nature and Culture. These identities are anything but uniform in the highly varied and rapidly changing rural and exurban West. Let us therefore turn our attention from the abstract theory of ecotransformation to examine the actual changes in economic and social structure that have occurred in the Range of Light over the past three decades.

ECOTRANSFORMATION OF THE GOLD COUNTRY

Within the Sierra Region, the Gold Country has undergone the most profound and complex social, economic, cultural, and ecological change over the past three decades. Its population growth and changing social, demographic, and economic structure illustrate the complexity of the process and the danger of making overly simplistic generalizations about the character of resource dependency in the rural and exurban West. The Gold Country subregion of the Sierra Nevada combines traditional commodity extraction, recreation and tourism, high-tech electronics manufacturing, retirement living, and commuting to the Sacramento metropolitan area. The income from these different activities then multiplies through the local economy to support a wide range of service-sector activities. The result is a social, demographic, and economic structure that looks more like the rest of California than the more remote regions of the Sierra Nevada. The Eastern Sierra subregion and the Lake Tahoe subregion, in contrast, depend much more heavily on recreation and tourism, while the Northern Sierra and Southern Sierra subregions depend more heavily on commodity extraction activities.

I will focus here on the Gold Country subregion in my exploration of the ecotransformation phenomenon, with a particular emphasis on Nevada and El Dorado Counties' transformation over the past three decades.[5] I will also demonstrate how that pattern of change is markedly different from that experienced by timber-dependent Plumas and Sierra Counties in the Northern Sierra subregion and recreation-dependent Mono and Inyo Counties in the Eastern Sierra subregion. Even these more remote counties show patterns of change consistent with my ecotransformation argument, however, for they generally exhibit increased economic dependence on amenity rather than commodity values. They are not likely to grow nearly as fast or to the degree that the Gold Country has over the

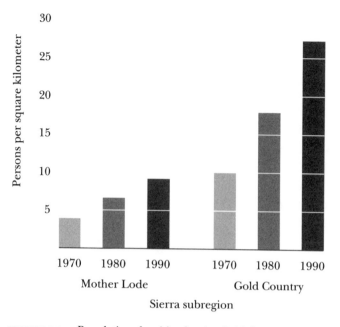

FIGURE 5.3.   Population densities for the Gold Country and
the Mother Lode subregions, 1970–90.

past three decades, however, so the increased diversification of their economies—
and the problems of managing growth—will not be as great for them.

Mother Lode residents in 1990 could look around their communities and see
many of the same things that Gold Country residents could see in 1970: very little
congestion, plenty of open space, thousands of unbuilt parcels, and enormous
potential for growth. Unlike the Gold Country, however, the Mother Lode lacks
four-lane freeway access to a growing metropolitan area. The world has changed
significantly since that time, however, making freeway access less critical for many
economic activities. The Mother Lode could therefore face population pressures
in the coming quarter century similar to those faced by the Gold Country since
1970. In fact, the average population density of the Mother Lode in 1990 was comparable to the Gold Country's density in 1970.

Therefore, let me turn to the structure of economic activity and growth over
the past three decades in the Gold Country subregion. My data sources are: 1) the
1970, 1980, and 1990 census at the county, CCD, and Block-Group levels; 2) state
Employment Development Department data for 1972–94 at the county level; 3)
state Department of Finance data for 1980–93 showing sources of local and
state tax revenue at the county level; 4) state Department of Forestry and Fire
Protection data for 1980–93 showing levels of timber harvest at the county level;
and 5) state Department of Finance data for 1980–93 showing levels of residential and commercial construction activity. Together, these data paint a vivid picture

of the ecotransformation that illustrates the complexity of the emerging exurban economy.

The census data paint a broad picture of the changes but fail to capture the year-to-year and month-to-month variations in employment that are so important to local economic stability and vitality. They nevertheless offer a useful "snapshot" comparison of the economic structure of the Gold Country subregion, the Sierra Region as a whole, and the rest of California. According to the 1990 census, more than 12 percent of the Gold Country workforce was employed in construction, for example, while only 10–11 percent of Sierra Region workers and less than 7 percent of Californians worked in the field. The Lake Tahoe and Northern Sierra subregions had about 9 percent working in construction. The Gold Country had only 11–12 percent of its workforce in manufacturing, however, while nearly 17 percent of Californians were employed in that sector. The Sierra Region employed about 10 percent in manufacturing, while the recreation- and tourism-dependent Lake Tahoe and Eastern Sierra subregions had only 3 percent in the sector. The manufacturing sector includes lumber mills in the timber industry. Expansion of the construction industry in the Gold Country has compensated for job losses in the timber industry there, while the absence of a comparable expansion has limited opportunities in the Northern Sierra. This shows up in unemployment statistics, where the Gold Country's rate was below both the Sierra Region and California's (slightly more than 6 percent in 1990) while the Northern Sierra's unemployment rate was 10–11 percent. Alpine County actually had the highest rate for an individual county (13 percent), but the Sierra Region portions of Butte, Fresno, Plumas, Sierra, Tulare, Tuolumne, and Yuba Counties stood out above both the Sierra Region and California averages.

In contrast, the Lake Tahoe and Eastern Sierra subregions depend very little on manufacturing, so they have not been seriously affected by mill closings. The Southern Sierra has an unusually high percentage of workers in agriculture (9 percent), while the Sierra Region has slightly more than 4 percent and the state has only 3 percent. The Northern Sierra (4–5 percent) and Eastern Sierra (5–6 percent) each has a slightly higher percentage of employees in agriculture than the Sierra Region overall, but the Gold Country looks a lot like California in terms of total agricultural employment. The agricultural designation lumps together "farming, forestry, and fishing," so it is difficult to detect employment rates for the forestry subsector alone from the census data. Timber industry employment includes both "agriculture" sector workers (foresters, loggers, reforestation technicians) and "manufacturing" sector workers (mill employees). For the SNEP report, Bill Stewart used additional sources to get a more accurate estimate of the timber industry's role in the regional economy, discussed below (Stewart 1996).

Roughly 17 percent of Sierra Region and Gold Country employment is in retail trade, which is slightly more than the average for California. Lake Tahoe (19 percent) and Eastern Sierra (20–21 percent) exceed the average as a result of their reliance on tourism. Wholesale trade is much higher for the state as a whole (4–5 percent) than for the Sierra Region (slightly less than 3 percent), however, and Lake Tahoe and Eastern Sierra have the lowest rates of wholesale trade employment. The Gold Country and Southern Sierra (both 3–4 percent) exceed the Sierra Region average but fall short of the California rate. All subregions except Lake Tahoe exceed the state's 4 percent rate of employment in government, however, with nearly 7 percent of the Gold Country workforce employed by the local, state, or federal government. This reflects both inefficiencies associated with smaller jurisdictions, a higher per capita education workforce in local schools, and the presence of state and federal land and resource management agencies. The Northern Sierra also stands out with less than 5 percent of its workforce in this sector, probably reflecting low numbers of school-age children.

The census data include four other broad industrial sectors: services; finance, insurance, and real estate; transportation and public utilities; and mining. Only Lake Tahoe stands out dramatically in regard to any of these sectors, with fully half of all employees working in services. The finance, insurance, and real estate sector is best represented in the Gold Country (7–8 percent), employing more than 5 percent in all subregions. The transportation, communication, and public utilities sector employs from 5 to 7 percent and mining approaches 2 percent of employment in the Mother Lode and the Eastern Sierra. The major mine in each of these two subregions has closed since 1990, however, a result of international competition (Diggles 1996). Other mines that have opened have experienced a boom-bust cycle, leaving the mining industry a nonexistent feature in a region once defined by it (Sneed 1995c; 1996d; 1996g).

Remember that census data reflect the employment characteristics of residents, many of whom now work outside the Sierra Region. These *jobs* are therefore not all within the Sierra Region or the Gold Country. The *income* from these jobs, however, does accrue to residents of the area. This is where the effects of equity refugees really becomes apparent: annual per capita interest, dividend, and rental income is actually higher in the Gold Country (nearly $1,500) than in the state as a whole (slightly more than $1,200), and only the Eastern Sierra ($1,000–$1,100), Lake Tahoe ($800), and Southern Sierra ($800–$900) are below the state average. All subregions except Lake Tahoe also have both retirement and Social Security income that exceeds the state averages of $500–$600 and $600 per capita, respectively. The Gold Country, Northern Sierra, and Mother Lode all top the Sierra Region average of $1,000 for retirement income, while the Gold Country and Sierra Region average about $1,000 per capita in Social Security.

The Northern Sierra has more than $1,400 per capita in Social Security income each year, however, suggesting that there may indeed be some retirees who are specifically seeking out the lowest-cost areas in the Sierra Nevada for retirement. A more detailed analysis of income by age class is necessary to test this hypothesis. In 1990 the Northern Sierra also reported more than $350 per capita in annual public assistance, while the Sierra Region average and the state average were both $200. The Gold Country had public assistance burdens of only $150 per capita, while Lake Tahoe's was slightly more than $100. Once again, different demographic characteristics interact with employment patterns to generate these patterns. Remember also that these are average values per capita; the average amounts actually received by those reporting income in each of these categories were higher.

Finally, the census data shows that nonfarm self-employment income is much higher in the Gold Country ($2,000), Lake Tahoe ($2,000), and Eastern Sierra ($1,800) than in the state overall ($1,400 per capita). The Northern Sierra has only $1,000 per capita and the Southern Sierra a little more than $1,100. This highlights the limitations of using EDD data to analyze the emerging economy of exurban regions like the Gold Country. The EDD data ignore both self-employment and income earned by commuters and do not address overall sources of income for residents of the Sierra Region or a given county.

The employment shift within Nevada County is nevertheless clear even from the EDD data.[6] Whereas employment in the timber industry stayed steady between 1972 and 1988, jobs in the service sector grew 400 percent during this period. Timber-sector jobs accounted for more than 6 percent of all jobs in 1972 but less than 2 percent in 1988. This is not the result of small timber harvests on public lands, though, because 1988 was the second highest timber harvest year on Forest Service lands in California during the forty-three-year period from 1952 to 1994.[7] Services (4,567) and retail trade (4,702) each provided nearly ten times as many jobs as the timber sector, while wholesale trade (485) and engineering and management services (572) provided comparable numbers. Finance, insurance, and real estate (1,536) and health services (1,525) each provided three times as many jobs, while other manufacturing (2,260) provided five times as many (Emmit 1992; EDD 1972; 1988). This latter category includes Nevada County's largest employer, the Grass Valley Group, which employed 1,000 local residents in the manufacture of high-technology television production equipment in 1988.[8] It is Nevada County's largest private employer.

The Nevada County economy was already highly diversified by 1988, but there have been important changes since then. In particular, lumber and wood products employment declined by half from 1988 to 1992, dropping to only 275 employees.[9] The loss of 275 lumber and wood products jobs was more than compensated for in the local economy, however, by the creation of nearly ten times as many new jobs (2,600) during the same four-year period: 650 in retail trade, 1,325 in services, and 625 in government. By 1992 the timber industry accounted for only .6 percent of all Nevada County jobs.[10]

The decline in the relative importance of timber therefore came *before* any new environmental restrictions were imposed to protect the California spotted owl and old-growth forests within the Tahoe National Forest. The decline of timber's relative importance was instead driven by other factors: population growth and diversification of the local economy and the substitution of capital for labor in the timber industry. That process has continued in the decade since, but the pattern was already clearly established by 1988. Since then the last mill in Nevada County has been closed—but a half dozen electronics firms have located in western Nevada County with both research and manufacturing facilities. They don't necessarily provide jobs that can replace those lost at the Bohemia mill or in the woods, but they do generate significant local employment through new construction and services that they generate. Construction is the new extractive industry of the Gold Country, and it is now driving the local economy.

Local construction activity in Nevada County is heavily influenced by interest rates, construction activity in Sacramento and Placer Counties, and the relative price of housing in metropolitan areas such as the San Francisco Bay Area and the greater Los Angeles area. None of these factors is a traditional focus of land and resource management policy. The controversy over the California spotted owl and forest management activities remains intense in both the Gold Country and the Mother Lode, however, despite the apparently diminishing importance of the timber sector in the local economy. This represents a rearview perspective of the economy that has failed to incorporate the effects of the ecotransformation.

The relative value of timber harvests and travel-related activity also changed dramatically in Nevada County from 1980 to 1993. Figure 5.4 shows this shift, but it understates the actual level and importance of tourism in the economy, because it records only the value of accommodations subject to the transient occupancy tax (TOT), or "bed tax." Accommodations account for only about 13 percent of travel-related expenditures by travelers in California, however, and 14 percent of Nevada County's estimated $175 million in travel-related spending (Dean Runyon Associates 1995, Table 8, p. 19). Transient occupancy taxes totaled slightly more than $1 million in 1992–93 in Nevada County, based on an average tax rate of 9.65 percent, so $10.4 million was directly spent on accommodations in the county. This would suggest total travel-related spending of only $75 million, however, if accommodations represent 14 percent of travel-related expenditures. The difference can be explained by the fact that only 20 percent of all travel-related expenditures in the county are attributed to those expenditures subject to TOT. Some visitors stay at private campgrounds (8 percent), public campgrounds (3 percent), private homes (19 percent), and vacation homes (26 percent). Another 23 percent of all expenditures are by visitors who don't stay overnight. The TOT revenues are therefore just the tip of travel-related spending in the county (Dean Runyon Associates 1995, Table 7, p. 11).

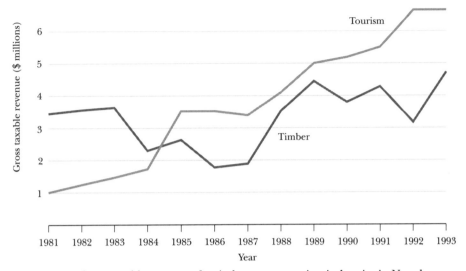

FIGURE 5.4.   Gross taxable revenues for timber versus tourism industries in Nevada County, 1981–93.

Even allowing for the undercounting associated with TOT revenues, however, direct expenditures on accommodations—which represented less than one-third the total value of timber revenues in 1980—climbed steadily throughout the period in Nevada County. The 1980 expenditures of $1.031 million had grown to $6.679 million by 1993, which was 41 percent higher than the total market value of all timber harvested in Nevada County in 1993 ($4.728 million). Spending on accommodations subject to the TOT therefore grew by 548 percent during the 1980–93 period, while total value of all timber harvested in Nevada County grew only 38 percent.

These total timber figures reflect the combined value of public and private harvests. The economic value of private harvests dropped dramatically from 1982 to 1986, while it actually increased for harvests on public land during the primary downturn from 1982 to 1985. Private harvests then increased in value from 1987 to 1990, held steady from 1990 to 1992 during the national economic recession, then increased in value (but not harvest levels) from 1992 to 1994 as prices shot up all over the West Coast. This increase in private timber values more than compensated for a drop in public timber harvests during the same period, although reductions since the adoption of CASPO have been more significant on public lands since 1992. The overall value of timber harvests in Nevada County was therefore fairly steady from 1987 to 1992.

These reductions in public harvests have hit the county's tax base harder and are as a result much more visible to the public because of important differences in how the gross values of those timber harvests translate into local tax revenues. Fully 25 percent of the gross value of federal timber harvests is returned to the

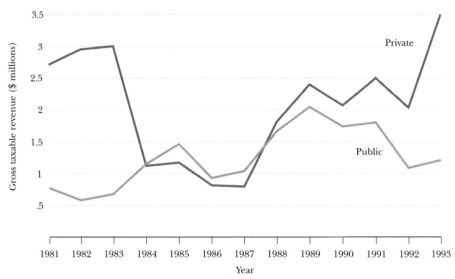

FIGURE 5.5.   Gross taxable revenues for public versus private timber harvest in Nevada County, 1981–93.

county for local roads and schools budgets, creating a strong incentive for local governments to support high levels of timber harvest on federal lands. In contrast, private timber harvests are taxed a much smaller yield tax at the state level. A portion of that tax is then returned to the county, but it is so small that it is dwarfed by the 25 percent gross receipts on federal harvests—even when the total value of private harvests far exceeds that of federal harvests.

County tax revenues from a million board feet of timber harvested on public lands were more than ten times higher than those gained by the county from a similar harvest on private land. "The net effect for Sierra Nevada counties," says Bill Stewart, "is that increases in private harvests do not make up for reductions in public harvests in terms of taxes."[11] Not surprisingly, this has made the U.S. Forest Service the whipping boy of local government in the Sierra Nevada and throughout the West in the 1990s. The effects of reduced timber harvests on roads and schools is always trotted out, pitting spotted owls against potholes and school children. That misplaced attention is purely an artifact of our current institutional arrangement, however, rather than a reflection of the true economic value of timber in the local economy. It also largely reflects assumptions about the relative value of recreation, tourism, and amenity-driven residential construction that have not been valid since at least the late 1970s.

Recreation and tourism are no longer the poor stepchild in relation to commodity extraction activities on public lands. Public campgrounds provide only 3 percent of the total travel-related expenditures in Nevada County, but public lands and resources are responsible for a much greater fraction of the county's economic activity. Those lands and resources provide many of the recreational ameni-

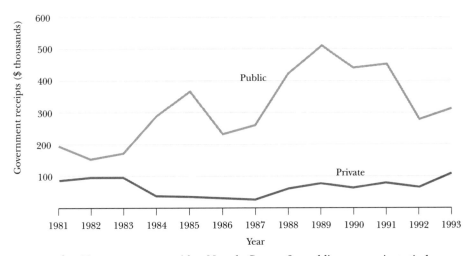

FIGURE 5.6.   Net tax revenues paid to Nevada County for public versus private timber harvest, 1981–93.

ties that occupy visitors during their time in Nevada County. There was an average of 50 to 60 million recreational visitor days on public lands in the Sierra Nevada from 1987 to 1993, and the vast majority of those visitors stayed and spent their money on private property (Duane 1996b). Recreation and tourism are now estimated to generate about $1.5 *billion* per year in the Sierra Nevada, making this the largest sector of the region's economy, with more than three thousand businesses and more than thirty-five thousand employees in the sector. About twenty-three thousand of these jobs are associated with serving tourists from outside the region (Stewart 1996, 1038). Nearly half of this employment in the recreation and tourism industry is located near Lake Tahoe and nearby ski resorts, however, with much of the rest concentrated near selected communities such as Mammoth Lakes and Yosemite's gateway communities (1039). Once again, those communities depend on maintenance of environmental amenities for their economic well-being.

Recreation and tourism now dwarf the timber industry in terms of total economic value, businesses, employees, and expenditures in the Sierra Nevada. The total value of timber harvests from both public and private lands in the region was $513 million in 1993, when stumpage values were unusually high (Stewart 1996, Table 4.2, p. 1023). This was only one-third of the total value of recreation and tourism in the region. Even county tax revenues from recreation and tourism are comparable to revenues from timber harvests, despite institutional arrangements that fail to capture many of the economic values associated with recreation and tourism. Sierra Nevada counties earned $7.46 million from federal timber revenues in 1980–81, another $1.88 million through federal payments in lieu of taxes, $1.16 million from private timber taxes, and $3.99 million from TOT. By

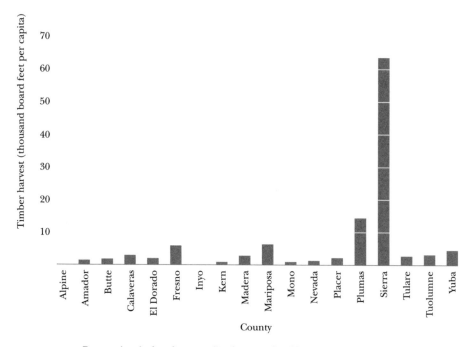

FIGURE 5.7.   Per capita timber harvest (in thousands of board feet) by county in the Sierra Nevada, 1989.

1992–93 the TOT revenues alone were $15.08 million and federal timber revenues were only $14.81 million. Payments in lieu of taxes totaled $2.94 million, and $2.82 million were collected in private timber taxes. Total county tax revenues from these sources therefore increased from $14.49 million to $35.65 million from 1980 to 1993 in nominal dollars. New TOT revenues grew at nearly three times the rate of federal timber revenues and accounted for about half the total increase in county tax revenues from these sources during this period (Stewart 1996, Table 6.2, p. 1046). These figures also exclude sales taxes, a significant fraction of which is associated with recreation and tourism activity. The total tax revenues from recreation and tourism are therefore much higher.

This pattern is not uniform throughout the Sierra Nevada, but nearly every county in every subregion has benefited economically from the growth of recreation and tourism. The Gold Country and Southern Sierra patterns are similar to that of the entire Sierra Nevada. Federal timber revenues and TOT were approximately equal in the Mother Lode in 1980, but TOT is now more than twice as high as federal timber revenues. The Eastern Sierra subregion has always had higher TOT than federal timber revenues. Only the Northern Sierra has continued to generate considerably more county revenue from federal timber sales than from TOT. The gap has narrowed even here, however, from a twenty-to-one ratio in 1980 to only eight to one in 1993 (Stewart 1996, Tables 6.3–6.7, pp. 1046–1048).

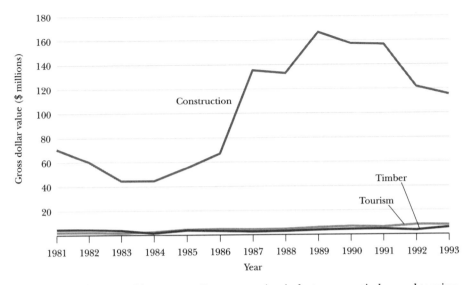

FIGURE 5.8.   Gross taxable revenues for construction industry versus timber and tourism industries in Nevada County, 1981–93.

County-level analysis of timber harvests show that only a few counties still notably depended on timber as early as the late 1980s. In particular, Plumas and Sierra Counties cut far more timber per county resident (sixty thousand board feet per capita in Sierra County and thirteen thousand board feet per capita in Plumas County), with higher value ($6,000 per capita in Sierra County and more than $2,000 per capita in Plumas County), than any other Sierra Nevada county in 1989. The Sierra Region of Yuba, Mariposa, and Fresno Counties also had higher than average values, but they are trivial compared with those of Sierra and Plumas Counties. Even other counties with mills in 1989—such as El Dorado, Amador, and Tuolumne—harvested relatively little timber per capita. Their economic dependence on timber is therefore directly tied to milling rather than logging.[12]

Nevada County does not similarly depend on timber harvests. In fact, merely the incremental value of the annual *change* in total construction activity exceeded the *total* value of *all* timber harvests the previous year in Nevada County in nine of the twelve years between 1981 and 1993. On average, the incremental annual *change* in total construction value was six times the total value of the previous year's timber value. The total value of construction was $114 million in 1993—*twenty-four times* the value of all timber harvests in Nevada County. Construction values ranged from a low of $43 million during the 1982 recession to a high of $165 million in 1988–89.

The volatility of construction-sector activity raises a number of concerns about the relative sustainability of an economy that has increasingly come to depend on

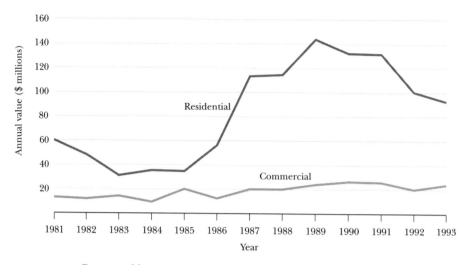

FIGURE 5.9.   Gross taxable revenues for residential construction versus commercial construction in Nevada County, 1981–93.

construction activity. This volatility was most pronounced between 1985–86 and 1986–87 (these data are for the state fiscal year, which runs from July 1 to June 30), when the total value of construction in the county more than doubled, from $66 million to $133 million. The $67 million boost in local construction activity was followed by another jump of more than $30 million two years later. Extremely high levels of construction activity continued for two more years, but then began to drop off as the statewide recession spread. The unsustainably high levels of activity led to a crash, with a drop of more than $30 million again between 1990–91 and 1991–92. The annual changes in construction value show a high degree of instability in construction-sector activity.

Decisions made by the Federal Reserve (and those other factors affecting both the employment opportunities in Placer and Sacramento Counties and the opportunities for equity gains in the Bay Area and Southern California) therefore have a much greater influence on local economic activity in Nevada County than federal land and resource management policies. These nonlocal influences include federal, state, and local policies outside Nevada County that affect defense-sector spending, public education, and public safety in urban areas. Public investments in infrastructure, public policies regarding land use regulation, and market factors also influence patterns of private-sector investment in construction. More recent hot spots for construction activity have been concentrated in the nearby cities of Roseville and Rocklin in Placer County and Folsom in Sacramento County, primarily reflecting the influence of Sacramento's proximity.

The relative importance of local employment versus residential location choices

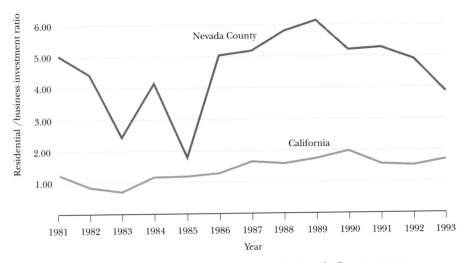

FIGURE 5.10.   Residential/business investment ratio for Nevada County versus California, 1981–93.

as a factor driving total construction investment is made clear by disaggregating the construction investments into residential and commercial components. Residential construction accounted for 82 percent of all construction investment from 1980 to 1993 in Nevada County.[13]

This investment pattern contrasts sharply with the statewide pattern, where residential and business investment are comparable (i.e., the residential/business investment ratio is closer to one). This highlights the current and ongoing deficiency of local employment-generating investments in commercial and industrial development to adequately employ the wave of exurban migrants. The investment in jobs to support the employed members of the new residents is occurring instead in Placer and Sacramento Counties. Review of the residential/business investment ratios from 1980 to 1993 for Nevada, Placer, El Dorado, and Sacramento Counties and for California shows that *residential* location choice—rather than new employment—is clearly driving development in Nevada County.

Construction activity is also highly variable on a seasonal basis. Time-series data are collected inconsistently by Nevada County and the incorporated cities of Grass Valley, Nevada City, and Truckee, but within each of these jurisdictions monthly variation in applications for building permits for new single-family homes is significant. Nevada County and Nevada City together issued a monthly low of 29 and a high of 236 permits from 1984 to 1991 (before Truckee became incorporated in 1993), while averaging 84 permits per month (1,008 per year). Single-family residential permits in Grass Valley varied from a monthly low of 0 to a high of 11 from 1989 to 1993, averaging 2 per month (24 per year). The town of

Truckee issued a low of 0 and a high of 56 single-family building permits each month from 1993 to 1996 (averaging 24 per month or 288 per year). Truckee only had one month out of 36 (3 percent) where no permits were issued, however, whereas Grass Valley issued no permits sixteen out of forty-nine months in the record (33 percent of the time). Truckee has now become the largest incorporated city in Nevada County.[14]

This seasonal variation is not a significant source of seasonal unemployment in the county, however, as a result of the diversification that has occurred over the past three decades. In fact, the Gold Country's average monthly unemployment rates from 1990 to 1995 were both quite steady and actually below the state averages. The timber-dependent Northern Sierra continues to have higher average unemployment rates and greater seasonal variation, however, with average winter rates from 1990 to 1995 more than 20 percent—comparable to Nevada County's seasonal unemployment rate in the late 1960s. The recreation-dependent and relatively isolated Eastern Sierra also has a higher unemployment rate than either the Gold Country or California, although it is much less seasonal; it actually peaks during the "shoulder season" after skiing has ended and before the Tioga Pass Road has opened through Yosemite National Park (Stewart 1996, 990).

My analyses above are based on employment and income data from the 1990 census and employment data from the EDD for 1972–94. They show that Nevada County and the Gold Country have been transformed over the past quarter century while the Northern Sierra subregion has an economy remarkably similar to Nevada County's in the late 1960s and early 1970s. Ray Rasker of the Wilderness Society has also compared personal income from all sources by county for all of the Sierra Nevada counties from 1969 to 1994, using the Regional Economic Information System CD-ROM produced by the Bureau of Economic Analysis. His conclusions for Nevada County are similar:

> In the last 25 years personal income (in real terms) has increased by more than fourfold.
>
> 44% of the growth in personal income has been from non-labor sources (money earned from past investments, retirement and other transfer payments).
>
> The largest and fastest growing sources of employment income are from "services and professional" sectors, construction, and government. Only farming income and resource extraction have declined in the last 25 years (Wilderness Society 1997, 81).

As Bill Stewart puts it, "The most significant economic changes in the Sierra Nevada over the past two decades have been driven by the large inflow of new residents attracted by the environmental and social amenities available in the region" (1996, 1039). This is less true for some subregions than for others, but this is clearly now the dominant economic driver in the Gold Country. The data for Nevada County illustrate that change.

THE RESIDENTIAL VALUE OF AMENITIES

These quantitative analyses help to explain the relative importance of different economic factors in the Nevada County economy, but they focus exclusively on those economic values that involve the exchange of dollars. As I noted in detail above, however, our current economic system fails to account for many other important economic values. The data nevertheless show that residential location choices are the dominant factor in the Nevada County economy, and that local employment in the commodity extraction industry is no longer the base of local economic activity and well-being. Moreover, it is clear that a wide range of external factors can have a dramatic effect on local economic activity. This analysis still fails to adequately capture the role of amenity values in determining the residential-location decisions driving the migration wave now transforming the rural and exurban West. This makes it necessary to turn to other sources to determine the relative importance of amenity values in the residential-location decisions of Gold Country residents.

Those values are readily apparent in a detailed survey of El Dorado County residents conducted in January 1992 as part of the El Dorado County General Plan update. The survey makes it clear that exurbanites are not attracted to the Sierra Nevada primarily by traditionally defined economic opportunities, but instead seek a way of life.[15] Less than one-fourth of the respondents said that "to work or to find employment" was a major reason for choosing to live in the county, while nearly half said it was to raise their family. "To get away from urban, city life" and "to live in a rural environment" were cited as major reasons by an overwhelming three-quarters of the respondents. Frequently cited reasons included open space (72 percent), air quality (65 percent), and views (62 percent). Only 36 percent considered "affordable housing" a major reason to live in the county. Slightly more than one-fourth listed "the quality of the public schools" and fewer than one-fifth mentioned water quality as a major reason for living in the county. Surprisingly, only slightly more than two-fifths of the respondents listed recreational opportunities as a major attraction. Nearly one-fourth of the residents specifically moved to the county to retire, and a little more than one-fourth mentioned the desire to be near their families as a major reason.[16] There were no questions about specific negatives or disamenities that local residents were trying to escape by moving from metropolitan areas to the region. These could include several of the factors mentioned earlier as the impetus for the exodus to exurbia: urban crime, poor schools, and racial heterogeneity.

The Sierra Business Council commissioned a subsequent survey across the entire Sierra Nevada in November 1995. Its results were published in July 1997, and they reinforce the findings of the El Dorado County survey. Both surveys were conducted by J. Moore Methods and followed generally accepted, statistically valid polling methods. The advantage of the regionwide survey is that it allows us to identify differences in attitudes, preferences, and values on a subregional and county level. The regionwide survey is weighted toward Gold Country and Tahoe Basin residents, however, with 55 percent of the respondents located in Nevada, Placer, or El Dorado County (whereas only 44 percent of Sierra Region residents lived in those counties in 1990) (Sierra Business Council 1997, Appendix A).

Respondents listed a familiar set of "major" reasons they had chosen to live in the Sierra Nevada: "to get away from city life" (81 percent), "the beauty and charm of [their] community" (81 percent), "to live in a rural area" (78 percent), "the quality of life" (76 percent), "to be part of a small community" (73 percent), and "the quality of the environment" (71 percent) dominated the list. Less important were "closer access to outdoor recreation, such as hiking, biking, backpacking, horseback riding, river rafting, or fishing" (48 percent), "closer access to developed recreation, such as skiing, golfing, and boatable lakes" (35 percent), "the quality of the schools" (35 percent), "the availability of affordable housing" (29 percent), "the cultural resources and activities" (25 percent), or the "lower cost of living" (22 percent). Nevada County respondents were generally consistent with these Sierra-wide averages, although "the cultural resources and activities" of the community were a major reason for 35 percent (versus 25 percent for the Sierra Nevada), and the "lower cost of living" was a major reason for only 15 percent (versus 22 percent for the Sierra Nevada). This last statistic is telling: only 17 percent of Gold Country residents listed it as a major reason, while at least one-fourth of Plumas, Calaveras, Amador, Alpine, Kern, Fresno, and Mariposa County residents listed the lower cost of living as an important factor (Sierra Business Council 1997: Appendix A).

The study also generated extensive cross-tabs that remain unpublished. These show that one's perception of whether the Sierra Region economy has "worsened" is correlated with length of residence: those answering yes represented 36 percent overall; 27 percent of those living in the area less than five years, 34 percent of those living in the area for 5 to 10 years, 38 percent of those living in the area for 10 to 20 and 20 or more years, and 40 percent of those who have lived in the area for their entire lifetime.[17] This suggests that the emerging economy of the Sierra Nevada is less friendly to the region's old-timers than its newcomers, although it could simply indicate nostalgia about a mythical past. The unemployment and income data for Nevada County clearly show that the economy was in worse shape in the late 1960s and early 1970s than it is today, for example, but people persistently long for the "good old days." Perhaps the boom of the late 1980s and early 1990s has colored their memories.

Sierra Nevada residents are also concerned more specifically with land use and development patterns. This appears to be important throughout the Sierra Nevada, but it is at the center of land and resource management conflicts in the

Gold Country and the Mother Lode subregions. Residents in Amador and Calaveras Counties have formed the Foothills Conservancy to promote local land use policies that maintain social and environmental amenities in their communities, and Tuolumne County residents have held public meetings to promote a sense of place in the community of Sonora.[18] The Rural Quality Coalition of Nevada County was formed to respond to proposed policies in the new General Plan update being considered by the county board of supervisors from 1990 to 1995. Materials disseminated by the coalition claimed that the new General Plan would determine the future path of a "County at a Crossroads," where the two alternatives led to either a "Rural" or a "Suburban" future. Stating it in these terms makes it clear that at least these migrants are not seeking to replicate the patterns of a suburban world. "The Rural Quality Coalition supports the text language (of the General Plan) that fosters rural quality," states the organization's information material. "However, the overall population and high city densities are a plan for suburbanization—not a rural community."[19] The characteristics of the physical environment are clearly important to the residents of exurban regions, yet continuing migration from metropolitan to exurban areas is placing enormous pressure on that environment. The primary political struggle in many rapidly growing communities is therefore over alternative policies and plans for mitigating the effects of growth on "community character," "environmental quality," and "rural quality of life." This is not unlike the conflicts that led to growth control and growth management ordinances in communities facing suburbanization in the 1970s and 1980s (Bradshaw 1993; Landis 1993a; Glickfeld and Levine 1992; Stein 1993; Schiffman 1989; Porter 1997).

The Sierra Business Council survey addressed some of these questions. A remarkable 66 percent of respondents indicated that their county should be "ensuring that new construction fits in with the historic character and scale of the community," 65 percent supported more work "conserving the natural environment in [their] county," and 60 percent favored "permanently preserving open space and agriculture lands" through stronger county action. When asked whether we "need to do a better job with land use planning" or if we "are already putting too much emphasis on land use planning," 68 percent supported better planning. Moreover, 65 percent specifically supported zoning over letting people "do whatever they want with their own property, without interference from government." Five out of every six respondents thought that "voters should have the right to determine how much growth they would like to have in their county," while 83 percent agreed both that "we need to protect wildlife habitat and ecosystems" and that "we should do more to permanently protect open space around towns in the Sierra Nevada to help agriculture survive and to keep our region beautiful" (Sierra Business Council 1997, Appendix A). Finally, 76 percent agreed with the statement that "maintaining the quality of life and the environmental health of the Sierra Nevada is one of the most important things we can do to attract new businesses to this region." The people of the Sierra Nevada know why they moved there, and they know that the future of the region's economy depends on its environmental assets.[20]

A CLEAR VIEW OF THE LAKE

The aspen trembled in the breeze as we dropped down from Echo Summit toward the lake; October's brilliant colors pressed against an endless sky of blue. My friends from England had never seen Lake Tahoe, and I was frankly a little bit embarrassed to be introducing it to them this way. I've always been partial to the west shore from Emerald Bay north, where the casinos and the scar of Heavenly Valley are just a distant distraction in the background. Here, we would soon be passing right beside those nuisances before catching a glimpse of Lake Tahoe's brilliant water. At least the crowds weren't bad on this autumn day in the middle of the week. We passed the state line and pulled into the parking lot at Harvey's casino and hotel near the water.

I made my way from the asphalt through the casino to the conference room, where two hundred people were gathered for the Tahoe Economic Summit. Technically, it was known as "Competition and Change: Creating an Economic Vision for Lake Tahoe," but everything had carried the addition *summit* since the Sierra Summit at Fallen Leaf Lake the year before. I had been invited to speak at this conference by the League to Save Lake Tahoe, only to have my name "rejected by the casinos" before finally being accepted after further negotiations by the League (Ames 1992). I didn't expect a big welcome reception: the speakers before me spent most of their time bashing the Tahoe Regional Planning Agency (TRPA) and bemoaning the stifling effect of excessive environmental regulation on the local economy. I could tell that my talk might not be popular.

I approached the podium with some trepidation. I was armed only with materials that the conference organizers had sent to me straight from the visitors' bureau. The glossy photos and text indirectly proclaimed the relationship between environmental quality and economic well-being, however, and it made my point for me. "The fairest picture the whole earth affords," I began, quoting Mark Twain from the cover of the visitors' bureau brochure (Twain 1871, 156). I held up the cover and displayed it to the audience. "Lake Tahoe's most important economic asset is its environmental quality," I said, "and if you lose that you lose your visitors." Behind me was a large mirror, and there were no windows to the lake anywhere in the room. "Instead of the back of my head," I said, "you should be looking at Lake Tahoe right now. We could just as well be in Las Vegas, Reno, or

Atlantic City. And if visitors didn't have Lake Tahoe to visit when they came here, why wouldn't they go to those places instead?" I pointed out that the TRPA's job of protecting the environment represented a means of protecting the region's primary economic development assets. Weakening the TRPA would undermine long-term economic sustainability.

"How many of you increased your salary when you moved to the Lake Tahoe area?" I asked. Fewer than ten hands went up. "How many of you gave something up economically in order to live here?" At least one hundred people raised their hands. "That represents real economic value," I added, "even if it doesn't always translate into dollars and cents. How many of you would still want to live here if Lake Tahoe were like any other lake and air quality and traffic congestion were like it is in most urban areas?" Nobody raised his or her hand.

They had come in search of an economic argument to weaken the TRPA's regulations, but they knew intuitively from their own personal experiences that such a move would eventually undermine their own well-being. Their own marketing materials identified the primary reason that visitors came to the area, and they knew from the economic data that the Lake Tahoe economy was driven almost entirely by recreation and tourism. They really had no choice now but to make the TRPA work and to reinvest in the natural capital of the region. Federal and state agencies had brought heavy-handed land use regulation to the basin, but the outsiders also had checkbooks and expertise that could help the basin through infrastructure, land acquisition, and restoration projects. It was time now for a partnership between the economic and environmental interests in the basin. I was not alone in this message, but the tone of the debate at Tahoe changed that afternoon.[21]

Five years later, President Bill Clinton and Vice-President Al Gore visited Lake Tahoe and applauded the community's collaborative effort to reconcile environmental quality and economic development. Developers were still suing the TRPA to weaken its regulations, of course, and users of personal watercraft, or jet skis, were challenging the TRPA's recent action to prohibit their use on the lake within a few years (J. Christensen 1997). The Tahoe Center for Sustainability was nevertheless the story of the day, for it offered a positive model for resolving conflicts over land and resource management in the West. Clinton and Gore promised more money for the basin and high-level attention to its needs as long as its residents would continue to work together (Purdum 1997).

The ecotransformation of the Lake Tahoe basin now appears complete, and its lessons have important implications for how we deal with the ecotransformation of the Gold Country. The appearance of consensus at Lake Tahoe masks important conflicts of both ideology and interest, but there is now widespread agreement about one thing: environmental quality is intimately linked to economic well-being in the region. The legacy of previous planning failures makes the task of restoring Lake Tahoe's environment both expensive and politically difficult, however, despite the commitment of state and federal taxpayers and the regulatory power of the TRPA. The Gold Country must avoid similar planning mistakes if it is to develop a consensus for action that does not fragment its social and ecological landscape.

∧∧∧

CHAPTER SIX

The Fragmented Landscape

Virtually all the great questions of our time involve land.

Richard Forman, 1995

Knowing who we are and knowing where we are are intimately linked.

Gary Snyder, 1995

My brother Danny and I were heading down to our tree house when we came across the stakes and flagging. Our bikes slid to a stop and we hopped off. I was twelve and Danny was ten years old at the time. We regularly took this trail to the home of some friends, where we had built a tree house the previous summer. We dubbed ourselves the "Squirrel Patrol," and had the usual collection of secret signs and rituals for membership. The only members were my brother, my older sister, Terrie, myself, and our friends Robin and Tracy MacDonald. The club and tree house both fell apart after Robin and Tracy moved, since we had built the fort high within a circle of five black oak trees on their property. The trails throughout the upper Wolf Creek and Deer Creek watersheds nevertheless remained our primary routes of travel in our summertime exploration of the countryside. We also ran our toboggan and sleds down the trails in winter, when that glorious white powder would close the schools for a "snow day" and release us to its wonders.

But here was a barrier to our travels. Only fifteen yards beyond our property line, behind a thick patch of blackberries and ponderosa pines, stretched a hot pink tape across the trail. It was held in place by a collection of freshly milled stakes that marked the corners of what was apparently destined to become the foundation for a house. It seemed a crazy place to put a house, though, right in the middle of a public trail.

Danny and I therefore did a public service and pulled up the stakes to clear the trail.

The builders returned, of course, and soon we awoke each morning to the sound of hammer and saw. Board by board, week by week, a house rose on the site.

We now went down a different trail and avoided the house site and builders as much as possible. There was still plenty of room to play along the ridge leading to Banner Mountain, but the proximity of the house surprised us. We thought we had moved onto a large lot—no, a large plot of land, which we measured in acres rather than square feet—in the "country." At some level, I don't think we had ever fully considered the implications of new houses ultimately being built on the empty parcels of Echo Woods. Our home had been built around 1960, as were most of the others in the neighborhood. It didn't feel like a subdivision under construction when we arrived in 1971. I guess we just assumed all that open space would remain open forever. Why would anybody want to cut down any more trees and replace them with houses? The trees, after all, were the reason we were all living there.

The next summer we were hit even harder. My buddies Dave Allstot and Ron Hufford and I were riding down a long dirt trail from Piney Woods and Madrone Way to our toboggan run and the Squirrel Patrol tree house. My odometer measured the downhill leg at more than a mile, culminating in a very steep descent down a slope where we could jump our bikes into the air. We often gathered there to have jumping competitions, with the winners typically keeping their rear wheel airborne for fifteen to twenty feet. The steep descent then bottomed out before a gentler ascent, which allowed us to dissipate all of the speed gained in the effort to clear some air. This also translated into a great toboggan run in the winter, although we once spilled the sled and tumbled down the slope when my brother, sister, and I hit a black oak tree after failing to make the last turn. That wasn't usually a problem with bikes, though, since we had brakes and knew the trail well. The biggest problem on this trail was dust, and I was choking on it that day while riding behind Dave and Ron. I gave them a short lead before heading through the haze with the sun angling through the trees and onto the mountain misery on either side. It was a majestic ride down what I would today call a single-track trail, now that the mountain bike has been "invented" and it dominates my exercise regime. This is the trail ride the mountain biker dreams of every winter.

We were ecstatic in our first major ride of the summer, because we hadn't been on this trail since our midwinter toboggan run a few months earlier. Unfortunately, the landowner at the site of our bike jump had been busy at the bottom of the trail in the meantime. I heard yelling as I approached the steepest section, then I saw an arm reaching out to pull a bike off the trail and into the mountain misery. I think it was Ron on the right, then I passed Dave on my left. "There's a cliff ahead!" one of them yelled. I swerved to the right as I saw a fresh road cut only fifteen feet ahead, creating a four-foot drop-off on our trail. My bike crashed through the kitkitdizze and crunched through the fallen oak leaves and pine needles. Suddenly, I hit a small downed log and was launched into the air. My bike smashed into a young madrone tree and my handlebars twisted ninety degrees. I found myself stuck in the tree six inches off the ground when the dust cleared.

The builders were back, and this time they had their sights on a major thoroughfare.

There were no stakes to pull this time, though, and our toboggan run and bike jump were already gone. The entire approach had been eliminated. Soon more trees were cleared nearby and an artificial pond was put in by the landowner, who happened to be the successor to the MacDonald family. Another house went up at the end of our deceleration "run-out," cutting off the backdoor access to the tree house. Still another went in just up the hill from the old MacDonald house, then another across the street. Lot by lot, driveway by driveway, tree by tree, the entire area was transformed. Our summer days were filled with the sounds of construction. Our newest neighbors, on whose property our kitchen and dining room windows looked out, preferred a large artificial lawn over all that dense forest. They cleared their land nearly to our property line, eliminating the natural screening that otherwise made one-acre lots somewhat private. Our house had been close to their property in order to maximize the distance from the one other house that was built (on the opposite side of our lot) around the same time as ours. Now we were facing the consequences of that siting decision. The other lots were now built out, and we could see houses in nearly every direction. What had once been hundreds of acres of open terrain for wildlife and exploration were laced now with roads, fences, driveways, houses, and an increasing number of "Keep Out!" signs. The unity of the landscape was fragmented by the ownership boundaries and imperatives of real estate development. What mattered were the lines on the assessor's maps and deeds, not the lines formed by waterways and social trails that connected our neighborhood.

That which had always technically been private property, but had functioned as public open space, had now been reclaimed by the exurban migrants seeking refuge from the city. The privatization of public space—in function, if not ownership—had finally reached the Sierra Nevada. And with that arrival came a loss of economic, ecological, and social value. Yes, the exchange value of our property went up despite all of these reductions in open space access. But we also faced new costs as a direct result of the construction of new houses in the area. Many use values were diminished. Our water supply, which had been provided by the open Cascade Ditch and then run through our on-site household chlorination and filtration system, was declared unfit for public consumption. This appeared to be a result of extensive development with inadequate septic systems upstream of the Cascade Ditch, which contaminated the ditch water as build-out occurred. There were simply too many houses relying on inadequate infrastructure for the natural capacity of the local soils to treat the septic system effluent adequately. Earlier planning and zoning decisions had resulted in too many lots of inadequate size (or inappropriate location) for the area. At first we dealt with it by collecting water on a regular basis at the public Bitney Springs (ten miles away), but that later proved impossible when we wanted to rent our house. We then called in the well-drilling rig, which eventually found a site on the far edge of our property. There are no true aquifers in the Sierra Nevada foothills, and finding groundwater in the fractured bedrock is highly uncertain (Swain 1994; Page et al. 1984; Wheeldon 1994; Hauge 1994; Fulton 1994). Often, multiple wells must be drilled in the hope of finding water. Ten thousand dollars later, we had "internalized" some of the cumulative costs of extensive upstream development.

Nevada City and Grass Valley had their own sewage treatment problems during the early 1970s. The basic problem was that they did not treat their sewage adequately. An old and decaying collector system gathered the effluent from city homes and businesses, then funneled it to a central point. Nevada City dumped its effluent into Deer Creek while Grass Valley dumped its into Wolf Creek. My seventh-grade social studies teacher, Charles Mumgaard, helped us organize a project on this problem around Earth Day in early 1973. Our local swimming areas were contaminated and unusable, and the smell of the raw sewage limited use of nearby trails and beaches. My classmates and I wrote letters, attended city council meetings, and generally demanded that the city address the problem by improving the sewage treatment plant. The city council had already pursued a federal grant to upgrade the system, but our civic activism helped to move things along.

That experience raised some fundamental questions for me about the relationship between humans, technology, development, local land use planning, and Nature. It was also my introduction to the world of public-sector economics and the politics of environmental policy. The bottom line, then as now, was money. People were willing to deal with the problem as long as they could get someone else to pay for it. A quarter century later, we still have much to learn about dealing with growth and the environment. Sewage treatment plants have been built for both cities, but we are still contaminating our waterways through inadequate operation of those systems and the cumulative effects of continued development of substandard parcels throughout the Sierra Nevada (Lauer 1995a; 1995e; 1995f; Hanner 1997). And we still deny the real costs that accrue from the negative effects of our current development approaches. Economic, ecological, and socially sustainable development remains an elusive goal in the Range of Light.

PRODUCING A LANDSCAPE OF CONSUMPTION

Ecotransformation of the Gold Country is shifting the role of land and resources in the region from a landscape of production to a landscape of consumption. Ironically, the process of *producing* that landscape of consumption may still have significant social and ecological consequences that threaten the long-run sustainability of the region.

The land use pattern in rural and exurban regions is mixed (Nelson 1992; Yaro et al. 1988; Arendt 1994b; J. Davis et al. 1994). High-density clusters of structures exist in pockets at critical crossroads and in small villages and towns, but most of the landscape is uninhabited or sparsely settled. Villages and towns often have population and structure densities comparable to urban metropolitan regions, but their *scale* (both in population and area) is significantly smaller. Rural and exurban villages and towns are typically home to 10^2 to 10^4 people, while metropolitan-area towns and cities range from 10^4 to 10^6 residents.[1] What differentiates a rural from an exurban landscape is the degree of human settlement outside the urban-density villages and small towns. Rural areas essentially maintain a working landscape outside the villages and towns, where those dwelling on that land are directly working it (Hiss 1990). The primary relationship of Nature to rural Culture is as a productive source of raw materials: it remains a landscape of production. In contrast, much of the land outside exurban villages and towns is inhabited by individuals and families who do not depend directly on the production of commodities on that land. The primary functional role of Nature has changed: it is now a landscape of consumption. This is a key difference between exurban and rural Culture.

This separation of settlement from the ongoing, productive economic exploitation of the land has also altered the economic viability of developing the landscape at higher densities. Rural land uses such as agriculture and related commodity production inherently limited the density and degree of settlement on the landscape because of the economies of scale in production that were necessary to maintain viable agriculture, or related commodity production activity, on the land. The exurbanites' economic independence from the immediate landscape allows a much smaller land area for each dwelling unit, while reducing the relative economic value of maintaining large working landscapes. The result is rapid fragmentation of the exurban landscape through settlement in low-density patterns that convert the land from productive to consumptive use.

This fragmentation is in part a function of economics, but it takes a particular physical form largely as a result of planning policies and land use regulations. Those policies in turn reflect some of the imperatives of the current real estate market, which demands standardized and simplistic ownership patterns to operate most efficiently. The dominant planning paradigm then reinforces that need, as real estate markets develop along that model. This is not unlike the series of developments that the capitalist economy brought to the standardization of corn and beef described by Bill Cronon in his book *Nature's Metropolis* (1991). The result is the commodification of the landscape (Lopez 1992) and the homogenization and standardization of place. This conceptual shift alone (to the abstraction of place in order to allow transfer of ownership rights in the elements of place through the market) has dramatically altered the exurban landscape.[2] Landscapes are viewed by the market primarily in terms of ownership patterns, often ignoring the ecological differences that may exist as a result of natural factors. Ownership boundaries then dominate over ecological boundaries when making planning policy.[3] As Frank Popper has noted, this reflects in part both the urban and the industrial origins of land use planning and zoning. These planning approaches appear poorly suited to the postindustrial context of emerging land use patterns in rural and exurban communities (1984; 1992; 1993).

Development in the Sierra Nevada is occurring primarily in the formerly rural, unincorporated areas near gold rush–era communities in the foothill zone. It is not city-centered, although the urban centers of the foothills often provide the essential services that the new exurban residents demand. The result is a pattern of low-density, land-intensive, large-lot exurban sprawl. Large-scale commercial service centers are also spreading across the landscape, robbing the historical downtown centers of their economic vitality and reducing their role in fostering social interaction and forging community identity (Beaumont 1994; Marois 1996c; National Public Radio 1996). This has altered both the ecological and the social landscape of the Sierra Nevada foothills. Nature and Culture are therefore coevolving as population growth transforms the relationship between them. Spatial diffusion and the expanded scale of the community have increased anonymity and decreased community identity. This pattern of exurbanization also causes significant fragmentation of ecosystems and tends to increase transportation distances—leading to decreased water and air quality locally and downstream. Some other countries are also experiencing a new pattern of periurban development, although most European countries have stricter land use controls, transportation pricing policies, and infrastructure investment strategies (including subsidies for public transit) that tend to encourage a more compact form of settlement. In the Sierra Nevada, unincorporated areas are absorbing most of the growth.

The reasons for this low-density pattern of development are manifold. The fundamental force is the desire of new residents to live in the "country" with wooded, open spaces shielding their "homestead" from the view of neighboring homes. This reflects the long-standing desire to have a country estate with privacy and tranquility, as described by Fishman in *Bourgeois Utopias* (1987). It can be achieved at densities less than an acre per unit with adequate vegetative cover, but it could take tens of acres per unit in a more open landscape. The resulting setting gives residents a sense of privacy and a connection with the natural world. Contact with the community comes through regular visits to the nearby town center, where daily employment and/or service needs are met. There is also limited neighborhood contact, although lower densities decrease opportunities for inadvertent interaction with neighbors. Often the center of informal social life in these areas

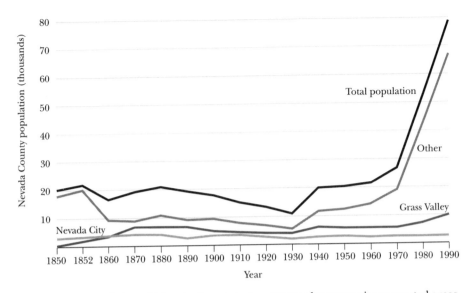

FIGURE 6.1.   Population of Nevada County in incorporated versus unincorporated areas, 1850–1990.

is the post office or the grocery store. These are "sacred spaces" within the community that serve a vital social function (Hester 1985; 1989; 1990).

For some of the migrants moving from metropolitan areas into gated communities, reproduction of the physical, spatial, and market aspects of the suburban landscapes they left may actually be desirable. They seek the market benefits of that physical and spatial pattern without the costs of scale diseconomies associated with the larger metropolitan pattern they left. Wal-Mart is fine for them, because the availability of a wide variety of goods at low prices is for them a desirable element.[4] What they want to leave behind are the traffic congestion, crime, graffiti, and homelessness they faced in their daily lives in the suburban communities of California's metropolitan areas (Garland 1997a). The suburban land use pattern of sprawl is therefore seen as a problem only if and when it begins to be associated with those disamenities. Within the tighter and more homogeneous social context of exurbia, however, traffic congestion is the first disamenity they will probably experience. By then, of course, the land use pattern will be very difficult to change.

Development in the Sierra Nevada foothills has generally occurred through an incremental process dominated by individual home construction, unlike the "new town" subdivision process common in metropolitan real estate markets.[5] Large parcels are often subdivided without simultaneous development of model homes and builder-originated construction. Instead, lots are sold to individuals without any requirement to choose a particular model home design or hire the subdivision developer as the home construction contractor. Moreover, many of the existing parcels were created through major subdivisions approved by local planners before the Subdivision Map Act of 1973 (*Grass Valley–Nevada City Union* 1970a; 1970b). These were often intended for second homes but have subsequently been developed for year-round residences. Quarter-acre lots with on-site septic systems are common among these subdivisions from the late 1960s and early 1970s. Just four major developments from this period account for 14,022 of the 57,963 parcels (24 percent) in Nevada County in 1992.[6] The land was subdivided and sold off parcel-by-parcel, but actual development has been incremental over nearly three decades. These rural lots have often been purchased by urbanites who hold them vacant until retirement or another personal (rather than a local real estate market) opportunity finally allows them to move. Each parcel is then typically developed individually in accordance with the needs of the lot owner. The size, style, and effect of each house on the environment therefore varies widely in exurban areas. The overall scale of the development and its eventual effects were consequently difficult to gauge during the early years of the projects. Individual landowners built their own houses without the mass-produced standardization so common to the large-scale suburban subdivision developments in California's metropolitan areas.[7] Most of the remaining lots have been and continue to be created through "minor" subdivisions of four or fewer parcels that are exempt from the Subdivision Map Act.[8] Concurrent subdivision and infrastructure investments (required under the Act) are therefore the exception rather than the rule in the exurban development process.

Nevada County had more than fifty-one thousand parcels when its general plan update began in 1990, but more than seventeen thousand of these (one-third of the total) had not yet been developed (Boivin 1991–96). One focus of the general plan update debate was the minimum parcel size in portions of the county designated as rural areas under the general plan. Allowing a ten-acre minimum parcel size in low-density rural areas not yet subdivided would have resulted in the creation of approximately twenty-five hundred new parcels, while a forty-acre minimum parcel size would have restricted new lot creation to only 1,500. The difference of a thousand new lots (40 percent of twenty-five hundred) seems significant within the context of new parcel creation, but it is trivial in light of the enormous backlog of presently undeveloped lots (it would represent only 6 percent of existing lots). Consequently, the central planning challenge is to address already created but presently undeveloped parcels that are typically owned by absentee urbanites. The planning debate has nevertheless focused on new lot creation, with existing parcelization grandfathered in and taken for granted (Boivin 1991–96; Nevada County Planning Department 1994c; Hanner 1997). Unfortunately, the general plan update process has for the most part failed to address how previous planning errors could be corrected through future policies. The existing pattern of parcelization has simply been presumed to be immutable.

In this way planning is an inherently contingent process, where land use decisions from one era influence and constrain the alternatives available and choices made in future eras. This is amply demonstrated for the Nevada County General Plan below, where I document how planning decisions made in the late 1960s and early 1970s still haunt the community in its planning debates today.

The reasons for this are primarily political. Controlling future land subdivisions will affect an abstract set of future landowners, who do not now vote in local elections. Limiting the development of existing parcels affects existing landowners, who do vote in local elections. Moreover, what is perceived to be *politically* acceptable land use regulation in these largely conservative counties falls far short of what is *legally* permissible. This reflects in part a presumption that regulatory restrictions on development will invariably constrain individuals' private property rights (Juvinall 1995a). That presumption is predicated on further assumptions that the regulatory tools available to government do not include the use of market-oriented incentives. As I discuss below, however, it is possible to construct an innovative approach to land use planning that goes beyond the density-control orientation of zoning to protect private property rights and market values. These include transferable development credits and performance zoning concepts (Schiffman 1989). Successful application of these more complex schemes requires careful development of sophisticated systems, however, and local officials have generally been unwilling to seriously consider these more innovative approaches. Land use planning and regulation have therefore continued to be hampered by continued reliance on simplistic and limited tools (ibid.).

Minimum lot sizes are usually set by the local government through a general plan designation and specific zoning ordinance. The minimum for rural residential lots typically varies from 1 to 5 acres, but there is no standard policy in the Sierra Nevada. As noted above, many of the existing parcels were approved for on-site septic disposal at densities up to four units per acre and were grandfathered in by subsequent general plans and zoning ordinances. The recent general plan updates by Nevada and El Dorado Counties now call for a minimum of 3–5 acres for on-site septic disposal systems with an on-site well water source (El Dorado County Planning Department 1994; Nevada County Planning Department 1994c). The 1980 Nevada County General Plan had a 1.5 acre minimum for the same configuration, but that standard has since been deemed inadequate in the new general plan adopted in 1995 (Nevada County Planning Department 1980).

Local government land use policy is usually set by a combination of five factors: existing parcelization (e.g., current land use designation); land uses on adjacent properties (e.g., typical densities); infrastructure availability (e.g., roads, water, sewers); environmental constraints (e.g., slope, soils, vegetation); philosophy, values, and ideology (e.g., the role of regulation).

Note that the third and fourth factors (infrastructure availability and environmental constraints) could lead to land use densities that are often inconsistent with the first two factors (existing parcelization and land use on adjacent properties). This heightens the importance of previous planning actions on current decision makers. Environmental constraints or a lack of infrastructure may limit the potential development density, for example, but the land may already be zoned for or adjacent to land already developed at higher densities. The final factor (philosophy, values, and ideology) seems to determine the relative weight given to the other factors and the range of alternative policies that elected and appointed officials are willing to consider (Juvinall 1995a).

Based on review of the general plan development processes in Nevada and El Dorado Counties, it appears that local officials often rely on the existing pattern of parcelization as the primary factor in designating land uses.[9] This is the primary reason that existing general plans and zoning designations in the Sierra Nevada are often inconsistent with the results of environmental analyses. Decisions have been made primarily based on adjacent land uses or existing zoning on adjacent parcels, rather than the availability of infrastructure or the environmental effects of development. Despite CEQA, the effects of development are therefore not fully mitigated in the county general plan and zoning processes. "Overriding considerations" are frequently invoked under CEQA to avoid mitigation for significant effects. This is demonstrated below in my case study of the Nevada County General Plan update. Planning clearly takes place in a highly politicized context. As Tuolumne County environmental activist Glenda Edwards puts it, "The name of the planning game at every bureaucratic level is politics" (1996).

Accordingly, it is necessary to develop innovative policies that address policymakers' political concerns. Land use planning is a politically potent issue in the Sierra Nevada and all rural regions facing rapid exurban growth pressure. Many residents (particularly those who have lived in the Sierra a very long time) have fervent views on the sanctity of private property, and among these same residents there is general resistance to government intervention in land development on private property. Constitutional guarantees against the "taking" of private property and the need for due process in government decision-making place both legal and political limits on local governments' ability to restrict private use of private land.[10] This is particularly true if previous government action has resulted in an expectation of a particular density or use. Local governments are therefore reluctant to downzone parcels. Local perceptions of vested rights differ markedly from legal findings in many cases, but perceptions dominate local politics.[11] As a result, local governments in rural and exurban communities are generally much less willing to restrict development on private property than they might legally do under state and federal law.[12] The relationship between private property rights and public responsibilities is discussed in detail below.

INFRASTRUCTURE AND
ENVIRONMENTAL CONSTRAINTS

The timing, location, and degree of urbanization in metropolitan regions are often determined by major capital investments in infrastructure systems: roads, water supply, sewage collection and treatment facilities, energy supply, and related systems such as storm water drainage. This policy tool—the ability of local governments to control the timing and location of investments in physical infrastructure—has significantly less influence on rural and exurban land development. As a result it is difficult to guide development patterns in rural and exurban areas, where relatively low land costs make site-specific on-site infrastructure investments economical. Indeed, most rural land development occurs without either centralized water supply or sewer systems. On-site wells and septic tanks are common. According to the 1990 census, among all Sierra Region housing units, nearly one in four has private, on-site well water supplies (versus about one in twenty-five for California), and nearly three out of every five housing units have septic tanks or cesspools for waste disposal (versus less than one in ten for California).

This has a direct bearing on the pattern of development that occurs in exurbia. Environmental and health factors dictate that on-site well water and septic tank systems be separated, resulting in zoning regulations that *require* low-density development patterns. This is in part the result of reliance on zoning (which is oriented toward density controls) as the primary means of regulating local land use. Local soil conditions, slopes, and hydrologic characteristics should all be considered when determining site-specific risks and appropriate standards (McHarg 1969), but comprehensive analysis of these natural factors has generally been weak in the exurban planning process. Rather than allow development only where environmental constraints are least limiting, however, local governments have relied on large-lot zoning to increase the likelihood that there will be at least *some* buildable site on a given parcel.

Undoubtedly, many one-acre parcels have multiple building sites and could support more than one house with an on-site septic system and on-site well water. Conversely, many one-acre parcels have poor soils, steep slopes, proximity to intermittent surface water sources, and very poor groundwater resources. Systematic analysis of environmental constraints would favor shifting development from the latter site to the former, with less overall environmental effect at the same level of development. The present reliance on large-lot zoning fails to require or depend on such analysis, so it promotes large-lot exurban sprawl and landscape fragmentation. Site-specific consideration of natural constraints tends to occur only through the building permit requirements of a percolation test (for septic systems) and minimum well water flows. There is rarely any site-specific evaluation of the risk of septic system failure or potential contamination of critical hydrologic resources as a result of failure.[13]

The large lot sizes that dominate the prevailing pattern of exurban development are therefore a direct result of the lack of infrastructure to serve the burgeoning population. This in turn is a function of both land market economics and the reliance of local land use authorities on low-density, large-lot zoning as the primary means of reducing the potential health risks associated with on-site well water and septic systems. These health risks, in turn, are a function of both on-site infrastructure technology and economics and the environmental constraints of the site. Large lots are not necessarily required to meet the market demand for homes. New residents might be just as satisfied with their quality of life on a half-acre lot as on a two-acre lot, for example, if the amenities they seek—privacy, clean water, wildlife, habitat, and possible room for a horse—are still available to them in that alternative configuration. The two-acre minimum leads to a development pattern that consumes four times as much land, while breaking up ecosystems and habitat into a pattern of unsustainable "islands" unconnected to related systems (Soule 1991a). The result may be considerably more environmental damage than would be necessary if the infrastructure allowed higher densities. *Lower density does not necessarily mean lower environmental effect.* The dominant pattern of exurban sprawl can cause significant environmental damage that could be mitigated through more careful land use planning and site design—including higher *net* densities on suitable sites.[14]

Is it possible to meet the growing demand for residential development in the Sierra Nevada foothills and other rapidly growing exurban regions with centralized water supply and sewage facilities? This is primarily a function of economics. Raw water supply in the foothills is often provided by irrigation districts, and treatment for domestic consumption is usually expensive.[15] Low densities tend to increase the per-household cost of delivering treated water, as each mile of pipeline must be paid for by fewer water accounts. This has discouraged treatment of raw water sources that would otherwise be available for rural development. Incorporated cities usually have distribution facilities that reach higher-density development, keeping the cost per household of treated water to a more economical level. Development on the immediate fringe of those exurban centers—or development at higher densities that will bring down the per-household costs—may be the only way to get treated water supplies to new residential development in the Sierra Nevada. The economics will otherwise continue to favor on-site wells.[16]

Like treated water supply, sewage collection and treatment is economical only when densities are high enough to lower the per-household cost to a level competitive with septic systems. Such densities are not achievable with exurban sprawl. Some exurban communities in the Sierra foothills, however, have sewage treatment plants and adequate collection facilities currently underutilized even as exurban sprawl continues. These communities could reduce exurban sprawl by encouraging denser residential development adjacent to the existing urban boundary.[17] Innovative wastewater treatment technologies could also be cost-effective for carefully designed developments that have higher net densities in some portions of the development site (where houses are "clustered") while maintaining overall (gross) densities comparable to development densities under sprawl. Such community systems could provide new flexibility in the spatial arrangement of lots, which have usually been dictated by the need to separate on-site wells from septic tanks on each lot. Clustered developments can utilize the "common" undeveloped areas adjacent to the privately owned lots for both wells and septic disposal fields.[18]

The relationship between the economics of providing centralized infrastructure systems and the pressure to continue exurban sprawl is difficult to assess at this point. Actual costs of alternative systems and the optimum system design for different densities and scales of development are often site-specific. The phased pattern of development in exurban areas also makes capital facilities financing costly. The economics of clustering are in part a function of infrastructure costs, but the relative importance of those costs to housing costs is a function of land values and construction costs. Increasing land values in the late 1980s and early 1990s dramatically changed the economics of on-site infrastructure. Declining well-drilling costs, together with increased land values, have led to much deeper well drilling in the Gold Country. Average maximum depths were between 200 and 300 feet before the early 1990s, but wells of 700 to 1,000 feet are now being drilled. Drilling costs average about $13.50 per foot, while pump costs run $1,700 for a 200-foot well and $4,000 for a 700-foot well. The total cost of a 200-foot well is therefore $4,400 while a 700-foot well would cost $13,450 (Ellis 1997). Land prices generally doubled in the Sierra Nevada foothills during 1991, however, dramatically increasing the value of finding water on marginal sites. The cost of drilling the deeper well was deemed prohibitive when the value of the finished home and land would be less than $100,000, but it is still only 3–4 percent of the total project cost when the finished home and land will be worth $300,000 to $500,000. It is therefore now worthwhile to spend an extra $9,050 to make a site buildable. The physical absence of readily accessible well water no longer makes a site unbuildable.[19]

This raises a fundamental point about the development process: the "unbuildable lot" is ultimately an *economic* concept. Human ingenuity and astronomical investments of capital, labor, and resources have allowed the construction of buildings time and time again on sites deemed unbuildable by a previous landowner. In some cases, the new capacity to build on a site reflected the development of new technologies. In others, it simply reflected the market perception that a lot was of low value—because it would be extremely expensive to build on. A combination of these two factors struck me while Teresa and I were looking for our first home when we moved to Berkeley in 1991. We visited nearly eighty homes in our search, and one of them still stands out in my mind. Built on a winding road in the Berkeley hills on the back side of a steep canyon, the narrow lot plunged down the steep face to the ravine below. The house sat high above the earth on steel pillars, with only the corner of the garage touching the ground. The difficulty of building on that site had precluded development for many years. But when land values finally rose high enough, the cost of engineering a steel frame support for the house was no longer an obstacle.[20] As the history of urban development clearly shows, what is unbuildable at one land value may be the site of a skyscraper at a higher land value. Indeed, the very presence of the skyscraper changes the probability of further development overcoming environmental constraints on adjacent land.

The economics of land development also depend heavily on transportation infrastructure. As a result of spatial dispersion of rural and exurban land uses, activity in the Sierra Nevada depends more on private transportation than in metropolitan areas, where it is more feasible to provide public transit. Rural and exurban road networks also cover vast distances, making maintenance and replacement costs a larger fraction of overall system costs. At the same time, transit systems are more expensive to operate in rural and exurban areas because of lower densities and a wider range of dispersed destinations. Yet the increasing importance of commuting by exurbanites to metropolitan regions makes public transit even more important for the alleviation of traffic congestion and associated air quality problems. Moreover, local traffic congestion is a disamenity that degrades the quality of life that exurban migrants have sought in moving from metropolitan areas. It therefore has an economic cost resulting from its effects on those amenity values. Rural and exurban regions have relatively little political clout, however, when it comes to the distribution of state and federal funds for transportation improvements. The general decline in both funding for and the condition of California's transportation system (coupled with major expenses associated with earthquake repairs and retrofitting following the 1989 Loma Prieta quake and the 1994 Northridge quake) has siphoned funds to metropolitan projects. Rural and exurban congestion affects relatively few people, so relieving such congestion is a relatively low priority for state and federal funding. Those projects most likely to receive funding are directly tied to metropolitan commuting. These same projects also typically provide significant air quality benefits that increase their total economic, ecological, and social value.[21]

Perhaps the greatest environmental effect of the transportation system is on air quality. The Sierra Nevada experiences excellent air quality at different times of the year and in different locations, but it is also sometimes in violation of state standards for ozone, carbon monoxide, and particulates (Knudson 1991; Cahill et al.

1996). Much of this air pollution is the result of transport from other regions, primarily the Central Valley and the San Francisco Bay Area to the west.[22] The importance of local emission sources is growing, however, and the transportation sector is primarily responsible for both ozone and carbon monoxide violations (woodstoves and forest fires appear to be the main sources of particulate emissions) (Cahill et al. 1996). In many cases this results from significant commuting between exurban communities and metropolitan areas up to sixty miles away. Much of it originates with local travel within the Sierra Nevada itself, however, for nearly all trips must be taken by private vehicle. Reductions in state funding for education have reduced school bus service, and many parents drive their children to and from their school bus stops.[23] This creates at least four additional trips per household per school day with long periods of idling while waiting for the bus to arrive. Modern county roads and subdivisions often follow the lines of old mining and logging routes, funneling traffic through older downtown areas originally designed for stage coach travel (Thomas 1994; Thompson 1995). The hilly terrain and limited funds have made alternative routes difficult to implement.

The transportation system is also important because of its significant environmental effects on land, water, and habitat. Roads act as important barriers to wildlife travel, fragmenting ecosystems and increasing the probability of extinction of local populations. This diminishes the native biological diversity of the local watershed, the entire Sierra Nevada, and the planet (Duane 1993c; Soule 1986; Noss 1991; Wilcove et al. 1986). Road construction in steeply sloped mountainous regions can also increase erosion, eliminating valuable topsoil and degrading water quality. Erosion is associated too with the loss of salmonid spawning habitat, critical to maintenance of salmonid species. Moreover, oils, heavy metals, and other pollutants are introduced to ecological systems through vehicle travel on roads. It is therefore important to minimize road construction and mitigate the effects of roads already built.

It may even be appropriate to close some roads to address fragmentation at the landscape scale and to reduce the negative effects on sensitive species and reduce biodiversity degradation. Road closures have been introduced on some federal lands to protect wildlife and promote greater integration between habitat patches that would otherwise be isolated by the roads (Trombulate 1997). This possibility has not yet been considered seriously for public roads adjacent to private lands in rapidly growing exurban areas. Preliminary analysis of habitat fragmentation in western Nevada County indicates that closure of several relatively short road segments could significantly reduce habitat fragmentation and promote connectivity between the largely privately owned Little Deer Creek watershed and Tahoe National Forest lands to the east. Such closures could also be accomplished in such a way that access would be only marginally reduced. Map 6.1 shows A) levels of fragmentation with existing paved roads, B) the increased fragmentation that

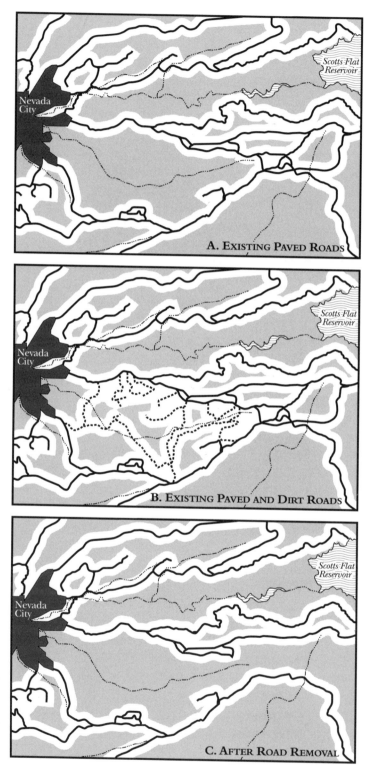

MAP 6.1. Habitat fragmentation and connectivity in the Little Deer Creek area near Nevada City, a) based on existing paved roads, b) based on existing paved and dirt roads, and c) after road removal.

would result from paving existing dirt roads and increasing their use, and C) the increased connectivity that would result from strategically selective road removal in the upper part of the Little Deer Creek watershed.[24]

Integration with an efficient transportation system is therefore necessary in exurban land use planning. With a few notable exceptions, however, little of that integration is now occurring.[25] Environmental analysis of the new Nevada County General Plan was conducted in late 1994 and early 1995 *before* the Regional Transportation Plan was completed, for example, raising serious questions about the reliability of the EIR's assessment of transportation and air quality effects. Moreover, the effects of the county road network on habitat fragmentation and water quality have not been analyzed by either the Nevada County Transportation Commission, Planning Department, or Transportation Department. Continuing population growth has also exceeded funding for transportation investments, so many of the costs of growth are now borne by the general public in the form of degraded levels of service standards—which then exacerbate both air pollution and the frustration associated with urban-style traffic delays (Norman 1982). As a result, total social costs are high under this system, even if the apparent direct financial costs seem low to local governments. The costs have simply been shifted to the environment and other parties (i.e., externalized). Rather than serve as a tool for managing and mitigating the environmental effects of growth, the current pattern of infrastructure investment is in many cases exacerbating environmental problems. Much greater coordination is required between land use planning and infrastructure investment to stop further degradation.[26] This will require more innovative planning approaches.

Water supply, sewage treatment, transportation, and power supply are the infrastructure systems that have had the greatest effect on exurban land use patterns and economic development to date, but future patterns may also depend on investments in telecommunications. Low densities may make it difficult to recover the fixed costs of major capital investment in some new technological innovations in telecommunications, such as fiber optics or ISDN lines, but other technologies, such as cellular telephones, have already reduced the relative importance of fixed locations to the system in doing global business (Richardson and Gordon 1989). Like photovoltaic (solar) cells, cellular phones make it increasingly possible to live "off the grid" while remaining connected to the outside world. Commercially available access to the Internet became available throughout Nevada County in late 1994 and early 1995 for just $25 per month and a local telephone call. Such access makes physical location in metropolitan areas even less important than it was before; this, in turn, may permit more information age "lone eagle" workers to relocate to exurbia. I know two telecommuters who live off the electrical grid on 160 acres near Nevada City but work for Xerox in Palo Alto (Mallgren 1994–95; Donaldson 1994–95). Like me, they communicate with coworkers by electronic mail, telephone, and fax. Periodic visits to the Bay Area allow them to maintain social contact with their company, while their Internet connection allows them to transfer electronic files for less than the cost of postage. My own e-mail correspondence regularly includes friends and colleagues across the country and in Portugal, Germany, New Zealand, Australia, and Japan. Continuing innovations in telecommunications technology—especially those that make teleconferencing more viable—will make it even more feasible to do business from the Sierra Nevada.[27]

HUMAN SETTLEMENT PATTERNS IN EXURBIA

As I noted above, much of the literature on rural and exurban land use has failed to distinguish between very different patterns of human settlement in the exurban landscape. Further distinctions are important to our understanding of land use and the effects of alternative patterns of human settlement. Exurban development patterns in the Sierra Nevada generally include five distinct types of settlement, each with different consequences for the exurban landscape, as described below.

Compact Small Towns of 10^2 to 10^4 Population

These communities are the core of exurban areas and the location of most commercial and service activities. In the rural and exurban West they usually date from the nineteenth century, making them compact in size and walkable.[28] These towns were built before the automobile had been invented and long before it had come to dominate urban form. Their architecture is usually a mixed vernacular, offering a variety of styles but relatively standard building scale of two to four stories (Jackson 1970; Groth and Bressi 1997). Many of these towns were built around mining or other commodity extraction industries, and their architecture reflects repeated investments and an evolution from tents to shacks to wood-frame buildings to masonry brick structures.

As Peter Owens notes, however, most of these places would be illegal under current zoning codes (1991–95). This is a striking indictment of our current zoning codes, for these places are both intuitively attractive and extremely practical forms of human settlement (Alexander et al. 1977). Recent "neotraditional" urban designers like Andres Duany and Elizabeth Plater-Zyberk have attempted to reintroduce the spatial patterns and urban form of these traditional patterns in new developments like Seaside, Florida (Duany and Plater-Zyberk 1991; Southworth 1997; Sexton 1995; Katz 1994). Similar proposals have been made by Peter Calthorpe for the Sierra Nevada foothills and elsewhere (1993). In theory, these neotraditional new towns promise both social and ecological benefits. In practice, the centrally planned neotraditional towns remain socially and economically segregated and lack much of the vitality of the organically developed traditional small towns (Harvey 1993; Southworth 1997). They are also limited in scale in terms of both population and land area, reducing their potential as models for handling the dramatic increases in population being experienced in the exurban West. They nevertheless provide a critical social and economic function and offer important lessons for urban design that could yield significant environmental benefits.[29]

Socially and culturally, there is daily interaction among residents in these small towns through shopping, attending school functions, or the rural ritual of picking up mail at the post office box. Volunteerism is quite common; in fact, many services provided by professionals in urban areas, such as fire fighting, are staffed primarily by volunteers in these communities. This is changing, however, as the ecotransformation occurs: commuters and retirees have little interest in or time for volunteer fire fighting, so taxes must be raised to pay for more full-time professional firefighters.[30] Social events still often revolve around participatory activities like Little League games and fund-raising pancake breakfasts rather than professional entertainment.

Population densities are urban within the city limits of these compact small towns—often from two thousand to five thousand persons per square mile (including significant commercial, industrial, and public lands). In many cases the towns are not incorporated but subject to county oversight for land use planning, regulation, and public services. Truckee was already a bustling town when C. F. McGlashan arrived in 1872, but it did not incorporate as a municipality with its own city council until 1993. Until then it was still officially known as "unincorporated Nevada County."

Often the most popular communities in exurbia are located in spectacular settings, making them attractive for tourists as well as residents. Examples around the West include Jackson, Wyoming; Aspen, Colorado; Park City, Utah; Santa Fe, New Mexico; Sedona, Arizona; Hood River, Oregon; Ketchum/Sun Valley, Idaho; Livingston, Montana; Bellingham, Washington; Incline Village, Nevada; and Nevada City, California. The mix of services in these communities therefore caters to a more cosmopolitan population—one that appreciates, for example, gourmet restaurants and espresso—than would be found in comparably sized small towns without the influx of tourism dollars. The "espresso and cappuccino index" is one rough measure of the degree of ecotransformation in a community,[31] as the greasy spoon is gradually being replaced by restaurants serving southwestern fare and California cuisine. A howling coyote or Kokopelli figure in the window is a sure sign that the exurbanites have arrived. The downtown gets a facelift, the marginal businesses fold, and many of the businesses providing traditional services, such as grocery and hardware stores, move out of the downtown to make way for tourist-oriented boutiques.[32] The role of the traditional small town as the center of social life then diminishes as daily activities become dispersed. This has occurred in Nevada City over the last decade or so and is also affecting Grass Valley and Truckee.[33]

Contiguous Exurban Subdivisions at Suburban Densities

Contiguous subdivisions built in the postwar period are often immediately adjacent to the pre–World War II, compact small towns. These subdivisions are usually connected to the small towns' water supply and sewer system, allowing densities comparable to suburban developments in metropolitan areas: anywhere from four to eight houses per acre, or a population density of five thousand to ten thousand per square mile of residential development after accounting for about 20 percent dedicated to public roads. Infrastructure is the key element defining these developments, which have architectural features and a layout that diverge sharply from the patterns in the historic small towns. Residences are typically single story, while they are often two levels in the historical pattern. Streets are much wider and the houses are set back from the streets and from each other with ample yard space. The social openness of the traditional front porch has been replaced by the fenced backyard, which isolates the modern family's leisure time and diminishes opportunities for casual interaction. The garage, a small and hidden addition to the lot in the traditional small town (if it exists at all), has moved from the backyard to the front of the house. The primary means of accessing the residential space is now through the automobile. These subdivisions are designed to maximize vehicle mobility and minimize social interaction. Michael Southworth, Peter Owens, and Eran Ben-Joseph have demonstrated that the evolution of subdivision design in America reflects a series of systematic changes by nonarchitects that seriously constrain urban form (Southworth and Owens 1992; 1993; Southworth and Ben-Joseph 1993).

Within the development, this settlement pattern is just like any other cookie-cutter subdivision; within the broader exurban context, however, it is often quite different. Its proximity to the old town often allows pedestrian or bicycle access to services, while its overall *scale* (10^1 to 10^2 acres) is usually much smaller than those developed in metropolitan regions (10^2 to 10^4 acres). This has an important social effect, for the residents remain familiar with their neighbors and connected to the immediately adjacent small town that is often absent in suburbia. These higher-density spaces are nevertheless very different from the traditional small town itself. They are often the only location in an exurban community where multiple-family housing is located. The poorest members of exurban regions tend to live either in subsidized multiple-family units or in trailers and mobile homes in the most rural (and lowest-cost) settings in the area. Gentrification of the quaint Victorian houses of the historic small towns has increased the need for this kind of housing, but state and federal funding for affordable housing has diminished recently and is generally concentrated in declining central cities. The ecotransformation of the rural and exurban West has nevertheless created a new affordability crisis. These contiguous urban subdivisions are therefore more important for their role as pockets of poverty in what is otherwise becoming a more affluent exurban landscape. Examples of this pattern are found in the Gold Country and the Mother Lode on the edges of Grass Valley, Auburn, Placerville, and Sonora.

Stand-Alone Gated Communities at Suburban Densities

The opposite condition exists in the many exurban areas that have independent gated communities, which are neither physically contiguous to nor socially integrated with the small towns that form the core of the exurban settlement pattern. Unlike the small towns, these private communities are usually homogeneous in ethnic (white), social (well-educated, former urbanites), demographic (older retirees), economic (wealthy relative to the rest of the region), and political (conservative) characteristics (Blakely and Snyder 1997). They are often built around significant recreational amenities such as lakes and golf courses, and they generally have larger lots and more expensive homes than the surrounding landscape. In some cases they have private community sewer and water systems, but many older subdivisions continue to depend on private septic systems and on-site wells. This dependence on private infrastructure has not diminished densities, however, for many of these older subdivisions were approved before land use and environmental planning laws required stricter standards. Densities range from one to four houses per acre, or one thousand to five thousand persons per square mile. The total population of these private communities at build-out is often comparable to the compact small towns (five thousand to ten thousand people). They are usually unincorporated, however, and do not provide many of the service functions of the compact small towns. They are therefore bedroom communities that insulate themselves from the rest of the exurban region except as the latter may provide necessary services such as shopping and medical care.[34]

The median assessed values of homes and median family incomes in these communities rival the highly inflated values of metropolitan California. They far exceed typical values for most of the rural and exurban West. Lake of the Pines had a median housing value of $368,500 in 1990, compared with median values of $155,685 in Nevada County, $128,678 for the Sierra Region and $195,500 for California. The median household income in the core Census Block Group of Lake of the Pines was $55,161 in 1990, compared with median values of $32,464 for all of Nevada County, $29,595 for the Sierra Region, and $35,798 for

California. Lake Wildwood's median house value was $226,800 and the median household income in Lake Wildwood was $52,359 in the core Census Block Group in 1990. The values are lower in Lake Wildwood than those in Lake of the Pines primarily because the latter has a much higher fraction of commuters who work outside Nevada County (53 percent) than Lake Wildwood (23 percent). Lake Wildwood also has a higher fraction of retirees, with 66 percent of its residents at least fifty-five years of age; 48 percent of the residents of Lake of the Pines are at least fifty-five years of age, which compares with 29 percent of Nevada County residents, 27 percent of all Sierra Region residents, and only 18 percent of all California residents who are fifty-five years of age or older.[35]

These high housing values and household incomes have supported what is effectively the privatization of public services without municipal incorporation. Lake of the Pines and Lake Wildwood now rival the incorporated towns of Grass Valley, Nevada City, and Truckee as population centers in Nevada County. Unlike those three incorporated cities, however, the privatized "public" sector of the gated communities is exempt from a wide range of laws guiding public policy in California municipalities. These include open-meeting laws and restrictions on mechanisms for controlling local land use and infrastructure decisions based on ownership rather than equal "one person, one vote" representation. Political jurisdictions are therefore less relevant to infrastructure and land use decision-making in privatized communities. Expansion of this pattern of gated-community development has implications for the land use planning process itself. It also has a direct bearing on the capacity to provide local infrastructure through general taxation.

Not surprisingly, many of the members of these communities see little reason to tax themselves to provide services for the larger community or the rest of the county. The privatization of the public sector through the gated community structure effectively segregates the broader exurban landscape by class. This in turn threatens some of the fundamental tenets of democracy and citizenship (Blakely and Snyder 1997). Gated communities clearly provide a market good with a particular set of characteristics that are highly valued by many consumers in the marketplace. In that sense, they provide room for many of the equity refugees fleeing metropolitan areas for exurbia. But as Ed Blakely asked about new towns proposed for the Central Valley in the early 1990s, "room for whom?" (1992). The marketing materials for these communities emphasize personal safety and social, demographic, economic, spatial, and architectural homogeneity. I tried to take a dozen graduate students through Lake Wildwood in 1993 while on a class field trip to study alternative patterns of human settlement in Nevada County, but the security officer wouldn't let us enter. I told him that we simply wanted to drive through the community and stop a few times to look at the street layout and home designs. I showed him my business card and explained that I had grown up in western Nevada County. "I'm afraid I just can't let you in here," he replied, "because I don't know for sure what you might do once you get inside. You might talk to some residents, and then they might complain to us."[36] Paranoia breeds paranoia, and gated communities replicate the mental attitudes their residents sought to escape when they left suburbia.

Other factors differentiate gated communities, however, in their relationship to the larger community. Lake of the Pines residents overwhelmingly voted to redirect local taxes toward roads in the March 1996 vote on Measure F in Nevada County, for example, while Lake Wildwood residents were split.[37] This reflects in part the closer integration of Lake Wildwood with the rest of the community, meaning that the Lake Wildwood residents would be more directly affected by shortfalls in other government programs such as libraries, social services, and so on. Lake of the Pines residents are more closely integrated with Auburn and Placer County, however, where many of them work and shop. Lake of the Pines also has higher household incomes and fewer retirees, and the community generally votes more conservatively than Lake Wildwood on a wide range of issues. It is therefore dangerous to generalize about gated communities without understanding their individual characteristics.

Large Single-Family Lots with Private On-Site Infrastructure

A plurality of exurbanites live in one of the first three settlement patterns described above, for 39 percent of Sierra Nevada residents lived on less than one acre in 1990 (but this totaled only 89 square miles of the 32,005 square miles in the region). Most of the land area, in contrast, is probably in the fifth settlement pattern described below: open space, agriculture, and forestry uses (74 percent of the Sierra Nevada land base had less than one housing unit per square mile). Most of the land area in exurban regions directly affected by human settlement is, however, probably settled in a pattern of large single-family lots with private on-site infrastructure. About 21 percent of Sierra Nevada residents lived within a density of one to four acres per dwelling unit in 1990 (on 209 square miles), while another 31 percent lived within an average density of between four and thirty-two acres per housing unit (affecting another 1,443 square miles). The latter therefore accounts for five-sixths of all land area settled in 1990 with at least one housing unit per thirty-two acres.[38] This is an extremely popular form of settlement, for it offers privacy as well as direct contact with the country ideal for the former urbanite.

Ironically, it can also have significant negative effects on the environment through habitat fragmentation and potential contamination from septic system operation. As described above, the large lot size is primarily a function of the public health need to separate on-site water supplies from on-site sewage disposal through septic tank and leach field systems. This requirement has resulted in minimum lot sizes of from one to five acres per dwelling unit (about three hundred to fifteen hundred persons per square mile).[39] Many of the grandfathered subdivisions approved under less stringent standards allow development at densities of up to four units per acre with on-site water and septic disposal, offering a bare minimum of adequate area for leach field drainage. Based on experience throughout the Sierra Nevada, however, many can now be expected to fail under soil, slope, or hydrologic conditions that are less than optimal (Lauer 1995a; 1995e; 1995f; Hanner 1997; Marie Davis 1994). In some cases this will preclude further development at the high densities allowable under current land-use designations. In other cases, septic system or well failures will lead to establishment of community water supplies and/or public sewer systems. This could then lead to higher-density infill development of these substandard lots. In either case there can still be significant social, economic, and ecological effects. Unfortunately, these are not analyzed in advance for most developments.

More than four thousand detailed test pits were dug at the Auburn Lake Trails subdivision in El Dorado County during the 1970s after septic failures raised concerns about the capacity of the local soils to support the proposed level of development. The tests determined that nearly fifteen hundred of the original lots could not support development. The original developers were then compelled to buy out landowners and consolidate lots to create feasible building sites (Marie Davis 1994). The scope of this testing and the degree of inadequate site design is not simply a relic of the early 1970s, however, or simply a function of lot sizes that are much too small. Fundamentally it reflects a failure to consider natural factors in the design of developments. The 7,771-acre Cinabarr development was once slated to produce thousands of houses on the old Cook Ranch in El Dorado County, but it was scaled back to 569 houses on five-acre lots in the early 1990s (McKuen 1994). Subsequent site analysis for the EIR required under CEQA determined that 40 percent of the field sites tested did not meet minimum soil percolation requirements (Fugro-McClelland [West], Inc. 1994). Moreover, water supply and access restrictions raised fundamental concerns about the capacity to protect public health and safety in the case of a wildland fire on the steep, dry site. Despite the designation of five-acre parcels in the general plan, therefore, serious questions remain as to whether Cinabarr can be developed safely at that density. This is true for many exurban parcels in this general size class.[40]

This pattern of development accounts for a significant fraction of the total land area developed to date in Nevada and El Dorado Counties. Parcels in the size class of one to five acres per dwelling unit accounted for 11 percent of the land area in improved parcels (7 percent of all land area) in Nevada County and 10 percent of the land area in improved parcels (5 percent of all land area) in El Dorado County in 1992. Proposed county general plan requirements call for minimum parcel sizes that would be in this range for on-site infrastructure, so this size class is expected to account for at least 12 percent of Nevada County's total land area and 3 percent of El Dorado County's total land area, under build-out of the 1994 draft general plan updates for each county. Parcels in the size class of five to ten acres per dwelling unit, ten to twenty acres per dwelling unit, and twenty to forty acres per dwelling unit account for a much smaller fraction of the total parcels but a much higher fraction of total private land in 1992 in the two counties. Each of these size and dwelling-unit-density classes has different ecological effects associated with development. Significant variation within each size class also exists because of different management practices and behavior of landowners, however, so it is difficult to generalize ecological effects by average density or average parcel size class (Duane 1993b; Fortmann and Huntsinger 1989). The SNEP assessment work by Joe McBride and his colleagues highlights some general relationships that suggest the scale of effects (McBride et al. 1996), but unfortunately we do not yet have a clear understanding of these relationships.

Because of the grandfathered substandard lots approved before current standards, however, any analysis based on allowable densities alone is likely to underestimate the number and land area of parcels with on-site well water and/or septic systems. Conversely, including all existing smaller parcels (which allow higher densities) is likely to overstate the dominance of this pattern, since many of them are unlikely to be developed as a result of other site constraints.[41] The effects of large-lot sprawl must be analyzed in relationship to the specific ecological features of an area.

Rural Agriculture, Natural Resource, and Open Space Lands

Less than 13 percent of Sierra Nevada residents lived at an average density of less than one unit per 32 acres in 1990, but most of the region's landscape (74 percent) is in lower-density land uses that are still managed primarily for agriculture or natural-resources-commodity extraction. Nevertheless, the primary economic value of these lands is increasingly in their function as part of a landscape of visual consumption rather than commodity production. Population densities on these lands are typically no more than one structure per 40 to 160 acres, or from ten to two hundred persons per square mile. Some rural ranches have as few as five people per 10,000 acres, or less than one person per three square miles.

Agricultural productivity on these lands is often threatened by the encroachment of exurban ranchette development, however, as the new exurban residents often impose new restrictions on traditional agricultural practices as a result of the spillover effects of those productive activities, such as noise and pesticides, on the consumptive enjoyment of amenities in the residential regions. This follows Rudel's model for increasing conflicts over land use practices with increasing density and development. These conflicts have led to the passage of "right-to-farm ordinances" in a number of rural counties, which restrict residents' rights to make nuisance complaints against long-standing agricultural practices. The economic viability of many agricultural lands is also threatened by exurban development, however, as rising land prices make agriculture an increasingly marginal activity when compared to the opportunity costs of subdividing and developing the land (Hargrave 1993; Hart 1992; American Farmland Trust 1995; Lapping et al. 1989). Moreover, diminishing agricultural activity in exurban regions can reduce the economies of scale in supplying remaining farmers, increasing the cost and decreasing the availability of farm equipment and related supplies, such as feed.[42] A similar phenomenon can occur with management of natural resources, such as timber, on private lands, although public land and resource management policy is often more important to the viability of local natural resources extraction industries in the Sierra Nevada and in general throughout the rural and exurban West.[43] Public land and resource managers clearly face a new and less supportive sociopolitical context for traditional commodity extraction activities as the private lands adjacent to public lands undergo ecotransformation.

Both agricultural and natural resources lands function effectively as de facto public open space for many of the new exurban residents, offering scenic and aesthetic as well as ecological benefits. These values are probably the primary driver of and value in agricultural preservation efforts in suburban and exurban regions. *Countryside* preservation is the real goal; *agricultural* preservation is simply a politically attractive rallying cry that invokes the self-sufficient, yeoman farmer and democratic ideals of Jefferson (Kemmis 1990). An inscription above Hilgard Hall on the University of California at Berkeley campus proclaims the purpose of the former College of Agriculture as "to rescue for human society the native values for rural life," for rural values are widely revered in our Culture.[44] The focus on agricultural production also taps into the folk economics that Thomas Power discussed: agriculture is considered primary, so it should and must be protected (1996a). Moreover, environmentalists often argue that the productive soils underlying agricultural lands are a nonrenewable resource that will forever be lost if an area is paved over for new subdivisions (Goldberg 1996). This is rarely the case in the Sierra Nevada foothills, however, even if it has been the case in places like the Santa Clara, Napa, Sonoma, and Central Valleys. It was also once true for the San Fernando Valley and Orange County, but the agricultural productivity of the Los Angeles basin was not enough to stem its loss (Davis 1990).

These amenity and ecological values are not easily captured by landowners, however, creating a conflict between long-term agricultural and natural resource landowners and other community members' interests. The greatest beneficiaries of countryside and agricultural preservation efforts are typically *not* the farmers or owners of agricultural land, but the rest of the community that derives public good benefits associated with the aesthetic and ecological goods and services provided by those private lands. Agriculturalists beyond the range of speculative development are also likely to support such efforts, for they yield marginal benefits, such as lowered property taxes, at very low opportunity cost.[45]

Large landowners within the range of speculative development—for example, those whose lands are likely to be developed within the next ten to twenty years—are likely to oppose such preservation efforts despite a long personal history in agriculture and/or natural resources and a commitment to agricultural preservation. Their children rarely want to continue in this difficult line of work, and they recognize that selling their land to developers is the most effective way to transfer its value to the next generation and relieve themselves of the uncertainties of agriculture. Despite their abstract support for preservation, then, their personal interest in realizing economic gains will often lead them to oppose such efforts. Social conflict is therefore likely to continue between the proponents of and the supposed beneficiaries of such efforts unless and until the true beneficiaries can structure mechanisms to compensate existing landowners for reduced speculative land values. The long-term landowners with speculative potential for land development often have significant social, economic, and political influence in county governments that control land-use decisions and are a key impediment to countryside preservation efforts. They are the core of the local GOP network and typically have disproportionate political influence on the board of supervisors.

Mechanisms for compensating private landowners for public benefits can range from direct monetary compensation for conservation easements to innovative open space development designs that still allow landowners to realize development values from their land. These and other approaches are discussed in more detail below.

CONSERVATION BIOLOGY AND LANDSCAPE ECOLOGY

Our ecological knowledge is both growing and changing, but there is much that we do not know or understand about the complex processes of ecology (Grime 1997). Like the word *economics,* the word *ecology* comes from the Greek root word *oikos,* meaning "household." But economics limits itself to analysis of activities within the human household, while ecology takes a broader perspective on what constitutes the household. Ecology is the study of the relationship between organisms and their environment, which includes both the physical environment and other biological components of the ecological system. The term was coined by Ernst Haeckel in 1866 and has a specific scientific meaning that is slightly different from that used by the popular ecology movement a century later.[46] The latter is more generally referred to now as the environmental movement, and its members are known as environmentalists (Gottlieb 1993). Ecologists, in contrast, are scientists who study the relationship between organisms and their environment. They may or may not be aligned with the broader social movement we know as the environmental movement. The ecological effects of human activities can therefore be studied systematically and scientifically without being colored by a political or social agenda. The selection of research questions and the interpretation of research results clearly have social and political consequences, of course, and they are undoubtedly influenced by the social and political context within which ecological questions are debated. But ecology is still a science, and its methods are subject to the rigorous rules of scientific methodology.

Several new branches of ecology and biology have emerged in the past decade. Conservation biology has blossomed as a subbranch of biology concerned specifically with the conservation of native biological diversity. The Society for Conservation Biology was founded in 1985 and now publishes a widely respected refereed journal, *Conservation Biology*, for more than six thousand members (Jasczak 1996). The field of landscape ecology has been evolving in Europe and the United Kingdom for some time, but it burst onto the American scene in 1986 with the publication of the book *Landscape Ecology* by Richard Forman and Michel Godron. The International Association for Landscape Ecology now sponsors an annual conference and publishes the refereed journal *Landscape Ecology*. Finally, the field of restoration ecology has had its own journal, *Restoration Ecology*, since 1993. The Society for Restoration Ecology was founded in 1989 and now has more than twenty-two hundred members. New college and university courses and textbooks have also been developed in all of these subfields. Systematic research is beginning to answer critical questions about how human activities affect ecological systems and individual biological components of those systems as well as how those systems can be restored after they have been degraded. It is an exciting shift in the direction of science toward the solution of environmental problems. That shift reflects growing concern by scientists about the effects of human activities on the global life-support systems of the planet (Clark and Munn 1986; Clark 1989).

This concern reflects the failure of traditional conservation approaches to protect and maintain native biological diversity. Much of the concern about biodiversity loss has focused on the tropics, where rain forest destruction accelerated the loss of species in the 1980s. E. O. Wilson estimated a .63 percent annual reduction in the area of tropical rain forest in 1992, which his model estimates will extinguish or doom .5 percent of the region's species per year. Half of the planet's tropical rain forests remaining in 1992 are expected to be gone by the year 2022, resulting in extinction of 10–22 percent of all existing rain forest species. Such a rate of species loss places us firmly in an extinction crisis that matches any other ecological crisis in the earth's history (Wilson 1988; 1989).

Many species are also threatened in the temperate zones, however, including the rural and exurban West (Newmark 1986). Despite passage of the Endangered Species Act (ESA) in 1973, the number of species facing likely extinction has grown at a faster pace than the U.S. Fish and Wildlife Service has been able to list species as threatened or endangered under the Act. The loss of global biological diversity is considered by many scientists (myself included) to be the most difficult and pervasive environmental problem on the planet (Wilson 1988; 1989). That concern led to development and adoption of a global framework treaty on biodiversity at the Earth Summit in June 1992. Under the Bush administration, the United States initially opposed the treaty, but President Bill Clinton signed it in 1993. The Senate later refused to ratify the treaty in 1994, so the United States is not yet an official party to the treaty.[47] The treaty creates incentives for the protection of biological diversity through technology transfer and funding for the protection of biologically rich landscapes.

Most of the debate about biodiversity has centered on avoiding the further loss of species. Biodiversity is not simply measured by the number of species, however, and the single-species focus of the ESA has distracted our attention from the importance of biodiversity in a variety of other dimensions. Biodiversity operates at multiple scales (Wilson 1989; Quammen 1996; Keystone Policy Dialogue 1991; California Resources Agency 1991). At the finest scale, genetic diversity within populations of a particular species is important. Within a particular species, it is important to maintain a diversity of populations of that species that may have adapted to a wide range of locally specific ecological conditions. Individual species are then important to the protection of overall biological diversity and are currently the focus of most of our attention. Finally, maintaining a diversity of ecological communities and their complex internal and external interactions with other communities is important. Only species diversity receives protection under the ESA. Moreover, the Act's policies and restrictions are triggered only after a species has been listed. This emergency-room-treatment strategy fails to include any preventative policies. The recovery of listed species has consequently been limited, with only six species delisted as a result of recovery since passage of the ESA in 1973. Another seven species have been delisted because of extinction (Cheever 1996), while the vast majority continue to flirt with extinction.[48]

Maintaining any two individual species is not enough, then, if their natural distribution and abundance are restricted in such a way that they no longer interact with each other within a local ecological system. There would be a loss of important information and functional relationships. This means that simply maintaining species viability is inadequate for long-term ecosystem health. Similarly, maintaining species viability but losing subspecies or population-specific genetic characteristics reduces the content of biological and ecological information in the overall ecological system (Millar 1996). This is why biologists and ecologists are concerned about the replacement of natural trout or salmon strains with hatchery-produced trout or salmon. Those hatchery-produced individuals contain less genetic variability because of the homogeneity of their gene source. They also contain less information about the relationship between trout or salmon and the local conditions of specific streams and aquatic systems. In the context of a highly variable and changing world, that information could be critical to the long-term survival of both the species and the overall function of an entire ecological system. Seasonal and annual climatic variations favor some subspecies over others, while global climate change could lead to conditions intolerable for all but a few populations of a particular species. Biological richness therefore exists at multiple scales, and its ultimate value to ecological function cannot be established in advance.

California's Biodiversity Council has prepared a nice graphic to illustrate these different levels of biodiversity. It shows that biodiversity occurs at multiple levels and that conservation of biodiversity requires protection at *all* levels: genetic, species, populations, communities, ecosystems, landscapes, and regions (California Resources Agency 1991). Focusing on species diversity alone is inadequate. The levels of biodiversity delineated in the biodiversity memorandum of understanding of 1991 are as follows:

GENETIC DIVERSITY
Diversity within and among populations
Variety of genotypes
Genetic flexibility
Genetic integrity

SPECIES/POPULATIONS
Diversity within and among ecosystems
Rarity
Demographics
Viability
Productivity
Habitat requirements
Spatial requirements (i.e., dispersal)
Temporal requirements (i.e., seasonal behavior)

COMMUNITIES/ECOSYSTEMS
Diversity within and among landscapes
Richness (i.e., number of species and/or habitats)
Structure (i.e., variety of successional stages)
Composition (i.e., variety of trophic levels)
Function (i.e., nutrient cycling, energy flow, species interactions)

LANDSCAPES/REGIONS
Variety and number of communities and ecosystems
Spatial patterns (i.e., mosaic of ecosystems)
Connectivity (linkages) among ecosystems
Catastrophe insurance (i.e., replication of ecosystems)[49]

The foundation for much of this current work in both conservation biology and landscape ecology was laid with the publication of the book *Island Biogeography* in 1967 by Robert MacArthur and E. O. Wilson. Island biogeography theory has been made accessible to nonscientists by David Quammen in his 1996 book, *The Song of the Dodo: Island Biogeography in an Age of Extinction*. The theory of island biogeography states that the viability of specific populations of organisms on island systems is a function primarily of the size of the island and its proximity to the mainland. Smaller islands support smaller populations, increasing the risks of extinction resulting from catastrophic events or inbreeding. Close proximity to the mainland increases the likelihood of recolonization following the collapse of an island's population and increases diversity within the island population's gene pool as a result of gene inflow and outflow between the island and mainland. This theory structured a framework for determining the minimum viable population that differentiates between these different sources of local extinction risk (MacArthur and Wilson 1967; Gilpin and Soule 1986). Empirical application of the theory to a data set of islands with varying sizes and distances from the mainland also allows the development of some generalized conclusions about the effects of size and proximity on both local extinction risk and local biological diversity. In general, the theory predicts that a reduction in island size (for a given proximity to the mainland) will reduce the number of species on the island. Changes in proximity will also affect the number of species and the probability of local extinction of a population. There is a complex relationship between island size and proximity to the mainland, however, so it is not a linear relationship between proximity and extinction risk. These are nevertheless the dominant factors for most species.[50]

Landscape ecology takes the theory of island biogeography and applies it to terrestrial landscapes. This is an important extension that has direct bearing on land and resource management decisions throughout the rural and exurban West. Like biodiversity and ecosystems (O'Neill et al. 1986; Bailey 1996), landscape ecology operates at a variety of spatial and temporal scales. Short-term, local phenomena may exhibit one type of pattern, for example, while another pattern emerges across a larger-scale (coarser-resolution) landscape over a longer period of time. These patterns are the heart of landscape ecology. With the shift of attention from the species to the landscape, structural characteristics are evaluated to determine their relationship to ecological function. Patches of habitat function like islands within a matrix of other patterns and processes, while patches of similar habitat types are connected through corridors. The edges between habitat types constitute rich ecotones that also have spillover effects from each habitat type into the adjacent patch of a different habitat type. The three dominant elements of landscape ecology are the *patch,* the *edge,* and the *corridor.* Following the principles of island biogeography, patches (islands) are connected to other, larger patches (the mainland) by corridors (proximity and contiguity) across a matrix of other habitat types (the ocean or surrounding sea). The important distinction in terrestrial systems is that a habitat type can function in multiple roles for different ecological functions. The "matrix" for one species may be a "patch" of primary habitat for another species, for example, while a linear or connecting system of habitat patches may constitute a "corridor" at a particular level of resolution. The "edge" of a patch or corridor also depends on the scale of resolution: a freeway may constitute an important edge of habitat for a mountain lion, for example, but it may not impede connectivity for a red-tailed hawk. The specific functional role of ecological elements therefore depends on species-level interpretations of the landscape. These in turn reflect scale-dependent characterizations of the landscape to discern patterns that affect processes at a variety of scales. A given landscape might be characterized differently for the mountain lion and the red-tailed hawk.

This scale-dependent approach to landscape characterization and analysis is the source of both power and uncertainty in landscape ecology. Organisms are clearly defined, self-contained physical units with clear boundaries. Species are less clearly defined, but the capacity to reproduce young who are in turn capable of reproducing has served as a useful threshold criteria for distinguishing between species. The criteria for determining the appropriate scale for landscape-scale characterizations and analyses are less clear. A two-by-four along the edge of a wet hiking trail constitutes a barrier and edge for a newt, yet many analyses rely on satellite imagery where the smallest pixel represents one square kilometer. There are no clear criteria for determining the appropriate scale for landscape-level analysis. At the same time, the lack of clear criteria encourages creative exploration of landscape ecology at a variety of spatial and temporal scales in a *search* for pattern and structure. This exploratory search may help generate new theories about ecological function and processes, which will in turn help to establish clear criteria for determining the appropriate scale for landscape characterization and analysis. This is still a young field, and we have far more questions than answers at this point. Those answers we do have reflect the narrow and limited scope of the questions we have asked and the tools we have for analysis. In many cases, our focus on the individual elements of the landscape or ecological system limits our ability to understand the landscape or ecological system as a whole.

Ecologist Greg Greenwood (1995) demonstrates this bias with his brilliant analysis of Vincent van Gogh's famous painting *Starry Night*. He deconstructs the complex painting into a series of images, each emphasizing either a different color or feature of the image (e.g., the moon and the stars, the sky, the clouds, or the terrestrial landscape). The painting loses something important when you see only the blues, for example, or only the yellows and oranges. Focusing on particular features also masks important information contained in the original painting. Each of the images helps us understand the role of the individual elements, but alone they still lack something. Van Gogh's brilliant painting is much more than the sum of its parts. The same is true of landscapes—for Greenwood has deconstructed the painting into its essential elements in the same way ecologists deconstruct landscapes into isolated elements. He demonstrates that we cannot understand or appreciate the subtle complexities of either paintings or landscapes by isolating their constituent elements and studying them independently.

The interactions between these elements are lost unless we can somehow integrate them into a coherent whole. It is impossible to appreciate the complex meaning of the painting without seeing the elements integrated in space and time. If this is true of paintings, why shouldn't it also be true of landscapes? Certainly landscapes are at least as complex as paintings. Art historians and painters would never approach analysis of art through the techniques that Greenwood uses, however, without also grounding those techniques in the context of an overall theory of art as an integration of those elements. Scientific reductionism, in contrast, has focused most of our historic attention in ecology on the individual elements of landscapes and ecological systems. As a result, we understand well how some individual species function but still do not fully understand how they interact within a landscape at multiple scales. Landscape ecology attempts to integrate those elements in order to understand the context in which they all occur and function.

Greenwood, who lives in the Sierra Nevada foothills in western El Dorado County, also illustrates the importance of spatial scale through another presentation that he calls "Falling into California." He illustrates how different features stand out in a landscape at different scales of resolution. At the coarsest scale, the Sierra Nevada mountains, the Central Valley, and the coastal areas stand out as separate regions. At a finer level of resolution, the urban areas stand out from the nonurban areas. The next level of resolution recognizes differences in vegetation within the nonurban areas. Individual trees can be distinguished at the most detailed level of resolution. This approach can be carried further to distinguish between young trees and old trees, spring growth from fall leaf litter, or nesting habitat quality or timber value. The key point is that sometimes we cannot see the forest for the trees—and likewise we sometimes see only the forest and fail to see the trees. Neither perspective is "right"; each reflects a particular spatial and temporal scale of resolution. All are necessary to understand the information contained in the landscape.

Limited application of minimum-viable-population analysis to extant populations of terrestrial species has yielded some alarming conclusions about the viability of many familiar species in the rural and exurban West. These analyses raise fundamental questions about the appropriate scale of conservation and strategies necessary to protect native biological diversity. In particular, William Newmark's Ph.D. dissertation and a subsequent article in *Nature* showed in 1987 that the loss of biodiversity at the species level in national parks of the American West was directly correlated with both the size of the parks and their age since establishment. Newmark examined fourteen western parks and park clusters, ranging from relatively tiny Bryce Canyon National Park, Lassen Volcanic National Park, and Zion National Park to the Yellowstone–Grand Teton cluster. The former three had lost close to 40 percent of their larger mammal species, while the latter—which is twenty times the size of Zion National Park—had lost only the wolf (Quammen 1996; Newmark 1995; 1987; 1986). Newmark's study quickly raised the specter of long-term depletion of the national park's ecological assemblages and functions just as other "island" studies showed similar results consistent with island biogeography theory (Verner 1997; Diamond 1984; Hope 1973). This raised new questions about how the "sea" of surrounding land was being managed as well as the viability of any biodiversity conservation strategy focused primarily on protected-area refugia (Verner 1997; Verner et al. 1992; Thomas et al. 1990).

For species protected under the ESA, such as the grizzly bear (*Ursus arctos horribilis*) in the Greater Yellowstone Ecosystem, the current levels of the population are probably insufficient to maintain the population over a hundred-year time frame with a 95 percent probability (Shaffer 1992a). These were the quantitative criteria selected by Mark Shaffer for his Ph.D. dissertation in 1978 when he used minimum-viable-population analysis to evaluate the probability of grizzly bear extirpation (Quammen 1996). Meeting these goals would require a minimum population of approximately two thousand individuals. The *effective* population size is much smaller, however, a result of the presence of nonbreeding individuals in the overall population size target (Shaffer 1978). This is an important distinction between the overall N and the effective N that drives up the number of individuals required in a population to achieve minimum viable populations. The land area required to support such a large population in the Greater Yellowstone Ecosystem is far in excess of the 3,472 square miles (2,222,000 acres) in Yellowstone National Park (Sunset Magazine 1970). Integrated management of federal, state, and private lands adjacent to the park is therefore necessary if grizzly bear viability is to be ensured. It may also be necessary to implement some of

MAP 6.2.   National park "islands" used in Newmark's study of island biogeography.

the principles of restoration ecology to create a landscape mosaic that can support grizzly bears in the Greater Yellowstone Ecosystem.

Similar efforts could be necessary to support far-ranging mammals in the Sierra Nevada, such as the fisher (*Martes pennanti*), marten (*Martes americana*), or wolverine (*Gulo gulo*) (Natural Resources Defense Council 1994; Graber 1996). Recent declines in the bighorn sheep (*Ovis canadensis*) population also illustrate the fragility of isolated populations in the Sierra Nevada (Nolte 1996). Such popula-

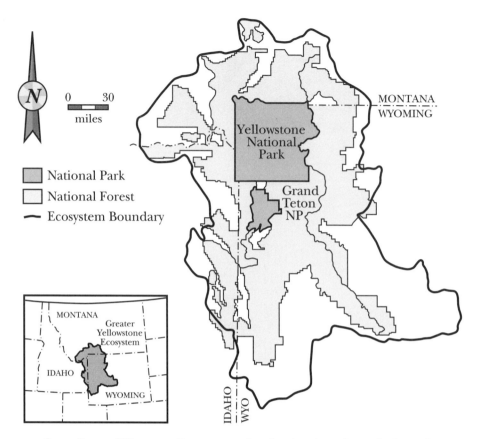

MAP 6.3.   Greater Yellowstone Ecosystem and national parks or forests in the region.

tions are vulnerable to a single catastrophic event because of their isolation from a metapopulation of genetic material that could revive the population following a collapse. Restoration of the bighorn sheep and other wildlife (including much smaller creatures, such as the California red-legged frog [*Rana aurora*]) therefore requires an integrated strategy that cuts across drainage basins and ownership boundaries and encompasses isolated populations.[51]

Restoration ecology integrates the biological and physical elements of ecological systems. While conservation biologists and most landscape ecologists focus on living systems, those systems function within a physical system structured by geology, soils, hydrology, climate, and a wide range of other factors underlying the ecological system. Much of the attention of restoration ecologists has focused on the relationship between those physical processes and the function of the biological elements in the overall system. Restoration ecology also goes beyond preservation or protection of native biodiversity to proactively restore the capacity of systems to support natural ecological systems. This was what the noted conservationist David Brower called for in the 1980s, as did John Berger in his summary of these ideas in *Restoring the Earth* (1985). Groups like the Urban Creeks Council have subsequently applied the concepts through the "daylighting" of formerly concrete-covered Cordinices Creek in Berkeley and the long-maligned Los Angeles River. A renaissance of social rediscovery of the historic ecological richness of urban areas and other degraded systems has accompanied the birth of restoration ecology.

The techniques of restoration ecology are in many cases quite decidedly unnatural, however, involving extensive and intensive intervention by humans to reverse and/or alter historical trends and conditions. This intervention is usually in the context of intervention in a system that has led to the degradation of natural processes in the past. The ultimate goal of restoration ecology is to reestablish natural systems that can function without continued human intervention. Until that occurs, however, human intervention is often required to restabilize systems that have been radically altered by humans. Culture helps to produce and reproduce Nature in accordance with Culture's needs.

Which brings us to the human element. There is one common thread in the nearly simultaneous emergence of and development of conservation biology, landscape ecology, and restoration ecology: an increasing recognition that humans have become a significant force in ecological systems at a variety of spatial and temporal scales. In some cases, human activity is the dominant force affecting the structure and function of landscapes. An example might be the influence of land development on the wetlands of a small drainage in the Sierra Nevada foothills of western Nevada County. In other cases, human activities have simply reached a scale and scope that makes them an important variable in all ecological systems. An example of this type of effect could be depletion of the stratospheric ozone layer resulting from the release of chlorofluorocarbons into the atmosphere. The potential effect on global climate change associated with greenhouse gas emissions is the most far-reaching of these more pervasive effects, leading writer Bill McKibben to declare that we have reached "the end of nature," in a book by that title and a series of *New Yorker* articles in 1989. Peter Vitousek and his colleagues at the Center for Conservation Biology at Stanford University calculated that human beings were directly appropriating nearly 40 percent of net photosynthetic productivity on the planet in 1986 (Vitousek et al. 1993). Since then the population of the planet has swelled by nearly a billion, placing further strains on ecological systems.

This represents a new phase in the relationship between Nature and Culture. We are no longer a minor player on the vast stage of a planet rich in natural ecological processes. We have taken on the additional roles of playwright, director, and set designer. And Nature is no longer just the setting for our performance, but a partner with unpredictable qualities and a tendency not to learn its lines as instructed. We must therefore turn more of our attention to the complex relationship between Nature and Culture. This deepening understanding must parallel the growth in our knowledge of ecological processes. Neither biology nor ecology can be studied in isolation from the relationship between those complex systems and human societies (Orr 1992). An integrated approach to the social and natural sciences is necessary to analyze processes driving the coevolution of Nature and Culture.

ECOLOGICAL IMPLICATIONS OF EXURBAN GROWTH

We must also break new ground to evaluate the ecological implications of exurban growth. Systematic field-based empirical work has been limited to a few poorly funded studies. In the early 1990s, Greg Greenwood and Robin Marose at the Strategic Planning Program of the California Department of Forestry completed an important landscape-scale analysis of the possible effects of human settlement on landscape patterns in the Sierra Nevada foothills, for example, but their analysis did not distinguish between different types or patterns of exurban development. All human settlement at a density of at least one dwelling unit per forty acres, which is the minimum polygon size that could be handled in the California wildlife-habitat relationships (WHR) model, was treated as urban in the study. A composite of several vegetation sources was then used to characterize the landscape in terms of twenty-two current vegetation and habitat types. Based on that definition, build-out of the former general plans for Nevada, Placer, El Dorado, Amador, Calaveras, and Tuolumne Counties would increase the urbanized area of the 4.8-million-acre region by more than 1,200 percent. The spatial analysis used a Geographic Information System (GIS) that allowed the researchers to identify which habitat types would be most affected by development. The study also introduced an important new tool (the "landscape evaluation module") for GIS-based landscape analysis that characterizes landscapes in at least four dimensions. These include 1) changes in area for different habitat types, 2) changes in the distribution of patch sizes within each habitat type, 3) changes in edge and adjacency relationships between each possible combination of habitat types, and 4) the contiguity or fragmentation of each habitat type at different levels of resolution. The results of the first-order analysis (of changes in land area) show that there could be significant changes in total area for each of twenty-two habitat types in the Sierra Nevada case study (Greenwood and Marose 1993).[52]

The second-order indicators show how the specific pattern of development is likely to change the distribution of habitat patch sizes, an important determinant of population viability. It is still difficult to interpret these metrics, but they show how the average patch size and the distribution of patch sizes may change as a result of modifications in land use. This may prove particularly important for

TABLE 6.1   Changes in Habitat Area by WHR Type under Gold Country
and Mother Lode General Plan Build-Out

Habitat Type	Build-Out Acres	Present Acres	Present % of Total	Build-Out % of Current
Alpine dwarf shrub	7,338	7,338	0	100
Agriculture	142,653	450,597	9	32
Annual grass	53,426	81,601	2	65
Barren	41,479	42,143	8	98
Blue oak–foothill pine	95,645	156,048	3	61
Blue oak woodland	32,188	59,488	1	54
Chamise-redshank	103,012	161,853	3	64
Interior and/or canyon live oak	224,685	485,871	9	46
Jeffrey pine	45,980	48,948	1	94
Lodgepole pine	54,536	56,336	1	97
Mixed chaparral	164,975	243,945	5	68
Mixed conifer	1,598,413	1,828,288	35	87
Montane chaparral	59,366	62,202	1	95
Montane hardwood	278,106	305,894	6	91
Nonforested wetland	2,427	2,678	0	91
Red fir	399,795	404,659	8	99
Subalpine conifer	30,528	30,558	1	100
Sagebrush	31,845	35,851	1	89
Urban-agriculture	10,391	30,536	1	34
Urban	1,287,459	104,574	2	1231
Valley-foothill hardwood	31,857	87,971	2	36
Water	160,199	163,012	3	98

SOURCE: Greenwood and Marose 1993 (Table 2).

species that require larger patches in order to make use of a given habitat. The total area of a given habitat may decrease by 50 percent, for example, but the total area in patches greater than some minimum size may decrease by 80 percent because the remaining patches of habitat are smaller and more isolated. This second-order indicator may therefore be more important than the first-order indicator, but it is difficult to interpret at this point except in a species-specific context.

The third-order indicators show how edge and adjacency relationships may change. These can be important determinants of the likelihood of particular types of effects from interaction between humans and particular habitat types. A blue oak woodland may be entered easily by humans on motorcycles for recreation or by dogs from a new subdivision chasing deer, for example, while a ponderosa pine

TABLE 6.2 Changes in the Edge/Adjacency Relationships
under Gold Country and Mother Lode General Plan Build-Out

Habitat Pair	Current Proportion (% of Total Edge)	Build-Out % of Current
Adjacency Decreased by More Than 50%		
Barren-nonforested wetland	0.01% of total edge	0% of current
Blue oak–mixed conifer	0.01% of total edge	0% of current
Montane hardwood–valley foothill hardwood	0.04% of total edge	0% of current
Agriculture–annual grass	0.81% of total edge	38% of current
Agriculture–interior and/or canyon live oak	2.79% of total edge	36% of current
Agriculture–mixed chaparral	1.36% of total edge	42% of current
Blue oak foothill pine–interior and/or canyon live oak	0.56% of total edge	46% of current
Blue oak–chamise redshank chaparral	0.78% of total edge	50% of current
Adjacency Increased by More Than 150%		
Urban–blue oak foothill pine	0.13% of total edge	892% of current
Urban–blue oak woodland	0.03% of total edge	1133% of current
Urban–chamise redshank chaparral	0.15% of total edge	693% of current
Urban–interior and/or canyon live oak	0.90% of total edge	388% of current
Urban–mixed conifer	1.62% of total edge	383% of current

SOURCE: Greenwood and Marose 1993 (Table 3).

forest may present a greater fire danger for an adjacent development than a foothill grassland habitat type. The model estimates changes in the total lineal distance of adjacent edge for each of the habitat combinations. Once again, their interpretation requires a context-specific question about the effects of specific activities along a specific ecotone type.

Finally, a fourth-order indicator of landscape structure is contiguity or connectedness. Depending on the level of resolution, of course, a given landscape may be characterized as highly fragmented or as having a high level of connectivity. Greenwood and Marose evaluated contiguity with grid cells of one square kilometer to identify larger landscape units. This analysis highlighted how larger landscape features, such as Interstate 80, U.S. Highway 50, and the steep, natural canyons of the American River, could isolate otherwise-similar habitat types. Only four large (but relatively isolated) blue oak woodland meta-patches of habitat would remain at build-out in comparison to a more connected landscape before development (Greenwood 1992–97). The implications of such isolation will vary with specific ecological processes, and connectedness will vary for different groups of species.

The scale of this analysis does not tell us very much about how alternative patterns of human settlement affect specific changes in habitat structure, composition, or function. Joe McBride has led several studies to characterize the effects of human settlement on forest structure and composition in South Lake Tahoe, Bear Valley, and several foothill communities in the Sierra Nevada (McBride and Jacobs 1979; 1986; McBride and Woodard 1990; McBride 1991–97; McBride et al. 1996). McBride and his colleagues have generally found that both the structure and composition of the forest changed dramatically after human settlement and that the real effects of settlement came through vegetative manipulation over a long period of time. Forest canopy and tree density generally decreased in all vegetation types, and species richness generally increased in the oak woodland and ponderosa pine types. Increased species richness was primarily associated with the planting of nonnative species for ornamental purposes (McBride et al. 1996).

McBride's work gives us important information about the influence of exurban settlement patterns on forest structure and composition, but it still leaves us far short of a comprehensive characterization of the ecological effects of alternative settlement patterns at a variety of housing densities. Considerably more fieldwork is necessary in order to determine how build-out of the exurban landscape would affect vegetation and habitat. Those studies will need to provide a better understanding of how behavioral differences among landowners may also affect variability in management regimes and ecological effects within each density size-class and vegetation or habitat type. We cannot presume the effects to be consistent based only on the common denominator of settlement density (Fortmann and Huntsinger 1989; Forero et al. 1992).

More detailed work has been completed in this regard for the Southern California coastal sage scrub, home of the coastal California gnatcatcher (*Polioptila californica californica*). The potential listing of the gnatcatcher under the ESA threatened to stop hundreds of millions of dollars of rapid real estate development in the late 1980s and early 1990s (Mann and Plummer 1995; Stevens 1996; 1997a). This led to greater interest in funding biological research as part of the habitat conservation planning efforts of developers, environmentalists, and local, state, and federal governments (Beatley 1994b; Stevens 1997a). Such a crisis has not yet precipitated similar interest in the Sierra Nevada foothills, despite the potential for saving money in the long run.[53] Ironically, there is very little funding support for proactive preventative analysis that could minimize the likelihood of a future crisis; most of the money spent to date on this type of analysis has been for Southern California. In some cases this has included multiple-species analysis, which has introduced a wide range of biodiversity concerns and concepts to planners. San Diego County funded a complex multiple-species study in the 1990s as

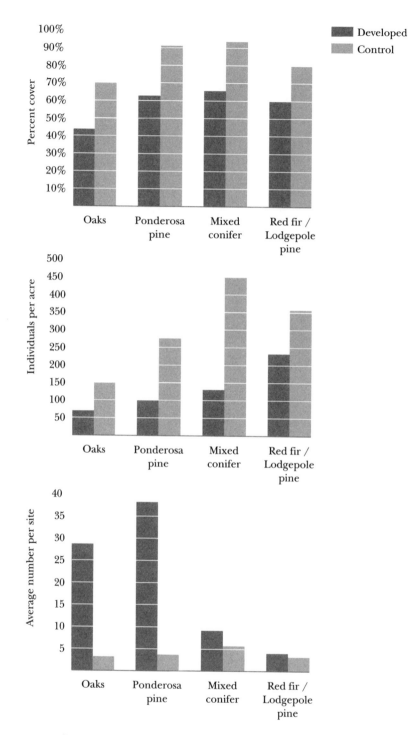

FIGURE 6.2. Differences between developed and control parcels by vegetation type for 1) percentage of canopy cover, 2) tree density per acre, and 3) species richness per site. Adapted from McBride et al. 1996.

part of its Clean Water Act compliance mitigation tied to expansion of its water treatment plant. This effort represents an important first step toward improved linkage between land use planning and the principles of conservation biology and landscape ecology (Soule 1991a; Forman 1995; Duane 1993b).

Michael Soule published an important study in 1991 of the effects of urbanization on wildlife in San Diego County that found empirical results consistent with conservation biology theory. Soule was the founder and first president of the Society for Conservation Biology (Quammen 1996). His article in the *Journal of the American Planning Association* reached beyond the usual audience of conservation biologists to introduce important concepts of conservation biology to planners (1991a). Sheila Peck and the California Department of Forestry and Fire Protection (CDF) subsequently published a guidebook to these concepts in her 1993 manual, *Landscape Conservation Planning: Preserving Ecosystems in Open Space Networks*, which was based on her professional project at UC Berkeley. Peck elaborated on these concepts in her 1998 book, *Planning for Biodiversity: Issues and Examples*. Soule (1991a, 319) outlined several of the key principles of conservation biology and demonstrated how they might be incorporated into planning for human settlements. He summarized the theoretical foundations of island biogeography theory for planners with five simple principles: a) more area is better than less area, b) a single large reserve is better than several small reserves, c) the presence of large predators is better than their absence, d) contiguous reserves are better than reserves fragmented by roads and trails, and e) reserves connected by corridors are better than isolated reserves.

Unfortunately, those principles have not been adopted by many planning practitioners. This is especially true in rural and exurban planning departments. Perhaps the most important effect of the large-lot settlement pattern in the Sierra Nevada is the fragmentation of terrestrial habitat and the edge effects of development on native biological diversity. Ironically, exurbanites' desire to live close to nature in a single-family home on a one- to five-acre lot has a *denaturation* effect that results in a pseudonatural matrix of native and exotic vegetation that is almost entirely "edge," rather than an intact matrix of larger habitat patches with the connectivity necessary to maintain native biological diversity. Relative to the metropolitan context from which they have just migrated, however, the landscape still appears natural to most former urbanites. It is necessary to educate the exurban public on the characteristics of native landscapes and some basic principles of conservation biology to affect this common misperception—possibly a necessary step before expecting broad public support for new policies necessary to reduce the effects of exurban growth. At present, there is only limited public perception that this is even a problem.[54]

The relationship between Nature and Culture is therefore critical to both definition of and resolution of the problem of biodiversity conservation. Do exur-

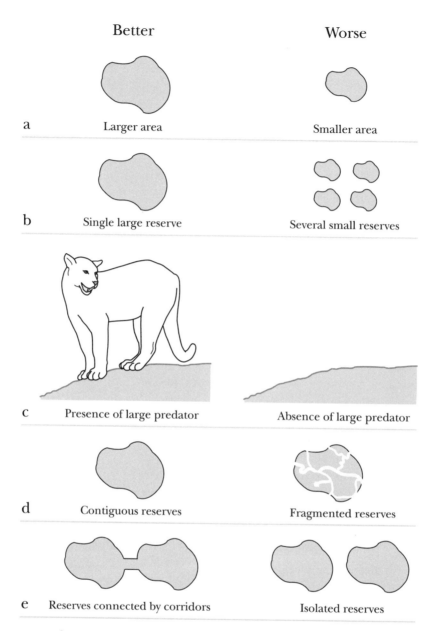

Better	Worse

a — Larger area / Smaller area

b — Single large reserve / Several small reserves

c — Presence of large predator / Absence of large predator

d — Contiguous reserves / Fragmented reserves

e — Reserves connected by corridors / Isolated reserves

FIGURE 6.3.   Biodiversity planning principles: a) more area is better than less area, b) a single large reserve is better than several small reserves, c) the presence of large predators is better than their absence, d) contiguous reserves are better than reserves fragmented by roads and trails, and e) reserves connected by corridors are better than isolated reserves. Adapted from Soule 1991a, 319. Reprinted by permission of the *Journal of the American Planning Association* 57, no. 3 (summer 1991).

banites desire a park, garden, forest, or wilderness? Each of these terms has different meanings that are both relative and context-specific.[55] Understanding the effects of exurban growth on ecological structure and function may help rural and exurban communities discuss the type of landscape they are both creating and desiring. Today this type of discussion is constrained by a failure even to recognize the full range of effects.

Exurban land conversion causes at least five direct effects on vegetation and wildlife, discussed below.

Reduced Total Habitat Area through Direct Habitat Conversion

This is the most apparent effect of development, but low-density development may not actually result in significant reduction in total habitat area. The actual building site and effects of associated construction may cover only one-fourth of an acre, for example, plus up to another quarter-acre for access roads, septic system leach lines, and a domestic well. This could indeed result in denaturation of up to 25–50 percent of a one-acre parcel, but only 5–10 percent of a five-acre parcel.[56] I estimate that the direct effect of low-density exurban development is probably a reduction in total habitat area by around 20 percent (10–30 percent). Some specific habitats are disproportionately threatened with area reductions, however, for they lie in the path of most exurban development. This reflects the underrepresentation of many vegetation types, such as blue oak woodland in the Sierra Nevada foothills, and the overrepresentation of a limited number of ecosystems in public ownership, such as "rocks and ice" of alpine wilderness preserves in the Sierra Nevada high country. The GAP analysis completed for SNEP by Frank W. Davis and David M. Stoms (1996) suggests specific vegetation types most likely to be affected by human settlement on private lands in the Sierra Nevada (most notably in the western foothills). Its implications are discussed further below. Direct reductions in total habitat area can also be significant for many rarer habitat types or those already suffering from significant reductions in total area.

Reduced Habitat Patch Size and Increased Habitat Fragmentation

Even when reductions in total habitat area are limited, the average patch size of remaining habitat is reduced significantly with low-density exurban sprawl. Depending on the evaluation of edge effects—for example, how large an area next to roads and structures is considered to be affected—average patch size can drop from thousands of acres to less than an acre (which happens when the entire area is fragmented into one-acre lots). The negative consequences of habitat fragmentation are well-known theoretically and documented in a number of specific cases for both tropical and temperate regions (Harris 1984; Adams and Dove

1989; Gilpin and Soule 1986; Wilcove et al. 1986; Lovejoy et al. 1986; Soule 1991b). The distribution of patch sizes is also typically shifted from one domi-nated by a few large-sized patches to one with only a small fraction of the total number of patches for any given habitat remaining large enough to support viable populations of many species. Those may be the only patches that remain effective habitat, despite the continued existence of many patches with similar vegetation and a relatively small reduction in total habitat area. As a result, total area *directly* converted from habitat to settlement uses may be only 20 percent, but *effective* area may decline by more than 90 percent at build-out. Roads are probably the single biggest source of habitat fragmentation and edge effects in exurban areas.[57]

Isolation of Habitat Patches by Roads, Structures and Fences

Neither total habitat area nor the distribution of habitat among patches of various sizes is an adequate measure of how the landscape matrix may change as a result of exurban sprawl. Connection of those patches with each other is also important, determining the effective habitat available for wildlife use and gene transport (Defenders of Wildlife 1989; Hudson 1991; Noss 1991; Soule 1991a). This is a critical determinant of population viability (Soule 1986; Gilpin and Soule 1986; Pimm 1986). One of the most significant effects of low-density exurban sprawl is therefore the isolation of habitat patches by roads, structures, and fences. Of course the effect of each depends on the specific life histories of the species affected. Most wildlife can avoid structures at densities of less than one unit per acre, and these do not constitute significant barriers if dispersed among adjacent parcels. Fences can serve as significant barriers for many mammals and reptiles, but appear to be relatively insignificant to the migration of birds and invertebrates or the transport of genetic material from most vegetation. Roads are probably the single most important barriers to both wildlife and genetic movement between habitat patches. Further research and education of both the public and trans-portation planners and engineers are necessary to develop alternative transporta-tion network designs that minimize these effects.

Harassment of Wildlife by Domestic Dogs and Cats

Even if wildlife can avoid residential structures, they are often subject to harass-ment by domestic dogs and cats. These pets extend the effective area of human set-tlements to a degree that development could form a significant barrier between, and/or reduce the effective habitat of, adjacent habitat patches. It is difficult to estimate the "dog-shed" or "cat-shed" associated with this effect, but it can be quite large. Many exurban properties have limited fencing, and leash laws are usually only loosely enforced. The result is that dogs and cats are able to roam freely throughout the exurban matrix as long as they avoid conflict with humans. The range of dogs can easily be several miles in a single day, making most of the settled portion of the exurban matrix subject to their effect. Michael Soule has documented the apparent effect of cat predation on birds in the urbanizing areas of northern San Diego County (1991a), and harassment from dogs is known to affect many species common in areas facing rapid exurban growth. Dogs and cats can also be a source of seed dispersal of nonnative plants (discussed below) and can be a source of disease for native wildlife. Other pets or domesticated animals such as cattle or sheep are also disease sources that can decimate native wildlife populations such as ungulates.[58] This could be especially important when seasonal migrations occur (Yuba County Community Services Department 1985; Peck 1993).

Biological Pollution from Nonnative Vegetation Alleles

Both invasive nonnatives, such as Scotch broom, and nonlocal stocks of species native to an area, such as Douglas fir, pose the threat of "biological pollution," or genetic contamination. In the first case, the invasive species can outcompete and displace some native species; this can then modify the vegetative structure to a degree that other species and the entire landscape matrix are affected. A sun-tolerant nonnative species may invade a recently opened forest area, for example, displacing an entire succession of species that would normally have occurred in the absence of that species. The species being displaced is therefore not the only one directly affected. The second instance is more subtle and much more difficult to evaluate: genetic hybridization may occur or the population with the nonlocal alleles may outcompete the local alleles. The apparent structure of the landscape matrix may not change as a result, but the genetic information contained in the resulting matrix will be different from that of the native matrix. This may then diminish the capacity of the entire system to respond to a significant future disruption such as global climate change. To the degree that populations are determinants of the long-term viability of Sierra Nevada ecosystems, it may be just as important to protect against nonlocal genetic contamination as to minimize the risk of invasive nonnatives (Millar 1996). Considerably more research must be completed before we can confidently determine the relative importance of particular populations (Medbury 1993).

In addition to these direct effects on vegetative composition, structure, and function (which in turn affect wildlife habitat and wildlife viability), land conversion for human settlement has several direct effects on hydrologic regimes that are ecologically important, as described below.

Increased Impervious Surface and Increased Peak Runoff

Conversion of wildlands for human settlement includes the construction of roads, parking areas, and structures, and has resulted in soil compaction and vegetation modification. In general, these changes are likely to increase the overall amount of impervious surface, decrease leaf canopy and its capacity to intercept precipitation, and decrease evapotranspiration on the site (Arnold and Gibbons 1996). A change in the local hydrograph often results, although intervening factors may mitigate the effects of these changes on sedimentation and downstream hydrological characteristics. Both the timing and volume of on-site water retention can be affected as well, so it is difficult to generalize the effects of land conversion for human settlement. Changes in vegetation can also increase evapotranspiration over time as planted vegetation matures.

Increased Heavy Metal and Oil Runoff from Impervious Surfaces

Many of the impervious surfaces associated with human settlement accumulate heavy metals and oils from vehicles and other machines, such as chain saws. Heavy precipitation during peak runoff periods is likely to wash these substances away. The degree to which they then enter surface water systems and affect hydroecological systems depends on the characteristics of both the local watershed and the aquatic ecological system. As a result it is difficult to generalize these effects from human settlement. The effects of commercial, industrial, and other nonresidential land uses are also likely to be greater on a per-acre basis than all but the highest-density pattern of human settlement (Thompson 1989).

Increased Risk of Groundwater and/or Surface Water Contamination through Septic Effluent Disposal

As noted above, the use of septic systems is significantly higher in the Sierra Nevada than for California as a whole. The potential risk of septic system contamination of groundwater is therefore much greater in the exurban landscape. That risk is a function of system operation, leach field characteristics, and groundwater characteristics (Marie Davis 1994)—highly site-specific features in the Sierra Nevada, where both soils and groundwater characteristics vary considerably. Historical failures of septic systems have led to building restrictions, groundwater contamination, and surface water contamination (Cranmer Engineering and Halatyn 1971; Marie Davis 1994; Lauer 1995a; 1995b; 1995c; Lenahan 1995). All these outcomes are possible results of failed existing or newly developed septic systems. They may also occur even if septic systems are operating normally, as densities or soil saturation following heavy storms increase to the point at which soils are unable to treat the septic effluent to an acceptable standard (Thompson 1989; Hanson and Jacobs 1989; Hanner 1997).

Decreased Groundwater Flow to the Surface Water System Resulting from Groundwater Pumping

On-site groundwater is a primary source of domestic potable water and irrigation water for most low-density exurban households in the Sierra Nevada (Turner 1973; U.S. Bureau of Census 1990).The region's groundwater system is characterized by highly variable and unpredictable storage in fractured bedrock, however, rather than a clearly delineated set of groundwater aquifers (Page et al. 1984; Wheeldon 1994; Hauge 1994; Fulton 1993; Ellis 1997; Swain 1994). This system is interconnected with the surface water system in complex and unpredictable ways. Groundwater pumping for water supply therefore has the potential to affect surface water flows. It is unclear how significantly this may affect surface water systems, for effects are likely to be site-specific.

Modified Surface Water Flow Resulting from Irrigation, Septic System Effluent Disposal, and Treated Wastewater Discharges

Human settlement requires access to water supplies, and providing them usually involves either importing water through interbasin transfers, or significant in-basin storage to accommodate seasonal differences between natural flow regimes and human uses (Turner 1973). Humans use water either to irrigate outdoors (this water can either recharge groundwater or enter the evapotranspiration cycle) or for internal domestic use. Most water used internally is discharged through septic system disposal or sewered wastewater treatment. Septic system disposal can affect groundwater and/or surface water hydrology within the local watershed (Hanson and Jacobs 1989), while sewered wastewater treatment can lead to either in-basin discharges or interbasin transfer to another watershed. Wastewater can then account for a significant fraction of surface water flow, altering both the seasonal timing and overall level of flows downstream of the point of discharge (Central Valley Regional Water Quality Control Board 1989; 1992).

FIRE MANAGEMENT IN THE EXURBAN LANDSCAPE

Land conversion resulting from human settlement can have a wide range of indirect effects on ecological structure and function. The most important of these in the Sierra Nevada is associated with influences on the fire regime in settled areas and adjacent wildlands. Human settlement affects the structure and level of fuel

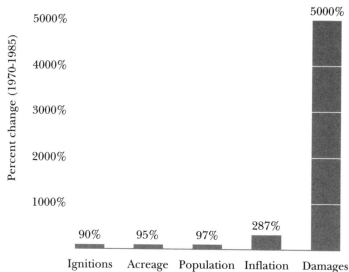

FIGURE 6.4.   Percentage increase in California wildfires, population, and economic damages, 1970–85.

loadings, the viability of presuppression fuels management strategies, the likelihood of ignition risk, the availability of suppression resources, and the allocation of those resources through suppression efforts. Each of these will in turn affect the future risk and characteristics of fire. Vegetation management in the "urban forest" of areas converted to human settlement can either decrease or increase fuels in the urban-wildland intermix zone (Doyle 1995). Further research is necessary to establish empirical relationships between alternative patterns of human settlement and each of these indirect effects.

The effects of exurban growth on fire regimes are less site-specific, but still very complex. Risk of fire ignition is associated with human activity, so the presence of humans in the exurban landscape increases the likelihood of a fire starting in the first place. Common sources of human-caused fires include chimney stovepipe (flue) problems, such as sparks from a woodstove fire igniting dry leaves on a neighboring tree; vehicle heat, such as a hot muffler igniting grasses underneath a parked and idling vehicle; sparks caused by metal scraping against rocks, as can occur when heavy equipment clears brush for a timber operation; unattended campfires, such as when flare-ups result from wind changes; escaped "controlled" burns when home owners burn brush, dead leaves, and other fuels; power-related sparking, such as when trees touch power lines or a transformer overloads; and children, who may, for example, play with matches or firecrackers. All of these ignition sources are present with exurban development. The historical relationship between fire ignitions, acreage burned, and population from 1970 to 1985 in

California shows that as the population rose by 97 percent, ignitions jumped 90 percent and burned acreage 95 percent. Inflation during this period totaled 287 percent (Barnhart 1997), but the economic cost of structural and natural resource damages from fire shot up a remarkable 5,000 percent! Fire losses therefore increased more than seven times the combined increases in inflation and population from 1970 to 1985. This is in large part the result of changing patterns of fires and the emergence of the urban-wildland intermix zone of exurban development. A mere 1 percent of all fires in 1985 accounted for 75 percent of the recorded damages. Those fires were dominated by structure losses in the urban-wildland intermix zone on the exurban frontier.[59]

The spatial pattern of ignitions in the Sierra Nevada is also highly correlated with settlement patterns. My research assistants and I prepared GIS coverage of 1990 housing density that aggregated more than fifty thousand Census Blocks in the Sierra Nevada into just eleven housing density classes. Greg Greenwood of CDF then completed an analysis showing that two-thirds of the spatial variation in fires from 1983 to 1993 could be explained simply as a function of housing density at the aggregated Census Block level in 1990.[60] This highlights the role of human settlement as the dominant factor driving fire ignitions and suppression efforts. We believe the addition of only two more variables—road density and a dummy variable for a lightning strike zone—would capture most of the remaining variation in low-density areas. The highest-density areas probably have relatively few wildfire ignitions and acreage burned, a result of both the dominance of the built landscape and the high level of suppression resources available locally to protect property values in the highest-cost settlement areas.

Increased ignition risks associated with exurban development change both the likelihood of fires occurring where development has taken place and the consequences of their occurrence. The spatial pattern of fires is therefore likely to threaten some public lands differently than before development, for those areas close to development, such as the Tahoe and Eldorado National Forests, are more likely to have fires on the private lands adjoining the federal lands than on public lands not near exurban growth. This affects the viability of strategies designed to protect important habitat or old-growth forests on the public lands. The proximity of high-valued exurban development to public lands also increases the potential cost of forest fires originating on the public lands, however, for an escaped public-lands fire could threaten lives and expensive private property. The higher economic value of exurban development places a new premium on fire suppression strategies that contain wildfires to public lands.[61]

Wildfire suppression techniques are also constrained after human settlement, however, for the higher value of the individual homes in the exurban landscape requires protection with different techniques. Some wildfire-fighting techniques, such as backburning, are not feasible if houses are located between the fire and the point at which firefighters believe they can contain the fire with a fire line and backburn. Fires in the urban-wildland intermix require new techniques that go beyond those used for either structural fires or wildland fires. The "49er Fire" burned thirty-three thousand acres in western Nevada County in September 1988, destroying nearly 200 homes and 356 other structures and causing $22.7 million in damages (Hedler 1988; Williams 1988). Another 4,000 structures were within the perimeter of the 49er Fire but did not burn. Firefighters were unable to really fight the fire because they were instead standing guard over individual houses, with an engine and crew stationed beside the house. This focus on protecting structures clearly limited their ability to fight the fire as they would have fought a wildland fire. In a wildland fire, they would have chosen to sacrifice some forest and fuels for tactical reasons in order to contain the fire in the most efficient manner.[62] This wasn't possible when individual home owners were refusing to leave their homes and stood in front of them with garden hoses spraying the roofs. Suppression resources were instead diverted to protect these individual structures and human lives. As a result, the fire was probably able to spread much more rapidly, and took much longer to contain, than if the area had not been settled. The 49er Fire burned for a week before finally being controlled (Hedler 1988; Williams 1988).

Homes that did burn may have also had an effect on fire intensity. Wildland fire models do not normally treat structures as potential fuels, but the behavior of the Berkeley-Oakland Hills fire of October 1991 appeared to have been exacerbated by natural gas pipelines as well as the intensity of burning of the houses themselves. Homes literally exploded as the fire engulfed them, sending burning debris into the air to cause additional spot fires as much as a mile downwind.[63] Based on this experience, several of my students (Nelia Badilla Forest, Malcolm McDaniel, and Lori Tsung) completed a detailed analysis in 1994 of the potential role of structures as fuels for the 7,771-acre Cinabarr development in El Dorado County. They found that the average twenty-five-hundred-square-foot house had a fuel content measuring between 685 million and 758 million BTUs. This is more than twice the BTU content per acre of the highest BTU-content fuels found on the Cinabarr site (the northern mixed, chamise, or serpentine chaparral). In comparison, an undeveloped acre of grassland or blue oak, interior live oak, or ponderosa pine forest has a fuel content of only 96 million to 210 million BTUs. Siting homes within these forest types at one dwelling unit per acre can therefore increase the potential fuel load by 443 to 851 percent. These estimates are, however, based only on the fuel content of the structures themselves, and do not include the additional fuel content of interior furnishings, household supplies of paints or other flammable materials, or gasoline in the fuel tanks of cars, tractors, chain saws, and motorcycles (Forest et al. 1994).

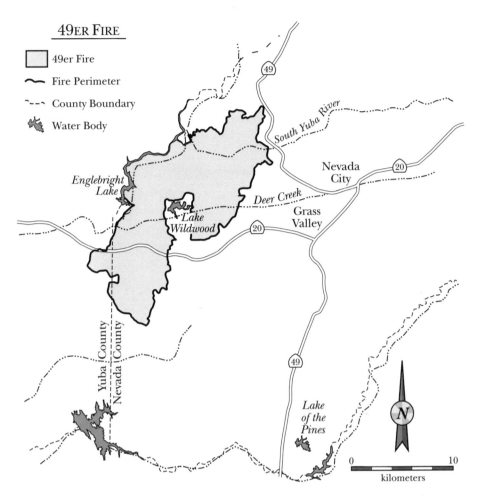

MAP 6.4.   Area within the perimeter of the 49er Fire, Nevada County, September 1988.

The ecological, economic, and social influences of exurban development on fire regimes are mediated through social processes and institutions such as fire suppression strategies. Fire risk, for example, may be mitigated by increasing fire suppression resources near exurban development. Higher property taxes for high-density development may actually increase the level of fire protection, more than offsetting the extra risk associated with the development. Such an effect is less clear with low-density exurban sprawl, where areas are covered by local, state, and federal fire agencies. Many of the homes built in exurbia are remote and inaccessible. Ingress and egress are often on small, scenic, substandard roads that will not allow an escaping home owner and an arriving fire truck to pass each other.

Similar conditions and a stalled vehicle led to the deaths of twenty-five people in the Berkeley-Oakland hills fire (Reinhold 1991; Paddock 1991), and it is only a matter of time before people get caught in a Sierra Nevada firestorm.

Consequently, new "fire-safe" regulations were adopted in 1991 by CDF that require new developments to have three critical features: roads wide enough to accommodate fire vehicle access and turnaround, water supplies adequate to support fire suppression on the site, and "defensible space" of at least thirty feet around homes to reduce the risk of high-intensity fires burning right up to, or being ignited from, the home.[64] The first requirement makes almost every road in any Nevada County development subdivided before the 1980s illegal. It also calls for extensive vegetative removal adjacent to the access road, which would affect both aesthetics and wildlife. The expense of maintaining such clearing is likely to mean that landowners will not maintain the clearance setbacks once the CDF and county building inspectors have signed off on the regulation. The second requirement calls for high-capacity gravity-fed water tanks to be installed on-site. This is a significant expense and may limit new development because of either site constraints or the increased costs. The third requirement is the only one that applies to existing parcels as well as new subdivisions. This means that it is likely to have the greatest potential effect, but could dramatically alter the aesthetic character of homesites as well as habitat values. Once again, enforcement will be difficult. Home owners are likely to resist implementing these vegetation changes if they will result in reduced privacy or loss of visual amenities. These site characteristics are often a central feature in residential location decisions, and they are especially important in the density size class of one dwelling unit per one to three acres.

The CDF is relying on a public education campaign, in cooperation with local Resource Conservation Districts, to promote voluntary home owner clearing of defensible space. The agency has also established a demonstration site in El Dorado County in an effort to show more attractive models of fire-safe houses. The fire-safe look may conflict directly with many exurbanites' desired landscape aesthetics, however, as may the fire-safe road standards that call for wider roadbeds and vegetative clearance. An innovative program in Nevada County lends a biomass chipper to any group of home owners thinning the fuels around their homes and access roads, but the program must be expanded significantly to encourage widespread landowner participation. Markets must also be found for the biomass, but biomass economics are now deteriorating in the face of electric utility deregulation and the decreased viability of biomass-burning electricity-generating plants. Continued persistence of highly combustible "ladder" fuels is therefore likely in the exurban landscape.

The ecological effects of exurban growth on vegetation, wildlife, water quality, and fire regimes could be partially mitigated through improved land use planning. Planning for future development is not a panacea, however, for we must also confront the implications of many previous decisions now bearing fruit. Some of that fruit has the potential to cost human lives and the enormous loss of both economic and ecological values. Many exurban residents and landowners nevertheless have compelling reasons to resist dealing with those costs. Those reasons and the processes driving planning are as important as ecology and economics in our exploration of the ecotransformation of the Sierra Nevada. The potential for and impediments to improved land use planning are discussed in detail below.

SPRING GROWTH IN THE HOME RANGE

My hundred-mile view of the Coast Ranges is now partially obscured by the new leaves of spring here in the Sierra foothills. They started as bright yellow-green buds, not far on the color palette from the brilliant yellow of autumn that preceded the bare browns and grays of winter. Now they are filling in with a shade that mixes well with the greens and grays of the foothill landscape. The digger, or foothill, pines have buds of yellow-gray pollen, while the ponderosa pines have already developed young cones among their light-green-tipped needles. The landscape is alive again with verdant growth. Our view through the woods is screened, and we lose sight of the individual trees as the overlapping branches and leaves of the forest envelop the trunks. Every square inch of warm sunlight is tapped as the process of photosynthesis begins anew. The oaks reach up through the pines and extend their crowns until they touch the sky. The nutrients gather in the roots and climb the trunk to the leaves for that remarkable chemical transformation that makes life possible. The leaves and the branches, in turn, will nourish the earth again when they fall with the rain and the wind of autumn and winter.

With the spring leaves also come the birds. Red-tailed hawks (*Buteo jamaicensis*) circle outside my window, perching on a dead ponderosa pine tree that offers a view over potential prey below. Two weeks ago a blue-and-gray scrub jay (*Aphelocoma coerulescens*) waited out the drizzle above the fresh blossoms of a five-foot manzanita, nest-building twigs in its beak. Today I looked out to see an acorn woodpecker (*Melanerpes formicivorus*) poking a hole in the bark of a black oak fifteen feet from my window. I was taken aback by his bright red head against the gray, brown, and green of the forest. I grabbed my camera before I could reach my *Birds of North America* book, but he darted away once my telephoto lens zoomed in on his brilliant hat. It made even the fresh spring leaves of the nearby poison oak look pale in comparison.

For each of these species, the landscape on the San Juan Ridge before us is still largely intact. The hand of humans is clearly present, but the natural environment dominates the built human environment. Changes in the landscape continue to reflect the seasons and an ecological system still basically functioning. That environment can be harsh, of course, but these birds can count on it being here each year when they return to build their nests and lay their eggs. That cannot be said of many places closer to Nevada City, Grass Valley, Alta Sierra, Lake of the Pines, and Lake Wildwood. Much of the wildlife habitat of western Nevada County is being radically transformed in the face of continuing human population growth and land development. Here on the ridge habitat is abundant in a landscape with larger parcels, less fragmentation, and fewer domestic predators. And as humans continue to settle this landscape, its capacity to support other species diminishes. These other species are then displaced through all of the processes described above. Growth is not always good.

This seems intuitively obvious, but much of our Culture seems to presume the opposite. Day after day, in television commercials and billboards, our well-being is linked through an inexhaustible set of messages to the never-ending expansion of both production and consumption. The president and his advisors become concerned when economic statistics indicate that the economy isn't growing, while local politicians complain about how the local economy and population are not growing as fast as they did in the late 1980s and early 1990s. In defiance of both common sense and most of our ecological knowledge, growth is equated with always being a good thing. It is even deemed a necessary thing, and those who question this wisdom are derisively labeled "no-growthers" or "antigrowth forces." This is the kiss of a radical identity in local political battles over growth control. Yet it is clear that growth is not always a good thing for every part of the ecological system. That includes humans, who continue to mature well after they've stopped growing. In fact, very few humans seem able to mature as long as they are still growing.

It may be the same with communities that live on the unnatural residue of, and in the abnormal state of, growth. They become so dependent on growth for their identities that they are unable to envision a future where they must live with who they are and do the best with it. Our challenge in the Sierra Nevada is to envision and ensure a future where growth can be managed in such a way that there will still be reasons to live here after the short-term boom of illusory growth has ended and our economy has matured. At this point growth is spreading like a cancer across the exurban landscape, engulfing both Nature and Culture in the process. We must find some way to manage it effectively if we are to avoid a shattered landscape of both social and ecological fragmentation in the Range of Light.

CHAPTER SEVEN

/\V.V\

Politics and Property

Because there are many different kinds of towns just as there are many different kinds of men; a development which is good for one kind can be death on another.

John Brinckerhoff Jackson, 1970

Don't it always seem to go that you don't know what you've got till it's gone?

Joni Mitchell, 1970

The First Amendment to the United States Constitution proclaims the separation of church and state, but there is a thematic center to our Culture that transcends religious, ethnic, racial, and spiritual differences. That common theme is a seemingly unquestioned belief that growth is good and the individual matters more than the community.[1] Growth is now God in America, and we worship it at an altar called economic progress. Economists are the new religion's clergy, and they hide the secrets of the faith in complex econometric models and a language not all that different from the Latin that once baffled my Celtic ancestors around the time St. Patrick allegedly rid their homeland of snakes. And like my Celtic cousins, the new parishioners have very few opportunities to question the basic tenets of the faith. Growth is good—end of discussion.

Economists like Herman Daly demonstrate the fallacy of this unquestioned belief and highlight how necessary it is to challenge many of the fundamental tenets of mainstream economics in order to achieve what he calls "steady-state economics" (1991; 1977), but this perspective has not yet made it into the mainstream discourse on planning and growth management. Environmental planners raise questions about the consequences of growth in graduate courses, of course, and environmental activists raise them before city councils and county boards of supervisors or commissioners. Main Street, however, continues to call for growth as the engine of economic development. Many elected and appointed officials turn to business people in the local Chamber of Commerce for advice on economic development issues, so it is not surprising that the company line continues to have great influence on those issues. These same public officials are the ones making local land use planning decisions. And this is where the unquestioned assumptions of our consumer society constrain the debate on land use planning. The landscape of planning is tilted heavily toward accommodating growth. Some have even argued that planning is primarily structured to promote efficient operation of capital markets in the conversion of natural landscapes into commodified elements of real estate (Logan and Molotch 1987). Planning's historical origins are much more complex than that, but it is true that planning is more effective at supporting development than environmental values. As Richard White has noted, planning is the exercise of political power (1996). And in our society, forces in favor of growth hold political power.

The focus of growth on material well-being also has broad support among the American population. Sociologist Robert Bellah and his colleagues noted the tensions between our dissatisfaction with the shallowness of "the packaged good life" and our willingness to change our lives to find meaning in other ways, in their remarkable 1985 study of American society, *Habits of the Heart: Individualism and Commitment in American Life:* "It is not clear that many Americans are prepared to consider a significant change in the way we have been living," they said. "The allure of the packaged good life is still strong, though dissatisfaction is widespread." The problem of moving beyond a simplistic growth-oriented public discourse on the relationship between economic activity, environmental quality, and social well-being is therefore not limited to economists and politicians. It is deeply embedded within American Culture.

Like most things, growth is inherently neither good nor bad. Some aspects of growth are good, and some are bad. In some cases, the same aspects may be good for some things (or people or interests) and bad for other things (or people or interests). This is why the "growth is good" fallacy is so dangerous: it tends to substitute a narrow conception of interests and values for the much richer and more complex suite of interests and values that represent the full community. And as long as that substitution is allowed to proceed, we can be sure whose interests and values will benefit from any analysis or policy decisions that depend on that substitution. And so we see many conflicts over land use planning and growth management that reflect more fundamental differences in interests and values. As Logan and Molotch have noted, those who favor exchange values over use values call for value-free development that in fact is not value free but instead reflects their own values—which they then clothe in "objective" and "neutral" analysis through the technocratic application of positivist utilitarian planning.

The dominant power structure attempts to control the debate by delegitimizing the interests and values of those who question the motherhood-and-apple-pie conventional wisdom that growth is good. Those who do question growth are painted as "radical, extremist, no-growthers," bringing to mind visions of selfish Luddites.[2] For the uninvolved public, these suggestions tap into a culturally constructed sense of what is good that often lies deep below consciousness. We are bombarded daily by the message, and it is difficult either to deny it or recognize its power. "Economic growth improves in the second quarter" shouts the headline, clearly associating growth with the idea of improvement. Remarkably, the connection between the indicators of economic growth and individuals' economic well-being is rarely made. "Unemployment figures up; Wall Street reacts with a rally" should give pause to anyone interested in a job. How could increased unemployment be good for Wall Street? Well, increased unemployment decreases pressures on wages, because more people are out of work and willing to work for less money or for fewer benefits. This increases company profits and decreases inflationary pressures (which could otherwise squeeze profits and devalue investments), which in turn increases the value of company stocks. Wall Street then stages a rally to celebrate the "good news." And in the end, we are told again, "growth is good."

The same principles apply in land use planning. Constraining rampant growth may maintain citizens' access to a wide range of nonmarket amenity values (use values) that have significant economic, social, and cultural value in citizens' lives, but it is also likely to diminish the potential for profits (exchange values) for developers. Constraining rampant growth may even increase the land and housing value of existing homes, increasing the material economic wealth (exchange values) of homeowners. The limitation on developers' profits will still represent a conflict between this apparent gain for existing residents and growth controls. Constraining the market is also likely to increase the cost of housing and decrease access to housing for many nonresidents (or renters, who may face increased rents without increased wealth), forcing them to live farther away from work and spend more of their time and other economic resources commuting to work, school, and the open space that may be maintained by the growth controls. Limiting growth therefore clearly does impose some costs on specific interests. It also yields real and tangible economic benefits, however, for many existing residents. And empirical studies of growth management demonstrate that the negative effects on affordable housing are usually limited by the "safety valve" availability of such housing in nearby communities (Landis 1992; Glickfield and Levine 1992). This spillover effect makes the worst predictions of the pro-growth advocates largely theoretical when growth controls are actually imposed. There is usually somebody else willing to feed the developers' appetite for additional profits.

The debate over growth management is complex, but popular singer-songwriter Joni Mitchell put her finger on key elements of it in her song "Big Yellow Taxi" in 1970:

> They paved Paradise, and put up a parking lot
> with a pink hotel, a boutique
> And a swinging hot spot

FIGURE 7.1.   Clear-cut construction site for a large-scale commercial development near Grass Valley.

> Don't it always seem to go
> That you don't know what you've got till it's gone
> They paved Paradise and put up a parking lot
>
> They took all the trees, and put them in a tree museum
> And they charged all the people a dollar and a half just to see 'em . . .
>
> Don't it always seem to go
> That you don't know what you've got till it's gone
> They paved Paradise and put up a parking lot.[3]

I will discuss more complex sociological explanations from the academic literature in a section below, but we should not underestimate the power of popular Culture to explain popular movements. All too often, I'm afraid, academics seek answers only from quantitative analysis of survey data and the census data, rather than the experience of living in a place with real people.[4] Joni Mitchell's song was popular not only because of its catchy tune. It was also popular because she captured a feeling widespread within American culture. Interestingly, she did so by saying "they" paved Paradise. Moreover, her return to the age-old theme that "you don't know what you've got till it's gone" makes it clear that the Paradise she's talking about is not in a distant and rarely visited national park. It is the Paradise that makes up the local landscapes of our everyday lives. And unless we notice it before it is gone, she makes clear, it could soon become another parking lot. In the process she challenges an entire system of planning and land development that designs and transforms landscapes into cities that more efficiently accommodate the automobile than the personal aesthetic and environmental values that can make a place Paradise. Mitchell implicitly calls for more citizen involvement in those decisions.

In 1976, another popular musical group, the Eagles, went beyond Joni Mitchell with their brilliant song "The Last Resort." Songwriters and band members Don Henley and Glenn Frey managed to address the complex relationships between migration, frontier myth, consumer culture, and religious rationalization in the destruction of any place perceived to be "Paradise." The recurring theme is that of frontier Culture and sequential migration: once a place has been developed, one can always move on to the next "Paradise." However, Henley and Frey document how, in place after place, our disposable society has transformed and then discarded each "new" landscape of Euro-American settlement "in the name of Destiny, and in the name of God." This has been a dominant theme in California's history, from the Los Angeles basin in the 1940s to the Sierra Nevada foothills in the 1990s:

> She came from Providence, the one in Rhode Island
> Where the old world shadows hang heavy in the air
> She packed her hopes and dreams like a refugee
> Just as her father came across the sea.
>
> She heard about a place where people were smiling
> They spoke about the Red Man's ways, and how they loved the land
> They came from everywhere to the Great Divide
> Seeking a place to stand, or a place to hide
>
> Down in the crowded bars, out for a good time
> Can't wait to tell you all what it's like up there
> They called it Paradise, I don't know why
> Somebody laid the mountains low while the town got high
>
> And then the chilly winds blew down across the desert
> Through the canyons of the coast to the Malibu
> Where the pretty people play, hungry for power
> To light their neon way and give them things to do
>
> Some rich men came and raped the land; nobody caught them
> Put up a bunch of ugly boxes; and Jesus, people bought 'em
> They called it Paradise, the place to be
> They watched the hazy sun sinking in the sea
>
> We can leave it all behind and sail to Lahaina
> Just like the missionaries did so many years ago
> They even brought a neon sign: "Jesus is coming"
> They brought the White Man's burden down;
>   brought the White Man's rain

> Who will provide the grand design; what is yours and what is mine
> 'Cause there is no more new frontier; we have got to make it here
> We satisfy our endless needs and justify our bloody deeds
> In the name of Destiny, and in the name of God
>
> And you can see them there on Sunday morning
> Stand up and sing about what it's like up there
> They call it Paradise; I don't know why
> You call someplace Paradise, kiss it goodbye.[5]

There are many who now view the exurban landscape of the Range of Light, where they are migrating in search of an amenity-filled lifestyle, as Paradise. There is even a town in the northern Sierra Nevada foothills in Butte County called Paradise, which makes an attractive postal address for equity refugees fleeing the city. (Consistent with Ed Blakely and Mary Gail Snyder's theme of *Fortress America*, Curte Meine reports that the word paradise originally meant "walled garden" [1997].) It is now in these places—in the rural and exurban West—that the vision or nightmare described by Joni Mitchell or the Eagles will be repeated if an alternative future vision is not developed.

CULTURAL IMPLICATIONS OF EXURBAN GROWTH

Ecotransformation and exurban growth involve both social and ecological change. Those changes have profound cultural implications, which in turn have ecological implications. The very essence of the relationship between Nature and Culture in rural areas is being transformed by exurban growth. We must therefore explore those cultural implications before considering what policies may be implemented to mitigate some of the social, economic, and ecological consequences of exurban growth. Some policy alternatives may be inconsistent with deeply held values of the community, while others may challenge conventional conceptions of the role of humans in the environment. Still others may reflect the historic urban/rural dichotomy rather than the emerging exurban reality. Some aspects of our cultural conceptions of Nature appear to be associated with social, economic, demographic, ethnic, and employment characteristics. Others may be more closely associated with the length of residence in the region.

What are these emerging values, and how do they affect exurban conceptions of Nature, space, community, and place? It is not easy to categorize the values of exurban residents, for they either come to exurban regions, or stay in them, for a variety of reasons. Many however share an interest in Nature that reflects their daily contact with it. Some—in particular, those who work in extractive industries—see Nature as both an obstacle to and a potential resource for their own economic well-being. In this view, Nature is meant to be conquered, and it exists to provide commodities to meet human needs. This viewpoint is consistent with the utilitarian philosophy dominant throughout American history and is the basis for much of the mythology of the western frontier. Whether through individual action or collective social organization (or, ironically, in many cases through significant subsidies by urbanites [Limerick 1988; White 1991]), the community identity of many rural towns in western North America is built around the conquest and control of Nature. Many rural residents have historically relied on the natural environment for employment in primary industries and therefore view Nature mainly as a provider of raw materials. From this perspective, natural resources are meant to be used by humans for production and consumption, and the historical necessity of a utilitarian approach to land and resource management seems self-evident. This "common sense" is sometimes further reinforced by a "dominion" interpretation of Christian belief, which emphasizes one aspect of Genesis and its call for humans to "subdue" the creatures of the earth. This leads to a familiar but simplistic call by some rural residents to, as the slogan says, "Put People First" in land and resource management policy.[6] Implicitly, the urban-dominated state and federal governments have gone too far in putting nonhuman creatures ahead of humans in policy: an inherent conflict is presumed to exist.

As William Cronon notes in his book *Nature's Metropolis,* the efficient operation of a capitalist economy requires the commodification of Nature through the abstraction of its elements and places into standard units or products that facilitate transport and exchange (1991). There is a tendency to view those elements and places as interchangeable over time. There are no sacred spaces in such a landscape, for all products entering the global system must be standardized to allow abstract exchanges of value. This raises an important question about the homogeneity of interests, values, and cultural conceptions among rural residents. While workers in commodity extraction industries generally support those activities, many of them also have a strong attachment to place that includes identification with specific elements of the landscape for noncommodity activities. These may include aesthetic and ecological values, but are dominated by recreational activities such as hunting and fishing (which, not coincidentally, reinforce their utilitarian conception of Nature). A favorite fishing hole or the site of an annual deer-hunting trip with one's buddies may indeed be sacred sites, and these local residents are likely to oppose Forest Service plans to conduct resource extraction activities that might damage them.

Indeed, the opportunity to go fishing every day after the mill shift is over is one of the primary nonpecuniary benefits that keeps these residents in the area. Greater incomes, less seasonality of employment, and greater material opportunities may exist "down the hill" in "the flatlands" of metropolitan regions, but most rural residents have explicitly rejected migration to those areas primarily for noneconomic reasons. Many rural residents are therefore likely to value Nature highly even for its noncommodity values. They may also see themselves as stewards of the land, following the principles established in professional forestry around the turn of the century. As a bumper sticker posted on an office door in UC Berkeley's former School of Forestry stated it, "A Natural Forest Is No Accident." This school of thought firmly maintains that nothing can be natural without human intervention. The risk of this view, of course, is that *any* human intervention may then also be viewed as natural. Nature becomes a pure construct of Culture (Evernden 1984), and there is no basis on which to distinguish "good" from "bad" actions.

Owners of capital in these rural and exurban communities may have a different set of values, interests, and conceptions of Nature. Indeed, the homogenization and commodification of Nature and place is essential to "efficient" operation of the economy. Moreover, these owners of capital may rely less on the nonpecuniary benefits of place than their employees do. Much of the capital in commodity extraction industries is actually held outside the local community.[7] Much of economic wealth generated through local resource extraction (and even local value-added milling into secondary products) is therefore exported outside the local community. Nonlocal owners of capital can reap the benefits of resource extraction without facing the local costs of such activity through negative effects on their own sacred sites. They can simply go fishing and hunting in another part of the Sierra Nevada if the local sites are damaged in some way. Their wealth also gives them far greater opportunities to go outside the Sierra Nevada altogether if extensive modifications take place. Money is a reasonable substitute in this case for nonpecuniary benefits; a private flight from San Francisco to Montana or Idaho for fly-fishing takes no more time than a long drive from San Francisco up to the Feather River canyon. The wealth generated by extracting resources from the Feather River can then pay for the Rocky Mountain vacation—although it may impose great costs on the residents of the Sierra Nevada. The interests of long-time rural residents may therefore diverge as a function of wealth. Indeed, the substitution of capital for labor in commodity extraction industries represents a direct conflict between the economic interests of workers and owners (B. Brown 1995). Both tend to see their well-being as tied to continuing commodity extraction, however, and their dominant conception of Nature is that of a resource waiting to be exploited for human benefit. As a result, they are likely allies against environmental and land use regulation or land and resource management strategies that emphasize amenity rather than commodity values.

This viewpoint contrasts with that held by many new residents from urban areas, whose experience with Nature has often been developed through recreational experiences in spectacular landscapes far removed from extractive industry or urban settlements. They often bring with them a romantic notion of nature as a benign source of aesthetic pleasure. Many of these exurbanites have moved to the mountains to "get away from it all," and they view Nature as a setting for leisure rather than the stage for an ongoing struggle. Nature is then a place for learning, and there is a spiritual component to the experience for many who seek to gain wisdom through a wilderness experience. It is therefore sacred. Despoiling the setting of such a retreat—even that surrounding the dispersed human settlements of exurbia, which are often significantly modified landscapes as a result of the presence of humans—is seen as an immoral act. For these people there is no place for benefit-cost analyses or land trades that treat different places as abstract, generic commodities; each place has a sacred spirit that must be above the capitalist marketplace. They are likely to support preservation strategies that reject all commodity extraction activities. This approach follows the model developed for both urban zoning (where industrial activities are explicitly separated from and excluded from residential areas) and the national parks (Popper 1984). The landscape of production is eliminated from the scene, to be replaced by a landscape exclusively reserved for aesthetic consumption.

This may ultimately lead to the "museumification" of the landscape, with a resultant attempt to halt successional processes and capture the landscape as initially encountered. Like a romantic landscape painting of the early West, the aesthetic pleasures of the landscape dominate the underlying (and dynamic) ecological functions (Robertson 1984). Ironically, fire suppression and attempts to maintain existing conditions may actually increase the likelihood that the entire landscape will be lost to a major disturbance—a catastrophic fire or an insect infestation during drought conditions. Ecological understanding of the role of succession in dynamic ecological processes may therefore actually be greater among long-time rural residents employed in commodity extraction industries. The newcomers often have very little experience with a dynamic Nature and only a limited understanding of how various human activities will in fact affect the local landscape. The old-timers have a stock of knowledge about local ecological processes that reflects decades of social memory. Unfortunately, the newcomers often reject the old-timers' knowledge as irrelevant because it is perceived to be biased by their utilitarian self-interest in commodity production. Interest-based politics, learned in the abstract through the media and the democratically inaccessible decision-making processes of large metropolitan governments, often dominate the way in which newcomers interpret statements by competing interests. There is then generally a failure to generate mutual learning opportunities between old-timers and newcomers that are built around their common interest in a specific place (Kemmis 1990).

There are also important differences *within* this group of newcomers. Economic and social class is one way to divide this group, but I find another classification more relevant: the motivations driving the decision to migrate to exurbia. My own assumptions about motivations, which were influenced most strongly by my personal experience and that of my friends, have been biased toward those motivations that appear to have dominated migration decisions in the early 1970s. In general, it appears that the first wave of exurban migrants to the Sierra Nevada moved *to* the Range of Light and had a primary desire to live in a landscape dominated by Nature. These migrants of the early 1970s included members of the back-to-the-land movement, which attempted to achieve some degree of self-sufficiency through solar power, organic vegetable gardens, and informal co-ops as substitutes for the market economy. They also included families like my own, who simply wanted to live a rural lifestyle surrounded by the natural world. We remained connected to the electrical grid and the market economy, but we made economic sacrifices (in the pecuniary sense) in order to achieve a particular quality of life. There was a wide spectrum of alternative settlement options that reflected different settlement densities, proximity to neighbors, proximity to town, and economic isolation. All were distinctly nonurban in character, however, and the built environment did not dominate the landscape. We called it rural living, although I can see now that it was exurban rather than truly rural.

This desire to move to a more natural landscape and achieve a rural lifestyle continued to be the primary motivation until the early-to-mid-1980s, when a new wave of migrants swept across the Central Valley and onto the shores of the Sierra Nevada foothills. An increasing fraction of this new wave was primarily moving *from* the urban ills of metropolitan California and was generally less interested in the Sierra Nevada's ecological landscape than its social and cultural homogeneity. Both motivations have been present throughout the past three decades, of course, and both continue to be part of the ecotransformation turning the rest of the rural West into the exurban frontier. This second motivation has, however, led to more gated communities that look a lot more like affluent, all-white suburban communities than the dispersed settlement patterns that resulted from the first motivation. Gated communities already existed in the 1970s, but they first experienced significant growth in actual development of vacant parcels in the 1980s. Higher-density residential subdivisions are more likely to be built—and more likely to accommodate the needs of the new exurban residents—if living within and among Nature is not a primary factor in residential location choices. Indeed, the expansion of employment opportunities in the greater Sacramento metropolitan region has reduced the degree of economic sacrifice necessary for newer residents to live in the Sierra Nevada. The residents of those new higher-density subdivisions are also likely to have a different conception of Nature that, in part, reflects the places in which they live. And through living in that environment, their conception of Nature is less likely to be influenced through daily interaction with a world that is not human-dominated. This in turn has important implications for how the exurban landscape will be managed.

In either case, however, the exurban landscape is being transformed into a landscape of consumption rather than production. The newcomers do not

depend on the land for a living, so they can afford this view. They may also desire
a natural environment that matches their TV-based expectations, rather than the
gritty world that one learns to appreciate through hard experience. The influence
of nonlocal, nonexperiential media images on our conceptions of Nature is therefore a more important factor for newcomers than old-timers. Barry Lopez has
addressed this issue for American society in general with great insight:

> In the attenuated form in which it is presented on television today, in magazine arti-
> cles and in calendar photographs, the essential wildness of the American landscape
> is reduced to attractive scenery. We look out on a familiar, memorized landscape that
> portends adventure and promises enrichment. There are no distracting people in it
> and few artifacts of human life. The animals are all beautiful, diligent, one might
> even say well behaved. Nature's unruliness, the power of rivers and skies to intimi-
> date, and any evidence of disastrous human land management practices are all but
> invisible. It is, in short, a magnificent garden, a colonial vision of paradise imposed
> on a real place that is, at best, only selectively known. The real American landscape
> is a face of almost incomprehensible depth and complexity. (1992, 116)

Other writers have also characterized Nature as a garden that can be managed
carefully by humans to retain naturalness without preservation and museumification. Michael Pollan suggests that we actually have an obligation to treat all of
Nature as a garden, because the definition of what is natural otherwise skids down
a slippery slope in terms of humans' historical role in the landscape. "If I've
learned anything in the garden up to now," he says, "it is that the romantic's blunt
opposition of nature to culture is not helpful. (Consider the popular usage: land
is 'virgin' until men 'rape' it.) The romantic idea might encourage me to revere
and preserve what trees I had, yet it didn't offer much incentive to plant new
ones" (1991, 199). Pollan argues for an approach to Nature that "is frankly
anthropocentric" and based on the idea that we have "a legitimate quarrel with
nature" (227, 229). Any other view, he argues, fails to recognize history. The
romantic view of preservationists is a recent anomaly, a luxury of the industrial age
that fails to recognize humanity's continuing struggle with the elements.[8]

Pollan also critiques the wilderness concept as "a profoundly alienating idea,
for it drives a large wedge between man and nature" (1991, 214). It has also protected only 8 percent of our landscape, he notes, leaving the other 92 percent as
a collection of sacrifice zones. In this respect Pollan is right that we need to
approach the landscape without facing extreme either/or choices between
"preservation" and destruction. I am less sanguine than he, however, about our
collective ability "to make distinctions between kinds and degrees of human intervention in nature" that still allow for Nature to exist in a form that maintains the
basis for its historical relationship to Culture. This is one of the paradoxes of the
problem: we need Nature in its wildest form (including that social construct
known as wilderness) in order to maintain our respect for and appreciation of

Nature, yet the very act of setting Nature aside to "preserve" it can shackle and undermine its essential character.[9] Such acts can also only occur within the context of a society able to meet its basic needs in a way that no longer exposes it to Nature's vagaries—the very thing we are trying to preserve through such acts! But what can we protect in Nature if it is purely a social construct of Culture? Perhaps more important, how can we determine what are acceptable or appropriate actions toward Nature? Is there any place to draw a line on the slippery slope? Moreover, how does the production of Culture itself affect how we answer these questions about Nature?

Lopez touches on this problem by critiquing "the packaging and marketing of land as a form of entertainment," which substitutes Culture for Nature far past the point of unacceptability:

> An incipient industry, capitalizing on the nostalgia Americans feel for the imagined virgin landscapes of their fathers, and on a desire for adventure, now offers people a convenient though sometimes incomplete or even spurious geography as an inducement to purchase a unique experience. But the line between authentic experience and a superficial exposure to the elements of experience is blurred. And the real landscape, in all its complexity, is distorted even further in the public imagination. No longer innately mysterious and dignified, a ground from which experience grows, it becomes a curiously generic backdrop on which experience is imposed.
>
> In theme parks the profound, subtle, and protracted experience of running a river is reduced to a loud, quick, safe equivalence, a pleasant distraction. People only able to venture into the countryside on annual vacations are, increasingly, schooled in the belief that wild land will, and should, provide thrills and exceptional scenery on a timely basis. If it does not, something is wrong, either with the land itself or possibly with the company outfitting the trip. (1992, 122–23)

This conclusion is supported by Bill McKibben in his book *The Age of Missing Information*, where he highlights the difference between the information presented in twenty-four hours' worth of television on nearly a hundred cable television channels in Fairfax, Virginia, and what he learned in twenty-four hours spent camping in the Adirondacks State Park in upstate New York. McKibben points out that if your only exposure to Nature has come through television, you would expect to see animals killing each other or having sex within the first minute of getting out of your car at the campground (1992). But Nature moves at a pace very different from television's, and it takes time and patience to experience it and understand it. In our increasingly urbanized society, however, a smaller and smaller fraction of our population is exposed to that pace or given the time as a child to discover its magical power. Joseph Collins's book *Sharing Nature with Children* has sold more than half a million copies,[10] but children growing up in rural areas need no guidance to find their own adventures of discovery (Cobb 1977; Nabhan and Trimble 1994). Television images dominate the conceptions of those children growing up without exposure to an un-"man-aged" Nature in their daily lives. This has the potential to profoundly affect their conceptions of it.

The tension between theme park expectations of a sanitized, predictable experience and the desire by former urbanites to move "back to the land" is captured in a recent real estate advertisement for a condominium in the "Snowcreek at Mammoth" development in the eastern Sierra Nevada: "Creekside three bedroom unit w/full 2 car garage in a one of a kind setting—it's like Disneyland!" (Prudential/Mammoth Sierra Properties 1993). While the designers of Disneyland once sought to simulate natural landscapes in their development of the Matterhorn and the tropical environment of the Jungle Cruise, developers are now simulating the Disneylandscape for the global market in real estate experiences. Since most skiers and exurban residents in the Mammoth Lakes area are from Southern California (the *Los Angeles Times* is available there on a daily basis), buyers can feel comfortable in Mammoth knowing that they could just as well be in Anaheim.

Sharon Zukin discusses the relationship between production, consumption, power, and Disney's manufactured images in her 1991 book *Landscapes of Power.* Her key point is that Disney has successfully substituted imagined memories for real experience in the collective unconscious in a way that supports consumerism while maintaining and enhancing inequitable power structures. The prototype of Main Street, U.S.A. is now the one found in Disneyland—whether such a place ever actually existed or not. Moreover, a ride on the "Matterhorn" has substituted for most Americans' real exposure to the thrills, excitement, and genuine danger of mountain sports. Now we see an extension of this approach into daily life with Disney's construction of a neotraditional "community" in Celebration, Florida. The town hall is just a facade, however, for the community's residents have no democratic authority over decision-making in Celebration (Rymber 1996). How will new residents in the exurban landscape project those Disney images of both Nature and Culture into their daily lives and decisions about the landscape? It is difficult to discern at this point, but the Disneyfication of Culture could have profound consequences.[11]

So far I have emphasized the different conceptions of Nature that may exist among new exurban residents. There are also important social differences between newcomers and old-timers that affect the power relationships within exurban society and political discourse. The newcomers generally have more education, more wealth, more mobility, and less economic dependence on the extractive development of the natural resources in their area (B. Brown 1995). The old-timers are often faced with little choice but to continue their traditional jobs. To them the alternative appears to be a shift into lower-paying positions servicing wealthier urbanites. This has negative social and economic implications for them *personally,* so it is not surprising that they resist. The current system of state and federal policies offers few ways for the economic value of preserving the region's natural resources *in situ* to translate into the hard-currency benefits of exploiting those resources as commodities in the marketplace. Until those policies change, then, the old-timers will have little reason to embrace the newcomers and the eco-transformation they represent. This is true even if they believe philosophically that the environment should be protected from further exploitation. Their immediate focus is on feeding their families and maintaining a way of life—a threatened Culture, if you will—that is all they have ever known on this land.

A third group actively participates little in this debate. Many in this third group are retirees with large equity stakes from their urban homes and very little interest in supporting the rest of the exurban community. As shown above for Lake of the Pines and Lake Wildwood in Nevada County, they often have household incomes and median housing values more than twice the median values for the counties in which they reside. They tend to vote against tax increases and focus on maintaining their own little worlds. There is no need to support education for tomorrow's generation if you have no ties to the community and your grandchildren go to a private school in distant suburbia. Moreover, there is no need to protect recreational areas in the nearby national forest if you spend your vacations driving to Arizona or Baja every winter in your Winnebago. This third group basically stays out of the ongoing debate over land and resource management, but they represent the swing vote in local elections. As former El Dorado County supervisor Bill Center has described it, this group also includes residents too busy commuting to take part in public meetings (1991–96). Their primary focus in the exurban landscape is to reproduce a *cultural* setting that offers the same thing that suburbia offered its residents in the 1950s when they were abandoning the urban core in the face of desegregation.

These differences in values are evident in the results of a survey conducted by J. Moore Methods as part of the El Dorado County General Plan Update in 1992. An overwhelming 63 percent of those resident for more than twenty years felt that things in El Dorado County were "seriously off on the wrong track," while only 27 percent felt things were "going in the right direction." In contrast, residents of less than five years were much more favorable: only 36 percent said things were "seriously off on the wrong track," while 42 percent thought things were "going in the right direction." Those who had been in the county for five to ten and ten to twenty years lined up along the continuum: the longer the residence, the more negative the feelings about how things were going (J. Moore Methods 1992, 6-1). When asked which two items under consideration as part of the general plan update were most important, the newcomers cited "land uses and zoning" (44 percent) and "natural resources and open space" (41 percent). The old-timers cited the same two, but less overwhelmingly (38 percent and 26 percent respectively). The difference was picked up in "job development," "housing," "public health and safety," "agriculture and forestry," and "public services." Newcomers cited "transportation and roads" more frequently than the old-timers, probably reflecting their expectations based on recent urban and suburban experience. The overall conclusion of this analysis is that old-timers tend to have a broader set of concerns about economic development and the provision of public services, while the newcomers are focused primarily on those things they did not have in urban areas.[12]

Extractive-industry representatives and environmental advocates have battled over the future of land use and resource management policy in exurban areas through major conferences and active lobbying of state and federal agencies. It is notable that environmental groups have now begun to focus on the issue of economic development, while, in at least one case, the extractive industries wrapped their conference binder in green with the subtitle *Sustainable Development in Harmony with Nature.*[13] A recurring theme of the Wise Use activists is their claim that they are now the true environmentalists. This claim recognizes that most Americans see themselves as environmentalists (Dunlap 1987; Kempton et al. 1995). These same "wise use" groups now label mainstream environmental groups as extremists who threaten the environment with policies that place unnecessary restrictions on land and resource managers.[14]

This highly polarized point-counterpoint debate may be necessary at the state and federal levels, but it does little to further either side's understanding of the issues or the true interests or values (rather than positions) of the opposing side. These are complex issues, and the people affected by them have complex identities and competing values both within themselves and within their respective communities. The state and federal debate is the only place where nonlocal communities of interest can participate in the policy discourse, for these communities are bound by interest in rather than residence in place. Within the emerging exurban landscape, however, there is still an opportunity to accomplish the genuine work of resolving conflicts within the context of place-based communities. This will require hard work and a leap of faith among participants from both sides, who have usually faced each other only in the context of the black-and-white, winner-take-all world of litigation.

It may be that the two sides hold such fundamentally different values and such fundamentally conflicting interests that they will be unable to find any common ground. I believe they have much more in common than they realize, however, for they share a place and a landscape they all care about deeply. That landscape and their shared affection for it is what may bring them together—if they recognize that it is unique. Only when individuals are able to relate their concerns to a specific place and specific effects on specific people will they be able to see their common interests. Unfortunately, my optimism is based more on theory and hope than any strong empirical evidence that exurban residents are willing to find that common ground (Jones 1996a). Much of the public discourse, even within place-based communities, has been strident and subject to the same patterns of labeling and position taking that occur at the state and federal level. Moreover, many are concerned that placed-based collaborative or consensus efforts will dilute the influence of urban environmental constituencies while strengthening industry's bargaining leverage (McCloskey 1996a; 1996b). In the Sierra Nevada there are few exceptions to this conflict in discourse.[15]

Unless exurban residents engage in this discourse as a dialogue, however, we will continue to see the commodification and homogenization of landscape and place and reliance on the market as the only legitimate determinant of value. This would result in a mechanism for resolution of the emerging conflict that relies on a logic that calls for elimination of cultural diversity and the establishment of a homogeneous landscape in both social and ecological terms. Neither the old-timers nor the newcomers in exurbia want that—they have stayed in these rural regions or moved to them specifically to avoid what they view as the featureless landscape of metropolitan America that James Kunstler calls "the geography of nowhere" (1993). They share a common interest in seizing control of their own destiny and the future of the exurban landscape by defining a new, sustainable relationship to the environment.

This will not occur, however, unless the politics of interest can be reconciled with the politics of community to protect the interests and values of everyone who lives in or cares about the future of the Range of Light.

COMMUNITY POLITICS: CONSENSUS VERSUS INTERESTS

The conflict-laden experience that now permeates land and resource planning and management in the Sierra Nevada contrasts sharply with the idyllic social and political interactions that we often associate with small-town life. For this reason it is useful to highlight an important distinction between two types of politics in American society described by Robert Bellah and his colleagues:

> In the first understanding, politics is a matter of making operative the moral consensus of the community, reached through free face-to-face discussion. The process of reaching such a consensus is one of the central meanings of the word *democratic* in America. This understanding idealizes an individualism without rancor. Citizenship is virtually coextensive with "getting involved" with one's neighbors for the good of the community. Often Americans do not think of this process as "politics" at all. But where this understanding is seen as a form of politics, it is the New England township of legend, the self-governing small town singled out by Tocqueville, that remains the ideal exemplar. We call this first type "the politics of community."

This is the politics one hopes to find in a community planning process in exurbia, although we will see that the politics of community often give way to the politics of interest:

> In sharp contrast to the image of consensual community stands the second understanding, for which politics means the pursuit of differing interests according to agreed-upon, neutral rules. This is the realm of coalitions among groups with similar interests, of conflicts between groups with opposing interests, and of mediators and brokers of interest—the professional politicians. We call this second type the "politics of interest." It is sometimes celebrated by political scientists as "pluralism," but for ordinary Americans the connotation is often negative. The politics of interest is frequently seen as a kind of necessary evil in a large, diverse society, as a reluctantly agreed-to second best to consensual democracy.

The latter is recognized by most as one dimension of community land use planning, but we still hope that resolution of our conflicts will occur in the spirit of the politics of community rather than the politics of interest—which are seen as primarily self- rather than community-oriented:

> One enters the politics of interest for reasons of utility, to get what one or one's group needs or wants, rather than because of spontaneous involvement with others to whom one feels akin. To the extent that many of those we talked to see politics as meaning the politics of interest, they regard it as not entirely legitimate morally. Hence the generally low opinion of the politician as a figure in American life. Politics suffers in comparison with the market. The legitimacy of the market rests in large part on the belief that it rewards individuals impartially on the basis of fair competition. By contrast, the politics of negotiation at local, state and federal levels, though it shares the utilitarian attitudes of the market, often exposes a competition among groups in which inequalities of power, influence, and moral probity become highly visible as determinants of the outcome. At the same time, the politics of interest provides no framework for the discussion of issues other than the conflict and compromise of interests themselves. Visibly conducted by professionals, apparently rewarding all kinds of inside connections, and favoring the strong at the expense of the weak, the routine activities of interest politics thus appear as an affront to true individualism and fairness alike. (1985, 200–201)

As we will see below, the Nevada County General Plan update process began with an emphasis on the politics of community while still recognizing the legitimate differences in interest among the community's members. The politics of interest then overwhelmed the politics of community, however, and this is more likely to occur as exurban communities grow larger. Traditional bilateral relational controls give way to trilateral controls, in Rudel's typology.

Daniel Kemmis makes a case that the politics of community can be strengthened by focusing a community's attention on the genius loci of its place (1990), but Bellah and his colleagues found that the politics of interest often lay beneath or behind the myth of the politics of community: "In the actualities of the first type of politics, the politics of community[,] . . . it is the politics of interest . . . that has emerged. And it is in situations such as these that even local officials can be accused of 'playing politics'—that is, acting more in terms of interests than consensus" (1985, 204).

This distinction between the politics of *consensus* and the politics of *interests* is critical to our understanding of the politics of planning in the exurban landscape. The literature on the political economy of growth management focuses primarily on an interest-based model of public policy and planning, often following the so-called public choice school of group decision-making. This approach highlights the role of each group in acquiring the spoils of public policy to maximize its own utility. Each group is therefore truly a "special interest" and can be thought of as acting in self-interest only. While this may be a reasonable model for political processes that are highly formalized and abstract, it is difficult to reconcile that model with the social considerations inherent in individual behavioral choices in smaller communities. In this context, individuals are identifiable within groups and will be held responsible for the actions of those groups. There are consequently social constraints on self-interested utility-maximizing behavior. This is why Ostrom's, Ellickson's, and Putnam's findings regarding the role of social capital represent potentially important additions to Logan and Molotch's model of the political economy of growth. Rudel's framework implicitly captures this by recognizing that social controls will vary with density, size, and linkages with extralocal institutions or communities of interest.

Together these theories suggest that the politics of community will initially hold in a community that relies primarily on bilateral relational controls. At this point most community members' interests are congruent and their use values are not threatened by allowing high exchange values for each other. Growth will alter this relationship, however, until the politics of interest will be played out as a conflict between community members emphasizing either exchange values or use values as structural speculators use the formal institutions of planning to alter the spatial arrangement of allowable land uses in their favor. Community groups will then form in response to this effort to protect use values through trilateral relational controls on further development. The degree to which these conflicts and trilateral intervention will be necessary will in part be a function of the availability of social capital—which in turn is a function of the norms of reciprocity and networks of civic engagement that exist in a given community. Those communities that have these elements of social capital will resolve their conflicts in such a way that all interests will benefit by emphasizing the broader community's interest. Those communities that lack these elements will move increasingly toward dysfunctionality and conflict as they squander their social capital and fight over outcomes in a zero-sum game.

This has certainly been true in Nevada County. The increasing heterogeneity and scale of the population have weakened traditional social constraints over time, making an interest-based model more relevant. A similar transition point is evident in the case of El Dorado County. Smaller and more socially homogeneous communities in the Sierra Nevada—such as the town of Quincy in Plumas County in the Northern Sierra (with its strong dependence on the timber sector) and the town of Bishop in Inyo County in the Eastern Sierra (with its strong dependence on the recreation sector)—continue to have stronger social constraints, suggesting that the politics of community may still be identified as a higher value within those communities than that of interests. Larger and more socially heterogeneous communities, such as the city of Roseville (which has more in common with Sacramento than with the rest of Placer County), appear to be dominated more by the politics of interest.

Bellah and his colleagues found that there is a deep longing for a "return" to the idealized politics of community in America, despite the fact that "local consensual politics . . . often partly obscures discordant and conflicting realities" (222). This desire is nevertheless an important factor explaining the migration to rural and exurban places over the past three decades—decades that coincided with significant erosion of the credibility of a wide range of political institutions. Bellah and his colleagues observe, "Lacking the ability to deal meaningfully with the large-scale organizational and institutional structures that characterize our society, many of those we talked to turned to the small town not only as an ideal but as a solution to our present political difficulties. Nostalgia for the small town and the use of its image in political discussion was common regardless of political views" (204). The perceived social homogeneity of small towns appears to be an important factor influencing this idealized vision, contrasting sharply with the deepening social, ethnic, religious, and racial differences that increasingly polarize American society. Despite that search for social homogeneity, however, the exurban migrant's idealized vision of small town political life must now be considered in the context of intricate linkages to the rest of American and global society through markets and many nonlocal institutions that undermine idealized small town life: "The American search for spontaneous community with the like-minded is made urgent by the fear that there may be no way at all to relate to those who are too different. Thus the tremendous nostalgia many Americans have for the idealized 'small town.' The wish for a harmonious community we heard from a variety of sources is a wish to transform the roughness of utilitarian dealings in the marketplace, the courts, and government administration into neighborly conciliation" (ibid.).

Many in the exurban landscape sincerely want to and are doing all they can to increase the relative importance of "the practices of the town meeting or the fellowship of the church" in their lives. If, as former House Speaker "Tip" O'Neill once said, "all politics is local," it is because people live their lives in real places and at a local scale rather than in distant capitals. Washington, D.C., and Sacramento seem too large and too far away for us to influence as individuals, making national and state-level politics an exercise in abstraction. Moreover, the deep cynicism of Americans for the politics of interest has largely ceded those forums to those interests.

In contrast, city and county governments are accessible and tangible. The Nevada City fire chief was a classmate of mine and he also works as a check stand clerk at the locally owned grocery store, SPD; we can discuss the fire department's request for a new fire station while I buy my beer. The mayor of Grass Valley was another classmate of mine and he runs Foothill Flowers with his mother; it's easy to stop by to see him when I'm in town if I want to talk to him about the proposed expansion of the wastewater treatment plant. Yesterday Teresa's parents hosted a dinner for a dozen people from Truckee, including the city's first mayor and the current mayor. The latter had just returned from a League of California Cities conference on redevelopment and asked our views on the issue as we looked across Donner Lake in the waning light. Individual votes really do count when elections are decided by tens of votes. The politics of community—"a matter of making operative the moral consensus of the community, reached through free face-to-face discussion"—is still possible in the exurban landscape (Bellah et al. 1985). I cannot imagine a similar degree of contact in Berkeley or with the Alameda County government, which services 1,279,182 people—more than the state of Maine, which has two U.S. senators for its 1,227,928 people (U.S. Bureau of Census 1990). The city of Berkeley itself has more people (104,900) in its nineteen-square-mile area than live in the 978 square miles of Nevada County, which is more than fifty times as large but has only 89,000 residents (Berkeley Chamber of Commerce 1997; McAdams 1997a).

The politics of community are nevertheless threatened by the rapid changes confronting exurban communities. The social, demographic and economic changes of the past three decades have diminished the social homogeneity of the exurban landscape while simultaneously making anonymity possible through the sheer numbers of people in the community. This is where the experience of western Nevada County supports Rudel's succession model of social controls (Rudel 1989). Christopher Alexander and his colleagues have described a "Community of 7000" as a maximum size for humanely scaled communities in their book *A Pattern Language: Towns, Buildings, Construction* (the companion to Alexander's book *The Timeless Way of Building*). "Individuals have no effective voice in any community of more than 5000–10,000 persons," they state (1977, 71), according to Paul Goodman's "rule of thumb, based on cities like Athens in their prime, that no citizen be more than two friends away from the highest member of the local unit" (72). Assuming that each person knows about 12 households in his or her local community, "an optimum size for a political community would be about 12^3 or

1,728 households or 5,500 persons" (ibid.). While the specific numeric optimum is arguable, this is approximately the order-of-magnitude for a maximum community size that can still allow for meaningful interaction among *all* citizens for a true politics of community. Allowing for personal relationships with 20 households per person yields an upper limit of about 25,000 people. Perhaps as many as 50,000 people in the community (the threshold used by the U.S. Census Bureau to declare a county "metropolitan" if a single city exceeds it) represents an upper limit; it is certainly far less than 100,000.[16]

Nevada County had slightly over 26,000 residents in 1970 and more than twice that number in 1980. It is perhaps no coincidence that it was around 1980—when the threshold of 50,000 had been crossed—that it also became possible to make a statement to the local press about someone with the knowledge that most people reading or hearing it would not know that person. By doing so, the political debates of community shifted from the post office—where we ran into each other while picking up our mail—to the newspapers and radio. Face-to-face interaction was then diminished, as was recognition of mutual interest. We lost our ability to confirm or deny accusations or claims through our own experience. It is no coincidence that the first commercial radio station in the community appeared around the same time.[17]

It is within this emerging social context that we must consider the politics of planning in the exurban landscape. The literature on metropolitan and state-level growth management is instructive about the politics of interest, while others have written about the politics of community. Gerrit Knaap and Arthur Nelson offer an excellent overview of the political economy of growth management in their 1992 book, *The Regulated Landscape,* where they complete both a class- and interest-based analysis of land use planning institutions in Oregon. Studies from California and Florida both show that class alone does not explain support for growth controls, but support for such measures is correlated with class *characteristics* such as income, occupation, education, gender, location, and home ownership (1992, 188). Support for Oregon's controls is also split along general interest characteristics: urban versus rural, service versus commodity employment, and renters versus homeowners. Two analyses of the 1976 Oregon Referendum reached contradictory conclusions about the importance of class as a determinant of growth control support, however. This may be explained by differentiating between class-based correlations at the individual level (which are weak) and similar correlations at the level of community aggregation (which are strong).[18]

Knaap and Nelson develop a useful framework for linking interest-based models of political processes with various regulatory structures. That system characterizes four distinct types of regulatory systems: distributive, where the general public allocates resources to selected groups; self-regulatory, where the general public allocates power to selected groups; redistributive, where specific groups transfer resources to other specific groups; and regulatory, where disparate individuals allocate power to centralized systems.

Because they require the identification of specific "winners" and "losers," both redistributive and regulatory systems are difficult to implement. Distributing the general public's resources or power to selected groups is considerably easier, however, because the specific groups are clear "winners" and the costs are borne by the broader public. This framework helps to clarify why some types of programs are strongly supported (e.g., expenditure of funds by the California Tahoe Conservancy, which come from the general public but generate specific localized benefits) while others face stiff resistance (e.g., the Tahoe Regional Planning Agency's regulatory process, which prohibits specific landowners from developing their parcels—while the benefits of such prohibitions are enjoyed by the general public). These and other growth management tools and institutions are discussed in more detail below.

In the context of land use planning and growth management, Knaap and Nelson identify three primary interest groups in pluralistic politics. A similar set exists for Nevada County politics: "developers, land speculators, builders, mortgage financiers, etc."; "highly organized groups interested in preserving environmental quality"; and "an amorphous collection of homeowners and neighborhood groups who prefer decentralized planning to preserve their social environment" (i.e., maintain social homogeneity) (195–96).

All three groups share similar upper-class origins, according to Knaap and Nelson, but they differ over which elements of the status quo should be protected. Successful policies therefore tend to provide something for all three groups, but those policies also tend to lack substance and to harm the unrepresented poor. Policies therefore tend to 1) have a procedural focus, as, for example, CEQA does; 2) have inconsistent objectives, leaving room for multiple interpretations of which ones should be emphasized; 3) be initially decentralized, reflecting the third group's power and the first group's preference for this; 4) become more centralized over time, reflecting the failure to achieve the second group's objectives as long as they are decentralized; 5) concentrate benefits; and 6) result in reduced social justice (196). This latter point reflects the general exclusion or nonparticipation in the politics of interest by nonelites, although their interests may sometimes correspond to those of some of the other groups. This result is, however, likely only if the resulting policies decrease affordable housing opportunities. Growth management systems that avoid, or even reduce, constraints on affordable housing development will not necessarily result in reduced social justice.

Knaap and Nelson observe that the interest-group coalitions changed over time in Oregon as implementation shifted from initially distributive policies to policies that were more redistributive. They also note that "the general thrust of state planning is determined by the general population, but . . . specific policy issues are resolved by competition among interest groups" (202). Among those interest groups, only some of them were ultimately successful: "environmentalists (in protecting environmentally sensitive areas), conservationists (in protecting farmland and forest land), and industrialists (in fostering economic development)." In contrast, some interest groups "ended up losers" by fighting the establishment of state-level growth management institutions: "county governments (on maintaining local control), farmers (on developing farmland), and exclusionists (on zoning out the poor)." Their conclusion focuses on state-level policy development rather than implementation, however, and Knaap and Nelson recognize that "it is clear that interest groups successful at the state level were not necessarily the same interest groups successful at land use politics at the local level" (ibid.).

This is also true in the Sierra Nevada: I never emphasize my title as a professor at UC Berkeley when I testify before the Nevada County Board of Supervisors or the Grass Valley City Council but instead highlight my family's long history in the community and my personal relationships with the decision makers. In contrast, I don't mention those things at all when I testify before a state or federal agency or the state legislature. Credentials and interests are what matter in those contexts, not a relational identity that emphasizes our mutual destiny and interdependence. Moreover, urban values dominate at the state and federal levels, whereas social and economic ties to traditional resource extractive industries have a greater influence at the local level through community mythology. "Resource-based industries and neighborhood groups are more effective at the local level," observe Knaap and Nelson, while "service-based industries and environmentalists are more effective at the state level. Developers, thus far, appear remarkably effective at both levels of government" (203). The same appears to be true in the Sierra Nevada.

Bellah and his colleagues note that national political parties in the United States function as "a party more of allied interests than, as in Europe, of ideology" and are the primary means of overcoming "the crazy quilt of conflicting and overlapping interests" to elect the president. The president then serves to unify national interests through symbolic interactions with the population and the exercise of an elusive quality known as "leadership." "In a variety of public rituals, in foreign relations, and above all in war, the sense of being part of a living national community colors the meaning of life. The politics of the nation is a positive image for most citizens. It is a notion that bypasses the reality of utilitarian interest bargaining by appealing for legitimacy to the first type of politics—the vision of consensual, neighborly community" (Bellah et al. 1985, 202).

These same opportunities to unify the identity of the people for a common purpose do not occur as readily at the state level. It may still be important, however, where citizens of a state identify with each other as sharing a common culture and way of life that deserves their mutual collaboration for protection, as occurred in Vermont and Oregon, both of which adopted strong state-level growth management systems in the early 1970s. This is generally not true in California, where its geographic scale, population size, and social heterogeneity diminish the likelihood of a singular commonly held identity as "Californian." The 32.6 million people residing on California's 100 million acres have difficulty identifying with each other as sharing a common fate. Indeed, even white middle-class suburbanites in Northern and Southern California—who have much in common in terms of social and physical environments—differentiate themselves from each other to such a degree that marketing campaigns have been developed to emphasize these differences.[19] I often note that I am from *Northern* California, for example, living far from the beaches of Southern California. There have also been repeated legislative efforts to divide the state into two or three new states (Smith and Di Leo 1983). Other large states, such as New York, have experienced a similar split between their urban and rural residents.[20] This has even been true in Oregon whenever land use planning has been on the ballot: rural areas in the state have rejected greater control, while the Portland area has endorsed it (Knaap and Nelson 1992).

Regional governmental structures usually represent an effort by state-level interests to impose some degree of coordination and control on local interests that would otherwise not behave in ways consistent with those interests who hold power at the state level. Not surprisingly, this has often been resisted. "Traditionally," says Dennis Machida, "local government has been at war with regional government—and the reason is that they thought it wasn't in their interests" (1995). This has been true in California with both the Tahoe Regional Planning Agency and the California Coastal Commission. Oregon's original Senate Bill 100 also included provisions to establish strong regional Councils of Government, but these were eliminated from the legislation before passage (Knaap and Nelson 1992).

The California Coastal Commission was originally established by passage of a state initiative in 1972 with 55 percent of the vote. Proposition 20 led to development of a statewide California Coastal Plan in 1975, but the state legislature viewed that plan as too specific for implementation by a state-level institution. Subsequent legislation in 1976 then modified the process so that Local Coastal Plans (LCPs) were developed by local governments. These LCPs were then subject to the review and approval of the state-level Coastal Commission, similar to Oregon's Senate Bill 100 process. Local implementing ordinances for the LCPs are also assumed to be vertically consistent with state-level policies unless rejected by the Coastal Commission within ninety days, placing the burden of rejection on the commission. Once approved by the commission, local governments retain responsibility to implement the LCPs. The commission has authority to review LCP implementation only if a "substantial issue" of statewide significance is raised, or if it involves an action affecting the land between the road nearest the coast and the shoreline (Fisher 1995; Rodriguez 1995).

This institutional model avoids the establishment of new regional institutions while maintaining the tension between state and local interests through policy formulation and implementation. This tension underlies many of the conflicts over recurring proposals either to delegate and decentralize or to consolidate and increasingly centralize regulatory power in land use planning and resource management. It also represents a desire to integrate the politics of community and the politics of interest—where some interests may not be aligned with the politics of community. Bifurcated institutional arrangements like the Oregon land use system and the California Coastal Commission represent an attempt to achieve this integration without the development of intermediate agencies like the TRPA that actually supersede "home rule" land use regulation by local jurisdictions. The TRPA tries to achieve that integration through the structure of its governing board rather than through a bifurcated state-local balance of power.

Several ideas could, however, improve community decision-making without moving to regional governance, by simply shifting the terms of political discourse within the existing institutional structure. Perhaps most important, solving the planning problems of rapidly growing exurban communities requires a community dialogue on community values that emphasizes *interests* and *ends* rather than *positions* and *means* (Duane 1992b; Fisher and Ury 1982). All too often the battle lines have been drawn to pit developers against environmentalists and residents against local businesses in a bipolar debate that *assumes* we face either/or choices between economic development and environmental quality. In many cases this is the result of our current planning paradigm in rural America: designed for urban areas and transplanted to a setting where decline was the dominant problem, rapidly growing exurban regions are ill-equipped to handle growth in a way that protects the rural character and environmental qualities of place. Environmental health is not a luxury in the emerging amenity economy of exurbia, however; it is the foundation of economic wealth. I will describe several creative alternatives below that can protect both. We should therefore not assume that protecting environmental quality is either inconsistent with (or in conflict with) economic well-being or that to protect it requires draconian regulatory restrictions on private property rights.

Unfortunately, this is how the debate has usually been framed: as a false choice between allowing unbridled free enterprise with unlimited private property rights and stifling governmental controls on land use that will destroy the local economy on the first step toward socialism. We clearly need to have a dialogue on the rights and responsibilities of both private property and government. It is time for the rhetoric to match the reality. An alternative framework for private property rights and public responsibilities is therefore necessary.

PRIVATE PROPERTY RIGHTS
AND PUBLIC RESPONSIBILITIES

Good plans and good planning principles are not enough to redirect the insatiable appetite of the growth machine: those good intentions must be coupled with legally binding policies that have the political legs to withstand the growth machine's inevitable attempts to turn good plans into hollow icons of planning's impotence. In the United States this means that we must address the meaning of private property as well as the legality and political viability of specific regulatory policies that may come into conflict with private property rights. Edward A. Williams recognized this reality when he wrote a report in 1965 on land use in California: "The traditional view toward private property that permits the temporary owner a proprietary interest has been outmoded by new knowledge of man's relationship to nature and to the community. This knowledge demands a new attitude toward ownership of land, substituting the concept of trusteeship for exploitation."[21]

Solving the planning problems of rapidly growing exurban communities requires a community dialogue on community values and the meaning of property, both public and private (Duane 1992b). Planning and public policy are not only about technical questions, but instead go to the heart of what our values are and what tradeoffs we are willing to make among them. Part of this dialogue must consider the relationship between private property rights and public values (Bellah et al. 1985). As Carol Rose notes in her 1994 book, *Property and Persuasion: Essays on the History, Theory, and Rhetoric of Ownership*, the rights one has to property are primarily a function of what the community agrees one has. The dialogue about those rights includes claims by purported owners, of course, and those claims are sometimes sufficient to allow exercise of proclaimed rights. The property rights regime itself remains a public good, however, which can be provided only if there is cooperation among those who will both claim and exercise property rights. This has led John Dwyer and Peter Menell to treat property rights regimes and property itself as "systems of governance" (1997). No rights inhere a priori in any *thing* that we call property, notwithstanding the rhetoric of some about natural rights. Rights instead reflect agreed-upon systems of social control that legitimize some actions and constrain others.

The concept of private property rights is well-established in both the Constitution and American political philosophy.[22] As Daniel Kemmis notes, however, the country's founding fathers also believed that those rights could exist only within a framework of broader social responsibility for the good of the community (1990). These *responsibilities* that come with the ownership and management of private property have received much less attention in the ongoing debate about the limits of regulation than private property *rights* have (Humbach 1992b). Even the exercise of the public prerogative to constrain private actions that might harm the greater community has been justified primarily under the theory of the *police power*, for example, where public action has been deemed allowable if it is necessary to avoid some *harm* that would otherwise occur. This approach is one fundamentally built on nuisance law.[23] The prevention of harm to others' private property rights therefore rationalizes regulation. The focus of such an approach is the restriction of some activities on private property in order to protect others' private property rights.

This approach places the burden on the public sector to identify the possible harm and justify any actions that may constrain private actions; the presumption is that private actions should otherwise be allowed without constraint. While the courts have taken a liberal view toward the exercise of the police power since the nineteenth century, they have recently moved toward a more restrictive stance. It is, however, arguable whether this reflects an emerging new social consensus on the appropriate role of government intervention or simply a concern that the scope of government regulation has reached unacceptable levels of interference with competing social values.[24] The Supreme Court, while recently shifting toward a more conservative makeup following twenty years' worth of Republican presidents in the twenty-four-year period from 1968 to 1992, is not necessarily any more conservative than many of the courts that previously upheld local governments' exercise of the police power.[25]

Indeed, private rights in property have never been absolute (Rose 1994). They have always been exercised within a social context that made some uses of property acceptable and others unacceptable. This has been true even for absolute monarchs, who had to consider the social costs of land use despite the absence of formal legal constraints on their actions. Social restrictions on use have always existed in fact if not in law. This social context sets the stage for our consideration of private property and the public's regulation of uses, for it is the social context that gave rise to our modern legal institutions and which fundamentally must underlie any analysis of the legal limitations to public regulation. This remains especially true in the social context of the exurban landscape, where the social distances and anonymity of modern metropolitan life make the abstract tools of litigation and legislation less absolute in their power to determine outcomes. Social controls still have a bearing on behavior in the exurban social context. This will be demonstrated below, where some groups with the *legal* power to constrain action on the Nevada County General Plan chose not to in 1995 because of the likely *social* consequences.

An alternative theory of property holds that the so-called *right* to develop private property is instead a *privilege*, granted by the public to private individuals under the *condition* that the individual receiving that public grant exercise *responsibility* to protect the public interest. The privilege of development therefore entails *obligations* to the community. This notion of community obligations under-lay even the granting of corporate charters until recently. Individuals were granted the right to organize themselves according to a corporate model (which gave them the benefits of individual immunity from liability for the corporation's debts) with an obligation to benefit society (Hawken 1993). Reciprocity compelled such an obligation; the grant of immunity from liability otherwise imposed costs on society without a corresponding benefit.[26] The parallel perspective on property rights views any government restriction as really an allowance of a certain level and type of development. The glass is then half full rather than half empty. Allowing a lower level or different type of development is then not a restriction, since there is no presumption of an unlimited right in the first place. As Aldo Leopold has sug-gested, we have both privileges and obligations to the land (1949). Even rights have responsibilities associated with them, for there is no unlimited right if one's actions cause harm to another. Under this approach property rights are instead sometimes described as property interests—which are held by both the commu-nity and the individual who holds title to the property subject to community con-straints on use (Strong et al. 1996; Emerson 1997; Pendall 1997; Jacobs 1997).

Embracing such a theory of private property rights—and private parties' responsibility to meet broader public objectives, as defined by the community—would go a long way to integrate innovative approaches into the prevailing land-use planning paradigm. Such an integration will be necessary to solve the prob-lems facing rapidly growing exurban regions. In short, it may be necessary for us to redefine our concept of the relationship between private benefit and the pub-lic good in a fundamental way. As Aldo Leopold suggested in his discussion of the need for a new "land ethic," "the mechanism of operation is the same for any ethic: social approbation for right actions: social disapproval for wrong actions."[27] Such social approbation and social disapproval can be institutionalized more for-mally through a land-use planning system that legally defines what is acceptable. We effectively do so already to protect our private interests from the nuisance of an irresponsible neighbor's private actions; we just have not yet structured a system to protect the *public* interest from such actions. Such an expansion of our con-ception of the role of planning and the responsibilities bundled with private prop-erty rights is now necessary.

This perspective affects whether or not land-use regulations can be thought of as a taking of private property without just compensation in violation of the Fifth Amendment to the United States Constitution. The Fifth Amendment has been the focus of recent attacks on environmental and land use regulation, and the 104th and then the 105th Congress introduced several so-called takings bills that would have required government compensation to any landowner whose land value was reduced by anywhere from 10 to 50 percent, that is, "taken" without due compensation, as a result of government regulation (Sax 1996a). Similar bills have been proposed at the state level in every state except Connecticut, and twenty states enacted some form of takings legislation from 1991 to 1996.[28] Many other bills were introduced and died either in state legislatures or by gubernatorial vetoes.

These bills have varied in their requirements but fall into one of three broad categories: 1) attorney general review laws, which require an opinion by the attorney general's office that regulations are consistent with takings jurisprudence; 2) assessment laws, which require agencies to conduct complex and expensive studies to determine how their programs might affect property owners; and 3) compensation laws, where compensation must actually be paid for reductions in property value attributable to the regulation or government action. This latter class of legislation has been adopted only in Florida, Louisiana, Mississippi, and Texas.[29] The governors of Colorado, Idaho, and Oregon have vetoed compensation bills, while 60 percent of the voters have rejected similar proposals in both Washington and Arizona. They did so at least in part because the bills would have required extremely costly and time-consuming efforts by public agencies to determine the loss of value resulting from regulation. Both the price tag and the potential for additional delays in the regulatory process scared many voters away (Frank 1996; Sax 1996a).

This flurry of initiative and legislative activity reflects a counterattack by the Wise Use movement against the expansion of government regulation to protect the environment over the past three decades (Jacobs 1995). The focus on legislative changes also reflects the relatively limited success that these parties have had in the courts, which have traditionally deferred to the legislative and executive branch and intervened only in the most egregious cases of unfair regulation. There has nevertheless been a series of court cases in the past decade that has begun to prescribe and circumscribe stricter limits on government regulation. It will be useful to review those cases briefly to see what is legally acceptable under current law.

The Fifth Amendment includes the following takings clause: "Nor shall private property be taken for public use without just compensation." Those twelve words were originally interpreted only so as to restrict the physical invasion of a private property owner's land and the taking of that property for a public use, such as for a public park or military armory. The rise of the regulatory state presented a different problem, however, that has since been the focus of takings jurisprudence: is it a taking if a government action, whether physical or not, results in a diminution of private property's value without just compensation? This latter concept is referred to as inverse condemnation, where the government does not formally condemn private property through eminent domain but may otherwise restrict its use in such a way as to "take" the value of its use from the private party for a public use. The inverse condemnation problem arises frequently in land use and environmental regulation, for both systems of social control invariably affect private property values while simultaneously generating benefits for, or avoiding harms that would befall, the broader public in the absence of such regulation. The problem of takings is not limited either to land use and environmental regulation or to the recent rise of the administrative regulatory state, however, so it is useful to trace the roots of takings jurisprudence across more than a century of American history.

One of the earliest cases in relevant takings law was *Mugler v. Kansas*, which demonstrated in 1887 the relationship between traditional nuisance law and modern government regulation.[30] Mugler owned a brewery whose value was significantly diminished when the state of Kansas adopted a constitutional amendment in 1880 that prohibited the production or sale of liquor. The focus of this federal litigation was on the Fourteenth Amendment's admonishment that "no State shall make or enforce any law which shall abridge the privileges or immunities of citizens of the United States; nor shall any State deprive any person of life, liberty, or property, without due process of law." (Note that "property" had taken the place of "the pursuit of happiness" between the signing of the Declaration of Independence in 1776 and adoption of the Fourteenth Amendment in 1868.)[31] The Court justified Kansas's exercise of the police power in this case by focusing on the potential nuisance consequences of unfettered private action. "While power does not exist with the whole people to control rights that are purely and exclusively private," noted the Court, "government may require 'each citizen to so conduct himself, and so use his own property, as not unnecessarily to injure another.'"[32] Modern takings law is therefore not limited to cases where society is limiting private property use in order to protect some environmental value (implicitly in conflict with the values of the marketplace). Whereas the social context of Kansas in the 1880s was concerned with the social costs of liquor manufacture and consumption, the principle established in *Mugler* applies equally today to widespread concern about the cultural and environmental consequences of land use and the unfettered exercise of private property rights.

Note also that the Fourteenth Amendment refers specifically to protection of *privileges* rather than *rights*. The *Mugler* court—certainly one not dominated by modern environmental interests, even if the Sawyer decision had just ushered in an early era of environmental litigation in 1884—also affirmed the notion that these powers include the power of the state to grant *privileges* such as the "right" to produce and sell liquor. "Such a right does not inhere in citizenship," noted the Court.[33] My proposed distinction between privileges and rights is therefore neither recent nor radical.

The Court made it clear that the range of regulations permissible under the police power, as long as they were otherwise constitutional, was quite broad: "Under our system that power is lodged with the legislative branch of the government. It belongs to that department to exert what are known as the police powers of the State, and to determine, primarily, what measures are appropriate or need-ful for the protection of the public morals, the public health, or the public safety." It added that "neither the [Fourteenth] Amendment—broad and comprehensive as it is—nor any other amendment, was designed to interfere with the power of the State, sometimes termed its police power, to prescribe regulations to promote the health, peace, morals, education, and good order of the people, and to legis-late so as to increase the industries of the State, develop its resources, and add to its wealth and prosperity."[34] As I demonstrated earlier, the "wealth and prosperity" of the Sierra Nevada now depends on the maintenance of its environmental amenities; environmental regulation could therefore easily fall within this scope.

Legal observers have recently focused on a distinction between regulations that prevent a public harm (as a legitimate use of the police power) and those that result in acquisition of a public benefit (as an unconstitutional use of the police power), but in *Mugler* the Court made no such distinction between policies intended "to protect the community, or to promote the general well-being."[35] This distinction has instead been introduced by more recent Court decisions.

The police power nevertheless still owes its origins to the common law of nui-sance. "It rests upon the fundamental principle that every one [*sic*] shall so use his own as not to wrong and injure another," stated the Court. "To regulate and abate nuisances is one of its ordinary functions." The Court added that compensation to private landowners under such regulation was not required "for pecuniary losses they may sustain, by reason of their not being permitted, by a noxious use of their property, to inflict injury upon the community." This is true even if such laws are enacted *after* landowners have purchased their properties and made investments in those activities that are otherwise lawful at the time. Mugler had made significant investments in his brewery property, "but the State did not thereby give any assurance or come under an obligation, that its legislation upon that subject would remain unchanged." This observation by the Court recognizes the changing nature of law and the social contract. Law is a creative process, and neither investors nor landowners can assume that the laws will remain as written forever. As the Court later said, "Circumstances may so change in time . . . as to clothe with such a [public] interest what at other times . . . would be a matter of purely private concern."[36]

This dynamic social process led to land use regulation and zoning in the face of expanding urbanization and industrialization in the twentieth century. Early applications of such regulation usually invoked the police power to promote eco-nomic development, although in some cases it is difficult to distinguish economic development from the protection of amenity values. In fact, in *Hadacheck v. Sebastian* in 1915 the U.S. Supreme Court supported strict land use regulation designed to protect economic development and "progress" through amenity-oriented residential development.[37] While the arguments in the case again focused on the equal protection clause of the Fourteenth Amendment, the case established several important legal principles that legitimated modern land use regulation. In particular, the Court found that the city of Los Angeles's prohibitions against Hadacheck's brickyard operation (which were designed to protect the amenity values of the region that underlay the city's rapid residential development) were acceptable under the police power despite an alleged 92 percent reduction in land value (the land was worth "about $800,000 for the entire tract for brick-making purposes, and not exceeding $60,000 for residential purposes or for any purpose other than the manufacture of brick").[38] The Court also noted the California Supreme Court's distinction between *Hadacheck* and another case, where the California court rejected as unconstitutional an ordinance in San Francisco "to absolutely deprive the owners of real property . . . of a valuable right incident to their ownership."[39] This distinction established an important principle that holds today: a regulation cannot eliminate *all* property value without violating either the Fifth or Fourteenth Amendment: *some* economic use must remain after imposition of the restrictions.

But the police power was reaffirmed by *Hadacheck* as a necessary power in a social world, where the uses of private property must be considered in the context of the broader community: "It is to be remembered that we are dealing with one of the most essential powers of government, one that is the least limitable. It may, indeed, seem harsh in its exercise, usually is on some individual, but the imperative necessity for its existence precludes any limitation upon it when not exerted arbitrarily. A vested interest cannot be asserted against it because of conditions once obtaining. To so hold would preclude development and fix a city forever in its primitive conditions. There must be progress, and if in its march private interests are in the way they must yield to the good of the community" (citations omitted).[40]

The Court also made it clear that the legislature (in this case, the Los Angeles City Council) was in the best position to determine what was necessary for the "good of the community." The burden of proof in challenging the Court's presumption of the ordinance's validity therefore lay with Hadacheck. "We must accord good faith to the city in the absence of a clear showing to the contrary and an honest exercise of judgment upon the circumstances which induced its action," stated the Court. This principle regarding the burden of proof in disputes over regulatory excess continued to hold until the *Lucas* and *Dolan* cases in the 1990s.[41]

There was considerable expansion of local, state, and federal regulation of land use on private property to protect social and environmental values in the time between *Hadacheck* and *Lucas*. The most ubiquitous of these controls came in the form of zoning, validated in 1926 by the Court as a legitimate exercise of the police power in *Euclid v. Ambler Realty Co.* This affirmation spawned widespread application of so-called Euclidian zoning, named after the town winning the case. Other important takings challenges included a successful repeal of statewide coal mining regulations in *Pennsylvania Coal v. Mahon* in 1922 and a claim against the United States government for a nonphysical taking resulting from the effects of low-flying aircraft over a farm in 1946 (*United States v. Causby*).[42] Both cases helped to clarify the boundaries and the limits of regulation and related government action. Neither fundamentally tipped the balance, however, against the general expansion of government that spanned the century between the Civil War and Johnson's Great Society. The Great Depression, FDR's New Deal, World War II, and the cold war all contributed to this expanded government role. By the 1970s government regulation affected nearly every aspect of social and economic life. Justice Oliver Wendell Holmes made the necessity of this clear even in his 1922 decision repealing the restrictive regulation in *Pennsylvania Coal v. Mahon:* "Government hardly could go on," he said," if to some extent values incident to the property could not be diminished without paying for every such change in the general law."[43]

He also cautioned, however, that "if a regulation goes too far it will be recognized as a taking."[44] This opened the door for so-called inverse condemnation claims against government regulations. The critical question remained, however, as to what constituted "too far."

It is in this social context that modern environmental regulation and growth management regimes began to affect land use on private property. These restrictions were applied in a wide range of development contexts, from downtown Manhattan (*Penn Central Transportation Co. v. New York City*) to exclusive suburban communities in Marin County, California (*Agins v. Tiburon*).[45] The former reaffirmed the *Mugler* and *Hadacheck* precedents that a regulatory taking did not occur unless the landowner was deprived of *all* economic value for his or her land, but it also established a reference to "distinct investment-backed expectations" as the basis for determining the degree of diminution. *Agins* established repeal of the regulation as the remedy for a regulatory taking. Both cases also made it clear that legitimate public interests must be advanced by the regulation. The *Loretto v. Teleprompter* case also established that a *physical* invasion of property (even for something as small as a cable TV connection) could not be compelled by the government without compensation.[46] From 1887 until 1987, then, governments were essentially free to enact regulatory restrictions under the following conditions: a clear public purpose was advanced by the regulation; there was no complete diminution of economic value;[47] there was no physical invasion of the property; there was consistent application of the restrictions to like-situated landowners.

Moreover, the governments faced no risk of having to pay economic compensation if the regulation was found unconstitutional. The remedy was instead the repeal of the regulation. This created a low-risk environment for imposing regulatory controls that flirted with the line of constitutional acceptability. The burden of challenging a regulation also lay with the landowner. This framework was largely supported as late as 1987, when the Court reaffirmed these principles in *Key Bituminous Coal Assn. v. De Benedectis:*

> Under our system of government, one of the State's primary ways of preserving the public weal is restricting the uses individuals can make of their property. While each of us is burdened somewhat by such restrictions, we, in turn, benefit greatly from the restrictions that are placed on others. These restrictions are "properly treated as part of the burden of common citizenship." Long ago it was recognized that "all property in this country is held under the implied obligation that the owner's use of it shall not be injurious to the community," and the Takings Clause did not transform that principle to one that requires compensation whenever the State asserts its power to enforce it.[48]

Moreover, the Court cited its decision in *Penn Central* to reaffirm that even complete diminution of value for one component of the full "bundle" of property rights did not constitute a taking under its previous decisions, and that the value of the full bundle of rights must still be considered when making the determination of whether or not *all* value had been eliminated: "Taking jurisprudence does not divide a single parcel into discrete segments and attempt to determine whether rights in a particular segment have been entirely abrogated. In deciding whether a particular governmental action has effected a taking, this Court focuses rather both on the character of the action and on the nature of the interference with rights *in the parcel as a whole*" (emphasis in original).[49]

Despite the Court's affirmation of Pennsylvania's regulations in the majority opinion, a dissenting opinion was entered by Chief Justice William Rehnquist and joined by Justices Lewis Powell, Sandra Day O'Connor, and Antonin Scalia. In particular, they challenged this final point that the constituent elements composing the bundle of property rights could not be disaggregated. In fact, they noted that Pennsylvania law specifically recognized transferable rights in the specific component in question. Complete diminution of the value of this component therefore represented a taking under the Court's precedents—even if that value represented only 2 percent of the total value of property held by the plaintiffs.[50] This distinction proves critical to planners when considering the relationship between subdivision regulations, zoning, and other restrictions. The subdivision act itself—when severable rights in individual parcels may be created—may now prove to be the most important step influencing the acceptability of other regulatory restrictions (Frank 1995).

The minority also emphasized the distinction between protecting against a public harm, that is, for which there is a nuisance rationale for police power, and acquiring a public benefit, that is, for which compensation must be paid. Noting the Court's *Pennsylvania Coal* decision of 1922 (which found a similar regulation unconstitutional) and its *Monongahela* decision from 1893, Rehnquist argued that the Fifth Amendment was intended to prevent "the public from loading upon one individual more than his just share of the burdens of government, and says that when he surrenders to the public something more and different from that which is exacted from other members of the public, a full and just equivalent shall be returned to him."[51] In those cases the public must exercise the equivalent of eminent domain and compensate the private landowner for public benefits.

This dissenting opinion set the stage for a series of four major decisions from 1987 to 1994 that modified the Court's position. The first case, *First English Evangelical Church v. County of Los Angeles,* established the new principle that the remedy for an unconstitutional regulation was economic compensation for a "temporary taking." (This had first been proposed in a dissenting opinion by Justice William Brennan in the *San Diego Gas & Electric Co.* case in 1981.)[52] This placed a new risk for planners contemplating regulatory regimes that might be challenged, for the public coffers do not generally carry reserves adequate to pay for the temporary loss of use of private property. The decision was signed by Chief Justice Rehnquist and he was joined by Justices Brennan, Byron White, Thurgood Marshall, Powell, and Scalia. It is striking to note that this new six-to-three majority did not represent a simple "swing" vote shift from the five-to-four minority opinion in the *Keystone Bituminous Coal* case. The complexities of takings law make it difficult to predict how the Court will respond by simply identifying stable and clearly defined coalitions on the Court. Justices Rehnquist, Powell, and Scalia were the only ones to find a taking in both *Key Bituminous Coal* and *First English* in 1987. Similarly, Justices John Stevens and Harry Blackmun were the only ones to find no taking by the government in both cases. The other justices found subtle distinctions between the cases that warranted different positions; four justices therefore represented "swing" votes.

The 1986–87 term was a busy one for the Court on takings issues, as *Nollan v. California Coastal Commission* established a stricter standard for regulatory review by the Court. This time the majority opinion was written by Justice Scalia, who subsequently led the charge against restrictive environmental regulation in the *Lucas* case in 1992. He also attacked the restrictiveness of the Endangered Species Act on takings grounds in his dissenting opinion in the *Sweet Home* case in 1995.[53] Scalia was joined in the *Nollan* decision by Justices Rehnquist, White, Powell and O'Connor. Brennan wrote the leading dissent, with additional dissents by Justices Stevens and Blackmun. In this case the focus was on the constitutionality of the conditions of approval of a permit rather than the complete denial of a proposed project.[54]

The Nollans owned a beachfront lot along the California coast and were required by the California Coastal Commission to provide a public easement across their property between a concrete seawall and the high tide mark of the ocean, which bounded their property. This easement was a condition of the agency's approval and would connect two public beach areas to the north and south of the Nollan property. While the Court did not find the requirement of a dedication necessarily unconstitutional, it declared that there was an insufficient nexus between the dedication requirement and the specific effects of the Nollans' development (construction of a single-family home). The Coastal Commission had argued that the dedication was intended to mitigate the effects of the Nollan home on public access to the beach, which was diminished as a result of reduced views, but the Court found this linkage too weak. Alternative remedies could have addressed that specific problem better:

> The condition would be constitutional even if it consisted of the requirement that the Nollans provide a viewing spot on their property for passersby with whose sighting of the ocean their new house would interfere. . . . The evident constitutional propriety disappears, however, if the condition substituted for the prohibition utterly fails to further the end advanced as the justification for the prohibition[;] . . . the lack of nexus between the condition and the original purpose of the building restriction converts that purpose to something other than what it was. The purpose then becomes, quite simply, the obtaining of an easement to serve some valid governmental purpose, but without payment of compensation.[55]

This issue of precision in defining the nexus has been a recurring theme in subsequent cases. Justice Brennan argued against a formulaic approach in his dissent to *Nollan,* noting that "such a narrow conception of rationality . . . has long been discredited as a judicial arrogation of legislative authority. 'To make scientific precision a criterion of constitutional power would be to subject the State to an intolerable supervision hostile to the basic principles of our Government.'"[56]

Brennan also argued that "the Court's insistence on a precise accounting system in this case is insensitive to the fact that increasing intensity of development in many areas calls for farsighted, comprehensive planning that takes into account both the interdependence of land uses and the cumulative impact of development."[57] Brennan quoted Joe Sax to place property in its modern social context, making a claim for the situational context of individual parcels that parallels Logan and Molotch's argument that property is idiosyncratic as a result of the importance of spatial relations: "Property does not exist in isolation. Particular parcels are tied to one another in complex ways, and property is more accurately described as being inextricably part of a network of relationships that is neither limited to, nor usefully defined by, the property boundaries with which the legal system is accustomed to dealing. Frequently, use of any given parcel of property is at the same time effectively a use of, or a demand upon, property beyond the border of the user."[58] Justice Blackmun also noted that "the land-use problems this country faces require creative solutions" and that "these are not advanced by an 'eye for an eye' mentality."[59] In an attempt to keep an avenue open for future parties, he also specifically argued that he did "not understand the Court's opinion in this case to implicate in any way the public-trust doctrine." Justices Stevens and

Blackmun then noted that the debate between the Court and Justice Brennan highlighted the complexity of land use regulation. "Even the wisest lawyers would have to acknowledge great uncertainty about the scope of this Court's takings jurisprudence," they noted, "yet, because of the Court's remarkable ruling in *First English* . . . local governments and officials must pay the price for the necessarily vague standards in this area of law." Stevens then added that "even if [Brennan's] position prevailed in this case . . . it would be of little solace to land-use planners who would still be left guessing about how the Court will react to the next case, and the one after that. As this case demonstrates, the rule of liability created by the Court in *First English* is a shortsighted one. Like Justice Brennan, I hope that 'a broader vision ultimately prevails.'"[60]

A narrower vision continues to dominate the Court, however, as reflected in the *Lucas* decision in 1992 and the *Dolan* decision in 1994. Scalia again wrote the majority opinion in *Lucas v. South Carolina Coastal Council*, which invalidated a coastal regulatory scheme that denied a proposed development of single-family homes on David Lucas's beachfront lots.[61] Lucas's "land" had periodically been inundated by shifting beaches and storm-related high tides over the years, but South Carolina's regulatory regime was deemed by the Court to have gone too far. Interestingly, the Court reached this finding primarily on the grounds that there had been a total diminution of value without ever ascertaining the value of alternative uses for the land under the restrictions—leaving open the question of whether a diminution comparable to that in *Hadacheck* (92 percent) would have withstood challenge today. Alternative uses such as a campground or boat ramp were not considered.[62] *Lucas* therefore reaffirmed a total diminution of value as a taking but offered no new threshold.

More important, Scalia advanced a much more restrictive theoretical rationale for acceptable governmental regulation through the *Lucas* decision. Harking back to *Mugler* from 1887, Scalia turned to nuisance law when he wrote that restrictions resulting in complete diminution of value can be applied "only if the logically antecedent inquiry into the nature of the owner's interest shows that the proscribed use interests were not part of his title to begin with." (Note that the *Lucas* case involved a complete project denial rather than permit conditions.) Scalia stated, "Any limitation so severe cannot be newly legislated or decreed (without compensation), but must inhere in the title itself, in the restrictions that background principles of the State's law of property and nuisance already place upon land ownership. A law or decree with such an effect must, in other words, do no more than duplicate the result that could have been achieved in the courts—by adjacent landowners (or other uniquely affected persons) under the State's law of private nuisance, or by the State under its complementary power to abate nuisances that affect the public generally, or otherwise."[63]

This renewed emphasis on nuisance law highlighted the Court's concern "that private property is being pressed into some form of public service under the guise of mitigating serious public harm." The Court also admitted, however, "the distinction between 'harm-preventing' and 'benefit-conferring' regulation is often in the eye of the beholder."[64]

The composition of the Court had changed between 1987 and 1992, however, and Justice Anthony Kennedy offered a dissent that highlighted the dynamic nature of the law. "Reasonable expectations must be understood in light of the whole of our legal tradition," he noted. "The common law of nuisance is too narrow a confine for the exercise of regulatory power in a complex and interdependent society. The State should not be prevented from enacting new regulatory initiatives in response to changing conditions, and courts must consider all reasonable expectations whatever their source. The Takings Clause does not require a static body of state property law; it protects private expectations to ensure private investment. I agree with the Court that nuisance prevention accords with the most common expectations of property owners who face regulation, but I do not believe this can be the sole source of state authority to impose severe restrictions."[65]

Justice Blackmun offered a lengthy dissent because of his "fear . . . that the Court's new policies will spread beyond the narrow confines of the present case. For that reason," he said, "I, like the Court, will give far greater attention to this case than its narrow scope suggests—not because I can intercept the Court's missile, or save the targeted mouse, but because I hope perhaps to limit the collateral damage." In particular, Blackmun noted that "in this case, apparently, the State now has a burden of showing the regulation is not a taking. The Court offers no justification for its sudden hostility toward state legislators, and I doubt that it could." Blackmun also criticized the Court's focus on the nuisance doctrine, noting that "*Mugler* was only the beginning in a long line of cases" that developed the Court's takings jurisprudence. He pointed out that conceptions of both nuisance and property have evolved over time:

> Arresting the development of the common law is not only a departure from our prior decisions; it is also profoundly unwise. The human condition is one of constant learning and evolution—both moral and practical. Legislatures implement that new learning; in doing so they must often revise the definition of property and the rights of property owners. Thus, when the Nation came to understand that slavery was morally wrong and mandated the emancipation of all slaves, it, in effect, redefined "property." On a lesser scale, our ongoing self-education produces similar changes in the rights of property owners: new appreciation of the significance of endangered species, the importance of wetlands, and the vulnerability of coastal lands shapes our evolving understanding of property rights.[66]

This analogy with slavery has particular relevance to the social problem of protecting public rights in cultural and environmental values—which have ethical, rather than simply economic, implications.[67] The takings jurisprudence established under *Lucas* focuses all attention on the economic values once held by our ancestors rather than the values we may hold today. It effectively limits ethical evolution as a foundation for social innovation, denying the institutional flexibility to accommodate changing social values. Not surprisingly, then, the law is a limited vehicle for institutional change.

Despite this narrow focus on the common law of nuisance on economic (rather than cultural or environmental) values, the limitations imposed under *Lucas* applied only to cases where *all* economic value had been taken. Two years later the Court extended the nexus principles of Nollan and increased the burden on the regulators in *Dolan v. City of Tigard*.[68] Chief Justice Rehnquist delivered the opinion of the Court, joined this time by Scalia, O'Connor, Kennedy, and Clarence Thomas. Stevens and Blackmun were joined by Ruth Bader Ginsburg and David Souter in dissent. The case involved a commercial landowner, Dolan, whose application to expand a store was approved by the city of Tigard, Oregon, conditional upon dedication of a public easement for a bicycle path along a stream corridor that crossed Dolan's land. In accordance with *Nollan,* the city made specific findings that this easement would both protect the public from flooding (it was within the hundred-year floodplain) and reduce the effects of traffic caused by the store expansion (by making bicycling an effective alternative to driving to the store).[69]

The Court found that alternative requirements, such as not allowing building within the floodplain, could have achieved the same result, however, and that "public access would deprive petitioner of the right to exclude others, 'one of the most essential sticks in the bundle of rights that are commonly characterized as property.'" This distinction proved critical. "The conditions imposed were not simply a limitation on the use petitioner might make of her own parcel," noted Rehnquist, "but a requirement that she deed portions of her property to the city." Referring to *Nollan,* he said that "the absence of a nexus left the Coastal Commission in the position of simply trying to obtain an easement through gimmickry, which converted a valid regulation of land use into 'an out-and-out plan of extortion.'" He then added that "no such gimmicks are associated with the permit conditions imposed by the city in this case" and that it is "obvious that a nexus exists."[70] The nexus was nevertheless not adequate in its specificity for the Court.

Instead, the Court called for establishment of a "rough proportionality" rule that would be applied once the *Nollan* nexus threshold was met. "No precise mathematical calculation is required," the Court added, "but the city must make some sort of individualized determination that the required dedication is related both in nature and extent to the impact of the proposed development." The question of quantification was not clear, however, for the Court went on to say that "the city must make some effort to quantify its findings in support of the dedication for the pedestrian/bicycle pathway beyond the conclusory statement that it could offset some of the traffic demand generated."[71] Apparently math is required, but it need not be a "precise mathematical calculation." Most important, however, is the call for "some sort of individualized determination" rather than generic guidelines.

Moreover, the Court reaffirmed the implicit direction of *Lucas* by establishing the burden of proof on the government agency when establishing both the nexus and rough proportionality. This was the focus of much of the dissent by Stevens, Blackmun, and Ginsburg: "The Court has made a serious error by abandoning the traditional presumption of constitutionality and imposing a novel burden of proof on a city implementing an admittedly valid comprehensive land use plan." They added that "a strong presumption of validity should attach to those conditions. The burden of demonstrating that those conditions have unreasonably impaired the economic value of the proposed improvement belongs squarely on the shoulder of the party challenging the state action's constitutionality. That allocation of burdens has served us well in the past. The Court has stumbled badly today by reversing it."[72]

Souter agreed with this in a separate dissent, also noting that "the Court concludes that the City loses based on one word ('could' instead of 'would'), and despite the fact that this record shows the connection the Court looks for ... *Nollan*, therefore, is satisfied, and on that assumption the city's conditions should not be held to fail a further rough proportionality test or any other test that might be devised to give meaning to the constitutional limits." Finally, Souter noted that "the right case for the enunciation of takings doctrine seems hard to spot."[73]

The combination of *First English*, *Nollan*, *Lucas*, and *Dolan* nevertheless offers a new doctrine that must guide planners and local governments in order to avoid takings claims:

> the regulation must substantially advance the public interest to prevent a harm;
> the government now faces the risk of paying compensation for "temporary takings";
> there must be a nexus between the regulation and its purpose of preventing harm;[74]
> there must be a rough proportionality between the likely harm and the remedy;[75]
> the regulation cannot result in a total diminution of value unless the use otherwise would have been prohibited anyway without regulation (under the state's background principles of property and nuisance, which vary state by state).

These guidelines place restrictions on regulation, yet they also indicate that a broad range of land use and environmental regulation is consistent with the Constitution. It is within this broader legal context—still dynamic and still evolving, to reflect our changing understanding of the world and our changing values—that the politics of planning have been and are being played out in the exurban landscape. We will see, however, that actual decision-making regarding property rights and interests is guided more by Culture than by the Court's change in takings doctrine.[76]

The implications of takings doctrine for a particular planning proposal or regulatory scheme depends in part on the relationship within the jurisdiction between comprehensive rural subdivision regulations, parcelization boundaries, and development limitations imposed by the general plan, zoning ordinance, or mitigation measures under CEQA. The "relevant parcel issue" is affected primarily by subdivision regulation, which makes the history of parcelization so critical to future planning discretion. Parcelization through subdivision (whether formally under the requirements of the Subdivision Map Act or not) is the critical act in the planning process that will determine the risk of a takings claim against a regulatory agency. Rick Frank describes the problem succinctly:

> The threshold issue of determining the relevant parcel or increment of property for purposes of analysis under the Takings Clause is deceptively complex. A simple example frames the issue: assume a property owner owns three rural, ten-acre parcels. One of those parcels consists of nine acres of developable uplands and one acre of fragile wetlands. Assume further that the landowner seeks to develop solely the one-acre portion of that ten acre parcel, but that the development would destroy a pristine marsh the government seeks to maintain as open space and wildlife habitat. The owner subsequently sues the government in inverse condemnation, alleging a compensable taking.
>
> What is the relevant parcel, or "denominator," for the reviewing court to assess in determining the economic impact and other relevant takings factors concerning the challenged government decision? The one acre of wetlands? The entire ten-acre parcel? Or the aggregate 30 acres of the three plots owned by the landowner?
>
> To a considerable degree, the answer to this question dictates whether an unconstitutional taking will be found to have transpired. (Frank 1995)

Planners must therefore be careful to coordinate the requirements of the general plan, zoning ordinance, and subdivision regulations in order to avoid the creation of undevelopable parcels. To do so requires comprehensive assessment of environmental conditions, however, which highlights the importance of good science as a critical component of good planning. Failing to complete such assessments in advance could lead to inadvertent creation of parcels that are effectively worthless under the regulatory restrictions that may subsequently be adopted by federal, state, and/or local authorities. This is a serious risk regarding many of the parcels created in the late 1960s and 1970s in the Sierra Nevada, and it remains a risk to the extent that further subdivision is allowed under any jurisdiction's general plan, zoning ordinance, or subdivision regulations without adequate environmental assessment. Completion of a water and sewer-septic suitability study, for example, should precede further approvals of subdivisions where unbuildable lots could be created. The prospects of a successful takings lawsuit increase without such a study.

This discussion has focused on the applicability of takings claims to land use planning and regulation, but other aspects of environmental law may provide protection from such claims because of their treatment of particular aspects of the environment. Examples include wildlife law, which includes influences from both the common law and statute, and the public trust doctrine as applied to waterways. C. F. McGlashan represented the Truckee Lumber Company in an important case on this topic in 1897, for example, when the state of California challenged the company for discharging milling wastes into the Truckee River in such a way as to harm the fishery. The state prevailed before the court because "by the repeated and continuing acts of the defendant this public property right [to fish in the river in a good condition] is being and will continue to be greatly interfered with and impaired; and that such acts constitute a nuisance, both under our statute and at common law, is not open to serious question." The court went on to emphasize the social and qualified nature of property rights: "This right in the owner of the land must be regarded as qualified to a certain extent by the universal principle that all property is held subject to those general regulations which are necessary to the common good and general welfare, and to that extent it is subject to legislative control. It is a well-established principle that every person shall so use and enjoy his own property, however absolute and unqualified his title, that his use of it shall not be injurious to the equal enjoyment of others having an equal right to the enjoyment of their property, nor injurious to the rights of the public."[77]

It would thus be difficult for a property owner to claim today that a land use regulation imposed by a city, county, or the state, if intended to protect an important fishery by restricting land use practices that might damage a stream on the owner's property, could not be anticipated as being one of the background principles that determine both the property rights that come with the land and the investor-backed expectations that a landowner should have. C. F. lost that battle a century ago, and additional statutory law has further clarified the matter. The public trust doctrine might also apply, although its usefulness in this regard is limited to navigable waterways.[78] Wildlife law, however, extends across terrestrial landscapes.

There is nevertheless still a potential conflict between statutory law designed to protect biodiversity and constitutional takings jurisprudence. Although the issue was a much narrower question of whether, under the ESA, destruction of habitat constituted a take of endangered species that depended on that habitat, Justice Scalia made it clear in his 1995 dissent in the *Sweet Home* case that the Takings Clause and the ESA may be on a collision course. "The Court's holding that the hunting and killing prohibition incidentally preserves habitat on private lands," wrote Scalia, "imposes unfairness to the point of financial ruin—not just upon the rich, but upon the simplest farmer who finds his land conscripted to national zoological use." This is clearly an unacceptable outcome for Scalia, and a takings challenge with a narrowly defined parcel "denominator" will inevitably come before the Court as long as the ESA remains in place.[79]

The door remains open for further legislative action to affect takings jurisprudence, but it remains unclear if it will withstand Supreme Court scrutiny in the wake of *Lucas.* The voters of Rhode Island attempted to clarify the relationship between regulation and takings in 1986 by overwhelmingly approving (by a two-to-one margin) an amendment to the state constitution to declare explicitly that environmental regulations are not takings. The amendment states: "Private property shall not be taken for public uses, without just compensation. The powers of the state and of its municipalities to regulate and control the use of land and waters in furtherance of the preservation, regeneration, and restoration of the natural environment . . . shall be an exercise of the police powers of the state, shall be liberally construed, and shall not be deemed to be a public use of private property."

That amendment may not be consistent with the U.S. Supreme Court's more recent declarations on takings jurisprudence, however, which from 1986 to 1994 substantially changed the requirements on governments. It therefore appears that the *Lucas* requirement for reliance on "background principles of the State's law of property and nuisance" could limit even a voter-initiated amendment to a state's constitution as the basis for clarifying the relationship between social and private interests in property and ecosystems. The Rhode Island example remains to be tested, however, and it could serve as a model for revision of *state* "background principles" that would then survive challenge in *federal* court on Fifth Amendment and Fourteenth Amendment grounds.[80]

THE RHETORIC OF RIGHTS: EXCHANGE VERSUS USE VALUES

Legal battles over the constitutionality of government regulation are fought in courts, but the political conflicts that ultimately determine the extent of local land use regulation—through the development of a property rights culture within a given community—take place in the letters-to-the-editor section of local newspapers. The op-ed pages of the *Grass Valley–Nevada City Union* are no exception, as local residents Todd Juvinall and June Jamerson squared off there in late 1995 to debate the meaning of private property in the context of the Nevada County General Plan update. It is the views of citizens such as these, rather than those of legal scholars, that most influence the political representatives and citizens that make policy at the local level.

Juvinall is a former county supervisor who chairs the local Republican Central Committee and founded a wise-use group called the California Association of Business, Property and Resource Owners (Marois 1995b; Juvinall 1995a; Juvinall 1995b). He is also a contractor and subdivision developer advocating a significant increase in allowable density for property he owns in the Glenbrook Basin area between Grass Valley and Nevada City (Lauer 1994a; 1994b; 1994c; 1994d; 1994e; 1994f; 1994g; 1994h; 1994j; 1994m). He is a strong advocate of exchange values over use values, emphasizing the unfettered right of any property owner to do as he or she pleases with his or her land. Juvinall "keeps a copy of the U.S. Constitution handy on his desk" (Marois 1995b), and the guest editorial he wrote for the *Grass Valley–Nevada City Union* is titled "Proponents of Strict Zoning Dishonor Constitution" (Juvinall 1995a). In it he paints the general plan update as a fundamental struggle between good and evil, with the very future of freedom and democracy at stake. He states that "those who control the most basic rights and freedoms can dictate the ultimate happiness of all," and he describes the general plan "as the battleground for opposing views on the importance of our basic individual rights."

The cold war may be over between the United States and the now-defunct Soviet Union, but the battle for freedom and democracy continues for Juvinall in the Sierra Nevada foothills. "The eco-socialists are part of a larger movement," he says, "which includes the environmental movement, that has attempted to destroy the principle of individual rights. The policies enacted by these earth worshippers are enmeshed in every aspect of our lives. Over time it becomes easier to control citizens through higher taxes, fees, assessments and other exactions." He then quotes from an article in *EcoSocialist Review* that calls for people to "identify themselves first as planetary citizens,"[81] adding that "obviously, when you become a planetary citizen, you must give up your national identity along with the rights and freedoms guaranteed in the Constitution." Juvinall then puts a conspiratorial spin on the relationship between local land use planning, the planetary "socialist agenda" and the complete loss of individual rights: "These attempts at planetizing us are being accomplished through the land use process. They know that local government is the easiest place to accomplish their agenda. Using 'greedy developers,' large landowners, and the desire for open space and wildlife as their springboard, they hope to convince us to become planetary citizens. Local general plans, bio-regional plans, regional government (with attendant regional planning) become justified mechanisms to them because they aren't concerned about individuals. They insist *we* take planetary responsibility which they can then control."

Ultimately, Juvinall sees any restriction on private property as part of this nefarious conspiracy, and so paints a stark picture of totalitarian rule versus individual freedom: "What this means is simple: control. The eco-socialists want to control land so they can control people. Landowners become uncompensated caretakers for the greater population. Add to that new fees, taxes, assessments and other government money raising schemes and you have a dependent, controlled populace. Our forefathers would not recognize the end product of their great sacrifice for our individual rights."[82]

Jamerson, however, frames the political debate in terms of interests rather than ideology. She is a home owner who has led the fight against Juvinall's proposed development in her neighborhood, where she has advocated protection of use values by emphasizing the private property rights of existing residents to maintain stable land uses and existing property values. Her guest editorial, which appeared in direct response to Juvinall's, is titled "Constitution Supports Residents over Developers" (1995). Jamerson argues that regulatory controls on land use are long-standing and derive from the common law concept of nuisance. She cites the U.S. Supreme Court in her argument, noting that "there are manifold restraints to which every person is necessarily subject for the common good." She then shows that zoning controls have been valid for three-quarters of a century and that extensive legislation during that period has curtailed unfettered property rights. "Real liberty for all could not exist," says Jamerson, quoting the Court, "under the operation of a principle which recognizes the right of each individual person to use his own, whether in respect of his person or his property, regardless of the injury that may be done to others."[83] The crux of her argument is that private property rights entail obligations and responsibilities to the broader community.

Moreover, Jamerson suggests that the protection of exchange values has come at the cost of sacrificing use values. "The property right of the neighborhood to protect its existing zoning does not appear to count," she says, "in the face of the developer's property right expectations." She adds that "most developers' requests for higher density have been approved despite the pleas of the neighborhood associations," citing "Todd Juvinall's infamous Glenwood Pines" project as an example. She then urges the public to attend public hearings scheduled before the board of supervisors on the new Nevada County General Plan. "Property rights will be an issue," she concludes; "*whose* property rights remains the question."

This remains the central question in all land use regulation and growth management efforts, and its resolution invariably involves social conflict between exchange and use values.

CHAPTER EIGHT

/.V.V.\

Managing Exurban Growth

Declarations of statewide policy do exist in the various state planning, zoning, and environmental statutes, but there is no direct connection between these policies and local plans or decisions.

Irving Schiffman, 1989

Some may say that Tahoe is planning nirvana, but it is also the best and the worst case of command-and-control regulation.

Bob Twiss, 1995

There are a wide range of policies available to manage population growth and mitigate the effects of human settlement in the Sierra Nevada. The appropriateness of specific policies depends on the consequences of concern, however, as well as the specific relationship between human settlement and its effects. A particular settlement pattern might, for example, have a significant effect upon native nesting songbirds that can primarily be traced to the presence of domestic dogs and cats. Alternative settlement patterns might all have a similar effect, therefore, while alternative pet management regimes could mitigate the effects on native nesting songbirds. In contrast, the influence of human settlement on hydrologic regimes may be either a linear or a nonlinear function of housing density. Perhaps there is an effect that is proportional to housing density only up to a "threshold" density, above which additional density does not change the effect. The specific form of these relationships is likely to vary, so we cannot now make a general statement about either effects or policies. Proper evaluation of alternative policies requires a better understanding of the relationships between alternative patterns of human settlement and a wide range of effects.

Despite this caveat, however, it is still possible to hypothesize likely relationships and evaluate the capacity of alternative policies to mitigate the likely effects of human settlement. Growth management tools have been in use since the first case of informal urban design, when incompatible activities were separated in order to reduce the likelihood of nuisances from affecting other uses (Kostof 1991). This approach has generally been formalized and institutionalized today through zoning ordinances and land use planning approaches that emphasize the spatial separation of incompatible uses. Zoning has been widely used in urban areas since the landmark Supreme Court case of *Euclid* in 1926,[1] but for many parts of the Sierra Nevada it was not adopted and applied to all land uses until the 1970s and 1980s. More innovative planning techniques have evolved recently to include a complex suite of general and specific tools for managing growth and mitigating its consequences. We therefore have an extensive literature to draw on when discussing growth management alternatives (Schiffman 1989; Innes et al. 1993; Stein 1993; DeGrove 1992). Because it is extensive, I will offer only a brief introduction here to some of the techniques that may have more specific application to the rural and exurban context of the Sierra Nevada. A more systematic consideration of growth management techniques and their capacity to mitigate the effects of human settlement in the Sierra Nevada requires a better understanding of the locally specific relationships between alternative patterns of human settlement and likely effects. Carefully targeted growth management tools can then be evaluated accordingly for application to the burgeoning communities of the Sierra Nevada.

In general, growth management tools can be characterized as one of three types: *spatial*, where the location of specific land uses is designated and constrained; *temporal*, where the timing of development is controlled; or *activity*, where the activities allowed on a particular site are controlled in their timing, duration, frequency, or intensity.

Any of these broad classes of tools might be adopted to address similar effects. Conversely, different approaches are likely to be appropriate and necessary to mitigate different types of effects. General public concern about the results of traffic from new development, for example, could lead to any of the following new policies: limitations on new commercial development near substandard intersections; requirements stipulating that new commercial development go forward only after intersections have been upgraded sufficiently to accommodate all forecast traffic flow; and requirements limiting business hours of new commercial developments in order to avoid exacerbating traffic problems at substandard intersections. These examples are simply illustrative, but they highlight how the term *growth management* can mean very different things to different people. Irving Schiffman outlines twenty-six different growth management tools in his 1989 book, *Alternative Techniques for Managing Growth,* and there are many variations on each of his themes. State-level growth management regimes have taken a variety of forms (Innes 1991), from Oregon's land-use (spatial) emphasis (Knaap 1991; Knaap and Nelson 1992) to Florida's infrastructure concurrency (timing) requirements (DeGrove 1992). Local jurisdictions have also adopted a wide range of growth management approaches within California (Governor's Interagency Council on Growth Management 1993; Landis 1992; Glickfeld and Levine 1992). The effectiveness of those measures is still subject to considerable debate, for it is difficult to control for the specific growth management policy alone (de Neufville 1981;

Landis 1988; 1992; Innes et al. 1993). Moreover, growth management policies may have the effect of increasing land prices and decreasing housing affordability (Dowall and Landis 1981; Dowall 1984; 1991). Spillover effects into adjacent jurisdictions are also difficult to capture, and many of the growth management systems have been in place only a short time or have been modified following legal challenges (Landis 1988; 1992; Glickfeld and Levine 1992). It is impossible to generalize about the likely effects of growth management tools on ecological, social, or economic conditions in the Sierra Nevada or other exurban landscapes.

The specific effects of human settlement in the Sierra Nevada will dictate which types of growth management tools, if any, are appropriate tools for impact mitigation. Urban limit lines alone, for example, are unlikely to have a significant effect if access to centralized infrastructure is not a primary determinant of settlement patterns. Moreover, concerns about maintaining rural character and the quality of life in the Sierra Nevada may make a highly concentrated pattern of human settlement undesirable for residents if it results in large-scale settlements. Specific effects on vegetation and wildlife however, could call for innovative growth management approaches not yet applied in other jurisdictions. These could include seasonal limitations on specific activities that could negatively affect rare and endangered or endemic native plants, for example, but in a way that would not necessarily limit the opportunities to develop adjacent areas for human settlement. The potential scope of such limitations could be identified for the Sierra Nevada through an overlay of local land use plans with the GIS databases prepared by SNEP for such resources (Shevock 1996; Millar 1996; Davis and Stoms 1996). Activity controls and management practices in sensitive areas—rather than land use designations—can then focus on the timing, intensity, and duration of activities affecting the threatened resources.[2]

Several rural areas *outside* the Sierra Nevada have pursued an innovative set of policies to maintain the rural character and quality-of-life amenities in the face of rapid population growth. These approaches draw on a long tradition in landscape architecture and site design, and they have recently been implemented in New England, the Mid-Atlantic states, and the Middle West. These techniques are summarized in separate sections below and described in more detail in Randall Arendt's 1994 book, *Rural by Design*. They build on the comprehensive guide to these techniques that was first published regionally by the Center for Rural Massachusetts in 1988 (Yaro et al. 1988). Other useful guides to these techniques have been published separately by researchers and by local jurisdictions that have adopted these policies.[3] High-altitude mountain environments (such as Truckee, the Lake Tahoe Basin, and Mammoth Lakes in the Sierra Nevada) also have special design problems because of their harsh weather conditions and steep slopes (Dorward 1990).

Growth management techniques have been most extensively applied in suburbanizing areas within metropolitan regions, however, rather than in the rural and exurban regions similar to the Sierra Nevada. We must therefore turn to the metropolitan and suburban experience to evaluate the promise and pitfalls of alternative growth management approaches. It has also often been the smaller communities that have moved first to establish controls on land use development within metropolitan areas. As Ted Bradshaw notes, this reflects the importance of *relative* rather than *absolute* changes in land use. *Perceptions of change* determine whether or not a political movement will arise to compel growth management systems:

> Growth as an issue of local concern is stimulated by traffic congestion and expanding urban construction. It is often perceived relative to land uses people remember and expect, rather than to some absolute level of density of urban development after which the land could not support anyone else. Thus rapidly growing small communities may feel more abused by development pressure than urban centers where the density is increasing more rapidly and the traffic is worse. Small town residents who value their smallness may think that growth is hurting them regardless of how inconvenient life really becomes. That's why Petaluma and Davis were land-use control innovators, but Los Angeles continued to grow with few successful controls. (Schiffman 1989, viii)

Growth management regimes have primarily been local, but there has also been a quiet revolution in land-use control through the establishment of many new state-level growth management systems since the early 1970s (Bosselmann and Callies 1972). Oregon, Vermont, Hawaii, New Jersey, and Florida have led the most comprehensive state efforts; California has not been among the states to adopt such a system. At the same time, there has been notably little regional or metropolitan-scale institutionalization of growth management regimes, leaving many of California's locally based systems without significant influence over regional patterns of growth. State-level systems have also suffered from lack of funding and technical support. Very few examples exist for well-integrated systems that coordinate local, regional, and state-level (or, in some cases, multistate) efforts.

This problem is particularly acute in California. Incremental changes to the institutional system have not fundamentally altered the regulatory system. "Rather than restructure the existing system to give a larger role to state agencies or policies," notes Schiffman, "the legislature has historically responded to land-use management concerns by strengthening the planning and regulatory capabilities of local governments and by expanding the criteria to be utilized in decision making" (1989, 2). Local cities and counties are therefore now required to adopt general plans that contain at least seven specific elements (land use, circulation, housing, noise, safety, conservation, open space) and conduct environmental reviews in accordance with CEQA. According to William Fulton, the state was "remarkably ahead of its time" when it first required general plans more than fifty years ago. Zoning ordinances were not required to be consistent with those general plans until 1971 (1993, 113–14), however, so the general plan has become an important regulatory tool only in the past quarter century. The general-plan guidelines issued by the Governor's Office of Planning and Research now total 368 pages (Fulton 1993; Office of Planning and Research 1987), and California courts have found that the general plan is intended to be "a constitution for all future developments within a city."[4] Zoning must therefore be consistent with general plans, which are controlling.

California's state-level requirements and case law provide the legal framework that has "permitted cities and counties to implement a wide range of growth management measures with considerable force," but Fulton points out that "the system provides little state oversight" (1993, 115). Schiffman summarizes by noting that "the changes have done little to reorient the essential character of the process: it continues to respond primarily to local objectives without consideration of state or regional needs" (1989, 2). This is primarily because "there is little in the way of substantive criteria" required by the state (ibid.) and because the system depends on citizen enforcement through the judicial process rather than state-level oversight or review to ensure achievement of statewide policy goals (Fulton 1993, 115–16). "Declarations of statewide policy do exist in the various state planning, zoning, and environmental statutes," observes Schiffman, "but there is no direct connection between these policies and local plans or decisions" (1989, 2). This has made both planning law and CEQA largely procedural. With the exception of affordable-housing goals, there are no substantive requirements in California for local governments to meet a "fair share" of state or regional goals. In fact, Schiffman notes that the fair-share housing requirements actually restrict land use control options:

> While the cost of housing is a serious issue in California, particularly in areas of employment growth, and land-use restrictions have played a role in the increase in housing costs, the legislative response has been a one-sided flow of legislation primarily designed to limit the ability of local officials to say "no" to developers. Valid community concerns with maintaining environmental amenities, preserving open space, financing public infrastructure, and slowing traffic congestion have been treated as secondary to the need to promote housing development. State legislation passed since 1980 places the burden of proof on communities to justify limitations on housing permits, reductions in housing densities or moratoria on residential growth. (5–6)

In California the only exceptions to this focus are where regional entities have been created to manage development with an emphasis on protecting environmental concerns in Lake Tahoe, the San Francisco Bay, and the California coast.[5] These regional entities have implemented innovative growth management regimes, but the strength of their regulatory enforcement powers has also been the source of significant political opposition to further establishment of regional agencies. Even simple efforts such as integration of the Association of Bay Area Governments, Bay Area Metropolitan Transportation Commission, and Bay Area Air Quality Management District have failed in recent years despite strong support from both environmental and business interests (Landis 1993). Local governments have effectively resisted any weakening of their strong "home rule" powers to determine land use within their jurisdictions.[6]

Resistance by local jurisdictions to greater state or regional control is not the only problem. Schiffman states that "the process of growth management in California is further complicated by the hostility that often exists between counties and their incorporated cities" (1989, 4). This hostility has been exacerbated since the passage of Proposition 13 in 1978, which created a more competitive environment among cities and counties for developments that could support local government through precious property and sales taxes. (The town of Truckee and Nevada County are now engaged in a lawsuit over the allocation of tax revenues, for example, which clearly affects their ability to plan land use cooperatively.) Fulton also notes that this increased "fiscalization of land use" unfortunately "coincided with the nationwide trend toward decentralization of job centers and the development boom fueled by easy credit from savings and loans and foreign investments" in the 1980s in California (1993, 118). Schiffman observes, however, that, despite the growing need for improved horizontal coordination, "neither city nor county is under any legal obligation to respect the other's general plan" in California today (1989, 5). Boundary disputes over land use designations within city "spheres of influence" are therefore common.

As noted above, most of the population in the Sierra Nevada resides in, and most of the growth in the region occurs in, the unincorporated rural areas subject to county land use jurisdiction. Most of the infrastructure necessary for denser and more compact patterns of development, however, is located in the incorporated or private, gated communities of the region. As a result, a jurisdictional gap exists between the areas where growth is now occurring and the areas that could positively direct where growth occurs through infrastructure investments in roads, sewers, and water supply. This is typical for exurbia and a central problem in the Sierra Nevada.

Cities and counties may therefore develop general plans and zoning ordinances that are inconsistent with each other's, and the conflicts between their plans may not be resolved until the time of annexation for specific parcels.[7] The lands where growth management policy could direct new development to reduce environmental effects are likely to be precisely where this overlap and potential conflict exists: land within the sphere of influence of a city but presently subject to county land use authority. It is therefore critical that cities and counties cooperate to develop consistent policies when one or the other is developing a new general plan or evaluating major amendments to a general plan. Without such cooperation, either entity might pursue land use or infrastructure policies detrimental to regional environmental quality. Even local growth management efforts by one jurisdiction are unlikely to be effective without cooperation and consistent policies from adjacent jurisdictions.

As a result, effective growth management appears to require more than just local growth management efforts. Despite the need for a regional perspective, however, local concern about growth had already led to the adoption of more than 850 local growth control or growth management measures in California by 1989 (Fulton 1993, 114), the majority of which were adopted by voter initiative at the ballot box (Fulton 1993; Glickfeld and Levine 1992). "Yet all these local efforts actually did little to truly manage and harness California's growth in the 1980s," notes Fulton. "Because they were local in nature, the growth management schemes only moved it around—often with disastrous consequences for the environment and the sustainability of the metropolitan area" (1993, 121). Fulton cites an agreement between the Irvine Company and environmental interests to preserve 70 percent of Irvine Ranch in Orange County as an example of this: "Although important undeveloped coastal areas were saved, the preservation of this land only made regional balance problems worse" because of the simultaneous development of high-density job centers in the area without adequate housing nearby (122). (An alternative perspective is that the fiscalization of land use under Proposition 13 has led to inappropriate approvals for the development of high-density job centers in the area without adequate housing nearby.) Fulton cites Madelyn Glickfeld and Ned Levine (1992) when he observes that "the state has, in effect, created a policy of suburban sprawl" by allowing local growth management systems independent of any framework for regional coordination (1993, 122).

Locally generated growth management regimes have also been remarkably simplistic and have generally failed to incorporate the most sophisticated planning and regulatory techniques. This may in part reflect the difficulty of getting voter approval for more complex schemes, while simpler, quantitative reductions in annual building permits or allowable build-out densities are clear and understandable in the voting booth. Such quantitative controls also limit the discretion of local governments to bypass the voters' preferences. This is not a trivial issue in the case of "ballot-box zoning," which has usually arisen after the failure of the local planning department and elected officials to restrict growth to a level acceptable to local voters (Glickfeld and Levine 1992). Initiatives are therefore often written so that those same planning department staff and elected officials have no ability to override the voter-enacted system through a complex and less-transparent system. "Indeed," says Schiffman, "it may well be that some of the anti-growth sentiment evident in California cities and counties is a reflection of their planning

systems' inadequate response to growth pressures that result in destroyed landscapes, monotonous subdivision, inappropriate densities, and the loss of historic
and architectural resources" (1989, 19). Accordingly, the adoption of crude and
simplistic growth management systems—many of which have generated new problems that are then difficult to remedy without another public vote—can be
blamed in part on the failure of planning staffs and elected officials to adopt more
complex and less rudimentary approaches. The bluntness of many growth management systems is not a *necessary* characteristic of more carefully developed
schemes using sophisticated regulatory tools. Yet, as a result of weakened credibility, many local governments are now unable to implement systems without "deal
making and arbitrary administration" (ibid., 129), which has diminished the willingness of voters to approve flexibility, innovation, or complexity (Heyman and
Gilhool 1964).

This problem has been evident ever since the city of Petaluma experienced a
stunning 1,510 percent jump from 59 building permit requests in 1971 to 891 in
1972 (Fulton 1993). The citizens' response was to enact a building permit cap of
500 per year (still an order-of-magnitude larger than the preboom rate), which
included a "beauty contest" that reviewed competing proposals each year. Santa
Cruz and Santa Barbara Counties and the cities of Redlands and Riverside adopted
similar measures after the Petaluma approach was validated by the courts in 1975.[8]
Fulton describes these as "rudimentary in nature, either restricting the overall
amount of growth (usually defined as population and/or housing units) or protecting agricultural areas from future development" (1993, 116). Only the San
Diego system (adopted when Pete Wilson was mayor in 1978) employed a complex package of incentives and regulatory tools. Developed by Robert Freilich, who
also wrote the ordinance for Ramapo, New York (which was upheld by the U.S.
Supreme Court in 1972),[9] the system established three broad land use classifications: urbanized areas, for which infrastructure fees are waived and permits
expedited to encourage infill; planned urbanizing areas, in which mandatory
assessment districts pay for infrastructure; and future urbanizing areas, where
development must pay the full costs of infrastructure plus an open space tax assessment. This system had two key features: it was *regional* and it was linked to *infrastructure costs*. These two features helped to direct 60 percent of growth from 1978
to 1993 to the urbanized areas and 30 percent to the planned urbanizing areas
and restricted only 10 percent to the future urbanizing areas (Fulton 1993).
Unfortunately, such complexity has been the exception rather than the rule.
Moreover, even the San Diego system implied that *all* land will eventually be urbanized. In doing so, it failed to adequately address the need to maintain viable, functioning ecosystems for the protection of native biodiversity, until multispecies
habitat planning efforts were conducted in the 1990s (Stevens 1997a).

Growth as a local political issue took on new fervor in the 1980s, as the

California Supreme Court opened up the ballot box for growth management advocates.[10] Glickfeld and Levine have documented that there were only 10–20 ballot box growth management measures per year in California in the early 1980s, but the number jumped to 50 in 1986 and more than 100 in 1990. Approximately 70 percent of these were approved by the voters. The adoption of local growth management ordinances without direct voter approval also skyrocketed, from fewer than 30 per year before 1983 to 70 in 1986 and 150 in 1988 (Fulton 1993; Glickfeld and Levine 1992). Many of these latter measures were no doubt intended by local officials to ward off the adoption of more stringent controls at the ballot box.

Despite all of this activity, however, Fulton notes that this "obsession with measuring and restricting growth quantitatively—building permit restrictions, for example—has distracted state and local planners from questioning the land use patterns that generate the harmful side effects of growth" (1993, 124–25). This is particularly evident in rural areas. "If zoning came late to rural communities," notes Schiffman, "land-use planning came even later" (1989, 16). First-generation Euclidian zoning and subdivision regulations were developed primarily in an urban context, and zoning was not required for agricultural lands in twenty-two states until well into the 1970s.[11] California did not require concurrent development of infrastructure with subdivision platting until 1973. By this time second- and third-generation techniques had been developed that recognized the limitations of zoning as a growth management tool. "By and large," observes Schiffman, "rural communities have not made use of the wide variety of second and third generation land-use control measures. As a result, for the most part, growth in the countryside continues to resemble early urban development: minimum size zoned lots, unimaginative layouts, and an insensitivity to natural features of the land" (1989, 16–17). This is a prescription for large-lot exurban sprawl.

Schiffman also agrees with Fulton that "the movement to limit growth has not been particularly innovative and has brought few new techniques or approaches to the task of growth management. Where the focus of the movement has been on absolute numbers of units to be built, it has often been on the reduction of density, using the traditional means of downzoning, increasing minimum lot sizes, and height limitations" (18). Moreover, "the expansion of the land-use planning process beyond its physical design origins and into a growth management process has rendered insufficient the traditional tools of land-use planning and control" (19). Consequently, Schiffman advocates consideration of a wide range of innovative techniques in order to increase flexibility for reconciling potential conflicts over competing goals. He also states that "innovation has been more apparent where attempts to control growth have been indirect and primarily concerned with the location of new development," such as "performance-type regulations or requirements for clustering and open space easements" (18).

It is these more sophisticated tools, *not* large-lot zoning, that have the potential to protect rural and small town character in the exurban landscape.

PROTECTING AGRICULTURE AND OPEN SPACE

This challenge of managing rural and exurban growth is not unique to the Sierra Nevada or the rural and exurban West. In fact, the most promising work in this field has been completed in the Connecticut River valley in rural Massachusetts, where the problem of rapid growth and the ecotransformation of the rural landscape parallel the phenomenon in the Range of Light. The Center for Rural Massachusetts completed an excellent study of the processes of change and potential policies for mitigating the effects in 1988 (Yaro et al. 1988). In it the authors describe conditions also found in the Sierra Nevada and throughout exurban regions in the western United States:

> Small towns are especially ill-equipped to deal with the challenge of rapid, unplanned growth which jeopardizes town character, natural resources, open space, public services and infrastructure, and the stock of affordable housing. Many of the debates on growth versus preservation have arisen because towns lack professional planning assistance and updated land-use techniques that allow for better management of needed economic development, reasonably priced housing, and transportation improvements. Most towns are governed by zoning by-laws which often unwittingly prescribe development patterns that are inappropriate for their rural areas. Suburban sprawl is spawned by large-lot development requirements and highway corridors zoned for unlimited commercial development—precisely the pattern mandated by many towns' bylaws. (7)

Indeed, the failure of rural zoning policies to address the problems of rapid growth reflects in part the historical focus among rural planners on the problems of rural decline rather than growth: decreases in population and perpetually open agricultural lands were assumed to be inevitable conditions (Getzels and Thurow 1979). Only recently have researchers recognized that rapid growth and environmental degradation are now major challenges for many rural planners (Lapping et al. 1989; Sargent et al. 1991). Adoption of zoning policies developed within a metropolitan context does not address the different relationship between private property development and public amenity values (which are the primary economic asset of the region) that often exists in rapidly growing exurbia. Zoning has been an abstract overlay to existing land use that has little meaning for most rural and exurban residents, because the *existing* land use is often quite different from the *allowable* land use under the zoning designation. This contrasts sharply with the typical condition in an urban setting, where zoning describes both what will be and what *is*. Frank Popper correctly argues that zoning is an urban concept often inappropriately applied in rural areas (1984). As John Humbach notes, "The ruralization of urban zoning makes it practically illegal to build anything *but* strips and sprawl" in rapidly growing exurban regions (1992c, 1). One of the reasons, he observes, is that "traditional zoning . . . was conceived as a management tool for cities and other areas expected to be built up, not for the open countryside" (ibid.). Rural residents typically find it difficult to imagine the degree of allowable change and development under an abstract zoning designation until important cultural and ecological resources have been destroyed—legally and without public recourse.

Randall Arendt, who was one of the primary authors of the Center for Rural Massachusetts study and is the leading advocate of alternative approaches, demonstrates the inevitable result of existing zoning policies by taking a map of the community and placing a red dot in each location where a housing unit could be built under existing policies. This usually shocks local residents at community meetings: he says that people declare that "it's like our town has the measles!"[12]

Most alternative development designs require more work and more risk to get approval even when they protect open space and public values while still allowing the same number of developed units. As a result, creative design solutions are discouraged by most existing regulations.[13] When not directly forbidden, pursuing these alternatives often increases uncertainty. Because the approval of alternative approaches is often discretionary, these more innovative designs are risky for developers to pursue. There are consequently strong incentives for developers to follow the path of least resistance by choosing low-density development—even when alternative design solutions would better serve the public interest while still meeting the developer's economic objectives. Not surprisingly, developers then follow the zoning guidelines to the letter in order to minimize the risk of permitting delays.

Humbach proposes that "existing-use zoning" be applied to "such economically vital and socially crucial open-land uses as agriculture and forestry, not to mention zoning to retain the overall character of nonurban areas" (1992c, 1). The concept, which would follow the normal practice of built-up urban areas, is already common in Europe and has been successfully applied in Oregon and Washington. It would also make use values paramount, however, which directly conflicts with both the growth machine's emphasis on maximizing exchange values and the cultural premises that growth is good and that undeveloped land is being wasted. It would be a decisive step toward protecting existing agricultural and open space uses threatened with development. Humbach states, "Existing-use zoning applied to rural areas would have essentially the same general effect as traditional zoning applied in already-developed urban areas: a tendency to stabilize neighborhood land-use patterns and character by establishing a legal presumption that people cannot necessarily change the uses of their land just because they might profit by doing so. Existing-use zoning is not, therefore, a departure from familiar zoning strategy. Rather, it is a logical adaptation of urban zoning to the rural context where (as in most already-built urban areas) the presumption is *against* substantial land-use change."[14]

Viewed in isolation, however, existing-use zoning would appear unable to accommodate the tremendous growth pressures now being exerted in exurban areas. Humbach recognizes this, and he recommends the adoption of urban growth boundaries together with existing-use zoning to encourage development in areas with adequate infrastructure and environmental capacity. He is not calling for an end to all growth in rural and exurban areas. He is instead arguing that growth should be directed to the most appropriate areas to improve the efficiency of the development process. In theory, this will also benefit developers, because "all (or at least most) of the development within an urban growth boundary can be 'as of right'" (ibid.). This would represent a major improvement over the current system, where every proposal for development must go through a similar level of confrontational and ad hoc review.

A variety of mechanisms can complement existing use zoning to create incentives for the protection of agriculture and open space lands. In California, the Williamson Act has been in place since 1965 to encourage the protection of agricultural and open space lands by ensuring that property tax assessments reflect only the value of the land in agricultural use rather than its value for speculative development. This economic incentive was designed to reduce the likelihood that rapidly rising real estate values would force farmers and ranchers to sell their land simply for the sake of making tax payments on that land. Landowners enter into rolling ten-year contracts to keep their land in agriculture or open space, and these are automatically renewed each year unless the landowner takes action to remove the land from the provisions of the Williamson Act. Premature removal for development (before the ten-year contract has expired) results in substantial penalties for back taxes. The relative tax advantages of Williamson Act land enrollment have eroded since the passage of Proposition 13 in 1978, however, which independently limits annual increases in all property tax assessments to 2 percent regardless of greater market appreciation. As a result, most long-time landowners face current property tax liabilities that reflect a property tax assessment well below market value, resulting in an opportunity to retain relatively low property tax payments *without* incurring Williamson Act restrictions.[15] Proposition 13 has therefore had the indirect effect of undermining the Williamson Act and contributing to the conversion of agriculture and open space lands without the ten-year "notice" provisions inherent in the removal of lands from the Act. (At the same time, however, lower property taxes under Proposition 13 have reduced the influence of rapidly appreciating land values on the conversion of land because of increasing property tax liability.)

Similar economic incentives have been established in California tax law through the establishment of Timber Production Zones (TPZs), formerly called Timber Preserve Zones. This designation allows landowners to avoid property taxation on the value of the timber on their property until it is harvested, at which point a severance tax is paid on the value of the timber. This avoids the cash flow problem of timber landowners growing trees over long periods while needing to make annual tax payments reflecting the increasing value of the merchantable timber—which would tend to encourage them to cut the trees after a short rotation period and/or to convert the land. Once again, however, Proposition 13 has diminished the relative effects of TPZ designation on land conversion decision-making. Penalties for TPZ withdrawal are also relatively small.

These indirect economic incentives represent attempts by the state of California to encourage the protection of agriculture and open space lands, but the historical record demonstrates their weakness as rapid conversion continues throughout the state. Los Angeles and Orange Counties were dominated by productive farmland through the 1940s, then underwent rapid conversion in the 1950s and 1960s (Davis 1990). This experience helped set the stage for adoption of the Williamson Act in 1965 and establishment of the California Coastal Commission in 1972. Santa Clara County then endured a similar fate *after* adoption of the Williamson Act, however, as apple orchards gave way to Apple computer factories and the area earned the name Silicon Valley in the 1970s and 1980s (Loma Prieta Chapter of the Sierra Club 1978–90; Peninsula Conservation Center 1978–83; Saxenian 1994). More recently, the productive farmland of the Central Valley has faced strong conversion pressure in the 1980s and 1990s (Johnson et al. 1993). Projections of future population growth suggest that existing policies are unlikely to stem the tide of agriculture and open space land conversion in California (Goldberg 1996; American Farmland Trust 1995).

Accordingly, more direct mechanisms have arisen in many communities facing continuing conversion pressure. Local, regional, and national land trusts, such as the American Farmland Trust, have worked with local governments to adopt "right to farm" ordinances and to acquire conservation easements to maintain working landscapes in places like the Sonoma and Napa wine country. These efforts have had broad local support as both residents and businesses have recognized the value of their agriculturally dominated open space to their tourism economy and local quality of life. In some cases, open space districts have been established to acquire threatened lands through fee-title purchase.[16] These efforts have been funded by local assessment districts that raise capital through voter-approved property tax assessments. Proposition 13 has made it difficult to establish these assessment districts, however, because of its requirement that all property tax increases be approved by a two-thirds majority.[17] In other cases, major landowners have donated conservation easements or fee-title ownership to local or regional open space districts.[18]

In most cases, however, a combination of techniques has been necessary for success: strict regulation in sensitive areas (e.g., existing use zoning), clear identification of targeted development areas (e.g., within an urban growth boundary), full infrastructure cost recovery (e.g., pricing policies that encourage more compact infill where infrastructure already exists), property tax incentives for preservation (e.g., Williamson Act and TPZ designations), conservation easements (e.g., through landowner donations as part of the development approval process or purchase by open space districts), and fee-title acquisition (e.g., by the city, county, or an open space district) all have a role to play. No single tool represents a "silver bullet," and most will be ineffective without complementary efforts. A comprehensive and integrated growth management system will draw on all these tools and more. Illustrations of such integrated growth management systems and their limitations are discussed below.

Moreover, even these coarse policy tools cannot address the finer-grain implications of subdivision layout and site design. It will therefore be helpful to look at additional design tools that address the pattern of subdivisions and design features that maintain the rural landscape.

CONSERVATION SUBDIVISION DESIGN

Comprehensive planning requires careful evaluation and consideration of both social and natural factors, and it must emphasize the cultural and ecological values not otherwise explicitly addressed by the marketplace. In the case of exurban sprawl, the primary cultural values that are degraded relate to visual and aesthetic qualities (Duane 1992b; 1993a; Yaro et al. 1988; Arendt 1994a; 1994b; Humbach 1989; 1990; 1992a; 1992b; 1992c). Native biological diversity is also threatened by habitat fragmentation and isolation of populations resulting from roads and development (Duane 1993c; Soule 1991a; Peck 1993; 1998). Consequently, alternative patterns of development must mitigate these effects while still meeting the social and economic needs of exurban residents. Good design need not deviate from market realities, however, and determination of the specific areas to be developed should include consideration of social, economic, and cultural criteria that include market land values.[19]

Randall Arendt and his colleagues make a compelling case for open space development or conservation subdivision design in rural areas, based primarily on an aesthetic rationale. Recognizing that the primary asset of rural communities is their ruralness, they argue for protecting rural character and scenic views by clustering development in patterns similar to the small towns and villages that drew exurbanites there in the first place. The neotraditional town planning movement has advocated a similar strategy for making places livable and pedestrian-friendly, although it has had mixed success in practice (Duany and Plater-Zyberk 1991; Calthorpe 1989; Katz 1994; Sexton 1995; Southworth 1997). (Rural clustering has also been criticized by Tom Daniels on the grounds that it continues to encourage rural development that threatens working agriculture [Sierra Business Council 1997, 28].) Traditional large-lot zoning destroys the very landscapes that have brought exurbanites to the country, while the same number of homes can be developed on a site in a way that retains landscape integrity through careful site design. This approach requires a reintegration across multiple spatial scales of city and regional planning (which has usually taken a macro-scale perspective to metropolitan and regional development) and landscape architecture (which has usually been applied primarily with a micro-scale perspective that emphasizes site design). Unfortunately, both disciplinary and professional differences have made this integration difficult and uncommon in practice.

As noted above, the problem is that most existing zoning ordinances have been transferred directly from urban and suburban settings without regard for the specific landscape features that make rural and exurban environments desirable and unique. Those planning tools reinforce the tendency of the market to homogenize and commodify the landscape. They also make design less relevant to the process of community development and marginalize important social, cultural, and ecological values (use values) relative to the economic values of the market (exchange values). These biases are deeply imbedded within the value-laden assumptions that belie their apparent innocuousness as technical tools meant to be applied by technocratic value-neutral, "objective" planners. They are instead a critical part of a complex development system designed to turn open or "empty" land into a readily transferable productive commodity for exchange in abstract capital markets.

Within this context, design matters to the marketplace only to the degree that it results in product differentiation in exchange values.[20] But design, as Arendt and his colleagues so clearly show, has enormous implications for the community character of small towns and rural regions facing the ecotransformation of the exurban boom. Louise Mozingo and others have described design as the tangible interface between Nature and Culture (1997). It is the primary mediator of our individual relationship to the planet through our daily lives. Design therefore matters in social, cultural, economic, and ecological terms not generally captured by the market. Use values are directly affected by design. Design must therefore be a critical element in landscape planning. We must move beyond the density and use-separation orientation of *zoning* and reembrace *design* if we are to maintain rural and small town character.

The power of creative site design is best demonstrated in the remarkable graphic images prepared for Arendt's books by Kevin Wilson, Elizabeth A. Brabec, and Harry L. Dodson. These pictures are indeed worth at least a thousand words each. They take a series of specific real-world sites and show how they look now and how they would look under both "conventional" and "creative" development designs. These approaches are then applied by Arendt and his colleagues more generally to the development of integrated planning strategies that maintain small town character while still allowing for development that can accommodate population growth (and protect the private property rights of landowners). These scenes from rural New England could easily be from the Sierra Nevada foothills or many other exurban regions in the West.

The *only* difference between these images is *design:* they have the same number of new units or commercial development (in area) in each of the development alternatives. A plan image of the development shows that the individual lots have also been decreased in size (and therefore increased in net density), while commonly owned open space areas have been increased dramatically. The average gross density for each development remains the same, but the lot lines have been redrawn to maximize the public open space on the site.

Note that careful design can still maintain comparable levels of privacy for individual homeowners. Long two-acre lots may offer only 150-foot separation between homes along the street, for example, while shorter three-quarter-acre lots may still offer 100-foot buffers between the homes (Arendt 1994b, 236). Careful use of vegetative screening and site design (at a more detailed scale than the overall subdivision design) can protect privacy at this distance. The 150-foot distance, despite the two-acre lot size, is unlikely to protect privacy any more than the 100-foot buffer if the neighbors are noisy.

Each of the homes can, however, be linked to the larger open space system of both the subdivision and the regional landscape under the creative design alternative. That open space system can in turn be designed to protect valuable views and ecological features that would otherwise be lost under the conventional development alternative. This is a win-win alternative that does not reduce the landowners' capacity to develop his or her property in terms of the number of parcels or homesites. It avoids any problem of taking private property while protecting the broader community interest.

It is possible, then, to achieve human settlement patterns in the exurban landscape that satisfy social, economic, and ecological criteria for sustainability. This directly challenges the notions that we can have *either* economic development *or* environmental quality but not both, or that we can protect *either* private property rights *or* community interests but not both. Those are false choices predicated on a conventional and popular wisdom that is simply wrong. That view is in turn predicated on a set of assumptions about our existing institutional mechanisms for

FIGURE 8.1a *(right).* Typical rural or exurban landscape before development. Site illustrations for figures 8.1a–c by Dodson Associates, Ashfield, Massachusetts. © 1988 The Center for Rural Massachusetts, University of Massachusetts, Amherst. Used with permission.

FIGURE 8.1b *(opposite).* Typical rural or exurban landscape after conventional large-lot development.

FIGURE 8.1c. Typical rural or exurban landscape after creative open space/conservation subdivision design development. Houses are clustered in the woods at bottom and right.

planning and development that are at least seventy years old and being applied out of context. Unless we challenge those assumptions, then, we are limited in our capacity to find innovative solutions to the dilemma facing small towns and rural regions on the exurban frontier.

Decreasing net development densities may therefore actually *degrade* both environmental quality and community character; *increasing* net densities in selected areas through smaller lot sizes could actually *protect* ecological and cultural resources—*if* large, permanent open space areas are established simultaneously to protect aesthetic values, environmental quality, and wildlife habitat.[21] This goes against conventional and popular wisdom, but the images presented above do not lie. We can indeed maintain rural and small town character while still accommodating some population growth in exurbia. The difficulty is that the current planning paradigm and its associated regulations and zoning designations are built on the flawed idea that lower densities always lead to lower impacts. It will therefore require significant changes to that approach and mindset to protect the values we care about in the exurban landscape.

These are not just abstract or academic ideas: they have been applied in real places by real people with results that we can evaluate. *Rural by Design* includes twenty-two residential cases, five town center commercial cases, and ten roadside commercial cases to illustrate successful applications (Arendt 1994b, 313–95, part

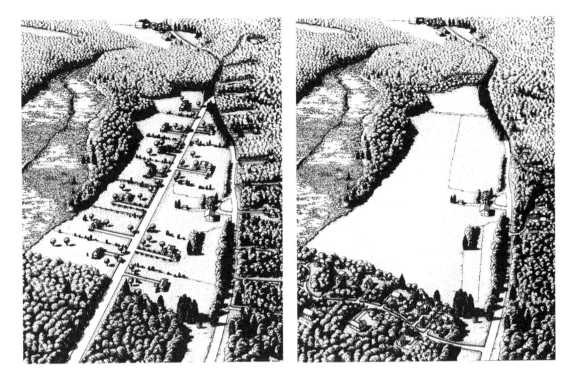

IV). It also includes examples of systematic efforts to implement these techniques at the county level as well as village design standards and architectural and site design principles that have been implemented. Most of the examples are from the Connecticut River valley of western Massachusetts, Vermont, New Hampshire, and Connecticut, as well as the mid-Atlantic states of Pennsylvania, Maryland, and Virginia. These techniques have also been applied in North Carolina, Michigan, Illinois, Washington, and Oregon. Marin County is the only jurisdiction in California to have adopted subdivision standards that require development of a conservation subdivision design, although other jurisdictions "encourage" such design.

One of the most comprehensive systems adopted to date is the PEARL program in Livingston County, Michigan. PEARL is the acronym for Protect Environment, Agriculture, and Rural Landscape (Livingston County Planning Department 1991). The program is described in detail by accessible materials distributed by the Livingston County Planning Department to citizens and prospective developers. These materials include summaries of the literature, examples of similar programs in other communities, comparisons for typical properties between build-out scenarios under traditional zoning versus the PEARL option, and excerpted articles addressing issues of economic valuation and the legal framework (Pivo et al. 1990). The PEARL documents also address citizens' commonly asked questions (Livingston County Planning Department 1991). This has helped to move exploration of these ideas out of the ivory tower and into public discourse in the rapidly growing exurban landscape. The Sierra Business Council has made similar information accessible to the public with its 1997 report, *Planning for Prosperity,* but local governments in the Sierra Nevada have not yet followed Livingston County's lead.

Consider for a moment a 150-acre parcel at the upper end of an environmentally significant drainage in the Sierra Nevada foothills—perhaps Little Deer Creek, where it spills off Banner Mountain before joining Deer Creek downstream in Nevada City. There is no potable domestic water supply or sewer service to the site, so a three-acre minimum lot size is required by county regulations. That means up to fifty units can be built on the site. The parcel would typically be subdivided into fifty three-acre parcels, then each parcel would be sold to individual home builders. Most of the homes would be built by general contractors (rather than the developer) for the people who will actually occupy them. They will be built individually over a ten-year period.

But what will that do to the landscape? Spread evenly among the fifty lots, the entire drainage will be developed. Half of the homes will be on north-facing slopes, while the other half will bask in sunshine all winter long—perfect for passive solar designs. The ecosystem will be fragmented by a maze of roads, and erosion will increase as road builders work their way down the steep slopes to the riparian edge. Fuel consumption and air pollution will both increase as residents travel long distances to town. Risk of water quality degradation is probably also higher with fifty separate septic systems than with one centralized system or a series of small community systems. Parcelization also tends to increase fencing, which limits wildlife movement while increasing habitat edges, and improve the dispersal of alien plant species associated with settlement. Finally, the dispersion of domestic dogs and cats throughout the landscape increases the risk of wildlife harassment that can kill many species through exhaustion (Duane 1993c; Soule 1991a; Peck 1993; 1998).

Consider next an alternative development scheme for the site using Arendt's open-space-development or conservation-subdivision design principles, where the *distribution* of new buildings is as important as the average density: instead of fifty three-acre parcels, the fifty units are distributed in ten five-unit "clusters" of houses along the ridge to the north of the waterway. They all have southern exposure, reducing wood burning and electricity use (and the associated emissions) for heating and lighting. Total length of roadways (and associated construction costs) is cut in half by this more compact design—allowing the roads to be engineered, thereby reducing erosion and amount of impervious surface contributing to runoff. Because the homes are built at a higher net density (but the same gross density), it may also be possible for sewer service and water service to be extended along the main access road. At the very least, septic leach lines can be located in the most suitable soils and away from waterways to reduce the effects of the units on the site.

The new homes each have about half an acre of land in private ownership immediately adjacent to their individual homes, and careful site design maintains their sense of privacy. The remaining land is held in common ownership with clear deed restrictions to protect its public value as an amenity resource for both the homeowners and the broader community. The developed portion of the site is only twenty-five acres, however, with another twenty-five acres affected by roads and leach fields. This leaves one hundred acres of open wildland for habitat and recreational use. A series of trails connects the ten housing clusters with each other and the riparian zone below, which is available for recreational use by the entire community. The ecosystem is largely intact for wildlife migration and habitat.[22] The one hundred acres of open space may not be adequate to maintain many native species, but it could be integrated with similarly sized parcels that are contiguous or nearby. An entire system of wildlife habitat and corridors could be established through careful planning. Four adjacent hundred-acre areas could be located to create a contiguous four-hundred-acre area—reducing edge effects and increasing interior habitat to protect threatened species (Duane 1993c; Soule 1991a; Peck 1993; 1998).

This alternative model of development requires comprehensive planning. It also requires institutional innovations that allow the fifty homeowners to share ownership of the hundred acres of common open space, and those owners (and their neighbors) must be assured that it will *never* be developed. They would otherwise lose the benefits of the arrangement. Concern about the risk of clustered developments leading to eventual infill of adjacent open space is one of the primary reasons neighboring residents often oppose clustered developments (Pivo 1992; 1988; Pivo et al. 1990; Arendt 1994a; 1994b). There must be *permanent* guarantees of open space protection. This can come through conservation easements, irreversible regulatory restrictions, or public ownership. Which approach is best depends on the specific local conditions. A local land trust could acquire and manage the land, for example, or it could be integrated into a larger public open space network through a local or regional open space district. The home owners themselves can also maintain control over and ownership of the open space, although they may prefer to transfer it in order to avoid liability and tax responsibilities.[23]

Arendt previously recommended that in all developments at least 50 percent of the land be retained in open space, but he now recommends that from 75 to 90 percent of the land in all developments in rural and exurban areas be dedicated to open space (Yaro et al. 1988; Arendt 1994a; 1994b; 1996a; 1996b). Other planning and design consultants have achieved similar reductions in developed area.[24] My example for Little Deer Creek (where 66 percent is retained as open space and 83 percent in common ownership or roads) is within this general range. The potential to protect open space and ecological function while ensuring privacy for individual homeowners will depend on site-specific characteristics, of course, so it is difficult to generalize for all sites. Preliminary analysis of a site to determine developable potential and a schematic site design is relatively easy, however, and could be accomplished by citizens and landowners relying only on the guidance of Arendt's 1994 book, *Designing Open Space Subdivisions,* or his 1996 book, *Conservation Design for Subdivisions.* Arendt has held workshops on his techniques and produced competent citizen designers by the end of two half-day sessions (Arendt 1992–94; 1994a; 1996a). More detailed design and engineering work can then be completed with professional assistance.

Of course this shift in the spatial distribution of settlement *within* each parcel alone is not likely to change the overall ecological effects of exurban development. *Site* design alone is therefore inadequate. Sites must also be linked to each other, then clusters of similar sites linked within a nested hierarchy of multiple spatial scales. Just as the location of each house on a parcel must be related to the other structures on the site, the relationship between the open space on a given parcel must be related to the open space on adjacent parcels. The open space on that clustered set of adjacent parcels must in turn be related to the next highest level of ecological integration—a riparian corridor (e.g., providing a connected habitat corridor from Nevada City up to Banner Mountain along Little Deer Creek), a watershed (e.g., the entire Little Deer Creek drainage, in order to assess the effects of development on water quality and runoff characteristics), or a vegetation or habitat type (e.g., all of the transition ponderosa pine forest in the region, which provides important habitat for wildlife species both within the Little Deer Creek watershed and in adjacent watersheds for Deer Creek, Wolf Creek, and Greenhorn Creek). This is why it is necessary to incorporate ecological design into land use planning as well as the site design process. The cumulative effect of hundreds of uncoordinated clustered developments is still likely to be a highly fragmented landscape. Site designs must relate to the larger landscape.

ENSURING ECOLOGICAL FUNCTIONALITY

As discussed above, the dominant pattern of exurban sprawl leads to a wide range of effects on both ecological integrity and quality of life. These direct effects suggest some principles for land use planning that could minimize the effects of low-density human settlement patterns in exurban regions. First, the direct reduction of habitat area must be minimized by limiting the footprint of buildings, roads, and associated development. Second, development should not occur in habitats that are rare or have already been significantly reduced. Third, development should be distributed in a way that minimizes the fragmentation of habitat. Fragmentation can be indicated in at least three ways: number of patches, average patch size, and the fraction of total area contained in patches of some minimum size. Fourth, connectivity of habitat patches must be assured through careful road network design, site development, and fencing requirements. Important linkages and corridors should be identified and protected from development that would isolate associated patches. Fifth, the public must be educated about the effects of dogs and cats on biological diversity. It is extremely difficult to monitor leash laws in low-density exurban areas, so we must rely on public education to reduce the effects of these domestic animals. Sixth, the public must also be advised about the effects of invasive nonnatives on biological diversity, and regulations can be implemented and incentives created to restrict their sale. Finally, septic systems and wells must be situated where they will avoid potentially affecting surface water and groundwater quality. This will generally require a much more comprehensive understanding of site capabilities associated with soils and slope constraints as well as the relationship between those and the hydrologic system. Together, these policies and actions could significantly reduce the effects of human settlement on both biological diversity and ecological structure and function in the exurban landscape.

These principles are not now being applied in most exurban areas. They call for careful planning and the application of design principles advocated in Ian McHarg's 1969 book, *Design with Nature*. Evaluation of natural factors and the relationship between settlement patterns and habitat fragmentation is a necessary first step, but one rarely completed by exurban planners. Clustered development patterns could minimize habitat fragmentation while promoting connectivity, but such a development scheme requires coordination among landowners and across multiple planning jurisdictions. California passed the Subdivision Map Act in 1973, requiring investments in infrastructure to be simultaneous with subdivision, but, as noted earlier, it applies only to subdivisions of more than four lots. Developers of minor subdivisions are not required to install infrastructure, and existing subdivisions were exempted from the requirements of the Subdivision Map Act. As a result, larger new subdivisions are usually the only ones in which development of infrastructure occurs simultaneously with parcel subdivision. The capital-intensive economics of infrastructure investment then compel immediate housing development in order to recoup the high fixed costs associated with site development. In contrast, the dominant pattern of development in the Sierra Nevada is one of sequential steps: initial parcelization of large properties into multiple lots by the original landowner (either through minor subdivisions or preexisting parcelization that preceded the Subdivision Map Act), the sale of each individual parcel to an owner by a real estate agent, then the individual development of each lot by each owner. The complexity of coordination seems to increase as a power function of the number of participants and transactions in the process. Improving integration of the prevailing exurban development process would therefore require dozens to hundreds of individual decisions to be coordinated.

It is often difficult to identify a single point in the planning process where conservation biology and landscape ecology can influence the ultimate pattern of development. The critical step, however, is the original subdivision of the land whenever the incremental subdivision process is not subject to government review and approval. Moreover, subsequent build-out of the parcels may occur incrementally over a ten- to thirty-year period (especially if many of the ultimate residents buy parcels in anticipation of retirement in future decades). This means that the full effect of the development pattern will not be evident to residents until it is too late to mitigate it. Like the frog in the metaphorical pot of water on a simmering stove, we will not react if the water is *gradually* brought to a boil. In contrast, contemplating a proposal for a massive subdivision that will be simultaneously developed is comparable to being dropped directly into hot water: we leap out quickly. We are more likely to suffer the effects of a multitude of small projects than one major one, since we have adequate legal mechanisms to evaluate and to influence major projects.

McHarg's approach to ecological analysis begins with an assessment of the natural factors, such as soils, geology, vegetation, and hydrology, affecting the capability and suitability of land for land development. Development is then directed toward those areas most suitable for development, while ecologically sensitive areas such as wetlands, steep slopes, and unstable soils are protected (possibly through existing use zoning and the other techniques described above). This analysis and design approach can be applied at a regional scale by, for example, protecting the hillsides and riparian corridors within a county, down to the site scale by, for example, placing the house on the sunny side of the lot. This approach effectively clusters development in those areas most suitable.

A number of researchers and planners have applied McHarg's ideas through comprehensive planning. Ecological analyses of constraints and land suitability are commonly employed by landscape architects at the site scale, and the general principles are sometimes applied at the regional scale by planners. All too often, though, the process founders on a lack of reliable ecological data for the region. Other factors, such as the market value of land under more intensive development designations, then dominate the decision process. The result is land use planning and regulation that protects neither important ecological resources nor public values central to community character.

The conservation of native biological diversity is not an explicit objective of the Arendt approach,[25] but his approach can be adapted to address that problem by applying it within a landscape ecology framework. This framework requires an integrated approach to regional planning that coordinates efforts at a variety of scales, which is consistent with the principles underlying conservation biology (Noss 1991; 1992). Essentially, the Arendt approach to site design and development should be nested within the McHarg approach to regional assessment and planning, with McHarg's ideas updated to reflect the principles laid out by Richard Forman in his book *Land Mosaics: The Ecology of Landscapes and Regions* (1995). Forman's new book updates the seminal book he published in 1986 with Michel Godron, titled *Landscape Ecology*. In the newer one, Forman highlights the relationships between landscape patterns and processes. McHarg also drew on such relationships (McHarg 1996a; 1996b), but the science of landscape ecology and conservation biology has given us considerable new insights since the original publication of *Design with Nature*.[26]

The result would be a pattern of human settlement built around a network of interconnected conservation preserves—rather than the matrix of fragmented habitat that results from our current approach. Human settlement can fit *within* ecological systems without disrupting their structure and function, but ecological systems cannot be maintained with only the scattered patches that remain *after* human settlement without regard for the structure and function of ecological systems. The spatial arrangement of wildlands is an important determinant of the long-term viability of maintaining ecological function in the landscape. We must shift from a planning perspective that considers wildlands as merely the leftovers that have not yet had the "opportunity" to be developed, to one that views them as an essential component of what Frederick Steiner calls "the living landscape" (1991): in the proper configuration, they constitute the highest and best use of land even if there is no market exchange value associated with that use.

COMPLETING THE ECOLOGICAL ANALYSIS

The technical aspects of completing the necessary ecological assessments have been well-known for several decades now,[27] but their application has been limited and relatively unwieldy. This reflects a variety of both theoretical and practical concerns. The theoretical problem is that we have a very poor understanding of the relationship between specific patterns of human settlement and ecological function. We do not know the precise relationship between "edge" and "area" for most species at the scale of exurban wildland patches, for example, and the Wildlife-Habitat Relationships model used by the California Department of Fish and Game assumes a minimum mapping unit of forty acres (Greenwood 1992–97; Graber 1994–97; Barrett 1992–96; Mayer and Laudenslayer 1988). We are therefore unable to use the WHR model to determine how one-, five-, ten-, or twenty-acre parcels may affect a particular wildlife species differently. Some species may be fine as long as all parcels are at least one acre and there are no major fences blocking migration, while other species may be adversely affected by domestic dogs and cats whenever the average density is greater than one housing unit per forty acres. We therefore need to complete significant additional field research to begin to document these relationships.

Why don't we have this data now, and why isn't research being conducted on this issue? This appears to reflect a conceptual difficulty on the part of conservation biologists and landscape ecologists when it comes to characterizing human-dominated landscapes. There is a tendency to treat all nonwildland areas as either urban or agricultural, with little differentiation within either of the latter two classes. This has changed recently for the agricultural class, however, as researchers have begun to document the influence of different agricultural practices on a wide range of wildlife species. The presence of synthetic fertilizers or pesticides, the presence or absence of woodlots or hedgerows, and the proximity of agricultural lands to riparian corridors or other bodies of water all have a potential effect on the viability of individual wildlife species and the ecological functionality of agricultural lands. As habitat, grazed grasslands are clearly different from rows of corn. The landscape ecology literature now reflects this and researchers can address policy questions affecting agricultural practices (Forman 1995).

Subclass differentiation is less well-developed for the urban landscape or habitat types. While dozens of papers at the 1995 conference of the International Association for Landscape Ecology differentiated agricultural landscapes, only one examined different degrees of habitat fragmentation in urban landscapes. Rather than distinguish different urban landscape types, however, that paper focused on how two different bird species of different body masses would view the same landscape differently (Hostetler and Holling 1995). This is an important distinction and can serve as the basis for characterizing urban landscape types. It may be that there are broad classes of urban landscape types that serve different classes of ecological function in relationship to species of a particular type (such as birds versus mammals versus reptiles versus amphibians) or particular body mass (such as eagles versus starlings, among birds, or mountain lions versus squirrels, among mammals). Such proxies hold promise for allowing us to find clusters of wildlife species characteristics that can then be related to landscape characteristics to generate broad subclasses for landscape classification. We may then need only to characterize a small subset of "urban" types to address the needs of broad classes of species (Marples and Holling 1995; Sendzimir and Holling 1995).

The availability of low-cost GIS technology and remote sensing data now makes comprehensive assessment of the relationship between human settlement patterns and landscape-scale ecological function much more feasible. This is especially true for the Sierra Nevada, where SNEP developed a detailed digital database on the spatial distribution of vegetation types, wildlife habitat types, rare and endemic plant species, significant natural areas (unfortunately, for public lands only), and hydrologic regimes with associated aquatic values, including an "index of biotic integrity" indicating the similarity of the aquatic fauna to native conditions.[28] It is therefore relatively straightforward now to overlay digital coverage of a local land use map on these other data layers in order to visualize (and analyze with quantitative indices) the potential effects of development build-out on ecological function. An example of this approach is illustrated below for El Dorado County. The land use mapping approach I used allowed me to differentiate the "urban" portion of the landscape into subclasses based on different allowable development densities. As noted above, however, we are still limited by our poor understanding of the relationship between those development patterns (e.g., clustering versus scattering) and ecological function.

The greatest difficulty at this point is making the public, and especially policymakers, aware of both the implications of the existing pattern of exurban sprawl and the alternatives available. Adoption of alternative techniques does not even require an explicit focus on biological diversity, for conservation subdivision design would also protect many things that local residents already see as in their own self-interest. Public participation in the process of planning to protect biological diversity could, however, bring such protection to the table, as well as precipitate the shift in ethical attitudes needed to protect biodiversity (Duane 1992b). There is widespread support for maintaining wildlife in the exurban landscape, but the technical tools of conservation biology and landscape ecology are poorly understood by most exurban residents.[29] Interactive application of GIS-based planning tools could therefore serve an educational as well as an analytic function. Citizens may then be willing to advance and support alternative settlement patterns—and the planning tools necessary to achieve them—once the implications of current practices become apparent.[30]

The technical aspects of comprehensive planning and analysis are relatively straightforward in theory (if highly uncertain in practice), but changing the actual pattern of exurban development will require much more than technical analyses. Significant institutional changes are also necessary. The first is creation of a climate in which people are willing to "look under the rock" to see what problems exist rather than hope that potential problems will go away long enough for them to become somebody else's responsibility. Many of our most heated conflicts over biological diversity reflect the persistent failure of existing institutions to identify potential problems and implement preventative policy solutions so as to avoid the "train wreck" conflicts that have resulted in stark either/or choices for society. This was true of the northern spotted owl (Stephen Yaffee has documented incremental development of the problem over two decades [1994]), and it was true for most of the other species for which HCPs have been prepared after the species was listed under the ESA (Beatley 1994b). The result has been a tendency to shoot the messenger—the biologists, environmentalists, and agencies charged with protecting biological diversity—as well as attempts to eliminate our very capacity to generate messages (e.g., weakening of the ESA and elimination of the National Biological Survey) that may require actions that modify current practices.

Current settlement patterns and land use planning practices will be difficult to change simply because they appear to protect the status quo. Rural residents now living on one- to five-acre parcels often resist the idea of clustered development for at least two reasons: they fear that the scale of clustering will be comparable to suburban subdivisions, which will lead to the traffic problems and high built/natural area ratios that they left when moving to the exurban region; and, as noted above, they fear that the remaining open space will eventually become a prime site for future development through infill that will destroy the aesthetic, recreational, and ecological benefits it may offer. It is therefore necessary to design clustered developments to match the scale requirements and primary motivation for exurban migration: they must maintain a sense of privacy through vegetative screening, protect viewsheds and recreational access, minimize the scale of any one development to reduce traffic and devegetation of an area, and avoid the site and architectural homogeneity of metropolitan subdivisions. Moreover, the development process must ensure permanent protection for associated open space. This should be articulated through planning policies such as the zoning ordinance and general plan, as well as through legal restrictions on deeds, such as permanent conservation easements and deeded restrictions on development.

Exurban residents also often view the existing pattern of development as already offering easy access to large areas of semipublic open space without the need for increased proximity to neighbors through clustering. As a result, they may be comfortable with their one-acre lot because it is surrounded by other, undeveloped one-acre lots, a circumstance that encourages perception of *actual* density that may be quite different from the *allowable* density. Residents are, in other words, quite comfortable with one-acre parcels as long as all of the adjoining parcels are not yet developed. Each home is then effectively in the center of a five- to ten-acre parcel, with at least a one-acre buffer between each of the developed parcels—until all of those parcels are developed. A clustered/open space development design, however, can ensure long-term protection of ecological and aesthetic values.

Finally, it is important to note another potentially significant advantage of clustered/open space development/conservation subdivision design: fire management. This design approach addresses two of the most significant problems facing fire management efforts in the urban-wildland intermix: it increases the possibilities for managing fuels in open space areas, either through mechanical means or prescribed burns; and it allows concentrated structural protection as well as some use of traditional wildland fire-fighting techniques, such as back-burning an area to reduce fuel available to the fire. Moreover, the reduced fire-fighting (and possible fire insurance) costs associated with the improved design could yield economic resources for the purchase of additional open space, especially in areas where *any* development would increase fire risk or be extremely difficult to evacuate or protect in the case of fire.[31]

This means that there could be an alliance between landscape ecologists, conservation biologists, fire management agencies, and insurance agencies, where the latter two institutions may be willing to pay for efforts that can simultaneously protect native biological diversity and functioning landscape-scale ecological processes.[32] Internalizing the fire management risks and costs of alternative settlement patterns could encourage greater use of clustered development through the establishment of economic incentives for developers. Such an effort would, however, require greater funding for "presuppression" activities, which are generally considered less pressing than emergency fire suppression and therefore expendable at budget time.[33]

INTEGRATED GROWTH MANAGEMENT SYSTEMS

The techniques described above can both preserve existing agriculture and open space lands and reduce the aesthetic, cultural, and ecological effects of new developments on open land. None of them can satisfy the complex goals of an integrated growth management system, however, for they generally fail to address the problems of existing parcelization and the spatial patterns of growth at a regional scale. They instead tend to focus only on individual parcels or structures and usually fail to link development patterns (or open space protection) on those individual parcels to adjoining parcels and regional ecological functions. Other tools are necessary to make the above techniques effective at a regional scale.

An integrated exurban growth management system requires ten complementary elements:

cultural and ecological inventory and assessment at the regional, community, and site scales (in order to determine which features are highly valued and should be protected);

designation of targeted development zones where development will be "as of right," with environmental and infrastructure or public service assessments already completed;

investment in public infrastructure to create incentives for compact development within the targeted development areas, with full-cost pricing disincentives outside these areas;

establishment of existing-use zoning in areas where agriculture and open space values are to be protected, with limited provisions for development of a single residence per parcel;

establishment of tax incentives to reduce conversion pressures on agriculture and open space lands (e.g., assessment of value for agriculture and open space, not development);

clustered/open space development/conservation subdivision design requirements, where such a design is at least required to be submitted as an alternative to any traditional large-lot subdivision;

streamlining of the subdivision review and permitting process so that clustered/open space development/conservation subdivision design options face no greater uncertainty or delay in permitting;

establishment of a regional system for the market transfer of development rights or development credits (TDR/TDC) from downzoned properties to designated development areas;

active acquisition of conservation easements and fee title lands (from willing sellers only) by an open space district (working within an integrated regional plan developed with other public land and resource management agencies);

stable sources of funding that capture some of the increased market value associated with the growth management program as well as the nonlocal benefits of ecological protection.

This ten-point approach includes both strict regulations and strong economic incentives, but relies on zoning as only a limited tool. It does not involve annual building permit restrictions or across-the-board downzoning to reduce developable densities, but instead depends on the comprehensive inventory and assessment effort to direct growth where it will have the least effect on social, cultural, and ecological values. This strategy has both economic costs and benefits, and it is designed to capture some of the economic benefits in order to cover some of the economic costs. Rather than rely on a static "plan" for managing growth, however, a community must develop and implement the plan with an eye toward the dynamic nature of land markets and our ever-changing knowledge base. Some investments in infrastructure or tax incentives may not generate the desired effect; in those cases, alternative tools must be applied and the original strategies modified to correct the program. In other cases, our knowledge about ecological needs may change and require more, less, or simply different habitat protection or different riparian corridor widths. The planning process must use an adaptive management approach that can respond to this new information in order to assure achievement of the program's goals (Holling 1978; 1995; Walters 1986).

It must do so with full recognition of equity concerns, however, and a degree of predictability that assures landowners of regulatory stability and reasonableness. Such assurances are necessary in order for the market to function properly. Existing-use zoning will not avoid speculation, for example, if developers believe zoning designations can be overcome with a general plan amendment. Similarly, clustered/open space development/conservation subdivision design require-ments will be successful only if buyers are assured of the permanence of open space. Finally, new requirements for downzoning that result in the elimination of development potential for existing landowners may require some kind of eco-nomic compensation—through either a TDR/TDC scheme or public acquisition of development rights on the land—in order to avoid concern about takings. This is necessary for fairness even if not mandated under constitutional protections against takings. Some kind of compensation or TDR/TDC market is certainly nec-essary *politically,* where existing zoning is often viewed as authorizing or validating a right to develop. As Jay Stein has observed, there must be an "ideological com-mitment" by the body politic to implement growth management successfully (1993, vii).

It is important to note that the act of targeting areas for future development will be of value to the development community as well as environmentalists and other concerned local citizens. The speculative value of lands zoned for existing uses will be reduced, but the reduction in supply on the land market should increase the value of those areas targeted for growth.[34] The resulting transfer in economic value between these two landholding groups creates an opportunity to structure incentives for compensating those who will lose economic value. A TDR/TDC scheme can then make all landowners whole while avoiding a problem of windfalls in value for some and wipeouts in value for others (Schiffman 1989, 111–14; Roddewig and Inghram 1987; James and Gale n.d.). "Upzoning" is the primary way in which speculators acquire increased market value for their lands, but the public should not give that value away when a TDR/TDC scheme could instead capture some of it to compensate other landowners whose development potential has been restricted by downzoning.

One of the major difficulties with establishment of a successful TDR/TDC mar-ket is that it should affect the entire subregional market for development, which often includes multiple jurisdictions. Failure to include the entire development market—which is quite common—will weaken the effectiveness of the TDR/TDC market, which depends on some scarcity of development credits in order to real-ize TDR/TDC prices that will encourage market transactions. Existing TDR/TDC holders, who may not be able to develop their properties under the new growth management regime, will otherwise not be compensated sufficiently to encourage their participation. Prospective developers, in turn, will have little incentive to acquire TDR/TDCs if they can simply "shop jurisdictions" to shift their develop-ment activities to an adjacent jurisdiction within the same development market. This will undermine both development activity within the TDR/TDC jurisdiction and the local tax base. The likely outcome would be a weakening of the growth management system by local authorities—because there would be significant slack in development rather than the spatial and temporal reallocation of that development. In this case growth "management" could mean "no growth." Consequently, horizontal cooperation and coordination is critical to the success of a TDR/TDC system if the development market includes multiple jurisdictions. An example of this would be the commuter market in southern Nevada County along Highway 49, Placer County near Auburn along Interstate 80, and perhaps even parts of El Dorado County along Highways 49 and 193.

Such a multijurisdictional approach to the establishment of a TDR/TDC system is rare, however, and Schiffman notes that "while a number of TDR programs have been initiated throughout the country, for various reasons relatively few of them have actually experienced TDR transfers" (1989, 113). The most successful example in California is in the Malibu and Santa Monica Mountains area, "where developers of coastal subdivisions have been required to 'retire'—through purchase of development rights—an equivalent area of environmentally detrimental small lot subdivisions" (ibid.). In that case the strict regulatory requirements of the California Coastal Act—which cuts across multiple local jurisdictions—compelled developers' participation in the program. A similar program has been effectively implemented by the Tahoe Regional Planning Agency "to retire the multitude of lots existing in sensitive areas of the Tahoe Basin; the rights transferred in this case are closely regulated sewer connection authorizations" (ibid.; Strong 1984; Branson 1996a; 1996b). Once again, a strict multijurisdictional regulatory scheme *compels* developers' participation in the TDR/TDC market in the Tahoe Basin. That system has subsequently been challenged on takings grounds, but the U.S. Supreme Court rejected a facial challenge on the TDR/TDC system in the *Suitum* case in 1997.[35]

Three characteristics of these two California examples stand out: 1) the multijurisdictional nature of the regulatory agency (which could therefore establish a TDR/TDC "market" cutting across city and county boundaries), 2) the presence of a strict regulatory scheme founded on detailed environmental inventory and assessment (and therefore able to withstand legal challenges), and 3) the complementary role played in the regional TDR/TDC market by regional conservancies with the funds to acquire development rights or credits.

The California Tahoe Conservancy and the Santa Monica Mountains Conservancy, together with the California Coastal Conservancy, have been active buyers and sellers of land and development rights in these markets (Machida 1994–96; 1995; Fisher 1995). They have been funded primarily by state and federal taxpayers, however, rather than the local community or developers. This infusion of external capital is a critical element of successful programs, for it gives the relevant regulatory agency, for example, the TRPA or the Coastal Commission, a compensatory mechanism for surviving legal challenges surrounding alleged regulatory takings. "I'm not sure that we're there yet," says Dennis Machida, executive officer of the California Tahoe Conservancy, "but I cannot think of any regulatory system that can be fully effective without a compensation scheme" (1995). He notes that acquisition and site improvement options are often necessary to resolve land use disputes "where there are tradeoffs that aren't necessarily accepted by the larger society"—that is, where prohibition of development could occur under regulation without compensation, which is anathema to the public's perception of fairness (ibid.). Conservancies must, however, be separate entities from the regulatory agencies in order to avoid self-dealing conflicts of interest, where, for example, a regulatory agency could downzone a property—thereby lowering its market value—that it was interested in acquiring through its conservancy arm (Fisher 1995).

Together with the state Wildlife Conservation Board, the Coachella Valley Conservancy (established to acquire habitat necessary to complete a habitat conservation plan near Palm Springs under the ESA) (Beatley 1994b; Moore 1997), and the San Joaquin River Conservancy, public agencies have spent more than $1 billion to acquire fee-title land or conservation easements and development rights in California (Machida 1995). Federal land and resource management agencies have also acquired hundreds of millions of dollars worth of property in the Lake Tahoe Basin and along the California coast (including in the Santa Monica Mountains) through purchases using Land and Water Conservation Act funds (usually facilitated by a nonprofit land trust such as the Nature Conservancy or the Trust for Public Land) or land trades for other public lands (Brown 1995). This represents an enormous investment by state and federal taxpayers in environmental protection. The conservancy model functions as an "environmental redevelopment agency" model rather than a regulatory model, making its actions less controversial than land use controls (Machida 1995; Fisher 1995). Conservancies can also be *proactive*, while regulatory agencies are largely *reactive*.

Far fewer transactions have occurred in TDR/TDC systems implemented by Marin and San Luis Obispo Counties in California, where the markets are much smaller and conservancy money must come primarily from local sources.[36] Despite the limited success of TDR/TDC markets to date, however, a TDR/TDC system appears to be necessary in order to correct the planning mistakes of the past—where unregulated substandard subdivisions have fragmented ownership patterns and created hundreds of thousands of "paper lots" through the parcelization of the Sierra Nevada. These lot splits occurred both before zoning and subdivision regulations existed (Gerstung 1970; 1973) and under current rules (Duane 1992a; 1992b; 1993a; 1993c). The result is that current planning efforts are constrained by existing parcelization and implicit development rights that result in demands for similar zoning designations on adjacent or like-situated lands within exurban jurisdictions. Planners who fail to address this problem of existing parcelization are forced to work at the margins of comprehensive planning, unable to influence the most important determinant of community growth patterns (Salvesen and Porter 1996). Existing *development* is difficult to change, but existing *parcelization* should be on the table in any comprehensive planning process. An innovative TDR/TDC system—combined with a strict regulatory system and direct acquisition of development rights for some parcels through a conservancy model—appears to be the only way to deal fairly with this problem of existing parcelization.

Several states have developed growth management systems that utilize elements of the ten-point approach outlined above. Oregon's system, for example, stands in sharp contrast to that of California with its strong protection of agriculture and open space through a combination of urban growth boundaries (UGBs), infrastructure investments and pricing policies, existing-use zoning, and tax incentives. "Unfortunately," says Schiffman, "there appears to be little interest in California of adopting—or even learning from—this comprehensive and, apparently, successful model of growth management" (1989, 9). Gerrit Knaap and Arthur C. Nelson have, however, made it much easier to learn from the Oregon case with their 1992 book, *The Regulated Landscape: Lessons on State Land Use Planning from Oregon*. Knaap and Nelson were both planning graduate students in Oregon as the state's system was adopted in the early 1970s, and they have continued to study its evolution since then as academic researchers. Their study calls attention to important lessons applicable to growth management and land use planning programs at the state, regional, and local level. Most important, it shows what can be accomplished when planning and growth management are coordinated across all of these levels.

Oregon was facing rapid growth in the early 1970s, having jumped from a population of 1,520,000 in 1950 to 2,091,000 by 1970. Those pressures led to adoption of Senate Bill 100 in 1973 under the leadership of Governor Tom McCall. As noted earlier, the original Senate Bill 100 would have created fourteen regional Councils of Government but this structure was eliminated from the bill before passage. Instead, a dual state-local structure was adopted that remains today (a preexisting regional Coastal Conservation and Development Commission, which was inadequately staffed and funded, was absorbed into the Senate Bill 100 structure in 1976). "The intergovernmental structure of Oregon's program," note Knaap and Nelson, "influences the objectives as well as the process of planning. Compared to purely local systems of land use control, combined state and local systems enfranchise a wider geographic constituency" (1992, 36). This has had an important effect on the politics of planning and the substantive outcomes of Oregon planning processes. Interests aggregate at multiple geographic scales to influence the planning process at different points: "comprehensive planning by local governments encourages participation in land use decision making by those most closely familiar with and affected by such decisions," while "review of local comprehensive plans by the state prevents local governments from adopting plans that would be detrimental to larger statewide interests" (35–36).

This structure includes designation of goals by the state Department of Land Conservation and Development and the Land Conservation and Development Commission (LCDC), adoption by local governments of local plans to implement those goals under LCDC guidelines, review and approval by the state LCDC, then implementation by the local governments. Counties serve as intermediaries between incorporated cities and the state LCDC, compelling some horizontal consistency within each county. There is nevertheless still "friction between the politics of planning at the state level and the politics of implementation at the local level," where Knaap and Nelson note that the group 1000 Friends of Oregon is concerned that implementation is under the direction of "guardian foxes" (201). LCDC decisions can be appealed before the state Land Use Board of Appeals, then the Court of Appeals, and finally the Oregon Supreme Court (1992). This back-and-forth system of state-local interaction exemplifies a theme of coordination and cross-acceptance—features that Judith Innes argues are politically necessary for successful implementation (1991). Other states, such as Florida and New Jersey, have pursued a similar dual model, although their guidelines (and substantive success in managing growth) have generally been weaker than Oregon's.

In particular, Oregon is the only state, other than perhaps Hawaii, that has truly implemented and effectively maintained strong UGBs. John DeGrove notes that the imposition of those firm UGBs has been accompanied by *increased* affordable housing. The UGBs have therefore generally *not* driven up housing prices in Oregon because of concurrent application of policies promoting housing.[37] Knaap and Nelson confirm that the Oregon system has decreased uncertainty and risk in the approval process for developments *within* the designated UGB: whereas they averaged eighteen months before Senate Bill 100, they now average only ninety days (1992, 5). "The evidence, though scarce," state Knaap and Nelson, "offers little to suggest that statewide planning harmed Oregon's economy. Instead the evidence suggests that statewide planning, by increasing certainty in the regulatory environment and by preserving environmental amenities, may actually foster economic growth" (ibid.). Indeed, the Oregon economy has been booming despite significant contraction of its traditional resource-extraction base.[38] Much of this new growth is amenity-driven and in part reflects the success of Senate Bill 100 in protecting landscape values (Power 1996a; 1996b). Oregon's population had grown to 2,842,000 people by 1990—a bit more than four times the population of the Sierra Nevada (Knaap and Nelson 1992, 18). Oregon has less than one-tenth of California's population, however, suggesting that citizen accessibility to Oregon's state-level program could be comparable to a regional program in the much more populous Golden State. It is difficult to imagine a dual state-local system like Oregon's in a state the size of California without some intermediary regional structure. California added more people to its population in the year 1990 alone (834,000) than Oregon did in the two *decades* from 1970 to 1990 (751,000) (California DOF 1996; Knaap and Nelson 1992, 18).

Vermont is another state with a strong growth management regime, and there are many similarities between that state and the Sierra Nevada: 25 percent of Vermont's employment base was in the commodity sector in the 1950s, followed by rapid growth pressures in the 1960s after completion of interstate highway links to Boston and New York City. Subsequent economic development has transformed the Vermont economy, pushing it, like the Sierra Nevada economy, toward services and other amenity-driven development. Unlike the Sierra Nevada, however, Vermont, with its 562,750 residents, has a single jurisdiction within which a systematic approach to growth management could be established. Its population is less than that of the entire Sierra Nevada, but it is distributed across only about one-third the land area. Vermont's Act 250, which was passed in 1970, called for a three-stage planning process: interim development restrictions, land capability analysis, and a state land use plan. Only the first two stages were adopted in 1972 and 1973, however, leaving Environmental District Commissions with the authority to review specific projects in a system that "lacked a planning context" within which to address cumulative effects or the growth pressures of the 1980s (Daniels and Lapping 1984; DeGrove 1992).

Those subsequent pressures led to the adoption of Act 200 in 1988, which modified Act 250 to increase the importance of economic development concerns in the planning process and finally established Regional Planning Commissions to complete comprehensive plans. State-funded planning grants created incentives for extensive participation in the planning process during Act 200's first year of implementation, although a well-organized backlash diminished participation in later years (ibid.). Knaap and Nelson note that Oregon's program also shifted its focus "from resource conservation and urban growth management to economic development and affordable housing" in the late 1980s, "largely in response to changes in the Oregon economy and to changes in the relative influence of interest groups" (1992, 201).

Florida adopted a state-level growth management system more recently that emphasizes concurrency requirements for the establishment of adequate infrastructure concurrent with development. As DeGrove notes, however, successful implementation of such a requirement also requires concurrent *funding* for infrastructure—which has generally been lagging in Florida (Stein 1997). Attempts to protect rural areas from sprawl have consequently required weaker standards for levels of service within urban growth boundaries and stronger ones outside UGBs in order to avoid migration of growth to rural areas with "slack" in their level-of-service capacity (where new infrastructure would not be required to meet those standards) (DeGrove 1992, 165). Florida's requirement that *vertical* consistency be established between land use and infrastructure *within* a jurisdiction is therefore inadequate; *horizontal* consistency is also required across jurisdictions in order to avoid growth displacement and spillover effects.

DeGrove observes that "growth management" can mean both to "manage growth" and "managing for growth," where economic development, rather than environmental quality, is the emphasis of policy. He makes it clear that most state-level growth management systems are decidedly neither "no growth" nor "slow growth," and they have been placing even greater emphasis on economic development since the late 1980s. Scott Bollens has noted that there is a tension here in state-level growth management systems because the states are in the "dual role of economic promoters and environmental protectors" (1993). Not surprisingly, this has sometimes resulted in strongly worded policies that then lack funding support for full implementation. DeGrove describes planning as the "software" of a comprehensive growth management system that still depends on the "hardware" of investments in infrastructure to operate (1992, 168). This hardware has not been forthcoming in Florida. Land trusts and conservancies play a similar role in relationship to successful TDR/TDC systems: without concurrent investments, regulatory programs are unlikely to operate well. Successful growth management requires economic commitments.

MANAGING GROWTH IN THE LAKE TAHOE BASIN

The Lake Tahoe Basin offers the most relevant example of an integrated growth management strategy for the Sierra Nevada, since it is located in the Range of Light and involves many of the local, state, and federal agencies that would participate in any similar growth management system in the Gold Country. Congress and the states of California and Nevada established the Tahoe Compact and the Tahoe Regional Planning Agency in 1969 following the emergence of strong public concern about the lake's declining clarity.[39] This public concern reflected a decade of field measurements by limnologist Charles Goldman and his colleagues in the Tahoe Research Group at the University of California at Davis that demonstrated a clear pattern of decline. Their analysis relied on a complex set of measurements, but the most powerful turned out also to be the simplest: a flat plate called a Secchi disk was lowered into the water to determine the lowest depth at which it could be seen, and Lake Tahoe's remarkable clarity was discovered to have decreased twenty inches per year since 1959 (Elliott-Fisk et al. 1996; Goldman 1995). The lake's clarity was probably even greater in 1875 when C. F. McGlashan and Charles Burkhalter used a weighted bottle to first accurately measure its depth

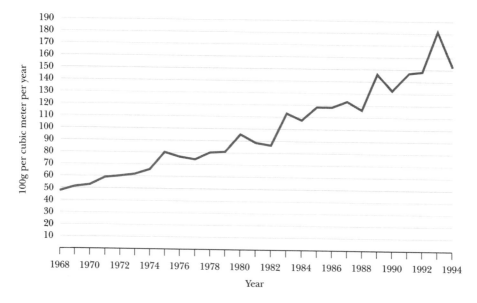

FIGURE 8.2.   Algal growth in Lake Tahoe (annual average growth per cubic meter), 1968–94.

at 1,645 feet (Scott 1957, 460). Algal growth over the past three decades has threatened to turn the largest alpine lake in North America into a mediocre body of water.

This decline in water clarity galvanized public attention and action by public agencies. The simple slogan "Keep Tahoe Blue" became emblazoned on bumper stickers as the ranks of the League to Save Lake Tahoe mushroomed, and the U.S. Forest Service consolidated its operations within the basin from three National Forests (the Tahoe, Eldorado, and Toiyabe) to form the Lake Tahoe Basin Management Unit. It also began acquiring private land: while 85 percent of the basin was private land in 1898, by 1995 more than 85 percent of it was in public ownership.[40] The private land includes twenty-nine thousand acres of developed area and forty-nine thousand subdivided but undeveloped lots. The California Tahoe Conservancy has spent $300 million over the past fifteen years to acquire development rights on the most environmentally sensitive parcels, while the Bureau of Land Management and the Forest Service traded valuable desert lands near Las Vegas for forested lands in the Lake Tahoe Basin (Sierra Nevada Ecosystem Project 1996, Vol. 1: 153).

These acquisitions, however, and the regulatory system that has compelled them, have been highly controversial (Machida 1995; Branson 1996a; 1996b; Twiss 1995). Local agencies were initially resistant to the TRPA's existence—Placer and El Dorado Counties even sued the TRPA to prevent compulsory financial contributions to support its operations. The California Supreme Court noted that counties are created by the state, however, and California had freely entered into the Tahoe Compact with Nevada and the approval of Congress. Justice Raymond Sullivan stated that "there is good reason to fear that the region's natural wealth contains the virus of its ultimate impoverishment," and that "the ecology of Lake Tahoe stands in grave danger before a mounting wave of population and development."[41] The population of the Lake Tahoe Basin had just increased tenfold in one decade from 1956 (when my parents first met in South Lake Tahoe) to 28,750 in 1966. The peak summer population increased during this same decade from 36,400 to more than 150,000. Squaw Valley hosted the Winter Olympics and the four-lane, all-weather Interstate 80 was completed across the Sierra Nevada to Truckee, only thirteen miles from Tahoe City, during that period. Lake Tahoe was now within a few hours' drive of the Bay Area. The judge noted that this "converted Lake Tahoe from a quiet summer resort to a year-round playground for water sports, skiing and entertainment."[42]

Justice Sullivan characterized the Tahoe Compact and the TRPA as "an imaginative and commendable effort to avert this imminent threat." He also described the Lake Tahoe Basin as "an area of unique and unsurpassed beauty"[43] and quoted Mark Twain's description of the lake as "a noble sheet of blue water lifted six thousand three hundred feet above the level of the sea[,] . . . with the shadows of the mountains brilliantly photographed upon its still surface[,] . . . the fairest picture the whole earth affords" (1871, 156). As noted above, this same quote appears on marketing materials for Lake Tahoe; the Chamber of Commerce knows that the lake's aesthetic and environmental qualites are economic assets.

On these values there was widespread agreement, and Lake Tahoe's international renown made it an iconographic image for protection. The goal—"Keep Tahoe Blue"—was easy enough to understand and agree on. The remedy, however—a complex system of environmental inventory and assessment, strict regulatory controls on future development, significant investments in water and sewage treatment infrastructure, continual monitoring of sediment and nutrient loadings and their effects on water quality, a TDR/TDC market in sewer connections, and public land acquisition—was more complex and imposed differential costs on different societal groups. The TRPA was "given broad powers to make and enforce a regional plan of an unusually comprehensive scope," noted the court, for the compact stated that the TRPA could "adopt all necessary ordinances, rules, regulations and policies to effectuate the adopted regional" plan.[44] These regulations and the regional plan itself preempted and superseded local land use planning and zoning by cities and counties within the TRPA area. Reflecting the primary focus on water clarity, the TRPA jurisdiction coincided with the lake's watershed boundaries (Twiss 1995). It remains one of the few formal governmental institutions in the nation with bioregional boundaries.

The TRPA board of directors was appointed to represent each of the local jurisdictions within the basin (El Dorado and Placer Counties and the city of South Lake Tahoe in California; Douglas, Washoe, and Carson Counties in Nevada) along with two members sitting ex officio and one member each appointed by the governors of California and Nevada. This structure ensured significant representation for residents within the basin, but the counties argued that it did not allow direct electoral influence on the board by those affected residents. The court rejected this challenge to the TRPA structure, however, noting the strong representation of local interests in the overall board composition.[45] The constitutionality of the TRPA governance structure is therefore solid and the agency serves as an important model.[46]

Following this initial challenge, the TRPA began the hard work of developing and then implementing a regional plan through an integrated growth management system. The initial steps relied on an exhaustive inventory and assessment of natural and social factors and the integration of those databases into a multi-attribute GIS system (Twiss 1995). In many respects, this amounted to classic McHargian analysis of the Lake Tahoe landscape (McHarg 1992). Much of this work was assisted by the U.S. Forest Service and was led by Bob Twiss at the University of California at Berkeley. This integrated GIS then allowed identification of sensitive development areas based on steep slopes, inappropriate soils, wetlands, and similar factors. This information was then used to determine where development should occur within the basin.

Threshold environmental quality targets were finally established in 1982. A regional plan, first adopted in 1984 and then revised and reissued in 1987, was created to keep development effects below those environmental thresholds (Frame 1997; Machida 1995; Twiss 1995). The new plan followed intensive negotiations following a court case that found the 1984 plan's environmental impact analysis inadequate.[47] The 1987 plan then withstood further court challenges in 1993 on takings grounds.[48] Recent proclamations of collaborative and consensus processes in the basin must be interpreted in the context of these important legal challenges that altered the power relations of the participants in the 1984–87 and 1993–97 negotiations. In short, the legal framework of trilateral relational controls gave the environmentalists a place at the table with significant bargaining power. Only after the power relationships were altered—by both the "stick" of regulation and the "carrot" of acquisition—was the table set for collaborative negotiations. Even then, it should be noted, the development community continued to challenge the TRPA in court.[49]

A monitoring program was established by the TRPA in the 1980s, but it has shown that lake water quality has responded little to the regulatory system to date. Sediment loadings are estimated to be two thousand times the natural rate; the degree of eutrophication that has occurred in the last forty years would have taken eighty thousand years to occur naturally (Machida 1995). Secchi depths have continued to decrease and the algal growth rate is increasing at a rate of 5.5 percent per year (although it slowed in drought years) (Goldman 1995).

This initial system allowed the TRPA to implement a program that prioritized development according to the basin's carrying capacity as determined by acceptable levels of water quality degradation. This was a necessary first step to understanding the regional dynamics of development and water quality. It did not allow clear resolution of parcel-specific development proposals, however, so a more detailed individual parcel evaluation system (IPES) was subsequently developed to include information of a finer grain than the regional information originally developed. The IPES approach, adopted in 1987, assigns individual development "scores" to each parcel in the basin, based on a model linking the various natural and social factors to the lake's sediment and nutrient loadings. Landowners can develop their parcels only if their scores exceed an identified target. The fact that the California Tahoe Conservancy is acquiring environmentally sensitive parcels will theoretically lower the acceptable IPES score over time.

Local realtors have complained about Conservancy purchases of lots with high IPES scores, however, and the apparent lack of the program's influence on the IPES threshold so far (Branson 1996a; 1996b). The Conservancy has responded that such acquisitions will have a beneficial effect on Lake Tahoe water quality and that many landowners with developable parcels want to sell them to the Conservancy. Doing so increases the value of adjacent parcels (ibid.). As of March 1996, the Conservancy had retired the development potential of 3,795 parcels considered too environmentally sensitive to build on. In addition, the organization had acquired 151 buildable lots and its board had approved purchases of 17 additional buildable lots. The Conservancy had contacted 897 landowners with buildable lots and 426 of those (47 percent) had expressed an interest in having the organization appraise their property for a possible sale to the Conservancy (Branson 1996b, 11A). Depending on funding available, this program could significantly increase public ownership of and access to land in the basin. At this point there are only 1,100 landowners along the seventy-one-mile shore of Lake Tahoe, where land costs ten thousand to thirteen thousand dollars per *foot* of shoreline frontage (Machida 1995).

The TRPA survived its greatest subsequent legal challenge to its authority in 1993, when its complex IPES approach and the associated regulatory system were validated by the Nevada Supreme Court.[50] There is still considerable controversy over the agency and its system, but Dennis Machida believes that "the culture of planning is changing at Lake Tahoe," away from a heated and adversarial setting to one built around consensus-oriented planning processes. "There's no single vision that's going to be right. However, there is a process taking place at Lake Tahoe that can help us arrive at a vision which can be supported by many in the Basin," he says. "After three decades of fighting in the basin[,] everyone knows at some level that their economic and environmental futures are intertwined" (1995). This is a recent development, however, and conflict continues over the parcel-specific decisions that the TRPA has to make every day.

"Some may say that Tahoe is planning nirvana," according to Bob Twiss, "but it is also the best and the worst case of command-and-control regulation" (1995). The TRPA system therefore pushes the limits of both legal and political accept-ability—which ultimately determine what is implementable in our society.

The TRPA is not the only player in the basin, however, and it is important to recognize that the agency's stick is complemented by the carrot of significant state and federal financial commitments to the basin. This is the real lesson from the Lake Tahoe experience: any successful growth management regime must be com-prehensive and must utilize incentives as well as regulatory controls. Only then can we expect to see true collaborative planning and development of a consensus about the economic necessity of environmental protection.

/.\.\.\

CHAPTER NINE

Planning and Politics

Spatial arrangements matter a great deal in human history. They reveal the social arrangements that produced them.

Richard White, 1996

Themes of power, coercion, and collective resistance shape landscape as a social microcosm.

Sharon Zukin, 1991

Planning is politics.

Manuel Castells, 1991

My grandparents' move to Penn Valley opened the door to Nevada County and exposed me to the earliest stages of the ecotransformation. The process was already under way by the time our family arrived for our first visit. Interstate 80 had been completed in 1964, creating four-lane access for commuters and tourists to the foothills and the Lake Tahoe region. The Golden Center Freeway then opened with great fanfare the day after New Year's in 1970 to connect Grass Valley and Nevada City, following much of the path of the old Nevada County Narrow Gauge Railroad. It sliced right through Nevada City but made the town much more accessible for tourists. Nevada City still had the feel of an old mining town when we moved to the area eighteen months later in the summer of 1971, with all of the overhead wires and neon lights that preceded the tourism-driven "cleanup" that soon followed. By 1973 the wires were underground, old-time gaslights had been installed, and city ordinances called for the phase-out of all neon lights. The seeds for preservation of the town's Victorian past had been sown five years earlier when the city council adopted a historic preservation ordinance on August 12, 1968, shortly after several historic structures were destroyed to make way for the new freeway (Nash 1997b). Nevada City ("the Northern Queen of the Mother Lode") was soon undergoing a facelift that would ultimately restore much of its Victorian aesthetic appeal—while simultaneously making the downtown much less useful to its residents.

FIGURE 9.1.   Downtown Nevada City, Banner Mountain, and the Little Deer Creek drainage.

My father went to work for Banner Mountain Realty at the corner of Brunswick Road and the old Nevada City Highway (only "old" by eighteen months, since it had been the main route for State Highways 49 and 20 until the Golden Center Freeway opened). "This area is going to boom," he told me, "because a lot of people are buying up lots and moving up here from the cities." Our neighborhood confirmed this view, because the kids I played with were a mix of natives born in the area and exurban migrants. Alisa and Kristi Proudfoot's father was a policeman in Los Angeles, where he continued to work while making a weekly flight to Los Angeles so that his kids could live outside the city. Brian Hogsburg and his brothers were from San Leandro in the Bay Area, where they returned the next year after the trials of long-distance commuting failed. Others were coming, though, and the local real estate industry was getting ready for them.

The second gold rush was on.[1] The gold mines had shut down only fifteen years earlier, in 1956, leaving the local economy in the doldrums. Timber mills and woods work employed many, but it was seasonal work and had high unemployment associated with it. The local unemployment rate reached the "winter average of 20 percent" in March 1970, which was low compared to the rate of 24 percent in March 1967.[2] These high levels of unemployment preceded both rapid population growth in the county and the laundry list of environmental laws that would be passed over the next decade. As a result, it is difficult to attribute more recent contractions of timber industry employment solely to modern environmental restrictions. These cycles have always been a part of rural, commodity extraction-dependent communities, and they probably always will be. One month later the *Grass Valley–Nevada City Union* noted that "the slump in the lumber market during the past year has cut 10 to 15 percent from the national forest revenues which Nevada [C]ounty shares." Even with that downturn, however, the 1970 harvest revenues on the Tahoe National Forest were forecast to exceed the 1968 revenues (*Union* 1970s). The national economy, together with the ongoing structural changes in the local economy, made Nevada County a tough place to make a living in the late 1960s and early 1970s.

Apparently there had been a mill closure in the area in the later 1960s,[3] but that simply confirms the basic point: dependence on extractive industry for local economic well-being subjected the area to cyclical upturns and downturns in the minerals and timber markets that were beyond local control. Public lands owned and managed by the state and federal governments were also experiencing increasing conflicts in use following a quarter century of postwar prosperity: recreational use among Americans had increased at twice the rate of population growth.[4] The U.S. Forest Service found demand for camping, fishing, and related recreational activities a potential source of new revenues for land and resource management. As a result, camping fees were charged on the Tahoe National Forest beginning in late May 1970 (*Union* 1970v). The revenues went straight to Washington, D.C., however, rather than into the local community, unlike timber harvest receipts—25 percent of the gross revenues from timber harvests went to fund local schools and roads (O'Toole 1988; Hirt 1994).

The emphasis of federal land and resource management policy therefore remained on timber in 1970, reflecting both the power of the timber industry and the continued reliance of most rural communities in the West on commodity extraction. The Public Land Law Review Commission even recommended in June 1970 "that timber production should 'dominate' national forest land over recreation and other uses" (*Union* 1970ac). This was consistent with the dominant view among foresters at the time. Carl Hawkes, deputy chief of the California region of the U.S. Forest Service, said, "Trees should be recognized as a crop and be farmed, using careful tree planting and harvesting practices" (*Union* 1970l). The Forest Service was, after all, part of the Department of *Agriculture* rather than the Department of the Interior (Hirt 1994; Wilkinson 1992a). This continuing emphasis on forests as merely timber-producing crops was in direct conflict with emerging social values about the environment, however, and the reforms that were later adopted in the National Forest Management Act of 1976 called for a planning process that balanced a far broader range of uses (Wilkinson 1992a; O'Toole 1988; Hirt 1994). It is a sign of how much has changed since 1970 that the public is now more concerned about the loss of old-growth forests than any potential shortage of wood products or rural communities' dependence on timber (Devall 1993).

But 1970 was still a time of new ideas, social turmoil, and the earliest stages of the environmental movement as a significant force in American politics. The *Grass Valley–Nevada City Union* actually carried the headline "Negro Is New Mayor of Newark" on page one, and it described Kenneth A. Gibson as "the first Negro mayor of a major Northeastern city" (*Union* 1970aa). Alabama Governor George Wallace had run for president of the United States only two years earlier on a thinly veiled segregationist platform, the same year that brought us the assassinations of Martin Luther King, Jr., and Bobby Kennedy (Schlesinger 1978). Contrast that climate with the August 1996 role for the African American mayor of Atlanta, Georgia—the cultural capital of the American South, in a state that still has the confederate emblem as an element of its state flag—as he opened the 1996 Olympics before a worldwide audience of billions. Nobody noticed or noted that he was black. We have come a long way since the world of 1970.

That year was also a year to remember for other reasons: the first Earth Day on April 22, the U.S. invasion of Cambodia, the near loss of Apollo 13, the killing of four unarmed protesters or bystanders by National Guardsmen at Kent State, and the first flight of the new Boeing 747. One of the last major reservoirs in the Sierra Nevada, Bullards Bar, opened on July 1 to provide recreation, flood control, and water supply in the Yuba watershed north of Nevada City (*Union* 1970ab). My father had his real estate development hopes set on Auburn Dam, which at that time was expected to soon be completed on the American River. Oroville Dam had recently been filled on the Feather River, in 1967, and the Los Angeles Department of Water and Power had just begun transferring water from the Mono Basin to its Owens Valley aqueduct, which had been doubled in capacity with a second "barrel" pointed south (Hart 1996; Walton 1992; Kahrl 1982). California's population reached 20 million in 1970—though 10 million more would augment that number over the next twenty years. It was still a time of boosterism and optimism, and few would have predicted that the swelling environmental movement would soon halt the Bureau of Reclamation's Auburn Dam project. Just a quarter century later, however, the Auburn Dam would still not be built and the environmental movement would achieve the unthinkable: a reduction in and reclamation of some of the city of Los Angeles's water rights in order to stabilize the level of Mono Lake in the name of the public trust (Hart 1996). Environmentalists would *become* part of the state's power structure during that period.

But this was not the social context in the late 1960s and early 1970s; instead, it was still a time of unfettered economic development dogma with few procedural or substantive requirements to consider the environmental consequences of growth or land use change. CEQA did not require the preparation of an environmental impact report (EIR) for nongovernmental projects until 1972, when the California Supreme Court determined in the *Friends of Mammoth* case that government agency permitting decisions required an EIR.[5] Compulsory general plans were not required until a new state planning law was adopted in 1971 (Fulton 1991). Subdividing a parcel into dozens of new parcels was a simple act until the Subdivision Map Act of 1973, which for the first time required that subdivision maps be approved by local government and that infrastructure be developed and in place before more than four lots could be sold (ibid.; 1993). "Paper" subdivisions made before 1973 could easily be created on steep slopes and across environmental features such as wetlands that would make development difficult if not impossible. Moreover, those lots could be sold quickly and without proper infrastructure investments by the developer.

It was a system designed to encourage the easy transfer of land into marketable assets rather than the conversion or retention of lands for socially desirable land uses. Exchange values dominated use values. Subsequent federal legislation, such as the Clean Water Act of 1972 and the Endangered Species Act of 1973, began to demonstrate greater social concern for environmental features that, like the wetlands, were otherwise unprotected. These state and federal legal frameworks would ultimately become the primary tools used by environmentalists to influence the design and development of land and resources throughout California and the country. They were largely nonexistent, however, from the time Nevada County adopted its first general plan in 1967 until 1972. That five-year window presented an enormous opportunity for land speculators and developers to subdivide the rural landscape of Nevada County for easy sale to future emigrants from the cities.

SUBDIVIDE AND CONQUER: "PLANNING" IN THE 1960S

Nevada County's first general plan was adopted in 1967 and theoretically could have directed the impending deluge of subdivisions and development. Instead it paints a colorful and hopeful picture of the county's future: four-lane freeways connect the population centers while productive timberlands continue to support the local economy. It was completed by the consulting firm of Williams, Cook, and Mocine under the direction of Nevada County Planning Director Bill Roberts (Nevada County Planning Department 1967), whose daughter was also a high school classmate of mine. The financial costs of realizing the plan, such as the cost of the transportation system, would be no constraint upon its vision, nor were the social and ecological costs of fulfilling this grand vision. It was simply an idealistic view of what the decision makers in the county hoped Nevada County would become by the year 1990. With no legal framework for procedural or substantive evaluation, however, there were no real challenges to the plan. The power structure of the county had a homogeneous set of beliefs about the world and the value of realizing a new county landscape that emphasized economic development. The mines had closed only a decade earlier, and seasonal unemployment of one out of every four or five workers in the county focused residents' attention on jobs. Neither retirees, tourists, nor commuters to Sacramento were evident on the planning radar screen of 1967. It was also almost impossible then to imagine the development and ultimate influence of the microcomputer, fax machine, electronic mail, or cellular phone: they were still the stuff of science fiction, not local planning.

Nor would it have made any difference to local land use patterns if the 1967 general plan *had* detailed a different vision. General plans had no legal power then, and Nevada County had no zoning ordinance in place to implement its plan. Individual landowners were basically free to propose whatever they wanted for the land outside the two incorporated cities, Grass Valley and Nevada City. As a result, the number of parcels in Nevada County ballooned from only 10,000 in 1960 to 43,000 by 1970. At first the increase was relatively gradual, with 487 new parcels created in 1964, 896 in 1965, and 604 in 1966 (*Union* 1970a). These totals primarily represented the aggregate effect of decisions by many individual landowners; there were very few large-scale developments proposed through 1966. And in keeping with the prevailing political philosophy of the area, there were no zoning designations restricting uses. Subdivision approvals were therefore relatively routine and rarely controversial. As a headline in the *Union* put it, the "planning commission rarely turns down subdivisions" (*Union* 1970c).

The scale of proposed developments changed dramatically beginning in 1967, when the first of the so-called recreation residential subdivision proposals came before the county. In that year Lake of the Pines was approved for the rolling hills around Magnolia Creek on the southern end of the county, establishing 1,800 more lots. Another 1,032 lots were created through other subdivisions that year (*Union* 1970a). Lake of the Pines was built by Boise Cascade and its predecessor, U.S. Land Company (*Union* 1970c), around three features: it boasted an artificial lake, a golf course, and half-acre or smaller lots that relied on on-site infrastructure. A similar model guided design of Boise Cascade's other large development in Nevada County, Lake Wildwood. The developers argued that the expected part-time use of these homes would result in sewage loads that could easily be accommodated by septic systems. Moreover, they claimed that the development model—where individual parcels would be sold to individuals, who would in turn build houses on their lots over a 20- to 30-year period—made up-front investment in centralized infrastructure uneconomic. These developments were therefore generally approved *without* centralized sewage treatment despite the proximity of the septic systems to recreation-contact waterways.

Another 1,312 lots were created in 1968 and an incredible 3,775 lots—more than the total for four of the five previous years combined—were created in 1969.

This latter set included part of Boise Cascade's 3,600-lot Lake Wildwood development on Deer Creek near Penn Valley, as well as the Glenshire subdivision near Truckee. Another 5,300 lots were being processed by January 1970 under tentative maps (about half in Lake Wildwood), and the preliminary subdivision review process had begun for 2,000 more lots at Glenshire and 6,000 lots at Lakeworld Development Company's Tahoe Northwoods development (later renamed Tahoe Donner) near Truckee (*Union* 1970a). The latter was ultimately approved in March 1970 for 8,320 units on 3,960 acres (*Union* 1970n). Lakeworld also established the Alta Sierra subdivision south of Grass Valley from 1967 to 1970. More than 14,000 of the 33,000 new lots created from 1960 through 1970 (42 percent) were therefore created in just four subdivisions (which were developed by just two companies): Lake Wildwood and Lake of the Pines (Boise Cascade) and Tahoe Northwoods and Alta Sierra (Lakeworld). Lakeworld's investors included San Francisco Mayor Joseph Alioto's family, and many of Alta Sierra's street names are Alioto family members' first names.[6]

By 1970 alarm bells were beginning to go off and the prevailing Gospel of Growth began to be challenged. "Does every square inch of Nevada [C]ounty have to be cut up into subdivisions?" asked Planning Commission Chair Bert Livingston (*Union* 1970b). Proposals for new land use controls—even zoning—began to circulate in public discussion. "Because the county is not zoned," noted Sharon Mahaffey of the Nevada County planning office, "there is nothing to say land can't be developed. It is unfair to tell a landowner he can't develop when there are no rules. We have to zone so we can tell them what to do" (ibid.). The subdivision process from 1967 to 1970 had already made the county's general plan completely irrelevant to what was happening on the ground: as the *Union* reported, "The designation for the Lake of the Pines area was rural agriculture; for the Cascade Shores site above Nevada City, the general plan recommended general forest" (*Union* 1970c). The rapid redesignation of Tahoe Northwoods from "forest environment" under the 1967 general plan to "urban density" only three years later also showed how toothless the 1967 plan really was (*Union* 1970n).

By this time Bill Roberts had left the county to become executive director of the Sierra Economic Development District, a four-county agency funded by the Economic Development Administration of the U.S. Department of Commerce to promote economic development in Sierra, Nevada, Placer, and El Dorado Counties. A new planning director, Stanley R. Mansfield, was hired in January 1970 to replace him. "Ironically," noted the *Union*, "he is the second new Nevada [C]ounty staffer who accepted a job here at a lower salary primarily to escape the crowded conditions of the southland. The supervisors said one of Mansfield's reasons for applying was to get away from southern California" (*Union* 1970d). Mansfield had worked with the Orange County town of Fountain Valley since its founding in 1959, then served as planning director of the town from 1966 to

1970, during which time it grew by 1,000 percent. Nevada County Supervisor William Thomas described Fountain Valley as "one of the most well planned communities in its area" (ibid.). Orange County had been best-known for its rural agriculture only two decades earlier, but it had already become suburbanized by 1970.

Mansfield would soon have his hands full with three critical planning challenges: 1) proposals to require centralized sewer systems rather than septic systems for large-scale subdivisions; 2) development of a lot-split ordinance to give the county a formal process for review of subdivisions and establishment of minimum standards; and 3) establishment of a zoning ordinance for the county. In all three cases he would find that the politics of planning can make strange bedfellows, as parties with conflicting interests cooperated to stifle significant regulation. The growth machine was alive and well in Nevada County, and exchange values would continue to have the upper hand in the local planning debate for the next two decades.

TOO LITTLE, TOO LATE: THE REGULATION OF 1970

Cascade Shores was already advertising its 296 half-acre parcels on billboards along Interstate 80 by January 1970. Unlike most development in the county, the Cascade Shores project had an on-site sewage treatment facility developed and operated by the developer. The Nevada Irrigation District found the facility inadequate in January 1970 (*Union* 1970f), however, and twenty-five years later state and county taxpayers were forced to bail out the system in order to mitigate continuing water quality problems associated with the substandard system (Lauer 1995d; 1995e). That subsequent bail-out translated into an $18,333 subsidy for each lot owner and a $30,000 subsidy for each existing home, which would otherwise not have been salable without the subsidy (ibid.).

Similar sewer systems were proposed for Lake Wildwood and Lake of the Pines. Each had at the heart of the development a large artificial body of water used for recreation, yet both had been approved with only septic systems (*Union* 1970e). "All of the engineering information we have indicates there is no reason not to allow septic tanks at this time," said Supervisor Thomas, in whose district Lake Wildwood was situated. "But the thought has been expressed that there could be a problem in the future. I want the board on record [as saying] that it recognizes there could be a problem in the future and wants a vehicle ready to put the project together" (ibid.). Others, such as District Attorney Harold Berliner, urged the supervisors to require sewers, more open space, and room for future community service buildings. The county's point of leverage was approval for relocation of two roads around Lake Wildwood, which was necessary for Boise Cascade to build the already approved subdivision. According to the *Union,* Supervisor Thomas "called the request 'blackmail' at this time because tentative and final maps for more than 1,000 lots already have been approved after planning commission hearings last year. In addition, the supervisors had made an oral commitment to relocate the road, he said" (*Union* 1970g). The supervisors deadlocked two to two on the road relocation vote when Board Chair Willie Curran disqualified himself. The *Union* noted that "the Truckee supervisor is a vendor to Boise Cascade's Incline Village development at Lake Tahoe. Voting to approve the relocation were Thomas and Robert Long. Voting against it were Ralph Buchanan and Dean Lawrence" (ibid.). Boise Cascade was converting much of its forested land from timber operations to residential development. The Fibreboard Corporation made a similar move with its development of Northstar-at-Tahoe midway between Truckee and Incline Village in Placer County. Northstar, like Tahoe Northwoods, fell outside the jurisdictional boundaries of the newly established TRPA.

By late March 1970 the Tahoe Northwoods project was caught in the middle of the sewers versus septic systems controversy. Supervisors had little legal leverage over the already approved subdivisions at Lake of the Pines, Lake Wildwood, and Alta Sierra, but Tahoe Northwoods still needed their formal approval to convert from "forest environment" to "urban density." Following heavy pressure from Truckee-area residents, the planning commission imposed thirty-six conditions on the Tahoe Northwoods subdivision. My classmate Teresa Berliner's father led the challenge from his official position as the county district attorney, as reported by the local paper: "District Attorney Harold A. Berliner called the subdivision the 'biggest land project ever in the county,' when he spoke on design. He contended that the proposed subdivision is 'over dense' and will create an 'impossible situation.' The district attorney reviewed county subdivision history and said in the past six years, 8,500 lots have been approved but that only 159 houses have been built. He charged 'speculation,' selling and buying. He described the subdivision as 'city lots at an alpine level'" (*Union* 1970m). They were "city lots at an alpine level" *without* city services, however, for the entire development was proposed to rely exclusively on household septic systems for waste disposal: "Dr. Roy Wiser of Truckee, the assistant county health officer, asked that sewage systems be installed in high density areas. He blamed septic tanks for contributing to infections of people in the Truckee area, and for a rise in the nitrate level of water. He said 'human refuse has made its way into the water supply.' One condition of approval does call for the entire subdivision to annex to the Truckee Sanitary District, and for construction of a complete sewer system in each unit" (ibid.).

These conditions helped turn the tide in the broader debate about standardizing conditions of approval in a new county subdivision ordinance. Once again, the father of a classmate of mine played a central role in the drama. But like many public servants in Nevada County in the 1970s, Lisa Hider's father would ultimately leave his post as director of public works under strong political pressure.

Others who did so included District Attorney Berliner and Planning Director Sharon Boivin (nee Mahaffey). The board didn't like it when their own staff substantiated their critics' claims. The local paper reported:

> Engineers representing developers have argued that sewers would not be needed until the lots are built up, and septic tanks could adequately handle effluent from the few homes expected in early years. They contended sewers would deteriorate if they are not used and it would be a waste to install them at the beginning. The supervisors' positions were solidified Tuesday when Public Works Director Harry Hider suddenly took a firm stand that sewers are practical at the start. Disagreeing with the view of development engineers, Hider told the supervisors that "vitrified clay pipe does not deteriorate." He added that the developer has to put up the money initially if sewers are required when a subdivision is built. If septic tanks are used, "the buyer has to put up the money for sewers later." Supervisor William Thomas said he was surprised at Hider's contention that the sewers would not deteriorate in light of contrary statements made by development engineers in the past. He wondered why this advice was not given the supervisors before to counteract the claims made by subdivision engineers. "You can get plenty of engineers to tell you that," Hider said. "But I do not happen to think it is valid. The problem is money." "That is the problem when we listen to subdividers instead of our own professional people," Supervisor Dean Lawrence said. (Bigham 1970b)

Berliner and Hider also received important support from the state and county health departments. The state's Porter-Cologne Act had become effective on January 1, 1970, establishing a new regulatory framework in California for the protection of water quality based on receiving water standards (Attwater and Markle 1988; Richardson 1992–94). In late March the State Health Department forced the board of supervisors to consider the relationship between land development and water quality by sending a letter saying that "our bureau will not recommend favorable permit action on water systems proposing to use sewage contaminated streams such as Deer Creek and Wolf Creek for domestic purposes. This decision is base[d] on the State Health Department's position that newly proposed water systems must meet all domestic water standards. The older sub-standard systems are to be upgraded as soon as practicable" (Bigham 1970a). The letter added that current discharge into those creeks by the cities of Nevada City and Grass Valley only had "limited dilution" at times, with no primary or secondary treatment of the effluent.

The state warned the county that the water in both Wolf Creek and Deer Creek was "so contaminated with sewage that they cannot be used as a source for domestic water" (*Union* 1970h). County Health Officer Peter Keenan then suggested that "it might be necessary to declare a moratorium on land development within this area, since the health department is of the opinion that there is insufficient in[-]ground water for any high density development" (ibid.). This was a direct reference to the Lake Wildwood development, which had originally proposed reliance on Deer Creek for its water supply. Nevada Irrigation District (NID) subsequently agreed to upgrade its Newtown Ditch to provide water to the development from other sources (*Union* 1970i). Keenan also noted that "a construction moratorium was imposed (by the state) on Glenbrook Basin a few years ago because of lack of sewers" (Bigham 1970a). Three weeks later the board of supervisors adopted a new ordinance compelling hookup to the new Glenbrook sewage collection system (*Union* 1970o; 1970p). The planning commission met the following week to discuss the issue, but not before approving two more subdivisions without adequate assurances of either water supply or wastewater disposal (*Union* 1970n).

Relying on wells for domestic water supply was also a problem. My classmate Kevin Sauers's father, NID's chief engineer Keith Sauers, suggested that the county should require that satisfactory wells be developed prior to the sale of lots. "We owe it to the people to speak out against development and sale of lots without an adequate water supply," said the NID manager, Frank Clendenon. "It's about time," said Planning Commission Chair Bert Livingston (ibid.).

The county sanitarian Hal Cox described the county's planning process in even more critical terms, saying that the commission met monthly and thought "how nice to chop up the county[,] and then went home" (ibid.). Earlier in that meeting, the planning commission had approved wells for two subdivisions not located in the creeks' basins. Commissioner Ted Waddell admitted to being "uneasy when we passed these two." He then recommended that the new planning director "prepare an ordinance regarding building permits" (ibid.). However, the primary goal of the members of the commission and board, with the exception of Planning Commission Chair Bert Livingston and Supervisor Dean Lawrence, was to subdivide the county as quickly and efficiently as possible. Regulations got in the way of that.

The county soon received a planning grant from the Federal Housing Administration to explore development of a regional wastewater treatment facility, but the subsequent report gathered dust instead of generating a regional solution (*Union* 1970q; Cranmer Engineering and Halatyn 1971). Sewage treatment was available only to the incorporated cities of Grass Valley and Nevada City and, on a case-by-case basis, large-scale subdivisions like Tahoe Northwoods. Many of those systems were also heavily subsidized by state and federal grants, including more than $5 million from the federally funded Economic Development Administration in 1970 alone (*Union* 1970x). Additional grants and loans under the Federal Water Pollution Control Act of 1972 (Clean Water Act) paid for most of the upgrades to the Grass Valley and Nevada City sewage treatment plants through the 1970s and 1980s.

The Tahoe Northwoods decision to require sewers established a new precedent and implicitly shifted county policy on new subdivisions, but it was still not formalized into law. Consequently, the county planning commission was confronted only seven weeks later with a conflict between its Tahoe Northwoods precedent and previous "commitments" it had made to other developers. Not surprisingly, the commissioners grandfathered the other developments and did not require sewers (*Union* 1970t).

The following Monday the board of supervisors passed an emergency ordinance in order to give the planning commission the legal leverage to require sewers during subdivision reviews "on all future lots of less than one acre." This was a simplistic approach to the problem, and it was likely to generate controversy. The *Union* noted:

> Representatives of General American Development Corporation, Lake World Properties, and Pat O'Brien urged that the commission decide sewerage requirements on a technical basis rather than by lot size. The General American representative claimed that he has no quarrel with attempts at control, but that "many many factors" influence sewage disposal. Lot size requirements "will not solve all problems," he said. He urged the commission "not to lock yourselves in a position that precludes good development." He contended that the proposed ordinance would limit planned open space developments and hoped that in its final stage it will consider "slopes, tree coverage, and soil suitability" rather than lot size alone. . . . Livingston wondered "if it would be better to go to some method where each piece of ground is examined on its own merit." . . . Apparently Chairman Bert Livingston does not anticipate placidity at the coming public hearing. His final words were: "I suggest you load your guns and come prepared for the next hearing." (*Union* 1970u)

This emergency ordinance was controversial, but it focused regulatory attention primarily on large landowners proposing large-scale subdivisions. Even the *Union* declared in its page-one headline that the "emergency ordinance on septic tanks was a necessary action" (Bigham 1970c). The ordinance did not seriously constrain existing expectations about development, although it certainly increased the infrastructure costs and decreased the profitability of some large developments that were caught "in the pipeline" while the new county policy was developed. Specific developers (and their attorneys, one of whom—Harold Wolters— was elected to a judgeship in Nevada County later that year) complained, but the policy reflected widespread public concern about the environmental effects of these large developments. The future residents of Lake of the Pines, Lake Wildwood, Alta Sierra, Cascade Shores, Deer Creek Park, Tahoe Northwoods, Glenshire, and Prosser Lakeview Estates were not yet here. They therefore had no vested interest yet in development of their properties without sewers and no political voice in the debate. That has since changed as these subdivisions have been built out and the few large corporations holding land in these developments have sold their interests to tens of thousands of landowners with individual parcels. Such a policy today would directly affect those thousands of landowners—who now externalize the environmental costs of their septic systems through water quality problems and the expenditure of emergency bail-out funds by county, state, and federal taxpayers.

Supervisor Thomas nevertheless faced significant political pressure to get Lake Wildwood from septic onto sewers, and he finally switched his position as the June primary election approached. Only thirteen days before the election, Boise Cascade agreed to build a sewer system for the new development and gave Thomas credit for the change. One of Thomas's opponents, Del Pharris, was running a campaign that painted Thomas as being in the pocket of the big developers and insensitive to local concerns about growth. "WHY was an EMERGENCY ordinance for sewers adopted only two weeks before the election," asked Pharris in a campaign ad in the *Union,* "when the recommendation had been made by the Nevada County Engineers Assoc. three years ago? WHY was this considered an emergency after approving [a] majority of over 18,000 lots in the past three years with provision for septic tanks only?" (*Union* 1970w). "WHY has the Nevada County General Plan received little consideration by Incumbent Thomas since its completion three years ago? WHY did Lake Wildwood officials agree to sewering so quickly (13 days before election) and give incumbent Thomas credit for the action?" (ibid.). Thomas was forced into a runoff with another candidate while Pharris finished fourth in the race.[7] Thomas was not required to report any campaign contributions from Boise Cascade and Lakeworld, Inc., however, because the Fair Political Practices Act was not adopted until 1974 in California. It is therefore impossible today to determine the financial relationship between Thomas and Boise Cascade. He did not recuse himself from votes involving the company, as Supervisor Curran did.

There was broad support for the sewers requirement of new large-scale subdivisions, but the residents of Nevada County came out of the woodwork against the proposed lot-split ordinance. "Lot Split Hearing to Draw Crowd: Could Set Minimum Land Rules," announced the *Union* in February 1970, noting that "a lot split ordinance—or record of survey as it is sometimes called—could impose some minimum regulations on division of land into four parcels or less. At present, the county has no regulations on this type of land division. Subdivisions, defined here as five parcels or more, are regulated with developers having to meet minimum county standards on roads, lot sizes and the like. A lot split ordinance could require minimum county road access to each lot and minimum size lots. The only regulations now covering these four-parcel splits are health department rules" (*Union* 1970k). Unlike the subdivision sewer requirements, however, these were regulatory actions that threatened to affect small landowners and "minor" actions as well as major developments. "The ordinance would encompass parcel divisions 'any one of which is less than 20 acres'" (ibid.). Subdivisions of parcels into four or fewer parcels were not subject to any regulatory review or approval at the time—regardless of how small the resulting parcels were. The paper went on to say:

> Perhaps the largest crowd ever to attend a supervisors' session packed the board room Tuesday to tell how they feel about a lot split ordinance. Most of them were 'agin [*sic*] it. . . . The audience—which totaled some 250 to 300 people—wanted to make certain the county wasn't going to enact legislation which would prevent them from dividing off parts of their acreage. Some undou[b]te[d]ly were worried because a previous board of supervisors did enact a lot split ordinance several years ago, then rescinded the action one week later after hearing a hue and cry from the citizenry. This time, the supervisors assured those in the audience that no attempt will be made to adopt such regulations without considerable study and consultation with affected local groups, such as Realtors and land owners. Mrs. [Dean] Lawrence [the supervisor who called the meeting] told the audience such an ordinance would not be intended to forbid people to sell their property. "You could sell, but maybe you would have to file a map or something." The intensity of the audience[']s opposition was indicated by the shrieks which followed that remark. Being forced to file a map, such as is required of subdivisions, is one of the regulations many oppose. Only a relatively few people spoke, but they made their point clear to the supervisors. . . . [Don Newton, a realtor]: "Employment of people in the land development business here is considerable." Supervisor Ralph Buchanan said that the meeting "was just to get a sampling of what people thought. You have told us in no uncertain terms" (ibid.).

And so a lot-split ordinance was killed again in Nevada County, this time before it was even formally proposed. Attempts were made later in the year to adopt an ordinance requiring a two-acre minimum for on-site water and septic systems, but this was effectively resisted (*Union* 1995f). It would take state-level action in the Subdivision Map Act, together with stricter minimum parcel size requirements in the Nevada County General Plan and Zoning Ordinance of 1980, before these minor subdivisions would be subject to discretionary county review. The "four-by-fouring" of the exurban landscape continued throughout the 1970s in Nevada County: 640-acre parcels were split into four 160-acre parcels, three of those 160-acre parcels would be sold by the original owner, each of those would be subdivided into four 40-acre parcels, and then three of those 40-acre parcels would be sold by each of the new owners. The process often continued down to parcels 5 acres or smaller. In this way many of the large parcels of 1960 were gradually converted to much smaller ones by the time zoning was adopted for all of Nevada County in 1980. Until then fully 40 percent of the county remained unzoned and unrestricted (Norman 1982; Boivin 1991–96). Following Rudel's model, exchange values continued to dominate use values as long as overall population density was low and most owners would benefit by retaining the widest possible options for developing their properties. Spillover effects from new development were also relatively minor, minimizing conflicts with use values among existing residents. The result was an effective political consensus for continued parcelization through the 1970s.

The parcelization of the 1960s and 1970s has, however, left a legacy that has seriously constrained planning options in the 1980s and 1990s. The county assessor's data is not available from earlier years for a time-series comparison, but 1992 data shows how fragmented the parcel base had become. Only 290 landowners owned more than 160 acres in Nevada County, and they controlled 53 percent of the private land in the county. These landowners still retained a lot of flexibility for good planning and conservation-oriented development design, although about 27 percent of that land was owned by industrial timber companies. There were 35,121 landowners with less than five acres, however, which accounted for 79 percent of the owners but only 8 percent of the land. There were a total of 57,963 parcels in Nevada County in 1992. El Dorado County showed a similar ownership pattern (Duane 1996c, 310–13). Most important, both counties had very few large parcels and thousands of small parcels in their central core development areas. This constrains planning and design options in the areas that have been most heavily affected by development.

The final planning challenge for the board of supervisors was to implement a zoning ordinance for the county. The board received considerable political support for such a step from the citizens' group that had assisted development of the 1967 general plan, which included prominent long-time local citizens and elected officials like Bob Paine.[8] "To my complete disappointment," said Paine at a town hall meeting sponsored by the American Association of University Women and the Nevada County Coordinating Committee, "it was not implemented." Paine called the current process "piece meal crazy-quilt planning" and proclaimed that the county was "a very sick patient who needs help." Finally, he charged that only "a band aid approach for the very ill patient" had been taken by the county to date (Trivelpiece 1970a).

The planning commission had asked the American Association of University Women to draft a preliminary zoning ordinance, and this draft was presented to the public for comment at the March 1970 meeting. The *Union* reported that Floyd A. Wright Jr., "who sat on the panel as a representative of the real estate interests, said, 'It is just possible that the landowners are happy with matters as they are. I suggest that someone find out.' He also said that 'zoning is the arbitrary imposition of a set of regulations on property owners regarding the use of their land.' He contended that people's wishes are rarely considered and that 'generally the people imposing the rules own none, or very little[,] of the property that will be affected by the rules.' He was critical of any proposal which could deprive a property owner of any rights" (ibid.). The specter of government control over individual landowners' decision-making authority was therefore invoked to present a political impediment to a zoning ordinance. Like the lot-split ordinance proposal,

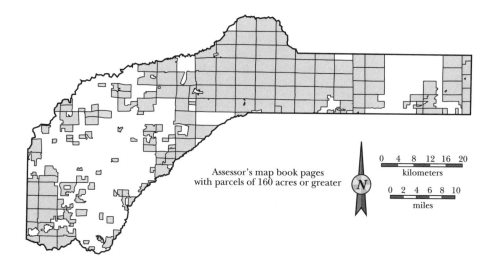

MAP 9.1.   Distribution of large parcels of 160 or more acres in Nevada County, 1992.

this was likely to generate significant opposition by current landowners who had acquired their lands with no zoning designations or restrictions. Bilateral relational controls still dominated land use planning, and this was the first step toward a rule-based system that could limit discretion by local decision makers. Ultimately, trilateral relational controls would have to be imposed by the state to protect environmental and amenity values.

Supervisor William Thomas offered the *Trust us; we would never do anything bad for the county* argument when he "asked the audience to 'Please separate what happened yesterday and what happens today.' He claimed that what took place six or seven years ago before 'some of us came to the county' could not take place today. He expressed concern for the future" (ibid.). Not surprisingly, this same argument has been made by many of Thomas's successors with the same sincerity: *That was then, this is now; nothing like that could ever happen again, so trust us!* goes the refrain. And for many members of the public—who want to protect the landscape but also hold a general suspicion of laws, lawyers, and especially planning regulations that could constrain their own choices—there is a strong desire just to trust officials who sound as if they mean well.

Mansfield, who had finally arrived in Nevada County on his first day of work as planning director, recognized the delicate line he needed to tread. "After hearing comments tonight," he said, "I had better have a presentation concerning zoning very soon." He added, "I look forward to the challenge in Nevada [C]ounty." "May God have mercy on your soul," commented Bob Paine (ibid.). Ten years and sev-

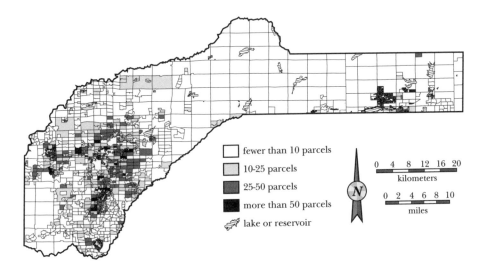

MAP 9.2.   Distribution of small parcels in Nevada County, based on parcel density, 1992.

eral planning directors later Nevada County would finally adopt a zoning ordinance that covered the entire county as part of the 1980 general plan—the first truly comprehensive plan developed in the context of new state laws that compelled substantive and procedural compliance with both CEQA and the Subdivision Map Act. Mansfield was long gone by then, and the social context had changed enough to place use values on the agenda at last.

Nevada County just wasn't ready yet in 1970 for a comprehensive, long-range, preventative approach to the problems of parcelization and development. As Harold Berliner had noted, the rush to subdivide had not yet translated into recognizable effects from new houses, new people, new cars, and new students in the schools. The conservatism of the local community and its historical ties to a rural way of life that relied primarily on commodity extraction had also engendered a community Culture that still viewed Nature primarily as a resource for exploitation. The first Earth Day presented a challenge to this viewpoint, but the local powers tried to quell it: high school faculty were "instructed that a handbook designed for last month's environmental teach-in is not to be used by students in class or purchased for the school library" because, according to Superintendent Gerald Gelatt, some of the material was "one-sided" and needed "maturity" to understand it (*Union* 1970r).

The 329 graduates of the Class of 1970 were therefore among the last from that historical Culture; their successors would graduate with a new society, new economy, and new ecological context developing right around them. Nevada

Union High School had 1,600 students when I arrived as a freshman in September 1974, and for the first time no students attending the school had been alive when the gold mines still operated in Grass Valley. The student population had grown 50 percent by the time I graduated in June 1978, to more than 2,400 students. I spent my junior and senior years in year-round school devised to accommodate the growth while the capacity of the school was expanded, but even that new capacity was exceeded by September 1978. Throughout that time the Nevada County Planning Department was developing a new general plan, but that planning effort had no effect on the lives of residents. And in my first election as an adult voter, California adopted Proposition 13 and put the brakes on local mechanisms for funding further school expansion. The fiscalization of land use would henceforth be a critical stumbling block to more rational planning through its creation of a competitive environment between cities and counties.

THE END OF INNOCENCE: THE ELECTION OF 1978

Nevada County had only two intersections with stoplights when I left home for Stanford University in September 1978. Palo Alto seemed like the big city to me, although I would later learn what a naive view of urbanity I had, coming from a small town in the Sierra Nevada. At that point it still seemed to me that western Nevada County was a coherent community of shared values and interests. This was certainly true on my first trip home to watch the Nevada Union Miners defeat our arch-rivals the Placer Hillmen of Auburn thirty-one to twenty-eight with a goal-line stand in the Sierra Foothill League's championship football game (Ray 1978). Our common opponent made the community seem united in common purpose and identity.

That facade was crumbling, however, in response to proposals to manage growth in Nevada County. A general plan update had been initiated in August 1974, but growth continued unabated as the update wore on. By 1977 even the *Union* was calling for the board of supervisors to place a series of growth-related measures on the ballot to get public input about the community's desired rate of growth. The supervisors took no action as the county continued to boom. From 1970 to 1978 the population jumped 62 percent, from twenty-six thousand to forty-two thousand (Mooers 1978).

A citizens' group had ultimately grown weary of efforts to adopt growth management ordinances through the planning commission and board of supervisors, so petitions were circulated to place Propositions A and B on the local ballot in late 1978. Except for the supervisor-specific elections of the previous decade, which rarely focused on development issues, this would be the first real test of the political will of the people. Supervisor Gene Covert had been elected in 1976 with the slogan "Give the Land a Vote," but his was a lone voice on the short end of many four-to-one board votes. He was sometimes joined by Supervisor Eric Rood on three-to-two votes, but Covert was the only supervisor to come out publicly in favor of strict controls (Carter 1978). His outspokenness on these issues threatened the power structure to such a degree that a recall effort was initiated against him just before the election. It failed to gather sufficient signatures to qualify for the ballot, but the effort managed to distract him during the campaign (*Union* 1979a).

Propositions A and B proposed to bypass the traditional power structure. Proposition A called for adoption of a new general plan and associated policies that would allow a population of no more than 50,000 by the year 1990. Proposition B called for a temporary moratorium on lot splits until the new general plan was adopted. Like most ballot-box planning and zoning measures, the two propositions represented crude tools for dealing with a complex problem. While the temporary moratorium made sense as a means of ensuring successful implementation of a new general plan, adoption of a simple population cap would not necessarily address the real problems facing local residents. These related as much to the rate, pattern, and location of growth as to the total population allowable at build-out in 1990. But like many ballot-box measures, the citizens' initiative also reflected deep frustration with the local government's inability to deal with the problem without simple and clear directives. As a result, the failure of official planning mechanisms gave rise to Propositions A and B.

The prospect of these initiatives nevertheless generated greater interest by the growth machine in expediting the languishing general plan update process. A new general plan could constitute a palatable alternative to swing voters who were concerned about growth but equally wary of strict development controls. Accordingly, the board of supervisors finally held its first public session on draft general plan alternatives one week before the November 1978 election. The new general plan promised to give much more policy direction and to protect the environmentally sensitive resources of the county. It would also allow for less population on build-out than the 1967 general plan. The *Union* helped to sell the new plan as an alternative to Propositions A and B by emphasizing how the new plan would be much stronger than the old one: "The draft Nevada County General Plan, while not a perfect plan, has 'more teeth' than the current document and is extremely important in that it will set the stage for future development of the county" (Mooers 1978). The likely effects of future development, the *Union* noted, would depend on the maximum allowable build-out or population capacity allowable under the adopted plan. The *Union* emphasized that these were maximum allowable rather than predicted population levels:

> Basically the three options offer a choice in population density determined by minimum parcels sizes of the various zoning classifications. Alternative "A," which pro-

poses the smallest minimum lot sizes, would allow a county population capacity of 197,000; Alternative "B" specifies parcel sizes which could accommodate 155,000 people; and Alternative "C" shows a population capacity of 125,000. The present plan is based on a population capacity of 240,000. These figures are capacities and not projections of what the population will be within the life of the plan. The projection of actual population used in the plan—State Department of Finance figures—is 83,400 by the year 2000, as compared to a current population of about 42,000. (ibid.)

Public hearings were scheduled by the board to begin January 25, 1979, with adoption of the new general plan not expected until the end of 1979. There had been very little public input before the formal presentation to the board, however, as staff planner Pat Norman completed a McHargian analysis of the county's "constraints and opportunities" for development. This represented a positivist "planners as value-free technocrats" model of planning practice. Norman, however, confronted two obstacles to full implementation of that approach in his admirable effort to make local environmental conditions and infrastructure availability the foundation of the new general plan: poor planning decisions from the previous decade, which had created thousands of parcels that were grandfathered and therefore exempt from most regulation under the general plan; and politically powerful landowners who exercised their power through the planning commission or the board of supervisors to limit future restrictions on use (and, in many cases, to increase allowable development for their properties under the new general plan). A third constraint, the new taxation limitations imposed by Proposition 13, meant that future development would now either have to "pay its own way" through development fees or else the level of service on existing infrastructure would decline as greater demands were placed on it. This made it almost impossible (because of the two-thirds voter approval required) to plan community-wide infrastructure initiatives to direct growth in ways that would minimize its effects. Sewers were largely controlled by the incorporated cities, while water supply was controlled by NID. Only land use and roads were within the county's control. As a result, the county's primary strategy for dealing with the growth expected under the new general plan became a predictable and continual degradation of the level of service on the transportation network (Norman 1982). The quality of existing residents' lives and use values, in other words, would continue to decline as they spent more and more of their time stuck in busy intersections or walking along increasingly dangerous roads.

Norman nevertheless did his best to reflect the landscape in his proposed land use designations for the general plan. Most designations retained a range of allowable densities, offering greater planning discretion to apply more information about site-specific constraints and opportunities through subsequent zoning decisions. This structure gave both planners and local citizens a greater opportunity for mitigating the effects of general plan build-out through zoning restrictions and the subdivision review process. Total maximum allowable build-out under the general plan that was ultimately adopted may have been between 215,000 and 240,000, but it is unlikely that the maximum ever would have been allowed in zoning decisions.[9] General plan amendments proved to be frequent, however, generally "upzoning" the land use designations for specific parcels in order to accommodate landowners' development desires. Rarely does a general plan amendment or zoning change *reduce* the developable potential.

But the details of the new general plan were not before the public in November 1978; instead, they faced a simple yes-or-no vote on Propositions A and B. The *Union* came out against the measures, arguing that they represented a simplistic approach that threatened private property rights. The growth machine successfully shifted the debate from whether the current system was adequately addressing the effects of growth to whether the proposed measures for dealing with that growth and its effects were perfect. The *Union* stated:

> While campaigns for political offices this year have generated considerable heat, they are but a candle to the bonfire of differing opinion on growth control. That rapid growth has spawned a myriad of problems, ranging from traffic congestion to crowded classrooms, is not at issue. It certainly has. Whether we in Nevada County must begin to deal more effectively with growth and its related and undesirable aspects is not at issue. We certainly must. Instead, the questions we face November 7 will be whether the ballot-listed proposals—Props. A & B—are the right solutions to current and future growth management. The answers are not clear-cut. They defy definition in terms of black and white, right and wrong, as the arguments of proponents and opponents tug at our reason and emotions. . . . Unfortunately, we are now faced with a false dilemma—a choice between two equally unfavorable alternatives—instead of a range of choices, each with differing advantages and consequences. This lamentable state of affairs, coupled with a strong reluctance to tell people where they can or can't live, prompts The Union to recommend a "no" vote on Proposition A. On the issue of Prop. B, which would halt land divisions until final adoption of the county's new General Plan, we have mixed emotions. While the logic of Prop. B is clearly a desire to ensure as many land use decisions as possible conform to the not-yet-adopted General Plan, several implications of the proposal bother us. (*Union* 1978a)

The proposals also generated considerable conflict in the press between the Nevada County Environmental Council (proponents of the measures) and Nevada County Citizens for Responsible Growth (who opposed the propositions). The controversies reached the point that Covert even filed a $1 million libel suit against the latter organization and two of its leaders on the Friday before the election. He was represented by Dick Ellers, who later teamed up with former District Attorney Harold Berliner to lead a successful environmental lawsuit against the development of Tahoe Donner by DART Industries, Inc. (successors to Lakeworld, Inc.). Ellers represented the interests of many of the recent migrants to the area, whose numbers would nearly double the county population from 1970 to 1980. He had also married Marcy Tremereaux, member of a longtime and prominent Grass Valley family, which gave him ties to the old-timer establishment despite his recent arrival in the area. Many others like him—young, smart, recent migrants to the Sierra Nevada—were the core of an emerging environmentalist minority in Nevada County that challenged the dominant local Culture's view of Nature.

Some of the ads in the *Union* opposing Propositions A and B suggested that developers would benefit from the ballot measures (thereby possibly capturing some of the pro-environment and pro-growth management sentiment cutting across the community), but the opponents relied primarily on time-honored scare tactics and a call to protect private property rights: "If . . . you value your private property rights [and] . . . you are concerned about the economic shutdown of Nevada County[,] . . . you do not want another bureaucratic layer of government. . . . You sincerely want to solve the problems of the community. . . . You want less government meddling in your life. . . . You are concerned about the high cost of goods and services. . . . Please be sure to VOTE NO on Propositions A & B" (*Union* 1978d).

The campaign was effective: Proposition A lost by a count of 11,535 to 8,036 (59 percent to 41 percent) and Proposition B lost 10,851 to 8,665 (56 percent to 44 percent). In the end it wasn't even a close contest (Fitzgerald 1978).

The winners were not sanguine, however, about the meaning of the vote. "'We did much better than we expected,' Realtor Steve DeSena, a spokesman for Responsible Growth said. . . . 'I had it [the winning margin] figured at about eight-tenths of a percent.' DeSena said however that the developers of the county shouldn't take the vote as 'pro-growth.' 'The voters that voted "no" on these two initiatives were not voting for growth,' DeSena said. 'It was a vote against bad law, and unworkable law. The problems are still there. Both the proponents and the opponents of A and B should attack these with the same enthusiasm and veracity that underscored the campaign,' he said. 'They have to'" (ibid.). DeSena recognized that there was strong public sentiment to manage growth and its effects more effectively in the rapidly changing exurban landscape.

Glen Cooley of the Environmental Council was less conciliatory, accusing the other side of distorting the language of Propositions A and B to make the voters believe that the initiatives represented what DeSena described as "bad law, and unworkable law." "I think we can be proud of the fact that we were always on the side of the truth," Cooley said. "There were so many statements made that were absolutely false, that's what defeated us." His fellow Environmental Council member Allan Johnson agreed that campaign tactics, rather than the merits of the propositions, had led to the defeat. "We had a 13–1 disadvantage as far as funds go,'" Johnson said. "I'm afraid a lot of people believed the literature that came out in the last week." Cooley also alluded to the personal cost of the hardball campaign tactics of the opposition that had led to the slander suit by Supervisor Gene Covert. "Our motives were continually questioned," he said, "but our motives were altruistic. We want to save a rural Nevada County. I think we were beaten by big money[,] and if this is what big money buys, I don't want any part of it" (ibid.).

Johnson may have actually underestimated the financial resources of his rivals: "over $88,000 had flowed into NCCRG [Nevada County Citizens for Responsible Growth] coffers as of late October" compared with slightly more than $5,000 for the pro-initiative forces of the Nevada County Growth Management Committee (Peiper 1978). This is greater than a seventeen-to-one ratio. "During its political life, NCCRG has attracted money from land sales and construction firms near and far. Donations between Sept. 24 and Oct. 23 were no exception. Of $13,523 in over-$50 contributions received by NCCRG during that period, $12,673 came from people and firms involved in land sales and building. Included in that amount is $5,000 from DART Industries of Los Angeles, developers of the controversial Tahoe-Donner Subdivision near Truckee. DART had earlier given another $5,000 to the anti-initiative cause. Excluded from the $13,523 figure is a $10,000 donation to the NCCRG war chest from a group listing itself as 'Issues Mobilization Political-Action Committee.' It, too, has a Los Angeles address. . . . The Los Angeles–based committee also gave $10,000 to Citizens for Sensible Growth, a group organized to oppose El Dorado County's Nov. 7 ballot measure limiting issuance of building permits" (ibid.). The final tally showed a fourteen-to-one advantage for the development interests that opposed the propositions, who spent $104,076 to the Nevada County Growth Management Committee's measly $7,542. The pro-growth forces supplied more than two-thirds of all money spent on all Nevada County election campaigns (including by all candidates for any office) in November 1978 ($153,790). Only $1,350 of the final $26,148 raised by the pro-growth campaign (5 percent) was from local residents (*Union* 1979b).

The pattern of campaign funding for and against Propositions A and B points to the difficulty of adopting regulatory systems that have diffuse winners but clearly identifiable losers. Everyone in Nevada County had an interest in the outcome of the vote, of course, but those in the real estate and construction industries would clearly face harder economic outlooks if the propositions had passed. Moreover, they could seek financial support from deep-pocket colleagues in other parts of the state who were concerned about the precedent-setting nature and balkanized market that could result from the adoption of many local growth management measures. Tens of thousands of dollars therefore poured into the Sierra Nevada foothill counties of Nevada and El Dorado from Los Angeles and other metropolitan areas in the state. The upstart city of Petaluma had clearly established in court that communities had a right to adopt these kinds of ordinances; the development industry recognized that it could not stop them in court. Preemptive investments in election outcomes was the industry's best insurance strategy. Proposition B was defeated in El Dorado County by a two-to-one margin (Fitzgerald 1978).

The *Union* included another story on the day of the election that was emblematic of what has happened in Nevada County since that remarkable victory over Placer's football team and all that it represented: the board of supervisors gave final approval to the county's first McDonald's the day before the election. They had voted four to one in August (Covert voted no) to rezone the land from "unclassified" to "neighborhood commercial," but imposed a condition calling for final approval of the sign. Their final approval on Monday, November 6, allowed construction to go forward (*Union* 1978b). The same day that article appeared, the artist Norman Rockwell—whose idealized images show a small town America where everyone knows everyone else through the local barber—died at the age of 84, although the *Union* did not relate these events to each other (*Union* 1978c). That day, Rockwell's America was well on its way toward the McDonaldization that has since become the homogenized and commodified landscape that fills the Glenbrook Basin.

Doc Dachtler was Gene Covert's appointee to the Nevada County Planning Commission when the McDonald's was first proposed for the Glenbrook Basin. "I made a long speech about traffic impacts, sewer impacts, about future development in the basin," Dachtler later recounted. "The six other commissioners listened politely and then voted 6–1 against me." And then, in a truly remarkable display, "the one seated next to me leaned over and whispered in my ear" that "'I agreed with everything you said, but I voted for it because I like their french fries'" (Dachtler 1990, 27).

LITIGATION AND LEVERAGE: THE GENERAL PLAN OF 1980

Losing at the ballot box did not end the quest for a new planning framework in the county. By 1978 state law provided legal leverage for the advocates of good planning, since an "inadequate" general plan could serve as the foundation for an injunction against further building permits. Moreover, approval of specific projects—or the new general plan itself—without adequate environmental impact assessment could be challenged under CEQA. Finally, the Subdivision Map Act made it much more difficult for the county to approve substandard subdivisions having inadequate infrastructure. None of these state-level requirements offered legal leverage for dealing with the problem of existing parcels, however, for they all affected only those actions taken by the county *subsequent* to their adoption into state law. The environmental community therefore focused its attention on preventing additional inappropriate parcelization.

Continuing delays in adoption of the new general plan presented new legal options despite the loss at the polls, and trilateral controls were invoked for the first time. In June 1979 the Nevada County Environmental Council filed a lawsuit challenging the county's approval of two major developments under the existing twelve-year-old general plan—one in the Glenbrook Basin and one in Truckee. The county board of supervisors had approved a proposal by the Glenbrook Basin developer Alan Brooks for a six-acre restaurant and office complex in May 1979 by rezoning his land from unclassified to neighborhood commercial. Once again, Richard Ellers represented the local environmental community (*Union* 1980a; 1980b; 1980c). He argued both that CEQA had been violated by a failure to consider the already congested traffic situation in the Glenbrook Basin, and that the conversion of Brooks's land failed to advance the goals of open space protection for the county—primarily because the open space element itself in the existing general plan was inadequate. Judge Frank Francis's "memorandum of intended decision" was released on February 22, 1980, after more than a year of delay in final action on the new general plan. Francis found in favor of the plaintiffs regarding both the Brooks development and Timberline Village in Truckee and sent the matter back to the board of supervisors (Mooers 1980).

Ellers quickly filed another suit seeking "to restrain the county and its agents from issuing permits." In the suit, Ellers asked the superior court decision in the Brooks case to apply immediately to all pending and future applications throughout the county. "The principle applies to every building permit, every zone change request, every general plan amendment, every subdivision map throughout the county," said Ellers, "so the new suit was brought merely to establish that principle for all applications." He added that "if the temporary restraining order is issued, that will stop all permits and so forth" (*Union* 1980a).

This raised the stakes dramatically and quickly got the attention of the board of supervisors, who had delayed adoption of the new general plan primarily in order to avoid establishment of more restrictive regulations on development. Judge Francis was considering Ellers's request for a temporary restraining order and had scheduled a hearing for the next week to consider a preliminary injunction when the supervisors scheduled a special meeting to adopt the new general plan (ibid.). The meeting was very clearly in direct response to Francis's decision and Ellers's suit. "The new general plan will contain an adequate open space element and open space plan," said the assistant county counsel Brad Ellsworth. "In fact, there are over 21,000-acres of open space in the plan. In the prior ruling, the judge indicated the matter was remanded to the board of supervisors until an adequate open space element was enacted together with an adequate designation of open space within the element. By adopting [the new plan] we're complying, in my opinion, with the order of the court" (*Union* 1980b).

The board agenda for the meeting called for a complex series of weighty decisions: changes to the plan itself (including repeal of the controversial grandfather clause, which had been incorporated in order to accommodate thirteen developments that had been pending but would not otherwise comply with the new plan), certification of the plan's EIR, making findings of "overriding social and economic concerns" (necessary under CEQA to approve a project with significant environmental effects), adoption of an urgency ordinance establishing an open space zoning district, and repeal of an earlier urgency ordinance that downzoned previously unclassified areas (ibid.).

The meeting was called for Wednesday, March 6, to beat the hearing before Judge Francis scheduled for Thursday, March 7. Francis nevertheless issued a temporary restraining order on Tuesday, March 5, halting all building permit or subdivisions map activities in the county (*Union* 1980c). Development did not literally shut down in the county, but the county was prohibited from issuing further building permits or approving subdivisions until the open space element of the general plan was revised. The board of supervisors then acted unanimously to do so on Wednesday, leading Francis to lift his temporary restraining order on Thursday morning. He also canceled the scheduled hearing, stating, "It looks like this matter need not be heard. I'm glad this matter has finally been resolved by the legislative body where I think these matters should be resolved" (ibid.). The outcome clearly satisfied Ellers, his partner Harold Berliner, and the members of the Nevada County Environmental Council. "We appreciate the speed with which they resolved this very serious problem—the preservation of open space in our county," said Ellers. The county counsel Brian Bishop had no public comment, but the assistant county counsel Brad Ellsworth said, "I think we have an outstanding general plan that meets all the requirements of the law—it's in the public interest" (ibid.). Everybody declared victory and the long wait for a new general plan—thirteen years after the first one was adopted in March 1967—was finally over.

The *Union* described the board of supervisors' meeting as "sometimes tense" before the board members reached final agreement on all points. In the end, though, they voted unanimously for the new general plan. The paper reported, "While most board members admitted they are not totally pleased with all items in the new general plan, Chairman Gene Covert said, 'We have learned a great deal through the process and we have reached many compromises'" (ibid.). Trilateral controls had changed the power balance in the county, and the threat of litigation—which was only possible because of changes in state law—altered the terms of the final compromises they made.

The board nevertheless acted primarily to meet the *procedural* requirements of the law rather than the plaintiffs' *substantive* concerns about the adequacy of

Nevada County's system for planning and managing growth. The 21,000 acres designated as open space represented only 3 percent of the county's 978-square-mile (626,000-acre) area. In the case of Brooks's Glenbrook Basin property, which was part of a larger, controversial, 23-acre neighborhood-commercial designation in an earlier version of the plan, the supervisors reversed their earlier decision only to recommend that the item be brought before the board again the next Monday as a general plan amendment—before the ink had even dried on the new general plan (ibid.). California law allows up to four general plan amendments per year, and many jurisdictions approve four per year—often in consolidated amendments that affect dozens of parcels. The board of supervisors encouraged another dozen property owners to seek similar amendments whose development proposals had been submitted consistent with the old general plan but would no longer be consistent with the new one (ibid.). Despite this encouragement, however, Brooks filed suit the next day to attempt to nullify the new general plan (Mooers 1980). He understood well that litigation had been the prime motivator of action by the board.

The new general plan withstood Brooks's legal challenge. The residents, developers, plants, and animals of Nevada County therefore had a new "road map" to guide development in the county over the next twenty years (although the twenty-year population target would be realized in merely half that time). Attention now turned to development of new general plans for the cities of Grass Valley and Nevada City, which held control over the key elements of infrastructure that could so strongly influence future development patterns.

INADEQUATE INFRASTRUCTURE: GRASS VALLEY'S GENERAL PLAN OF 1982

The cities of Grass Valley and Nevada City ultimately adopted new general plans emphasizing objectives and policies that reflected their respective circumstances and personalities. Grass Valley went first in 1982, with a boosterist plan developed by the consulting firm of WPM Planning Team of Sausalito under the direction of Bill Roberts, who had taken over as planning director for the city after his stint at the Sierra Economic Development District (Grass Valley Planning Department 1982). Nevada City adopted a much more cautious general plan in 1985 that reflected the strong community sentiment to retain the special character of both the town and its surrounding landscape (Nevada City 1985). The latter approach, while invoking design guidelines and regulatory mechanisms usually associated with liberal values, was, ironically, the most conservative, in that it conserved the town's heritage and maintained the status quo. Grass Valley's general plan, in contrast, relied on a conservative political philosophy in terms of government oversight and regulation—which could lead to a much less conservative outcome in terms of changes to the townscape and landscape.

I was hired as assistant city planner by the city of Grass Valley for the summer of 1982 to assess the implications of the new general plan for future infrastructure needs—something that my planning professors told me should have been done much earlier in conjunction with development of the land use plan. How could they have already adopted a plan, I wondered, without first understanding the effects of future growth on infrastructure capacity? That relationship is a critical determinant of both the economic feasibility of the plan and the environmental consequences of development under the plan. It seemed impossible to comply with CEQA—which requires both identification and mitigation of significant environmental effects—without that information. Yet the city already had a new general plan and a certified EIR when I started work in June 1982 to investigate these relationships.

Remember, though, that "it is an adage of California planning law that your General Plan is in compliance unless and until somebody successfully sues you over it." This philosophy certainly held true in Grass Valley, where Bill Roberts kept a low profile and left the tough political choices to the elected city council. His job would be threatened if he did not do what the elected officials wanted. An assistant fire chief was complaining a bit loudly about the city employees' pay package as I first arrived, and there was even talk of unionizing the employees. He soon found his position eliminated from the next year's budget and himself out of a job. The city council cited budgetary savings as the rationale and then promptly budgeted more than his annual salary to hire a replacement via contract. This tactic sent a very clear message to all city staff: do not rock the boat, or you will be fired.

The town's citizens, for the most part, went along with it. Planning issues rarely generated much interest, and the city council became accustomed to making its deals without much fear of intense public scrutiny. Grass Valley was a working-class town, and its citizens inherited a legacy of vertical social networks dating from its hardrock gold mining days as a virtual company town. The county's political elite and the noisy newcomers generally lived in Nevada City or somewhere in the county's jurisdiction. Those other people and places were also much more concerned with rapid growth and its effects on quality of life, while Grass Valley was trying to hang on to its economic vitality in the face of new commercial and residential development outside its control. The town was withering on the vine financially while Proposition 13 took its steady toll against the inflationary pressures of operating business in a city with infrastructure dating back to the 1850s. Nevada City had new businesses and increased tax assessments because of its booming tourist traffic, while Nevada County could count on new construction to increase tax assessments. Nevada County also controlled the booming commercial "sacrifice zone" of Glenbrook Basin, situated strategically between Grass Valley and Nevada City. It was known locally by the derisive labels "junk food junction" and "garbage gulch," but it was nevertheless where most local residents now did their shopping. And sales tax revenues were the key to fiscal health with property taxes constrained by Proposition 13.

That is one of the reasons Grass Valley's general plan of 1982 sounded eerily familiar: like the Nevada County General Plan of 1967, it focused on fostering greater economic growth rather than growth management. It also called for major transportation improvements that threatened to alter the character of some neighborhoods through increased traffic. The Squirrel Creek Homeowners Association recognized this, and its members began to rattle their sabers with threats of a lawsuit. The residents of that neighborhood probably understood the implications of the new general plan better than the city council did, but with the exception of that one neighborhood group, no organized opposition developed against the plan. Perhaps everyone simply viewed it as another rosy vision for the future, where all of the traffic would flow freely and somebody else would fix the infrastructure.

There should have been considerably more concern. My summer research determined that the growth projections in the plan would require a new wastewater treatment plant by around the year 1990, which was only eight years away. The Reagan Revolution had, however, brought an end to the free-flowing money of the 1970s that had funded most of the local sewage treatment capacity through a combination of state and federal grants. The new funding regime called for local communities to pay the cost through some combination of general taxation, development impact fees, and user charges. Paying for a new treatment plant under those terms could have a direct financial effect on existing city residents and taxpayers that they might prefer to avoid. Similar investments could be necessary for fire, police, parks, and storm drainage services.

The pro-growth city council feared these costs would discourage growth, however, so the council established an advisory committee of local developers to determine what was politically acceptable to their interests. The nation's economy was in the midst of recession in 1982, and the city council was not about to adopt impact fees that would be blamed for keeping the city's economy in the doldrums. Besides, those fees would alleviate problems that everyone acknowledged would not become acute for many more years—the impending crises would occur well beyond even the next election cycle: eight more years represented two full city council terms. It was doubtful any of the decision makers of 1982 would still be around to face the music by the time 1990 rolled around.

And so they punted. My summer reports gathered dust in the city's archives while new subdivisions were approved for connection to the city's wastewater treatment plant. One of those projects was actually outside the Wolf Creek drainage, requiring even greater costs for pumping effluent to the treatment plant. Several years later the city council approved a massive redevelopment project on the south periphery of town in hopes of capturing some of the sales and property tax benefits that were continually going into the county's coffers. That action gave the go-ahead for the leveling and clear-cutting of a magnificent ridge leading into town in order to build the "Pine Creek Shopping Center." Following a long tradition in American real estate development, it was of course named after the natural features destroyed by its creation. Many locals call it the "Pineless, Creekless, Shopping Center."

Ironically, the "redevelopment" project helped seal the decline of Grass Valley's historical downtown. Downtown's biggest retail establishment, J. C. Penney, subsequently closed its doors and moved out to the new shopping center (Nash 1997a). The city therefore captured some of the "new" development potential for tax purposes while simultaneously undermining its own efforts to restore vitality to its main street. This action generated a lawsuit charging noncompliance with CEQA, but the challengers ran out of money and had to drop their suit (Roberts 1997; Johnson 1997). Subsequent controversies over the firing of the Grass Valley police chief led to a recall election, however, where the voters removed four of the five council members by a four-to-one margin in November 1988 (Eberle 1988a). Once they had been removed from office, the district attorney dropped grand jury charges that had been pending against the four for inappropriate use of public funds and violations of the state's open meeting law, the Brown Act (Eberle 1988b; 1988c). The fifth council member had voted against the firing and was not recalled. The other four managed to spend $103,152 of city funds defending themselves from the accusations in the weeks leading up to the election (Eberle 1988b).

And so a different city council held office when the Regional Water Quality Control Board (a state agency) finally issued an order in 1989 for the city of Grass Valley to cease and desist its continuing discharge of effluent into Wolf Creek in violation of its permit.[10] This order came after the wastewater treatment plant had violated standards for biochemical oxygen demand and suspended solids for two consecutive three-month periods, placing the treatment plant on the Environmental Protection Agency's priority list. The state and federal government orders then forced the city to constrain its sewer hookups while renovation of the system was completed in order to avoid further problems, which were especially acute during storms. The storm-related problems reflected the fact that the city's collection system was riddled with holes as a result of age or the geologic structure of the city. According to one engineer, the ground under Grass Valley "is like a big piece of Swiss Cheese." The problem is exacerbated by upstream development in the Wolf Creek watershed, however, most of which is outside the city limits. Increases in impervious surface and reductions in vegetative cover generally increase the peak storm water flows, overwhelming the city's storm water collection system. The excess then makes its way into the aging sewer system to over-whelm the treatment plant.

"We didn't want to call it a moratorium," says city engineer Rudy Golnik, so the city instead instituted a "connection restriction program" (1995). A special "hookup" committee approved hookups for a senior center and a low-income housing project during the moratorium ("connection restriction program"), but individual home owners generally had to wait for the order to be lifted before get-ting a building permit that would require a new sewer hookup. Another cease-and-desist order was nevertheless issued by the Regional Water Quality Control Board in 1992.[11] The required improvements to the wastewater treatment plant were finally completed in 1995, and the moratorium was lifted (Shigley 1995a).

This saga illustrates the perils of poor planning and inadequate attention to the costs of growth. The treatment plant and sewer system improvements have cost $10.1 million since I completed my analysis in 1982, but the city's general plan has not been updated since then to reflect the treatment plant problems. Those costs have been covered primarily through increased rates over the past few years and the sale of "Bond Anticipation Notes" that were subsequently repaid through a Federal Housing Administration loan (Golnik 1995). At this point the system is again accepting hookups, so no resident of 1982 (when the general plan was adopted) is being denied the right to develop because of new development allowed by the plan (EIP Associates 1996). The existing wastewater treatment plant, however, does not have the capacity to handle full development of existing parcels within the city limits in accordance with the general plan's land use desig-nations. Consequently, the city has proposed a significant expansion of the treat-ment plant's capacity to accommodate an additional 5,500 connections at a cost of another $10 million (EIP Associates 1995; Shigley 1995b). This would permit a more than doubling of Grass Valley's population over the next twenty years at a pace of 275 new connections per year—versus an average of only 150–200 in recent years (Johnson 1997). Taxpayers could therefore end up subsidizing new development in the short-term if rates and hookups are insufficient to cover the cost of the treatment plant expansion.

This expansion will also be a critical determinant of settlement patterns in western Nevada County and could be used to mitigate the effects of population growth that would otherwise take place throughout the county. Despite this oppor-tunity, however, there has been absolutely no coordination between the city's plan-ning and decision-making processes regarding the treatment plant and the county's land use planning. The city's own general plan is more than fifteen years old, and the treatment plant expansion calls for a major reconsideration of the city's future expansion. Yet only four people submitted public comments on the draft EIR for the treatment plant in 1995, and only three people testified on the final EIR before the city council (EIP Associates 1996). And even though participation was minimal, the mayor at the time, DeVere Mautino, was persistent in cutting off public comment on the matter and was clearly irritated that the council had to listen to anyone criticize the project or question its need.[12] The spirit of open inquiry into the city's future is therefore still missing, although I am hopeful that the current mayor, my high school classmate Mark Johnson, can change that. He must convince the city council to overcome its long-standing resistance to opening up the planning process to the public. So far, though, the risks of "looking under the rock" to see what is there have simply been too great.[13]

And failure to look is legally adequate as long as nobody bothers to take the city to court over it.[14]

THE POLITICS OF CITIZEN PLANNING: 1990–95

The 1980 Nevada County General Plan estimated that it would take two decades to reach a population of 83,000 in accordance with the state Department of Finance's projections for the year 2000. What it didn't count on was having the county reach that population in only one decade. And once that population was reached, the likelihood of a successful suit challenging the adequacy of the existing general plan increased with each and every day. The board of supervisors therefore authorized another update of the general plan in February 1990 (Lauer 1995b; *Union* 1995a). Little did the board know that this new update would take as long as the last one and cost nearly $2 million in the process. It would also cost some of them their jobs, because land use planning would again become the focus of politics at the polls. Not a single Nevada County supervisor was reelected during the nearly six years that the general plan update was under development.

This time, however, the board took a different approach by establishing a citizen steering committee composed of the representatives of major interest groups. It was an approach that explicitly recognized for the first time that the politics of interest was an important element of the local planning process. At the same time, it sought to resolve the inherent conflicts of interest through a forum emphasizing the politics of community. Unlike most appointed advisory groups, the board invited specific groups to name their own representatives to the steering committee. This reduced the board's ability to control the composition of the steering committee. It was a bold move toward citizen participation, and the Nevada County Board of Supervisors was justly awarded recognition by the American Planning Association for its approach.

Seventeen members were appointed to the steering committee to represent the real estate and construction industries, natural resource (commodity extraction) industries, neighborhood groups, environmental groups, local business interests (both small and large), and local agencies, such as NID. Geographic diversity ensured that land use issues in specific parts of the county could be addressed by somebody knowledgeable about that area. The committee was established in August 1990, and nearly five hundred other citizens then volunteered to work on special subcommittees examining specific topics. These subcommittees worked throughout the next year to develop preliminary reports on everything from well water supplies to habitat fragmentation and open space management. It was the steering committee's job to digest those subcommittee reports and develop a vision to guide the planning department staff and its consultants. The county had entered into a contract with Harland Bartholemew and Associates of Sacramento to develop the new general plan. This company was originally established around 1920 in Philadelphia, and it had a long-standing reputation for its general-plan work, but it had little experience in California.

Katie Burdick was named project manager by Harland Bartholemew and Associates, and she expertly facilitated the steering committee's deliberations. Most important, she had a talent for focusing their attention on areas of agreement rather than disagreement.[15] The steering committee chair, Alan Halley, had a similar talent, and he combined his experience as a Nevada County native with the sharp thinking that got him through Harvard Law School and his skills of persuasion honed while a successful appellate attorney. The steering committee and its subcommittees represented a fine example of the politics of community that first year, as everyone approached the task in a spirit of cooperation. The inherent tension between exchange values and use values had not yet become evident.

There were no difficult choices to be made at that time, however, and the citizens involved in the process could emphasize their common vision for maintaining rural character and the quality of life that made Nevada County special (Burdick 1997). Rural quality may have meant different things to different people, but they all agreed that they wanted to retain it—whatever it might be. The computer consultant Peter Van Zant described rural quality as "a community rural in look, and characterized by small towns and a lifestyle consistent with a natural setting" (Lauer 1995c). Karen Knecht, who represented the Nevada County Contractor's Association, believed that could be achieved on one-acre parcels. Steve Beckwitt, however, lived on forty acres on the San Juan Ridge situated among much larger parcels and a lot of public land. He believed a forty-acre minimum was necessary to maintain rurality. Steve also ran the Sierran Biodiversity Institute with his son Eric and believed much larger parcels were necessary to protect biodiversity and ecological function in the area. This led him, armed with his own sophisticated GIS capabilities, to be particularly concerned with the spatial pattern of development and its effects on Nature. Karen Knecht focused much more on a Culture of rurality that her neighbors at Lake of the Pines valued. Their homes were largely in a suburban pattern within that gated community, but its placement within the broader community gave them a sense of a rural rather than metropolitan living.[16]

I first attended a steering committee meeting in August 1991, after most of the subcommittee reports had been completed and preliminary general plan ideas were being considered. Unfortunately, Katie Burdick had just left Harland Bartholemew and Associates to work with the Alliance for the Wild Rockies in Missoula, Montana.[17] I spoke with her by phone about her experience and she told me she was very concerned that the steering committee was being held together by the most tenuous of threads. It would take great leadership to continue to forge a sense of common purpose among the members, who shared a love for the place but many deep philosophical differences. Unfortunately, Alan Halley had also resigned his position as chair in 1991 because of family and professional commitments, creating a leadership vacuum. Halley too expressed frustration with some of the steering committee members, who he believed were firmly set in their views and unwilling to listen to others' views or to compromise (Halley 1992). Karen Knecht was selected to chair the steering committee after Halley resigned.

It was a disastrous choice. Knecht clearly approached her role on the steering committee from an interest-based model of politics, and she focused on the potential effect of any prospective regulation on her prime constituency, the construction industry. Perhaps more important, however, Knecht emphasized the *differences* between the steering committee members rather than the *commonality* among them. As chair she had a great deal of authority to direct both the agenda and the discussion. She also had the prerogative to frame the debate in terms that might lead to compromises rather than conflict. She rarely did this. I was struck instead by many discussions among steering committee members that suggested 90 percent agreement on a point—only to have Knecht call for a vote between two competing approaches that differed only over the remaining 10 percent. Separating the issues into areas of agreement and disagreement would have resulted in many more near-unanimous votes on the 90 percent of the issues where there was widespread agreement. Instead, steering committee votes quickly degenerated into split decisions because of deep disagreement about some aspect of the issue that was attached to the areas of agreement in the motion.

This approach polarized the steering committee and led to its near-breakdown. In essence, there were always three votes that would oppose almost anything that could dictate in any way what landowners could do with their property. These three votes were out of synch with the dominant values of the community, however, and a fourteen-to-three outcome on most votes would have sent a clear message to the board of supervisors when a draft general plan was to be forwarded to them from the steering committee. But Knecht's approach to the issues led to many votes that were instead split ten to seven or nine to eight, eliminating any sense of consensus or clear direction from the steering committee. At one point there was a rancorous debate on one of these votes, and a motion was made to separate the issues. Knecht did not agree with this approach, however, and she felt slighted by the way the motion was presented. She literally crossed her arms, turned away from the group toward the side, and said she would simply not allow a vote on that motion. The steering committee vice-chair, the Grass Valley businesswoman Fran Grattan, then took over the meeting as Karen Knecht sulked. Grattan had served on the planning commission since 1987 and was much more effective at both running a meeting and finding common ground. The tone had been set, though, by Knecht's behavior.

Knecht's approach struck me as highly bizarre, and I was deeply disappointed at the end of that meeting. Why had it fallen apart so completely when these people had so much in common and there was such an opportunity to focus on common ground? A likely answer came to me as I walked out the door and overheard a consultant to one of the county's largest developers talking to one of the steering committee members who represented environmental and neighborhood interests. "Well," the development consultant said, "I guess if the steering committee is going to be split on everything it will just be up to the board of supervisors to make all of these decisions."[18] Now it was clear to me why the process had emphasized disagreement rather than agreement: a split steering committee allowed the board to act on the update without the political constraints that would be imposed by steering committee consensus. The developers knew that they couldn't control the steering committee, whose shared vision would emphasize use values, and that their best bet for maximizing exchange values and development discretion was with the board. Accordingly, they ensured that the steering committee was highly polarized.

I do not know if it was deliberate on Knecht's part, and I do not want to ascribe malicious motives to her. It is clear to me that some parties had an obvious interest in seeing the steering committee break up. There was a conflict between the implicitly delegated power of the steering committee and the official power of the board, and this tension was made explicit by Planning Director Tom Parilo when the steering committee asked him to complete further analysis of an innovative policy option. "You don't understand," he said while telling them that he couldn't direct his staff to analyze that topic. "I don't work for *you*—I work for the Board of Supervisors." He explained that unless *the board* wanted him to do something, he couldn't spend time or money on it—even if the steering committee requested it.[19] Several members of the steering committee were deeply troubled by this statement, for they—like me—held a naive notion of democracy in their heads. Didn't the board of supervisors work for *them*, not the other way around? Wasn't this process about citizen empowerment in planning? The realpolitik of local land use planning meant that the board called all of the shots.

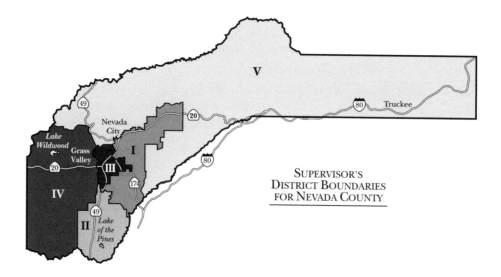

MAP 9.3.   Supervisor's district boundaries for Nevada County.

The steering committee nevertheless indicated its preference for a new general plan with a build-out population of only 146,000 when it submitted its report in July 1992. Public sentiment at hearings in September seemed to support that cap. The board then voted in October 1992 to use the 1980 zoning as the basis for the new general plan, but it also added a new-town proposal for an 8,232-acre area west of Penn Valley. The site was composed of twenty-four contiguous parcels and was owned by a combination of large local landowners and out-of-county investors. It was their representative who had made the remarks about the inevitable outcome of a split steering committee. Dozens of other individual landowners had also submitted specific requests for "general plan designations" that would be considered later by the board.

Karen Knecht quickly turned her steering committee experience into a successful political campaign. She was elected to the board of supervisors the following month when she defeated incumbent Jim Callaghan by a vote of 4,716 to 4,363 in conservative District II.[20] Environmentalist incumbent G. B. Tucker, who held Gene Covert's old District V seat, was also defeated, while Nevada City Council Member Dave Tobiassen won Todd Juvinall's former District I seat despite garnering only 44 percent of the vote. Former Supervisor Isle Barnhart and City Council Member Paul Matson split the remaining vote, giving Tobiassen the victory. The pro-growth forces now had solid control of the board.

The new board then voted in February 1993 to dissolve the steering committee and all of its subcommittees. The task of preparing the draft general plan was given to Harland Bartholemew and Associates and the planning department. It was released several months later, and I had my graduate students analyze early drafts of the general plan in my environmental planning studio during spring 1993. In May, after the students completed individual papers analyzing specific portions of the general plan, I met with county planners Sharon Boivin and Pat Norman to give them copies of the reports and an offer to assist them on the general plan. I was told by Boivin and Norman that the board of supervisors wasn't interested in our input.[21] Even the staff was largely being kept out of the process, while the consultants continued to function as the perfect target for any criticism of the plan (Boivin and Norman 1993). The planning commission held public hearings from June through September.

By that time the writing was on the wall. Several members of the disbanded steering committee gathered in the spring of 1993 to form a new group, the Rural Quality Coalition (RQC), to focus local attention on their concern that the board would hand Nevada County a suburban future rather than a rural one. They believed that the board's actions directly conflicted with the preferences of the steering committee and community. Several RQC members contacted me in late 1993 and asked me to give a presentation to the RQC and the local community.[22] They arranged radio interviews with me on local stations KNCO (AM) and KVMR (FM), as well as a public presentation in late 1993. I found myself stepping into the political crossfire, however, when a reporter for the *Union* called me and said he heard I was upset about the draft general plan. I was surprised by his tone, which emphasized the potential conflict in the issue. "I'm not upset," I said, "but I think it has some problems." I then proceeded to explain how I thought the draft general plan could be improved and that my students' reports proposed specific steps that would cost very little to implement. He wasn't interested in policy prescriptions, however, for he thought the real story lay in the fireworks of conflict. "Planning Professor Attacks General Plan" was the headline the next day. The opening line of the article said, "Tim Duane is coming home, and he's angry" (Taylor 1993). Everyone's focus was on the simmering political conflict in the community.

In December 1993 the board adopted by unanimous vote a draft general plan allowing a build-out population of 176,000 (Lauer 1995b; *Union* 1995a). That estimate ignored existing parcelization that would have resulted in a much higher build-out population (Duane 1996a). The planning department and Harland Bartholemew and Associates had failed to analyze that issue, so the charade of a general plan that lowered the apparent development potential in the county was maintained. This represented a significant omission in direction given by the board to Parilo and the consultants. The 1980 general plan allowed for a build-out population of between 215,000 and 240,000.[23] The apparent reduction to 176,000 people represented a 27 percent reduction in total population at build-out, but this figure was still 30,000 people above the steering committee's recommendation—and fully twice what the county's population was in 1990. The 176,000-person build-out target was expected to be reached in twenty to forty years and would radically transform the region. Not surprisingly, it included development of the new town proposed by Gold Country Ranch west of Penn Valley. It did not include any TDR/TDC mechanism to use the development of the new town as a means of solving problems with substandard lots in other parts of the county. Steering committee member Steve Beckwitt, who was proficient in sophisticated GIS analysis, also showed that the site lay in the heart of the largest block of contiguous oak woodland in the county.[24] Moreover, the new town threatened to increase traffic congestion and radically alter the character of the landscape near Penn Valley and Lake Wildwood.

Several speakers at the December 1993 hearings made it clear that the board would soon face the wrath of the voters at the ballot box. Exchange values dominated the board of supervisors while use values had no direct influence in the decision-making process. The RQC realized then that political action was necessary.

A POLITICAL AWAKENING: 1994 – 95

The year 1994 began with new political energy in Nevada County.[25] The board had finally indicated its preferences through its adoption of the draft plan, and many of the disenfranchised members of the now-defunct steering committee felt as if most of their work had been discarded. Their attention therefore turned to the upcoming supervisorial elections for District III (which included most of Grass Valley and parts of Alta Sierra), District IV (which included the proposed new town site, Lake Wildwood, and Penn Valley), and District V (which included Truckee, the San Juan Ridge, and areas near Nevada City). District IV incumbent Bill Schultz faced challenger Rene Antonson, who campaigned against the new town and handily won with nearly two-thirds of the votes (3,690 to 1,933) in the June primary. District V incumbent Bob Drake of Truckee, who had been appointed to the position by Governor Wilson, faced Sam Dardick from the San Juan Ridge. Dardick was the only registered Democrat in the supervisorial races and was well-known to the liberal community on the ridge and in Nevada City. RQC members were also active in his campaign. He garnered 56 percent of the vote and defeated Drake by a margin of 2,782 to 2,184 in the June election, even carrying the votes of newly incorporated Truckee.

All eyes now turned to the District III election, where incumbent Jim Weir faced his own former planning commission appointee, Fran Grattan, in a November runoff. The election of Antonson and Dardick meant that the District III race would decide which side would hold a three-to-two majority on the board of supervisors. Weir had been uneven in his planning positions, but he had also once been a registered member of the Green Party. As a result, he had some environmental credentials that Grattan could not claim. The RQC membership reluctantly threw its support behind him despite his unreliability on environmental issues. Grattan was the clear favorite of the development community, which poured money into her campaign coffers. The future of the general plan and development in the county was at stake.

Only the voters of District III would be voting, of course, but the entire county took a keen interest in the race. Both candidates recognized the importance of planning and land use issues to the voters. "*Responsible, balanced* growth," said Fran Grattan's campaign signs, which promised to "Save jobs *and* taxes." Her opening statement at the big candidates' debate emphasized her "outsider" status against a two-term incumbent. "I am a business owner and a homeowner, not a politician," she said. "This is my first run for public office." She also tapped into concerns about the rapidly changing landscape. "Nevada County is not what it once was . . . we must protect our rural quality of life and historic qualities. . . . Let's face it: people are going to continue to move to Nevada County[, and] . . . our roads are a disgrace. Let's fix our roads." Finally, the apparent culprit emerged: "We are burdened by excessive regulation, a lack of affordable housing." She also indicated that the draft general plan was a good document.[26]

Differences between Grattan and Weir emerged when forest management came up for discussion. "I favor conserving our natural environment to the extent we can," said Grattan, but she added, "I do not favor extremists" who "are detrimental to the citizens of our county." Weir then indicated that federal plans should increase logging slightly. "I am a woodworker; I do woodworking for relaxation," he said. "To say I'm not going to support . . . logging just isn't true. I've cut too many trees . . . I've burned too much wood for that to be true." Grattan nevertheless called Weir an "extremist" by association. "Mr. Weir is very much in line with the extremist groups," she said, then he asked her "to name some specific groups." "The Sierra Club," she responded. "Of course I have friends in the Sierra Club," said Weir, "and I have friends in the Business Association[,] . . . but to say I support the Sierra Club hook, line and sinker is not true."[27]

This characterization of the Sierra Club as an extremist group nevertheless highlighted fundamental differences between the candidates. Grattan was a classic small-town business-owning Republican, and she carried herself professionally. Weir was an unpredictable liberal who had already served eight years on the board. That was probably enough to make a difference in the election of November 1994, when Republicans regained control of Congress for the first time in forty years. Grattan also managed to paint herself as a reasonable moderate who was just as concerned about "rural quality" as the electorate. She beat Weir by just 49 votes out of 5,939 cast (while 477 voters abstained and 33 wrote in candidates).[28] The developers had retained a slim three-to-two majority on both the planning commission and the board of supervisors despite Dardick and Antonson's election. Antonson also proved to be philosophically aligned with his fellow Republicans when it finally came down to board votes on the general plan, leaving Dardick in Weir's old position of being on the short end of four-to-one votes. This led Dardick to pursue a strategy of compromise to minimize damage.

Many of the compromises had first been reached by the so-called resolution committee established by the board of supervisors during the two months before the 1994 election to try to reach agreement on some of the issues that still polarized the community. Forming the committee had been an excellent idea, but it suffered from both a lack of time and inadequate technical knowledge on the part of the facilitators. It also represented a political attempt to lower the build-out estimate for the new general plan to a level that would improve both sides' chances in the November elections. The new politically acceptable number, which had emerged in public testimony during the previous summer, was 140,000 people. Accordingly, the resolution committee members struggled to reach agreement before the election on a general plan that would yield that number at build-out. They did so by removing the new town development (a clear political necessity, given Antonson's strong opposition to it in his June 1994 campaign) and reducing allowable densities in a number of areas. But like the earlier estimate of 176,000 people, the new 140,000 estimate failed to account for existing parcelization and the built-in momentum of the subdivisions of 1967–80. It ultimately represented a symbolic rather than a substantive reduction.

The resolution committee was composed of two supervisors (Knecht and Dardick, who had taken office immediately after his election in June), two representatives from the business and development communities (Dale Creighton of Sylvester Engineering and Ken Myers of the Grass Valley Group), and two representatives from the RQC (Laurie Oberholtzer, a planning consultant and city council member in Nevada City who had served on the steering committee) and the Federation of Neighborhood Associations (Peter Van Zant, who had helped to found the RQC and had also served on the steering committee). Creighton was a planner who represented the interests of Ed Sylvester, who was seen by many in the RQC as the most powerful political broker in Nevada County. Sylvester served as chair of the Nevada County Transportation Commission, helped found the Nevada County Business Association (whose executive director, Joanne Owens, was chair of the planning commission), and was later named to the State Transportation Commission by Governor Wilson in March 1996 (Marois 1996a). His daughter was a high school classmate of mine. Myers represented the largest private employer in the county and was more conservative than Creighton on regulatory and property rights issues.

This group of six tirelessly met eleven times from August 29 to October 26.

They generally entered the room and, apparently unconsciously, sat on opposite sides, with the more liberal Dardick, Oberholtzer, and Van Zant appropriately on the left and the more conservative Knecht, Creighton, and Myers comfortably on the right. Pat Norman and Acting Planning Director Tom Miller (who replaced Tom Parilo after he left to become El Dorado County Planning Director in April 1994) provided technical support to the group as it went through the draft general plan and associated land use maps. Their efforts were assisted by two professional facilitators whose expenses were originally funded by the League of Women Voters and then supplemented by the board. They were well-trained as facilitators, but their focus on *process* often meant that opportunities to link multiple issues of *substance* for innovative compromise were overlooked. They simply did not understand the terminology of planning or the specific details of the draft general plan. This dramatically reduced the likelihood of reaching far-ranging agreement on many issues. The resolution committee nevertheless accomplished its task of resolving some controversies, giving both Knecht and Dardick public credibility for their efforts. Knecht performed much more effectively in this role than she had as steering committee chair. Their recommendations were submitted to the board of supervisors one week after the election (Miller 1994).

The draft EIR on the new general plan was also released shortly after the 1994 election, and the planning commission began hearings on it in January 1995. This state-mandated review under CEQA presented a new opportunity for the RQC, since the EIR highlighted both the effects likely under the draft as well as a range of mitigation measures that could be adopted to reduce them. Antonson and Grattan also took office in January, with Antonson appointing Elizabeth Martin to the planning commission. Martin joined Dardick appointee Barbara Green of Truckee in the minority. Grattan retained Bob White, who had been appointed by Weir to replace Grattan when she announced her intention to challenge Weir for his board seat (Sneed 1995e). White showed his stripes as a hardcore conservative on property rights by reading into the record position statements on the takings question prepared by the Pacific Legal Foundation. He was also closely aligned with Todd Juvinall's organization, the California Association of Business, Property and Resource Owners (CABPRO), which was and is the primary organized opposition to protection of environmental values. My sister once dated Juvinall, and CABPRO's chair is Maskey Heath, who was my Little League coach in 1972. White was supported in his prodevelopment position by Chair Joanne Owens and Amos Seghezzi, whose daughter grew up near me on Banner Mountain. Seghezzi had been retained by Tobiassen after first being appointed to the planning commission by Todd Juvinall when he took office as a supervisor in 1985.

The results were predictable, with each individual playing his or her role according to script (Staneart 1995). The outcome was preordained; this was merely a procedural exercise for compliance with CEQA. The RQC submitted thirty pages of written comments, while Dale Creighton submitted a counterbalancing twenty pages for Sylvester Engineering; individuals added specific, passionate comments on either side, but the basic positions were already well-known. The only difference was that the debate now focused on the specific mitigation measures proposed in the draft EIR, which included many elements proposed during steering committee deliberations and then rejected from the draft general plan by the planning commission and/or the board of supervisors. These included development of a habitat management plan, establishment of an open space district, mandatory clustering in subdivision design, mitigation fees for road impacts, and completion of a water and sewer study to determine the capabilities of different areas to accommodate on-site infrastructure development. Developers thought they had gotten rid of these ideas two years earlier, but here they were again as the result of a distant consultant's recommendations.[29] Now they had to deal with them again, and it was preferable not to have to do so in public via an EIR.

The planning commission entertained these mitigation measures in the draft EIR, but quickly moved to eliminate them in the final EIR by making findings of overriding considerations under CEQA. Availability of the final EIR was announced April 1, it became available April 4 through a local copy shop, and it was then the subject of a public hearing before the planning commission on April 6 (*Union* 1995d). Chair Joanne Owens gave the forty-five to fifty people in the audience the option of testifying the next week, however, by continuing the hearing because of the late availability of the final EIR. At least half the members of the public at the first hearing wore large, purple buttons saying "Put People First!" These were being distributed by Todd Juvinall and Margaret Urke, who had recently taken over for Juvinall as executive director of CABPRO. The planning commission obliged the CABPRO constituency in early May when they finally certified the final EIR. The version they certified had nearly all of the substantive mitigation measures that appeared in the draft EIR removed, on the grounds of overriding considerations under CEQA. Martin and Green were repeatedly outvoted three-to-two on individual changes to the EIR.[30]

This action was immediately followed by the first public hearing on the final version of the general plan. About ninety to a hundred people were present plus planning department staff and planning commissioners, and it was in this forum—where the new general plan, rather than the EIR, was subject to consideration—that repeated calls were made for the politics of community rather than the politics of interests. This call generally came from those advocating greater attention to use values, while those focused on exchange values called for reduced regulatory oversight. Michael Fox acknowledged philosophical differences with the majority of commissioners when he spoke while challenging the divide-and-conquer tactics of CABPRO. "When we wear buttons that say 'People First,' what we are really saying is 'Me First,'" he said. "The present patterns of development and population pressures ensure prosperity for a minority at the expense of the majority. Once you lose your community, you cannot get it back. We are not some faceless enemy; we are your neighbors, we are your community." Richard Thomas also pleaded for the politics of community. "I'm not wearing any buttons today," he said, although he was officially representing the local Sierra Club group. Many RQC members were wearing green buttons that said "I Love Nevada County." The issues were much more complex than buttons could capture, however. "Life is not green, life is not blue; life is shades of gray," added Thomas. "We really need to be working toward middle ground today." "This is not an ideological battleground," said Peter Van Zant. "What I urge you to do is turn out a good plan."[31]

Dale Creighton disagreed. "I have to disagree with Mr. Van Zant that this is not an ideological battle," said Creighton. "It has always been an ideological battle." Todd Juvinall went even further, making it clear why the general plan update had brought out such passionate emotion in the community. He recalled his father, who had fought in World War II. "One of those things he fought for was private property rights," said Juvinall, "and some people tend to forget that when they get up to the podium, and they substitute community vision for private property rights. We shouldn't allow those rights to be squashed because the majority wants to squash them. And that's why we have the Constitution. This is an ideological battle. It has been since the beginning."[32] Juvinall's ideology won; the commission stood behind him three to two.

The RQC and others (fifteen groups and 165 individuals) appealed the planning commission's decision on the final EIR to the board of supervisors, but the board rejected the appeal by a four-to-one vote. Antonson was sick and tired of the delays, and only Dardick supported the appellants' concerns. Dick Ellers and Harold Berliner represented them before the board. I firmly believe that the EIR would have been found inadequate in court, but the appellants ultimately decided not to sue. The social cost was simply too high; they were burned out and tired of being accused of being obstructionists. Kerry Gameau, a volunteer planner with Ananda Village on the San Juan Ridge, accused the RQC of making false statements. "The politics of intimidation that has surrounded the General Plan process has to come to an end," added her husband, Dave Gameau. "Quality of life means more than just trees," he said, but includes "civility among neighbors."[33] The politics of interest had severely polarized the community.

The battle over the general plan had also exhausted it. Dave Tobiassen, supervisor from District II and the son of a former county sheriff, literally collapsed the morning after the final hearing and died in his car parked by the side of his road. His widow later received a significant insurance settlement from the county, after arguing that the stress of his job had contributed to his death. The remaining board would have split two to two if Antonson had followed the advice of his planning commission appointee, Elizabeth Martin, but it was clear to Dardick after the EIR appeal hearing in late July that Antonson wanted to end the general plan update. The new town had been replaced by a "special development zone" designation, and Antonson was more interested in efficient government than additional analysis or regulations. Accordingly, Dardick did his best to get the compromises of the resolution committee adopted, and he voted with the majority when the board finally approved the general plan in October 1995 (Mooers 1995a). "I had gotten agreement on too many compromises," said Dardick, "to vote against it in the end" (Dardick 1995). The time had come to move on and deal with the difficult task of implementing the new framework.

The RQC had also learned an important but difficult political lesson: it takes a majority on the board of supervisors to implement a vision, even if that vision is agreed to by a majority of the population. The RQC had mistakenly believed that good analysis, eloquent testimony, and broad public support for their position would be enough. It wasn't. What they needed was a majority on the board of supervisors and a majority on the planning commission. Defeated in the planning process, they turned their attention next to the 1996 reelection of Dardick, the defeat of Knecht in her reelection bid, and the opportunity to fill Tobiassen's seat with the crucial swing vote they needed. And this time they were not about to let the votes of only twenty-five people determine the outcome of the election.[34]

CHANGING OF THE GUARD: THE ELECTION OF 1996

Fran Grattan was elected by far more than only twenty-five voters in 1994, however: she also had twice as much money as Jim Weir, and she received significant support from interest groups outside the county. The California Forestry Association—an industry group that called itself the Timber Association of California before 1992 (MacFarquhar 1996)—directly supported Grattan in an attempt to, as its slogan advised, "Produce New Friends in Local Government." This represented a major shift from the politics of community to the politics of interest in the local election process, last seen to this degree in the November 1978 battle over Propositions A and B. Nonlocal environmental groups did not get involved, however, and their interests were consequently compromised by Grattan's win. The California Forestry Association said of its own efforts:

> Taking a new tack in the recently concluded election cycle[,] the California Forestry Association (CFA) jumped into the crossfire of local politics by contributing both expertise in campaign management and financial resources to targeted county races. Choosing hotly contested challenges where incumbents and open seat opponents represent[ed] the philosophies of extremist environmentalists, CFA set out to

send the message that common-sense environmentalism and job protection were the new messages of the majority of people living in rural communities. In all but one of the campaigns, we were proven right!

Most notably, in Nevada County, two-term incumbent Jim Weir was defeated in a huge come-from-behind victory by local businesswoman Fran Grattan. Industry Affairs Vice-President Donn Zea and his wife[,] Lisa[, both of whom live in Nevada County,] provided the political strategy and management for all facets of the campaign, including research, direct mail and radio production. CFA's political action committee, as well as individual contributions from various members helped fund the effort.[35]

Campaign finance records show that Grattan received $55,864 in contributions in 1994—more than twice the annual salary for the job—to Weir's $21,929. Grattan's total included a $2,110 loan to herself. Weir also had $7,143 in outstanding loans to himself from his 1986 and 1990 campaigns.[36] Both candidates raised roughly one-third of their total funds from donations exceeding $250 each. Only seven of Weir's donations exceeded $250 in cash, however, while another three purchased more than $250 in goods and/or services at a fund-raising yard sale and nine donated goods and/or services worth at least $250 for that yard sale. He received a total of $7,303 in value from these large donations, averaging $348 each. Grattan brought in twenty-eight donations that were more than $250 each, totaling $18,553 and averaging $663 each.[37]

The CFA directly donated only $500 in cash, but Sierra Pacific Industries owner Red Emmerson of Redding donated another $1,000. Maskey Heath of Superior Propane—chair of CABPRO—matched Emmerson's large donation. Various members of the Smith family, owners of Vectra Engineering—which was representing Emperor Gold Corporation in its controversial proposal to reactivate the Idaho-Maryland Mine at the time—donated a total of $1,115. Another $1,274 were donated by various members of the Fowler family, owners of the local Builders and Consumers Lumber Company and the Fowler Center, a large shopping center that included an Albertson's.[38] Other large contributors included real estate and timber interests. The largest donation, however, came from Cletus Rogers of Smartville, located just across the Yuba County line. Rogers listed his business as a mining equipment supplier and donated a whopping $3,400 to Grattan's election. In sharp contrast to Grattan's contributors, few of Weir's contributors had a direct financial stake in the outcome. Grattan owed her victory to timber, mining, and development industries.[39]

Grattan's campaign success inspired continued investments by CFA in supervisorial races. Donn and Lisa Zea, Grattan's former campaign consultants, advised Karen Knecht in her 1996 campaign, which received donations from Landsburg Logging employees ($996), Sierra Pacific Industries ($500), Vector Engineering employees ($349), Sha-Neva Aggregate of Truckee ($249), and Siskon Gold

Corporation ($249). The developers Fred and Ruth Sacher topped the list with $998 in contributions while Joseph Slouber gave $550, the Hopkins Trust (which was trying to develop an eight-hundred-acre parcel near Truckee) contributed $500, and R. E. and Margaret McCollum donated $498. Knecht had spent only $22,317 to defeat an incumbent in 1992, however, and she faced a much less difficult race than Grattan in 1996 when former Supervisor Callaghan challenged her to a rematch. Knecht easily won reelection in the March 1996 primary with 61 percent of the votes cast (3,356 to 2,170, with 452 casting abstentions). She spent only $18,772 in the 1996 elections as the RQC decided not to challenge her in conservative District II.

Dave Tobiassen's sudden death had created a new opportunity for the RQC in July 1995, however, for he had barely won the District I seat in a three-person race in 1992. In fact, Tobiassen had won only 20 percent of the vote in the June 1992 primary and had beaten Paul Matson by only 78 votes in the November 1992 general election. Matson and Ilse Barnhart—both of whom were supported by the RQC, but neither of whom would pull out of the race until it was too late, when Barnhart withdrew after the ballots had been printed—gained 1,050 more votes between them (out of 9,556 votes cast) than Tobiassen in the general election.[40] Todd Juvinall had beaten Barnhart for the same seat in 1984 by 335 votes (out of 6,119 votes) and then successfully defended his win by a margin of only 44 votes over Matson (out of 7,457 votes) as an incumbent in 1988. The seat was clearly winnable by an RQC-supported candidate, for the residents of the area placed a high value on their rural quality of life. District I included most of Nevada City and the Banner Mountain area, and it extended along the Colfax Highway to Chicago Park, as well as along Highway 20 east of Nevada City. It was the second-most liberal supervisorial district in the county by party registration, after Sam Dardick's District V.

A small group of RQC activists had already begun meeting to consider prospective candidates shortly after the heart-breaking loss by Weir to Grattan in November 1994. Matson and Barnhart had both run twice and lost twice, so they were never seriously considered. Peter Van Zant's name was circulated early on, but he initially failed to generate strong support because of concern that he would be negatively associated with the appeal of the general plan EIR. By July 1992 an apparent favorite had emerged: computer expert Dave Denney, a Republican who had lived in the Nevada City area since 1984. He had also served as foreman of the 1986 grand jury and was one of the original founders of the Federation of Neighborhood Associations, which Van Zant represented in the general plan update process. Denney was also an Annapolis graduate, Vietnam War veteran, member of the Deer Creek Park Water Board, and president of the Deer Creek Park Homeowners Association (Mooers 1995b). He had virtually no name recognition, however, and Carol Johnson of Peardale announced that she was also running. Another loss resulting from a divided majority loomed over them, so the RQC power brokers made efforts to persuade Johnson to withdraw.

The development community was much more systematic and well positioned for naming and promoting its preferred candidate. In fact, that process began well before the campaign began. Before his death, concern about Tobiassen's health had already led to widespread speculation that he would not seek reelection, so the search for his successor began soon after the November 1994 election. Nevada City Council Member Christine Wilcox quickly emerged as the clear favorite. Her fiancé, George Foster, was president of Eigen Video (a high-technology manufacturer located in the district) and chair of the subcommittee assigned to recruit political candidates for the Nevada County Republican Central Committee. Todd Juvinall was committee chair. By late winter Wilcox had quietly been anointed and a subtle political marketing campaign had begun.

The first step was to get better name recognition, and the Nevada County Board of Realtors quickly obliged by naming her the winner of their Community Service Award in 1994. More important, the *Gold Country Real Estate Showcase* was published for the first time in March 1995 as an insert to the *Union*. Page three featured an article titled "Spotlight: Christine Wilcox, 'A Woman of Substance'" (*Union* 1995b). (It was positioned immediately next to another article describing how the National Association of Realtors strongly supported the Private Property Protection Act of 1995 [H.R. 925] before Congress. That bill would have required compensation for any diminution in real estate value of more than 10 percent resulting from government action of any type.) The same insert then repeated its performance with another article—this time, with photo—in July 1995 (ibid.). No explanation was given as to why she was featured twice within four months.

Two weeks later Tobiassen died, creating an opportunity to have Wilson appoint Wilcox (who had since married George Foster and now went by Wilcox-Foster). The local GOP committee went through the motions and interviewed both Wilcox-Foster and Denney, but endorsed Wilcox-Foster by a vote of eighteen to five (Mooers 1995c). Governor Wilson then appointed her to the post in mid-October 1995—more than six months before the March 1996 primary, assuring plenty of time for developing name recognition—and she immediately began fund-raising for the primary. She had previously been appointed to a seat on the Nevada City Council when Dave Tobiassen gave up his city council seat upon being elected supervisor in 1992. She had been the top vote-getter among the losing candidates, but had never been elected to office. The 1996 elections would be the first real test of the voters' willingness to *elect* her to office or to *keep* her in office.

The RQC realized at this point that they needed a strong candidate with name recognition and the ability to generate enthusiasm. Denney did not seem likely to beat Wilcox-Foster with the advantages of incumbency on her side, and Johnson

could only take votes from Denney. They turned again to Peter Van Zant and per-
suaded Denney and Johnson to withdraw. Van Zant officially announced his can-
didacy in late 1995, and the head-to-head race was on (Niedorf 1995). This would
be a true test of the voters' positions on land use and growth management issues
in District I. Wilcox-Foster and Van Zant clearly represented different visions for
the county.

This time the RQC supporters opened up both their checkbooks and their cal-
endars. "We weren't about to let Peter lose by thirty-seven votes,"[41] said Brian
Bisnett, head of the RQC. (Grattan beat Weir by just thirty-seven votes in the original election returns, but the final tally increased to forty-nine votes after a
recount.) "Everyone I know spent every hour we had working on this campaign.
We weren't going to end up losing and wondering if we could have talked to
another twenty people about the importance of this election" (Bisnett 1996a).
They also made sure that Van Zant was not at a disadvantage in fund-raising and
campaign spending. Two weeks before the election Van Zant had raised $34,899
and spent $18,294. Wilcox-Foster had received just $25,221 and spent $14,472. In
the end Van Zant spent $42,155 and Wilcox-Foster spent $43,122 on the hard-
fought election.

Much of Van Zant's money came from noncash donations that totaled $15,278
in value. These were then auctioned off to generate cash for signs, fliers, mailings,
and other campaign costs. Only eleven individuals or families donated more than
$250 each for a total of $8,586 (averaging $781 each—more than twice the 1994
average for Weir).[42] I wrote a check for $100 to the campaign, which typified the
much smaller contributions that Van Zant received. He had a broad base, however,
which allowed him nearly to equal Wilcox-Foster's spending.

Wilcox-Foster's campaign generated twenty-five donations of $250 or more,
totaling $13,822 to average $553 each. She also received a $4,000 donation from
her husband, George Foster, after the election, to retire her remaining debt. The
largest contribution came from the developer Fred Sacher, who donated $1,400 to
her campaign and who is also a major contributor to conservative political candidates at the state and federal level. The Los Angeles–based California Real Estate
Political Action Committee of the Board of Realtors donated $1,200; Judy and
Francis (Jerry) Cirino, who ran a restaurant in Nevada City, donated $1,000 to the
campaign. Monty East (one of the board members of the Nevada County Business
Association) gave Wilcox-Foster $874, and Sierra Pacific Industries donated
$500.[43] Wilcox-Foster also received noncash donations totaling $10,714.

With the exception of Sierra Pacific Industries' donation, however, the only
significant cash contribution from commodity extractive industry was Siskon Gold
Corporation's $249 donation. Neither the Zeas nor the nonlocal California
Forestry Association participated visibly in Wilcox-Foster's campaign. They were
focusing instead on the reelection of Knecht, where they knew they had a strong

supporter. Wilcox-Foster's loyalties were more likely to lie with the real estate industry and high technology companies like her husband's. The problem with those high technology companies, of course, was that many of their employees shared use values with the RQC. Wilcox-Foster's interests were not necessarily the same as CFA's interests.

Assemblyman Bernie Richter of Chico (whose district included Nevada County) tried to give Wilcox-Foster's campaign a boost by naming her "Woman of the Year" for his assembly district in a thinly veiled political ceremony just one week before the election (Mooers 1996), but she couldn't overcome Van Zant's clear advantages. He won 4,088 votes to Wilcox-Foster's 3,136 votes—a stunning margin of 952 votes. Van Zant's victory made it very clear that the voters of District I wanted a new supervisor who would protect neighborhood character and rural quality (Sneed 1995h). His 57 percent to 43 percent win was accompanied by an even stronger victory by Sam Dardick (3,409 votes to 1,800, a margin of 1,609) against his challenger Bill Mecorney.[44] The new board of supervisors would therefore have two firm pave-it-and-build-it votes (Knecht and Grattan), two firm protect-rural-quality-and-character votes (Van Zant and Dardick), and one protect-it-but-don't-regulate-it-too-much swing vote (Rene Antonson) in January 1997. Antonson's planning commission appointee, Elizabeth Martin, was nevertheless likely to vote consistently with Barbara Green and Van Zant's new appointee, Lee Good, to take control of the commission on planning issues. The developers' long-standing lock on the positions of power had finally been broken.

The lessons of the election of 1994 had finally come home for victory in 1996. "It's a sweet victory," said Peter Van Zant on election night as his lead over Wilcox-Foster widened (Van Zant 1996). It was only March, though, and Van Zant still had the rest of 1996 remaining before he would be seated to represent the voters' will.

CHAPTER TEN

᠕᠕᠕

Habitats and Humanity

I moved to the West because of the spectacle: the mountains, their streams, the canyons those streams cut, the summer flowers in high meadows. I stayed because of the landscapes[:] . . . sage flats, mining towns whose tiny houses are perched on switchbacks, trailer parks, eroding gullies. . . . When these scenes vanish from the West, when it becomes "full color" everywhere and not just in the ski towns and the discovered villages, then the West will no longer be worth living in, any more than Disneyland is worth living in.

Ed Marston, 1996a

The March 1996 election changed the face of Nevada County politics, but it did not end the debate over the general plan. All efforts now turned to the rezoning effort following Van Zant's election, for the lame-duck majority still had nine months to make policy before Van Zant would replace Wilcox-Foster on the board of supervisors. The focal point of the new battle was the build-out estimates for the general plan: which "carrying capacity" of allowable population would guide zoning decisions under the new general plan? The ensuing debate illustrates how technically complex land use and environmental planning analyses can be overwhelmed by the adoption of symbolic policies that placate the citizenry while maintaining the growth machine's control over both the level of government regulation and the spatial structure of the market. In this way exchange values can be promoted while use values receive symbolic support.

The build-out estimates had become highly politicized during the November 1994 election campaigns, when both supervisorial challenger Fran Grattan and incumbent Jim Weir embraced a 140,000-person build-out number for the new general plan. This then became the basis for the resolution committee's deliberations, which included Supervisors Karen Knecht and Sam Dardick (both of whom would face reelection campaigns in 1996). The resolution committee modified land use designations on the draft general plan maps, allowable densities for specific land uses, assumptions about the number of persons per household, and assumptions about how much of the gross land area under each land use would ultimately be developed. This brought the *estimated* build-out population down to 140,000–150,000 without fundamentally changing either the land use map or the general plan policies. Peter Van Zant and Laurie Oberholtzer supported the effort, however, because they believed the new agreement on a maximum build-out population could serve as the basis for further limitations on development during the implementation phase. Dale Creighton and Ken Myers supported it because they believed it would produce a more "realistic" build-out estimate without imposing any significant new restrictions on the development potential for most parcels. Acting Planning Director Tom Miller therefore satisfied both constituencies by providing an analytic basis for the symbolic result. Like Bill Roberts in Grass Valley and Tom Parilo before him, Miller knew who was in charge.

The agreement took on more than symbolic significance after Van Zant's resounding defeat of Christine Wilcox-Foster in the March 1996 supervisorial election. The new general plan had been adopted in late 1995, but zoning designations had not yet been changed and implementing ordinances had not yet been adopted. This is where the rubber hit the road: the general plan's policies and land use maps were important, but zoning designations and implementing ordinances would determine the actual development densities and pattern of land use on the ground. The new political calculus showed that the Rural Quality Coalition and its allies, who emphasized use over exchange values in the political economy of land use planning and regulation, would gain control of the board of supervisors and the planning commission at twelve noon on January 7, 1997. Delaying adoption of the zoning ordinance and implementing regulations would favor the RQC; accelerated adoption of the same would favor the pro-growth majority on the board and the commission. Accordingly, the lame-duck board pushed Miller to get them both done in 1996.

He responded quickly. The entire zoning ordinance was scheduled to be adopted by the planning commission in May 1996 after only one day of hearings, which put it on a fast track for approval by the board of supervisors in 1996 even if there were appeals. The planning commission approved the initial draft of the new zoning ordinance with only minor changes.[1] The RQC and its allies responded by challenging the planning department, the planning commission, and the outgoing board of supervisors every step of the way. A new group, the Nevada County General Plan Defense Fund, was formed to challenge the new general plan through either litigation or possible circulation of a referendum for the November 1996 ballot. I was asked to participate in this effort but declined and was not involved in the process directly. I believed that the critical window for legal action had closed following the board's adoption of the final EIR for the general plan in July 1995, which I considered legally deficient. I also felt that further delays would not be enough to stop the new regulations before Van Zant would take office.

I had not, however, anticipated that my work for the Sierra Nevada Ecosystem Project would become a central part of the political debate. The SNEP report was delivered to Congress in "prepublication" form in June 1996, and a two-day conference was held on the SNEP effort that same month at the El Dorado County Fairgrounds in Placerville. Earlier in the month, the California Biodiversity Council had held its quarterly meeting in Nevada City. I presented the results of my general plan build-out analysis at both meetings, since they were now public information after delivery of the report to Congress. Supervisor Fran Grattan made positive reference to my presentation when she spoke at the Biodiversity Council dinner, suggesting that my analysis was a solid foundation for land use planning in Nevada County. I approached her afterward both to thank her and to challenge her. "I appreciate your comments," I said, "but I really think you should read my report to see the problems with the new general plan that was adopted last fall." She told me she would be happy to read it, and I promised to send her a copy as soon as I had the final page proofs (Grattan 1996).

A few weeks later I received an urgent e-mail message from RQC President Brian Bisnett, saying that the board was about to consider the new zoning ordinance and that he wanted me to testify at the public hearing. I told him I could not attend, but that I would contact the supervisors in advance. I then photocopied my SNEP report at a local Truckee copy shop and sent copies to all five supervisors via express mail. I also sent copies to Tom Miller, the *Union*, Peter Van Zant, and the Nevada County Library. My cover letter was to Fran Grattan (then chair of the board) and it referred specifically to our conversation in early June. Neither the board nor the planning department could deny the availability of my report and its underlying data at the time they took the critical step of adopting a zoning ordinance to implement the new general plan.

The Nevada County General Plan Defense Fund had meanwhile decided to fight the general plan politically through the one number that everyone in the county could understand: the build-out "goal" of 140,000. There was wide political agreement on that goal, and the concept was understood easily enough to sell in the papers and at the polls. They therefore took my SNEP analysis—which showed a build-out of anywhere from 93,991 to 152,080 housing units (Duane 1996a: Table 11.A7, p. 357), translating into anywhere from 197,381 to 364,992 people[2]—as the basis for arguing that the new general plan violated the agreed-upon 140,000 cap on Nevada County population at build-out. My SNEP analysis was based on the 1994 Final Draft General Plan, however, and the resolution committee's changes had clearly reduced the build-out estimate somewhat. I nevertheless estimated that the general plan adopted in late 1995 would have a build-out of at least 200,000 (Willis 1996a; 1996b). This estimate was supported by an independent analysis by former UC Davis physics professor Jim Hurley, a local resident and RQC activist who estimated a build-out of at least 207,161 (Hurley 1996).

None of this should have been news to the planning department, the planning commission, or the board of supervisors. I first raised the issue during the resolution committee meetings in October 1994, and I presented my preliminary analysis to Miller in a draft copy of the SNEP report in July 1995. I also commented on it as a citizen of the county during public hearings on both the general plan and the draft EIR before both the commission and the board throughout 1994 and 1995. My analysis was never refuted, however, for that would have made the validity of the estimates a point of debate. Instead, my concerns were simply ignored. It was not until the Nevada County General Plan Defense Fund rallied behind the issue in the summer of 1996 that the planning department was compelled by politics to analyze the question.

The advent of the microcomputer and the spreadsheet has made it much easier to choose assumptions that generate an "answer" that matches the desired result, and the planning department was able to give its political masters what they wanted by selecting generous assumptions where they were helpful, as well as conservative assumptions where those were helpful. The planning department's new estimates ranged from 154,953 residents to 162,726 residents at build-out (averaging 158,870), with 7,900 of the increase attributable to build-out changes within incorporated cities (Willis 1996b; Nevada County Planning Department 1996). The new county build-out estimate (excluding the city-induced changes) was therefore only 7,000 to 15,000 over the 140,000 goal. This was probably within the range of both legal and political acceptability.

However, my own analysis of these estimates identified two significant sources of error in the planning department's projections: they estimated "net" build-out for a given land use, rather than the *allowable* build-out under the general plan; and they estimated "likely" parcelization (based on historical patterns of parcelization), rather than the *allowable* parcelization. Their build-out analysis, in other words, did not actually calculate how much could be built under the general plan (i.e., the "capacity" of the land use designations under the adopted general plan)! There may have also been additional errors, but these two errors alone increased the build-out estimate by an average of 17,092 across the three alternatives considered. The true build-out (accepting the reliability of every other aspect of the planning department's analysis, which I was unable to evaluate) would therefore range from 169,135 to 185,288 (averaging 175,962) (Duane 1996c).

The implications of this higher build-out number are significant. Based on a 1994 population of 86,700, a build-out estimate of 175,962 would result in 41 percent more *new* residents than a 150,000 goal (89,262 versus 63,300 new residents, or a difference of nearly 26,000 more residents—roughly the population of Nevada County in 1970).[3] Ironically, it was political reaction to the 1994 build-out estimate of 175,200 in the Final Draft General Plan that had originally led to the formation of the resolution committee and widespread agreement on the 140,000 build-out goal. Similar "net" and "likely" estimation errors were made in the planning department's original 1994 analysis of the plan's build-out, however, that would have increased its true build-out to 223,224. Consequently, the net effect of the resolution committee's actions was to reduce the *perceived* build-out estimate from 175,200 down to 140,000 in time for the November 1994 election—while the *actual* build-out possible under the subsequently adopted changes in fact dropped from 223,224 to 175,962 (Duane 1996c). The real build-out capacity of the plan ultimately ended up near the original bargaining position that was rejected as too high in late 1994—when the growth machine's lock on the decision-making apparatus appeared threatened during the Grattan-Weir campaign.

In the end, however, it was perception that won the day. The growth machine still controlled the planning department, the planning commission, and the board of supervisors; as long as the debate remained a political one, it could control the outcome in favor of exchange values. Trilateral relational controls did not move beyond local political venues to the courts, which were not controlled by the growth machine. The *Union* came down in favor of the growth machine, arguing that the debate was "nonsensical navel-gazing" and that "while the chattering classes continue to pretend that they can foresee the future with clarity, the residents of Nevada County live without a functioning general plan—and any number of people's hopes to create homes and business opportunities for themselves and their families are delayed and delayed again" (*Union* 1996a). This reflected the growth machine's recurring emphasis on an economic model built on commodity and exchange values rather than amenity and use values, of course, for those delays had real value for those who saw rural quality as an economic asset. "The issues surrounding growth are probably the most important questions that face Nevada County," said the *Union,* "but the argument about build-out numbers is diverting our attention" (ibid.).

I could not agree more: build-out numbers are much less important than the critical choices embedded within the new general plan that define the spatial organization of future development. It is through spatial patterns that structural entrepreneurs realize gains, and it is through spatial patterns that effects can be mitigated—at the potential cost of those gains. That conclusion is clearly supported by my analysis of the El Dorado County General Plan, where two alternatives—both accommodating approximately the same total population at build-out—are likely to have dramatically different consequences for biodiversity in the region. Those are the differences that should have been part of the debate, but they were never fully considered. The same is true for the social, cultural, and economic consequences of alternative plans.

The RQC therefore lost the debate when it allowed build-out to become the primary indicator of the potential effects of the new general plan, for the build-out estimates were easily co-opted and then manipulated. The public eventually could not understand the "chattering classes." That left things in the hands of the growth machine, and they had time to finish the job. The outgoing board of supervisors adopted the new zoning ordinance on the morning of January 7, 1997. Peter Van Zant was sworn in as a Nevada County supervisor less than three hours later.

POPULATION GROWTH AND BIODIVERSITY
IN THE SIERRA NEVADA

The ultimate effects of various build-out scenarios under the Nevada County General Plan must be placed in the broader context of population growth throughout the Range of Light. The Sierra Nevada is likely to undergo significant land conversion resulting from continued population growth over the next half century. Total land area converted to human settlement to accommodate that growth will depend on the spatial pattern and average density of settlement, which will in turn depend on a complex interaction of public policy, infrastructure, and land economics. Strict development controls, significant expansion of water and sewer systems, and higher land prices would likely lead to a more intensive pattern of development with less land conversion than would occur in the absence of those conditions. Continuing existing patterns of development would consume more land than under those conditions.

Three out of five Sierra Nevada residents lived on less than 300 square miles (less than 1 percent of the Sierra Nevada) in 1990, but human settlement was spread across nearly 1,741 square miles at an average density of at least one housing unit per 32 acres. This area accommodated seven out of every eight Sierra Nevada residents and constituted 5.44 percent of the entire Sierra Nevada, or nearly 14 percent of all private land (including industrial timberlands). Up to one-eighth of the entire Sierra Nevada (3,905 square miles) may have been affected by human settlement in 1990 at an average density of at least one housing unit per 128 acres, however, for the remaining one-eighth of Sierra Nevada residents were spread across the landscape at lower average housing densities. These lower densities could negatively affect some ecological functions.

Without assuming any specific linkages to specific policies or market conditions, I developed twenty-four future growth scenarios as part of my SNEP work and then simplified the set into four scenarios in order to estimate the range of likely land conversion from 1990 to 2040:[4]

    A. Low population growth with compact human settlement patterns (Low-Compact);

    B. High population growth with compact human settlement patterns (High-Compact);

    C. Low population growth with sprawling human settlement patterns (Low-Sprawl);

    D. High population growth with sprawling human settlement patterns (High-Sprawl).

Based on these four scenarios, the additional land conversion required to accommodate Sierra Nevada population growth forecast for 1990 to 2040 (in *addition* to the land area already converted for human settlement as of the 1990 census) is estimated to range from:

106 to 579 square miles at an average density of at least 640 units per square mile;

299 to 875 square miles at an average density of at least 160 units per square mile;

480 to 1,655 square miles at an average density of at least 80 units per square mile;

477 to 2,957 square miles at an average density of at least 40 units per square mile;

134 to 5,105 square miles at an average density of at least 20 units per square mile.[5]

The social, economic, and ecological ramifications of future development will depend on specific spatial patterns of human settlement in relationship to existing communities, infrastructure services, vegetation and habitat types, and watershed boundaries. As discussed above, scientific understanding of those relationships is still poor at this time, making it impossible to characterize the specific effects that population growth and human settlement will have in the Sierra Nevada. The range of effects could be quite significant, however, if existing development patterns continue. Continuing the existing pattern of sprawl development with a high-growth scenario could result in human settlement on nearly half the private land in the Sierra Nevada (6,846 square miles) at an average density of at least one housing unit per 32 acres. A low-growth scenario with the existing pattern of sprawl development would reduce that figure by 44 percent, to just 3,817 square miles. This is still significantly greater than the 1,741 square miles affected by human settlement at that average housing density in 1990.

Even modified settlement patterns are forecast to result in significant land conversion from 1990 to 2040, suggesting that the scale of population growth alone could lead to significant effects. A high-growth scenario with a more compact form of settlement would result in nearly a doubling of land converted to human settlement, from 1,741 square miles to 3,363 square miles at an average density of at least one housing unit per 32 acres. A low-growth scenario with a more compact form of settlement, however, could nearly be accommodated within the land area already converted to human settlement at an average density of at least one housing unit per 32 acres in 1990. Through infill and carefully targeted density transfers, the low population forecast for 1990 to 2040 would require only a total of 1,875 square miles (only 8 percent or 133 square miles more than in 1990). Both the scale and pattern of human settlement will therefore affect—and must be considered by—local, state, and federal land and resource management agencies with responsibility for the health and sustainability of Sierra Nevada ecosystems.

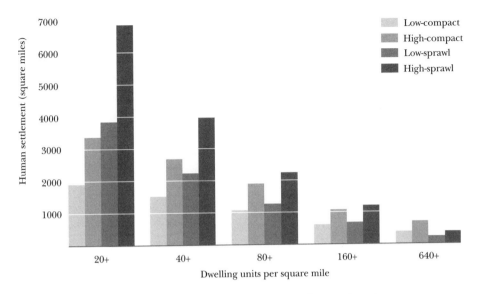

FIGURE 10.1.   Additional land area required to accommodate projected 1990–2040 population growth in the Sierra Nevada for four alternative development scenarios, by threshold settlement density.

These estimates of land conversion associated with human settlement from 1990 to 2040 are not uniform throughout the Sierra Nevada. They reflect the distribution of population forecast by the DOF for each county and the allocation of that population by my allocation models to each of the County Census Divisions in my analysis. In general, land most likely to be converted to human settlement is primarily in the western foothills and within commuting distance of rapidly growing cities in the Central Valley. Some specific vegetation (Holland) types and WHR types are therefore more threatened by human settlement than others, reflecting the nonrandom spatial distribution of growth, private ownership, and vegetation. More spatially explicit analysis is necessary to determine the effect of specific patterns of human settlement on specific vegetation (Holland) types and WHR types.[6]

A starting point for this analysis is the GAP vegetation analysis completed by Frank Davis and David Stoms in the SNEP report (Davis and Stoms 1996). Recall that GAP analysis "assesses the distribution of plant community types among land classes defined by ownership and levels of protection of biodiversity. Gap analysis helps to identify which plant communities and species might be especially vulnerable to different human activities that can lead to habitat conversion or degradation," including human settlement. Davis and Stoms analyzed a portion of the Sierra Nevada covering 24,367 square miles, which is only about three-fourths of the area covered by the CCDs in our demographically defined Sierra Region. Approximately 37 percent of that land area is in private hands, and only 10 percent is in national parks (671).

Eighty-eight plant community types were analyzed in the Sierra Nevada, sixty-seven of which covered an area at least 9.65 square miles (25 square kilometers). These plant community types are not distributed randomly across the landscape, however, so some types are more likely to be located on private lands. Moreover, private land ownership is not distributed randomly across the landscape. As a result, "less than [1 percent] of [the] foothill woodland zone is in designated reserves or otherwise managed primarily for native biodiversity, and over 95 percent of the distribution of most foothill community types is available for grazing" (ibid.). Those foothill community types are also prime locations for human settlement. In particular, the twenty-seven Holland plant community types listed in Table 10.1 occur on land that is at least 50 percent privately owned and therefore most likely to bear the brunt of human settlement in the Sierra Nevada (676–77).

Although these Holland types are not well represented on public land, local governments do not afford them any special consideration when evaluating the consequences of alternative land use plans or development proposals. In fact, my SNEP evaluation of the general plan update processes for both the Nevada County and El Dorado County General Plans shows that biodiversity was only explicitly and systematically considered by local governments for plant or animal species listed under the ESA. Impact assessment under CEQA was otherwise left to broad generalities; the plans suggested that implementation of the plans would cause significant effects on biodiversity but then failed to adopt mitigation measures because of overriding considerations. Nevada and El Dorado Counties together spent approximately $4 million from 1990 to 1995 on their general plan updates, and SNEP presented an opportunity to use updated data that would have allowed a systematic analysis of these effects. Moreover, the availability of digital data and GIS technology allowed the counties and their consultants to evaluate the relative effects of alternative general plan land use designations, general plan policies, zoning designations, and mitigation measures through both the planning process and the CEQA-required EIR process. Neither county did so.[7]

The GAP analysis tells us only what is "at risk" because it lies in the *potential* path of development on private lands. Spatially explicit analysis of general plan maps, however, shows the "official future" for land development, giving us the opportunity to assess how specific Holland and WHR types are *likely* to be affected by future population growth. General plans are easily changed, of course, and I am not naive about whether these land use designations will hold. They nevertheless allow us to assess the likely consequences of official land use policy. Moreover, comparisons among alternative plans allow us to determine how a shift from the dominant patterns of sprawl to a more compact form of human settlement could modify the effects of a given level of population growth on specific Holland and WHR types in the Sierra Nevada. Accordingly, I completed a more detailed analy-

TABLE 10.1   Holland Communities in the Sierra
at Least 50 Percent Privately Owned

Great Basin montane meadow (100%)*	Interior live oak woodland (71%)
Valley oak woodland (98%)	Mojave mixed woody scrub (71%)
Great Valley valley oak riparian forest (97%)	Scrub oak chaparral (71%)
Ione chaparral (96%)	Interior live oak chaparral (71%)
Transmontane alkali marsh (92%)	Mojavean juniper woodland and scrub (67%)
Blue oak woodland (89%)	Great Valley mixed riparian forest (63%)
Nonnative grassland (88%)	Shin oak brush (60%)
Alkali meadow (82%)	Open foothill pine woodland (58%)
Foothill pine – oak woodland (82%)	Black oak woodland (55%)
Valley needlegrass grassland (80%)	Chamise chaparral (52%)
Tan oak forest (77%)	Mojave creosote bush scrub (50%)
Interior live oak chaparral (76%)	Upper Sonoran subshrub scrub (50%)
Deer brush chaparral (75%)	Knobcone pine forest (50%)
Great Valley cottonwood riparian forest (73%)	

*This is an addition to the Holland classification. Davis and Stoms 1996, p. 676.

sis of two very different alternative land use maps that were explicitly considered in the El Dorado County General Plan update process.[8] This analysis was completed subsequent to my work for SNEP, but the underlying data from the SNEP report and databases are available to the public.[9]

Coverages are available for both Holland and WHR classifications, but we used the WHR coverage because it includes fewer classes and is therefore less likely to identify areas of significant conversion resulting from human settlement projected under the general plan. El Dorado County includes twenty WHR types. Those twenty types were intersected with eleven broad classes of housing densities, ranging from zero dwelling units per square mile to 640 or more dwelling units per square mile (at least one unit per acre). Changes in housing density under general plan build-out therefore translated into changes in total area in each of the WHR and housing-density-class subcategories. This allows us to determine which type of development affects which habitat types.

The spatial pattern of general plan build-out varies significantly between the two El Dorado County General Plan alternatives, which are referred to as the "Project Description" (Project) and the "General Plan Alternative" (Alternative). These two alternatives were considered equally in the plan's EIR process under CEQA, because El Dorado County Supervisors Bill Center and Sam Bradley convinced their colleagues (who favored the Project) that the county would be vulnerable to litigation under CEQA if the EIR did not consider the Alternative

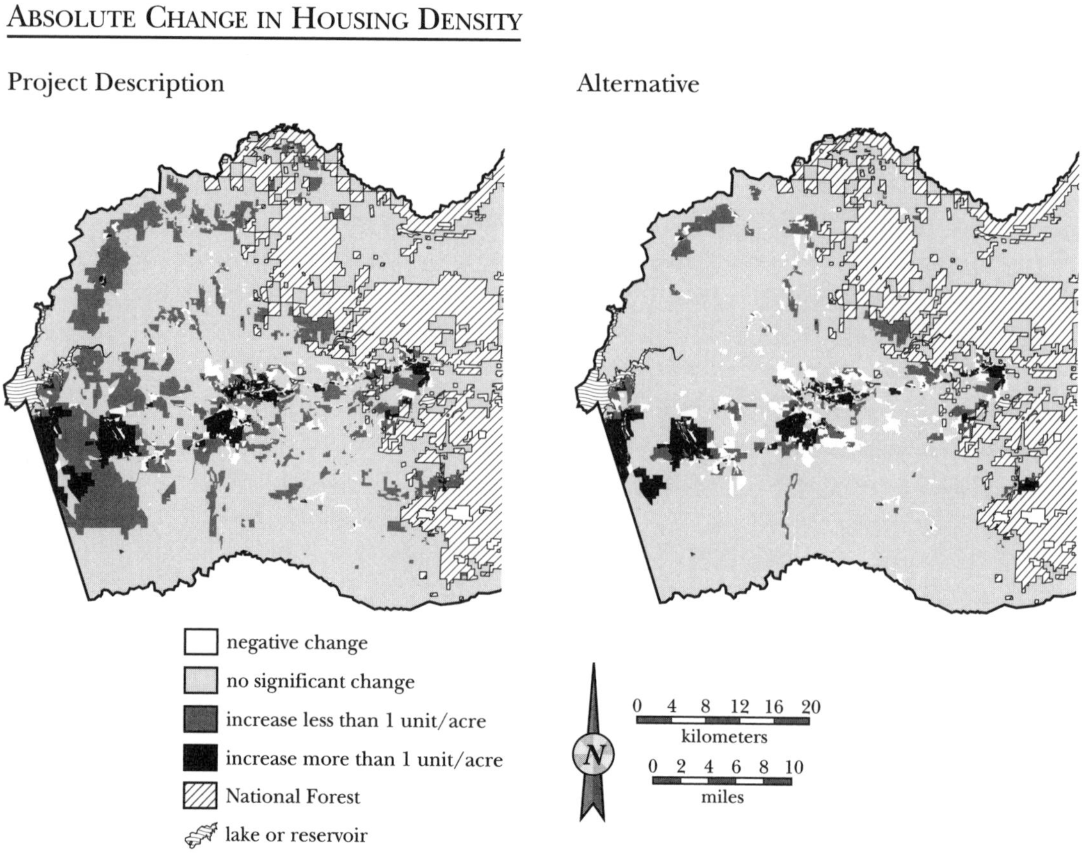

ABSOLUTE CHANGE IN HOUSING DENSITY

Project Description   Alternative

negative change

no significant change

increase less than 1 unit/acre

increase more than 1 unit/acre

National Forest

lake or reservoir

| 0 | 4 | 8 | 12 | 16 | 20 |
kilometers

| 0 | 2 | 4 | 6 | 8 | 10 |
miles

MAPS 10.1 and 10.2.   Absolute change in housing density for the El Dorado County General Plan Project Description and El Dorado County General Plan Alternative, from 1990 to build-out.

comprehensively. The three-to-two majority therefore agreed to conduct an analysis of both alternatives, allowing me to examine them without having to generate my own "alternative" to the officially adopted Project. My analysis reflects the Project and Alternative descriptions used in the draft EIR analysis in 1994 and 1995, but the 1994 elections resulted in Bill Center's replacement by a pro-growth supervisor. The new four-to-one majority weakened many of the environmental protections in the original Project version of the general plan and rejected most of the mitigation measures considered in the draft EIR (Hoge 1995; *San Francisco Chronicle* 1998). As a result, my analysis probably understates the adopted general plan's true effects on habitat conversion.

The differences are nevertheless striking. Map 10.1 shows the *absolute* change in housing density from 1990 to build-out for the Project, while Map 10.2 shows the absolute change for the Alternative. Both maps show what appears to be a rel-

RELATIVE CHANGE IN HOUSING DENSITY

Project Description   Alternative

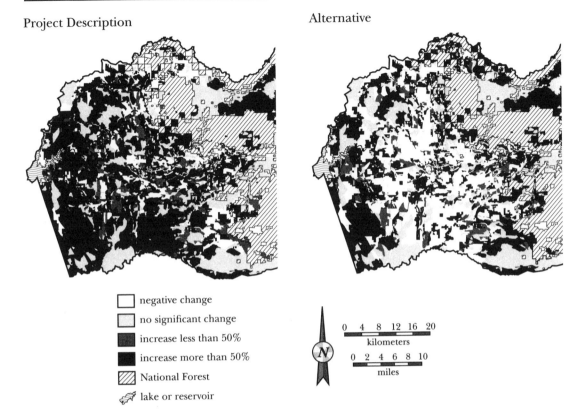

☐ negative change

▨ no significant change

▨ increase less than 50%

■ increase more than 50%

▨ National Forest

🦋 lake or reservoir

0 4 8 12 16 20
kilometers

0 2 4 6 8 10
miles

MAPS 10.3 and 10.4.   Relative change in housing density for the El Dorado County
General Plan Project Description and El Dorado County General Plan Alternative, from
1990 to build-out.

atively concentrated pattern of development under the Alternative and a slightly
less concentrated pattern under the Project. Both alternatives accommodate
approximately the same total number of housing units and population, but the
Alternative attempts to concentrate future development while protecting rural
character and environmental features. The Project allows continuation of current
sprawl patterns of settlement.

Even these maps understate the *relative* degree of change, however, which may
prove to be more important both for social and ecological reasons. Map 10.3 shows
the relative change in housing density from 1990 to build-out of the Project, and
Map 10.4 shows the relative change for the Alternative. In this case the Project
clearly has a much more pervasive influence on the landscape and is likely to affect
a wider range of WHR types.

Quantitative analysis of changes for specific WHR types confirms this conclu-

TABLE 10.2   Reduction in Habitat Area
under Each of the El Dorado County General Plan Alternatives

WHR Class (Habitat Type)	Project (low)	Project (high)	Alternative (low)	Alternative (high)
Annual grassland	38.3%	92.4%	36.6%	48.9%
Blue oak–foothill pine	34.3%	88.5%	35.0%	51.2%
Blue oak woodland	37.0%	94.3%	43.8%	59.3%
Chamise–redshank chaparral	37.1%	86.4%	38.7%	48.7%
Cropland (agricultural)	(42.6%)*	73.7%	(12.7%)*	71.2%
Montane hardwood	20.9%	68.6%	26.5%	40.5%
Valley foothill riparian	54.7%	100%	54.7%	54.7%

*Increase in cropland land use *classification* in average densities below 32 acres per dwelling unit; the actual area of cropland at this density is unlikely to increase because of existing parcelization effects.

sion. Seven of the twenty WHR types experience at least a 50 percent reduction in total area at an average housing density of less than one unit per thirty-two acres, which was selected as a threshold because of its significance for winter deer habitat and because the WHR system assumes a minimum mapping unit of forty acres.[10] The degree of change was also a function of zoning designations, however, because many of the general plan land use designations allow a range of densities depending on further zoning analysis. The maps above are based on the average allowable density, but I also evaluated the effects of adopting either the low or high densities within the designated range. This choice turns out to have a significant effect on the total conversion of WHR types. In fact, adopting the low allowable density under the Alternative results in only one WHR type having at least a 50 percent reduction in total area, while the medium or high zoning designations for that particular WHR type would result in a 99 percent and 100 percent reduction in area, respectively, under the Project.

Table 10.2 summarizes the percentage reduction in habitat area for each of the alternatives. These results make it clear that the effects of a given level of population growth are ultimately a function of both land use designations through the general plan process and zoning designations used to implement the general plan. Annual grassland could be reduced by 92 percent under the Project, for example, if zoning designations support the highest allowable density under the Project. Only 38 percent of the annual grassland will be converted, however, if the lowest allowable density is the basis for build-out. This is comparable to the 37 percent reduction that would occur under the Alternative at the lowest density, and it is below the 49 percent reduction that would occur under the Alternative at the highest density.[11]

Similar policy choices can be made to address the influence of future build-out

TABLE 10.3   Number of Species (Number of Sensitive Species)
Potentially Affected by Habitat Type Conversion

WHR Class (Habitat Type)	Amphibians	Birds	Mammals	Reptiles
Annual grassland	9 (5)	57 (19)	52 (16)	19 (9)
Blue oak–foothill pine	10 (5)	76 (17)	52 (19)	21 (11)
Blue oak woodland	11 (6)	71 (16)	52 (19)	22 (11)
Chamise–redshank chaparral	5 (2)	39 (13)	50 (16)	17 (9)
Cropland*	4 (1)	5 (4)	42 (11)	7 (3)
Montane hardwood	9 (5)	67 (16)	51 (20)	19 (10)
Valley foothill riparian	10 (5)	87 (19)	58 (18)	20 (11)

*Increase in cropland land use *classification* in average densities below 32 acres per dwelling unit; the actual area of cropland at this density is unlikely to increase due to existing parcelization effects.

on the other WHR types shown above. In fact, selection of the Alternative and adoption of zoning designations at the lowest allowable density would reduce conversion of all WHR types to less than 50 percent, except for valley foothill riparian habitat. This habitat—which serves an especially important function because of its double duty as nesting habitat for some species and as a corridor connecting other habitats for a wider variety of species—could then be protected under other general plan policies, the zoning ordinance, and subdivision regulations. A buffer-zone setback could be required for all riparian areas, for example, to protect all riparian habitats (including many that may not be mapped at the level of resolution used in the WHR coverages). We cannot know what to protect and how to protect it, however, unless we go through this type of analysis to determine the *specific* consequences of policies.

All other things being equal, adoption of the Project version of the general plan by El Dorado County Supervisors—together with their general support for the highest allowable development densities for most areas—will result in much more significant effects on the biodiversity of the Sierra Nevada than would have occurred under the Alternative. Table 10.3 shows the potential number of wildlife species that will be detrimentally affected. The numbers of special-status species (threatened, endangered, protected, special concern, or sensitive) are listed in parenthesis, based on the WHR model database version 5.2.[12]

The total number of species that could be affected by human settlement is a function of the degree of overlap among the WHR types above, since many species (in particular, mammals and birds) have home ranges and life cycle habits that transcend multiple WHR types. The highest number for each wildlife type (amphibians, birds, mammals, reptiles) across all of the WHR types is nevertheless a minimum estimate of the number of species likely to be significantly affected: 11 amphibian species, 87 bird species, 58 mammal species, and 22 reptile species. Of these, at least 5 amphibian species, 19 bird species, 20 mammal species, and 11 reptile species are currently facing threats to their viability and have been officially recognized under either the federal ESA, the California ESA, or the California Native Plant Protection Act, or have been listed as "sensitive" by the Forest Service or Bureau of Land Management.

Remarkably, these sensitive species generally received no special attention in either the El Dorado County General Plan or the mitigation measures adopted under CEQA in the EIR.[13] This is not atypical in rapidly growing exurban jurisdictions: Nevada County also failed to conduct this type of analysis, and these two counties have more planning staff and resources than any other Sierra Nevada county except Placer. Rural counties basically ignore this issue unless the ESA forces them to address it, yet it is their very failure to address it at this stage that could lead to future restrictions under the Act. When that occurs, local political leaders will then invariably blame the federal government for intervening in local land use decisions in a way that threatens the local economy! Such an intervention is preventable, however, with systematic analysis of the general plan itself.

This WHR-level analysis, which uses only first-order indicators of change in total land area, should be viewed as merely a first step in a comprehensive assessment of the effects of development on biodiversity. Additional analysis of the *spatial* characteristics of each habitat type—including its edge-to-edge relationships both to human settlement and other habitat types—is also necessary in order to develop a biodiversity protection system that would incorporate the principles of conservation biology and landscape ecology. As described above, the framework developed by the California Department of Forestry and Fire Protection would be a good place to start for this type of analysis. I was unable to complete such an analysis as part of SNEP, but Greg Greenwood has been working with a local task force in El Dorado County to complete a similar analysis at a finer level of spatial resolution (Greenwood 1997). There is presently no requirement that the county undertake such analyses, however, and, where such analyses have been completed, there is no requirement that decision makers act on their findings. Analysis of these effects therefore depends at this time on either enlightened leadership at the local or state level or a crisis similar to that which finally led to the Natural Communities Conservation Planning program (NCCP) effort to preserve coastal sage scrub habitat (Mann and Plummer 1995; Stevens 1996; 1997a). Ironically, the latter is widely touted as preferable to the harsher restrictions that could be imposed under the ESA—yet it is clearly less preferable than preventative planning.

In addition to Holland and WHR classifications, moreover, there are many rare and endemic plants whose distribution is more confined and whose precise locations are not well documented. Jim Shevock's analysis of these plants shows that there are approximately 405 vascular plant taxa endemic to the Sierra Nevada, fully 218 of which are considered rare. In addition, 168 other rare taxa are present in the Range of Light. The Sierra Nevada has 50 percent of California's flora represented on only 20 percent of the state's land base (Shevock 1996). Shevock generated tables showing the spatial distribution of these taxa at the level of WHR types, river basins, counties, and 7.5-minute U.S. Geological Survey quad sheets. The latter data are now available in digital form and can serve as the basis for more systematic field investigations by private, local, state, and federal biologists evaluating the potential effects of human settlement and land use. This represents a level of spatial resolution beyond that of my general plan analysis. Shevock's data show that El Dorado County has 103 taxa, 89 of which are Sierran endemics and 45 of which are rare taxa. In fact, five of those are endemic to El Dorado County (700). Only these have received detailed treatment by the county in the general plan process, for they have additional legal protections at the state or federal level (Deck 1993). Nevada County has no special programs to protect rare and endemic plants, although it has four species that are endemic to the county and fifty-five considered rare. Nevada County has 75 plant taxa and 59 Sierran endemics.[14] Their distribution and the likely effects of future development were not evaluated in the Nevada County General Plan update.

CARRYING CAPACITY AND "FAIR SHARE" HABITAT PROVISION

The debate over a maximum build-out population under the Nevada County General Plan reflected social values and the political consequences of choosing different numbers as the ultimate cap on growth in the county. These figures were not, however, based on systematic analysis of constraints on development that could serve as the basis for establishing a true carrying-capacity limitation for human settlement. The presumption has instead been that the allowable build-out growth under a given general plan will still be below the true carrying capacity of the region, making any build-out cap under a given general plan merely an interim limitation on future development. This approach reflects the frontier ethic that underlies growth machine philosophy: land only has value for exchange purposes, and Nature only has value as a commodity, a viewpoint inconsistent with an ecological view of Nature and its relationship to Culture. We must consider a more appropriate approach based on limits to growth and carrying capacity.

Carrying capacity is a concept well understood both in ecological and social contexts. In ecological contexts it refers to the capacity of a given environment to support a population of a species under specified conditions. The population may depend on a variety of habitat conditions, for example, which in turn are a function of soil conditions, nutrient loadings, sunlight, rainfall, and other natural factors. Those factors may affect the maximum level of the population through direct means, such as by limiting grazing forage for an herbivore, or indirectly, such as by limiting the availability of prey for a carnivore by limiting grazing forage for an herbivore. Social crowding may also affect carrying capacity as it affects reproductive behavior and social behavior, such as aggression, among members of the population. Classic ecological models of carrying capacity demonstrate that populations that overshoot their carrying capacity may degrade their environment to the point that carrying capacity of the area is lowered, resulting in a lower population level after post-overshoot stabilization (Krebs 1978). These models have been the basis both for understanding ecological phenomena and managing resources such as fisheries (McEvoy 1986).

The extension of these models to social systems has generated considerable controversy. The most famous is the Club of Rome's 1972 study, *Limits to Growth,* which argued that human population growth threatened to exceed the carrying capacity of the planet through overconsumption of resources (Meadows et al. 1972). That perspective has been challenged by many economists, however, who argue that social systems can respond to resource scarcity by substituting technology, labor, or other resources for the exhausted resource (Howe 1979; Dasgupta and Heal 1979). The leading proponent of this viewpoint is Julian Simon, who claims that human population is "the ultimate resource" and that "natural resources and energy are getting less scarce, pollution in the U.S. has been decreasing, the world's food supply is improving, [and that] population growth has long term benefits" (Simon 1981, cover). His position has in turn been challenged most eloquently by Herman Daly, whose *Steady-State Economics* remains the definitive book on the topic by an ecological economist (1991). Donella Meadows and some of her Club of Rome colleagues also updated their 1972 study in 1992 with the book *Beyond the Limits,* in which they shifted their emphasis from resource scarcity to the negative externalities associated with overpopulation (Meadows et al. 1992).

I will not attempt to resolve this global debate here. Instead, I want to draw attention to the importance of carrying capacity as a concept that has clear applicability to land and resource planning and management in specific places where some of the resources that may limit development are nonsubstitutable. In particular, this is relevant for preserving native biological diversity at the level of communities and populations. As Logan and Molotch (1987) and Sax (1971) have noted, land is a unique resource (and commodity) in that every point on the landscape is in a unique spatial relationship to every other point. This feature of land makes land economics different from resource economics: substitutability is constrained by location, making some locations more valuable in the marketplace regardless of similarities in soils, slope, size, and so on. Commodity outputs produced on those lands may be substitutable in the market, and the same principle may make some levels of biodiversity protection substitutable, for example, within a single species across space and time. Communities and populations are, however, tied to particular places and have location-specific structural and functional relationships that seriously limit their transferability across space and time.

Consequently, we may face some "hard" limits to growth in specific places, meaning that they cannot be modified through further investments of labor, capital, or resources. Other factors influencing carrying capacity may be "soft," meaning that they can be modified through substitution as a function of the economics of technology. This is why the "buildable lot" concept is an economic, rather than physical, concept. The history of urbanization is full of such substitutions, and the history of development is largely one of overcoming "soft" constraints. Small parcels can still generate large profits if the value of locational advantage warrants investments in high-rise steel skyscrapers; distant oil deposits may still be transported to markets if their value is high enough to warrant the investment and risk. This could be true even if the markets for those resources fully internalized their environmental externalities.

The same cannot be said for biodiversity: there is only so much valley foothill riparian habitat in the Sierra Nevada, and build-out according to the El Dorado County Plan Project Description threatens to convert 100 percent of it to human settlement with a density of at least one dwelling unit per 32 acres. The consequences of that development pattern could include further declines and even extirpation of local populations of some portion of the 175 amphibian, bird, mammal, and reptile species found in the valley foothill riparian habitat type. Already 53 of these species are considered sensitive. The El Dorado County resident and deep ecology philosopher George Sessions argues that we need to "draw the line" and establish a carrying capacity for the Sierra Nevada. He and many other Sierra Nevada residents also argue that our current policies are accommodationist and fail to address the underlying problem of population growth, which is driving species extinctions throughout the world (Sessions 1996). Other Sierra Nevada residents have criticized my own proposals to reduce the effects of human settlement on the grounds that reducing the effects will simply defer full recognition of the consequences of growth.[15]

I agree with Sessions on the point of establishing a "hard" carrying capacity for the Sierra Nevada. I would do so based on *effects*, however, rather than population levels. It remains true that good design, coupled with intelligent infrastructure, can support many more people than poor design and resource-intensive infrastructure systems. Accordingly, we should define limits to growth based on achievement of environmental thresholds both within the region and through the ecological footprint of consumption patterns and infrastructure system operation.

The place to start on that is to protect Holland vegetation communities and WHR types in sufficient number, size, and spatial distribution so as to maintain a healthy, functioning ecological system. That is clearly not happening now.

It is also not going to happen if we continue to rely on local governments to "do the right thing." We must instead create strong incentives for them to protect biodiversity, for the loss of biodiversity has regional, state, national, and global consequences. The same arguments that we use in the Amazon rain forest apply to the Sierra Nevada foothills: people should protect biodiversity, even if that requires them to modify their settlement patterns and economic activities in ways that will no longer maximize their own short-term economic gain. Both the carrot and the stick must be employed to protect biodiversity. The carrot can take the form of technical assistance, tax incentives, and possible "bonus" development credits for exceeding protection targets. The stick must take the form of state and federal regulations enforceable by both agencies and communities of interest monitoring biodiversity protection.

Already a clear precedent for this type of approach exists in local land use planning law, in the area of exclusionary zoning and requirements in state law for the "fair share" provision of affordable housing by all the state's communities. The fair-share obligation arose from the Mount Laurel, New Jersey, discrimination case described by David Kirp, John Dwyer, and Larry Rosenthal in their 1995 book, *Our Town: Race, Housing, and the Soul of Suburbia.* Fair-share requirements compel local jurisdictions to provide adequate affordable housing proportionate to each community's projected absorption of a state or region's future population growth. This limits the use of exclusionary zoning, which could otherwise be used by communities in a discriminatory way. The Mount Laurel cases specifically revolved around racial discrimination, but class discrimination is also intimately bound together with race when it comes to exclusionary zoning practices in suburbs (Kirp et al. 1995).

Today California planning law specifically requires only the housing element of each jurisdiction's general plan to be updated every five years, and every community has a fair-share housing target in specific income classes that it must demonstrate it is trying to meet. I have been involved in this effort over the past few years as a member of the board of directors of a nonprofit community development corporation called Common Ground Communities, whose tax-exempt status is based on helping Nevada County meet its burden for providing affordable housing. Providing land use and zoning designations that are not exclusionary is only part of the puzzle; communities must also assist the market to ensure that affordable housing actually gets built. This challenge therefore offers an apt basis for structuring a fair-share requirement for the provision of habitats, vegetative communities, and ecological function: it requires both top-down regulation and bottom-up institutional support for successful implementation.[16] Distribution of such responsibilities across multiple local jurisdictions has also been a central feature of the NCCP process in Southern California, which involves dozens of cities and five counties (Stevens 1996; 1997a). The "ends" of policy are then set by regional, state, and/or federal authorities while the "means" of achieving those policy goals are determined at a more local level.

A fair-share requirement for the provision of protected ecological values would actually be easier to achieve than affordable housing goals, however, for the de facto result in the absence of affirmative action by a local jurisdiction would be achievement of the goal. Protecting habitats, in other words, may be as simple as ensuring that no development occurs on them. That is within the purview of local governments through well-crafted general plans, zoning ordinances, and subdivision regulations. Protecting habitats and ecological functions in a given jurisdiction may also conflict with other policy goals, however, if one relies only on regulatory tools. Acquisition strategies and coordinated management efforts—in particular, with other land and resource management agencies—may be necessary in order to reduce those conflicts. These agencies could trade some public lands of low ecological value but high development potential for other lands with low development potential and high ecological value, for example, thereby expanding the total land base in public ownership and protection while simultaneously promoting economic development. Some of the economic benefits from development can then be the basis for funding (e.g., through increment tax financing) the acquisition and management of what Mark Shaffer has called a "lifelands" system of publicly owned ecological reserves and ecologically functional private lands (1994).

None of this will happen, however, unless a systematic assessment of ecological function and gaps in protection is completed first. We should therefore create strong incentives for local jurisdictions to participate in such efforts by providing technical assistance by state and federal agencies and universities. The SNEP data, for example, presents a perfect opportunity for systematic application of these ideas, but local jurisdictions presently have neither the resources nor the motivation to use it. The NCCP process is the model; what is missing are the funding and the legal incentives that brought the key players to the table in the case of Southern California coastal sage scrub. State and federal funding for technical assistance to Sierra Nevada cities and counties would create an incentive for participation and avoid the political costs of having such participation appear to be another "unfunded mandate" that must compete with other local priorities for general fund appropriations. Habitat conservation planning through an NCCP process should not be pitted against libraries, sheriff's deputies, or fire protection. Multiagency teams should instead be funded through existing state and federal agencies who can work with local land use planning staff to develop multispecies habitat conservation plans that reflect both local priorities and ecological realities.

Fair-share requirements should dictate *what* must be achieved, but they do not have to prescribe *how* those targets will be met. This approach gives local communities some discretion as to how they meet state and federal goals.

We cannot rely exclusively on voluntary participation from local jurisdictions, however; the state must also compel participation by law and regulation. Those jurisdictions that do not meet state-mandated fair-share targets must face potential cease-and-desist orders from state agencies with the power to stop issuance of building permits, just as Regional Water Quality Control Boards can now stop sewage hookups for noncompliance with water quality regulations. Moreover, third parties should be given the authority to challenge nonenforcement by state agencies under both planning law and CEQA. Provision of fair-share ecological functions should be deemed adequate mitigation under CEQA, but failure to meet such responsibilities should presumptively reflect inadequate mitigation. Third-party litigation under CEQA could then delay implementation of any development project that could affect ecological functions if a local jurisdiction has failed to provide fair-share habitat in its general plan. This will create a strong constituency for sound planning among developers, who will want to ensure that general plans protect adequate habitat in order to avoid costly CEQA litigation.

The most appropriate place to address that provision would be in the "conservation" and "open space" elements of the general plan, which currently tend to focus on maintaining commodity production ("conservation") and recreational opportunities ("open space"). Potential effects on species listed under the ESA are generally the only ecological effects considered in general plan updates, and it is clear from the Nevada County and El Dorado County General Plan case studies that CEQA has failed to ensure systematic assessment of effects or mitigation even for these listed species (Duane 1996a; Thomas 1995a; 1995b). Conservation and open space elements must therefore address the complex and difficult problem of ensuring ecologically functional landscapes.

The SNEP effort developed an analytic tool that can help jump-start consideration of these suggestions by California Biodiversity Council members, the state legislature, and local governments. Buried in "Selecting Biodiversity Management Areas," the last chapter of volume 2 of the *Final Report to Congress*, Frank Davis and his colleagues offer a useful basis for identifying those subwatersheds that can best achieve representation of Holland vegetation communities across the Sierra Nevada (or a subregion within the Sierra Nevada) at minimum expense in land area, opportunity cost, social or economic disruption, or a variety of other indicators (Davis et al. 1996). The analytic technique is built on "a conservation strategy whose objective is to represent all native plant communities in areas where the primary management goal is to sustain native biodiversity," and those areas are referred to as "biodiversity management areas" (BMAs). These are defined as "specially designated public or private lands with an active ecosystem management plan in operation whose purpose is to contribute to regional maintenance of native genetic, species and community levels of biodiversity, and the processes that maintain that biodiversity" (1503). The BMA selection model is spatially explicit, and it allows a multiobjective function that can reflect different constraints on BMA selection, different weights for each of those constraints, different boundaries around the subregion being used to select BMAs, and different representation objectives for the subregion. It therefore allows policymakers to conduct explicit tradeoff and sensitivity analyses.

Application of the BMA model in the SNEP study region shows, as the GAP analysis suggested, how poorly public lands now protect the incredible biodiversity of the Range of Light. The SNEP report documents the results of twenty-three different BMA strategy alternatives to achieve target-level representation of either 10 or 25 percent of the current distribution of all Holland vegetation communities across three subregions (north, central, south) of the Sierra Nevada. Initial BMA area assignments by the model vary from zero land to all park and wilderness lands in the GAP analysis classification system (Davis and Stoms 1996; Davis et al. 1996). The total BMA area required to meet the objectives in the subregions ranged from 555,427 acres (868 square miles) to 1.88 million acres (2,938 square miles) under this range of conditions. This upper estimate is more than the total land area in Yosemite, Sequoia, and Kings Canyon National Parks combined (1.628 million acres) (Palmer 1988, 293). Notably, solutions that depended only on public land not only required more land area to meet the BMA objectives, but were generally unable to meet the objective for many Holland types because of inadequate representation of those types on any public lands in the Sierra Nevada (Davis et al. 1996, Table 58.1, p. 1509). This highlights the importance of addressing the relationship between public and private lands in any conservation strategy designed to protect biodiversity and ecological function.

The BMA selection model is only a starting point for biodiversity planning, but it is an important start. SNEP scientists Jerry Franklin and Jo Ann Fites-Kaufmann used different criteria to develop strategies for maintaining ecological structure and function in late successional/old growth forests, for example, that resulted in a model network of Areas of Late-Successional Emphasis on the public lands of the Sierra Nevada (1996). Fisheries biologist Peter Moyle developed a parallel concept of Aquatic Diversity Management Areas for the hydrologic network of the Sierra Nevada that included factors such as an Index of Biotic Integrity (1996b). The Areas of Late-Successional Emphasis framework could guide public land and resource managers in their forest management practices, while the Aquatic Diversity Management Areas network might primarily influence decisions by water policymakers. A separate mapping effort led by Connie Millar identified Ecologically Significant Areas and Significant Natural Areas on public lands based on other criteria (Millar et al. 1996). Each of these approaches has strengths differ-

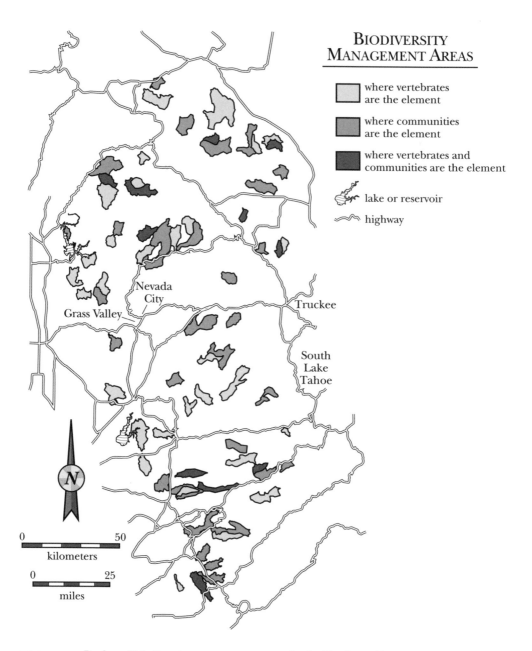

MAP 10.5. Preferred biodiversity management areas in the Northern Sierra, Gold Country, and Mother Lode subregions based on the distribution of vertebrates, plant communities, or both.

Within the map:

BIODIVERSITY
MANAGEMENT AREAS

where vertebrates
are the element

where communities
are the element

where vertebrates and
communities are the element

lake or reservoir

highway

Nevada
City

Grass Valley

Truckee

South
Lake
Tahoe

0   50
kilometers

0   25
miles

N

ent from those of the BMA model, and all can contribute to the development of an ecologically based conservation strategy for protecting biodiversity. They are not mutually exclusive.

These approaches will, however, remain merely academic models unless there is an institutional framework for their implementation. That is where my proposed revisions to general plan and CEQA law (to compel development of an NCCP effort in local land use planning *before* a crisis occurs) could put these models to work in the field. Public land and resource management agencies should also be part of that effort in order to minimize the total social and economic costs of meeting these ecological objectives. The agencies must also make those ecological objectives their primary management goal, for public good will not be adequately provided on the private lands alone. The public lands must therefore take the lead in protecting these public values.

The SNEP team explored the relationship between these approaches (together with other analyses focusing on fire risk and erosion risk associated with forest management) in a limited case study of El Dorado County and the Eldorado National Forest (SNEP 1996, Vol. 1: 87–89). Our effort illustrates that models and all analytic tools are ultimately only heuristic devices for exploring relationships and identifying problems in representation and goal specification (Steinitz 1990). The availability of digital GIS coverages for the SNEP region, however, allows us to complete powerful analyses that would be difficult if not impossible in most other rapidly growing exurban landscapes. As a result, we have the potential to build on the intellectual capital of SNEP in the Sierra Nevada to implement a proactive and preventative NCCP effort before an endangered species crisis compels preparation of a more formal HCP under the mandate of the Endangered Species Act. Such an effort must go beyond local jurisdictions, however, to encompass the full Range of Light. Regional, state, and federal involvement is necessary.

As Bob Twiss has suggested, a good GIS can serve as the focal point of a "war room" where all of the stakeholders in a planning exercise can interact with and debate the meaning of information using visually powerful maps and analytically powerful spatial models (1995). Research by Judy Innes and others emphasizes the importance of shared experience with data, assumptions, models, and each other in order to generate the conditions for the social construction of a problem and its possible solutions in a way that may represent "communicative rationality" (Innes 1991; 1995; 1996a; Innes et al. 1994). The SNEP team members who participated in the El Dorado case study (Frank Davis, Doug Leisz, Jonathan Kusel, Greg Greenwood, and myself) found that our interaction with the various data layers and models generated a number of questions about their validity in a localized planning context. However, we also came up with a number of creative solutions to apparent conflicts that would have been unlikely to emerge through independent application of the different models. Planning processes that use good information and good technical tools are likely to generate better solutions through the consensus-oriented "communicative rationality" planning model described by Innes (Innes 1995). The focus of those processes should be on defining the *means* of achieving already specified *ends,* however, which should primarily reflect ecological criteria.[17]

PLANNING PRINCIPLES FOR
MANAGING EXURBAN GROWTH

Concern about the effects of unmanaged population growth has spread throughout the Sierra Nevada in the 1990s, gaining a visible place in the panoply of issues featured in Tom Knudson's "Sierra in Peril" series in 1991, the Sierra Now conference in 1992, the *Los Angeles Times*'s front-page "Sierra Nueva" article in 1996 (Clifford 1996), and the SNEP report in 1996. The Sierra Business Council (SBC) also conducted research on the issue in 1996–97, releasing an excellent and accessible report in 1997 titled *Planning for Prosperity: Building Successful Communities in the Sierra Nevada* (Griffith 1997). The organization was motivated to complete a "planning audit" both because of concerns about planning practice and inefficient government bureaucracy (expressed by the SBC membership, which is composed primarily of environmentally oriented businesses within the Sierra Nevada) and the negative effects of dominant patterns of development on the assets measured in the SBC's previous *Sierra Wealth Index* (Blake 1993–97; Grubb 1995–97; Sierra Business Council 1996; Marois 1996b; Christensen 1996c). According to the council's report,

> More than any fact or figure . . . the dramatic beauty and majesty of the Sierra landscape define our region in the public's imagination and in the minds of business owners throughout the Sierra. In a recent survey of Sierra Nevada business owners, 82% identified "the high quality of life" as one of the most significant advantages of doing business in this region. Considerations like "fewer regulations than urban areas" and "lower cost of doing business" were ranked by only 8 percent and 11 percent as a significant advantage of doing business in the region. When asked to define "quality of life," business owners identified "the rural character of the overall region," "access to high quality wildlands," and "the landscape surrounding my immediate community." (Sierra Business Council 1997, 7)

The SBC report then describes ten "principles for sound development" for "building successful communities." These principles primarily address the policy goals that should guide local land use planning and desirable patterns of development, rather than the planning process itself:

Safeguard the rural character of the Sierra Nevada by maintaining a clear edge
between town and country.
Preserve historic assets.
Build to create enduring value and beauty.
Enhance the economic vitality of our small towns through ongoing reinvestment
in the downtown core.
Anticipate and address the housing needs of all community residents.
Conserve and showcase each community's natural assets.
Maintain the economic productivity of our region's agricultural lands and forests.
Do not place people and structures in harm's way.
Maintain the health of the natural systems which support life in the Sierra Nevada.
Expand local and regional transportation options to reduce traffic congestion and
the intensity of public dependence on the automobile.

The SBC report also lays out six "principles for involving and serving business and
the public" that support "building customer satisfaction" with the local land use
planning *process:*

Invest public resources and direct private investment to maintain and expand
each community's social, natural and financial capital.
Integrate land use planning with other planning for community development.
Create efficient and meaningful ways to engage the public in shaping local land
use plans.
Ensure that general plans and plan implementation documents are thorough,
current and consistent.
Build customer satisfaction through efficient and predictable plan
implementation.
Reach across jurisdictions and plan cooperatively for the future.

Together, the principles in the SBC report offer a useful basis for evaluating
current planning practice, planning institutions and processes, and the development patterns that result under them. In many ways they echo a set of recommendations I first made at the Sierra Now conference in 1992, although my
principles are more specific and do not address the efficiency or the unpredictability of the planning process itself. I also did not need to reach agreement
with a committee of SBC members, so I could afford to take a stronger position
than the SBC. Many of the SBC members would probably support many of my
exurban planning principles but may disagree with some of the specific institutional mechanisms I recommend for achieving them:

Villages and towns should have distinct boundaries, be spatially separated from
each other so as to retain community identity, and their scale should be no
larger in either population or physical area than is considered desirable by
area residents.

Compact, community-centered development in villages, small towns, and distributed exurban clusters should be encouraged instead of widely dispersed, sprawling development in the traditional pattern of one- to five-acre lots.

Infrastructure investments should encourage a pattern of higher density development in clusters, reducing the need for road grading, long travel distances, and the fragmentation of open space that would otherwise occur through large lot development with private on-site well water and septic systems.

Development should be timed to occur only when adequate infrastructure exists to handle the effects of new growth without degrading the quality of service for existing residents. This concurrency criteria will ensure that growth "pays its own way" without burdening local governments financially.

Transportation systems planning should be integrated with land use planning to reduce trips, travel distance, and emissions. Because of the lower densities and greater distances in rural areas, this may require approaches very different from those applied in a metropolitan context. Any new-town developments should reduce, rather than exacerbate, existing air quality problems associated with long, drive-alone commute patterns to nearby metropolitan centers.

Clustered developments should be built around adequately sized open space for the protection of habitat and water quality. Wildlife corridors and linked trails should connect these areas, and they should be part of an overall habitat protection network structured within a nested hierarchy of habitat, watershed, and ecosystem scales.

Land use policies should provide mechanisms for transferring development credits from highly sensitive lands (which may presently be zoned for more intensive development than is appropriate, given the ecological sensitivity of the site or lack of infrastructure) to lands suitable for higher density (e.g., areas on the fringe of existing development with adequate water, sewers, and roads).

Environmental considerations and public values, such as aesthetic values, rather than existing general plan and zoning designations, should be the primary determinants of where future development will be encouraged and restricted. Reduction of any perceived vested rights in development can be addressed by establishment of a market for transferable development credits and the purchase of conservation easements.

A two-tier zoning approach should be developed for local cities and counties that presently have general plans and zoning designations allowing significant development in environmentally sensitive areas. This approach would allow the transfer of density credits from entitlement zones, where an inappropriately high level of development is presently allowed, to development zones, where development will be encouraged by the new planning guidelines.

Existing-use zoning should be used in areas where existing agriculture, timber, or open space uses are to be maintained. Minimum lot sizes adequate to maintain the desired activity should encourage such use, and those minima will depend on both the characteristics of that use and environmental factors. No development should be allowed in areas with steep slopes, unstable soils, wetlands, or critical habitats for threatened or endangered species.

Serious consideration should be given to establishment of a target carrying capacity for the Sierra Nevada and its subregions, watersheds, counties, and communities. This ultimate capability of a region to accommodate continued growth and urbanization is a function of environmental constraints, financial costs of providing needed services, and social desires. The latter are culturally defined, and the community character desired by residents of exurbia is clearly not urban or metropolitan in character.

Intergovernmental cooperation must be improved within exurban regions, through either simultaneous consideration of general plans or some regional integration. Regional integration may occur through bilateral or multilateral agreements between adjacent or overlapping jurisdictions or the establishment of a regional authority.[18] Flexible arrangements are encouraged over top-down control from regional government, but some redefinition of existing jurisdictional boundaries may be appropriate.[19]

Legal institutions must recognize that private property rights entail important public responsibilities, and that the "right" to develop is a privilege conferred by the action of the general public that is conditional upon meeting certain obligations. This community conception of the relationship between private property development and public values should be the basis for comprehensive planning in exurban areas.

We must carefully consider the relationship between the *scale* of urban settlements and the quality of experience, sense of place, and community character that its residents and visitors attribute to it. Scale matters to the quality of life in exurbia; if it did not, its residents would not have chosen to live in these communities.[20]

Planners must address the conflict between these principles and prevailing patterns of development in the exurban landscape through innovation and creativity. The specific form of planning practice will therefore vary from community to community, from land use to land use, and from issue to issue. In combination, however, these principles can guide exurban growth and protect the cultural and ecological values of the "middle landscape"—while still accommodating much of the population pressure now pushing beyond the metropolitan fringe into exurbia.

LESSONS FROM LOS ANGELES:
THE LIMITED POWER OF PRINCIPLES

We should not, however, be too sanguine about the likely effects of these policies. Principles and policies have been a part of planning practice at least since Ebenezer Howard published *To-Morrow, a Peaceful Path to Social Reform* in 1898, which was republished as *Garden Cities of To-Morrow* in 1902 (Kostof 1991, 75). Howard's vision responded to the dramatic increase in Europe's population from 180 million to 400 million in the nineteenth century (Calthorpe 1986), which also inspired responses by the landscape architects Frederick Law Olmsted, Andrew Jackson Downing, and Robert C. Phillips (Kostof 1991, 73–75). Their legacy was carried into the twentieth-century design of suburban communities in the United States by Olmsted, architect Ray Unwin, and the visionaries Patrick Geddes, Benton MacKaye, and Lewis Mumford (15–16). Other notable new-town designers have included Toni Garnier and Le Corbusier, who advocated modernist visions that emphasized centralization and control, and Frank Lloyd Wright, whose low-density vision of decentralized single-family homes has dominated twentieth-century American settlement patterns (Calthorpe 1986).

"For Howard," says architect Peter Calthorpe, "the focus and building block of the community was the neighborhood; for Corbusier, it was the high-rise; and for Wright, the individual home and the family that it represented" (217–18). Calthorpe himself is the author of the 1993 book *The Next American Metropolis: Ecology, Community, and the American Dream,* and he is part of a contemporary movement of architects and planners who have organized themselves as the "Congress of New Urbanism" (Calthorpe 1993). Other leaders of this neotraditional movement include Andres Duany and Elizabeth Plater-Zyberk, whose 1991 book, *Towns and Town-Making Principles,* has guided the successful development of Seaside, Florida, and the Kentlands, Maryland (Duany and Plater-Zyberk 1991; Katz 1994; Sexton 1995). Calthorpe's "transit-oriented development" at Laguna West, near Sacramento, has been less successful and it illustrates the conflict that often exists between market realities and design principles (Southworth 1997). Good ideas on paper do not always work in real communities on the ground.

That conflict is best demonstrated in Mike Davis's brilliant history of planning in Los Angeles. His 1990 social history and cultural critique, *City of Quartz: Excavating the Future in Los Angeles,* explains the political economy of Southern California development and how the "Octopus" of nineteenth-century California (the Central Pacific and then the Southern Pacific railroad) (Norris 1901) has been replaced by a twentieth-century version in the land development industry (Mike Davis 1990, 130). His most sobering story, though, is told in two other pieces titled "Cannibal City: Los Angeles and the Destruction of Nature" (1994) and "How Eden Lost Its Garden: A Political History of the Los Angeles Landscape" (1996), which were published separately as chapters in edited volumes.

To quote noted philosopher Yogi Berra, it felt like "deja vu all over again" when I read Mike Davis's work. Much of what the SBC and I propose for the Sierra Nevada today was tried first in Los Angeles a half century ago, and the landscape of Southern California does not conjure the image of "good planning" in the minds of most Americans. It certainly doesn't in the Sierra Nevada, where the former demon of "Los Angelization" has been replaced sequentially by demonized images of San Jose, Sacramento, and now Roseville. Recall that Nevada County's new planning director, hired in 1970 to quell the minority revolt against unfettered parcelization in the late 1960s, came from an Orange County community that had grown by 1,000 percent during the previous four years. Nevada County Supervisor William Thomas nevertheless described Fountain Valley then as "one of the most well planned communities in its area," despite (or perhaps because of) the wholesale conversion of a rich agricultural landscape into a neat and well-ordered bedroom community (*Union* 1970d). The planning experience of Southern California is therefore directly relevant to both the history and future of planning in the Sierra Nevada. Both are deeply embedded in a similar institutional and cultural context.

Charles Mulford Robinson first outlined the deficiencies in Los Angeles's provision of open space and parks in a 1907 report to the Los Angeles Municipal Art Commission. His proposals called for the city to "become a land developer in its own right" (Mike Davis 1996, 161), however, which even the Progressives were unwilling to take on in the face of downtown power and the financial gains to be realized through real estate syndication. Like many of us in the Sierra Nevada today, Robinson argued that a failure to maintain the desirable qualities of the Los Angeles landscape could lead to the incidence of "more beautiful" cities gaining an economic advantage over Los Angeles in the future. Within two decades, however, another 2 million people (the equivalent of Philadelphia) had moved into the region. Parks comprised just .6 percent of the metropolis by 1928 (162).

The design firm of Olmsted Brothers and Bartholomew and Associates (predecessor to the consulting firm that developed Nevada County's general plan in the 1990s) was then hired by "the most distinguished citizens committee in Los Angeles history," and it transmitted its final report to local governmental officials in March 1930. The Citizens' Committee on Parks, Playgrounds, and Beaches claimed that the situation was "so disquieting as to make it highly expedient to impress upon the public the present crisis in the welfare of Los Angeles."[21] As Davis describes it, "Accessible open space was the foundation of an economy capitalized on climate, sports, and outdoor leisure. But the region's scenic beauty was being eroded on all sides by rampant, unregulated private development. Los Angeles's future prosperity was directly threatened by the increasing discrepancy between tourists' buoyant expectations and their disillusioning experiences in the Land of Sunshine" (160). This description sounds a lot like the SBC reports of 1996 and 1997; substitute "the Sierra Nevada" for "Los Angeles" to hear the echo.

It is also a theme that has been repeated every generation since in Southern California. The 1930 report failed to generate significant change, but by World War II the impending expansion of Los Angeles into the San Fernando Valley presented a new opportunity to apply sound land use planning principles to an as-yet-unplatted landscape. (In 1930, in contrast, 175 square miles of Los Angeles lay already subdivided but undeveloped because of the speculative frenzy and precipitous collapse of the 1920s oil boom [163].) Planning Commissioner Robert Alexander and Planning Director Charles Bennet devised a scheme that would make both Ebenezer Howard and the neotraditional "new urbanists" proud: rather than continue to allow undifferentiated subdivision and development of the valley without reference to either social or ecological values, their proposed zoning strategy "concentrated new development at medium-density levels around sixteen existing suburban nodes permanently separated by eighty-three square miles of citrus and farm greenbelts" (168). This again sounds like much of what many of us advocate today: each of the sixteen town centers "formed a small, compact, self-sustaining community, surrounded and separated from other country towns by agricultural greenbelts."[22]

These were not merely an academic's vision for the "garden cities of tomorrow," however; "greenbelt zoning for the valley was actually passed into law by the city council at the end of the war" (ibid.). It did not last long, however, for "it lacked the broad political support to survive the relentless counterattack of developers and landowners" (169). Land developers simply "obtained options for practically nothing to buy the cheapest land zoned for agricultural use and applied for changes in zone" to residential use.[23] This is perhaps the most sobering lesson of the Los Angeles experience: without strict limitations on business-as-usual, the growth machine can bypass the policies and land use designations of a well-developed general plan and zoning ordinance through piecemeal changes that generate windfall profits. In fact, the plan and zoning designations adopted in 1945 actually increased the likelihood of leapfrog development through their influence on land values. The agriculture-zoned lands were worth less in the marketplace in part because of their zoning designations, creating a greater disparity between market value as raw land and market value after development. The difference was pure profit—some fraction of which could be used to gain the support of a majority of the board of supervisors or the city council. And this is exactly what happened. "By the early 1960s," concludes Davis, "instead of a 'balanced self-sufficient constellation of communities' bordered by greenbelts, the San Fernando

Valley had become a paved-over 'undifferentiated slurb' of nearly one million people" (ibid.). Exchange values had overwhelmed use values once again.

The rhetoric and rationale for good planning also parallels today's debate in the Sierra Nevada, as "the 1945 County Citizens Committee—reminding political leaders that the quality of the recreational landscape was 'the goose that lays our golden eggs'—proposed extensive open-space conservation" in the hills around the Los Angeles basin (171). Once again, however, their warnings were largely unheeded. Davis documents the consequences in the history of postcard imagery of the region, which captures shifting popular images of Southern California:

> Before 1940, the most common postcard image of the Los Angeles region was a sunny panorama of orange groves at the base of snowcapped Mount Baldy. Often a mission or Mission revival residence was included in the foreground. The scene's huge popularity undoubtedly derived from its unification of three classical landscape ambiances: the "wilderness sublime" of the wild mountain, the "Hesiodic idyll" of the well-ordered orchard, and the "romantic nostalgia" of the medieval ruin (or, rather, its local equivalent, the mission). By the mid-1960s, however, the citrus-and-Mount Baldy motif had totally disappeared from the postcard racks. In its place, the most popular postcard view of Southern California had become (and remains today) an image of Mickey Mouse cavorting along Disneyland's Main Street. Old Baldy—now obscured by smog for much of the year—has been replaced by a stucco replica of the Matterhorn.[24]

And so Disneyland's Main Street, modeled after the idealized and romanticized memories of Walt Disney's boyhood town Marceline, Missouri, has replaced the real Main Streets that once existed in the San Fernando Valley, the San Gabriel Valley, and Orange County. "This mock-up in fact idealized the vernacular architecture Disney remembered from his childhood," says Sharon Zukin, in a way that "both restored and invented collective memory." Moreover, Zukin notes, the fantasy "memory" that Disney created "paralleled the creation of a mass consumption society" (1991, 222). Today that image-driven society is homogenizing the exurban landscape in the same way real estate development did in Southern California in the 1950s and 1960s.

Southern California's growth in the 1950s gave us two words relevant to the Sierra Nevada today: *amenity,* which drove the great migration to the promised land in the Mount Baldy postcard (R. Alexander 1966; Nelson 1992), and *sprawl,* which obliterated the postcard landscape and left us only the remnant of Disney's virtual memories (Whyte 1958; Mike Davis 1994). Agricultural land in the San Gabriel Valley fell from 300,000 acres in 1939 to merely 10,000 acres by 1970; bulldozers felled a thousand citrus trees per day in the 1950s (Mike Davis 1996, 170–71). According to Davis, "More than one-third of the surface of the Los Angeles region was dedicated to car-related uses: freeways, streets, parking lots, and driveways" by 1970—totaling 3 billion tons of concrete or 250 tons per resident (171).[25] Physical geography may prevent a similar fate for the Range of Light, but the lessons of Los Angeles loom large for any land-use planning proposals in California.

Planning principles were involved in one more attempt to save the Southern California landscape in 1965, when the landscape architecture and planning firm of Eckbo, Dean, Austin, and Williams completed several studies of the region that predicted the loss of all remaining Mediterranean valleys and foothills along coastal California.[26] The report specifically critiqued local governments and their misuse of zoning powers and a tax system that rewarded speculators and punished farmers, which led to passage of the Williamson Act of 1965. Eckbo, Dean, Austin, and Williams also drew explicit links between sprawl at the fringe of the metropolitan area and urban decay, which Davis (1990) traces more directly to racism and exclusionary zoning practices that supplanted deed restrictions when the latter were declared unconstitutional by the U.S. Supreme Court in 1948. The 1965 report called for greater infill development, public acquisition of parkland, and willingness to "treat the area as a total system of air, land and water relationships, not simply as real estate to be developed."[27]

The landscape architecture and planning firm conceded, however, that development of suitable designs for the region was probably "beyond the capability of [existing] planning processes."[28] Similar calls for reform were made by Ray Dasmann in his 1965 book, *The Destruction of California,* and by Richard Lillard in his 1966 polemic, *Eden in Jeopardy.* Lillard's book was subtitled *Man's Prodigal Meddling with the Environment (the Southern California Experience).* Davis identifies Lillard's contribution as representative of suburban home owner elites trying to defend their property values through exclusionary zoning policies (1990), but that does not make the environmental dimension of Lillard's argument irrelevant. In 1959 fully two-thirds of the Los Angeles landscape was considered urban; by 1995, the fraction had increased by one-fourth to 84 percent (1996, 179). The natural landscape is now an island archipelago in an ocean of urbanization, which threatens both the individual islands and the network.[29]

The most recent wave of resistance to the growth machine has focused on the social strains that have followed the Proposition 13 "tax revolt" in 1978, the effects of Reaganomics, and the dramatic transformation of the global economy. The Los Angeles region has recently reeled under the pressure of defense industry cutbacks, the riots that engulfed the city following the Rodney King police acquittals in 1992, the Northridge earthquake in 1994, and the usual spate of fires and floods. Yet of all the post-riot proposals for rebuilding South Central Los Angeles, only the joint proposal of the Crips and the Bloods specifically addressed the physical space of the region and the need to improve its condition (Laurie 1992; West 1992). The parks deficiency first recognized by Robinson in 1907 was now finally coming home to roost; for all of the "open space" in private backyards in Westwood or the San Fernando Valley, there remains a fundamental inequity in access to open space from South Central or East Los Angeles. East Los Angeles residents must now take their soccer games two hours away to Bureau of Land Management lands in the desert, simply because they do not have enough fields within their neighborhoods (Laidlaw 1992). Once again, the fate of California's wildlands is inextricably linked to the fate of its cities.

The Los Angeles region now evokes a *Bladerunner*-like image of chaos and fragmentation, far from the idyllic scenes that once drew Americans along Route 66 to the promise of the Golden State (Schrag 1998). Ironically, however, futuristic technology may yet allow Hollywood to repackage that image for continuing consumption. The palm trees of In-N-Out Burger stands come to mind: they can be transplanted to any site adjacent to a California freeway, as if it were still the 1950s. The first In-N-Out Burger stand was built in a Southern California suburb in 1948, but by the late 1990s the company's home range had extended into the Sierra Nevada foothills in Auburn (In-N-Out 1996; Yollin 1997). This makes the fate of Los Angeles over the past half century a poignant reminder of one potential future for the Range of (B)Light. The virtual landscape of Disneyland now tries to recreate the real landscape that it destroyed, and the Anaheim City Council turned the city's last remaining orange grove into a parking lot in 1994 (Mike Davis 1996, 179–80). Joni Mitchell was right.

It is all a bit far-fetched today to imagine a similar fate for the amenities of the Sierra Nevada, but I am sure this outcome was also unimaginable to Southern Californians fifty years ago.

POWER, PROCESS, AND THE
PROSPECTS FOR PLANNING

Peter Van Zant's election placed the exchange value-oriented growth machine in a minority position for the first time in the history of any Sierra Nevada county. Van Zant and Sam Dardick were also in a minority in their representation of use values, however, while Fran Grattan and Karen Knecht continued to represent exchange values with equal power. Swing vote Rene Antonson therefore held the reins as he began 1997 as the new chair of the board of supervisors (Marois 1994; Spencer 1994; Willis 1997d). Antonson has been an unpredictable decision maker on land use issues, however, making it difficult to characterize the new planning regime in terms of either interests or ideology. Instead we must turn to an analysis of *power* to understand what has happened since then. The source of power has also proved to be important, for many of the most important planning decisions since January 1997 have turned on the state's institutionalization of tri-lateral controls through legal mandates that have bypassed the local power structure of the growth machine. By the end of 1997, this structure had given the Rural Quality Coalition powerful authority to protect use values in local planning. That result was not solely the result of the institutional structure, of course, but the institutional structure was a *necessary* condition that allowed the RQC to achieve influence.

The year began less auspiciously when the board of supervisors approved a "negative declaration" on a three-to-two vote for the three-hundred-home Dark Horse development near Lake of the Pines. Such a declaration is a statement made under CEQA that the project in question has no likelihood of significant negative environmental effects, making an EIR unnecessary. The EIR, as I have noted above, is both costly and time-consuming—but, more important, it generates information that is then publicly disclosed and can be used to organize political and process-oriented legal opposition to a project. Negative declarations are common in rural and exurban regions, but the Nevada County Board of Supervisors had explicitly promised comprehensive project-level environmental reviews when it weakened the general plan EIR in 1995. Final action by the outgoing board also effectively eliminated such review at the zoning stage, making project-level review even more critical than if adequate environmental analysis had been completed for the general plan and zoning decisions. Consequently, the RQC felt that it had to act in the Dark Horse case—if it did not, it would set a dangerous precedent for future projects.

Van Zant's election had not been enough; Antonson had continued to side with the growth machine to support exchange values without adequate consideration of how use values would be affected. It would also be two more years before the next new supervisor could be seated, making electoral politics irrelevant to the crisis at hand. The RQC retained a leading environmental law firm from San Francisco and quickly filed suit against Nevada County and the Dark Horse developer for failure to comply with CEQA and state planning law. They also joined forces with the Sierra Club, Friends of Placer County, and project neighbors to gather nearly 6,300 signatures on a referendum petition to place the supervisors' action before all Nevada County voters. This far exceeded the 3,821 needed to place the issue on the ballot (Oberholtzer 1997–98; Boivin 1997). It also delayed any further board action on the project until the voters could decide the matter in the June 1998 election. This altered the power relationship between RQC and the developer in the lawsuit.

Within months the RQC had achieved all of its goals on the Dark Horse EIR: the board repealed its ordinance altering the zoning for the project "rather than wait for a June election," and "the developer told the Board . . . to have an EIR prepared" (Boivin 1997). This changed the terms of the CEQA and planning debate in western Nevada County. The RQC clearly had both the organizing capability and the financial resources to challenge land use decisions inconsistent with their interests. This elevated use values to a place at the table equal to that of exchange values. All large projects proposed before the county would henceforth have EIRs prepared on them, no matter how secure the supervisors' vote against preparing one might be (Van Zant 1998).[30]

RQC President Brian Bisnett saw the Dark Horse victory as having set a clear precedent:

> The difference this effort has made on County government is tremendous. We have sent a clear signal to the supervisors, the planning department and the development community that development in Nevada County must be done according to the rules, and that shortcuts, preferential treatment and cursory environmental review will no longer be tolerated. Already two other major South County projects, Quail Lake Estates and Wolf Ranch Estates, have announced that they too will be preparing EIRs. The EIR process will provide everyone who will be affected by these developments the opportunity to participate fully in the discussion of what the impacts will be and how those impacts can be mitigated. This is why EIRs on major projects are so essential—we will all be living with these projects for a long, long time. We need the in-depth studies and the opportunities for public review and comment that an EIR provides to make sure that these projects, which will have such a lasting impact on our homes, our neighborhoods, and our quality of life, are designed as well as they can possibly be.[31]

The lesson had not yet been fully learned, however, for the city of Grass Valley was still actively considering negative declarations for three major annexation agreements as the RQC celebrated its Dark Horse victory. These three projects would nearly double the land area of the city in one fell swoop—despite the inadequacy of the fifteen-year-old general plan. The proposed annexation agreements were based on the new Nevada County General Plan and Zoning Ordinance, but no environmental analysis had yet been completed by the county for build-out of the 643 dwelling units allowed on the 1,573 acres involved: Northstar could add 363 dwelling units on its 760 acres, Loma Rica Ranch could develop 180 dwelling units on 450 acres, and Kenny Ranch (also known as "Hell's Half Acre" because of its unusual soils and profusion of native wildflowers) could build 100 dwelling units on its 363 acres. The three projects were also zoned for a total of 240 acres for mixed-use business park development, 168 acres for industrial use, 42 acres for commercial use, 50 acres for recreational use, and 528 acres of open space. None of the environmental effects of such large-scale development—on transportation, wastewater treatment, or biodiversity—had yet been analyzed. The RQC therefore called on the city of Grass Valley to complete a comprehensive EIR on the cumulative effects of the three annexations. They also wanted a community-based urban design process to ensure community input on the ultimate character of the community. "Instead of leaving the dreams up to the minds of a few developers," suggested RQC member Nik Kelly, "why not have community input on creative future developments?" (1997).

At first the city resisted, arguing that an EIR could be completed for each project after specific development proposals were presented (Johnson 1997; Oberholtzer 1997–98). The RQC persisted, however, suggesting that a referendum signature campaign in Grass Valley would be much easier than for Dark Horse because of the smaller number of registered voters. Grass Valley Mayor Mark Johnson, who was then considering a run for county supervisor against Fran Grattan, was also told in no uncertain terms that the RQC would not support him with either campaign funds or grassroots volunteers if the annexations went forward without an EIR (Oberholtzer 1997–98). The RQC correctly understood that it would be much harder to modify any individual project after annexation if the permissive standards of the county were the basis for the annexation agreement. Future city councils would have their hands tied by the agreement, limiting the potential influence of public input or environmental analysis. Large-scale development on these parcels would also not be possible without access to the city's wastewater treatment plant, and expansion of the treatment plant would not be possible until higher levels of development were likely. These annexations therefore held the potential to generate specific effects on the community by ensuring treatment plant access, as well as to induce significantly more development in the Grass Valley area by making the treatment plant expansion feasible. The annexation agreements were therefore not to be entered into lightly.

In the end, Johnson and the city of Grass Valley accepted the RQC's arguments and/or their power to enforce their position. Johnson also decided for personal reasons not to run for supervisor (Van Zant 1998), weakening the RQC's chances of gaining a majority on the board but ensuring that he would remain a force on the city council to see the annexations through the long EIR process. A second term would also give him time to support a community design process and a comprehensive update of the 1982 general plan before committing to rapid expansion of Grass Valley through large-scale projects. Truckee had just completed a very successful model of such a process for its downtown area, and Grass Valley could learn from Truckee's experience to protect the community's character while growing. In the short run, Johnson was disappointed in the EIR delay because he would not be able to secure several economic development opportunities for the city (1997). In the long run, though, a longer and more complex planning process could lead to articulation of a community vision that could accommodate both exchange and use values—and might therefore be implemented in the twenty-first century through the politics of community. The Nevada County General Plan was clearly an inadequate basis for doing so.

The Rural Quality Coalition finally proved in the 1998 elections that it had the political power to implement its vision, when it secured a clear majority on the board of supervisors that would take office in January 1999. Incumbent Fran Grattan was ousted in the primary election by RQC-backed candidate Bruce

Conklin, a forester and lawyer who received 51 percent of the votes cast. He received 2,647 votes to Grattan's 1,842, while Grass Valley City Council Member Gerard Tassone—who withdrew from the race and threw his support behind Conklin—was supported by 659 voters (13 percent). Grattan therefore received only 36 percent of the votes, an astounding 1,464 fewer votes than her opponents. This meant that beginning January 1999, Dardick, Van Zant, and Conklin would have at least a clear three-to-two majority on the board.

Rene Antonson was also thrown out during the June primary after his former planning commission appointee, Elizabeth Martin, waged a remarkable *write-in* campaign that garnered 39 percent of the votes. The RQC had initially backed Nancy Keil in the race, but she withdrew after the filing deadline had passed. Antonson's other challenger on the ballot was Jeff Ingram, an attorney who favored development of the new town site. Ingram picked up 31 percent of the votes, while Antonson received only 23 percent and Keil continued to be supported by 7 percent. Martin could count on Keil's supporters in the November runoff, but that still left her short of a clear majority. The growth machine, stunned by Grattan's defeat, would now throw its weight behind Ingram—who had paid for 40 percent of his campaign expenses out of his own pocket until just two weeks before the election. He spent $18,279 on the primary, while Martin spent $14,935, Antonson $3,088, and Keil $13,975. Antonson also spent only $3,995 to win his seat the first time, in 1994. The political landscape had changed dramatically since then, though, and no candidate could afford to be as disengaged from either the RQC or the growth machine again. Both financial support and grassroots organizing were now necessary to win an election in Nevada County. Antonson was too unpredictable to be reelected. Martin beat Ingram by only 188 votes in the November 1998 run-off election, winning 4,200 votes (51 percent) to Ingram's 4,012 votes (49 percent). Victory in the close race gave the RQC a solid four-to-one majority on the new board of supervisors in January 1999.

Grattan had again engaged Lisa Zea as a campaign consultant, but this time her campaign's $23,422 was not enough to win. The RQC was both organized and highly motivated, whereas the group had been new to the election process during the Grattan-Weir race of 1994. Conklin raised $35,882 and ended his campaign with a mailer that highlighted votes Grattan had made to increase density within District III. "Is Fran Grattan's 'Smart Growth' really a 'Smart Bomb'?" asked the cover of the campaign piece. Inside, voters were shown an aerial photograph of the Grass Valley area with "upzoned" areas shaded in red. Grattan could no longer count on the rhetoric of moderation to get her into office; this time, she had a voting record to account for. She responded by painting Conklin as an extremist because of his previous support for a "Nuclear-Free Zone" in Nevada County, but her mailer's photo of a violent arrest of a longhaired protester didn't resonate with voters. Her votes on land use, however, were a clear and present danger. The growth machine was left gasping for breath the day after the election. Laurie Oberholtzer, in contrast, answered her telephone with an elated "Are you happy?" She clearly was.

Only time will tell if the Rural Quality Coalition's newfound political power will make a difference on the ground and in the lives of the people who live in the Sierra Nevada. The institutional structure of CEQA and California planning law is, after all, largely procedural. The litigation and referenda strategies that thwarted Dark Horse in 1997 therefore represent only pesky sources of delay to the growth machine unless the RQC is able to make use values the dominant basis for land-use decision-making in local government. For at least two years, 1999 through 2000, the RQC will have the majority it needs on the board of supervisors and the planning commission to accomplish this. Those values will hold political potency only as long as they are held by both a majority of Nevada County citizens and a majority of those with decision-making authority. Accordingly, the RQC must translate its political victories at the polls into lasting political support for changes in policy and land use controls. This will be a more difficult task, but the eco-transformation of the past three decades has generated the conditions for a relationship between Nature and Culture that *should* emphasize use values over exchange values. Nevada County is now the leading test case of whether use values *will* be the basis for decision-making.

CHAPTER ELEVEN

.۸.۷.۸.

Reinhabiting the West

Angry as one may be at what heedless men have done and still do to a noble habitat, one cannot be pessimistic about the West. This is the native home of hope. When it fully learns that cooperation, not rugged individualism, is the quality that most characterizes and preserves it, then it will have achieved itself and outlived its origins. Then it has a chance to create a society to match its scenery.

Wallace Stegner, 1969

The mud is thick and the rain is hard, and visibility is down to less than a few hundred feet. Misty rain drifts by the window and across the canyon in waves, suddenly gusting in a full-force attack on the side of the house. Every square inch on the deck is soaked. To anyone who has moved to western Nevada County in the past eight years, this is an unfamiliar experience. It reminds me of winters past, however, when I sat by the fire in the living room as the thunder and lightning crashed among the pine trees and rolled in a deep echo down the spine of Banner Mountain. This weather is good for the mind but bad for the body; I've been outside to exercise only twice in the past two weeks. I try to take advantage of the gaps between these heavy storm fronts, but they have been few and far between. It looks like a good weekend for reading by the fire.

We've had seven years of drought during the past ten, emptying the reservoirs and drying up the earth and its springs. In some ways, that respite is the reason this current wave of weather has been able to soak into the ground and gather behind the dams before easing down to the floodplains below. Flooding in the larger rivers has not been a big problem so far. What has surprised everyone, however, has been the ease with which small creek beds have become raging torrents and jumped their banks to fill suburban streets and homes in the valley. The town of Roseville, on the western edge of Placer County, has been inundated by floods emanating from what are usually unremarkable trickles with names like Dry Creek. Suddenly there is a new awareness in the neighborhood about the links between the built environment and the natural environment. Where the developers and residents once thought their neighborhood ended at the edge of the cul-de-sac, they are now realizing that Dry Creek is also part of the neighborhood. It is as if the neglected, channelized creeks have reached out to say, "Hello there, neighbor!"

The South Yuba River, one of my biggest neighbors, has been tearing down the canyon this week in a frothy, muddy, boiling torrent of raw natural power. It has been a remarkable display of how quickly western rivers can transform themselves. In addition to furnishing the local rain, the warm storm front raised the snow level to nearly seven thousand feet. It rained in Truckee for two solid days. Snow was being melted by the high country rain, feeding the river with stored moisture that had accumulated in the heavier-than-usual snowpack to date. A similar rain-on-snow event had triggered much of the widespread flooding that hit northern California in February 1986, although the failure of human systems to deal with the runoff adequately can be blamed for much of the resulting flood damage (South Yuba River Citizens League 1993). A friend and neighbor stopped by the river in the height of the downpour the other day to marvel at the sight. "Isn't this Wild Nature at her best!" she said with positive excitement to a stranger standing near her on the old Highway 49 bridge. "I think it's Nature at its worst," responded the glum woman. Downstream, the levees held and the Yuba caused no flooding in the valley.[1]

Californians and other westerners are obsessed with water. In the arid country beyond the hundredth meridian, there is always either too much or too little to be of immediate use. It is also usually in the wrong place at the wrong time. As a result, we have constructed complex and expensive systems to transport the water through both space and time to make it less damaging and more useful for economic production. There are limits to our capacity to transform the entire hydrologic system, however, for we face both economic and ecological constraints (Reisner 1986). The marginal costs of building more and bigger dams and canals are increasingly beyond the economic value of the water or flood relief gained, and pork barrel money from Washington is getting harder and harder to come by. Drought and flood therefore continue to plague us.

There is no such thing as normal rainfall or normal snowpack in California. As David Beesley has noted, "Drought is *normal* in the west" (Beesley 1994b). There is such a thing as average rainfall and average snowpack, but even those values are being challenged by the seemingly increasing occurrence of extreme events that change the average values. Annual precipitation averaged 51 inches per year in Nevada City from 1951 to 1975, but approached nearly 63 inches per year from 1975 to 1996. This increase occurred despite the drought years of 1975–77 and 1984–92 because of the disproportionate influence of nearly 71 inches per year during the wet cycle of 1992–96.[2] The 1951–75 low of 37 inches was shattered by a low of only 20 inches of precipitation during the 1976–77 drought, while the 1951–75 annual high of 79 inches was overwhelmed by this year's total of more than 100 inches of precipitation. Three of the past four years were close to or well over the 1951–75 high, making short-term weather data a poor basis for predicting the future.[3] "Average" conditions are actually *abnormal.* It takes a long memory of a place to keep the individual fluctuations and degree of variation in perspective.

That memory of place is explicitly rejected as relevant to the expertise-oriented model of land and resource management that dominates state and federal agencies. Instead, the bureaucracies of modern land and resource management were structured around the idea of a neutral scientific expert and his or her knowledge of a discipline and its methods, rather than familiarity with and knowledge about specific places (Hays 1959; Smith 1987; Wilkinson 1992a; Langston 1995; Yaffee 1994). The modern Forest Service employee or park ranger is therefore likely to move from place to place every few years as if in the military. The system is specifically designed to promote employee experience across a given agency and minimize the opportunity for remote, rural communities to unduly influence the decisions of local federal officials. Consequently, memories of place rarely enter into the planning process and policy decisions for state and federal land and resource management agencies, who control between three-fifths and two-thirds of the Sierra Nevada landscape.

Despite the boundary-breaking promise of "ecosystem management," those agencies still focus their attention on the land and resources directly under their management control (Grumbine 1994; Duane forthcoming). The result is that many places that span multiple jurisdictions and resources are managed in a fragmented manner. Ownership boundaries tend to divide the landscape and decrease the degree of integration in land and resource planning and management that affect a given place or resource. This institutional fragmentation is at least partly to blame for the failure of our existing institutions to stem the loss of biodiversity and ecosystem function throughout the world. A sockeye salmon hatched at Redfish Lake in the Sawtooth National Recreation Area of Idaho passes through the jurisdictional responsibility of dozens of different federal, state, tribal, and local agencies during its long and arduous journey up the Columbia, Snake, or Salmon River drainages to spawn at the end of its life. Is it any wonder that policies enacted by one agency work at cross purposes with many of the policies enacted by another? Our jurisdictional boundaries themselves are inconsistent with the underlying relationships of ecological systems. Our attempts at reconciling the two therefore have profound institutional implications.

As Lynton Caldwell suggested in 1970, using ecosystems as the basis for public land policy would require that the conventional [political] matrix be unraveled and rewoven in a new pattern (Caldwell 1970). Such an unraveling and reweaving may now be necessary in the Sierra Nevada, however, and bioregionalism may be the paradigm that can lead to a sustainable future.

BIOREGIONALISM AS A PLANNING PARADIGM

The principles of bioregionalism have developed through an eclectic movement composed of multiple individuals, philosophies, and texts advocating its adoption (Parsons 1985; Andruss et al. 1990; Sale 1991). As with the terms *sustainable development* and *ecosystem management,* there is no definitive definition of *bioregionalism* (Andruss et al. 1990). Despite this complexity, however, the basic approach of bioregionalism is summarized well in Kirkpatrick Sale's 1991 book, *Dwellers in the Land: The Bioregional Vision.* Other books on the topic have been written by Peter Berg, Ray Dasmann, and Seth Zuckerman of the Planet Drum Foundation, poet Gary Snyder of the Yuba Watershed Institute (YWI), and Van Andruss, Christopher Plant, Judith Plant, and Eleanor Wright of British Columbia (Berg 1978; Snyder 1974; 1990). Northern California (or, in the term of the bioregional movement, the Shasta Bioregion) and British Columbia (the North Pacific Coast Bioregion) seem to be focal points for the development of the bioregional movement (Van Andruss et al. 1990; Carr 1994). The collection of articles in the 1990 book *Home! A Bioregional Reader,* however, demonstrates a wide geography of bioregional interest in North America, from the prairies of Kansas to the streets of New York City.[4]

The bioregional movement has evolved over the past few decades through newsletter articles, letters, and biennial gatherings at the North American Bioregional Congress. The following statement was adopted by consensus at the first North American Bioregional Congress in 1984 and reaffirmed by subsequent gatherings:

> Bioregionalism recognizes, nurtures, sustains and celebrates our local connections with: Land; Plants and Animals; Springs, Rivers, Lakes, Groundwater & Oceans; Air; Families, Friends, Neighbors; Community, Native Traditions, Indigenous Systems of Production and Trade. It is taking the time to learn the possibilities of place. It is mindfulness of local environment, history, and community aspirations that leads to a sustainable future. It relies on safe and renewable sources of food and energy. It ensures employment by supplying a rich diversity of services within the community, by recycling our resources, and by exchanging prudent surpluses with other regions. Bioregionalism is working to satisfy basic needs locally, such as education, health care and self-government. The bioregional perspective recreates a widely-shared sense of regional identity founded upon a renewed critical awareness of and respect for the integrity of ecological communities. (Van Andruss et al. 1990, 170)

In contrast with ecosystem management, bioregionalism truly is a grassroots movement.[5] As Carolyn Merchant puts it, "Bioregionalism advocates a new ecological politics of place" (1992, 220). It is rooted in the advocacy of the back-to-the-land movement of the late 1960s and early 1970s, when a broader set of questions about mainstream industrial American society were being asked. Many chose to drop out of urban life and reinhabit the country. They have since found each other to form a loose network of bioregionalists, and there are now nearly a hundred local groups who identify themselves with some bioregion (ibid.).

Many of the central ideas of bioregionalism, however, predate the current generation of advocates and practitioners. The noted regional planners Patrick Geddes (1854–1932), Benton MacKaye (1879–1975), and Lewis Mumford (1895–1990) were central figures in the development of bioregional ideas, although they did not use the term (Luccarelli 1995; Carr 1994). Mike Carr argues that the Regional Planning Association of America and MacKaye's vision for the Appalachia Trail were "a wilderness-inspired planning framework" that embraced many of the values of today's bioregionalists (1994, 4). "Bioregionalism," says Carr, "is in good part the rediscovery of the regional ideas of Geddes, Mumford, MacKaye and others." He adds, however, that "this movement of people has reclaimed the concept and knowledge of an earlier regionalism, reframed them and begun to apply them to our contemporary reality. Yet, bioregional thought also goes beyond the vision of MacKaye and Mumford. As we shall see, bioregionalists have deepened and enhanced the vision of MacKaye and Mumford" (8). Mark Luccarelli also argues that Mumford and MacKaye's vision of regional planning based on the ecological region represents a foundation for new approaches to planning and development that could lead to sustainable development: "In the modern industrial world, where the perfection of *technical reason* means the subjugation of nature and regimentation of society, there is vital 'need' to create a culture capable of extending and nurturing life in all its forms. This requires public deliberation on the ends to which modern technology is applied. To this end, Mumford sought to cultivate a sense of place necessary to community and to bring the built environment into balance with the natural region" (Luccarelli 1995, 61).

The roots of bioregionalism lie in ecology as the science of relationships among and between organisms and their physical environment. In a strict ecological sense, bioregionalism is concerned with "home" regions defined according to physical and biological interactions that describe ecosystem dynamics. Bioregionalism therefore has a strong orientation toward the natural systems that humans inhabit, which are bound by watersheds, elevation, slope, aspect, temperature, and the other biophysical factors determining the distribution and abundance of organisms in an ecosystem. In the most limited definition of bioregionalism, *place* is usually defined in ecological rather than social terms.[6] There is no clear standard for determining the appropriate scale of bioregions by this criteria, and they may range in size from a small drainage basin (measured in hundreds of acres) to an entire mountain range or contiguous vegetation type (measured in tens of millions of acres). The watershed appears to be the most common organizing unit. Seth Zuckerman suggests four different criteria that can be used to define the bioregion: hydrology, geology, vegetation, and cultural distribution (1992). He notes that all four result in different maps of the bioregions of California—and that none of them matches a map of existing institutional arrangements for land and resource management or local government.

As Carolyn Merchant notes, however, bioregionalism is about much more than physical geography. It is also about how humans conceive of their relationship and interaction with the rest of the natural world. "Beyond the geographical terrain," she says, "is a terrain of consciousness—ideas that have developed over time about how to live in a given place."[7] This introduces a human dimension that includes the social, economic, political, cultural and institutional. Bioregionalism, therefore, integrates both Nature and Culture. It also emphasizes environmental history as the interaction of humans and their environment. A community may technically be on the "wrong" side of the watershed divide, for example, but it may have historical ties to a nearby river because of its proximity and its role as the trading center for placer gold mining in the area. Another community, while situated in a forest type similar to that of the first community and the nearby watershed, may not have transportation access to either of them. Its social isolation may then place it outside the boundaries of some commonly-agreed-upon bioregional identity— the people in this "outside" community may even speak a different language and practice different customs because of this separation and the lack of appropriate human systems. Existing institutional arrangements may also be relevant— although the boundaries of most political jurisdictions have rarely been drawn along bioregional lines.[8] They nevertheless help to determine social identity through elections, postal zip codes, football rivalries, telephone directories, economic relations, and those other social factors that originally determined the boundaries of the jurisdiction.[9] Identity with place is central to bioregionalism, and identity is influenced by social, cultural, and economic—as well as ecological—ties.

Throughout human history, Culture has been heavily influenced by the physical landscape, and many cultural practices reflect those ties to place and biophysical realities. Only recently—through the use of fossil fuels—have we been able to break the bonds of place to ignore (temporarily) the deeply rooted historical and evolutionary relationship between Nature and Culture.[10] The emergence of the bioregional movement is in many respects a reaction against modern industrial society and its severed relationships with the land (Castells 1997). Bioregional thinking has been the norm for the vast majority of human history. Bioregionalism simply seeks to reclaim a traditional way of knowing and relating to the natural environment, to overcome our industrial separation.[11] In doing so, however, it challenges many of the tenets of the modern industrial age.

BIOREGIONAL ECONOMICS
AND SELF-SUFFICIENCY

Indigenous people were the original bioregionalists. The acorn-collecting practices of the Miwok Indians in the western Sierra Nevada foothills near Yosemite contrasted sharply with, for example, the brine fly-larvae diet of the Paiute Indians who lived near the brackish Mono Lake on the east side of the Sierra Nevada. Those cultural differences reflected the biophysical realities of their respective ecological conditions. Were these two groups still practicing bioregionalism, then, when they met in mountain passes to trade the fruits of their respective regions? For some, bioregionalism is a call for self-sufficiency that does not rely on export trade to maintain economic livelihood. Bioregionalism does not necessarily call for self-sufficiency or complete isolationism, however, and there is a debate within the bioregional movement about the relative merits of trade. There is general agreement within bioregionalism that economic activity must maintain a high degree of sensitivity to the ecological conditions of the local area and the seasonal rhythms of the bioregion. Most bioregionalists say that only surpluses should be traded, after basic local needs have been met. Self-sufficiency comes first, to be supplemented by trade.

Complete economic self-sufficiency within each bioregion would be a complete reversal, however, from the market globalization that is now sweeping the world (Linton and Greco 1990). In many ways, the bioregionalist calls for such self-sufficiency reflect a belief that stopping the expansion of the existing industrial system is necessary for the long-term health of the planet. In his 1997 book, *The Power of Identity*, Manuel Castells links a wide range of social movements of resistance to environmentalism, and to antienvironmental calls for "local control" by the Wise Use movement. For all of these groups, localization is a natural counterresponse to what Castells calls the "globalization" and "informationalization" of the economy. In its extreme form, localization would constitute complete self-sufficiency.

A shift toward self-sufficiency would clearly reduce some environmental effects, but it might also increase the effects of other activities and possibly exacerbate inequities. Natural resources are not evenly distributed about the earth, which creates inherent advantages for some regions over others. It does not really make sense for every area to be self-sufficient if one region can produce a particular product with less labor, energy, capital—and, potentially, with fewer detrimental environmental effects—than an adjoining region. Moreover, the adjoining region may have a comparative advantage in other areas. Trade between these two would then make both groups better off—without necessarily causing greater environmental degradation than would occur if each were left to produce both products independently. There is an extensive literature on trade and markets that demonstrates that efficiency is improved when they are allowed. Should all opportunities for such efficiency gains be ignored, *regardless* of the potential environmental impact?[12] Answering this question requires bioregionalists to recognize the *specific* consequences of *specific* trading relations, some of which are beneficial.

It therefore probably makes more sense to define *conditions* of trade—rather than *prohibit* all trade—that reflect specific requirements for ecological integrity in each bioregion.[13] This modified bioregionalism is an approach that is neither complete laissez-faire nor self-sufficiency without trade. It maintains opportunities for cultural exchange and development of increased interdependencies among and between different peoples. It also recognizes that ten thousand years of trade have already transformed the landscape and our consumption patterns dramatically. It is unlikely that we will now be able to go back to a lifestyle that depends only on indigenous production. (Moreover, there is no clear and consistent set of criteria that can determine the appropriate scale of the bioregional boundaries within which self-sufficiency should be achieved. Larger-scale units generally have more heterogeneity and therefore need less trade with external units, because internal trade satisfies needs within the unit. There is no sound theoretical basis for establishing the scale of the units within which self-sufficiency would need to be maintained.)

This position is consistent with that of MacKaye and Mumford, who Luccarelli notes did *not* advocate "the creation of economically self-sufficient regions." In Mumford's words, "No region is rich enough or varied enough to supply all the ingredients of our present civilization."[14] Trade is therefore necessary if the full range of human needs is to be met in complex societies.

The critical point of bioregionalism is that the natural capacity of the landscape should dictate the degree and type of cultural activity within a bioregion. Culture is, as a result, bound by Nature rather than the other way around. The sun and the soil are the foundation of ecological function, and renewable, regenerative processes are the bioregional goal. Extensive dependence on nonsustainable imports of energy and resources creates the conditions for a complex but brittle system.[15] As noted by Holling, this often leads to a crisis condition (1995). Bioregionalism calls for greater simplicity, greater flexibility, closer connections to the land, and decreased dependency on external inputs. This is consistent with Holling's observation that system resilience is associated with not being overconnected through strong vertical networks (ibid.), which Putnam observes are also associated with low levels of social capital. The horizontal networks of bioregionalism, however, are consistent with Putnam's necessary conditions for the generation of social capital through norms of reciprocity and civic engagement (1993).

The issues of trade and economic self-sufficiency bring up another important concern: the relationship between urban settlements and the rural regions that cities and their inhabitants depend on. Sale discusses the work of such luminary urban thinkers as Mumford and Jane Jacobs on the topic, arguing that true regional planners have always recognized this dependency (1991). The city does not exist in isolation from its counterpart, the country. William Cronon has also highlighted how dependent the country is on the city for its identity. He demonstrates that the pattern of natural resource use and trade within and between urban areas is a critical determinant of the pattern of rural land use and natural resource conditions (1991).

It is only through the emergence of economic surpluses and greater leisure time among the urban population that recreation in the nonurbanized landscape has been made possible. This is true of both the physical act of recreating and our very conceptions of recreation itself. Moreover, the resource inputs of a capitalist economy directly link this same landscape to urban centers and industrial processes in myriad social, economic, cultural, and institutional ways. From second-home developments to ancient forest preservation, rural regions are directly affected by the success or failure of urban areas.[16] Moreover, the national political debate about the fate of public lands lies largely in the hands of institutions dominated by easterners and urban westerners.[17]

Bioregionalism must therefore explicitly recognize the importance of urban centers. A "green city" program has developed recently to address the ecological effects of cities. "The way we live in cities today is probably the greatest threat to our survival," writes one group of urban bioregionalists. "Cities unconscionably consume resources and spit out horrendous waste. The green city program does not face this reality by turning to the countryside. It recognizes that most of us live in cities and will continue to do so for some time. It faces up to the reality that cities are basically anti-nature; but instead of writing them off, it looks to ecologize them" (Cholette et al. 1989, 103). Green city programs have been developed for San Francisco, New York, Seattle, Chattanooga, and other cities. A sustainable cities program has also been spreading, following the bumper-sticker slogan "Think Globally, Act Locally."[18] Finally, Richard Register and the group Urban Ecology in Berkeley have led a successful "eco-cities" movement that has held conferences in the United States and Australia.[19] This has coincided with a serious reconsideration among urban design professionals of the social and ecological consequences of our dominant patterns of urban form (Van der Ryn and Calthorpe 1986; Calthorpe 1993; Beatley and Manning 1996; Katz 1994; Duany and Plater-Zyberk 1991). From urban creek "daylighting" to tree planting, and from transit system design to energy conservation ordinances, green city programs have even become the foundation for some successful political coalitions in U.S. cities. In other cases, sustainability has remained simply an abstract concept.[20]

Wackernagel and Rees's "ecological footprint" concept is a useful technique for estimating the environmental effects of specific activities. It allows every activity to be translated into an estimate of the land area required to support it on a renewable basis, allowing a common basis for comparing the environmental effects of different activities and settlement patterns (Wackernagel and Rees 1996). A more sophisticated accounting system would, however, be necessary to capture effects that are not land-based, such as air quality, water quality, biodiversity, and exposure to toxic contaminants (which may all have effects disproportional to their "footprint" on the land). Such an accounting system could then be combined with an approach modeled on Leontief's technique for economic input-output analysis, which relates specific economic activities in one sector to multiplier consequences in other sectors of the economy (Leontief 1986). Environmental input-output analysis could then be used to generate an environmental impact matrix that would relate specific trade transactions to likely environmental consequences through a generalized estimate of those relationships.[21] The trade transaction could then be evaluated with full consideration of the environmental consequences of the trade.[22] This information could inform the terms of trade between bioregions.

It is all a bit abstract, however, to talk about urban and rural areas without reference to physical geography or specific places. The bioregional perspective attempts to incorporate these relationships to the spatial dimension through a place-based discussion: the fate of *specific* rural areas is tied to the activities in *specific* urban places. Again, the globalization of trade makes it difficult to trace these ties. Increased sales of Macintosh computers to the Iowa Writer's Workshop puts cash in the pockets of Silicon Valley engineers, who then go to Nordstrom's—based in Seattle, Washington—to buy teak furniture imported from Malaysia. A Japanese shipping company delivers the furniture, putting additional revenues into a Tokyo household that buys a dinner at a restaurant—where corn, grown in Iowa in the shadow of the Writer's Workshop, is served. Each of our actions reverberates around the global marketplace, affecting dozens if not hundreds of bioregional economies and ecosystems.

It is hard to imagine isolating or tracing all of those effects—both the positive and negative—for any bioregion. Bioregionalism must be adapted to the technological and economic realities of global trade and the opportunities as well as the problems they present. It will therefore require resources and systematic accounting mechanisms that go far beyond the bioregion. Ultimately, bioregionalism's success will depend on suprabioregional institutions to protect bioregional interests.[23] A complex nested hierarchy of institutions must exist for bioregionalism to be practiced in our emerging age of informationalization and globalization (Castells 1997).

BIOREGIONAL POLITICS AND A SENSE OF PLACE

"Bioregionalism," says the Pulitzer Prize-winning poet Gary Snyder, "is the entry of place into the dialectic of history."[24] Emphasis on *place*—and being *in* place—is central to the bioregional vision. "We must consciously fully accept and recognize that this is where we live," says Snyder, "and grasp the fact that our descendants will be here for millennia to come. Then we must honor this land's great antiquity— its wildness—learn it—and work to hand it on to the children (of all beings) of the future with its biodiversity and health intact."[25] Snyder calls for us to reinhabit the spectacular and still-wild continent of "Turtle Island" (a Native American name for North America), in his poetry, in his essays, and in his books *The Practice of the Wild* and *A Place in Space: Watersheds, Aesthetics, Ethics* (1990; 1992a; 1992b; 1992c; 1995). He emphasizes one simple but powerful act of commitment by individuals within each bioregion: "Don't move. Stay still. Once you find a place that feels halfway right, and it seems time, settle down with a vow not to move any more" (1990). Over time, this simple act should influence both policy and the effects of human activities on the landscape in subtle but profound ways. This reinforces the importance of Merchant's comment on the "terrain of consciousness": bioregionalism is as much about how we *think* about place as it is about how we draw lines on a map (1992). To truly *know* a place, we must also live there on a daily basis for a long, long time.[26]

There are potentially important political ramifications to place-based identity and a commitment to a place. While he does not say that a "bioregional" identity is required, Daniel Kemmis argues in his 1990 book, *Community and the Politics of Place,* that physical interaction among people in and around a spatially defined, geographic community has the potential to transform democratic political processes. This is also consistent with the theories of social capital as a critical factor in collective action developed by Ostrom (1990), Ellickson (1991), and Putnam (Putnam et al. 1993). Kemmis argues that the principles of Jeffersonian democracy are best served in appropriately scaled social and political institutions tied to place-based communities. He challenges the trends toward centralization and economies of scale that have tended to reinforce the Madisonian vision of a powerful elite making decisions on behalf of the citizens (which is consistent with the dominant agency-led model of ecosystem management) and calls again for a government of normal people making decisions locally when issues can be resolved at that level (Kemmis 1990; Lovins and Lovins 1982). In contrast with Madison and the Federalists, who structured the U.S. Constitution on a "policy of providing by opposite and rival interests, the defect of better motives," Jefferson believed it was possible to build a republic on the "civic virtue" of its citizens—and that such virtue would be enhanced by a connection to the land through working it (Kemmis 1990, 54). "Cultivators of the earth," said Jefferson, "are the most valuable citizens. They are the most vigorous, the most independent, the most virtuous, and they are tied to their country, and wedded to its liberty and interests by the most lasting bonds."[27] Madison's structure has become characterized by what Michael Sandel has called the "procedural republic and the unencumbered self,"[28] where individuals attempt to maximize their self-interest through formal trilateral relational controls. These procedure-oriented institutions do not recognize either norms of reciprocity or networks of civic engagement, however, and therefore undermine the generation of social capital (Putnam et al. 1993).

Regular interaction over noncontroversial or nonadversarial issues and events, such as Little League picnics and volunteer fire department fund-raisers, create a mutual dependency, a stake in the community and the networks of civic engagement that cannot be generated through occasional, conflict-ridden encounters. The result, according to Kemmis, should be less adversarial processes that tend to emphasize consensus and the search for win-win solutions. This is what Bellah called the politics of community: one is less likely to call someone nasty names if the community context will ensure regular encounters following the conflict. This contrasts sharply with the divide-and-conquer politics of interest that now dominate American political discourse. Much of what passes for political discussions today constitutes a form of "drive-by debate,"[29] where each side fires off a volley of attacks at the other side but never listens to the other side's position. Kemmis argues that the politics of community can still triumph over the politics of interest in small towns (Bellah et al. 1985).

As we have seen in Nevada County, however, the two do a delicate dance together under the pressures of rapid change now sweeping the landscape. Continued growth is likely to displace the politics of community with the politics of interest, just as bilateral controls are likely to give way to rules and then trilateral controls. Maintaining social capital in this context is difficult and ultimately depends on a willingness to compromise for some greater good.

In many cases, the two "sides" in a debate may actually share common values and a common vision for the future. They may disagree about the *means* for achieving that vision, however, and that is usually where the debate emphasizes conflict. All too often the common vision is never articulated. As Robert Hass puts it, "*Imagination* makes communities" (Clines 1996). Moreover, our present land and resource planning and management processes do not allow room for discussion about our fundamental *values*, which are often at the heart of the conflicts. It is difficult to deal with such emotionally charged issues under the positivist guise of objectivity and through a formally structured process before "experts," who profess to hold and favor no values (Bimber 1996; Logan and Molotch 1986). Yet this appears to be the path of both ecosystem management and land use planning favored by the bureaucracy. The dominant approach to public participation is built on a model of adversarial legislation and trilateral relational control: competing interests present their positions to an agency, which then acts in an adjudicatory capacity, like Solomon, to reach a decision to resolve the conflict between the competing parties' positions. This encourages extremist positions and grandstanding, yet the parties in apparent conflict are rarely able to interact directly. No social learning occurs, no social capital accumulates and the bad will left by the process affects both the parties and the agency (Putnam et al. 1993; Ostrom 1990). The one thing both parties usually share in common at the end of the process is unhappiness with the result, for the agency often "splits the baby down the middle" to find a middle ground. The traditional approach therefore emphasizes the *differences* between the parties' positions rather than any common ground they may share.[30]

This is where the principles of communicative rationality and communicative action come into play (Innes 1995). Innes does not discuss bioregionalism per se, but bioregionalism emphasizes two aspects of place-based community problem-solving that differ significantly from the dominant model in agency-based ecosystem management: human-scale institutions (Sale 1980) and consensus-based decision-making (Estes 1986). The former is necessary for the latter to be possible, so one cannot discuss consensus processes without addressing the context within which they occur. The key to Kemmis's politics of place is a place-based community that is of a scale that ensures three things: regular social interaction, a shared sense of mutual dependency, and limited opportunities for anonymity. These conditions are consistent with the findings of Ostrom, Ellickson, and Putnam regarding the conditions that generate social capital.

Kemmis (1990) discusses the importance of these elements in the development of political discourse in his native rural and small-town Montana, where he has served as minority leader in the state legislature and as mayor of Missoula. Much of today's ongoing discontent with Washington and national politics may in part reflect a concern that critical decisions have moved away from the citizenry and become locked up within the control of special interests and powerful elites inside the beltway. While we often depend on large, complex institutions that have constituencies numbering in the tens or even hundreds of millions of people, they often must be disaggregated to the neighborhood or village scale to allow active participation by the citizenry. There is a general sense of separation between individuals and Washington or Sacramento that is not present when dealing with local government in a small town or neighborhood. In small towns and neighborhoods, there is a genuine feeling that one's vote makes a difference in local elections.[31] This is an important factor to consider in the design of planning institutions.

What is the appropriate scale to allow this level of interaction and influence among community members? There is no clear standard, although it appears difficult to maintain regular community-wide interaction beyond somewhere between 10^3 to 10^4 residents. This estimate is consistent with Christopher Alexander and his colleagues' call for five thousand to ten thousand persons per neighborhood or community (Alexander et al. 1977, 70–74). Some would place the threshold at 10^2 to 10^3 residents, while others might argue for 10^4 to 10^5 residents. This is within the limits of Ostrom's case studies, and it is notable that few examples of larger-scale efforts have been successful.[32]

For consensus-based decision-making, however, the manageable threshold may be as low as 10^1 to 10^2 individuals (Estes 1986). Larger groups do not allow interaction at a level that allows all parties to be heard and to participate fully in the discussion. Even within human-scale communities, then, it may be necessary to disaggregate further to allow full participation in decision-making. Consequently, some bioregionalists call for alliances of smaller bioregional decision-making units into "tribes" that can act at a larger scale, with confederations of "tribes" forming "nations" (Mollison 1988). These "nations" would presumably be formed along bioregional boundaries, representing aggregations of watersheds or other ecological and cultural units (ibid.). In general, this approach to hierarchical institutions of government focuses on the principles of self-government and devolution of authority to the smallest possible unit, with nation-states being unimportant relative to local groups (except on matters affecting the interests of the larger units). It would, of course, completely reverse the recent trend toward centralization of authority and power in the federal government within the United States (Fairfax and Cowart 1984; Fairfax et al. 1984). Full embrace of these particular bioregional ideas therefore has potentially radical political implications.[33]

The point here is not to define a maximum or optimum level at which social interaction can promote a sense of shared identity and norms of reciprocity, but to recognize that the success of different models of public participation depends partially on the scale of the community and the complexity of its institutions. Other factors, such as homogeneity of values and interests, also have a clear bearing on both the appropriate scale and the likelihood of conflict resolution.[34] The opportunity for anonymity seems to be the most important factor, however, for individuals can be more readily attacked and true discourse denied if both the attacker and the subject of the attack are mere abstractions. Lies can be told about abstract symbols for ideologies or movements, while they will be discounted and the liar will lose credibility if community members know from personal experience the individuals being attacked.

ETHICS AND THE EXPERIENCE OF PLACE

Strengthening the "sense of place" in human-built environments appears to tap into a basic human need (Hiss 1990; Tuan 1974). This is true for both urban and rural places. For many people, there is an empty space in their lives not being filled by our mobile, urban, isolationist, separatist society. This is a function of many social factors that have developed over decades, and they have converged to leave us with an alienated society that has lost much of its sense of place. Moreover, expanding urbanization and the scale of urban communities are increasingly reducing the degree of contact individuals have with Nature. The emergence of lifestyles with long commutes, gated communities, and ready access to communities of interest via electronic means has led to a feeling for many that there is no need ever to get to know either one's human neighbors or the flora and fauna of one's local bioregion. Besides, aren't the Nature programs on PBS or the Discovery Channel more interesting than what one can experience easily in one's own backyard?

This indeed appears to be the general attitude of many Americans (McKibben 1992; Lopez 1992). Our postwar prosperity has brought us many material, cultural, and psychological benefits, but the promise of industrial, metropolitan America has also cost us dearly in biological diversity. There were more than 650 species listed as threatened or endangered under the ESA in the United States from 1973 to 1994 (Clark et al. 1994). California's contribution to that total included 65 species of birds, 52 species of mammals, 11 species of fish, and 5 species of invertebrates (Jensen et al. 1993; BioSystems Analysis, Inc. 1994). It is doubtful that we can reverse this trend by continuing to delegate responsibility for it to our centralized, professionalized institutions of land and resource management. Some form of direct personal and community involvement by the people who live on the land will also be necessary to ensure on-the-ground success.

Although he is also associated with the centralized watershed planning of the Tennessee Valley Authority and the Bonneville Power Administration, Lewis Mumford made it clear that we need as well an active community of citizens directly engaged in both the knowledge generation and management decision-making of their own local regions:

> We must create in every region people who will be accustomed, from school onward, to humanist attitudes, co-operative methods, rational controls. These people will know in detail where they live and how they live: they will be united by a common feeling for their landscape, their literature and language, their local ways, and out of their own self-respect they will have a sympathetic understanding of other regions and different local peculiarities. They will be actively interested in the form and culture of their locality, which means their community and their own personalities. Such people will contribute to our land-planning, our industry planning and our community planning the authority of their own understanding, and the pressure of their own desires. Without them, planning is a barren externalism.[35]

Mumford's approach emphasizes a model of relevant knowledge very different from that which imbues the organizational and professional Culture of most state and federal land and resource management agencies. Fundamentally, it challenges the dominant ideas of professionalization, expertise, and the transferability of knowledge from place to place in the absence of local knowledge. It places a premium on experiential ways of knowing that do not necessarily come from a classroom, and it highlights the importance of relationships that are not reducible to linear equations and quantitative analysis. In short, it challenges both the assumptions and tools of land and resource management that have guided most of the existing planning institutions in this century. Mark Luccarelli (1995, jacket) notes that "instead of standing against modernity," however, "Mumford linked [a tradition of ecological] thinking to the potential of science for recovering a healthy relationship to nature through the rubric of a participatory democracy." Mumford also recognized that "we must start a regional movement before we can have regional planning,"[36] for he was "always distrustful of what he considered the overly technical focus of many planners," according to Luccarelli (175). "As a way to package expertise," Luccarelli adds, "science has become the tool of managers and professionals, a means of consolidating their exclusive hold on power by limiting public debate" (190). Mumford and MacKaye therefore called for democratic planning that would give the residents of the ecological region as much influence as the "experts": "Planning should build on a shared sense of responsibility. Urban and regional design cannot be separated from the capacity to create a public sphere, a commons, and the sense of place associated with commonality and community" (ibid.).

"The language of technological experts," says Neil Evernden, "cannot accommodate the radical novelty of wildness: indeed, that is just what it has been fashioned to deny. The insinuation of a vocabulary of economy ensures our bondage to the literal and obstructs our access to otherness" (1992, 123). Artists, in contrast, are still able to speak in the language of metaphors to convey the possibility of wildness to stir our imagination. It is no coincidence, then, that artists like the poets Gary Snyder and Robert Hass have been articulate spokespersons for bioregionalism. It is also no coincidence that indigenous cultures widely cited by bioregionalists as exemplary are well-known for integrating art into daily life. The Balinese, for example, are said to have no separate word to distinguish *art* from *life* (Abram 1992). Artists are noticeably absent, however, from the ecosystem management efforts that still dominate formal land and resource management institutions. Artists may nevertheless be an important voice in the development of strategies for collective action because of the importance of Culture as a foundation for and constraint on conceptual problem formulation.

"If we would protect nature from the perils of the 'environmental crisis,'" says Evernden, "we must first acknowledge that those perils arose as a consequence of conceptual imprisonment. If we would save the world, we must set it free" (1992, 130). In the language of Holling, our focus on reducing the variability of ecological systems has generated brittleness and a loss of resilience, which threatens to undermine both the system and our dependence on it through a crisis and subsequent reorganization process beyond our direct control (1995). Yet to "set [Nature] free," in Evernden's words, "is a frightening prospect. As members of twentieth-century industrial societies, and as functionaries of technological thought, what we fear most is the loss of control (or at least of the illusion of control). To contemplate actually letting something be is very nearly beyond our ability" (1992, 130). As Charles Bergman notes, however, "Endangered species are not simply accidents of our way of living. They are the necessary consequences of our way of knowing animals."[37] Evernden quotes Gifford Pinchot as stating unequivocally that "the first duty of the human race is to control the earth it lives on."[38] Pinchot's perspective, I am afraid, still dominates agency approaches to land and resource management.

As Aldo Leopold also noted in 1949, in our highly urban, industrial society we have largely separated ourselves from the natural world and those other ways of knowing. To remedy that, Leopold articulated and argued for development and adoption of what he called a land ethic. "The land ethic," wrote Leopold in his classic book, *A Sand County Almanac*, "simply enlarges the boundaries of the community to include soils, waters, plants and animals, or collectively: the land" (239). "In short, a land ethic changes the role of *Homo sapiens* from conqueror of the land-community to plain member and citizen of it. It implies respect for his fellow-members, and also respect for the community as such" (240). Leopold emphasized as well that such an ethic would not emerge unless it was grounded in a personal, experiential knowledge of place:

> An ethic to supplement and guide the economic relation to land presupposes the existence of some mental image of land as a biotic mechanism. We can be ethical only in relation to something we can see, feel, love, understand or otherwise have faith in.
> It is inconceivable to me that an ethical relation to land can exist without love, respect, and admiration for land, and a high regard for its value. By value, I of course mean something far broader than mere economic value; I mean value in the philosophical sense.[39]

Leopold's personal relationship to a particular place—to the land as an entity, rather than a mere abstraction—had an enormous influence on his view of Nature (Meine 1988; Callicott 1987). *A Sand County Almanac* is the story of his relationship to a particular place rather than to an abstract concept of Nature. His essays also describe specific incidents and specific ecological relationships that he observed in the field. I have walked across his farm by the Wisconsin River in Sauk County, and Leopold's spirit was evident in the forests and the rain. He knew this soil, this water, this sky, this place; he could tell the change in seasons by the coming and going of the sandhill cranes. Ultimately he died on that land fighting a wildfire at the age of sixty-one (Meine 1988). His greatest work had not yet been published, but his personal transformation was complete. He had moved from having an anthropocentric and utilitarian view of Nature to an ecocentric outlook.[40]

Leopold summarized his call for adoption of a new land ethic with a simple plea and a simple test for determining what is right: "The 'key-log' which must be moved to release the evolutionary process for an ethic is simply this: quit thinking about decent land-use as solely an economic problem. Examine each question in terms of what is ethically and esthetically right, as well as what is economically expedient. A thing is right when it tends to preserve the integrity, stability, and beauty of the biotic community. It is wrong when it tends otherwise" (Leopold 1949, 262).

This last statement by Leopold is his most-quoted, but it has confounded philosophers with its apparent absolutism. Is it still "wrong when it tends otherwise," for example, if to do so would protect some other values—such as the right of an individual not to experience pain, or to continue living? This is where Leopold's land ethic has given rise to a charge of "environmental fascism" by Tom Regan (1983, 361–62). Noted Leopold philosopher Baird Callicott addresses the charge in two ways: by demonstrating that individual suffering is an inherent part of ecological systems; and by admitting that the land ethic is not an absolute basis for action but must be applied in the context of other ethical considerations.[41] He argues that the land ethic would not sacrifice a human life, for example, in order to "maintain the integrity, stability, and beauty of the biotic community." Perhaps Leopold's statement would have been more usefully stated as "A thing tends to be right when it preserves" rather than "A thing is right when it tends to preserve."

Unfortunately, Leopold died before it was published so he has been unable to clarify his words.[42] Callicott has nevertheless done an admirable job of defending them, although Joseph Des Jardins suggests that "it is not always clear where Leopold's work leaves off and Callicott's begins" (1997, 195, note 20). Des Jardins also offers an excellent overview of the critiques of Leopold's land ethic, but he notes that "it may be unfair to ask more of Leopold than what we ask of philosophers," for "philosophers still much debate" the need to supply "categorical imperatives" (as advocated by Immanuel Kant) as opposed to an ethics based "on the feelings, attitudes, or sentiments of the individual" (as advanced by David Hume and attributed to Leopold's work by Callicott) (192). The specific philosophical critiques of Leopold's land ethic and their potential counterarguments are discussed in detail in Des Jardins, where he also summarizes Callicott's philosophical defense of Leopold's land ethic: "Callicott has offered a thoughtful and provocative account of the ethical foundations of the land ethic. Mainstream Western philosophy has no doubt judged that foundation to be unstable, at least when compared to the possibility of a more categorical imperative. Perhaps Western philosophy has asked too much of ethics. Perhaps the best we can hope for is an ethics based on sympathy, compassion, and love. It might not be a bad place to start" (ibid.).

Des Jardins concludes by highlighting the heuristic value of Leopold's land ethic within the broader context of social discourse and social action, placing the academic debate among philosophers in appropriate perspective. I agree with his emphasis on its *practical* implications, for Leopold's land ethic is widely cited and has generated important discussion among citizens outside the halls of academia. Des Jardins asks,

> What are we to make of these debates? It seems that we have gone far afield from the elegance of Leopold's inspiring and original work. Seeking to defend it from challenges, we find ourselves deep within philosophical debates that seem quite removed from environmental and ecological concerns[;] . . . serious philosophical challenges to the land ethic remain. Nevertheless, Leopold's work holds promise for philosophical reflection on the environment. Without question, his writing provides inspiration for everyone concerned with environmental ethics. Perhaps his greatest contribution lies in focusing attention on ecosystems and relationships—in short, to take ecological wholes as worthy of serious moral consideration. Whether this consideration turns out to be in the form of direct or indirect moral standing, after Aldo Leopold this issue can no longer be ignored. (ibid., 194–95)

Leopold's land ethic is both simple and radical in its implications for social organization and how we might solve dilemmas of collective action involving Nature. Leopold therefore recognized that the land ethic would not be adopted easily. He believed that social interaction around issues of conservation would be the ultimate basis for the development of a collective land ethic that would permeate individual actions. Indeed, some community-level consensus on the values that should guide individual action is necessary in order to implement the land ethic. He states: "I have purposely presented the land ethic as a product of social evolution because nothing so important as an ethic is ever 'written.' . . . The evolution of a land ethic is an intellectual as well as emotional process. Conservation is paved with good intentions which prove to be futile, or even dangerous, because they are devoid of critical understanding either of the land, or of economic land-use. I think it is a truism that as the ethical frontier advances from the individual to the community, its intellectual content increases. The mechanism of operation is the same for any ethic: social approbation for right actions: social disapproval for wrong actions" (1949, 263–64).

Leopold's reliance on the social consequences of action as the mechanism of "enforcement" of the land ethic highlights the importance of both formal institutional arrangements, such as the ESA and the Fifth Amendment to the U.S. Constitution, and the more informal determinants of social capital generation that dominate Ostrom's, Ellickson's, and Putnam's work. Norms of reciprocity and horizontal networks of civic engagement will influence the interdependence of individuals in a community or of those in conflict over a public policy issue, as well as the likelihood that the individuals will care about their reputations. Similarly, the generation of social capital accumulated during formal institutionalized processes such as consensus-based planning processes can determine the influence of social approbation on individual behavior. These formal processes, as Innes notes, can serve as the foundation for generating social capital among communities that may transcend both place and interest. The degree to which the stakeholders in these processes reach agreement, of course, will depend in part on the formal institutional structure within which their agreements are developed. Formal institutional arrangements can therefore either thwart or foster the development of Leopold's land ethic, for the land ethic is one that must be practiced by *society* to have meaning.

This is where ecosystem management can learn from the bioregional planning movement, for the latter explicitly recognizes the importance of social capital in overcoming dilemmas of collective action. Bioregionalism offers an ecocentric emphasis on community well-being at a scale that could promote the development of the land ethic as envisioned by Leopold. Without some "social approbation for right actions; social disapproval for wrong actions," the analytic results of ecosystem-scale analysis will not result in on-the-ground changes in management applied throughout the landscape on public and private lands. This is particularly true for management of private lands, which have generally been outside the scope of land and resource management agencies' jurisdiction. Adoption of some elements of bioregionalism into planning, together with development of a new land ethic (or, at least planning and management processes that explicitly recognize the importance of differences among values as well as the value-laden assumptions of existing utilitarian approaches), is therefore imperative for successful ecosystem management. We are otherwise likely to continue down the path of ecological decline now degrading the planet's biological diversity and ecological function every day. Whether economically tenable or not, the current path is unethical by almost any responsible criteria.

BUILDING A BIOREGIONAL COMMUNITY

Many bioregionalists today echo the call of both Leopold and so-called deep ecologists (Devall and Sessions 1985; Naess 1989) for the reestablishment of rituals to reduce the separation between human experience and "wildness." Among these rituals is the Council of All Beings, where individuals in the group represent different species and components of the ecosystem before the rest of the group to engender greater understanding (Fleming and Macy 1990). These rituals have become a regular element of bioregional gatherings (Grumbine 1992). While dismissed by some as irrelevant to the "hard" world of expert-driven decision-making, they are symbolic of a deeper commitment to a connection with the land. They also often translate into community gardens and working directly with the earth, which strengthens the ties that bind between humans and the other citizens of a bioregion.

At the very least, bioregionalism calls for a knowledge of place based on direct personal experience. "Bioregionalism means a return to life," says Snyder. "People should hike their land to know it" (McHugh 1992a; 1992b). (Snyder advocates *crawling* across the land to improve one's understanding and appreciation of chaparral communities, through which it is impossible to walk. This is how one gets to know the land intimately—face-to-face from just inches away [Snyder 1992d].) Bioregionalism also calls for an intimate *relationship* with a *specific* landscape, not just abstract ecological knowledge. This is what I sought in my hikes on the shoulders of Banner Mountain, and this is what keeps bringing me back to the same home territory that lies within sight of it. It has taken me a long, long time to get to know this landscape, and much of my knowledge of it has come from living here day-to-day, season-to-season, year-to-year. I never could have come to know this place from the academic isolation of Stanford or Berkeley.

There are very few successful examples of bioregionalism in action on the public lands, but one of the most promising is here on the San Juan Ridge. It involves an innovative manager at the Bureau of Land Management (BLM) and a community of dedicated citizens who live here in the 'Inimim Forest—the Nisenan (Southern Maidu) word for ponderosa pine. Together they are creating a model that integrates bioregional planning into ecosystem management while addressing the social, economic, and ecological needs of the community. The model also stands in sharp contrast with most other efforts at ecosystem management, which continue to emphasize the values of scientific utilitarianism rather than ecocentric democracy (Grumbine 1994). The 1,813 acres that comprise the 'Inimim Forest are therefore among the most important fragments of public lands in the Sierra Nevada if not the entire United States (Duane 1997a).

The 'Inimim Forest experiment originated in the conflict between traditional land and resource management practices and the emerging social values that were not adequately reflected in that paradigm. The BLM proposed a timber harvest on some of its lands and several land trades in the late 1980s that met strong local opposition. Nearby residents used the forest for recreation and it provided important habitat for wildlife. They were also concerned about water quality degradation from soil erosion and herbicide use that would occur if the logging were to go forward. The dirt and gravel roads of the ridge are lined with hand-painted signs saying "No Spray, Please," demonstrating local concern about herbicide use. Hundreds of residents protested the BLM proposals either in writing or by attending a public hearing process conducted under the Federal Land Policy and Management Act of 1976 and NEPA.[43]

Folsom District BLM manager Deane Swickard says that "the land use planning process, as we were exercising it, was bankrupt. The products were being rejected in the form of appeals and lawsuits" (1997). Swickard observed that public "participation" occurred much too late in the planning process to either influence agency actions or generate long-term support for them, placing the agency and citizens at loggerheads. "Most of the public felt they weren't involved," he says. "They thought they were being dictated to [by the agencies;] . . . the royalty of the federal agencies would come to present something, the peasants would come in to comment, then they would go out, then they'd come back in the EIS process" (ibid.). This represented mere tokenism in public participation (Canter 1996, 591; Arnstein 1969), which may meet the letter of the law but is generally not helpful.

As a result, the BLM management system faced a crisis, in Holling's model, and Swickard played the visionary role of loyal heretic, working within agency guidelines to seek a more meaningful alternative. Swickard was a catalyst for innovation by being both willing to listen to the community's concerns and willing to try something daring that would reduce the BLM's direct control over planning and management decisions.[44] "We affect the quality of the community's life," Swickard says, "so why not involve them in this process?" He noted that the Federal Land Policy and Management Act "says the public would be involved in the planning and decision-making," yet "the truth is, they weren't" (1997). With the support of California State BLM Director Ed Hasty, Swickard approached members of the community and asked them how they would approach management of ten scattered parcels totaling 1,813 acres on the San Juan Ridge (ibid.). The BLM staff then worked with local residents and the Timber Framers Guild of North America, whose seven hundred members (from more than three hundred companies) rely on high-quality old-growth forests to produce larger timbers that are difficult to produce from smaller trees (Lin 1996, 14; Brackett 1993–96). Local residents saw an opportunity to produce timber on the land in a responsible way that would both protect old-growth habitat values and support value-added wood-products manufacturing that could provide jobs in the local community. They established the Yuba Watershed Institute (YWI) as a nonprofit organization to develop a detailed plan, manage the forest, and implement the alternatives. The BLM then entered into a shared management agreement with the YWI and the guild, which still complies with all federal laws (Yuba Watershed Institute et al. 1994; Bureau of Land Management 1994; 1995a; 1995b).

The YWI has generated community involvement in both the planning process and ongoing management decisions through public lectures, field trips, work days, the quarterly newsletter *Tree Rings,* book publications, and monthly board meetings that are open to the community. They often cosponsor events with the North Columbia Schoolhouse Cultural Center, which is also located at the heart of the dispersed rural community. Extensive horizontal networks of civic engagement characterize the San Juan Ridge, as well as norms of reciprocity that reflect in part the rural character of the community.[45] The community also shares an ecocentric value structure that nevertheless recognizes the legitimacy of woods workers' need to make a living.

Together the partners have agreed to manage the 'Inimim to produce a sustainable supply of old-growth timber for specialized wood products (Yuba Watershed Institute et al. 1994; Bureau of Land Management 1994; 1995a; 1995b). Maintaining ecological processes and biological diversity is also an explicit goal of the effort (ibid.). "One of the concerns I had was that the community might try to maximize short-term yields," says Swickard, "but in this case they didn't." He believes there is a continuum of community conceptions of multiple use and sustained yield conditions, and that "some will tend toward the preservation end and some will tend toward the commodity end" (1997). The ridge community is preservation-oriented, reducing the likelihood that their proposals would be inconsistent with either other state or federal laws or the values and interests of other parties external to the community. As a result, the 'Inimim experiment has not generated opposition from state or national environmental groups. This, I believe, stems from the fact that it has satisfied three criteria that distinguish it from many other efforts, such as the Quincy Library Group proposal for management of 2.2 million acres of Forest Service land in the Northern Sierra: 1) environmentalists are not disproportionately less represented in the community than in the state or nation, 2) the agreements and plans are consistent with existing state and federal environmental laws, and 3) it is an incremental experiment encompassing less than 1 percent of the area affected by the Quincy proposal. The latter proposal, in contrast, would affect a vast area and is opposed by more than 140 state and national environmental groups (Duane 1997a; Marston 1997; Margolis 1997).

The 'Inimim Forest Plan is nevertheless not a classic preservationist management strategy that makes the forest off-limits to human activity. The ridge community clearly recognizes that the 'Inimim embodies both Nature and Culture through significant alterations in the landscape evident today that resulted from historical mining, timber harvest, and fire suppression practices. Community members have therefore advocated active management strategies that are more likely to "grow big trees fast" than passive preservation would. This challenges many mainstream environmentalist approaches to public lands management, but it suggests that there is room to find innovative agreements to achieve social, economic, and ecological goals in public lands management by using timber harvests as a means to an end rather than an end in themselves. National environmental groups can support this strategy: as long as "the highest and best use of those lands is to protect their natural values," says the Natural Resources Defense Council attorney David Edelson, logging and grazing can be used "as a means to an end" in public lands management (1997a).

The result of the 'Inimim effort is now a model partnership between the grassroots locals and a professional federal land and resource management agency. "There's no question anymore" as to whether this approach has worked, says Swickard, and he has initiated similar dialogues in two other communities within the three-hundred-thousand-acre Folsom Resource Area along the western slope of the Sierra Nevada foothills (1997). In one of those cases, on nearby Round Mountain across the South Yuba River, the process appears to be going well, having tapped into preexisting social capital generated through the development of the Lake Vera/Round Mountain Neighborhood Association planning effort during the Nevada County General Plan update process (ibid.; Scull 1996). This neighborhood was the only one in the county to produce its own alternative land use plan and present it to the planning commission and board of supervisors. It included an excellent analysis of existing parcelization, alternative build-out projections, fire risk and safety corridors, and a survey of residents' attitudes about alternative levels of future development (LVRMNA 1995). It is also the site of a highly visible dedication of conservation easements on four forty-acre parcels by Robin Mallgren and Janaia Donaldson to the Nevada County Land Trust (Sneed 1995f; 1995g; Mallgren 1994–95; Donaldson 1994–95), which has highlighted the role of area landowners in providing critical winter range habitat for the Nevada City deer herd (Faulstich and Xio 1993). Finally, like the 'Inimim lands, the Round Mountain area benefits from widespread local interest by both citizens and government agencies in protecting the scenic, ecological, and recreational values of the South Yuba River corridor (South Yuba River Citizens League 1993). This has helped to place the 'Inimim and Round Mountain efforts into a broader regional context of an interconnected system of social, economic, ecological linkages.

My year on the San Juan Ridge taught me that the YWI is deeply embedded in this complex series of social relations, which reinforces and supports the ecocentric values of the community. The YWI is both a descendant and an antecedent of bioregional thinking within the broader community, where Nature and Culture are coevolving to give rise to new institutions such as the YWI and its partnership with the BLM. Deane Swickard's visionary role was certainly a critical catalyst in the 'Inimim Forest story, but it would not have made a difference without the hard work of YWI board members like Bob Erickson, Bruce Boyd, Len Brackett, Don Harkin, Gary Snyder, and Eric Beckwitt. Perhaps much more important than these individual contributions, however, is the fact that the Culture on the ridge embraces Leopold's land ethic. This has been true since the "back to the land" movement brought most of the YWI board members to the ridge at the same time that Boise Cascade was carving up the lower (and more accessible) foothills for Lake Wildwood and Lake of the Pines. Cultural production on the ridge is therefore distinct from much of the rest of western Nevada County and may even be unique within the Range of Light. The practices that nurture such a Culture are therefore important to its continued viability and replicability.

Three practices on the San Juan Ridge stand out. One is the annual Sierra Storytelling Festival, which supports and nurtures an ancient craft that ensures a voice for ways of knowing a place and its people through narrative and metaphor rather than spreadsheets and satellite images. The annual event fills the last weekend in July with lawn chairs, fine food, moving stories, good music, and fuzzy feelings that last well after the "professional" storytellers have caught their planes back to their respective homes. Stories reinforce the importance of vision, perception, experience, and the little details that constitute a life well lived. Much of the ridge community participates in the weekend by either working at the festival or housing visiting storytellers. The result is a community still steeped in oral tradition and less easily overwhelmed by the homogeneity of the mass-marketed symbols of mainstream consumer society. I notice details now that I never would have noticed before I heard some of those stories, and I am sure that others in the community have had similar revelations.

The second practice is regular cultural and educational events at the North Columbia Schoolhouse Cultural Center, where YWI has its office. Some of these events are sponsored by YWI; others are sponsored by the Cultural Center. Many of them involve the relationship between Nature and Culture, for the community is filled with artists who have emphasized this relationship. Gary Snyder encourages the pursuit of watershed-conscious poetry; Bob Erickson and Holly Tornheim the craft and beauty of local woods. "A Celebration of Sierra Woods," for example, was a brilliant exhibit that ranged from Tornheim's delicately carved wood bowls and spoons (alas, I could afford only a small but beautiful manzanita spoon) to Erickson's spectacularly functional yet fashionable wooden chairs (exhibited at the Smithsonian the next year, when Erickson was one of just two American furniture makers selected for the honor). Handmade guitars sat next to oak rolltop desks, each declaring its relationship to the landscape through the tracing of the home source of its wood. In this way, these cultural events link both utility and beauty to ecological health. This approach has helped to bridge the gap between economy and ecology that permeates so many discussions in the Sierra Nevada.

Finally, the community practices rituals acknowledging its relationship to Nature. Every May a private meadow becomes the site of a May Day celebration of spring that is both festive and sensitive to the land. For example, the event was canceled this year for the first time, because the meadow was too wet to support the trampling that accompanies the gathering. The community did manage to hold its annual harvest celebration near the end of October, however, heralding the end of the gathering season and the beginning of winter. In some respects it was like any other small-town social event in a rural community: people shared stories, food, and laughter while they caught up with visiting friends and family who had left the ridge to pursue other dreams. Unlike the typical village gathering, however, the event also included both a highly ritualized dance of residents dressed as animals and a symbolic offering of seeds at a harvest altar. More than three hundred people circled the altar, passed through a blessing ritual, and experienced the power of a social—rather than only a personal—declaration of the seasons and our thanks for abundance. Teresa and I introduced our son, Cody, to the community at this gathering one month after his birth. He will return in future years, and may someday join the archers as they fire arrows toward the east (Dachtler 1990, 57–59). It would be impossible to remain unaware of the connection between Nature and Culture with these twice-yearly rituals, and they have given me a new appreciation for those connections.

We no longer depend on the grace of Nature to ensure a good harvest or good health through the winter, but the rituals of the ridge remind us that we continue to depend on Nature for many other things. Those gatherings have strengthened my appreciation for those things while simultaneously linking me with my neighbors through shared experience. That is how Culture is constructed, and it is something that distinguishes the ridge from any other community I have ever encountered in the rural West. Whether or not it can be reproduced in different contexts and at different scales may prove to be one of the critical determinants of whether we will successfully reinhabit the Range of Light over the next seven generations. At the very least, however, we can learn from its success as we confront the problem of sustainability elsewhere.

RETHINKING INSTITUTIONAL BOUNDARIES

If the principles of bioregionalism are to be the basis for planning, what is the proper scale for bioregional institutions? This is probably the wrong question, for it presumes that there is a correct perspective. It is more appropriate to evaluate the effects of human activities at a *variety* of scales and to respond to them with institutions that match the effects and activities that generate them. The CDF, for example, may be interested primarily in how forest management under its jurisdiction may affect the viability and biological diversity of the state's forest species. That emphasis on a state-level scale, however, does not exempt the agency from considering how biological diversity might be affected at the higher scale of western North America, the Pacific Rim or the Western Hemisphere, temperate montane forests, or the entire planet. Similar consideration should be given to effects on the biological diversity of the lower scales of the Sierra Nevada, the Yuba watershed, or the ponderosa pine forests of the South Yuba canyon. Asking these questions at different spatial and temporal scales will often yield different answers and insights as well as actions. Bioregionalism therefore requires multiple institutions operating at multiple scales.

This seems to be a reasonable set of spatial scales for comprehensive analysis:

1. global: for example, global biodiversity or global ecological system function;
2. ecosystem: for example, temperate forests or wet tropical forests;
3. continental: for example, the Pacific Rim or North America or the Americas;
4. ecoregional: for example, California or the Pacific Coast of North America;
5. bioregional: for example, the Sierra Nevada or Klamath Province or Central Valley;
6. watershed: for example, the Yuba River or Yuba-Bear or Yuba-Feather drainages;
7. community: for example, western Nevada County or the San Juan Ridge;
8. population: for example, the ponderosa pine forests of the South Yuba canyon;
9. family: for example, the extended Duane and McGlashan families (relatives of my son, Cody);
10. individual: for example, you or me or Cody as we connect to all the levels above us.[46]

This typology represents a nested hierarchy of scales, which has also been recognized for both urban design and landscape ecology. For example, the pathbreaking 1977 book by architect Christopher Alexander and his colleagues, *A Pattern Language*, relies on this principle in development of a framework for Alexander's *The Timeless Way of Building*, published in 1979. He advocates designing "one pattern at a time," but these patterns are nested within a "language" of form that gives meaning to individual elements through a spatial semiotics. "The structure of the language," says Alexander, "is created by the network of connections among individual patterns: and the language lives, or not, as a totality, to the degree these patterns form a whole" (385, 305). More specifically, the pattern language is built around the idea that "independent regions within each region work toward those regional policies which will protect the land and mark the limits of the cities" (Alexander et al. 1977, xix) and which "through city policies, encourage the piecemeal formation of those major structures which define the city." Those elements then "build up these larger city patterns from the grass roots, through action essentially controlled by two levels of self-governing communities, which exist as physically identifiable places" and that in turn depend on a series of elements that "connect communities to one another" (xx). Other "fundamental principles" at a finer-grain scale "establish community and neighborhood policy to control the character of the local environment," which "encourage the formation of local centers" for a rich urban life "both in the neighborhoods and the communities, and in between them, in the boundaries" (xxi).

"Based on face-to-face human groups," this structure provides "for the growth of housing in the form of clusters" around these centers, while "work communities" are developed "between the house clusters, around the centers, and especially in the boundaries between neighborhoods." Alexander and his colleagues then suggest that designers should "allow the local road and path network to grow informally, piecemeal" to reflect patterns of social activity, and that we should also "provide public open land where people can relax, rub shoulders and renew themselves," as well as "the smaller bits of common land, to provide for local versions of the same needs" (xii, xxi, xxii, xxiii). Ultimately, Alexander and his colleagues believe, a livable community will emerge if these patterns are followed and nested within the appropriate pattern at the next higher spatial and temporal scale. They then apply similar principles to the arrangement of a group of buildings, the design of buildings, and the design of individual building elements. Each element finds meaning within its nested linguistic context: context determines content.

Richard Forman discerns a similar structure of nested hierarchy in the patterns of landscapes in his 1995 book, *Land Mosaics,* as does Robert Bailey in his 1996 book, *Ecosystem Geography.* Holling's four-stage model of ecological systems recognizes further that ecological processes function at a variety of spatial and temporal scales (1995, 23). Forman, Bailey, and Holling demonstrate that the relationship between processes and patterns at different spatial and temporal scales may be discontinuous and therefore nonuniformly distributed. One of the problems with modern land and resource management, it appears, has been its focus on phenomena that operate at a particular level in the hierarchy while ignoring equally important processes operating at other spatial and temporal scales (Holling 1995). Increasing the mean outputs at one scale, such as occurs in timber harvests, then narrows the range of variability at that scale while decreasing system resilience because of structural and functional changes in the operation of the system at other scales. It is therefore necessary to manage ecosystems at a variety of scales simultaneously.

Note that there are multiple social identities and ecological relationships within each of the ten spatial scales that I have outlined above, and that the boundaries may overlap and sometimes cross between higher or lower spatial scales. This place that I am writing from, for example, is both within the Yuba River drainage and the Sierra Nevada Bioregion. The Yuba River drainage extends beyond the Sierra Nevada, however, linking me to the Central Valley (another bioregion within California). Moreover, the headwaters of the Yuba River are in snowfields adjacent to waters that drain down the eastern slope of the Sierra Nevada into the Truckee River and the Great Basin ecoregion. The southernmost waters of the Sierra Nevada flow into the Caliente drainage of the Great Southwestern Desert, still another ecoregion within the North American continent. It is precisely this complexity that makes the community level and the population level so important: the ponderosa pine forests of the South Yuba canyon I see out my window have ecological influences in their evolutionary history very different from those of many other coniferous forests in the Sierra Nevada. As a result, it is inadequate to evaluate the effects of a human action at only the level of the Sierra Nevada or the state of California. Locally specific conditions make populations important for the genetic information they carry and the ecological relationships they may have developed by adapting to those local conditions.

This complexity makes it very difficult to classify and categorize landscapes, and it challenges the taxonomic orientation of many scientists and academics. A failure to classify something makes it extremely difficult to measure, which then makes it hard to test hypotheses where relationships among measurable variables are postulated. But this is an ambiguity in the real world, not just in our theories about the world. Just as I have multiple identities—as professor, husband, father, son, brother, friend, mountain biker, photographer, musician—so can a place have multiple relationships to, and contextually determined identities with, the rest of the world. Below the level of the bioregion, three of those relationships between each place and its attributes stand out.

The first relationship is defined by the boundaries of the watershed or drainage basin.[47] Each of us and each place we are part of is connected to other people and other places through the hydrologic system. Every place is part of a watershed, however, so there is no correct level at which we can draw a line around the hydrologic process and say that it constitutes a watershed. Each watershed is composed of countless subwatersheds, each composed of countless other sub-subwatersheds. But no matter what the level of the watershed hierarchy, recognizing one's position in the watershed requires a parallel recognition of one's connection to places upstream and downstream. It also raises the importance of recognizing relationships at a variety of spatial and temporal scales. This house is perched on the edge of the Shady Creek watershed, which then feeds into the South Yuba River. But at different spatial and temporal scales, it is also part of the Sacramento River watershed and the pulse of water that flows through the Carquinez Straits each year to cleanse the San Francisco Bay.

The size and number of the major river basins within the Sierra Nevada are— perhaps coincidentally—roughly comparable to the size and number of counties. Identifying a relationship to a watershed that is tangible and similar to a familiar social institution is therefore possible. The only difference between most counties and most watersheds is that the boundaries of the watershed follow topography and hydrology and are visible without a sign or a map. Therein lies an important conceptual difference, however, for county boundaries drawn along watershed boundaries would regularly signal to us that we live in a biophysical universe of ecohydrological processes.

The second important relationship is defined by the vegetation. Each of us lives within, and each place we are part of supports, an assemblage of vegetation also found in other places with similar conditions. The conditions supporting that vegetation include elevation, slope, aspect, precipitation, and soils. The vegetation,

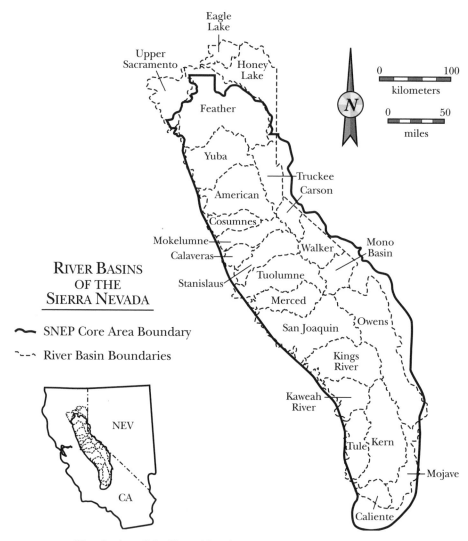

RIVER BASINS
OF THE
SIERRA NEVADA

〜 SNEP Core Area Boundary

‑‑‑ River Basin Boundaries

MAP 11.1.   River basins of the Sierra Nevada.

in turn, supports a variety of wildlife species that inhabit the place with us. Understanding the vegetation is therefore an entrée into a better understanding of both our neighbors and the forces that shape our environment. Just as we are connected upstream and downstream to all who share our watershed, we are connected through vegetation to all who share the conditions of our place. This place is in the Yuba watershed, but it is also in the transition zone between the oak–foothill pine forests of the foothills and the midelevation coniferous forests of the Sierra Nevada. Similar areas are found at a similar elevation to the north and south of us in the Sierra Nevada. We might therefore look north and south along an elevational band in the foothills of the Sierra Nevada to find a set of ecological connections within this vegetation type that transcend our watershed boundaries. Both plants and animals of our vegetation type migrate between watersheds and share each others' genes. The particular mix of plant species and their ratios may be specific to our particular place, but there are similarities with other areas that bond us in our experience of the natural world. Both the forces that shaped our place and the conditions we experience are similar within our vegetation type. Understanding our vegetation therefore links us to the rest of the natural world in a way that the watershed does not.

Finally, each place has an ecological relationship to human activities. Some communities depend on the land for resource extraction, while others have built their economies around recreation and tourism. Still others, like the rapidly changing Gold Country, have a mixed economy with a complex set of dependencies on the landscape, each other, and metropolitan economic activity. Each of us has a set of relationships to other people, moreover, that includes both personal ties and institutional affiliations. County boundaries, city and town limits, school district boundaries, and newspaper distribution networks all affect our connections to each other and our place. Nevada City may be on Deer Creek, and Grass Valley may be on Wolf Creek, but they share a history through mining, marriage, governance, and economic exchanges that transcends the watershed divide. They therefore find themselves together in western Nevada County, which has a set of county boundaries that reflect social and economic ties. Those social, economic, and institutional relationships are all part of the identity of any particular place and our relationship to that place. Today's county boundaries reflect the conditions of the 1850s, however, rather than those of the 1990s.

Our existing institutional boundaries are nevertheless limiting our ability to integrate Nature and Culture in a sustainable way. We should therefore consider changing some of those boundaries. Watersheds (at the river basin scale) could be the basis for new county boundaries in the Sierra Nevada and throughout California to establish a closer relationship between land use planning, water resources quality and management, and the functional ecological relationships that dominate ecosystem management. Such a change would not be a panacea, of course, and adoption of any new county boundaries must also reflect the dimensions of vegetative communities and social, cultural, and economic relationships. The latter include existing institutional arrangements, such as county and city boundaries that currently allocate governmental responsibilities as well as determine identity. School districts, for example, are an important determinant of community ties.

Many of these social institutions are constrained by existing jurisdictional boundaries, however, and a shift to watershed-based counties would actually strengthen community identity and relationships to other communities. The Tahoe-Truckee High School Wolverines, for example, compete in athletics with

Nevada state high schools, and many residents in Truckee work or shop in Reno. The *Sierra Sun*, also based in Truckee, recently won several state press awards—for Nevada. Similarly, the residents of the Carson, Walker, and Owens River watersheds on the eastern Sierra do much of their shopping in Carson City, Gardnerville, or Tonapah, Nevada. The Reno paper is delivered along the eastern Sierra front as far south as Bishop, while the *Los Angeles Times* is delivered as far north as the colonial outpost of Mammoth Lakes. These "circulation-sheds" help to identify and define existing social relationships that are clearly not tied to existing county boundaries. The residents in Truckee, for example, have much more in common with the residents of Squaw Valley, Tahoe City, and South Lake Tahoe than they do with the residents of Nevada City and Grass Valley. Yet those eastside residents are all now residents of three different California counties (Nevada, Placer, and El Dorado) and have a grand total of three county supervisors representing them as minority members of their respective boards of supervisors. It is no wonder then that Truckee's incorporation in 1993 was driven primarily by desire for local self-determination in land use decision-making, which had been abused for decades by the developer-controlled board of supervisors in Nevada City. Today the community is engaged in a remarkable effort to develop a "downtown vision plan" that will further the community's goals as adopted recently in its first general plan. The Truckee River, not surprisingly, has emerged as a centerpiece in that downtown-vision exercise, as a sacred landscape for the community (Truckee 1997; Eddins 1994–97; Lashbrook 1994–97).

Leaving aside the significant problem of the California-Nevada state border—which is not likely to be changed any time soon because of the economic significance of the boundary to the gaming industry and tax-haven refugees seeking exemption from California income tax—the twenty-two major river basins identified in the SNEP analysis approximate the nineteen California counties in the Sierra Nevada. They could therefore serve as the basis for drawing new county boundaries without fundamentally altering either the average size, income, or land use characteristics of existing counties. Only three of the watershed-based counties would include more than one existing county seat, but twelve of the twenty-two river basins do not now have a county seat within them.

Some of these watersheds are very large and would probably be better served by being split, while others are quite small and could be consolidated with an adjacent watershed to form a new county that would be above a minimum threshold of population and/or area for viability. I have considered these factors to develop a preliminary proposal for watershed-based counties in the Sierra Nevada shown in Table 11.2. This proposal would maintain all existing county seats, establish four new county seats and counties, and make several existing counties smaller to reflect geographic differences between the Sierra Nevada, the Central Valley, and desert regions nearby. This approach would minimize disruption and the cost of

TABLE 11.1   Existing River Basins, Counties,
and County Seats in the Sierra Nevada

River Basins	Counties	County Seats
Eagle Lake	Lassen	
Honey Lake	Lassen	Susanville
Sacramento	Tehama, Butte	
Feather	Plumas, Butte, Tehama	Quincy, Oroville
Yuba/Bear	Sierra, Yuba, Nevada, Placer	Downieville, Nevada City
American	Placer, El Dorado, Alpine	Auburn, Placerville
Truckee/Tahoe	Nevada, Placer, El Dorado	
Cosumnes	El Dorado, Amador	Jackson
Mokelumne	Amador, Calaveras, Alpine	
Calaveras	Calaveras	San Andreas
Stanislaus	Calaveras, Tuolumne, Alpine	
Tuolumne	Tuolumne, Mariposa	Sonora
Merced	Tuolumne, Mariposa	
San Joaquin	Mariposa, Madera, Tulare	Mariposa
Kings	Tulare, Fresno	
Kaweah	Tulare, Fresno	
Tule	Fresno, Kern	
Kern	Fresno, Kern	
Mojave	Kern, Inyo	
Owens	Mono, Inyo	Independence
Mono	Mono	
Walker	Mono	Bridgeport
Carson	Alpine	Markleeville

delineating new county boundaries that would reflect the ecological realities of the watersheds as bioregional units.

The Tuolumne River watershed demonstrates one of the difficulties with using river basins as the basis for delineating county boundaries: the town of Sonora itself rides the divide between the Stanislaus and Tuolumne River basins, and Highway 108 follows that divide into the upper reaches of the Stanislaus watershed to Sonora Pass north of Yosemite National Park. The SNEP GIS data layers apparently treated most of these residents as being within the Stanislaus River basin (Duane 1996a, Table 11A4), although closer study of land use patterns suggests that most of the population is actually in the watershed of a tributary to the Tuolumne River. I have proposed inclusion of Sonora in the Tuolumne water-

TABLE 11.2   Proposed New Watershed-Based Counties
and County Seats in the Sierra Nevada

New County	SNEP River Basins Included	County Seat
Lassen	Honey, Eagle	Susanville
Plumas	Feather, Upper Sacramento	Quincy
Sierra	North Yuba	Downieville
Nevada	Middle and South Yuba, Bear	Nevada City
Placer	North American	Auburn
El Dorado	Middle and South American	Placerville
Amador	Cosumnes, Mokelumne	Jackson
Calaveras	Calaveras, Stanislaus	San Andreas
Tuolumne	Tuolumne	Sonora
Mariposa	Merced	Mariposa
Minarets*	San Joaquin	Oakhurst†
Sequoia	Kings, Kaweah, Tule	Three Rivers†
Golden Trout*	Kern	Lake Isabella†
Inyo	Owens, Mono Basin	Independence
Walker	Walker	Bridgeport
Carson	Carson	Markleeville
Tahoe	Truckee	South Lake Tahoe†

*Named for the respective Wilderness Areas that dominate the upper watershed area
(Minarets Wilderness was renamed the Ansel Adams Wilderness upon his death).
†New county seat (all other county seats are already county seats of existing counties).

shed, moreover, because of economic links to Yosemite and the conflict with San Andreas as a county seat in the Stanislaus River basin. The town of Sonora is also already the county seat of the existing Tuolumne County.

I have used a similar logic to propose expanding Inyo County to include Mono Basin in order to reflect the social, economic, and institutional ties that link water resources management, forest management, and recreation and tourism activities in the region. The region looks southward toward Los Angeles and is all part of the Inyo National Forest, managed from Bishop. The Walker River basin, in contrast, looks northeasterly toward Nevada and is institutionally tied to the Toiyabe National Forest based in Nevada. In addition, two "remnant" SNEP river basins could be incorporated into adjacent regions to reflect the social and economic links that bind these areas to nearby communities: the Caliente and Mojave River basins face southward to the desert and are both presently in Kern County. I propose splitting Kern County and making the desert community of Ridgecrest a new seat for a county that would include the Caliente and Mojave watersheds. I would also remove Roseville from Placer County and include it in an expanded

Sacramento County to more accurately reflect its social and economic links to the metropolitan area. This is consistent with Pacific Bell's recent decision to split the 916 area code and apply it only to the greater Sacramento region, including Roseville (McAdams 1997b).

John Wesley Powell first proposed the organization of western communities, local governments, and reclamation projects along watershed boundaries in 1878 (Powell 1878; Stegner 1954). His vision for a rational development approach to the arid West was rejected in favor of the more "efficient" system of delineating boundaries according to the surveyor's grid, which marched across the western landscape oblivious of the ecological realities of place. Gary Snyder proposed a more limited reorganization of Sierra Nevada county boundaries in his 1990 book, *The Practice of the Wild,* where he suggested a "Truckee River County" that would extend from the Sierra Valley to north Lake Tahoe (with Truckee as the county seat), and another county from the west shore of Lake Tahoe down through areas south of Lake Tahoe (including the upper Truckee River watershed). His proposal would also combine western Sierra County, eastern Yuba County and northwestern Nevada County (north of the South Yuba River) to form "Nisenan County," while the rest of Nevada and Placer Counties would be combined. This would place the San Juan Ridge outside of the jurisdiction of the Nevada County Board of Supervisors (Snyder 1990, 47).

These suggestions make sense to me in social, economic, and cultural terms that reflect the differences between places like Lake of the Pines and the San Juan Ridge (which would remain together in the same county in my proposed boundaries). Having smaller counties might also be necessary to reflect the difficulties of mountain travel in the winter, which would continue to isolate Truckee residents from county decision makers in South Lake Tahoe. I offer my initial list simply as a starting point for discussion. The citizens of the Sierra Nevada are themselves in the best position to determine if different county boundaries would work better. New county boundaries should reflect today's ecological and social realities, however, rather than the nineteenth-century patterns of resource use, transportation networks, and communications technologies that determined our current county boundaries.

Pacific Bell recently discovered this reality when it proposed splitting the 510 area code along county lines, intending to retain the 510 area code for Alameda County and give Contra Costa County the new 925 area code. Residents overwhelmingly objected to the proposal and offered an alternative that reflected social, economic, and ecological realities: a division along the watershed boundary of the East Bay Hills, which kept the inner-ring suburbs along the San Francisco Bay shore together in the 510 area code (regardless of county) while placing the socially linked newer suburban communities east of the hills together in the new 925 area code. This watershed-based approach has now been adopted, and it probably makes sense at this time to reconsider Alameda and Contra Costa's county boundaries as well.

Robert Hass used his term as poet laureate of the United States during 1995 to 1997 to promote the idea of watersheds as the basis for both community and identity through relationship to place, and the poetry his effort inspired takes us further toward recognizing our "place in space" (Clines 1996). A similar poetic effort titled "counties" instead of "watersheds" would have evoked far less inspiration and more of an institutionally defined identity that would have invariably focused almost exclusively on social relations. Watersheds compel us to think about people, place, plants, animals, soils, weather, and how they all interact to affect our lives. Watersheds are therefore a useful foundation for new institutional boundaries. Our boundaries reflect our "terrain of consciousness" (Merchant 1992).

Institutions are not immutable. They nevertheless influence how we look at and interact with Nature. Consequently, our institutional structures, jurisdictional boundaries, and the identities we develop in response to them are important reflections of our Culture. J. B. Jackson suggests that the term "boundary" is often thought of as that which *separates* things, but its roots lie in the idea of "binding" things together (1984, 13–16). Our boundaries represent both borders of exclusion and the limits of inclusion. Marking our county boundaries along the watershed divide may help us recognize our relationship to all that flows and lives within the river basin included therein.

WATER, WEALTH, AND WATERSHED HEALTH

Water runs downhill in its natural state, but we all know that in the arid West it runs uphill toward money. The human institutions that make this true are inherited from a frontier past when resources seemed infinite and water seemed always to be in the wrong place at the wrong time (Wilkinson 1992a). Our predecessors in the Sierra Nevada landscape were remarkably effective at developing new institutions to "correct" that problem by creating incentives for labor and capital to convert the energy and resources of the Sierra Nevada into the wealth that gave rise to what is now known as California. As Gray Brechin (forthcoming) has shown, "Imperial San Francisco" had a reach that transformed its hinterland and extracted the wealth of the Sierra Nevada for its own benefit. In large part this continues to be the case today, although Los Angeles and the rest of California have also placed their claims on the Range of Light. Today the Sierra Nevada is closely linked to every human activity in California.

We now have the opportunity to reform our land and resource management institutions to address the problems of the region in the context of the ongoing ecotransformation, and there is ample precedent for this in California history. By 1880 there were more than two thousand miles of ditches, canals, and flumes in Nevada County to supply water to the hydraulic mines on the San Juan Ridge and the emerging communities that depended on them and the hardrock mines of Grass Valley (Thompson and West 1880). The primary water institution guiding the allocation of water resources was the simple "first in time, first in right" idea of the prior appropriation doctrine. This system led to significant environmental damage, however, including the dramatic transformation of the Yuba watershed as whole mountains were washed into the canyons and valleys below. Farming and navigation interests were repeatedly threatened by flooding and debris, leading to intense conflict between agricultural and mining interests. These conflicts culminated in the 1884 decision by Judge Lorenzo Sawyer to curtail hydraulic mining unless it was conducted in a way that limited its effects on other parties downstream. The social institutions guiding water policy therefore adapted to reflect new social values (Kelley 1959).

We can see parallels between that controversy and more recent conflicts over the effects of water resource projects on environmental values. Nobody ever thought a ragtag band of UC graduate students would ever be able to challenge the water rights of the thirstiest city on the continent, but that is exactly what happened when the Los Angeles Department of Water and Power was recently compelled to surrender some of its water rights in order to return Mono Lake to an environmentally acceptable condition. It took a long time, of course, but the 1983 decision of the California Supreme Court in favor of the Audubon Society and the Mono Lake Committee established the public trust concept as a legal foundation for transforming the allocation of water and power in modern society (Hart 1996). A dozen years later the State Water Resources Control Board finally implemented the court's decision after additional scientific studies and public hearings. A similar transformation has occurred with the San Joaquin and Sacramento Rivers through the Central Valley Project Improvement Act of 1992, which requires the release of eight hundred thousand acre-feet of water per year and an aggressive recovery plan for fisheries affected by Central Valley Project operations. The Environmental Protection Agency's strict position on bay-delta water quality also compelled the parties to come to the table in 1994 to hammer out the bay-delta agreement. Now it looks like implementation of these programs will be supported by nearly $1.5 billion in state and federal funding.[48] We are finally moving toward restoration of California's tragically degraded aquatic ecosystems for the first time in California history since Euro-American settlement. This is a major shift.

But something is still missing. To date, all of the analysis and policy effort has been directed at restoring the ecological system *downstream* of dams and diversions. There has been very little attention paid to the relationship between *upstream* watershed conditions and the overall health of the ecohydrological system. Moreover, the rural communities that inhabit the forested watersheds of the Sierra Nevada have been largely ignored in this debate.[49] Yet it is from the forests of the Sierra Nevada that the waters of the bay and delta flow; both the economic and ecological well-being of urban and agricultural California therefore depend on the well-being of those forests and their associated communities. We must link the water users of California to watershed restoration and stewardship programs. The cost of doing so is small, while the benefits are enormous.

The direct economic value of water from the State Water Project's Oroville Dam and Pacific Gas and Electric Company's Feather River Project illustrates the scale of the wealth that accompanies water transfers in the state. The State Water Project yields an average of 2.5 million acre-feet from the Feather River watershed (California Department of Water Resources 1994), and 5.4 billion kilowatt-hours of power are generated by PG&E or the State Water Project in that watershed (California Energy Commission 1993). The water exports are worth anywhere from $25 million at low agricultural wholesale rates ($10 per acre-foot) to $1.3 billion per year at higher municipal water rates ($500 per acre-foot) (Policy Implementation Planning Team 1994). An additional $652 million in hydroelectric value is generated by Feather River water each year at average retail market rates (California Energy Commission 1993). As a result, the total commodity value of Feather River water is between $677 million and $1.9 billion. Yet not a single dollar of that value is returned on a regular basis from the direct beneficiaries of those water resources to the upper watershed specifically for management or restoration.[50] The environmental and social costs of the water system therefore largely remain externalities to both producers and consumers.

Total retail price increases of less than 10 percent for all water originating in the Sierra Nevada would begin to internalize those costs and fund a significant level of watershed restoration. A flat fee of $8 per acre-foot would generate $160 million in revenue (assuming zero elasticity of demand, since California's projected population increases would probably drink up any price-induced reductions in demand), while an increase of only $1.50 per acre-foot for agricultural users and $35 per acre-foot for municipal and industrial users (or a flat fee of $43 per acre-foot for municipal and industrial users only) would generate about $150 million in revenue (Policy Implementation Planning Team 1994). A 10 percent tax on the hydroelectric power would generate another $65 million per year. The *total* value of all timber harvested on public lands in the Sierra Nevada is only $300 million per year (Stewart 1996). "Lost" timber revenues get all of the attention in the press, but water is the key to generating wealth in the Sierra Nevada. Water is also the link that directly ties Sierra Nevada communities to the rest of California. Moreover, we already have an institutional mechanism in place for collecting revenue without creating a new bureaucracy—everybody already pays a water bill and a power bill, so a small surcharge to fund watershed management and restoration could be collected easily without high overhead or transaction costs.

The recent SNEP report shows that there is plenty of work to do, and we know from the 'Inimim Forest experience that restoration of ecologically functional landscapes takes both commitment and funding. Fuels management, prescribed fire, wildlife inventories, stream bank stabilization, intelligent planning, innovative development patterns, and public education all represent investments in the natural capital that sustains environmental quality and economic well-being for those who reside in and depend on the Sierra Nevada. It will probably take at least one year of restoration work for every year of degradation, so it is time to get started on the task of restoring the Sierra Nevada landscape. Perhaps then we can begin to fulfill Wallace Stegner's vision of "a society to match its scenery" in the rural and exurban West.

We need a partnership between the people of the nation, state, bioregion, and local communities in the Sierra Nevada to realize that vision. Water is what links us, for watershed health is ultimately the true measure of our wealth. This is a reality that cannot be captured in the cash-flow accounting systems that now dominate our financial and governmental accounting systems. It is time, as it was for Judge Sawyer in 1884, to recognize that reality. We must make ecosystem health a priority that will receive the sustained funding it needs in order to be viable.

Both the social and ecological systems of the Sierra Nevada stand at a critical juncture. In Holling's model, we are near the end of the "conservation" phase and are experiencing crises in specific elements of the socioecological system because brittleness in those elements has led to a loss of resilience (Holling 1995). The crises have in turn generated a remarkable release of energy and creativity since the early 1990s, the result of a train of events that began with the "Sierra in Peril" series. Some of these events, such as founding of the Quincy Library Group and the Yuba Watershed Institute, have helped to compound social capital within communities; others—such as the Central Valley Project Improvement Act of 1992 and Proposition 204 funding for the CalFed Bay-Delta effort in 1996—have generated financial capital that could be applied to solve ecological and social problems. SNEP has also raised intellectual capital, which can serve as the foundation for new agreements that can further development of political capital.

The SNEP data and analyses are now languishing, however, because of the absence of either political leadership or an overarching crisis that would galvanize action across the region. The state and federal governments are "waiting" for grassroots action, while communities of interest and of place are waiting for leadership from the state. Political capital must be expended to mobilize additional financial capital and deploy the technical resources necessary to solve the crises facing the region—but it is still being hoarded by all sides.

FROM THEORY TO PRACTICE

We often talk about the desirability of collaborative planning and ecosystem management, but the bottom line is that the growth machine, the timber industry and the water development industry are all unwilling to give up business-as-usual unless there are strong incentives to come to the bargaining table. Why should they pay for habitat conservation plans or voluntarily accept a surcharge on water and power use if their current approach to these problems is unthreatened? The prospect of future listings under the ESA is too uncertain and the discount rate too high to worry about them now. They are therefore following the time-honored path that has given us every other "train wreck" blamed on the ESA to date: poor planning invariably leads to predictable outcomes, usually including a no-win confrontation between a species' viability and the economic livelihood of a region. In the year 2020 we will lament the lost opportunity of this time, however, just as with twenty-twenty hindsight we now critique the forestalled action of other crises. By then we will face a further loss of resilience in both our social and ecological systems, all of which will translate into degraded quality of life in the Range of Light. Where will we go then?

The answer can no longer be "the next frontier." Those days are over: we must learn to live in place without the benefit of an untapped frontier waiting to be mined. Sustainable development requires clear vision, sensitive monitoring, hard choices, experimental learning, and adaptive management if it is to survive the test of time among a people committed to place. We must seize this moment of crisis to reorganize the system in a new way. As Holling's model shows us, the process of reorganization will determine the conditions of the next phase of exploitation and ultimate conservation (1995). This is the critical step.

What should we do with this tremendous opportunity? Some of the preliminary elements of a successful reorganization are already in place, although they have not yet been fully utilized: the California Biodiversity Council and the biodiversity memorandum of understanding stand out as the skeletal framework for implementation of truly adaptive, collaborative ecosystem management—although the California Biodiversity Council remains hampered by its focus on information-sharing rather than goal-setting and implementation of policies that will actually protect biodiversity. The Bioregional Councils that were originally authorized under the memorandum of understanding at the bioregional level have also not been established, while watershed groups and landscape associations remain scattered. Even reorganization of existing state and federal agencies to reflect bioregional boundaries has generally not been implemented. This leaves individual watersheds, vegetation communities, habitat types, and species with little more protection than they had before the biodiversity memorandum of understanding was signed in 1991. We all know a lot more about the state of biodiversity in

California now, but not a lot more is getting done in a systematic manner to arrest its decline or begin its restoration.

Action on the issue of biodiversity must still take place today primarily through traditional application of the ESA or through CRMP efforts (California Association of Resource Conservation Districts 1990). The CRMP process is an admirable means of eliciting private landowner participation in conservation, but it is still voluntary and ad hoc. It is also not oriented specifically toward biodiversity protection, as a result of the historical Culture of commodity production in the Soil Conservation Service (now the Natural Resources Conservation Service) and the Resource Conservation Districts in the U.S. Department of Agriculture.[51] Those agencies offer an important entrée into a critical landowner community, and I would not replace them with any other agency. However, their role needs to be complemented by multiagency and multidisciplinary participation from other state and federal agencies that will both emphasize biodiversity values and be able to provide management expertise that goes beyond traditional U.S. Department of Agriculture concerns. We also need systematic application of CRMP efforts throughout the entire Sierra Nevada. Efforts to date by both Resource Conservation Districts and CRMPs have been built on patchwork funding that has seriously limited the ability to plan long-term projects that will generate serious commitments. As a result, participants have had to waste too much time on fundraising and focus too narrowly on short-term projects.

These project-specific efforts must take place within the context of other larger-scale biodiversity management efforts that assess the relative contribution of individual CRMP efforts to the protection of biodiversity and restoration of ecological systems at the watershed, community, subregional, bioregional, and state levels. Such an integrated approach cannot occur under the current ad hoc CRMP program. Application of a BMA-type model should therefore be completed at the bioregional and subregional scales in order to identify priorities for management actions within specific watersheds and communities and among specific landowners. Ultimately CRMPs should be nested within an NCCP effort that includes both public and private land, with public land and resource management plans and local general plans designed to incorporate the results of such an NCCP effort.

Even the NCCP has been applied only under the umbrella (and threat) of the federal ESA, however, making claims of its effectiveness as a new model of proactive or preventative action hollow. A truly proactive and preventative application of the NCCP model would be to compel its application in the Sierra Nevada and its subsequent incorporation into the general plans of Sierra Nevada counties and the land management plans of state and federal agencies. The SNEP data and the BMA model allow a less costly application there than anyplace else in California. Nobody is taking the bull by the horns, though, and applying an NCCP to the Range of Light.[52] Consequently, we need new state legislation, a public commitment to funding, and a governor and administration committed to implementing comprehensive biodiversity planning throughout the region and the state. The dominance of the federal government as a landowner in California and the importance of biodiversity as a public good with national and international values also compels federal participation. Similar efforts in the past have mobilized social, financial, intellectual, and political capital to develop infrastructure, industry, and agriculture in the history of California (McWilliams 1949; Starr 1996); certainly we have the capacity to do the same for protecting our ecological heritage.

We can even do it without bankrupting our economy or increasing taxes. A trivial reallocation of our state and federal spending patterns would easily pay for a systematic biodiversity planning effort for the entire West, eliminating the risk of future "train wrecks" of untold financial risk. The *total* cost of SNEP ($7 million), the Forest Ecosystem Management Assessment Team (which produced President Clinton's Northwest Forest Plan [$15 million]) (FEMAT 1993), the Interior Columbia River Basin Ecosystem Management Project (which covers all Forest Service and BLM lands east of the Cascades in Washington, Oregon, Idaho, and Montana [$20 million]) (Steubner 1997; Steubner and Larmer 1997), and the coastal sage scrub NCCP ($4–7 million) was only $46–$49 million—about half the $97 million spent by *all* state and federal agencies on endangered species in 1990.[53] Total expenditures for endangered species protection from 1973 to 1990 averaged only $41 million, and the Fish and Wildlife Service received an appropriation of only $36 million for related work in 1992.[54] Perhaps more to the point, this level of funding is comparable to the cost of a single *mile* of new four-lane interstate highway in the United States in 1992 (Shaffer 1992b), or a single *lane-mile* of the $1.35 billion expansion of Interstate 80 between the Carquinez Straits and the San Francisco–Oakland Bay Bridge.[55] Application of a SNEP-level assessment to the entire land area of the eleven western states (slightly over 1 million square miles) would therefore cost only $280 million on a proportional basis—which is only *1 percent* of the total cost of the thirteen B-2 Stealth bombers recently acquired by the U.S. government. The cost of a *single* B-2 bomber (costing $2.2 billion, or $2,200 *million*) could have paid for 314 SNEP studies (*Union* 1997a).

It is time that we systematically assess the conditions of the federal lands and the rest of the West for their ecological significance and the role they can play in preserving biodiversity. This task would have fit well with the original purposes of the National Biological Survey before it was downsized by the 104th Congress into the National Biological Service and then the Biological Resources Division of the U.S. Geological Survey. Like the majority of most rural boards of supervisors in the Sierra Nevada, too many GOP Congressmen simply did not want the National Biological Survey to look under the rock. Yet it is these same political "leaders" who decry the stark choices presented by an ESA that kicks in only after a species has gone far down the slope of precipitous decline. It is therefore ironic that the

National Biological Survey now languishes in the U.S. Geological Survey, which was established to survey the resources of the nation as it expanded westward into the land beyond the hundredth meridian. Today we face a new challenge of uncharted terrain, for our systems of measuring and monitoring the landscape have failed to capture the important information that constitutes what we call biodiversity. Like the maps of the Geological Survey and the records of John Wesley Powell, that information has public value that belongs to all of us and will promote the well-being of us all. Accordingly, Congress should appropriate a steady funding stream of $28 million (in real terms) over the next decade to conduct SNEP-level assessments of the entire western United States. The federal government owns 48 percent of the West, and it needs to know what it owns and how it relates to the greater western landscape if it is going to manage those lands to our benefit. Public trust values of the public domain must be considered and protected systematically (Duane forthcoming).

ECOSYSTEMS AS INFORMATION

Neither the federal, state, nor private lands of the rapidly changing West can continue to be managed with the assumptions and tools that we have relied on for the past century, however, for the relationship between Culture and Nature is fundamentally different today than it was when our existing institutional arrangements were established. The Pacific Northwest region of the Forest Service had only two biologists on staff in the postwar timber heyday of the 1950s, and their primary function was to identify means of reducing the negative effects of wildlife on timber production (Hirt 1997). (Wildlife ate saplings and otherwise reduced the efficiency of plantation forestry, and these biologists produced reports on their effects and possible means of controlling them.) Three decades later the northern spotted owl became the focus of concern, and by the 1990s wildlife and biodiversity concerns dominated forest management in the region (Yaffee 1994). The Gospel of Efficiency (Hays 1959) failed to address the consequences of a narrow utilitarian focus on a wider range of social and ecological values, and today the Pacific Northwest finds itself struggling even to maintain viable native salmon populations.

The Forest Service is now filled with many "ologists" who were first hired in the wake of the National Forest Management Act two decades ago in an attempt to incorporate broader social and ecological concerns in the forest planning process. The planning approach established by the Act continued to rely on the paradigms of control and expertise, however, failing to recognize the social dimension of the Act's genesis in public demand for a new forestry that emphasizes ecosystems as *information* rather than industrial inputs. Today the Northern Rockies region of the

Forest Service has more than three thousand employees, but the regional forester has only two bona fide social scientists on the regional staff (Salwasser 1997). These social scientists undoubtedly find themselves in a position within the agency today similar to that of wildlife biologists in the Pacific Northwest in the 1950s: their primary task is to help the agency succeed in its mission to convince the public of the efficacy of its policies, rather than to learn from that public why the agency may be pursuing the wrong policies altogether. It should be no surprise, then, if future historians of the Forest Service find the demise of the agency in the late 1990s or early twenty-first century to have been driven by a failure to understand changing social values (Marston 1993b). Congress shares much of the blame, of course, but there is no doubt that the agency is now firmly in the crisis phase of Holling's four-stage model of ecological and social systems (1995). Even the General Accounting Office (1997) now agrees that the Forest Service is an aimless agency torn between competing social objectives and ambiguous evaluative criteria.

The agency's future—and that of the public lands generally, since the Forest Service is the key public lands manager throughout most of the West—will therefore be determined by the actions of loyal heretics, such as members of the Association of Forest Service Employees for Environmental Ethics, and visionaries (e.g., from nongovernmental environmental organizations) who are willing to step "outside the box" to frame innovative solutions. These catalysts will frame the alternatives for decision makers. Epistemic communities and shadow networks are increasingly important to the development of these alternatives (Gunderson et al. 1995, 531; Clark 1995), for it is across the skeletal remains of existing institutional structures that institutional reorganization will occur. Such reorganization will then allow the exploitation phase again, but the reorganization process itself will determine the shape of future conservation (Holling 1995; Clark and Minta 1994).

This is why the paradigmatic underpinnings of our conceptual framework are so important to the challenge at hand: unless we recognize the profound consequences of the ecotransformation of the West and the new role of ecosystems as *information* rather than mere industrial resource inputs, we run the risk of failing to address the emerging relationship between Nature and Culture. That relationship determines the desirability of both the ends and means of land and resource management, environmental policy, and land use planning.

This can best be summarized with a matrix showing the means and ends of an industrial versus an informational view of Nature, for they each give rise to a different combination of means and ends primarily associated with particular viewpoints. Commodity outputs are the ends of policy in the industrial paradigm, while the dominant means for achieving those ends is centralized control. This has given us the institutional structure of the centralized federal agencies such as the

Forest Service, designed during the Progressive era and oriented toward efficient commodity outputs (Smith 1987; Hirt 1994; Wilkinson 1992a). The information paradigm, in contrast, views ecosystem structure and function as the primary ends of policy because of uncertainty surrounding the value of ecosystem information and the irreversibility of biodiversity loss. Centralized means, which reflect historical industrial-paradigm institutional structures, give rise to the "structural reformers" of the mainstream modern environmental and conservation movements (Dryzek and Lester 1989). These interests seek to use centralized mechanisms of control, such as federal agencies and federal courts, to achieve different management outputs. An information-oriented approach to both the means and ends of policy would, however, call for more decentralized institutional structures consonant with bioregionalism and the deep ecology movement. Industrial ends and information means have given rise to what has been tagged the Sagebrush Rebellion and its call for decentralized management of federal lands in accordance with the Wise Use movement's goal of maximizing commodity outputs.

TABLE 11.3   Information versus Industrial Means and Ends
in Land and Resource Management

	Ends	
Means	Industrial (Commodity)	Information (Ecosystem)
Industrial (Centralized)	Progressive utilitarianism	Structural reformers
Information (Decentralized)	Local control and Wise Use	Bioregionalism and deep ecology

This framework clearly needs further development, but it is a starting point for exploration of the potential implications of ecosystems in the Information Age rather than the Industrial Age. The critical point is that the ecotransformation from industrial to information economies and societies has implications for both the ends and means of planning and management, and it is the combination of the two that will determine the specific form of institutional innovation that is appropriate. Local control under a wise-use framework may be very appropriate if the ends of policy are primarily to produce industrial commodity outputs, for example, but neither the Sagebrush Rebellion nor the utilitarian Progressive models are appropriate if social values now view ecosystem integrity, that is, information retention, as the primary management objective. This is precisely what has happened at the local and regional levels through the ecotransformation of the

Range of Light over the past three decades. It is also driving social change and policy conflict throughout the West. Continuing to value the western landscape according to nineteenth-century notions dooms us to protracting that conflict.

For all of our theory and technical analysis, then, philosophy and values are at the heart of reforming land use planning, human settlement, commodity extraction, recreational development, and ecosystem management in the rural and exurban West. We must therefore transform our Culture if we are to mature in our relationship with Nature. We can no longer presume to conquer the western landscape, extracting Nature's riches before moving on to another place; instead, we must choose to reinhabit the landscape as if we and our descendants will stay. Only then can we build a society that can reconcile Nature and Culture. Only then can we build social capital and create new social institutions that respect and reflect the noncommodity values of the Range of Light. Only then can we move beyond seeing Nature as the unconquered "other" that is here only to serve humanity, regardless of how our actions may affect the land itself (Evernden 1984). Only then can we, as individuals and as a society, develop a land ethic—in relation to real places through daily living.

"In its most profound sense," says Mark Luccarelli, describing Benton MacKaye's approach to planning based on the idea of the ecological region, "environmental planning is not about limiting human destruction of the environment or providing 'natural preserves' that may stand apart from 'human use' areas: it is about 'exploring' the terrain and permitting what we find to suggest how we use the land" (1995, 100). Through that exploration—and a willingness to relinquish our obsession with control over Nature—such a relationship to the landscape might develop.

This relationship cannot be promulgated by statute or edict, of course, although the broader institutional framework will have important consequences for how individual communities, scattered across their respective watersheds, address the challenges of reinhabitation. Instead, it must occur through individual commitments to build a life here that will sustain the social, economic, and ecological values of the Range of Light across the next seven generations. We must work together, then, to realize that future in every aspect of our daily lives, no matter where we are or what our relationship to the Sierra Nevada may be.

Our destiny, and that of the Range of Light, depends on such a commitment.

NOTES

1. In-N-Out had only 18 outlets when its founder, Harry Snyder, died in 1976, but it had grown to 93 outlets in 1993 and 118 outlets by early 1997. Cofounder Esther Snyder still works as bookkeeper for the privately held company, which has been managed by her sons since 1976. Yollin 1997, pg. A14.

2. Wiley and Gottlieb 1982. See Turner 1906; Limerick 1987; and White 1991 about the West, which has constantly been changing and challenging existing economic and social interests in response to population growth and technology.

3. Many architects would argue that all of the professional fields in the College of Environmental Design can trace their roots to architecture, and many architects engage in site planning (often the province of landscape architects), city planning (with urban designers often coming from all three professions), and even regional planning (although architects invariably encounter a need for social, economic, and ecological information at this scale that often transcends their training).

4. Luccarelli 1995, 24. Luccarelli's focus is on Mumford's contribution, but MacKaye was clearly a critical influence on his "imaginative exploration of the environment" (1995, 79–80). Luccarelli noted, "It was MacKaye's Appalachian Trail, though, that established the model for the RPAA: the linkage of regional development and planning to the recovery of regional consciousness" (79–80), and that "for MacKaye, planning began with exploration" (90–91).

5. The GIS field is now increasingly defining itself as Geographic Information *Science* rather than just *Systems*.

6. Luccarelli 1995, 53. The quote from Mumford within the quote from Luccarelli is not cited by Luccarelli.

7. Also see Brown 1995 for a discussion of the social costs.

8. An important exception is Dubbink 1984.

CHAPTER ONE

1. The BLM has critical landholdings here, and there is a Nevada Irrigation District ease-ment for access along the Cascade Ditch.

2. Englebright Dam was built by the Army Corps of Engineers to stop the downstream flow of hydraulic-mining debris, but it now serves primarily as a narrow training ground for waterskiers.

3. That dependence is highlighted by the ongoing "CalFed" process to implement a December 1994 agreement between state and federal regulatory and resource manage-ment agencies in order to address problems of water quality and ecological conditions in the San Francisco Bay and the Sacramento–San Joaquin Delta. See CalFed 1995a; 1995b; 1996; 1997.

4. The Lake Tahoe Basin Management Unit is administered independently, but it is technically composed of portions of the Tahoe, Eldorado, and Toiyabe National Forests.

5. The remaining public lands are administered primarily by the California Department of Parks and Recreation, the U.S. Department of the Interior Bureau of Land Management, the U.S. Department of the Interior Bureau of Reclamation, and the Army Corps of Engineers. Public utilities also own significant land area associated with reservoirs in the Sierra Nevada.

6. Palmer 1988. These figures do not include any additions under the California Desert Protection Act of 1994.

7. Hays 1959. The Raker Act authorizing the city of San Francisco to dam the Hetch Hetchy Valley passed the Senate on December 6, 1913, and was signed by President Woodrow Wilson on December 27, 1913. Turner 1985, 342.

8. Muir 1988. Muir took in this view from a part of the Coast Ranges southeast of the city of San Jose, his first view of the Sierra as he hiked from San Francisco to Yosemite fol-lowing his arrival in San Francisco on April 1, 1868. The final clause of the quote does not appear in the excerpt reproduced in Reid 1983 but is taken from a quote in Whitney 1979.

9. Schoenherr 1992. This was comparable to having more than one hundred inches of rainfall.

10. The final Native American to leave the Sierra Nevada wilderness and to be taken in by Euro-American civilization, Ishi, came out of the foothills of the northern Sierra Nevada in the Feather River country on August 29, 1911. Webster 1972, 256.

11. As another incentive, the Central Pacific received significantly higher payments for "mountainous" terrain, defined as any area more than five thousand feet in elevation — which included all of the flat regions of Nevada and Utah.

12. Coleman 1952. Recent mergers and acquisitions in the electric utility industry in the late 1990s may quickly change the company's current status.

13. A historical plaque documents this history near French Corral, northwest of Nevada City, California, near the South Yuba River.

14. This fact continues to plague the Marin Municipal Water District, which relies pri-marily on local supplies. The lack of adequate water supply for expansion has been a pri-mary constraint on growth in Marin County. Environmentalists have even actively opposed expansion of the system as a way to protect open space.

15. Stewart (1996) estimates 20.58 million acre-feet from the Sierra Nevada; California Department of Water Resources 1994 estimates 73 million acre-feet for all of California.

16. Stewart (1996) estimates that more than 18 million acre-feet per year of the 20.58 is consumed, while California Department of Water Resources 1994 estimates that urban

uses consume 6 million acre-feet and agricultural uses consume 24 million acre-feet in the state.

17. This has changed recently with application of the Public Trust Doctrine to existing water rights.

18. The Mokelumne River salmon runs exceeded forty thousand salmon before 1900; now, fewer than one hundred return each year.

19. Lynn White (1967) has claimed that the modern ecological crisis traces its roots to Judeo-Christian traditions, but I am making a much broader *cultural* claim, rather than a specific point about the role of Christian beliefs.

20. Watt left under fire on October 9, 1983.

21. It is also important to note that, unlike in the 1960s, when powerful industrial forces were viewed as primarily responsible for urban air and water pollution, the negative environmental and social effects of land and resource management policies today are not concentrated where most Americans live and work.

22. The bumper sticker was sighted at Sorensen's Resort on Highway 88, in Alpine County, in 1992.

23. It was Knudson's second Pulitzer Prize in six years and the first in fifty years for the *Sacramento Bee* (Knudson won his first Pulitzer Prize while reporting for the *Des Moines Register*).

24. See Palmer 1988, although he also does not address issues in the foothills of the Sierra Nevada.

25. This conclusion is based on conversations with at least five people who attended the Quincy meeting.

26. The observation is based on personal attendance at the Placerville workshop and conversations with other attendees.

27. You can see this on-line (http://www.ceres.ca.gov).

28. I was on the steering committee for the Sierra Now conference, and I cochaired the task force and panel presentations at the conference on "Urbanization and Local Economic Development" with Bill Center.

29. U.S. Bureau of Census, 1970, 1980, 1990 census files.

30. These changes are described in more detail in Duane 1993a.

31. I personally dislike the "battlefield" and "war" metaphors, for these presume that mortal combat is the only feasible means of resolving what must be irreconcilable differences. This is, however, the terminology used by many members of both the environmental and Wise Use movements, so I also use it here.

32. Verner et al. 1992; Wildland Resources Center 1994. The ballot initiatives were known as the "Forests Forever" and "Big Green" initiatives.

33. This is based on my personal observations during a summer 1990 trip to Oregon, Washington, and British Columbia.

34. Exceptions to this were the Carson and Bridgeport Ranger Districts of the Toiyabe National Forest, administered from a supervisor's office in Sparks, Nevada, and a regional office in Ogden, Utah.

35. *Bruce Babbitt v. Sweet Home Chapter of Communities for a Great Oregon, et al.*, 1995 U.S. LEXIS 4463, No. 94–859

36. Ibid.

37. This remains true even under the NCCP approach, of course, where habitat is reduced even further.

38. The HCP approach was developed to allow development to proceed in spite of an

ESA listing, rather than as a comprehensive strategy to avoid reaching the point of listing a species under the ESA. See Beatley 1994b; Deck 1993.

39. I am indebted to Dale Sanders for this term. As my colleague Matt Kondolf has noted, however, this phenomenon is not limited to biologists. He cites cases among geologists, hydrologists, and soil scientists.

40. Many of us believe that integrity is essential for business reasons as well as ethical reasons, however, and many consultants are highly sought specifically because they are respected for their integrity. Credibility is an asset founded on integrity as well as credentials, and it does have a market value.

41. The county planning staff is too small to allow me to reveal who made this statement.

42. Budget of the United States Government, Fiscal Year 1996, Appendix: 587.

43. HR 5503, Sierra Nevada Ecosystem Project 1994.

44. HR 6013, Sierra Nevada Ecosystem Project 1994.

45. This concept is discussed in more detail in Duane, forthcoming; also see Grumbine 1994; and Grumbine 1997.

46. I first gave a presentation to the SNEP team in October 1993, and I formally served as a special consultant to SNEP from February 1994 through completion of the final report to Congress in June 1996.

CHAPTER TWO

1. Canter 1996. This perspective still dominates the environmental planning field, despite widespread evidence to the contrary.

2. Logan and Molotch adopt these terms from Marx "as clarified through David Harvey's (1973, 1982) writings" (1).

3. Specifically, they cite Charles Tiebout (1962).

4. Ellickson 1991, 1 (quoting Phil Ritchie).

5. Nelson (1992) offers a detailed discussion of the literature on exurban development and suggests criteria for defining exurban regions within the constraints of U.S. Census Bureau data collected at the county level. His definition emphasizes the role of the central city in metropolitan regions as an employment center for exurban households. I argue that exurban development should be construed more broadly to include patterns of economic activity that depend on and are integrated with urban centers but are not physically proximate. This means that some exurban households can be located well beyond commuting distance to cities, in areas that would otherwise be considered rural based on their overall appearance or their apparent physical relationship to the nearest metropolitan region.

6. See Duane 1993c for a proposal for research on the spatial relationship between western exurban development and the network of ecologically important public lands necessary to conserve biological diversity. Also note that my definition of exurbia is broader than Nelson's (1992) and encompasses many areas that may be classified as rural by his criteria or could be classified as metropolitan by the Census Bureau. An example of the former would be Calaveras County; an example of the latter would be Placer County.

7. Some recent data suggest that rural areas again experienced a small net in-migration from 1990 to 1991 (Barringer 1993). Surprisingly, nonmetropolitan areas had a lower unemployment rate than metropolitan areas in fiscal year 1992 (for the first time in thir-

teen years, since the supposed end of the rural renaissance of the 1970s). The factors driving this shift are discussed in detail below. Also, note the 1996 study by Beal and Johnson described in Johnson 1996.

8. Some writers have challenged the idyllic representation of small-town life and "the demonization of city life" (Zukin 1993) as unrealistic; the "latent preference" cited by Nelson, Blackwood, and Carpenter may indeed reflect a romantic vision of nonmetropolitan living. It is nevertheless a genuine preference for many Americans, and they are now able to pursue it.

9. These technologies have also affected the availability of other media, such as same-day publishing through telecommunications of the *New York Times* and *Wall Street Journal* throughout the country. See Riebsame and Robb 1997, 116, for a map of various cultural amenities now available in nonmetropolitan areas of the "New West."

10. Power 1996a. Cohen and Zysman (1987) argue that manufacturing jobs may now be offshore.

11. This general comment about exurban areas is based on a detailed analysis of Sierra Nevada data and development of a more detailed cohort survival model for Nevada County by Collados and Griffiths (1993).

12. Note that the 1997 federal budget agreement eliminated this disincentive for gains up to five hundred thousand dollars.

13. Assuming an 8–10 percent interest rate and typical insurance and taxes in California, the monthly (before tax) cost of a mortgage is approximately 1 percent of a thirty-year, fixed-rate mortgage. Annual costs of $10,000–$20,000 for private schools equal $833–$1,667 per month. Avoiding those costs therefore frees a comparable amount for a mortgage, allowing one to acquire a mortgage of approximately $83,300–$166,700 (average = $125,000) without a reduction in net cash flow. The median owner-occupied household housing value in the Sierra Nevada was $128,678 in 1990. Lower current interest rates for mortgages translate into even greater home purchasing power for each dollar of savings from education.

14. These claims were made in real estate marketing and advertising for Lake Wildwood in 1993.

15. According to a survey conducted by the U.S. Fish and Wildlife Service, Americans spent some $14 billion on "primary nonconsumptive wildlife recreational pursuits" in 1985 (Vickerman 1989). The actual value of those recreational experiences was probably much higher, since there is only a limited "market" for these activities. This means there was, in the jargon of economics, a large uncaptured consumer surplus.

16. Ibid.; they cite Mark Granovetter's work and anticipate the work of Evans (1995).

17. The Nevada County General Plan update process shows that the establishment of a citizen's steering committee initially enhanced social capital, but its dissolution and the election battles that followed consumed social capital. The Sierra Nevada Research Planning process and SNEP's "key contacts" group built social capital on the scale of the entire Sierra Nevada, but the Forest Service's controversial proposals for reduced timber harvests in 1992 and increased timber harvests in 1996 failed to build on that social capital and therefore threatened to undermine it. The Sierra Business Council's 1995 *Sierra Wealth Index* and 1997 *Planning for Prosperity* report have both enhanced social capital, as have the Sierra Nevada Alliance's annual conferences. Each of these is described below.

18. Ellickson (1991) offers a generalized theory of social control that parallels the findings of Ostrom (1990) and Putnam et al. (1993), although his inductive approach

relied primarily on a single case study rather than the range of cases that the other authors used.

19. Creighton 1981 (cited in Canter 1996, 610).

20. Canter 1996, 591; Arnstein 1969 (cited in Canter 1996).

21. Central Sierra Wilderness Areas Public Involvement Team process, Inyo National Forest, Bishop, California, 1994, and the Mammoth-to-June Ecosystem Management Project, Inyo National Forest, Bishop, California, 1994.

22. For specific examples in the Sierra Nevada, see Beesley 1994a; 1996.

23. This is a critical point, because there seems to be a blind, headlong plunge into consensus and collaborative processes as the solution to environmental conflicts, without an understanding of the deep political divisions and legal hammers that constrain and influence local participants' willingness to compromise. Also note county control movements (Jacobs 1995; T. Davis 1996) and Wise Use efforts that are inconsistent with national interests, including the so-called Sagebrush Rebellion and the proposed transfer of 50 million acres from the federal government to the state of Nevada during the 1980s.

24. Seelye 1997. The 1995 population of the United States was 262.8 million; the 2050 forecast is 393.9 million.

25. See Duane forthcoming for a detailed discussion.

26. Michael Fainter and Robert Thompson both contributed to my understanding of these influences.

27. C. F. McGlashan's granddaughter, M. Nona McGlashan, is an even more direct link. She was raised by her grandparents in their Truckee home following the death of her mother, Ann Maqueda, in 1909. Nona authored two books about C. F. McGlashan that served as sources for much of this discussion: McGlashan 1977 and McGlashan 1986. Nona served as grand marshal for Truckee's Fourth of July parade in 1997.

28. Cronon 1983, 19 ("settlement began in the 1620s" in New England).

29. The commodification of Nature also standardized its value outside the context of place. See Cronon 1991.

30. Ibid., 85; *People vs. Truckee Lumber Co.,* 116 Cal. 397 (1897).

31. Nona McGlashan describes this as the Assembly Mining Committee, but it was probably either the Committee on Mining Debris and/or the Committee on Water Rights and Drainage (there was no "Mining Committee").

32. The National Park Service was formally established in 1916, the Forest Service in 1905, and the Bureau of Land Management in 1946.

CHAPTER THREE

1. Data for the state of Nevada were unavailable at the time of the analysis, so the results presented here refer only to those portions of the Sierra Nevada within California. Because Nevada was not a signatory to the biodiversity memorandum of understanding, the focus of the policy recommendations is on California.

2. Griffiths 1993; Duane 1993a. The final SNEP analysis includes a more detailed community-level social assessment that includes the Nevada side of the Lake Tahoe Basin. These data show why the enclave of Incline Village is sometimes called "Income Village" by locals, for it is home to many former California residents seeking refuge from state income taxes while remaining relatively close to Sacramento and the San Francisco Bay Area.

3. All figures are cited from an analysis of the 1990 census; these are cited in detail in Griffiths 1993. Note that these data are only for those persons five years of age and older, since younger ones were not alive in 1985!

4. This analysis is based on Table 3.1 of Griffiths 1993.

5. Collados and Griffiths 1993, 7–8. Also note that the model has not been adjusted to account for Nevada County's crime-related death rate among young males, which is lower than the statewide average.

6. The state grew by 386,000 people in 1996, for example, despite net emigration of 16,000. More recent migrants have higher reproductive rates, and the age structure of the existing population has generated enough demographic momentum to ensure continued population growth through natural increase for several decades.

7. Benton 1997. These figures include one prison in Amador County (3,638 inmates, of which 1,291 were white), one prison in Tuolumne County (5,905 inmates, 2,129 white), and three prisons in Kern County (14,634 inmates, 3,876 white).

8. These characterizations of changes since 1990 are based on personal observation and conversations with residents of the Lake Tahoe subregion (including Truckee, in Nevada County) and the Eastern Sierra subregion. Employers in the tourism and construction industries commented on the increase in their utilization of a Latino workforce since 1990. This increase appears to have occurred in both large and small businesses. Based on these conversations, it appears that there is very little employment of illegal aliens in the formal sector. Stricter penalties against employees and Proposition 187, together with tighter federal border controls, appear to have minimized the role of illegal aliens in the economy of the Sierra Region.

9. This excludes the western portion of Placer County (the cities of Roseville and Rocklin) located in the Sacramento Valley. The CCD boundary is roughly between Sierra College and the town of Loomis.

10. These counties include portions of Yosemite National Park, where National Park Service personnel live.

11. Those portions of the Nevada counties of Washoe, Carson, and Douglas in the Lake Tahoe Basin are not included.

12. Those portions of Lassen County covered by the SNEP study could be included here, but they do not appear in the summary statistics described below. The Butte County data includes Oroville and Paradise, but excludes Chico.

13. Alpine County is a bit problematic: part of it is on the west slope (Bear Valley) and part of it is on the east slope (Markleeville). Moreover, winter closure of Monitor Pass isolates even the east slope portions of Alpine County from Mono and Inyo Counties. The east slope economy is closely tied to both the Lake Tahoe economy (over Luther Pass) and the Carson Valley towns of Genoa and Minden in Nevada.

14. The CCD boundary for these four counties is the most problematic. It is roughly a southeasterly extension of the western boundary of the Mother Lode counties along the Friant-Kern Canal.

15. This was noted in a presentation at the California Biodiversity Council, El Portal, California, held in September 1994.

16. The California Tahoe Regional Planning Agency was established in 1967, but the bistate Tahoe Compact that established the agency was not formally approved by Congress and signed into law until December 18, 1969. Strong 1984, 117–47.

17. A new proposal was advanced in 1997 to develop a major destination resort on the

site of the existing parking lot at Squaw Valley (according to owner Alex Cushing, "The valley just cries out for development").

18. The Spainhowser Ranch of Lone Pine hosted tourists on its cattle drive to Olanche in June 1996.

19. This estimate is based on average-year water yields of approximately 2.5 million acre-feet by the State Water Project (valued at $150 per acre-foot) and 5,431 gigawatt-hours of hydroelectric production by PG&E and the State Water Project (valued at $0.12 per kilowatt-hours retail). California Department of Water Resources 1994; California Energy Commission 1993.

20. Fresno County is the largest agricultural county in the United States; Kern County is the largest oil- and gas-producing county in the country. Johnson et al. 1993; Goldberg 1996; American Farmland Trust 1995.

21. These weighted average median incomes were derived by taking the median income estimate for each CCD and dividing the population of each CCD by the total population of the Sierra Region to derive a weighted average median value for the Sierra Region.

22. Griffiths 1993, Table 4.1. Also note Hoffmann and Fortmann 1996 for a county-level time-series analysis.

23. Because of the concentration of both residents and employment outside the Sierra Nevada bioregion, data for the three Sierra Nevada counties in Nevada (Washoe, Carson, and Douglas) were not analyzed. Lassen County in the northern Sierra Nevada is also outside the boundaries of the Sierra Nevada as defined by the biodiversity memorandum of understanding, so it was also excluded from my analysis. The SNEP effort included Lassen County in its social assessments as a result of the inclusion of Lassen National Forest in other SNEP analyses (while technically outside the Sierra Nevada, Lassen County includes several resource-dependent communities that rely extensively on timber harvests from federal national forests in the Sierra Nevada). My analysis also excluded a small part of Plumas County in the Sierra Region census analysis for similar reasons, but county-level data from the EDD are for all of Plumas County.

24. No adjustments are made to the wage and salary incomes reported in the 1990 census, because they are consistent with the county-level LAPI data from the IRS. This assumes that wage and salary incomes are accurately reported, which may or may not be a valid assumption. There is a significant under-the-table economy that is not reported to the IRS in the LAPI figures or in the census data. The barter economy is also unaccounted for. Note that transfer payments are likely to be concentrated in particular communities and among residents with particular social, demographic, and economic characteristics, of course, so this is not the same as saying that half the residents of the Sierra Region do not depend on income from wages and salaries. Once again, regional variation within the Sierra Nevada is quite significant. Even differences among groups of residents within a single county or community can be significant in this regard.

25. Calculation: 10% x 58% = 6%; 6% + 21% = 27% of total wage and salary income.

26. Calculation: 27% x (50%–60%) = 14–16%; 14% + 50% = 64%; 16% + 40% = 56%.

27. Median housing values in the areas with the highest levels of commuting are two to three times weighted average median housing values for the entire Sierra Region. This suggests that commuters are actually bringing in a much larger share of total personal income than assumed in this simple analysis.

28. Just as California boomed under the excessive military spending of the Reagan and early Bush years, it suffered a bigger bust than most other states with the cutbacks of the 1990s. This is true in part because of base closures (twenty-one major base closings and one

realignment, resulting in a direct loss of 82,127 jobs from 1988 to 1993), but defense contractor spending cuts have been more significant. The three Southern California counties of Los Angeles, Orange, and San Diego lost an estimated 162,000 jobs in the defense sector between 1988 and 1992, and another 125,000 were projected to be lost from 1993 to 1997. These three counties accounted for five out of every six aerospace jobs lost in California. See Bradshaw et al. 1994.

29. This means that home buyers in the late 1980s and early 1990s purchased their homes at high prices and have seen slow or negative growth in their equity since then. This reduces the future potential for significant equity gains that could then free another wave of equity refugees to migrate to exurbia.

30. The final version of the Nevada County General Plan and the last draft of the El Dorado County General Plan stated that maintaining rural quality and environmental quality is an essential goal for each county. The El Dorado County Board of Supervisors deleted some of this language following the 1994 elections and before adopting the final plan.

31. This assumes that the lower-bound DOF forecast is 6 percent greater than the CCSCE forecast, and that the higher-bound DOF forecast is 8 percent greater than the lower-bound DOF forecast ($1.08 \times 1.06 = 1.14$).

32. The DOF estimates for 1990 differ slightly from the 1990 census figures, which are from April 1990.

33. The San Francisco Bay Area referred to here includes the nine counties that are members of the Association of Bay Area Governments: Alameda, Contra Costa, Marin, Napa, San Francisco, San Mateo, Santa Clara, Solano, and Sonoma. Population figures are taken directly from census data for 1940, 1950, 1960, 1970, 1980, and 1990.

34. This has become less true in the 1990s, as the expanded capacity of Interstates 580 and 205 and Highway 120 now link residences in San Joaquin and Stanislaus Counties to employment in the periurban Bay Area.

35. These amenities include the Bureau of Reclamation's Folsom Lake, on the edge of the foothills.

36. Two of the three homes listed for sale in the classified ads section of the May-June 1994 issue of the internal *Intel Folsom News* were in El Dorado County, while the third was in nearby Placer County. This is clearly an inadequate sample, but it is suggestive. Intel would not release data on the residency of its employees.

37. The San Joaquin Valley town of Merced may also grow significantly when it becomes the site of the University of California's tenth campus. Recent closure of the nearby Castle Air Force Base threatens at present to stall economic development in the area, but a new UC campus would likely serve as an incubator for a wide range of employment opportunities both in research and in the private sector.

38. The Bay Area Rapid Transit system has recently completed a feeder line out to Livermore that connects potential commuters directly to downtown San Francisco. This in turn is likely to increase commuting from bedroom communities in the Central Valley to the San Francisco Bay Area metropolitan region.

39. See Stockton Record 1997 for a thorough overview from the perspective of a Central Valley population center.

40. A simple bivariate regression analysis of the data has an r-squared of 0.97, which means that 97 percent of the variation in one variable is explained by variation in the other variable. This is based on only six observations, however, so we cannot attribute any statistical significance to this finding. It nevertheless illustrates that growth in these areas appears to be closely linked.

41. The relationship appears weaker, with an r-squared value of only 0.92 for the 1940–1990 data, but that appears to be the result of a split in the data around 1960. This is also when Interstate 80 was completed, so we have a plausible explanatory variable consistent with the general theory of commuting as a primary factor in determining population growth in these counties. The r-squared value for the 1960–1990 regression is 0.99, although there are only four data points.

42. California Department of Water Resources 1973. The report was prepared by DWR's associate engineer Kenneth M. Turner, who provided a preliminary review edition of the report to SNEP in March 1995.

43. Based on the sum of all Sierra Region CCDs within the ten-county study area, the Sierra Region of those counties had a population of 436,426.

44. An excellent letter to the editor on this topic by Linda L. Beeson was published on March 28, 1995, on pg. A4 of the *Grass Valley–Nevada City Union,* in which she lamented decreasing community support for local agriculture.

45. The one exception was the John Woolman School, a residential Quaker school that had few local attendees.

CHAPTER FOUR

1. The relationship between power and knowledge is also critical, of course. See Foucault 1980; Fillingham 1993.

2. Flood Control Act of June 22, 1936, cited in Grant et al. 1976, 132; emphasis added.

3. This characteristic is usually associated with high "transactions costs," which means that it would be very expensive to control access to the public good and charge the beneficiaries for using it. Transactions costs are in part a function of technology, however, so new technologies could potentially reduce the public-good characteristics of a resource. A lighthouse is the classic example of a public good, because it is difficult to limit sailors' ability to see it and derive its benefits. New radio navigation technologies could be encoded, however, and it might be possible to charge all beneficiaries of such encoded signals through new technologies that record usage and relay that information to the transmitting tower. A new radio-based "lighthouse" could therefore replace the traditional lighthouse and its nonexclusive attributes.

4. The degree to which a public good is "nonrivalrous" is also sometimes a function of the level of demand for that good or service. A new freeway may be so uncrowded that additional users do not reduce the capacity for existing users to benefit from the freeway, for example, but existing users may face additional congestion costs if new users are allowed access to an already crowded freeway. In the latter case, there is clearly "rivalry" among competing users seeking access to what was formerly a nonrivalrous public good.

5. Lack of adequate transportation, water supply, telecommunications systems, civil aviation traffic control, flood control, and gas and electricity supply could all limit the operation of private markets.

6. The title of Richard White's brilliant book *It's Your Misfortune and None of My Own* (1991) comes to mind.

7. An example of a positive externality might be the fine smell of freshly baked bread that wafts through a neighborhood near a bakery. The residents gain the benefits of this aroma, but neither the producers nor the consumers of the bread are compensated for the

benefits that the residents gain. A similar but negative externality would be toxic emissions from a battery factory located near the same neighborhood.

8. Lauter 1992. Summers was subsequently named undersecretary of the Treasury.

9. Daily 1997. This estimate has been criticized by some economists, however, for failing to incorporate consumers' willingness to pay as a factor affecting the ultimate value of the environment to consumers.

10. This was demonstrated when the Biosphere II project needed significant modification in order to maintain the internal ecological system and the health of its human occupants.

11. *Comic Press News* n.d., 18, citing *EcoNews,* journal of the Northcoast Environmental Center, Arcata, California.

12. This is an important protection, although other, less strict protections might also be developed. See the discussion below on the U.S. Constitution's Fifth Amendment protection against government takings.

13. There have been several encouraging local efforts to develop indicators at several scales, however, including *Sustainable Seattle,* Urban Ecology's *Blueprint for a Sustainable Bay Area,* and the Sierra Business Council's *Sierra Wealth Index.*

14. Cecilia Collados (1997) has also developed a useful theoretical framework for differentiating among different types of natural capital to determine the sustainability of various paths of development. Her approach leads to stricter criteria for sustainability that go beyond the "weak" sustainability (where capital is constant or increasing, but substitutions can be made across different types of capital) and "strong" sustainability (where natural capital is constant or increasing, so that technology cannot be substituted for natural capital) discussed in the literature.

15. The Sierra Economic Development District in Auburn, California, continues to rely primarily upon EDD data to complete base analyses for Sierra, Nevada, Placer, and El Dorado Counties that ignore other sources of income. See Reeves 1995.

16. SNEP economists Bill Stewart and Norm Johnson specifically rejected my proposal to complete a contingent valuation study as part of the SNEP report, and the rest of the SNEP Science Team deferred to their judgment.

17. An example is the Forest Inventory Assessment plot system operated by the U.S. Forest Service, which collects information about forest characteristics that primarily allows modelers to project future tree size and timber harvest yields—but those characteristics do not provide important information about wildlife habitat conditions.

18. O'Toole (1988) claims that this drives all agency decision-making.

19. Fortmann and Huntsinger (1989) differentiate "large" versus "small" landowners using a much higher threshold.

20. Examples include Pacific Lumber Company's land and resource management practices before and after its acquisition by Maxxam Corporation (see Harris 1995) and differences between Collins Pine Company and Sierra Pacific Industry's land and resource management practices on private industrial forestlands in Plumas and Lassen Counties. Both pre-Maxxam Pacific Lumber and Collins Pine relied upon much more sensitive practices.

CHAPTER FIVE

1. Power 1996a. Power is professor and chairman of the Economics Department at the University of Montana, and his book offers a number of examples that apply these concepts to the northern Rockies.

2. Stewart 1993; 1996. This figure is for new mills; the average is higher, and even the new mills could require more labor inputs depending on the size class of the timber and the flexibility of the mill.

3. Power 1996a. See also U.S. Department of Labor (1975 to 1992); of these years, only 1992 showed a rate less than twice the national private sector average for the lumber and wood products industry and a lower-than-average rate for the mining industry.

4. See Tuan 1974, 104–5, for an excellent depiction of the shifting image of Nature; also note Evernden 1992 for a more nuanced discussion.

5. Nearly two-thirds of Placer County's population lived outside the Sierra Region in 1990, so county-level data is not very useful for exploring the impacts of the ecotransformation on the Sierra Region portion of the county.

6. For this discussion, I have relied on Daniel Emmett's 1992 summary of EDD data for 1972 and 1988. Philip Griffiths assisted me with analysis of 1989–92 data.

7. In 1972, 2.22 billion board feet were harvested, and in 1988 2.18 billion board feet; the highest year was 1968, when 2.36 billion board feet were harvested (and seasonal spring unemployment in Nevada County was 20–25 percent).

8. That figure has since dropped by half following significant reorganization by the Group's parent company, Tetronix of Beaverton, Oregon, in the competitive electronics industry. See Marois 1996f.

9. The estimate of 550 employees in this sector is higher than the estimate of 400 above because it includes lumber industry workers employed by the Bohemia mill in Grass Valley, which closed during this period.

10. See Yassa and Diamant (1995) and Zackman (1993) for a detailed analysis of the timber industry's declining importance in the Sierra Region counties.

11. Stewart 1996, 1044. Note that this estimate includes federal Payments in Lieu of Taxes and property taxes, which have remained low on private lands since Proposition 13 was adopted in 1978. This has increased the relative advantages of public versus private timber harvests for county governments: the ratio of revenues per million board feet of timber harvested was less than four to one in 1985.

12. California Department of Conservation 1991. Many residents of these counties may still be woods workers, however, because of the presence of mills in those counties. They may then harvest timber outside their county.

13. This is in nominal dollars, so the real investment in residential construction would be slightly less because the nominal value of residential construction increased much more in later years than it did for commercial construction.

14. Building permit records, County of Nevada (Nevada City, California), City of Grass Valley (Grass Valley, California), Town of Truckee (Truckee, California), January 8, 1997. With the exception of Truckee, each time series had significant gaps.

15. J. Moore Methods 1992. While the survey did not make use of an unbiased sample or unbiased method, my own informal surveys at presentations in Nevada, Placer, El Dorado, Amador, Tuolumne, Inyo, and Mono Counties support these results.

16. J. Moore Methods 1992, 2. These results are for the entire sample of 748 respondents. More detailed cross-tabulations are also available by supervisorial district, age, hous-

ing status, income, school children, education, occupation, political ideology, length of residence, Sacramento commuters, area, acreage of parcel, June 1990 voter status, political party, and sex. These cross-tabulations reveal some significant differences among subgroups, especially differences in values between newcomers and old-timers.

17. Sierra Business Council, Truckee, California. Unpublished data reviewed February 6, 1997.

18. I gave presentations on population growth and land use alternatives to each group in May 1993.

19. Rural Quality Coalition of Nevada County n.d. These materials were widely distributed to the public in 1993.

20. Unpublished survey data also suggest that they exaggerate the relative importance of the timber industry to the Sierra Nevada economy, however, while underestimating the importance of amenity-based economic activities.

21. The local paper opened its front-page story on the conference with a description of the windowless room and my observation that the large wall mirror failed to capitalize on the Lake Tahoe region's environmental quality assets.

CHAPTER SIX

1. These values indicate the order of magnitude of the population, rather than the absolute number. Villages usually hold hundreds and up to maybe thousands of people, for example, while towns hold thousands and possibly tens of thousands. Rural and exurban regions usually do not have communities larger than maybe ten thousand to twenty thousand people, but there may be some centers that hold up to twenty to fifty thousand. Note that the U.S. census would treat any county with a community larger than fifty thousand in population as "metropolitan."

2. This idea needs further exploration in the context of the rapid transformation now occurring in rural and exurban areas. Rural areas previously linked to the global economy already had altered landscapes, of course, and some degree of standardization and commodification had occurred to ensure the abstraction of resources and place in the global market. The shift to an exurban economic base changed that relationship, however: the location preferences of individuals for residences now determine the dominant land use (rather than the global market for agricultural or other natural resource commodities).

3. Political jurisdictions also establish boundaries, which often overlap or ignore ecological reality. This tends to reinforce the assessment of planning problems in terms of human rather than natural systems.

4. The siting of "big boxes" like Wal-Mart has nevertheless generated intense opposition in the Sierra foothills as a result of both their impact on the physical environment and their negative effect on existing downtown businesses (Marois 1996c; National Public Radio 1996).

5. This is changing now in accordance with Rudel's model (1989), however, as out-of-town developers are entering the market with proposals for large-scale new towns where amortization of internalized infrastructure costs compels more centralized development of the houses themselves rather than lot sales alone. See Garland 1997b and Fugro-McClelland (West), Inc. 1994 for recent examples. Southworth (1997) notes that turn-of-

the-century streetcar suburbs were also often developed by individual home builders within a master-planned subdivision's infrastructure.

6. These subdivisions are called Lake of the Pines, Lake Wildwood, Alta Sierra, and Tahoe Donner.

7. Homes built by speculators have become more common in the Gold Country since the boom of the late 1980s, although the market appears to have been overbuilt in the early 1990s. Future "spec" home activity is therefore likely to be dampened by the significant losses incurred by speculators in the early 1990s.

8. A "minor" subdivision typically involves a parcel split that results in four or fewer lots, thereby avoiding detailed planning and environmental review under the state Subdivision Map Act of 1973.

9. This conclusion is supported by review of the 1980 Nevada County General Plan, 1982 Grass Valley General Plan, 1994–95 Nevada County General Plan update, and 1994–95 El Dorado County General Plan update. Local officials are consistently unwilling to downzone below existing parcelization because of concerns about takings.

10. This issue is discussed in detail below.

11. "Landowners have no vested right in existing or anticipated zoning regulations." See *Tahoe Keys v. Water Resources Control Board, HFH Ltd. v. Superior Court* (cited in Sierra Business Council 1997, 112).

12. As Humbach (1992c; 1993) notes, this is true even after the Supreme Court's ruling in *Lucas v. South Carolina Coastal Council*, 112 S. Ct. 2886 (1992).

13. This is based on a detailed review of general plan documents for Nevada County and the city of Grass Valley and preliminary review of general plan documents for Placer, El Dorado, Tuolumne, Inyo, and Mono Counties and the cities of Nevada City and Mammoth Lakes. The Lake Tahoe region is an exception because of the detailed environmental thresholds established by the TRPA.

14. This discussion should not be construed as a recommendation for half-acre lots. The higher density can also be quite destructive environmentally if not integrated with appropriate open space and protection of ecologically sensitive resources through careful site design. The critical point here is that *design matters*.

15. According to Nicholson (1995), it is not economical to deliver treated water to lots larger than two acres.

16. In many cases local residents have historically relied on raw water from irrigation ditches for domestic purposes. Increased development of the watersheds serving the irrigation canals has increased public health risks for this source, however, as a result of non-point-source pollution from septic systems and increases in impervious surfaces associated with development. This has necessitated a shift to private on-site wells.

17. There may then be tradeoffs with congestion and traffic impacts, though, without adequate transportation planning.

18. Examples of this spatial arrangement are illustrated in Yaro et al. 1988 and Arendt 1996b, Figure 5.

19. For further information on well water sources in the Sierra Nevada foothills, see Swain 1994; Page et al. 1984; Hauge 1994; Wheeldon 1994; Fulton 1994; California Department of Water Resources 1991; 1992; 1993.

20. I wish I could include a photo of this house, but it was destroyed just three months later in the tragic fire that swept the Berkeley and Oakland hills in late October 1991.

21. The western portions of both Placer and El Dorado Counties are part of the Sacramento Area Council of Governments (SACOG) and the Sacramento Air Pollution

Control District. Nevada County is part of the Northern Sierra Air Pollution Control District and has resisted any direct affiliation with SACOG. The link to SACOG increases the political leverage for projects on Interstate 80 or U.S. Highway 50.

22. In many cases ozone levels are higher in the Sierra Nevada than at the emission sources in the valley. This results from the fact that some ozone precursors (e.g., nitrogen oxides, or NOx) interact with ozone in the absence of sunlight to reduce ozone levels overnight. This breakdown occurs in metropolitan regions where NOx is emitted, but ozone builds up in the Sierra Nevada without nighttime breakdown by local emission sources. Cahill et al. 1996; Knudson 1991.

23. This has primarily occurred since the passage of Proposition 13 in June 1978.

24. Access to this area would remain via either Red Dog Road or Banner Lava Cap Road after such a closure.

25. The California Air Resources Board, the Local Government Commission, and Pacific Gas and Electric Company jointly sponsored a workshop, "Planning for Clean Air," in Placer and El Dorado Counties in Auburn, California, in February 1993. Both counties are in the Sacramento commute-shed.

26. Coordination between land use planning and infrastructure investment is a cornerstone of the Florida state growth management program's concurrency requirement, which theoretically does not allow development to go forward unless infrastructure investments are made concurrently to avoid degradation of levels of service. Implementation has been difficult, however, causing both leapfrog development and degraded levels of service. See Stein 1997 regarding schools.

27. Teleconferencing costs are already dropping rapidly. By early 1995, a simple system with a camera, microphone, and software for showing a small image on a computer monitor was less than fifteen hundred dollars per site. This system provided images that reminded me of the early Apollo transmissions, where the astronauts moved jerkily. Improved processing speeds, greater memory and storage capacity, and standardization of communications and software protocols should bring this cost down dramatically while making interactive teleconferencing much more effective. Whether it will be feasible to teach my classes in Berkeley from the Sierra Nevada will probably depend on nontechnological factors, however, such as the need to have spontaneous and informal student meetings.

28. Many similar villages that dot the New England countryside date from the eighteenth century.

29. See Beatley and Manning 1997 for a critique that proposes additional elements to the new urbanism.

30. Increasing state training requirements for fire fighting volunteers have also diminished volunteerism.

31. I have not researched this index in quantitative terms, but I think it would be a good proxy for the cultural changes occurring as rural communities become exurban through in-migration.

32. Alpha Hardware ("Since 1878") converted to a set of boutiques in downtown Nevada City in the late 1980s.

33. The evidence is in the sidewalk in Truckee, where a large coffee cup design now lies in front of a boutique.

34. See Blakely and Snyder 1997 for a more general overview of the gated community phenomenon in the United States.

35. All data are from the U.S. Bureau of Census STF 3A, Population and Housing,

1990 Census. Because of underreporting errors described in chapter 3, however, these estimates of median total income are therefore lower than actual median incomes (Stewart 1996).

36. The supervisor of security then approved our tour of Lake Wildwood the next day, when we returned to tour it without any restrictions (Findley 1993).

37. Nevada County Elections Office data at the precinct level, which I then summarized by community, based on GIS coverage.

38. Duane 1996a, 352, Table 11.A3. These figures are based on average housing unit densities rather than parcel-specific information about lot sizes, however, so this is only an approximation of parcel size distribution.

39. Minimum lot size requirements vary widely with jurisdictions, reflecting both the high uncertainty and lack of detailed analysis of septic or well system risk associated with various soils, slopes, and other natural factors. Higher minimum parcel sizes of ten or twenty acres per dwelling unit are often required to maintain the rural character of a place or to protect some sensitive area (e.g., steep slopes or an adjacent wetland), but those larger parcel sizes are not usually required to meet public health requirements. It is important to note that the general application of a minimum lot size requirement means that the site-specific capability to accommodate water and septic needs is usually not evaluated.

40. Environmental activists in El Dorado and Amador Counties successfully sued to stop the Cinabarr project in early 1998 because of an inadequate EIR (Foothill Conservancy 1998; *San Francisco Chronicle* 1998).

41. See Duane 1996a for a detailed analysis of the subdividability of existing parcels and the build-out implications of developing existing substandard lots in Nevada and El Dorado Counties (excluding the Lake Tahoe subregion).

42. Note that a shift in the mix of agricultural supplies may also occur, rather than an overall reduction in the total value of such supplies. Many ranchette activities require significant expenditures that may actually increase the overall level of total economic activity in the agricultural supply sector.

43. The Pacific Northwest may be an exception, where industrial forest landowners are extremely important. Decreased timber harvests on federal lands in the 1990s have also decreased their importance in the Sierra Nevada.

44. I have been unable to trace the source of the quotation in the inscription or to determine who selected it for the site.

45. Note that Proposition 13 reduced the tax advantages of the Williamson Act and similar conservation programs.

46. Haeckel 1866. The term was adopted in its modern spelling as *ecology* after the International Botanical Congress of 1893.

47. Barry and Cook 1994. The United States is likely to be in a similar position following the Kyoto negotiations on global climate change, where the Clinton administration has agreed to a treaty with elements opposed by the Senate.

48. Several additional species were proposed for delisting by the U.S. Fish and Wildlife Service in 1998, including several populations that were deemed sufficiently recovered from endangerment.

49. California Resources Agency 1991, p. 6 (based on Keystone Policy Dialogue 1991).

50. See Soule 1986 for a detailed discussion of the minimum-viable-population estimation problem and potential sources of extinction risk. Also note that recent research (Grime 1997) raises important questions about the species-area curve and its relationship to ecological function (Wardle et al. 1997).

51. Sneed 1996a. The U.S. Fish and Wildlife Service proposed listing the red-legged frog as threatened under the ESA in May 1996, just one day after the Jumpin' Frog Jubilee that made it famous was held in Angels' Camp of Calaveras County in the Sierra Nevada foothills. There were hundreds of thousands of these frogs in the Sierra Nevada when Mark Twain wrote his famous story about them in the 1860s, but today there are only 350 or fewer adults in the Range of Light—in an isolated drainage of the Feather River, more than a hundred miles from Angels' Camp.

52. These are not firm projections of future growth or landscape change, but instead illustrate one possible scenario based on the general plans of the time.

53. It was exactly this type of *potential* listing of the California spotted owl, however, that precipitated significant research on the habitat needs of the owl and management changes in the mixed-conifer zone on federal lands.

54. I must admit that I always thought my own region's matrix was entirely native until I studied the subject in greater depth. In fact, the invasive plant Scotch broom (*Cytisus scoparius*) is so common in the Sierra Nevada foothills that I always assumed it was native to the area! The species is even carried by some local nurseries, which increases the likelihood of it spreading further in the area.

55. See Tuan 1974; Evernden 1984; Nash 1967; Spirn 1984; Oelschlaeger 1991; and Cronon 1995.

56. This is consistent with McBride et al. 1996, who found that an average of 41 percent of the lots less than one acre were covered by impervious surfaces, versus an average of 7.5 percent for the larger lot size classes. Table 46.2, p. 1196.

57. Their effect on the distribution of patch size (and total patch area) is a function of both their geographic distribution and the "edge effect" assumed to extend to them from the roadway into the interior of adjoining patches. A four-lane freeway and a two-track dirt road probably have significantly different effects, and they should be considered accordingly. Much more research needs to be done on the ecological edge effect of different road types and uses.

58. Native wildlife can also transmit disease to cattle or sheep, of course, and this concern has led to brutal "culling" of the Yellowstone bison herd by Montana Wildlife officials. *San Francisco Chronicle* 1997e.

59. Irwin 1987. Summary fire data for the 1986–97 period are unavailable from either the CDF or state Office of Emergency Services.

60. Sapsis et al. 1996. The correlation was much lower, however (r-squared = 0.31), using unclassified data.

61. Unfortunately, it also constrains the implementation of prescribed burning to reduce fuel loadings.

62. I was an assistant fire dispatcher for the Tahoe National Forest in Nevada City during the summer of 1978.

63. I base this conclusion on both personal observation and participation in the expert team on infrastructure organized by the Oakland Metropolitan Forum and the mayors of Berkeley and Oakland following the disaster.

64. Barclay's California Code of Regulations: Title 14, Division 1.5, Chapter 7, Subchapter 2, Article 1.5.

CHAPTER SEVEN

1. This is usually expressed as belief in rugged individualism, and it reflects our history as a people who sought freedom from the state. See de Tocqueville [1835] 1980; and Lipset 1997, for a discussion of American Culture.

2. Although, as Sale (1995) argues, the much maligned Luddites also attempted to protect others' interests as well.

3. "Big Yellow Taxi," written by Joni Mitchell. Copyright © 1970 Siquomb Publishing. ALL RIGHTS RESERVED. Used by permission.

4. Anthropologists are an exception, of course, but even they often feel compelled to quantify their findings.

5. "The Last Resort," written by Don Henley and Glenn Frey. Copyright © 1976 Cass County Music/Red Cloud Music. ALL RIGHTS RESERVED. Used by permission.

6. These buttons were distributed by the California Association of Business, Property and Resource Owners at public hearings on the Nevada County General Plan in March 1995.

7. Sierra Pacific Industry controls the timber industry in the Sierra Nevada, for example, from Shasta County. See Graebner 1994; and Stewart 1997.

8. See McPhee 1989.

9. See Cronon 1995b; Nash 1967; Oelschlaeger 1989; Evernden 1984; and Tuan 1974, regarding the degree to which various social constructions of "nature" and "wilderness" affect the very qualities we attribute to those things.

10. Cornell 1979; 1987. The book had sold 250,000 copies by 1987 and more than 500,000 by 1995.

11. This influence could be even more pervasive now that Disney also owns the ABC television network.

12. J. Moore Methods 1992, 6-3. There were also differences between Sacramento commuters and noncommuters.

13. Personal communication with various board members of the Sierra Nevada Alliance, 1992–93. I cochaired the panel discussion and task force report, "Urbanization and Local Economic Development," at the Sierra Now conference in August 1992, and I appeared on behalf of the Sierra Nevada Alliance to discuss these issues at two news conferences announcing the formation of the organization in February 1993. *The Sierra Economy: Sustainable Development in Harmony with Nature* was produced by the Nevada County Business Association and California Forestry Association (1993). I spoke at this conference on the Sierra Nevada Alliance panel. The Wilderness Society, the Natural Resources Defense Council, and the Sierra Business Council all completed studies on the Sierra Nevada economy from 1994 to 1996. The Sierra Club began such a study in 1997.

14. *Grass Valley–Nevada City Union* 1995h. The advertisement specifically said, "Sierra Residents Are About to Get Burned: Federal bureaucrats and environmental extremists develop a plan to protect the owls. The next thing you know, millions of acres of once productive forests are shut down, thousands of jobs are lost and communities struggle to survive." It went on to argue that, as a result of taking forests out of production, the environment becomes threatened by increased fire risk and the likelihood of catastrophic fires.

15. Recent debate over the Quincy Library Group's proposed strategy for management of 2.2 million acres of Forest Service land in the Northern Sierra subregion highlights the

fact that even "collaborative" efforts within a community can be controversial (Christensen 1996a; Marston 1997; Blumberg 1997a; 1997b; Blumberg et al. 1997).

16. Promising examples of successful 50,000-person communities include Davis, Santa Cruz, and Petaluma. Most of the incorporated cities in the Sierra Nevada range from 10^3 to 10^4 in population, which is a very manageable size.

17. KNCO-AM was established in late 1978; previously, the closest "local" station was twenty-four miles away in Auburn.

18. Ibid., 190–94. Compare results in Medler and Mushkatal 1979 with Knaap 1987.

19. Honda broadcast a television campaign for the Civic in 1995 that said, "Are we different, or what?" emphasizing the fact that Northern California is culturally distinctive from Southern California.

20. This is particularly true between New York City and "upstate" legislators in state-level politics.

21. EDAW 1966, 21 (cited in Davis 1996, 172). Williams was echoing Leopold's (1949) call for a new "land ethic," discussed in detail in Callicott 1987a; 1989; 1996; and Duane forthcoming.

22. Most of the literature on private property in the United States emphasizes its utilitarian exchange value, and Demsetz (1967) has argued that rights in property are both clarified and enforced more systematically as a given type of property becomes more scarce. I will emphasize instead the public-good aspects of property.

23. Note that the extent of governmental discretion for exercising that police power has been determined through a long series of Supreme Court decisions and case law, from the *Euclid* decision authorizing zoning in 1926 through the *Lucas* case in 1992. The acceptability of governmental regulation has evolved in parallel with developments in the common law regarding nuisance.

24. The degree to which the *Lucas* decision restricts policy is hotly debated. See Humbach 1993.

25. I recognize that the court is generally more conservative, but more conservative courts established takings jurisprudence that was generally consistent in its deference to government regulation from 1887 to 1987.

26. It could, however, be argued that such immunity was necessary to undertake investments that benefit society.

27. Leopold 1949, 263. All page numbers cited for quotes are from the 1970 Ballantine edition.

28. Arizona, Delaware, Florida, Idaho, Indiana, Kansas, Louisiana, Maine, Michigan, Missouri, Mississippi, Montana, North Dakota, Tennessee, Texas, Utah, Virginia, Washington, West Virginia, and Wyoming.

29. Some of these, such as Mississippi's, are restricted to specific activities, such as forestry and agriculture.

30. *Mugler v. Kansas,* 123 U.S. 623 (1887)

31. The original phrase, modified in the Declaration of Independence, referred to property rather than the broader concept of "pursuit of happiness."

32. *Mugler v. Kansas,* 123 U.S. 660 (quoting *Munn v. Illinois,* 94 U.S. 113, 124).

33. Ibid., 662.

34. Ibid., 661; 663 (quoting *Barbier v. Connolly,* 113 U.S. 27, 31).

35. Ibid., 669.

36. Ibid., 667, 669; *Block v. Hirsh,* 256 U.S. 135, 155 (1921), quoted in *Keystone Bituminous Coal Ass'n v. DeBenedictis,* 480 U.S. at 488 (1987).

37. *Hadacheck v. Sebastian, Chief of Police of the City of Los Angeles,* 239 U.S. 394 (1915).

38. *Hadacheck v. Los Angeles,* 239 U.S. 405 (1915).

39. Ex parte Kelso, 147 California, 609; cited in *Hadacheck v. Los Angeles,* 239 U.S. 405 (1915).

40. *Hadacheck v. Los Angeles,* 239 U.S. 410 (1915).

41. Ibid.; *Lucas v. South Carolina Coastal Council,* 112 S. Ct. 2886 (1992); *Dolan v. City of Tigard,* 114 S. Ct. 2309 (1994).

42. *Euclid v. Ambler Realty Co.,* 272 U.S. 365 (1926); *Pennsylvania Coal v. Mahon,* 260 U.S. 393 (1922); *United States v. Causby,* 328 U.S. 256 (1946).

43. *Pennsylvania Coal v. Mahon,* 260 U.S. 393 (1922) at 413.

44. Ibid., at 415.

45. *Penn Central Transportation Co. v. New York City,* 438 U.S. 104 (1978); *Agins v. Tiburon,* 447 U.S. 255 (1980).

46. *Penn Central Transportation Co. v. New York City,* 438 U.S. 104 at 124 (1978); *Loretto v. Teleprompter Manhattan CATV Corp.,* 458 U.S. 419 (1982).

47. Following *Penn Central,* the reference for diminution was "distinct investment-backed expectations" rather than whatever the maximum (perhaps unreasonable) theoretical economic value of the land.

48. *Keystone Bituminous Coal Ass'n v. DeBenedictis,* 480 U.S. at 491 (quoting *Kimball Laundry Co. v. United States,* 338 U.S. 1 at 5 [1949] and *Mugler v. Kansas,* 123 U.S. at 665).

49. *Penn Central Transportation Co. v. New York City,* 438 U.S. at 130–31 (1978), cited in *Keystone Bituminous Coal Ass'n v. DeBenedictis,* 480 U.S. at 497 (emphasis in original).

50. *Keystone Bituminous Coal Ass'n v. DeBenedictis,* 480 U.S. at 506–21, 517–21 (Rehnquist, dissenting).

51. *Monongahela Navigation Co. v. United States,* 148 U.S. 312 (1893); *Keystone Bituminous Coal Ass'n v. DeBenedictis,* 480 U.S. at 512 (quoting *Monongahela*); *Pennsylvania Coal v. Mahon,* 260 U.S. at 415 (1922); *Penn Central Transportation Co. v. New York City,* 438 U.S. at 123–25 (1977); and *Armstrong v. United States,* 364 U.S. 40, 49 (1960).

52. *First English Evangelical Church v. County of Los Angeles,* 482 U.S. 304 (1987); *San Diego Gas & Electric Co. v. San Diego,* 450 U.S. 621 (1981).

53. *Nollan v. California Coastal Commission,* 483 U.S. 825 (1987); *Lucas v. South Carolina Coastal Council,* 112 S. Ct. 2886 (1992), *Dolan v. City of Tigard,* 114 S. Ct. 2309 (1994); *Bruce Babbitt v. Sweet Home Chapter of Communities for a Great Oregon, et al.,* 1995 U.S. LEXIS 4463, No. 94–859 (Scalia, dissent).

54. This distinction is important, for regulators have a potential conflict of interest when they have an opportunity to bargain away permit approval in exchange for other concessions such as land, easements, money, or infrastructure investments. Such a conflict is less likely to exist if permit approval or denial is the only choice before the regulators. I am indebted to Rick Frank (1997) for making this distinction, which is often ignored in the literature.

55. *Nollan v. California Coastal Commission,* 483 U.S. at 836–37.

56. Ibid., at 846. (Brennan, dissent) (quoting *Sproles v. Binford,* 286 U.S. 374, 388 [1932]).

57. Ibid., at 847 (Brennan, dissent).

58. Sax 1971, 152. Quoted in *Nollan v. California Coastal Commission,* 483 U.S. at 863–64 (Brennan, dissent).

59. *Nollan v. California Coastal Commission,* 483 U.S. at 865 (Blackmun, dissent).

60. Ibid., at 866, 867 (Stevens, dissent).

61. *Lucas v. South Carolina Coastal Council,* 112 S. Ct. 2886 (1992).

62. It should be noted that similarly situated parcels on either side of Lucas's already had single-family homes on them, however, raising a fundamental question of fairness in allowing them to remain while denying Lucas.

63. *Lucas v. South Carolina Coastal Council,* 112 S. Ct. at 2899, 2900.

64. Ibid., at 2895, 2897.

65. Ibid., at 2903 (Kennedy, dissent).

66. Ibid., at 2904, 2909, 2910, 2921–22 (Blackmun, dissent).

67. Aldo Leopold made a similar argument regarding his land ethic (1949), and Roderick Nash has argued that the evolution of social values regarding the environment parallels the abolitionist movement (1989).

68. *Dolan v. City of Tigard,* 114 S. Ct. 2309 (1994).

69. As Dolan's attorneys suggested, however, it was difficult to visualize many of the customers of this plumbing and electrical supply store arriving by bicycle.

70. *Dolan v. City of Tigard,* 114 S. Ct. at 2316, 2317–18.

71. Ibid., at 2320, 2322.

72. Ibid., at 2326, 2329–30 (Stevens, dissent).

73. Ibid., at 2331 (Souter, dissent).

74. Frank (1997) notes that this is technically a requirement only for permit conditions or exactions, but the nexus requirement is widely interpreted to apply more generally to the relationship between the regulation and its goals.

75. Frank (1997) argues that the rough proportionality standard, like the "nexus" requirement, applies primarily to permit conditions or exactions. The Court has not applied the *Nollan* and *Dolan* standards to a permit denial case.

76. Rolf Pendall (1997) has suggested that rural and urban areas have different "property rights cultures."

77. *People v. Truckee Lumber Company,* 116 Cal. 397 (1897) at 400; 402 (entire quotation is from *State v. Roberts,* 59 N.H. 256; 47 Am Rep. 199; 59).

78. Sax 1980b; Stevens 1980; *National Audubon Society v. Superior Court,* 33 Cal. 3d 419 (1983).

79. *Bruce Babbitt v. Sweet Home Chapter of Communities for a Great Oregon, et al.,* 1995 U.S. LEXIS 4463, No. 94–859. The Interior Department and state resource agencies would like to avoid such a confrontation before Scalia, of course, and they have been settling some takings claims out of court. See *Corvallis (Ore.) Gazette-Times* online, 1996 ("The three-year-old suit—formerly set to go to a US District Court—was 'supposed to be a landmark test of the Endangered Species Act' but was instead 'quietly settled' with the buyout"); Sax 1996b; Margolis 1997.

80. California law (constitutional, statutory, and common) generally supports strong public property interests.

81. Juvinall is citing "A WORLD PARTY?" by David Scwartzman in the spring 1992 *EcoSocialist Review.*

82. Juvinall's phrase "uncompensated caretakers for the greater population" is bound to generate a number of strong racial associations in Nevada County, which is 97 percent white and harbors many former urban refugees.

83. Jamerson is quoting 197 U.S. at 26.

CHAPTER EIGHT

1. *Euclid v. Ambler Realty Co.* 272 U.S. 365 (1926).

2. Shevock 1996 emphasizes this point in regard to rare and endemic plants.

3. Examples of the former are Arendt 1994a; 1994b; 1996a; 1996b; Pivo et al. 1990; 1988; and Wolfe 1990; examples of the latter are Redman 1992; Montgomery County 1992b; 1992a; and Livingston County Planning Department 1991.

4. *O'Loane v. O'Rourke,* 231 Cal. App. 2d 774, 782 (1965); Fulton 1993, 115.

5. The Bay Conservation and Development Commission was established by the legislature in 1965. The Tahoe Regional Planning Agency was established by a bistate Tahoe Compact in 1969. The Coastal Zone Conservation Act was adopted by California voters as Proposition 20 in November 1972; then the Coastal Act of 1976 was adopted by the legislature to modify the structure of the California Coastal Commission.

6. The Bay Vision 2020 "Blue Ribbon Commission" had many *former* local officials on it but no current elected local officials (Heyman 1991–93).

7. All annexations must be approved by the Local Agency Formation Commission, which includes representatives from the county, incorporated cities, and special districts within each county. Each commission can address jurisdictional issues only *within* a county, however, and none has power to act across county boundaries.

8. *Construction Industry Ass'n of Sonoma County v. Petaluma,* 424 U.S. 934 (1976).

9. *Golden v. Planning Board of Town of Ramapo,* 409 U.D. 1003 (1972).

10. *Arnel Development Co. v. City of Costa Mesa,* 28 Cal. 3d 511 (1980).

11. More than 40 percent of Nevada County was still unzoned until adoption of a general plan and zoning ordinance in 1980.

12. Arendt 1992–94; 1994a; 1994b. Arendt was the project manager for the report written by Yaro et al. (1988), and he led an excellent workshop, "Making Rural Clustering Work," at the May 1992 conference of the American Planning Association in Washington, D.C.

13. It appears that well-designed clustered or open space development designs are often favored by the market. Arendt (1994a; 1994b; 1996a; 1996b) demonstrates that homes in a clustered or open space development in a town in Massachusetts appreciated faster than those in a conventionally developed subdivision nearby.

14. Humbach 1992c, 1 (emphasis in original).

15. As an example, my wife's parents sold their home in Palo Alto for more than three times the value of our home in Berkeley—yet, because the Proposition 13 constraint on assessed valuation had increased their valuation by only 2 percent per year since 1980, they paid lower property taxes than we did from 1991 to 1996.

16. Northern California examples include the East Bay Regional Park District and the Midpeninsula Regional Open Space District.

17. Many proposed assessments have failed despite majority approval, having won less than the required two-thirds supermajority.

18. Examples include the agreement by the Irvine Company to keep 70 percent of the Irvine Ranch in open space (Fulton 1993).

19. McHarg's (1969) approach has been criticized for failing to adequately consider how the real estate market values different uses on different lands, reflecting locational value or the costs of development on them. Various multiattribute weighting schemes have been proposed to determine both capability and suitability, and digital Geographic

Information Systems allow rapid quantitative assessment of these values. This discussion does not prescribe a specific weighting scheme, but emphasizes the principle of clustering.

20. Even the marketplace may be undervaluing and underproviding open space amenities, however. According to recent market research, 78 percent of prospective home buyers are willing to pay to have such open space accessible—while only half as many are willing to do the same for access to golf courses. See Sierra Business Council 1997, 27.

21. This idea needs more research for its applicability to the Sierra Nevada, and we need to identify the site-specific characteristics that determine the appropriate levels of density, distribution, and spatial relationships between contiguous open space.

22. More research needs to be conducted to determine how human use of open space, such as for recreation, affects different species. Edge effects could still be significant if habitat patches are small.

23. This has been true in negotiations between the Nevada County Land Trust and the home owners' association for Banner Mountain Woodlands to acquire an easement or fee title for a recreational trail along the Cascade Ditch.

24. Examples were presented at the American Planning Association conference workshop titled "Making Rural Clustering Work," held in Washington, D.C., in May 1992.

25. This is less true of Arendt 1994b, which was funded in part by the U.S. Environmental Protection Agency, and Arendt 1996a, which was published by Island Press and includes explicit descriptions of ways to protect biological diversity.

26. Steiner (1991) has drawn on McHarg to develop similar themes—with an emphasis on landscape planning and design, rather than landscape characterization and analysis. Also see Thompson and Steiner 1997; Steinitz 1990; and Steinitz et al. 1996 for examples of more recent analytic frameworks and approaches to ecological planning.

27. I am referring here simply to the process of inventorying and assessing the characteristics of the natural factors of a region as part of the planning process (Marsh 1991; Canter 1996; Ortolano 1997; McHarg 1992). I recognize that there is still considerable uncertainty and debate about how one should approach the protection of native biological diversity, but at this point information is not even being collected. I believe environmental planners and conservation biologists can work together to develop integrated conservation/development strategies that can be applied to exurban development. The research is already under way.

28. The database on the spatial distribution of vegetation types was developed by Davis and Stoms (1996); for wildlife habitat types by Davis and Stoms (1996) and Graber (1996); for rare and endemic plant species by Shevock (1996); for significant natural areas by Millar et al. (1996); and for hydrologic regimes by Moyle (1996a), Kattelmann (1996), and Kondolf et al. (1996).

29. As noted earlier, Quammen (1996) makes the theory of island biogeography very accessible.

30. Of course they may also decide that protecting biological diversity is not worth the changes it requires (see Kanigel 1996 for a review).

31. Structural losses to wildfires still account for a relatively small portion of insurance losses, however, making it difficult to develop insurance premium structures that would favor improved urban-wildland intermix site designs.

32. The Forest Service and the California Department of Forestry and Fire Protection have funded some research on this topic, but it has generally been at the landscape scale, such as determination of which forest resources are most likely to be developed in the future, or at the structural scale, such as research on how fast shake rooftop materials burn.

The missing link is site design and the possibility for integrating development patterns with fuels management and protection needs.

33. Expenditures for fire suppression and related disaster relief expenses among government agencies totaled $735 million in California in the 1993–94 fiscal year. Federal taxpayers paid $299 million of the total cost, while the state spent $266 million and local governments spent $170 million. Initial efforts to suppress fires cost $510 million, major fires cost $130 million, and disaster relief for California wildfires cost another $105 million. The new state fire plan calls for such a redirection of funds, as well as an innovative GIS-based public participation process for identifying presuppression management alternatives. These could and should include land use planning approaches that minimize conflicts between development patterns, fire risks, suppression costs, and ecological needs. See State of California 1995. Direct losses from California wildfires reached as high as $1 billion in the East Bay Hills fire of 1991, and another billion in the fires that ravaged Southern California counties in 1993 (State of California, n.d.).

34. Assuming that the total number and type of housing units constructed under the alternative scheme remains the same as that which would have occurred under existing zoning, housing prices should be comparable under either planning approach. Reductions in the housing supply could increase prices.

35. *Bernadine Suitum v. Tahoe Regional Planning Agency*, No. 96–243, U.S. Sup. Ct. decided May 27, 1997 (65 LW 4385). The court voted six to three against the TRPA on a procedural point regarding the ripeness of Suitum's claim, overturning the decision by the Ninth Circuit Court of Appeals and sending the case back to the district court for consideration of the takings claim (Greenhouse 1997). The minority opinion called for expansion of takings jurisprudence to find the system unconstitutional on its face, however, because of the loss of economically viable *use* of Suitum's actual land. The Court essentially gave the TRPA a victory on the substantive issue at hand.

36. Schiffman 1989. The Marin Agricultural Land Trust has, however, received significant state and federal funding in areas that directly affect the Point Reyes National Seashore. See Hart 1992.

37. DeGrove 1992, 165. Housing prices in the Portland area have increased significantly since the adoption of UGBs, but they have increased less in the Portland area than in other similarly sized metropolitan areas in the West facing similar growth pressures, such as Denver and Salt Lake City. The UGBs therefore do not appear to be primarily responsible for the increased housing costs; higher prices come with growth (Nelson 1998).

38. Toulan (1997) argues that the region's remarkable growth in the 1990s is now pushing it up against the UGB, however, driving up land prices and threatening both affordability and the region's future economic development.

39. U.S.C. section 66801, P.L. 91–148 (Tahoe Compact); Elliott-Fisk et al. 1996; Strong 1984.

40. The federal government owns 78 percent of the land base, while state and local governments own about 7 percent (Elliott-Fisk et al. 1996).

41. *People ex rel Younger v. County of El Dorado*, 5 Cal. 3d 480 at 485, 486.

42. Ibid., at 486, note 3.

43. Ibid., at 485, 487.

44. *People ex rel Younger v. County of El Dorado*, 5 Cal. 3d 480 at 487; Section 66801, art. VI, subd. (a) as cited at 488 of the court's decision.

45. *People ex rel Younger v. County of El Dorado*, 5 Cal. 3d 480.

46. As Bob Twiss notes, however, the initial language in the Tahoe Compact made it a

weaker agency than the San Francisco Bay Conservation and Development Commission. Subsequent revisions to the compact have since strengthened the TRPA with stronger legislative findings regarding its mission and a shift in rebuttable presumptions (Twiss 1997).

47. Elliott-Fisk 1996, 241; *Van de Kamp v. Tahoe Regional Planning Agency,* 766 F.2d 1308 (1985).

48. *Kelly v. Tahoe Regional Planning Agency,* 855 P.2d 1027 (Nev. 1993).

49. The *Suitum* case was set to go to trial in 1998 after being remanded to the District Court by the Supreme Court in 1997. Other cases are also pending against the TRPA.

50. *Kelly v. Tahoe Regional Planning Agency,* 855 P.2d. 1027 (1993) [169 Nev. 638]. As noted above, the U.S. Supreme Court rejected a facial challenge on the TRPA's TDR/TDC system in the *Suitum* case in 1997. The *Suitum* case could still result in a successful takings claim against the TRPA.

CHAPTER NINE

1. This term was also used by Johnson (1993) to describe the growth of the East Bay Area during World War II.

2. *Grass Valley–Nevada City Union* 1995f (the publication is identified as the *Union* in citations that follow).

3. This was mentioned in comments by Nevada County Supervisors Karen Knecht and Fran Grattan at a hearing by the Nevada County Board of Supervisors regarding the California spotted owl draft environmental impact statement, 1 May 1995.

4. Recreational visits grew from 10 million in 1948 to 190 million in 1976 (Wilkinson 1992a). According to McHugh (1996), visits were up to 730 million by 1993.

5. *Friends of Mammoth v. Board of Supervisors,* 502 P. 2d 1049 (1972).

6. This history was discussed in meetings in 1996 when the Nevada County Board of Supervisors was considering naming a new road connecting Alta Sierra with Highway 49 "Karen Drive" after area Supervisor Karen Knecht.

7. *Union* 1970z. Supervisor Dean Lawrence came in third behind Wolters for judgeship. See *Union* 1970y.

8. Paine served on the Nevada City Council for a total of fifteen years between 1960 and 1980. He was elected twice, appointed twice, and served as mayor from April 1978 until February 1979.

9. This estimate of 215,000 is the official estimate given by the Nevada County Planning Department. As noted in detail below, however, these build-out estimates are highly politicized and have been manipulated in the 1995 general plan to mean something other than the maximum population allowable under the general plan.

10. CVRWQCB, Central Valley Region, Order No. 89–005, NPDES No. CA0079898.

11. CVRWQCB, Central Valley Region, Order No. 92–112.

12. Transcripts of the public hearing on the draft EIR are published in EIP Associates 1996. I attended the public hearing on the final EIR on March 26, 1996.

13. The city council finally agreed in 1998 to begin an update of its general plan, more than three years after the treatment plant expansion was first formally proposed.

14. Ironically, Mark Johnson and one of the city council members were among the plaintiffs who challenged the city's EIR adequacy regarding the Pine Creek Shopping Center (Roberts 1997).

15. Several members of the steering committee commented to me on Burdick's skill during interviews in 1992.

16. This discussion of the views of Karen Knecht and Steve Beckwitt is based on a conversation between them during a steering committee meeting in 1992, subsequent discussions with Steve Beckwitt, and comments made by Karen Knecht during public hearings and resolution committee meetings on the general plan in 1994–95.

17. She has returned to consulting work in California; see Burdick 1997 regarding her approach to facilitation.

18. The person in question was part of a group introduced to the steering committee as representing the proponents of the "new town" proposed for land owned by Gold Country Ranch, Inc. I do not know the name of the individual, but the entire group was there to observe the steering committee and answer their questions. I heard the comment myself.

19. July 15, 1992, steering committee meeting.

20. Elections Office, Nevada County Clerk-Recorder, Nevada City, California.

21. In retrospect, I should have just mailed copies of every graduate student paper to the planning commission and submitted them formally as public testimony. Ultimately I sent a letter to the board of supervisors in November 1993 listing the titles of the student papers and calling for their consideration of the information contained in them before they adopted a draft general plan. This prompted Supervisor Karen Knecht to have a staff member of the county send a letter to my dean at UC Berkeley challenging my use of UC letterhead for my letter to the county (Ward 1994–95). I have since been very careful always to make clear that my opinions do not represent the University of California.

22. The RQC members had seen a video of a presentation I had given in Sonora that was broadcast on local cable TV.

23. These estimates were given in the 1980 Nevada County General Plan and have not been independently verified.

24. SNEP's subsequent application of the biodiversity management area model also identified this area as ecologically significant because of its relatively low level of existing development and its contributions to biodiversity.

25. I lived in Nevada County during 1994–95 and developed material for this section and the rest of the chapter through interviews, newspaper accounts, and attendance at public meetings regarding the update of the general plan. For further background documentation, see the many articles published in the *Grass Valley–Nevada City Union* by reporters Susan Lauer, David Sneed, Judith Mooers, Michael Marois, Shawn Neidorf, Paul Shigley, Tim Willis, and Mark Spencer, listed in the bibliography. Other sources (i.e., op-ed pieces and letters to the editor, as well as public hearings) are cited below.

26. The debate was held at Nevada Union High School and broadcast on KNCO on October 11, 1994.

27. October 11, 1994, debate notes.

28. Elections Office, Nevada County Clerk-Recorder, Nevada City, California (after a recount had been completed).

29. The EIR consultant was Amy Skewes-Cox, who is married to my colleague Bob Twiss and is president of the Association of Environmental Professionals. I did not know she was involved in that contract, however, until after the draft EIR was released. She was also unfamiliar with the recommendations for mitigation I was making.

30. Hearings were held April 6, April 13, and April 14; the planning commission certified the EIR on May 11.

31. Public hearing for the Nevada County General Plan, Nevada County Planning Commission, May 11, 1995.

32. Public hearing for the Nevada County General Plan, Nevada County Planning Commission, May 11, 1995.

33. Public hearing for appeal of the Nevada County General Plan EIR, July 22, 1995.

34. If twenty-five people had voted for Weir instead of Grattan in the Grattan-Weir election, Weir would have won by one vote instead of losing by forty-nine votes.

35. California Forestry Association n.d. Fax copy of article provided by Harley Greiman, U.S. Forest Service (Sacramento) via the California Supervisor's Association of California. Greiman was a longtime resident of Nevada County whom I first met in 1978 while I was a dispatcher for the Tahoe National Forest and he was the Downieville district ranger. He later worked with the SNEP team before dying tragically in an accident while working at his Lake Wildwood home in June 1996.

36. These figures are based on review of the campaign finance filings at the Elections Office, Nevada County Clerk-Recorder. According to Lauer (1995j), however, Weir spent a total of $30,470 on the campaign. This is $1,398 more than the sum of $21,929 in contributions and $7,143 in outstanding loans that I report here, but does not change the total significantly. Grattan still spent more than twice as much as Weir in direct expenditures on the 1994 campaign.

37. All totals reported here have been culled from the campaign finance files of the Elections Office, Nevada County Clerk-Recorder.

38. According to Dale Creighton (1994) and Dan Landon (1994), Ed Sylvester had refused to work on that particular project when it was first proposed for Glenbrook Basin on the grounds that it did not fit in with the community.

39. Weir's contributor's list was much less interesting. The largest donation of $779 came from Linda Rachmal through her purchases at the yard sale. Another $645 came in the form of a rug from the Magic Carpet, a local business owned by RQC activists Paul and Eileen Jorgensen. Kent Gallagher donated $550 worth of goods or services, while Michael Killegrew, who lives on the San Juan Ridge and has been an active environmentalist—and whose efforts include establishment of conservation easements on much of his land—donated $425 in kind. Local dentist Stephen Smith donated $250 in services and then purchased $251 worth of goods or services at the yard sale fund-raiser. Harold Berliner and Richard Ellers donated $250 each.

40. Barnhart did formally announce her withdrawal from the race and support for Matson just days before the election, but it was too late to change the ballots and she drew 1,078 votes—primarily away from Matson.

41. Weir lost to Grattan by only thirty-seven votes in the initial tally, but a recount gave her a forty-nine-vote margin.

42. They were led by Paul Jorgensen of the Magic Carpet with $1,151, Richard Kat with $1,360, Eric Prudhomme with $1,335, and Lawrence Lansburgh with $1,238. With the exception of a $2,000 donation from Rena DeWitt, who is the mother of Van Zant's wife, Mary, only three cash contributions exceeded $250 (totaling $1,100 and averaging $370): the Nevada County Employees Association donated $500, Kent Gallagher gave $350, and Janaia Donaldson gave $260.

43. Wilcox-Foster received $950 from John Estes, $875 from David Jones, $750 from Morgan Stoltz, $700 from local auto dealer Jim Keil, and $650 from local engineer Mark Smith. Kathleen Christensen, Charles Litton, the Western Mobile Home Parkowners, Graphic Label Group, Kent Boothby, Kenneth Smith, and Ivan Kochan all donated $500

each, while Amos and Beverly Seghezzi (Wilcox-Foster retained Amos Seghezzi as her planning commission appointee when she took office) donated $498.

44. Elections Office, Nevada County Clerk-Recorder, Nevada City, California.

CHAPTER TEN

1. The final vote to approve the zoning was three to one after Commissioner Barbara Green left the meeting for Truckee.

2. This is based on 2.1 to 2.4 persons per household.

3. The Nevada County Planning Department estimated that the build-out population of the adopted general plan, using its old planimetric methodology (which did not account for existing parcelization patterns) and including the additional 7,900 population attributable to the incorporated cities' build-out potential, would equal 150,300.

4. See Duane 1996c for a detailed discussion of the methodology and underlying assumptions for each scenario.

5. The Low-Compact scenario (A) always represented the lower bound of the range and the High-Sprawl scenario (D) always represented the higher bound of our range, with the exception of the threshold of 640+ dwelling units per square mile. These two extreme scenarios resulted in approximately the same land area conversion in the latter case, while the Low-Sprawl (C) scenario resulted in the least land conversion and the High-Compact (B) scenario resulted in the most land conversion. This primarily reflects the fact that the compact scenarios concentrate 71.34 percent of the total population into the highest housing density class. The compact scenarios therefore result in more land area converted to human settlement in the highest housing-density class, but they still result in less land area converted to human settlement in all of the other housing density classes. This is clear at all of the other density thresholds.

6. The Holland classification system focuses on vegetation types, while the WHR system focuses on the habitat needs of wildlife (Jensen et al. 1993).

7. Duane 1996a. I provided my digitized general plan GIS coverage to Nevada County in July 1995, along with my draft SNEP report. At that time the county did not have a functional GIS for analysis of the general plan.

8. The original GIS-based analysis was completed in 1995 by Karl Goldstein to generate tabular summaries of the overlay of land use plans and habitat types, then these tabular data were analyzed in Excel in 1997 by Will Caldicott.

9. The method, assumptions, and results were also presented to the California Biodiversity Council in November 1997.

10. Greenwood and Marose (1993) used one dwelling unit per forty acres in their analysis for the CDF. See Yuba County Community Services Department 1985; Faulstich and Xoi 1993; Finn 1994; and Lehr 1995, regarding deer habitat and the impact of human settlement on winter breeding success.

11. These quantitative results are meant to be illustrative of the analytic technique. The density of thirty-two acres per unit is somewhat arbitrary, of course, and different thresholds of significance would lead to different estimates of habitat conversion.

12. A new version of the WHR system (5.3) was released in early 1997, which could modify these results slightly.

13. The one exception is a small set of rare endemic plants confined to Gabbro ser-

pentine soils, which are inconveniently located in prime development areas along Highway 50 near Cameron Park. See Deck 1993.

14. Shevock 1996, 700. With the exception of Kern and Tulare Counties in the extreme southern Sierra Nevada, each of the other counties in the Sierra Nevada harbors zero to seven plant taxa endemic to each county and six to seventy rare taxa.

15. This comment was made by an audience member at a presentation I gave to the Rural Quality Coalition, Nevada City, California, December 1993.

16. Malcolm McDaniel suggested to me the connection between fair-share requirements in California housing law and the possibility of similar responsibilities to protect wildlife habitats through local jurisdictions' general plans. Bob Johnson and Mary Madison (1991) also suggested a similar link between general plan law and habitat protection efforts in a report to the CDF.

17. I recognize that this statement reflects my own values, and that others may prefer other objectives; Innes calls for a planning process that would also define the *ends*.

18. An example is the Coordinated Resource Management Planning (CRMP) process, which brings together state and federal land and resource management agencies in ad hoc arrangements for specific resources. To date, local land use planning has not been very well integrated into the CRMP process, however, but state and federal agencies are increasingly seeking the participation of local government in new CRMP projects.

19. These could include modifying local government boundaries or agency field offices along bioregional or watershed lines. See California Resources Agency 1991 for an example in the case of biodiversity.

20. This list was originally developed for the Sierra Now conference in 1992 (Duane 1992b), which was then published in part in Environment Now 1993 and presented in Duane 1993a; 1993b; and 1993c.

21. Olmsted Brothers and Bartholomew and Associates 1930, xiv (cited in Mike Davis 1996, 160).

22. Alexander 1990, 80 (quoted and cited in Mike Davis 1996, 168).

23. Alexander 1990, 82 (quoted and cited in Mike Davis 1996, 169).

24. Mike Davis 1996, 179–80. For an excellent overview of shifting attitudes toward different types of landscapes, see Tuan 1974.

25. As Shoup (1997) notes, however, statistics like these are difficult to verify. The land area statistics cited by Davis seem reliable, but the concrete estimate seems high.

26. Williams 1969; EDAW 1972 (both cited in Mike Davis 1996).

27. EDAW 1965, 45 (cited in Mike Davis 1996, 174).

28. Ibid.

29. As Mike Davis notes (1997), Los Angeles now has the largest urban-wildland interface of any city in the United States except perhaps Miami, Florida. He estimates that the city's edge with Nature exceeds a thousand miles.

30. The draft EIR for Dark Horse identified eighteen "unmitigable" significant effects of the project, confirming the RQC's critiques of the original negative declaration (Oberholtzer 1997–98).

31. Bisnett 1997. Quail Lake Estates involves 91 lots on 808 acres, while Wolf Creek Ranch Estates would create 229 lots on 691 acres. Together with Dark Horse these developments would create more than 600 new parcels.

CHAPTER ELEVEN

1. Two years later, however, they broke, flooding the area along the Feather River near Olivehurst. The New Year's storms of 1997 pounded the Feather River watershed, and the Oroville Dam was little protection for downstream communities. Ironically, most of the serious flooding that year occurred downstream of major dams.

2. Data are from a 1952–96 daily-rainfall record spreadsheet prepared by the *Grass Valley–Nevada City Union*. These data do not include the incredible storms that pelted the region between Christmas 1996 and New Year's Day 1997 or the wet El Niño weather of 1997–98, which was the wettest year in San Francisco since 1862.

3. In statistical terms, the coefficient of variation for precipitation in Nevada City is high: a standard deviation of just under 18 inches divided by a mean of just over 56 inches per year yields a coefficient of variation of .32 for the 1951–96 period.

4. According to Paul Starrs (1994), "The intelligence and influence of bioregionalists is far in excess of their numbers." It remains to be seen if he is correct on either count, although I am inclined to agree with him on both.

5. Some have called the Wise Use movement an "astro-turf" movement, claiming it is not really based upon genuine, authentic grassroots concerns (National Public Radio 1995). I think the movement originally sprang from a genuine concern by real people who have been directly affected by real decisions, but it is not grassroots in its organized form.

6. Ecological concepts are also socially defined, of course. See Evernden 1992.

7. Merchant 1992. Her comment draws on the writings of Ray Dasmann and Peter Berg (most notably in publications by the Planet Drum Foundation) from the early 1970s through the early 1990s.

8. As noted above, this is one of the primary concepts imbedded in ecosystem management—that there is a need to coordinate policies and land and resource management activities across jurisdictions and ownerships.

9. It is important to note that people can have multiple regional identities simultaneously. Starrs (1994) discusses six broad regional categories today: ecosystems; regional authorities; vernacular regions; bioregions and watersheds; cultural areas, ethnic regions, and homelands; and nodes in the global exchange.

10. There is a long, ongoing debate among geographers and anthropologists, of course, about the relative importance of physical geography to the development of culture. It is generally accepted, however, that modern industrial society in the era of fossil fuels has at least weakened the dependence of cultural development on physical geography, if not the relationship between the two. See Starrs 1994.

11. See Goldsmith (1993) for a more detailed discussion of the dominance of an ecological worldview in human history throughout the world.

12. This is a central question in the ongoing debate over the effect of so-called free trade agreements, such as the North American Free Trade Agreement and the General Agreement on Tariffs and Trade. Of course, in the absence of some system for evaluating impacts and internalizing those costs, the negative consequences of trade are not now considered by the market or buyers and sellers when making decisions.

13. Opportunities to do so are constrained by the terms of the General Agreement on Tariffs and Trade, however, as implemented by the World Trade Organization. In contrast, environmental "side agreements" make such considerations an explicit part of the North American Free Trade Agreement.

14. Mumford 1938, 345 (quoted in Luccarelli 1995, 97).

15. For an exploration of the degree of flexibility in complex systems, see Lovins and Lovins 1982; and Tainter 1988. For a discussion of regeneration see Van der Ryn and Cowan 1996.

16. This is true both for rapidly growing rural areas—whose new residents largely come from urban areas because of a perceived decline in the quality of life in those urban areas— and economically depressed rural areas, where market prices for agricultural goods are largely determined in urban markets for those goods.

17. The exception is western U.S. senators, who wield influence on public lands and resource management policy disproportional to the populations of their respective states.

18. This project involved dozens of cities in the United States around Earth Day 1990 and has continued to spread.

19. Register 1987. Richard Register is no longer with Urban Ecology, but has founded a new group called Ecocities.

20. Former Seattle Mayor Norm Rice built a new metropolitan political coalition around his Sustainable Seattle proposal, while the Portland metropolitan area has embraced sustainability as a theme for planning. See Beatley and Brower 1993; Throgmorton 1994; and Berke and Manta 1997, for examples of municipal sustainability efforts.

21. Environmental impact matrices have been developed for many activities for use in environmental impact assessments. See Canter 1996; and Ortolano 1997.

22. I recognize that the institutional arrangements for doing so would require significant changes and may distort markets, but those institutions could also rely on price signals such as taxes to internalize the costs of specific types of trade transactions and therefore discourage them except when their benefits are otherwise significant.

23. This point is not widely accepted or recognized in the bioregional literature. The emphasis of that literature is on decentralization and devolution of authority to watershed-scale self-government. Larger geographic areas and larger institutions are necessary, however, both to trace the effects of trade (e.g., through environmental and resource accounting systems) and to address ecological phenomena that transcend bioregional boundaries, such as air pollution. Any border, even if drawn along ecological lines, creates transboundary issues. Watersheds are fine for hydrologic processes, but they do not address vegetation or habitat. We must therefore consider several overlapping units of analysis and pay as much attention to what transpires between those units as within them, at multiple scales.

24. One could also argue that it is the *re*-entry of place into the dialectic of history, since place and its biophysical features have been central to human history for the vast majority of human existence. Also see Luccarelli 1995.

25. Snyder 1994–98. I have been unable to find the source of this quote, but Snyder agrees that he wrote it. For more on Snyder, see D. Duane 1996; McHugh 1992a; and Sneed 1996b.

26. Wendell Berry has also made this point eloquently in his writings. See Berry 1977; 1989.

27. Thomas Jefferson to John Jay, August 23, 1785, in Jefferson 1952, 426 (cited in Kemmis 1990).

28. Sandel 1984 (cited in Kemmis 1990, 54).

29. Sheldon Hackney, former president of the University of Pennsylvania, in Guiner 1994b and 1994c.

30. This discussion is based on observation of decision processes at the federal (Forest

Service, National Park Service, Bureau of Land Management), state (California State Water Resources Control Board, California Energy Commission, California Public Utilities Commission, California State Board of Forestry), and local (city and county general plan and zoning debates) levels over two decades.

31. Note the Grattan-Weir election, which was initially decided by just thirty-seven votes (forty-nine following a recount). A voter can imagine influencing twenty to twenty-five members of the community to change their votes, making the outcome of such an election within one's direct influence. Sierra County voters decided one election in 1994 by just three votes.

32. Ostrom 1990; she does not discuss larger-scale cases in detail, but the need to maintain a smaller scale is consistent with the design principles she developed, as well as with those of Ellickson (1991) and Putnam et al. (1993).

33. Once again, it is important to note that the bioregional movement is composing a tapestry from many different weavers. All bioregionalists do not necessarily embrace all aspects of any bioregional viewpoint. Interestingly, however, this perspective on decentralization is also shared by many on the political right who would not otherwise identify with many of the basic values or stated goals of bioregionalism.

34. These ranges appear to be appropriate in both rural and urban settings, as they correspond roughly with the typical population ranges of small towns and urban neighborhoods. This has important implications for urban design, for it suggests that larger urban centers could be structured as hierarchies of smaller neighborhoods to promote social interaction within place-based communities. It also has implications for the relative participatory success of political institutions in larger urban centers, however, for the formal institutional mechanisms for public participation in decision-making are usually linked to the aggregated mega-unit. This may partially explain stiff local resistance to proposals for regional governments. Those apposed to regional control prefer the politics of community to that of interest.

35. Mumford 1938 (quoted in Andruss et al. 1990).

36. J. Thomas 1990, 81 (quoted in Luccarelli 1995, 111).

37. Bergman 1990 (cited in Evernden 1992, 105).

38. Pinchot 1967, 45 (cited in Evernden 1992, 131).

39. Leopold 1970, 251, 261. Leopold's use of the term *biotic mechanism* reflects a Cartesian and Newtonian view of nature as a mechanistic clock, which has been challenged by developments in both physics and ecology since 1948. See Capra (1975) and Botkin (1990).

40. See Pister 1987 for a wonderful discussion of Pister's own shift from what Leopold described as type "A" to type "B."

41. His defense is much more elaborate, of course, but there is no room here to discuss its finer philosophical points. See Callicott 1989 for a thorough discussion and Des Jardins 1997 for a discussion of Leopold's critics.

42. Even the published version might have been modified by Leopold before publication, for he intended to solicit reviews of the draft and to revise it accordingly in the summer of 1948. See Meine 1988, 523–24. I know from my own experience that specific phrases do get modified in the editing process!

43. Snyder 1990; McHugh 1992a; 1992b; Lin 1996; and personal communication with board members of the YWI. I also attended the BLM public hearings on the proposals during 1987–88.

44. Gunderson et al. (1995b) and Clark and Minta (1994) note the importance of such individuals to institutional innovation.

45. I have been an active member of YWI since 1994, and I lived in the community from 1994 to 1995.

46. See Bailey 1996 for a systematic approach based solely on ecosystem geography; my structure includes considerations of social and economic system networks and hierarchies, as well as those of ecosystem geography.

47. The word *watershed* originally meant the divide between two drainage basins (e.g., "it was a watershed event" suggests a boundary or divide), but generally means the same thing as *drainage basin* in today's usage.

48. California voters approved Proposition 204 in November 1996 ($995 million), and the Clinton administration has pledged another $400 million in federal commitments toward the effort during the 1997–2000 budget years. See CalFed Bay-Delta Program 1995a; 1995b; 1996; 1997, for a description of the CalFed Program, its funding, and the scope of its proposed projects.

49. The Regional Council of Rural Counties has recently been very active in the CalFed Bay-Delta process under the leadership of the Plumas County attorney Michael Jackson and several Plumas County supervisors. They are seeking transfer of funds from downstream water users to upstream watershed source counties for restoration and forest management projects that will protect or enhance water quality and/or quantity.

50. There have been some special agreements between PG&E and the Plumas Corporation to pay for upstream watershed management activities that will reduce PG&E's reservoir dredging costs, but they are not permanent (Wills 1992).

51. In at least one case, however, the CRMP approach has been tried in an urban environment. See Small 1996.

52. The Sierra Business Council has initiated development of a NCCP-type planning process for Placer County, however, that is expected to be completed by the year 2000. Placer County Planning Director Fred Yeager has been supportive, and all relevant agencies are being included. This represents the first proactive NCCP.

53. Fish and Wildlife Service 1991 (cited in Shaffer 1992b, 6). This estimate is clearly too low, of course, if one considers the opportunity cost associated with foregone power revenues, timber harvests, or mineral extraction that might have been constrained by efforts to protect endangered species. Expenditures have also increased since 1992.

54. The figure on expenditures is from Bean 1991; the second figure, $36 million, comes from Reid 1992. Both are cited in Shaffer 1992b, 7.

55. This cost estimate was publicized during a lawsuit by the group Urban Ecology (Berkeley, California) against the California Department of Transportation. Urban Ecology argued that public transit should be funded instead.

BIBLIOGRAPHY

Abram, David. 1992. "The Ecology of Magic." In Sauer 1992.

Adams, Lowell W. and Louise E. Dove. 1989. *Wildlife Reserves and Corridors in the Urban Environment: Guide to Ecological Landscape Planning and Resource Conservation.* Columbia, Md.: National Institute for Urban Wildlife.

Alexander, Christopher. 1979. *The Timeless Way of Building.* New York: Oxford University Press.

Alexander, Christopher, Murray Silverstein, Sara Ishikawa, Ingrid Fiksdahl-King, and Max Jacobson Shlomo Angel. 1977. *A Pattern Language.* New York: Oxford University Press.

Alexander, Robert E. 1966. *Environmental Quality and Amenity in California: An Analysis of State Development Decision Procedures Affecting Visual and Other Qualitative Characteristics of the California Environment.* Sacramento: California Office of Planning.

———. 1990. "The San Fernando Valley." Manuscript, p. 80. Cited in Mike Davis 1996, p. 168.

Allen, P. Geoffrey, and Thomas H. Stevens. 1983. *Use of Hedonic Price Technique to Evaluate Wetlands.* Amherst: University of Massachusetts, Water Resources Research Center.

Alterman, Rachelle. 1994. "Can Farmland Preservation Work? Lesson [sic] for the USA from a Six-Nation Comparative Perspective." Paper presented to the Association of Collegiate Schools of Planning, 3–6 Nov., Tempe, Ariz.

Altschuler, Alan. 1965a. *The City Planning Process: A Political Analysis.* Ithaca, N. Y.: Cornell University Press. Cited in Innes 1996a.

———. 1965b. "The Goals of Comprehensive Planning." *Journal of the American Institute of Planners* 31 (3): 186–97. Cited in Innes 1996a.

American Farmland Trust. 1995. *Alternatives for Future Urban Growth in California's Central Valley: The Bottom Line for Agriculture and Taxpayers.* Washington, D.C.: American Farmland Trust.

Ames, Laurel. 1992–95. Executive Director, Sierra Nevada Alliance and Former Executive Director, League to Save Lake Tahoe. South Lake Tahoe, Calif. Personal communication.

Anderson, H. Michael and Jeffrey T. Olson. 1991. *Federal Forests and the Economic Base of the Pacific Northwest: A Study of Regional Transitions.* Washington, D.C.: Wilderness Society.

Andruss, Van, Christopher Plant, Judith Plant, and Eleanor Wright. 1990. *Home! A Bioregional Reader.* Philadelphia: New Society Publishers.

Appelyard, D. and K. H. Craik. 1979. *Visual Simulation in Environmental Planning and Design.* Working Paper No. 314. Berkeley, Calif.: University of California, Institute of Urban and Regional Development.

Arendt, Randall. 1992–94, 1997. Vice President, Natural Lands Trust, Media, Penn. Personal communication.

———. 1994a. *Designing Open Space Subdivisions: A Practical Step-by-Step Approach.* Media, Penn.: Natural Lands Trust.

———. 1994b. *Rural by Design: Maintaining Small Town Character.* Chicago: American Planning Association.

———. 1996a. *Conservation Design for Subdivisions: A Practical Guide to Creating Open Space Networks.* Washington, D.C.: Island Press.

———. 1996b. *Open Space Design Guidebook.* Media, Penn.: Natural Lands Trust.

Arens, Karla. 1996. "Planners' Wisdom and Experience Make NC What It Is," *Grass Valley–Nevada City Union,* 10 August, p. A7.

Arnold, Chester L., Jr., and C. James Gibbons. 1996. "Impervious Surface Coverage: The Emergence of a Key Environmental Indicator." *Journal of the American Planning Association* 62, no. 2 (spring): 243–58.

Arnstein, S. R. 1969. "A Ladder of Citizen Participation." *Journal of the American Institute of Planners* 35, no. 4 (July): 216–24.

Attwater, William R., and James Markle. 1988. "Overview of California Water Rights and Water Quality Law." *Pacific Law Journal* 19:957–1030.

Aune, Phil. 1995. U.S. Forest Service, Redding, Calif. Personal communication.

Austin, Debbie. 1994. Inyo National Forest, Bishop, Calif. Personal communication.

Austin, Mary. [1903] 1988. *The Land of Little Rain.* New York: Penguin.

Axelrod, R. 1984. *The Evolution of Cooperation.* New York: Basic Books.

Baden, John A., and Tim O'Brien. 1994. "Economics and Ecosystems: Coevolution in the Northwest." *Illahee* 10 (3): 192–204.

Bailey, Robert G. 1996. *Ecosystem Geography.* New York: Springer-Verlag.

Baker, Deborah. 1998. "Taos Has Down Side for Low-Income Residents." *San Francisco Examiner,* 4 January, p. E6.

Baker, Mark, and William Stewart. 1996. "Ecosystems under Four Different Public Institutions: A Comparative Analysis." In *Sierra Nevada Ecosystem Project Final Report to Congress: Status of the Sierra Nevada,* 2:1347–68. Davis: Center for Water and Wildland Resources, University of California.

Bakker, Elna. 1971. *An Island Called California: An Ecological Introduction to Its Natural Communities.* Berkeley and Los Angeles: University of California Press.

Baldassare, Mark. 1981. *Trouble in Paradise: The Suburban Transformation of America.* New York: Columbia University Press.

Bank of America, Greenbelt Alliance, California Resources Agency, and the Low Income Housing Fund. 1994. *Beyond Sprawl: New Patterns of Growth to Fit the New California.* San Francisco and Sacramento: Bank of America, Greenbelt Alliance, California Resources Agency, and the Low Income Housing Fund.

Barbour, Michael, Bruce Pavlik, Frank Drysdale, and Susan Lindstrom. 1993. *California's Changing Landscapes: Diversity and Conservation of California Vegetation.* Sacramento: California Native Plant Society.

Barfield, Owen. 1973. *Poetic Diction.* 3^d ed. Middletown: Wesleyan University Press. Cited in Evernden 1992.

Barnard, Jeff. 1998. "Former Timber Mill Converted into Trendy Village District: Fast-Growing Bend Becomes Bustling Burg." *San Francisco Examiner,* 4 January, p. E6.

Barnhart, Jason. 1997. California Department of Finance, Economic Research Unit. Personal communication, 10 March.

Barnum, Alex. 1996a. "Culture Clash as Sprawl Nears Sierra: Pro-Growth vs. Slow Growth." *San Francisco Chronicle,* 27 May, p. A1.

———. 1996b. "Growing Pressure on the Sierra: Urbanization, Logging Cited in U.S. Report." *San Francisco Chronicle,* 7 June, p. A1.

———. 1996c. "GOP Lawmakers Question Sierra Report." *San Francisco Chronicle,* 11 June, p. A2.

———. 1997. "Endangered Species Found to Frequently Share 'Hot Spots.'" *San Francisco Chronicle,* 24 January, p. C1.

Barrett, Reginald. 1992–96. Professor, Forestry and Resource Management, Department of Environmental Science, Policy and Management, University of California at Berkeley. Personal communication.

Barringer, Felicity. 1993. "Population Grows in Rural America, Studies Say." *New York Times,* 25 May, p. A1.

Barry, Daniel A., and Kenneth Cook. 1994. "How the Biodiversity Treaty Went Down." Washington, D.C.: Environmental Policy Group.

Barry, John Byrne. 1997. "Stopping Sprawl." *Planet Special Report, Planet: The Sierra Club Activist Resource* 4 (3).

Bates, Robert H. 1988. "Contra Contractarianism: Some Reflections on the New Institutionalism." *Politics and Society* 16:387–401.

———. 1990. "Institutions as Investments." Duke University Program in Political Economy, Papers in Political Economy, Working Paper 133, December. Cited in Putnam et al. 1993.

Baumol, William J., and Wallace E. Oates. 1979. *Economics, Environmental Policy, and the Quality of Life.* Englewood Cliffs, N. J.: Prentice-Hall.

Baxter, Jane. 1992–96. Range Watch, Posey, Calif. Personal communication.

Beale, Calvin. 1975. *The Revival of Population Growth in Nonmetropolitan America.* Washington, D.C.: U.S. Department of Agriculture, Economic Research Service.

Bean, Edwin F. 1867. *Bean's History and Directory of Nevada County, California.* Nevada [City, Calif.]: Daily Gazette and Job Office.

Bean, Michael J. 1991. "Issues and Controversies in the Forthcoming Reauthorization Battle." In *Endangered Species Update* 9 (1) and *Endangered Species Update* 9 (2). Ann Arbor: University of Michigan. Cited in Shaffer 1992b.

Bean, Walton. 1978. *California: An Interpretive History.* New York: McGraw-Hill.

Beatley, Timothy. 1994a. *Ethical Land Use: Principles of Policy and Use.* Baltimore: Johns Hopkins University Press.

———. 1994b. *Habitat Conservation Planning: Endangered Species and Urban Growth.* Austin: University of Texas Press.

Beatley, Timothy, and David Brower. 1993. "Sustainability Comes to Main Street Planning." *Planning* (May).

Beatley, Timothy, and Kristy Manning. 1997. *Beyond the New Urbanism: Planning for Environment, Economy and Community.* Washington, D.C.: Island Press.

Beaumont, Constance E. 1994. *How Superstore Sprawl Can Harm Communities and What Citizens Can Do about It.* Washington, D.C.: National Trust for Historic Preservation.

Beedy, Edward C., and Stephen L. Granholm. 1985. *Discovering Sierra Birds: Western Slope.* Yosemite National Park, Calif.: Yosemite Natural History Association.

Beesley, David. 1994a. "The Opening of the Sierra Nevada and the Beginnings of Conservation, 1827–1897." Manuscript, Sierra College, Rocklin, Calif.

———. 1994b. "Sierra Celebration." Presentation given on Earth Day, 22 April, at Sierra College, Rocklin, Calif.

———. 1996. "The Opening of the Sierra Nevada and the Beginnings of Conservation in California: 1827–1900." *California History* 75, no. 4 (winter): 322–37.

Bellah, Robert N., Richard Madsen, William M. Sullivan, Ann Swidler, and Steven M. Tipton. 1985. *Habits of the Heart: Individualism and Commitment in American Life.* Berkeley and Los Angeles: University of California Press.

Belzar, Dena, and Cynthia Kroll. 1986. *New Jobs for the Timber Region: Economic Diversification for Northern California.* Berkeley, Calif.: Institute of Governmental Studies.

Benedict, Ruth. [1934] 1959. *Patterns of Culture.* Boston: Houghton Mifflin.

Benjamin, Walter. 1990. Cited in Mike Davis 1990, frontispiece.

Benton, Cory. 1997. Data Analysis Unit, California Department of Correction, Sacramento, Calif. Personal communication, 10 March.

Berg, Peter, ed. 1978. *Reinhabiting a Separate Country: A Bioregional Anthology of Northern California.* San Francisco: Planet Drum Foundation.

Berger, John J. 1985. *Restoring the Earth: How Americans Are Working to Renew Our Damaged Environment.* New York: Knopf.

Bergman, Charles. 1990. *Wild Echoes: Encounters with the Most Endangered Animals in North America.* Anchorage: Alaska Northwest Books. Cited in Evernden 1992.

Berke, Philip, and Maria Manta. 1997. "Planning for Sustainable Development: Measuring and Explaining Progress in Plans." Paper presented to the Association of Collegiate Schools of Planning, 9 November, Ft. Lauderdale, Florida.

Berkeley Chamber of Commerce. 1997. Brochures on the city of Berkeley. Berkeley: Berkeley Chamber of Commerce.

Berry, Wendell. 1977. *The Unsettling of America: Culture and Agriculture.* San Francisco: Sierra Club Books.

———. 1989. "The Futility of Global Thinking." *Harper's,* September, pp. 16–22.

Bigham, Joe. 1970a. "State Health Concern with Sewage in Creeks Expressed." *Grass Valley–Nevada City Union,* 22 March, p. 1.

———. 1970b. "Subdivision Lot Sewer Ordinance Ordered: Could Become County Law within Weeks." *Grass Valley–Nevada City Union,* March 25, p. 1.

———. 1970c. "Emergency Ordinance on Septic Tanks Was a Necessary Action." *Grass Valley–Nevada City Union,* May 20, p. 1.

Biging, Greg S. 1994. "The Design of the Old-Growth Mapping Project." Letter submitted to the Sierra Nevada Ecosystem Project Steering Committee, vol. 4 of public records. Center for the Assessment and Monitoring of Forest and Environmental Resources, Department of Environmental Science, Policy, and Management, University of California at Berkeley, February 21.

Bimber, Bruce. 1996. *The Politics of Expertise in Congress: The Rise and Fall of the Office of Technology Assessment.* Albany: State University of New York Press.

BioSystems Analysis, Inc. 1994. *Life on the Edge: A Guide to California's Endangered Natural Resources*. Santa Cruz, Calif.: BioSystems Books.

Birch, Dean Nelson. 1986. "Water Resources and Rural Growth: A Policy Analysis of Water Resource Management in the Sierra Nevada Foothills (California)." Ph.D. diss., University of California at Santa Barbara. Dissertation Abstracts International, Vol. 47/11-a, p. 4185.

Bisnett, Brian. 1996a. President, Rural Quality Coalition, Nevada City, Calif. Personal communication, 26 March.

————. 1996b. "Rezoning Proposal Needs More Thought." *Grass Valley–Nevada City Union*, 3 May, p. A9.

————. 1997. "Message from the President." *Rural Quality News* (Rural Quality Coalition of Nevada County, Nevada City, Calif.) (November): 1.

Black, Donald. 1976. *The Behavior of Law*. New York: Academic Press. Cited in Ellickson 1991.

Blackburn, Thomas C., and Kat Anderson, eds. 1993. *Before the Wilderness: Environmental Management by Native Californians*. Menlo Park, Calif.: Ballena Press.

Blackwood, Larry G., and Edwin H. Carpenter. 1978. "The Importance of Antiurbanism in Determining Residential Preferences and Migration Patterns." *Rural Sociology* 43 (1): 31–47.

Blake, Lucy. 1993–97. Executive Director, Sierra Business Council, Truckee, Calif. Personal communication.

Blakely, Edward J. 1992. "Room for Whom?" Presentation to informal rural and small town planning seminar, Department of City and Regional Planning, University of California at Berkeley.

Blakely, Edward J., and Mary Gail Snyder. 1997. *Fortress America: Gated Communities in the United States*. Cambridge, Mass.: Lincoln Institute of Land Policy; Washington, D.C.: Brookings Institution Press.

Blaug, M. ed. 1986. *Who's Who in Economics*. Cambridge: MIT Press.

Blumberg, Louis. 1997a. Assistant Regional Director, the Wilderness Society, California-Nevada Office. Testimony on H.R. 858 before the House Resources Committee, Forests and Forest Health Subcommittee. March 5.

————. 1997b. Assistant Regional Director, the Wilderness Society, California-Nevada Office. Statement before the U.S. Senate, Committee on Energy and Natural Resources, Subcommittee on Forests and Public Land Management, Workshop on Community-Based Approaches in Conflict Resolution in Public Lands Management. May 22.

Blumberg, Louis et al. 1997. Letter to Senator Barbara Boxer and Senator Diane [*sic*] Feinstein re: Quincy Library Group Legislation. Signed by representatives of the Wilderness Society, Natural Resources Defense Council, Central Sierra Environmental Resource Center, Tule River Conservancy, Yosemite Area Audubon, Sierra Club, California Wilderness Coalition, Plumas Forest Project, Friends of the River, Friends of the Inyo, Friends Aware of Wildlife Needs, Environmental Protection Information Center, Cal Trout, Klamath Forest Alliance, Northcoast Environmental Center, Willits Environmental Center, Mendocino Environmental Center, and Citizens for Better Forestry. 26 February.

Blumenfeld, Hans. 1954. "The Tidal Wave of Metropolitan Expansion." *Journal of the American Institute of Planners* 20 (1): 3–14.

————. 1986. "Metropolis Extended." *Journal of the American Planning Association* 52 (3): 346–48.

Bobker, Gary. 1997. Comments at the conference "Ecosystem Management: Law, Science and Policy," 15 February, School of Law, University of California at Davis.

Boivin, Sharon. 1991–96. Nevada County Planning Department. Personal communication.

———. 1997. "What's Happening." *Rural Quality News* (Rural Quality Coalition of Nevada County, Nevada City, Calif.) (November): 3.

Boivin, Sharon, and Pat Norman. 1993. Meeting with Nevada County Planning Department to present results of LA 205 analyses by students, May, Nevada City, Calif.

Bollens, Scott A. 1993. "Integrating Environmental and Economic Policies at the State Level." In Stein 1993, pp. 143–61.

Bonfante, Jordan. 1993. "Boom Time in the Rockies: More Jobs and Fewer Hassles Have Americans Heading for the Hills." *Time*, 6 September, p. 20–25.

Borchers, Jim. 1994. United States Geological Survey, Sacramento. Personal communication, 29 June.

Bosselman, Fred P., and David Callies. 1972. *The Quiet Revolution in Land Use Control*. Washington, D.C.: Council on Environmental Quality.

Botkin, Daniel B. 1990. *Discordant Harmonies: A New Ecology for the Twenty-first Century*. Oxford: Oxford University Press.

Bowman, Chris. 1994. "Placer Plan Predicts Freeway Tie-Ups." *Lincoln News Messenger*, p. 1.

Brackett, Len. 1994–96. Timber Framer and Board Member, Yuba Watershed Institute, Nevada City, Calif. Personal communication.

Bradshaw, Ted K. 1993. "Growth Control and the Failure of Planning." *California Policy Choices* 8:61–81.

———. 1994–95. Institute of Urban and Regional Development, University of California at Berkeley (now in the Department of Human and Community Development, University of California at Davis). Personal communication.

Bradshaw, Ted K., and Edward J. Blakely. 1981. *Resources of Recent Migrants to Rural Areas for Economic Development: Policy Implications*. Berkeley: University of California, Division of Agricultural Sciences.

Bradshaw, Ted K., Cynthia A. Kroll, Mary Corley, Josh Kirschenbaum, Lyn Harlan, Rokaya Al-Ayat, and Jason Moody. 1994. *Defense Industry Conversion, Base Closure, and the California Economy: Critical Issues for a Statewide Strategy*. Berkeley: University of California, Institute of Business and Economic Research.

Bradshaw, Ted K., and Brian Muller. 1994. "Mapping the California Exurbia: Patterns of Non-Metropolitan Population Growth." Paper presented to the Association of Collegiate Schools of Planning, 3–6 Nov., Tempe, Ariz.

Bramlette, Bill. 1994. Recreation Officer (now Deputy Forest Supervisor), Inyo National Forest, Bishop, Calif. Personal communication.

Branson, Tanya. 1996a. "Buildable Lots at a Premium." *Tahoe World* 34 (28) (Tahoe City, Calif.), 11 July, p. A1.

———. 1996b. "Realtor Board Criticizes Conservancy Purchases." *Tahoe World* 34 (28) (Tahoe City, Calif.) 11 July, p. A1.

Brechin, Gray. Forthcoming. *Imperial San Francisco: Urban Power, Earthly Ruin*. Berkeley and Los Angeles: University of California Press.

Breheny, M., and A. Hooper, eds. 1985. *Rationality in Planning: Critical Essays on the Role of Rationality in Urban and Regional Planning*. London: Pion.

Brennan, Andrew. 1988. *Thinking about Nature: An Investigation of Nature, Value, and Ecology*. Athens: University of Georgia Press.

Briscoe, Maphis, Murray, Lamont, Inc. 1978. *Managing Growth in the Small Community*. Prepared for Region 8, U.S. Environmental Protection Agency, Denver, Colo. EPA-908/4-78-005. Washington, DC: Government Printing Office.

Brissenden, John. 1993–94. Supervisor, Alpine County, Calif. Personal communication.

Brooke, James. 1995. "Colorado Tries to Keep Lid on Population Boom." *New York Times*, 5 November, p. 9.

———. 1996a. "Boom Times Hit Utah, and Sticker Shock Follows." *New York Times*, January 31. p. A6.

———. 1996b. "Montana Mining Town Fights Gold-Rush Plan." *New York Times*, 7 January, p. 8.

Brown, Beverly A. 1995. *In Timber Country: Working People's Stories of Environmental Conflict and Urban Flight*. Philadelphia: Temple University Press.

Brown, Corey. 1995. Trust for Public Land. Presentation to the Environmental Law and Resource Management class (IDS 233), November, University of California at Berkeley.

Brown, Lester. 1981. *Building a Sustainable Society*. New York: W. W. Norton and Company.

Browning, Peter. 1986. *Sierra Nevada Place Names from Abbot to Zumwalt*. Berkeley: Wilderness Press.

Brush, R. O. 1976. "Perceived Quality of Scenic and Recreational Environments." In Craik and Zube 1976.

Brush, R. O., and E. L Shafer. 1975. "Application of a Landscape Preference Model to Land Management." In Zube et al. 1975.

Buckley, John. 1993–97. Executive Director, Central Sierra Environmental Resource Center, Twain Harte, Calif. Personal communication.

Buitenkamp, M., H. Venner, T. Wams, eds. 1992. *Action Plan Sustainable Netherlands*. Amsterdam: Friends of the Earth Netherlands.

Bullard, Robert D. 1994. *Dumping in Dixie: Race, Class, and Environmental Quality*. Boulder, Colo.: Westview Press.

Burdick, Katie. 1997. "Being in the Middle at the Beginning—Pre-emptive Mediation." *AEP Monitor* (Association of Environmental Professionals) (spring): 6–8.

Bureau of Land Management. 1994. *Environmental Assessment (Draft), 'Inimim Forest Draft Management Plan*. Folsom Resource Area. Folsom, Calif.: Bakersfield District, Bureau of Land Management, U.S. Department of the Interior.

———. 1995a. *Environmental Assessment, 'Inimim Forest Draft Management Plan*. CA-018–95–17. Folsom Resource Area. Folsom, Calif.: Bakersfield District, Bureau of Land Management, U.S. Department of the Interior.

———. 1995b. *Record of Decision: 'Inimim Forest Management Plan*. NEPA CA-018–95–17. Folsom Resource Area. Folsom, Calif.: Bakersfield District, Bureau of Land Management, U.S. Department of the Interior.

———. 1995c. Transcripts of public hearing on the 'Inimim Forest Plan (held in North San Juan, Calif.). 8 April, Folsom Resource Area. Folsom, Calif.: Bakersfield District, Bureau of Land Management, U.S. Department of the Interior.

Burkhardt, Larry. 1997. "Nevada County: Are We Ready to Choose Success in Business?" *Grass Valley–Nevada City Union*, 22 March, p. C2.

Cahill, Thomas A., John J. Carroll, Dave Campbell, and Thomas E. Gill. 1996. "Air Quality." In *Sierra Nevada Ecosystem Project Final Report to Congress: Status of the Sierra Nevada*. Vol. 2. Davis: Center for Water and Wildland Resources, University of California.

Caldwell, Lynton. 1970. "The Ecosystem as a Criterion for Public Land Policy." *Natural Resources Journal* 10 (2): 203–21.

CalFed Bay-Delta Program. 1995a. *Program Background.* June. Sacramento: CalFed Bay-Delta Program.

———. 1995b. *Program Process.* September. Sacramento: CalFed Bay-Delta Program.

———. 1996. *Update.* September. Sacramento: CalFed Bay-Delta Program.

———. 1997. *Moving Ahead, Maintaining Momentum.* January. Sacramento: CalFed Bay-Delta Program.

Calhoon, F. D. 1977. *49er Irish: One Irish Family in the California Mines.* Hicksville, N.Y.: Exposition Press.

California Association of Resource Conservation Districts. 1990. *California Coordinated Resource Management and Planning Handbook.* Sacramento: California Association of Resource Conservation Districts.

California Biodiversity Council. 1997a. "HCPs: Planning Strategy Offers Incentives to Conserve Habitat." *California Biodiversity News* 4, no. 3 (spring): 1.

———. 1997b. "Council Supports Sierra Nevada Network to Utilize Sierra Nevada Ecosystem Project (SNEP)." *California Biodiversity News* 4, no. 3 (spring): 6–7.

———. 1998. "Fish and Game Issues NCCP Guidelines." *California Biodiversity News* 5, no. 3 (spring): 9.

California Department of Conservation. 1991. Sierra Summit maps and data tables. Distributed at the Sierra Summit, Fallen Leaf Lake, Calif. November.

California Department of Finance. 1993. *Population Projections by Race/Ethnicity for California and Its Counties, 1990–2040.* Sacramento: Demographic Research Unit, California Department of Finance.

———. 1996. *California Demographics.* Sacramento: Demographic Research Unit, California Department of Finance.

———. 1997. *California Demographics.* Sacramento: Demographic Research Unit, California Department of Finance.

California Department of Fish and Game. 1993. *The Natural Community Conservation Planning Program.* Sacramento: California Department of Fish and Game.

———. n.d. *Living with Mountain Lions.* Sacramento: California Department of Fish and Game.

California Department of Forestry and Fire Protection. 1995. *Fire Management for California Ecosystems.* Sacramento: California Department of Forestry and Fire Protection.

California Department of Water Resources. 1973. *Sierra Foothills Investigation, Central District.* Sacramento: California Department of Water Resources, Central District.

———. 1991. "Ground Water in Fractured Hard Rock." *Water Facts,* Number 1. Sacramento: California Department of Water Resources.

———. 1992. "California Well Standards Questions and Answers." *Water Facts,* Number 5. Sacramento: California Department of Water Resources.

———. 1993. "Ground Water." *Water Facts,* Number 6. Sacramento: California Department of Water Resources.

———. 1994. *California Water Plan Update: Bulletin 160–93.* Sacramento: California Department of Water Resources.

California Energy Commission 1993. *Electricity Report Technical Appendices,* table III-1C. Sacramento: California Energy Commission.

California Forestry Association. 1995. "County Supervisorial Races Produce New Friends in Local Government." *California Forests Today,* p. 7.

California Resources Agency. 1991. *California's Coordinated Strategy to Conserve Biological Diversity, Memorandum of Understanding (The Agreement on Biological Diversity)*. Sacramento: California Resources Agency.

———. 1992a. *Sierra Summit Workshop Materials*. Distributed at public workshops.

———. 1992b. *The Sierra Nevada: Report of the Sierra Summit Steering Committee*. Sacramento: California Resources Agency.

California Spotted Owl Federal Advisory Committee. 1997. *Final Report of the California Spotted Owl Federal Advisory Committee (Evaluation of the "Revised Draft Environmental Impact Statement [RDEIS] Managing California Spotted Owl Habitat in the Sierra Nevada National Forests of California")*. Portland, Ore.: Pacific Northwest Research Station, United States Department of Agriculture.

California, State of. 1995. *California Fire Plan: A Framework for Minimizing Fire Costs and Losses from Wildland Fires*. Sacramento: Board of Forestry, Department of Forestry and Fire Protection, and California Resources Agency.

———. n.d. *OES Disaster Information Fact Sheet*. Unpublished document. Sacramento: Office of Emergency Services.

Callicott, J. Baird, ed. 1987a. *Companion to* A Sand County Almanac: *Interpretive and Critical Essays*. Madison: University of Wisconsin Press.

———. 1987b. "The Land Aesthetic." In Callicott 1987a.

———. 1989. *In Defense of the Land Ethic: Essays in Environmental Philosophy*. Albany: State University of New York Press.

———. 1996. "Do Deconstructive Ecology and Sociobiology Undermine Leopold's Land Ethic?" *Environmental Ethics* 18 (4): 353–72.

Calthorpe, Peter. 1986. "A Short History of Twentieth Century New Towns." In Van der Ryn and Calthorpe 1986, pp. 189–234.

———. 1989. *The Pedestrian Pocket Book: A New Suburban Design*. New York: Princeton Architectural Press.

———. 1993. *The Next American Metropolis : Ecology, Community, and the American Dream*. New York: Princeton Architectural Press.

Calthorpe, Peter, and Mark Mack. 1988. "Pedestrian Pockets: New Strategies for Suburban Growth." *Northern California Real Estate Journal* 2 (11).

Campbell, Scott. 1996. "Green Cities, Growing Cities, Just Cities—Urban Planning and the Contradictions of Sustainable Development." *Journal of the American Planning Association* 62 (3): 296–312.

Canter, Larry W. 1996. *Environmental Impact Assessment*. 2^d ed. New York: McGraw-Hill.

Capra, Fritjof. 1975. *The Tao of Physics: An Exploration of the Parallels between Modern Physics and Eastern Mysticism*. New York: Random House.

Carlino, Gerald A. 1985. "Declining City Productivity and the Growth of Rural Regions." *Journal of Urban Economics* 18:11–27.

Carlino, Gerald A., and Edwin S. Mills. 1985a. *The Determinants of County Growth*. Philadelphia: Research Department, Federal Reserve Bank of Philadelphia.

———. 1985b. "Do Public Policies Affect County Growth?" *Business Review* (July-August).

Carr, Mike. 1994. *Toward an Ecophilosophical Approach to Community and Regional Planning: A Bioregional Framework*. Policy Issues and Planning Responses PI#2. Vancouver: University of British Columbia, Center for Human Settlements, School of Community and Regional Planning.

Carson, Rachel. 1962. *Silent Spring*. Boston: Houghton Mifflin.

Carter, Dave. 1978. "Message from Props A and B? Board Answers." *Grass Valley–Nevada City Union,* 2 November, p. 1.

Casey, John. 1995. Chair, Caseywood Corporation, Grass Valley, Calif. Personal communication.

Castells, Manuel. 1989. *The Informational City: Information Technology, Economic Restructuring, and the Urban-Regional Process.* New York: Basil Blackwell.

———. 1991. Biographical statement in student orientation materials, Department of City and Regional Planning, University of California at Berkeley.

———. 1996. *The Rise of the Network Society.* Cambridge, Mass.: Blackwell Publishers.

———. 1997. *The Power of Identity.* Cambridge, Mass.: Blackwell Publishers.

———. 1998. *End of Millennium.* Cambridge, Mass.: Blackwell Publishers.

Center, Bill. 1991–96. Supervisor, El Dorado County, Calif. Personal communication.

Center, Bill, John Cassidy, Bea Cooley, Mo Daley, Marc Davis, et al. 1989. *The American River: North, Middle, and South Forks.* Auburn, Calif.: Wilderness Conservancy.

Center for the Continuing Study of the California Economy. 1995. Data Tables for County-Level Projections from 1995–2005. Palo Alto, Calif. Personal communication.

Central Valley Regional Water Quality Control Board (CVRWQCB). 1989. *Order No. 89–005 (NPDES No. CA0079898): Waste Discharge Requirements for City of Grass Valley Domestic Wastewater Treatment Plant (Nevada County).* Sacramento: Central Valley Regional Water Quality Control Board.

———. 1992. *Order No. 92–112 Requiring the City of Grass Valley (Nevada County) to Cease and Desist from Discharging Waste Contrary to Waste Discharge Requirements.* Sacramento: Central Valley Regional Water Quality Control Board.

Cervero, Robert. 1986. *Suburban Gridlock.* New Brunswick, N.J.: Center for Urban Policy Research.

———. 1991. *Suburban Employment Centers: Probing the Influence of Site Features on the Journey-to-Work.* Berkeley: University of California Transportation Center.

———. 1993. "Changing Live-Work Spatial Relationships: Implications for Metropolitan Structure and Mobility." Paper presented to the *Fourth International Workshop on Technological Change and Urban Form: Productive and Sustainable Cities,* April, Berkeley, Calif.

Chapel, Mike, Ann Carlson, Diana Craig, Terry Flaherty, Chris Marshall, Mark Reynolds, Dave Pratt, Leo Pyshora, Steve Tanuay, and Wendy Thompson. 1992. *Recommendations for Managing Late-Seral-Stage Forest and Riparian Habitats on the Tahoe National Forest.* Nevada City, Calif.: Tahoe National Forest.

Cheever, Frederico. 1996. "The Road to Recovery: A New Way of Thinking about the Endangered Species Act." *Ecology Law Quarterly* 23:1–78.

Chinitz, Benjamin. 1990. "Growth Management: Good for the Town, Bad for the Nation?" *Journal of the American Planning Association* 56 (1).

Cholette, Kathryn, Ross Dobson, Kent Gerecke, Marcia Nozick, Roberta Simpson, and Linda Williams. 1989. "Green City: An Introduction." In Andruss et al. 1990, p. 103.

Christensen, Jon. 1996a. "Everyone Helps a California Forest—Except the Forest Service." *High Country News* 28, no. 9 (May 13): 16.

———. 1996b. "The Shotgun Wedding of Tourism and Public Lands." *High Country News* 28, no. 24 (December 23): 12–13.

———. 1996c. "High-Country Common Ground: In the Sierras, Growth and Preservation Are Not at Odds." *New York Times,* 30 November, pp. N21, L39, col. 2.

———. 1997. "The Greening of Gambling's Golden Boy." *New York Times,* 6 July, sec. 3, p. 1.

Christensen, Norman L. 1996. *Report of the Ecological Society of America Committee on the Scientific Basis for Ecosystem Management* (http://www.fs.fed.us/eco2/execsum.htm).

Christian Century 113 (26): 843 (11 September 1996).

Clark, Tim. 1995. Comments at the conference "At the Crossroads of Science, Management, and Policy: A Review of Bioregional Assessments," 8 November, Portland, Oregon.

Clark, Tim W., and Steven C. Minta. 1994. *Greater Yellowstone's Future.* Moose, Wyo.: Homestead Publishing.

Clark, Tim W., Richard Reading, and Alice Clark. 1994. *Endangered Species Recovery: Finding the Lessons, Improving the Process.* Washington D.C.: Island Press.

Clark, William C. 1989. "Managing Planet Earth." *Scientific American,* special ed. (September): 51.

Clark, William C. and R. E. Munn, eds. 1986. *Sustainable Development of the Biosphere.* New York: Cambridge University Press.

Clements, F. E. 1916. "Plant Succession: An Analysis of the Development of Vegetation." *Publication of the Carnegie Institute of Washington* 242:1–512. Cited in Gunderson et al. 1995.

Clifford, Frank. 1996. "Sierra Facing a Mountain of Trouble." ("The New Californias: Sierra Nueva; First in an Occasional Series.") *Los Angeles Times,* 21 June, p. A1.

Clifford, Harlan C. 1993. "Aspen: A Colonial Power with Angst." *High Country News* 25, no. 6 (April 5): 8–11.

Clines, Francis X. 1996. "A Poet's Trip along Main Street, U.S.A." *New York Times,* 9 December, p. A1.

Cloer, Carla. 1992–93. Teacher, Porterville, Calif. Personal communication.

Clow, Deborah, and Donald Snow, eds. 1994. *Northern Lights: A Selection of New Writing from the American West.* New York: Vintage Books.

Coase, Ronald H. 1960. "The Problem of Social Cost," *Journal of Law and Economics* 3:1.

Coates, Bill. 1994. Comments at the Sierra Nevada Alliance Conference, 16 July, Mammoth Lakes, Calif.

Cobb, Edith. 1977. *The Ecology of Imagination in Childhood.* New York: Columbia University Press.

Cohen, Stephen S., and John Zysman. 1987. *Manufacturing Matters: The Myth of a Post-Industrial Economy.* Washington, D.C.: Carnegie Forum on Education and the Economy.

Coleman, Charles M. 1952. *PG and E of California: The Centennial Story of Pacific Gas and Electric Company, 1852–1952.* New York: McGraw-Hill.

Coleman, James S. 1990. *Foundations of Social Theory.* Cambridge: Harvard University Press.

Collados, Cecilia. 1997. "Natural Capital and Quality of Life: A Regional Perspective." Diss. prospectus, Department of City and Regional Planning, University of California at Berkeley.

Collados, Cecilia, and Philip Griffiths. 1993. "Implications of Age Composition and Migration for the Nevada County General Plan." Paper prepared for Prof. Timothy P. Duane, University of California at Berkeley.

Collins, Adam R. 1996. *The Story of the Gold Country, California.* Lake Arrowhead, Calif.: Gold Mountain Books.

Comic Press News. n.d." Eco-Shorts," *Comic Press News* 5 (3): 18

Corliss, Donovan, and Timothy P. Duane. 1998. "The Pollution Problem Revisited: Rethinking Air Pollution Regulation." Manuscript, University of California at Berkeley.

Cornell, Joseph. 1979. *Sharing Nature with Children.* Nevada City, Calif.: Dawn Publications.

————. 1987. *Listening to Nature.* Nevada City, Calif.: Dawn Publications.

Corvallis (Ore.) Gazette-Times. 1996. "Species Act: Owl Protection Suit Settled with $3.5M Buyout," 7 October (online).

Costanza, Robert. 1990. *The Ecological Economics of Sustainability: Making Local and Short-Term Goals Consistent with Global and Long-Term Goals.* Washington, D.C.: World Bank, Sector Policy and Research Staff, Environment Department.

————, ed. 1991. *Ecological Economics: The Science and Management of Sustainability.* New York: Columbia University Press.

Costanza, Robert, Bryan G. Norton, and Benjamin D. Haskell, eds. 1992. *Ecosystem Health: New Goals for Environmental Management.* Washington, D.C.: Island Press.

Cowart, Richard, ed. 1976. *Land Use Planning, Politics, and Policy.* Berkeley: University Extension Publications, University of California.

Cozzers, Christine S. 1996. "A Cabin, a Lake, a Memory." *New York Times Book Review,* 8 September, p. 33.

Craighead, F. 1979. *Track of the Grizzly Bear.* San Francisco: Sierra Club Books.

Craik, K. H. 1972. "Appraising the Objectivity of Landscape Dimensions." In Krutilla 1972.

Craik, K. H., and E. H. Zube, eds. 1976. *Perceiving Environmental Quality: Research and Application.* New York: Plenum Press.

Cranmer Engineering and Harry Halatyn. 1971. *General Water and Sewer Plan: Nevada County, California.* Nevada City, Calif.: Nevada County, California.

Creighton, Dale. 1994–95. Senior Planner, Sylvester Engineering, Inc., Nevada City, Calif. Personal communication.

Creighton, J. L. 1981. "Acting as a Conflict Conciliator," in *Public Involvement Techniques: A Reader of Ten Years' Experience at the Institute of Water Resources,* ed. by J. L. Creighton and J. D. Delli Priscoli, 454–55. IWR Staff Report 81–1, U.S. Army Engineer Institute for Water Resources, Fort Belvoir, Va. Cited in Canter 1996, p. 610.

Cronon, William. 1983. *Changes in the Land: Indians, Colonists, and the Ecology of New England.* New York: Hill and Wang.

————. 1991. *Nature's Metropolis: Chicago and the Great West.* New York: W. W. Norton and Company.

————. 1992. "A Place for Stories: Nature, History, and Narrative." *Journal of American History* 78 (1): 1347–76.

————. 1995a. "The Trouble with Wilderness: Wilderness Is No More 'Natural' Than Nature Is—It's a Reflection of Our Own Longings, a Profoundly Human Creation." *New York Times Magazine,* 13 August, p. 42.

————, ed. 1995b. *Uncommon Ground: Toward Reinventing Nature.* New York: W. W. Norton and Company.

Cronon, William, George Miles, and Jay Gitlin, eds. 1992. *Under an Open Sky: Rethinking America's Western Past.* New York: W. W. Norton and Company.

Cunniff, John. 1995. "Jobless Rate Doesn't Tell All: Factory Jobs Decline for Third Month." *Grass Valley–Nevada City Union,* 13 July, p. A5.

Cushman, John H., Jr. 1996. "G.O.P. Backing Off from Tough Stand over Environment." *New York Times,* 26 January, p. A1.

Dachtler, Doc. 1990. *Waiting for Chains at Pearl's.* Austin: Plain View Press.

Daily, Gretchen C., ed. 1997. *Nature's Services: Societal Dependence on Natural Ecosystems.* Washington, D.C.: Island Press.

Daly, Herman E. 1977. *Steady-State Economics: The Economics of Biophysical Equilibrium and Moral Growth.* San Francisco: W. H. Freeman.

———. 1991. *Steady-State Economics.* 2^d ed. 1977. Reprint, Washington, D.C.: Island Press.

———. 1996. *Beyond Growth: The Economics of Sustainable Development.* Boston: Beacon Press.

Daly, Herman E., and Clifford W. Cobb. 1989. *For the Common Good: Redirecting the Economy Toward Community, the Environment, and a Sustainable Future.* Boston: Beacon Press.

Dana, Samuel Trask, and Sally K. Fairfax. 1980. *Forest and Range Policy: Its Development in the United States.* 2^d ed. New York: McGraw-Hill.

Daniels, Thomas L., John W. Keller, and Mark B. Lapping. 1995. *The Small Town Planning Handbook.* Chicago: American Planning Association.

Daniels, Thomas L., and Mark B. Lapping. 1984. "Has Vermont's Land Use Control Program Failed? Evaluating Act 250." *Journal of the American Planning Association* 50, no. 4 (autumn): 502–8.

Dardick, Sam. 1995. Supervisor, Nevada County, Calif. Personal communication, October.

Darrow, George. 1993. "How the West Was ~~Won~~ Liquidated." *High Country News* 25, no. 6 (April 5): 16.

Dasgupta, P. S., and G. M. Heal. 1979. *Economic Theory and Exhaustible Resources.* Cambridge: Cambridge University Press.

Dasmann, Raymond F. 1965. *The Destruction of California.* New York: Macmillan.

Davidoff, Paul. 1965. "Advocacy and Pluralism in Planning." *Journal of the American Institute of Planners* 31 (4): 331–38.

Davis, Frank W. 1996. "Comparison of Late Seral/Old Growth Maps from SNEP versus the Sierra Biodiversity Institute." In *Sierra Nevada Ecosystem Project Final Report to Congress: Status of the Sierra Nevada,* 3:745–58. Davis: Center for Water and Wildland Resources, University of California.

Davis, Frank W., and David M. Stoms. 1996. "Sierra Vegetation: A Gap Analysis." In *Sierra Nevada Ecosystem Project Final Report to Congress: Status of the Sierra Nevada,* 2:671–89. Davis: Center for Water and Wildland Resources, University of California.

Davis, Frank W., David M. Stoms, Richard L. Church, William J. Okin, and K. Norman Johnson. 1996. "Selecting Biodiversity Management Areas." In *Sierra Nevada Ecosystem Project Final Report to Congress: Status of the Sierra Nevada,* 2:1503–28. Davis: Center for Water and Wildland Resources, University of California.

Davis, Judy S., Arthur C. Nelson, and Kenneth J. Dueker. 1994. "The New 'Burbs." *Journal of the American Planning Association* 60 (1): 45–59.

Davis, Lawrence S., and K. Norman Johnson. 1987. *Forest Management.* New York: McGraw-Hill.

Davis, Marie. 1994. Assistant Manager, Georgetown Divide Public Utility District, Georgetown, Calif. Personal communication, 8 July.

Davis, Mike. 1990. *City of Quartz: Excavating the Future in Los Angeles.* New York: Verso.

———. 1994. "Cannibal City: Los Angeles and the Destruction of Nature." In Ferguson 1994, pp. 39–57.

———. 1996. "How Eden Lost Its Garden: A Political History of the Los Angeles Landscape." In Scott and Soja 1996, pp. 160–85.

———. 1997. "Maneaters of the Sierra Madre," Avenelli Lecture, October 7, University of California at Berkeley.

Davis, Tony. 1996. "Catron County's Politics Heat Up as Its Land Goes Bankrupt," *High Country News* 28, no. 12 (June 24): A1.

Dean Runyon Associates. 1995. *California Travel Impacts by County: 1993.* Prepared for the California Trade and Commerce Agency, Division of Tourism, Sacramento, by Dean Runyan Associates, Portland, Ore.

Deck, John. 1993. "Habitat Planning in California: Suggestions for the County of El Dorado Based on an Analysis of Recent Endangered Species Habitat Plan Case Studies." Master's professional project, Department of Landscape Architecture, University of California at Berkeley.

Defenders of Wildlife. 1989. *Preserving Communities and Corridors.* Washington, D.C.: Defenders of Wildlife.

DeGrove, John M. (with the assistance of Deborah A. Miness). 1992. *The New Frontier of Land Policy: Planning and Growth Management in the States.* Cambridge, Mass.: Lincoln Institute of Land Policy.

Demsetz, Harold. 1967. "Toward a Theory of Property Rights." *American Economic Review* (Papers and Proceedings) 57:347. Cited in Rose 1994.

de Neufville, Judith I., ed. 1981. *The Land Use Policy Debate in the United States.* New York: Plenum Press.

de Saussure, Ferdinand. 1959. *Course in General Linguistics.* New York: Philosophical Library. Cited in Fainter 1996.

Des Jardins, Joseph R. 1997. *Environmental Ethics: An Introduction to Environmental Philosophy.* 2^d ed. Belmont, Calif.: Wadsworth Publishing.

de Tocqueville, Alexis. [1835] 1980. *Democracy in America.* New York: A. A. Knopf.

Devall, Bill, ed. 1993. *Clearcut: The Tragedy of Industrial Forestry.* San Francisco: Sierra Club Books, Earth Island Press, Foundation for Deep Ecology.

Devall, Bill, and George Sessions. 1985. *Deep Ecology: Living as If Nature Mattered.* Salt Lake City: Gibbs M. Smith.

Diamond, Henry L., and Patrick E. Noonan. 1996. *Land Use in America.* Washington, D.C.: Island Press.

Diamond, Jared M. 1984. "'Normal' Extinctions of Isolated Populations." In *Extinctions,* ed. by M. H. Nitecki, 191–246. Chicago: University of Chicago Press. Cited in Verner 1997.

Diffenderfer, Mark, and Dean Birch. 1997. "Bioregionalism: A Comparative Study of the Adirondacks and the Sierra Nevada." *Society and Natural Resources* 10:3–16.

Diggles, Michael. 1996. U.S. Geological Survey, Menlo Park, Calif. Personal communication.

Diringer, Elliot. 1994. "Crowd on the New Frontier: Elbow Room Running Out." *San Francisco Chronicle,* 15 December, p. A1.

———. 1996. "Clinton to Name New Panel to Study Logging in the Sierra," *San Francisco Chronicle,* 6 September, p. A6.

Doak, Sam C., and Jonathan Kusel. 1996. "Well-Being in Forest-Dependent Communities, Part II: A Social Assessment Focus." In *Sierra Nevada Ecosystem Project Final Report to Congress: Status of the Sierra Nevada,* 2:375–402. Davis: Center for Water and Wildland Resources, University of California.

Dobrzynski, Judith H. 1996. "The New Jobs: A Growing Number Are Good Ones." *New York Times,* 21 July, section 3, p. 1.

Donaldson, Janaia. 1994–95. Programmer, XEROX Palo Alto, Nevada City, Calif. Personal communication.

Doolittle, James. 1994–95. Consultant to El Dorado County, Placerville, Calif. Personal communication.

Dorward, Sherry. 1990. *Design for Mountain Communities: A Landscape and Architectural Guide.* New York: Van Nostrand Reinhold.

Dowall, David E. 1984. *The Suburban Squeeze: Land-Use Policies in the San Francisco Bay Area.*

Berkeley and Los Angeles: University of California Press, California Series in Urban Development.

———. 1991. *Less Is More: The Benefits of Minimal Land Development Regulation.* Working Paper No. 531. Berkeley: University of California, Institute of Urban and Regional Development.

Dowall, David E., and John D. Landis. 1981. *Land-Use Controls and Housing Costs: An Examination of San Francisco Bay Area Communities.* Working Paper No. 81–24. Berkeley: University of California, Institute for Urban and Regional Development.

Doyle, Jim. 1995. "Fear Fuels Mill Valley Fire Plan: Vulnerable Town Learns from Oakland Hills, Inverness." *San Francisco Chronicle,* 16 October, p. A1.

Drace, Richard. 1993–97. Executive Director, Common Ground Communities, Nevada City, Calif. Personal communication.

Drummond, Mike. 1996. "Coping in the Country: Burning Brush Piles Preferable to Burying Whole County in Sawdust." *Grass Valley–Nevada City Union,* 17 January, p. A6.

Dryzek, John S. 1987. *Rational Ecology: Environment and Political Economy.* New York: Blackwell.

———. 1990. *Discursive Democracy: Politics, Policy and Political Science.* Cambridge: Cambridge University Press.

Dryzek, John S., and James P. Lester. 1989. "Alternative Views of the Environmental Problematic." In Lester 1989, pp. 314–30.

Duane, Daniel. 1996. "A Poem, 40 Years Long," *New York Times Magazine,* 6 October, p. 62.

Duane, Timothy P. 1989. "The Risk-Adjusted Cost Evaluation of Electric Resource Alternatives." Ph.D. diss., Energy and Environmental Planning, Resources Planning Program, Department of Civil Engineering, Stanford University, Stanford, Calif.

———1992a. "Environmental Planning and Policy in a Post-Rio World." *Berkeley Planning Journal* 7:27–47.

———. 1992b. "Urbanization and Local Economic Development: Strategies for a Sustainable Sierra Nevada." Paper presented to the Sierra Now Conference, August, Sacramento.

———. 1993a. "Managing the Sierra Nevada." *California Policy Choices* 8:169–94.

———. 1993b. "Exodus to Exurbia: The Threat of Population Growth in Rural 'Buffer Zone' Regions to the Conservation of Biological Diversity." Paper presented to the Society for Conservation Biology, Tempe, Ariz.

———. 1993c. "Managing Exurban Sprawl in the Sierra Nevada Foothills." Paper presented to the Association of Collegiate Schools of Planning, Philadelphia, Penn.

———. 1995. Testimony before the California State Water Resources Control Board for the California Sportfishing Alliance, 19 April, Sacramento, Calif.

———. 1996a. "Human Settlement, 1850–2040." In *Sierra Nevada Ecosystem Project Final Report to Congress: Status of the Sierra Nevada,* 2: 235–59. Davis: Center for Water and Wildland Resources, University of California.

———. 1996b. "Recreation in the Sierra." In *Sierra Nevada Ecosystem Project Final Report to Congress: Status of the Sierra Nevada,* 2:557–609. Davis: Center for Water and Wildland Resources, University of California.

———. 1996c. Letter to the Board of Supervisors, County of Nevada, and associated "Summary of Errors in Nevada County Planning Department's 'Buildout' Analysis of the Nevada County General Plan," October 21.

———. 1996d. Letter to the Board of Supervisors, County of Nevada, identifying deficiencies in CEQA analysis of adopted Nevada County General Plan and transmitting a copy of SNEP Report, vol. 2, chap. 11, for consideration. July 26.

———. 1997a. "Community Participation in Ecosystem Management." *Ecology Law Quarterly* 24 (4): 771–97.

———. 1997b. "Water, Wealth, and Watershed Health," *Tree Rings* (journal of the Yuba Watershed Institute, Nevada City, Calif.) 10: 3–4.

———. Forthcoming. *Wolves, Water, and Wilderness: Ecosystem Management in the Changing West.* Berkeley and Los Angeles: University of California Press.

Duane, Timothy P., and Jennifer L. Krauer. 1996. *Recreational Use Patterns and Visitor Characteristics for the Mammoth Lakes and Mount Whitney Regions of the Inyo National Forest.* Bishop, Calif.: Inyo National Forest.

Duany, Andres, and Elizabeth Plater-Zyberk. 1991. *Towns and Town-Making Principles.* Ed. by Alex Krieger. New York: Harvard Graduate School of Design.

Dubbink, David. 1984. "I'll Have My Town Medium-Rural, Please." *Journal of the American Planning Association* 50 (4): 406–18.

Dunlap, Riley E. 1987. "Public Opinion on the Environment in the Reagan Era: Polls, Pollution, and Politics Revisited." *Environment* 29 (6).

———. 1991a. "Trends in Public Opinion toward Environmental Issues, 1965–1990," *Society and Natural Resources* 4 (3): 285–312.

———. 1991b. "Public Opinion in the 1980s: Clear Consensus, Ambiguous Commitment." *Environment* 33 (8): 104.

Durbin, Kathie. 1994. "Ambitious Ecosystem Management Advances East." *High Country News* 26, no. 17 (September 19): 8–12.

Durham, William H. 1979. *Scarcity and Survival in Central America: Ecological Origins of the Soccer War.* Stanford, Calif.: Stanford University Press.

Durning, Alan T. 1992. *How Much Is Enough?: The Consumer Society and the Future of the Earth.* 1st ed. New York: W. W. Norton and Company.

Dwyer, John P., and Peter S. Menell. 1997. *Property Law and Policy: A Comparative Institutional Perspective.* Westbury, N.Y.: Foundation Press.

Eastside Ecosystem Management Project. 1994. "News from E.E.M.P. (Walley-World)." Memorandum from E.E.M.P. July 1.

Eberle, Todd. 1988a. "Councilmen Swept Out of Office by Nearly 4–1 Margin." *Grass Valley–Nevada City Union,* 9 November.

———. 1988b. "D.A. Drops Misconduct Case against GV Councilmen." *Grass Valley–Nevada City Union,* 10 November.

———. 1988c. "GV Recall Vote Likely to Decide Court Fight, Too." *Grass Valley–Nevada City Union,* 2 November.

Eckbo, Dean, Austin, and Williams (EDAW). 1972. *State Open Space and Resource Conservation Programs for California.* Sacramento: California Legislature Joint Committee on Open Space Lands. Cited in Mike Davis 1996.

Ecological Economics: The Journal of the International Society for Ecological Economics (New York).

Ecological Stewardship Workshop. 1995. *Toward a Scientific and Social Framework for Ecologically Based Stewardship of Federal Lands and Waters.* Interim Report. Tucson, Ariz.

Economic and Planning Systems. 1993. *Sierra Region Economic Profiles.* Berkeley, Calif.: Economic and Planning Systems.

Eddins, Elizabeth. 1994–97. Town Planner, Town of Truckee, Calif. Personal communication.

Edelson, David B. 1997a. Comments at the *Ecology Law Quarterly* symposium "The Ecosystem Approach: New Directions for Land and Water," 21 February, at Boalt Hall School of Law, University of California at Berkeley.

———. 1997b. Senior Attorney, Natural Resources Defense Council, San Francisco. Personal communication.

Edelson, David B., Louis Blumberg, John Buckley, and Deanna Spooner. 1997. *The Forest Service's Revised Draft Environmental Impact Statement for Managing the California Spotted Owl: A Critique.* Submitted to the California Spotted Owl Advisory Committee on behalf of the Sierra Nevada Forest Protection Campaign, July 28.

Edwards, Glenda. 1992–93. Tuolumne County 2000, Sonora, Calif. Personal communication.

———. 1996. "Politics of Growth in Tuolomne County." *Linkages: Newsletter of the Institute for Ecological Health* no. 3 (fall): 6.

Egan, Timothy. 1995. "The Serene Fortress: Many Seek Security in Private Communities." *New York Times,* 3 September, p. A1.

———. 1996. "Urban Sprawl Strains Western States." *New York Times,* 29 December, p. A1.

Ehrlich, Paul R., and Anne H. Ehrlich. 1970. *Population, Resources, Environment: Issues in Human Ecology.* San Francisco: W. H. Freeman and Company.

Ehrlich, Paul R., and Edward O. Wilson. 1991. "Biodiversity Studies—Science and Policy." *Science* 253 (5021): 758–62.

EIP Associates. 1995. *Draft Environmental Impact Report: Grass Valley Wastewater Treatment Plant Expansion.* SCH #93042024. Grass Valley, Calif.: City of Grass Valley.

———. 1996. *Final Environmental Impact Report: Grass Valley Wastewater Treatment Plant Expansion.* SCH #93042024. Grass Valley, Calif.: City of Grass Valley.

Elazar, Daniel Judah. 1987. *Building Cities in America: Urbanization and Suburbanization in a Frontier Society.* Lanham, Md.: Hamilton Press.

Elazar, Leora, Steven Lewis, and Perl Perlmutter. 1993. "Biodiversity Policy Options for Nevada County." Paper prepared for Prof. Timothy P. Duane, University of California at Berkeley.

El Dorado County Community Development Department. 1994. *Final Draft El Dorado County General Plan.* Placerville, Calif.: El Dorado County Planning Department.

El Dorado County Water Agency. 1994. *Preliminary Assessment of Water Demand and Supply Balance for El Dorado County.* Placerville, Calif.: El Dorado County Water Agency.

El Dorado Irrigation District. 1994. Personal communication with staff in Placerville, Calif. and review of CAD-based digital files.

Ellickson, Robert C. 1991. *Order without Law: How Neighbors Settle Disputes.* Cambridge: Harvard University Press.

Elliott-Fisk, Deborah, Rowan A. Rowntree, Thomas A. Cahill, Charles R. Goldman, George Gruell, Robert Harris, Doug Leisz, Susan Lindstrom, Richard Kattelmann, Dennis Machida, Ray Lacey, Penny Rucks, Debra A. Sharkey, and David S. Ziegler. 1996. "Lake Tahoe Case Study." In *Sierra Nevada Ecosystem Project Final Report to Congress: Status of the Sierra Nevada,* addendum: 217–76. Davis: Center for Water and Wildland Resources, University of California.

Ellis, Wendell. 1997. Diamond Well Drilling, Auburn, Calif. Personal communication, 7 March.

Emerson, Kirk. 1997. "Why States Adopt Private Property Protection Measures: Looking beyond the Rhetoric for Evidence." Paper presented to the Association for Collegiate Schools of Planning, 6–9 November, Ft. Lauderdale, Fla.

Emmett, Daniel. 1992. "Economic and Industry Trends in the Sierra Nevada Mountains."

Senior thesis, Environmental Studies–Economics, University of California at Santa Cruz.

Encyclopedia of California. 1997. New York: Somerset Publishers.

Environment Now. 1993. *A Vision for the Future: Sierra Now Conference Summary, Sacramento, August 7–9, 1992.* Malibu, Calif.: Environment Now.

Erickson, Bob. 1994–95. Furniture Craftsman and Board Member of the Yuba Watershed Institute, Nevada City, Calif. Personal communication.

Erman, Don C. 1991. Director, Wildland Resources Center. University of California at Berkeley. Personal communication.

———. 1997. Director, Centers for Water and Wildland Resources, University of California at Davis. Letter to Senator Dianne Feinstein regarding H.R. 848. March 12.

Estes, Caroline. 1986. "Consensus." *New Catalyst* no. 3 (spring). In Andruss et al. 1990, pp. 165–69.

Evans, Peter. 1995. *Embedded Autonomy: States and Industrial Transformation.* Princeton, N.J.: Princeton University Press.

Evernden, Lorne Leslie Neil. 1992. *The Social Creation of Nature.* Baltimore: Johns Hopkins University Press.

Ewing, Robert. 1995. Director, Strategic Resources Planning Program, California Department of Forestry and Fire Protection, Sacramento. Personal communication, 22 February.

———. 1997. Director, Strategic Planning, Weyerhauser Corp. Presentation to the William Main Lecture Series, 25 March, University of California at Berkeley.

Fainter, Michael Ryan. 1996. "Exposing the Scaffolding: The Need for Self-Reflexivity in Environmental Planning Theory." Paper prepared for Prof. Timothy P. Duane, University of California at Berkeley.

Fairfax, Sally K. 1997. Comments at the conference "Ecosystem Management: Law, Science and Policy," 15 February, at the School of Law, University of California at Davis.

Fairfax, Sally K., Barbara T. Andrews, and Andrew P. Buchsbaum. 1984. "Federalism and the Wild and Scenic Rivers Act: Now You See It, Now You Don't." *Washington Law Review* 59:417–70.

Fairfax, Sally K., and Richard Cowart. 1984. *State-Federal Relations: A Practitioner's Guide to the Law and Politics of Federalism.* Berkeley: University of California, Institute of Governmental Studies and California Policy Seminar.

Fairfax, Sally K., and Carolyn E. Yale. 1987. *Federal Lands: A Guide to Planning, Management, and State Revenues.* Western Office, Council of State Governments; Washington, D.C.: Island Press.

Farquhar, Francis Peloubet. 1965. *History of the Sierra Nevada.* Berkeley and Los Angeles: University of California Press.

Faulstich, Robert, and Ming Xio. 1993. "Central Nevada County Deer Habitat Study." Paper prepared for Prof. Timothy P. Duane, University of California at Berkeley.

Ferguson, Russell, ed. 1994. *Urban Revisions: Current Projects for the Public Realm.* Cambridge: MIT Press.

Fillingham, Lydia Alix. 1993. *Foucault for Beginners.* New York: Writers and Readers Publishing.

Findley, Jeff. 1993. Chief of Security, Lake Wildwood, Penn Valley, Calif. Personal communication, 23 March.

Finn, Jeff. 1994. Presentation to the Yuba Watershed Institute, 1 December, North Columbia Schoolhouse Cultural Center, Nevada County, Calif.

Fish, Stanley. 1980. *Is There a Text in This Class? The Authority of Interpretive Communities.* Cambridge: Harvard University Press.

———. 1989. *Doing What Comes Naturally: Change, Rhetoric, and the Practice of Theory in Literary and Legal Studies.* Durham, N.C.: Duke University Press.

Fish and Wildlife Service, U.S. 1991. *Federal and State Endangered Species Expenditures, FY 1990.* Washington, D.C.: U.S. Department of Interior, Fish and Wildlife Service. Cited in Shaffer 1992b.

Fisher, Anthony C. 1981. *Resource and Environmental Economics.* New York: Cambridge University Press.

Fisher, Michael. 1995. California Coastal Conservancy. Presentation to the Environmental Law and Resource Management class (IDS 233), November, University of California at Berkeley.

Fisher, Robert, and William Ury. 1982. *Getting to Yes: Negotiating Agreement Without Giving In.* London: Hutchinson.

Fishman, Robert. 1987. *Bourgeois Utopias.* New York: Basic Books.

Fitzgerald, Michael. 1978. "Voters Reject Growth Controls." *Grass Valley–Nevada City Union,* 8 November, p. 1.

Fleming, Pat, and Joanna Macy. 1990. "The Council of All Beings." In Andruss et al. 1990, pp. 95–99.

Foothill Conservancy. 1996. "Sierra Study Makes Its Debut." *Foothill Conservancy Focus* (Pine Grove, Calif.) (fall): 1

———. 1997. "SPI to Close Martell Sawmill," *Foothill Conservancy Focus* (Pine Grove, Calif.) (winter): 1

———. 1998. "Victory in Cinnabar [*sic*] Suit." *Foothill Conservancy Focus* (Pine Grove, Calif.) summer: 2.

Foreman, Dave. 1995. *Confessions of an Eco-Warrior.* 1st ed. New York: Harmony Books.

Foreman, Dave, and Howie Wolke. 1992. *The Big Outside: A Descriptive Inventory of the Big Wilderness Areas of the United States.* Rev. ed. New York: Harmony Books.

Forero, Larry, Lynn Huntsinger, and W. James Clawson. 1992. "Land Use Change in Three San Francisco Bay Area Counties: Implications for Ranching at the Urban Fringe." *Journal of Soil and Water Conservation* 47 (6): 475–80.

Forest, Nelia Badilla, Malcolm McDaniel, and Lori Tsung. 1994. "Hazard Management Analysis in the Context of an Urban-Wildland Intermix Scenario: The Cinnabar [*sic*] Site." Paper prepared for Timothy P. Duane, University of California at Berkeley.

Forest and Rangeland Resources Assessment Program. 1988. *California's Forests and Rangelands: Growing Conflict over Changing Uses.* Sacramento: California Department of Forestry and Fire Protection, Forest and Rangeland Resources Assessment Program.

Forest Ecosystem Management Assessment Team (FEMAT). 1993. *Forest Ecosystem Management: An Ecological, Economic, and Social Assessment.* Portland, Ore: Forest Ecosystem Management Assessment Team.

Forester, John. 1989. *Planning in the Face of Power.* Berkeley and Los Angeles: University of California Press.

Forman, Richard T. T. 1995. *Land Mosaics: The Ecology of Landscapes and Regions.* New York: Cambridge University Press.

Forman, Richard T. T., and Michel Godron. 1986. *Landscape Ecology.* New York: Wiley.

Forstenzer, Martin. 1997. "What's Wrong in the Sierra? A Look at an Ecosystem in Trouble." *Audubon* (March-April): 14–18.

Fortmann, Louise. 1988. *Locality and Custom: Non-Aboriginal Claims to Customary Usufructuary*

Rights as a Source of Rural Protest. Berkeley: University of California, Institute of Governmental Studies.

Fortmann, Louise, and Lynn Huntsinger. 1989. "The Effects of Nonmetropolitan Population Growth on Resource Management." *Society and Natural Resources* 2:9–22.

Foucault, Michel. 1980. *Power/Knowledge.* New York: Pantheon Books.

Fox, Stephen R. 1981. *John Muir and His Legacy: The American Conservation Movement.* Boston: Little, Brown.

Frame, Julie. 1997. Tahoe Regional Planning Agency. Personal communication, 13 March.

Frank, Richard M. 1995. "The Relevant Parcel Issue from the Government Lawyer's Perspective. Inverse Condemnation and Related Governmental Liability." ABA-ALI, May 4–6, p. 367.

———. 1996. "Bibliography of Recent Cases, Statutes and Secondary Sources [on Takings]." Presentation to the Environmental Law and Resource Management class (IDS 233), 3 October, University of California at Berkeley. (Bibliography prepared for Land Law Section, California Attorney General's Office, Sacramento.)

———. 1997. Presentation to the Environmental Law and Resource Management class (IDS 233), 18 November, University of California at Berkeley.

Franklin, Jerry, and Jo Ann Fites-Kaufmann. 1996. "Assessments of Late-Successional Forests of the Sierra Nevada." In *Sierra Nevada Ecosystem Project Final Report to Congress: Status of the Sierra Nevada,* 2:627–62. Davis: Center for Water and Wildland Resources, University of California.

Friedman, John. 1987. *Planning in the Public Domain: From Knowledge to Action.* Princeton, N.J.: Princeton University Press.

Freidman, Lawrence M., and Harry N. Scheiber. 1996. *Legal Culture and the Legal Profession.* Boulder, Colo.: Westview Press.

Friends of the Earth Netherlands. 1994. *Sustainable Netherlands.* Amsterdam: Friends of the Earth Netherlands.

Friends of the River. 1996. "Range of Problems in the Range of Light." *Headwaters* 20, no. 3 (fall): 1.

Fugro-McClelland (West), Inc. 1994. *Cinnabar [sic] Planned Development Project (Rezone 92–25), Draft Environmental Impact Report.* Placerville, Calif.: El Dorado County Planning Division, Community Development Department.

Fulton, Dave. 1994. Presentation to the Yuba Watershed Institute, 8 December, Nevada City, Calif.

Fulton, William B. 1991. *Guide to California Planning.* Point Arena, Calif.: Solano Press Books.

———. 1993. "Sliced on the Cutting Edge: Growth Management and Growth Control in California." In Stein 1993, pp. 113–26.

Garchik, Leah. 1997. "High Praise and High Stakes." *San Francisco Chronicle,* 3 December, p. E8.

Garcia, Kenneth J. 1996. "Staking a Claim on Education: Nevada County Schools Give Parents a Choice." *San Francisco Chronicle,* 17 October, p. A1.

Garland, Francis P. 1997a. "New Settlers after Peace in the Lode." *Stockton Record,* 19 October. In *Stockton Record* 1997, p. SR2.

———. 1997b. "Huge Development Planned for Small Town." *Stockton Record,* 19 October. In *Stockton Record* 1997, p. SR4.

Garreau, Joel. 1991. *Edge City: Life on the New Frontier.* New York: Doubleday.

Garrow, David J. 1996a. "The Rehnquist Reins." *New York Times Magazine,* 6 October, p. 65.

————. 1996b. "One Angry Man: Antonin Scalia's Decade." *New York Times Magazine,* 6 October, pp. 68–69.

General Accounting Office. 1997. *Forest Service Decision-Making: A Framework for Improved Performance.* GAO/RCED-97–71. Washington, D.C.: General Accounting Office.

Gentry, Curt. 1968. *The Last Days of the Late, Great State of California.* Sausalito, Calif.: Comstock Editions.

Gerstung, Eric R. 1970. *A Brief Survey of the Impact of Subdivision Activity on the Fish and Wildlife Resources of Nevada County.* Sacramento: California Department of Fish and Game.

————. 1973. "Land Development and Fish and Wildlife Protection." *Cal-Neva Wildlife,* pp. 134–37.

Getzels, Judith, and Charles Thurow. 1979. *Rural and Small Town Planning.* Chicago: Old West Regional Commission, American Planning Association.

Gilpin, Michael, and Michael E. Soule. 1986. "Minimum Viable Populations: Processes of Species Extinction." In Soule 1986, pp. 19–34.

Giusti, Gregory A., and Pamela J. Tinnin, eds. 1993. *A Planner's Guide for Oak Woodlands.* Berkeley: University of California, Department of Forestry and Resource Management, Integrated Hardwood Range Management Program.

Glance, Natalie S., and Bernardo A. Huberman. 1994. "The Dynamics of Social Dilemmas." *Scientific American* (March): 76–81.

Glick, Dennis. 1997. "The Greater Yellowstone Ecosystem Case Study: Overcoming Boundaries in a Managed Landscape." Paper presented to the Society for Conservation Biology, 9 June, Victoria, B.C.

Glickfeld, Madelyn, and Ned Levine. 1992. *Regional Growth . . . Local Reaction: The Enactment and Effects of Local Growth Control and Management Measures in California.* Cambridge, Mass.: Lincoln Institute of Land Policy.

Goldberg, Carey. 1996. "Alarm Bells Ring as Suburbs Gobble Up California's Richest Farmland." *New York Times,* 20 June, p. A6.

Goldman, Charles. 1994. "Lake Tahoe: A Microcosm for the Study of the Impact of Urbanization on Fragile Ecosystems." In Platt, Rowntree, and Muick, pp. 93–105.

————. 1995. Presentation to the conference "At the Crossroads of Science, Management, and Policy: A Review of Bioregional Assessments," 7 November. Portland, Ore.

Goldsmith, Edward. 1993. *The Way: An Ecological Worldview.* Boston: Shambala.

Goldsmith, William W., and Edward J. Blakely. 1992. *Separate Societies: Poverty and Inequality in US Cities.* Philadelphia: Temple University Press.

Goldstein, Bruce. 1992. "Can Ecosystem Management Turn an Administrative Patchwork into a Greater Yellowstone Ecosystem?" *Northwest Environmental Journal* 8 (2): 285–324.

Golnik, Rudy. 1995. City Engineer, City of Grass Valley. Personal communication, March.

Goodavish, Martha. 1994. Environmental Applications, Inc. Personal communication, September.

Gore, Albert. 1992. *Earth in the Balance: Ecology and the Human Spirit.* Boston: Houghton Mifflin.

Gottlieb, Robert. 1993. *Forcing the Spring: The Transformation of the American Environmental Movement.* Washington, D.C.: Island Press.

Gottlieb, Robert, and Margaret Fitzsimmons. 1991. *Thirst for Growth: Water Agencies as Hidden Government in California.* Tucson: University of Arizona Press.

Governor's Interagency Council on Growth Management. 1993. *Strategic Growth: Taking Charge of the Future: A Blueprint for California.* Sacramento: Governor's Office of Planning and Research.

Graber, David M. 1994–97. Research Scientist, National Park Service, Three Rivers, Calif. Personal communication.

———. 1996. "Status of Terrestrial Vertebrates." In *Sierra Nevada Ecosystem Project Final Report to Congress: Status of the Sierra Nevada,* 2:709–33. Davis: Center for Water and Wildland Resources, University of California.

Graebner, Lynn. 1994. "Michigan-California: Anatomy of a Failed Mill." *Business Journal* (Sacramento) 10, no. 51 (March 14): 1.

Granholm, Stephen L. 1987. *Tuolumne County Wildlife Project.* Sonora, Calif.: Tuolumne County Planning Department.

Grant, Eugene L., W. Grant Ireson, and Richard S. Leavenworth. 1976. *Principles of Engineering Economy.* 6th ed. New York: John Wiley and Sons.

Grass Valley–Nevada City Union, 1970a. "10,000 New Lots—3,000 More Coming," 9 January, p. 1.

———. 1970b. "Planning Commission Rarely Turns Down Subdivisions," 10 January, p. 1.

———. 1970c. "Some Favor Planning Controls; Some Don't," 11 January, p. 1.

———. 1970d. "Orange County Man Hired to Head Local Planning Office," 23 January, p. 1.

———. 1970e. "Sanitation District for Wildwood Suggested," 30 January, p. 1.

———. 1970f. "Cascade Shores Sewer Plant Not Acceptable—NID," 23 January, p. 1.

———. 1970g. "Two Subdivisions on Supervisors' Agenda," 9 February, p. 1.

———. 1970h. "Lake Wildwood Water Moves a Step Closer," 12 February, p. 1.

———. 1970i. "NID to Bring Subdivision Water," 12 February, p. 1.

———. 1970j. "Lot Split Hearing to Draw Crowd: Could Set Minimum Land Rules," 16 February, p. 1.

———. 1970k. "Lot Split Ordinance Draws Opposition from Majority," 18 February, p. 1.

———. 1970l. "Harvesting of Timber Defended," 27 February, p. 1.

———. 1970m. "Tahoe Northwoods OK, with Conditions: Hearing Room Crowded but Subject Limited," 24 March, p. 1.

———. 1970n. "Water Problems Occupy Planners," 28 March, p. 1.

———. 1970o. "Deadline on Glenbrook Basin Sewer Hookup," 15 April, p. 1.

———. 1970p. "Ordinance on Sewers Goes to Planning Board," 15 April, p. 1.

———. 1970q. "$26,000 Sewer System Plan Grant: County to Pay $5,500 of Cost," 29 April, p. 1.

———. 1970r. "Earth Day Handbook Banned as Class Text," 4 May, p. 1.

———. 1970s. "Slump in Lumber Market Cuts Forest Revenues," 13 May, p. 1.

———. 1970t. "Sewer Public Hearing Scheduled Monday," 16 May, p. 1.

———. 1970u. "Supervisors Pass Emergency Ordinance on Subdivision Sewers," 19 May, p. 1.

———. 1970v. "Camping Fee Starts Monday in Tahoe Forest," 22 May, p. 1.

———. 1970w. "Your Write-In Candidate for Supervisor, District 4" (Advertisement), 28 May, p. 3.

———. 1970x. "EDA Grants $5 Million for County," 1 June, p. 1.

———. 1970y. "Brown, Trauner Win; Todd, Wolters in Finals," 3 June, p. 1.

———. 1970z. "Long Winner; Filer, Thomas Make Runoff," 3 June, p. 1.

———. 1970aa. "Negro Is New Mayor of Newark," 17 June, p. 1.

———. 1970ab. "Bullards Bar Due to Open to Public July 1," 20 June, p. 1.

———. 1970ac. "Land Report Proposes Priority for Timber," 30 June, p. 1.

———. 1978a. "Growth Control a Tough Choice," 1 November, p. 19.

———. 1978b. "Golden Arches on the Way: McDonald's Sign OK'd," 8 November, p. 3.

———. 1978c. "Artist Norman Rockwell Dies: Career Spanned Six Decades," 9 November, p. 3.

———. 1978d. Advertisement, 6 November.

———. 1979a. "Efforts to Recall Covert Stall; His Opponents Promise Second Try," 31 January, p. 1.

———. 1979b. "Growth Money Led in Campaign," 2 February, p.1.

———. 1980a. "Supes to Adopt Plan, Sidestep Ban," 3 March, p. 1.

———. 1980b. "Suit Proceeds in Face of General Plan," 4 March, p. 1.

———. 1980c. "Supervisors Approve New General Plan," 6 March, p. 1.

———. 1994a. "Gold Rush-Era Ship Found in S.F.," 7 December, p. A3.

———. 1994b. "Grattan Remark Riles Sierra Club," 26 October, p. B1.

———. 1995a. "How Time Flies: Milestones of the General Plan," 4 February, p. B1.

———. 1995b. "Spotlight: Christine Wilcox, 'A Woman of Substance'" (insert), 11 March, p. 3.

———. 1995c. "The Union's Opinion: Forest Idea Deserves Applause," 30 March, p. A4.

———. 1995d. "General Plan EIR Ready for Review," 1 April, p. 1.

———. 1995e. "Retirement Community a Success in Roseville: Sun City's New Development Cost-Effective," 1 April, p. B7.

———. 1995f. "As Years Go By: 25 Years Ago, April 13, 1970," 13 April.

———. 1995g. "Board Condemns 'Extremist' Label by Herger: Supervisors Lend Mutual Support," 26 April, p. B1.

———. 1995h. Advertisement, 26 April, p. A6.

———. 1995i. "Computer Makers Flock to California's Capital," 10 October, p. A1.

———. 1995j. "Tiny Canary Island Rebuffs Tourism and Development," 22 September, p. C1.

———. 1995k. "Writer Tells Virtues, Trials of Country Life," 8 July, p. B4.

———. 1995l. "Ore. 'Silicon Forest' Attracts Investment," 19 July, p. A7.

———. 1995m. "Squaw Valley Founder Isn't Ready to Slow Down," 14 April, p. B7.

———. 1995n. "Costa Rican Ban to Aid Sport Fishing" 13 July, p. D4.

———. 1995o. "Juvinall Resigns as CABPRO's Leader," 1 February, p. A1.

———. 1996a. "The Union's Opinion: Clarity, Not Clairvoyance Needed," 31 October, p. A6.

———. 1996b. "Tourism Rebounds Statewide," 10 May, p. A1.

———. 1996c. "Court: No Exemption for Small-Timberland Owners," 21 March, p. A3.

———. 1996d. "The Union's Opinion: No Easy Solution on Tree Issue," 17 July, p. A6.

———. 1996e. "State Courts Overturn Three-Acre Exemptions for Timber Cuts," 14 June, p. A1.

———. 1996f. "The Union's Opinion: Will We Hear the Wake-Up Call for New Jobs Locally?" 14 June, p. A1.

———. 1997a. "Three Years Later, Stealth Bombers Finally Ready for Combat," 31 March, p. A1.

———. 1997b. "White House: Taxpayers Lose Money on Logging," 19 February, p. A1.

———. 1997c. "Salmon Release: Students Raise Chinook Fry," 15 March, p. A1.

———. 1997d. "Longtime NC Attorney Wins '96 Kilroy Award," 6 January, p. A3.

Grass Valley Planning Department. 1982. *Grass Valley General Plan.* Prepared by WPM Planning Team, Sausalito, Calif. Grass Valley, Calif.: City of Grass Valley.

Grattan, Fran. 1996. Chairwoman, Nevada County Board of Supervisors. Personal communication at the California Biodiversity Council meeting, June, Grass Valley, Calif.

Greater Yellowstone Coalition. 1997. *Tools for Managing Growth in the Greater Yellowstone Area.* Bozeman, Mont.: Greater Yellowstone Coalition.

Green, Bryn. 1981. *Countryside Conservation: The Protection and Management of Amenity Ecosystems.* London: G. Allen and Unwin.

Green, Frank. 1996. "El Dorado." Film produced by Green TV, San Francisco.

Greene, Carol. 1991. *John Muir, Man of the Wild Places.* Chicago: Children's Press.

Greenhouse, Linda. 1997. "Supreme Court Roundup: Court to Decide If Customs Can Seize Undeclared Cash," *New York Times,* 28 May, pp. A11 (N), A17 (L).

Greenwood, Gregory B. 1992–97. Research Manager, California Department of Forestry and Fire Protection, Sacramento. Personal communication.

———. 1995. "Managing Wildlands for Biodiversity: Paradigms and Spatial Tools." In West 1995, pp. 92–108.

———. 1997. Presentation to the California Biodiversity Council, 20 November, Davis, Calif.

Greenwood, Gregory B., and Robin Marose. 1993. "GIS Tools for the Assessment of Land Use Impacts on Biodiversity." In Keeley 1993, pp. 61–68.

Grese, Robert. 1992. *Jens Jensen: Maker of Natural Parks and Gardens.* Baltimore, Md.: Johns Hopkins University Press.

Griffith, Dorsey. 1997. "Poor Policies Hurt Sierra, Study Says: New Land-Use Guidelines Offered," *Sacramento Bee,* 10 July, p. A1.

Griffiths, Philip. 1993. *The Sierra Now: A Compendium of Social and Economic Statistics Describing California's Sierra Nevada Region.* M.C.P. Professional Report. Berkeley: University of California at Berkeley, Department of City and Regional Planning.

Griffiths, Ray. 1995. Former Planning Commissioner, El Dorado County, Calif. Personal communication.

Grime, J. P. 1997. "Biodiversity and Ecosystem Function: The Debate Deepens." *Science* 277 (29 August): 1260–61.

Groth, Paul Erling. 1994. *Living Downtown: The History of Residential Hotels in the US.* Berkeley and Los Angeles: University of California Press.

Groth, Paul Erling, and Todd Bressi, eds. 1997. *Understanding Ordinary Landscapes.* New Haven, Conn.: Yale University Press.

Grubbs, Tracy. 1995–97. Assistant Director, Sierra Business Council, Truckee, Calif. Personal communication.

Gruell, George. 1995. *Understanding Sierra Nevada Forests.* Sacramento: California Forest Products Commission.

Grumbine, R. Edward. 1992. *Ghost Bears: Exploring the Biodiversity Crisis.* Washington, D.C.: Island Press.

———. 1994. "What Is Ecosystem Management?" *Conservation Biology* 8 (1): 27–38.

———. 1997. "Reflections on 'What Is Ecosystem Management?'" *Conservation Biology* 11 (1): 41–47.

Guiner, Lani. 1994a. *The Tyranny of the Majority: Fundamental Fairness in Representative Democracy.* New York: Free Press.

———. 1994b. Presentation at Black Oak Books, 27 April, Berkeley, Calif.

———. 1994c. Presentation at the National Press Club, Washington, D.C. (broadcast on National Public Radio on 30 November).

Gunderson, Lance H., C. S. Holling, and Stephen S. Light, eds. 1995a. *Barriers and Bridges to the Renewal of Ecosystems and Institutions*. New York: Columbia University Press.

———. 1995b." Barriers Broken and Bridges Built: A Synthesis." In Gunderson et al. 1995a, pp. 489–532.

Gupta, Anil. 1994. "Social and Ethical Dimensions of Ecological Economics." Paper presented to the International Society for Ecological Economics, 24–28 October, San Jose, Costa Rica.

Habermas, Jürgen. 1984. *The Theory of Communicative Action*. Boston: Beacon Press.

Hadaway, C. Kirk, Penny Long Marler, and Mark Chaves. 1993. "What the Polls Don't Show: A Closer Look at US Church Attendance." *American Sociological Review* 58 (6): 741.

Haeckel, Ernst. 1866. *Oecologie*. Cited in Worster 1977.

Halley, Allan. 1992. Attorney, Former Chair of the Nevada County General Plan Citizens' Steering Committee, Nevada City, Calif. Personal communication.

Handley, Bruce, and Peter Grenell. 1995. *Stewardship Plan for the Grass Valley-Spenceville Area*. Prepared for the California Institute for Man in Nature. Sacramento: California Institute for Man in Nature and California Department of Forestry and Fire Protection.

Hanemann, W. Michael. 1994. "Valuing the Environment through Contingent Valuation." *Journal of Economic Perspectives* 8 (4): 19–43.

Hanna, Susan S., Carl Folke, and Karl-Goran Maler, eds. 1996. *Rights to Nature: Ecological, Economic, Cultural, and Political Principles of Institutions for the Environment*. Washington, D.C.: Island Press.

Hanner, Richard. 1997. "Rancho Calaveras Subdivision Defines Crisis." *Stockton Record,* 19 October. In *Stockton Record* 1997, SR4.

Hannon, Bruce M., and Matthias Ruth. 1994. *Dynamic Modeling*. New York: Springer-Verlag.

Hanson, Mark E., and Harvey M. Jacobs. 1989. "Private Sewage System Impacts in Wisconsin: Implications for Planning and Policy." *Journal of the American Planning Association* 55 (2): 169–90.

Hardin, Garrett. 1968. "The Tragedy of the Commons." *Science* 162 (13 December):1243–48.

Hargrave, Tim. 1993. "The Impact of a Federal Grazing Fee Increase on Land Use in El Dorado County, California." Paper prepared for Prof. Timothy P. Duane, University of California at Berkeley.

Hargrove, Eugene C., ed. 1992. *The Animal Rights/Environmental Ethics Debate: An Environmental Perspective*. Albany: State University of New York Press.

Harkin, Don. 1994–95. Forester and Board Member, Yuba Watershed Institute, Nevada City, Calif. Personal communication.

Harland Bartholemew and Associates, Inc. 1994. *Draft Environmental Impact Report*. Nevada City, Calif.: Nevada County Planning Department.

Harrar, Paul. 1996. "County Residents to Buy Radio Stations." *Grass Valley–Nevada City Union,* 22 March, p. A3.

Harrar, Paul, and Shawn Neidorf. 1996. "Bob Paine Dies at 88." *Grass Valley–Nevada City Union,* 25 July, p. A1.

Harris, David. 1995. *The Last Stand: The War between Wall Street and Main Street over California's Ancient Redwoods*. New York: Times Books.

Harris, Larry D. 1984. *The Fragmented Forest: Island Biogeography Theory and the Preservation of Biotic Diversity*. Chicago: University of Chicago Press.

Harris, Tom H. 1991. *Death in the Marsh*. Washington, D.C.: Island Press.

Harrison, Robert Pogue. 1992. *Forests: The Shadow of Civilization.* Chicago: University of Chicago Press.

Hart, John. 1992. *Farming on the Edge: Saving Family Farms in Marin County, California.* Berkeley and Los Angeles: University of California Press.

———. 1996. *Storm over Mono: The Mono Lake Battle and the California Water Future.* Berkeley and Los Angeles: University of California Press.

Hart, John Fraser. 1991. "The Perimetropolitan Bow Wave." *Geographical Review* 81 (1): 35–51.

Harvey, David. 1973. *Social Justice and the City.* London: Edward Arnold.

———. 1993. Comments at the Western Humanities Conference, October, Stanford University, Stanford, Calif.

Hatcher, David. 1993. "Mill Dies; Town Comes to Life." *High Country News* 25, no. 6 (5 April): 13.

Hauge, Carl. 1994. Presentation to the Yuba Watershed Institute, 8 December, Nevada City, Calif.

Hawken, Paul. 1993. *The Ecology of Commerce: A Declaration of Sustainability.* New York: HarperBusiness.

Hawkins, Bob. 1994. Mammoth-to-June Ecosystem Management Project Director, Inyo National Forest, Bishop, Calif. Personal communication, June and September.

Hays, Samuel P. 1959. *Conservation and the Gospel of Efficiency: The Progressive Conservation Movement, 1890–1920.* Cambridge: Harvard University Press.

———. 1987. *Beauty, Health, and Permanence: Environmental Politics in the United States, 1955–1985.* New York: Cambridge University Press.

Healy, Robert G., and James L. Short. 1981. *The Market for Rural Land: Trends, Issues, Policies.* Washington, D.C.: Conservation Foundation.

Heath, Maskey. 1995. Chairman, California Association of Business, Property, and Real Estate Owners, Nevada City, Calif. Personal communication, 29 March and 11 April.

Hedler, Ken. 1988. "County up for Federal Disaster Label." *Grass Valley-Nevada City Union,* 23 September, p. A1.

Hendler, Sue, ed. 1995. *Planning Ethics: A Reader in Planning Theory, Practice, and Education.* New Brunswick, N.J.: Center for Urban Policy Research.

Hester, Randolph T. 1985. "Subconscious Landscapes of the Heart." *Places* 2 (3): 10–22.

———. 1989. "Social Values in Open Space Design." *Places* 6 (1): 68–77.

———. 1990. *Community Design Primer.* Mendocino, Calif.: Ridge Times Press.

Heyman, Ira Michael. 1991–93. Professor and Chancellor Emeritus, University of California at Berkeley. Personal communication.

Heyman, Ira Michael, and Thomas K. Gilhool. 1964. "The Constitutionality of Imposing Increased Community Costs on New Suburban Residents through Subdivision Extractions." *Yale Law Journal* 73 (7): 1119–57.

High Country News. 1993. "Small Towns under Siege" (special issue), 25, no. 6 (5 April).

———. 1994a. "Shame and Threats Impel Eastside Plan," 26, no. 17 (19 September): 9.

———. 1994b. "Grappling with Growth," 26, no. 16 (5 September): 16.

Hinkle, George and Bliss Hinkle. 1987. *Sierra-Nevada Lakes.* New York: Bobbs-Merrill, 1949. Reprint, Reno: University of Nevada Press.

Hirt, Paul W. 1994. *A Conspiracy of Optimism: Management of the National Forests since World War Two.* Lincoln: University of Nebraska Press.

———. 1997. "A Conspiracy of Optimism: Management of the National Forests since

World War Two." Paper presented to the Energy and Resources Group Colloquium, 5 February, University of California at Berkeley.

Hiss, Tony. 1990. *The Experience of Place: A New Way of Looking at and Dealing with Our Radically Changing Cities and Countryside*. New York: Vintage.

Hoffmann, Sandra A., and Louise Fortmann. 1996. "Poverty in Forested Counties: An Analysis Based on Aid to Families with Dependent Children." In *Sierra Nevada Ecosystem Project Final Report to Congress: Status of the Sierra Nevada*, 2:403–38. Davis, Calif.: Center for Water and Wildland Resources, University of California.

Hoge, Patrick. 1995. "Rural Growth: Promise or Threat? Plans Causing Tension in Booming Sierra Counties; Development in El Dorado Pleases Some, Worries Others." *Sacramento Bee*, 16 October, p. B1.

Holbert, Will. 1995a. "GV's Volunteers Discover Training Time Consuming." *Grass Valley–Nevada City Union*, 15 February, p. A1.

———. 1995b. "GV Volunteer Firefighters Seek Funding." *Grass Valley–Nevada City Union*, 16 February, p. A1.

Holliday, J. S. 1981. *The World Rushed In*. New York: Touchstone.

Holling, C. S. 1978. *Adaptive Environmental Assessment and Management*. New York: John Wiley and Sons.

———. 1995. "What Barriers? What Bridges?" In Gunderson et al. 1995a, pp. 3–36.

Hooper, David U., and Peter M. Vitousek. 1997. "The Effects of Plant Composition and Diversity on Ecosystem Processes." *Science* 277 (29 August): 1302–5.

Hope, J. H. 1973. "Mammals of the Bass Strait Islands." *Proceedings of the Royal Society of Victoria* 85:163–96. Cited in Verner 1997.

Horner, Edith R., ed. 1996. *Almanac of the 50 States*. Palo Alto, Calif.: Information Publications.

Hostetler, Mark, and C. S. Holling. 1995. "Using a New Ecological Technique to Measure Scale-Specific Impacts on Landscape Structure in Urban Environments." Paper presented to the International Association of Landscape Architecture, April, Minneapolis, Minn.

Howarth, Richard B., and Richard B. Norgaard. 1992. "Environmental Valuation Under Sustainable Development." *American Economic Review* 82 (2): 473–77.

———. 1995. "Intergenerational Choices under Global Environmental Change." In *Handbook of Environmental Economics*, ed. by Daniel W. Bromley. Oxford: Basil Blackwell.

Howe, Charles W. 1979. *Natural Resource Economics*. New York: John Wiley and Sons.

Howe, Elizabeth. 1994. *Acting on Ethics in City Planning*. New Brunswick, N.J.: Center for Urban Policy Research.

Hudson, Wendy E., ed. 1991. *Landscape Linkages and Biodiversity*. Washington, D.C.: Island Press.

Hughes, T. P. and A. C. Hughes, eds. 1990. *Lewis Mumford: Public Intellectual*. New York: Oxford University Press. Cited in Luccarelli 1995.

Humbach, John A. 1989. "Law and a New Land Ethic." *Minnesota Law Review* 74, no. 2 (December): 339–70.

———. 1990. "Law and a New Land Ethic." *Exchange, the Journal of the Land Trust Alliance* (fall): 13–15.

———. 1992a. "Defending the American Land." *Audubon* (May-June): 112.

———. 1992b. "What Is Behind the 'Property Rights' Debate?" *Pace Environmental Law Review* 10, no. 1 (fall): 21–42.

———. 1992c. "Existing-Use Zoning." *Zoning News* (American Planning Association, Chicago) (December): 1–2.

———. 1993. "Evolving Thresholds of Nuisance and the Takings Clause." *Columbia Journal of Environmental Law* 18 (1): 1–29.

Hundley, Norris Jr. 1992. *The Great Thirst: Californians and Water, 1770s—1990s.* Berkeley and Los Angeles: University of California Press.

Hurley, Jim. 1996. "Chief Causes of Statistics Are Smoking, Politics." *Grass Valley–Nevada City Union,* 1 November, p. A6.

Hyman, Jeffrey B., and Kris Wernstedt. 1993. "Recovery Planning for Endangered Species: Ambiguous Science and Hidden Values." Paper presented to the Association of Collegiate Schools of Planning, 28–31 October, Philadelphia.

In-N-Out Burgers. n.d. Corporate communication materials summarizing the history of the chain. N.p.: In-N-Out Burgers.

Inman, Bradley. 1992. "Haven on Earth." *San Francisco Focus* (April): 59–67.

Innes, Judith E. 1987. *Knowledge and Public Policy: The Search for Meaningful Indicators.* New Brunswick, N.J.: Transactions Press.

———. 1991. *Group Processes and the Social Construction of Growth Management: The Cases of Florida, Vermont, and New Jersey.* Working Paper No. 542. Berkeley: University of California, Institute of Urban and Regional Development.

———. 1995. "Planning Theory's Emerging Paradigm: Communicative Action and Interactive Practice." *Journal of Planning Education and Research* 14 (3): 128–35.

———. 1996a. "Planning through Consensus Building: A New View of the Comprehensive Planning Ideal." *Journal of the American Planning Association* 62 (4): 460–72.

———. 1996b. "Indicators for Collective Learning and Action: Rethinking Planning for Complex Systems." Draft paper prepared for delivery at 50th Anniversary Conference, University of Newcastle, Department of Town and Country Planning, 25–27 October, Newcastle, England.

Innes, Judith E., Judith Gruber, Michael Neuman, and Robert Thompson. 1994. *Coordinating Growth and Environmental Management through Consensus Building.* Berkeley: California Policy Seminar.

Innes, Judith E., John D. Landis, and Ted K. Bradshaw. 1993. *Issues in Growth Management: Reprints of Recent Growth Management Writings by IURD Associates.* Berkeley: University of California, Institute of Urban and Regional Development.

Institute for Ecological Health. 1996. "The Future of the Sierra Foothills." *Linkages* 3 (fall): 1.

Intel Corporation. 1994. *Intel and Its Folsom, California, Site.* Folsom, Calif.: Intel Corporation.

Irwin, Robert L. 1987. "Local Planning Considerations for the Wildland-Structural Intermix in the Year 2000." In *Symposium on Wildland Fire 2000 in South Lake Tahoe, California.* Albany, Calif.: Pacific Southwest Forest and Range Experiment Station.

———. 1989. *A Discussion of the County General Plan and the Role of Strategic Fire Protection Planning.* Sacramento: California Department of Forestry and Fire Protection.

J. Moore Methods, Inc. 1992. *El Dorado County General Plan Survey.* Sacramento: J. Moore Methods, Inc.

Jackson, John Brinckerhoff. 1970. *Landscapes: Selected Writings of J. B. Jackson.* Ed. by Ervin H. Zube. Amherst: University of Massachusetts Press.

———. 1984. *Discovering the Vernacular Landscape.* New Haven, Conn.: Yale University Press.

Jackson, Kenneth T. 1985. *Crabgrass Frontier: The Suburbanization of the United States.* New York: Oxford Press.

Jackson, Michael. 1997a. Comments at the *Ecology Law Quarterly* symposium "The Ecosystem Approach: New Directions for Land and Water," 21 February, at Boalt Hall School of Law, University of California at Berkeley.

———. 1997b. Attorney, Quincy, Calif. Personal communication, 13 June.

Jacobs, Harvey M. 1995. "The Anti-Environmental 'Wise Use' Movement in America." *Land Use Law* 47, no. 2 (February): 3–8.

———. 1997. "*Those* Laws and *My* Land! The Impact of State Property Rights Laws on the Security of Individual Land Tenure." Paper presented to the Association of Collegiate Schools of Planning, 6–9 November, Ft. Lauderdale, Fla.

Jacobs, Jane. 1984. *Cities and the Wealth of Nations: Principles of Economic Life.* New York: Vintage Books.

———. 1992. *The Death and Life of Great American Cities.* New York: Random House, 1961. Reprint, New York: Vintage Books.

Jain, R. K., L. V. Urban, G. S. Stacey, and H. E. Balbach. 1993. *Environmental Assessment.* New York: McGraw-Hill.

Jamerson, June. 1995. "Constitution Supports Residents over Developers," *Grass Valley–Nevada City Union,* 26 September, p. A4.

James, Franklin J., and Dennis E. Gale. n.d. *Problems and Promises of Transferable Development Rights for Land Use Planning* (draft). Washington, D.C.: Urban Institute.

Jansson, AnnMari, Monica Hammer, Carl Folke, and Robert Costanza, eds. 1994. *Investing in Natural Capital: The Ecological Economics Approach to Sustainability.* Washington, D.C.: Island Press.

Jaszczak, Sandra, ed. 1996. *Encyclopedia of Associations.* 31st ed. Detroit, Mich.: Gale Research.

Jefferson, Thomas. 1820. Letter to William Charles Jarvis, September 28, in *The Writings of Thomas Jefferson.* Memorial ed., vol. 15 (Washington, D.C.: Thomas Jefferson Memorial Association of the United States, 1904). Washington, D.C.: National Archives. Cited in Bimber 1996.

———. 1952. *The Papers of Thomas Jefferson,* ed. by Julian P. Boyd. Princeton, N.J.: Princeton University Press. Cited in Kemmis 1990.

Jensen, Deborah, Margaret S. Torn, and John Harte. 1993. *In Our Own Hands: A Strategy for Conserving California's Biological Diversity.* Berkeley and Los Angeles: University of California Press.

Jensen, Jens. [1939] 1990. *Siftings.* Baltimore, Md.: Johns Hopkins University Press.

Johnson, Dirk. 1996. "Influx of Newcomers Part of a Rural Upturn." *New York Times,* 23 September, p. A1.

Johnson, K. Norman, Richard Holthausen, Margaret A. Shannon, and Jim Sedell. 1995. "Developing a Forest Plan for Federal Forests of the Pacific Northwest: FEMAT and Its Aftermath." Draft paper presented to the conference "At the Crossroads of Science, Management, and Policy: A Review of Bioregional Assessments," 7 November, Portland, Ore.

Johnson, Kenneth M. 1993. "Demographic Change in Nonmetropolitan America, 1980–1990." *Rural Sociology* 58 (3): 347–65.

Johnson, Marilyn. 1993. *The Second Gold Rush: Oakland and the East Bay in WW II.* Berkeley and Los Angeles: University of California Press.

Johnson, Mark. 1997. Mayor, City of Grass Valley, Calif. Personal communication.

Johnson, Stephen, Gerald Haslam, and Robert Dawson. 1993. *The Great Central Valley: California's Heartland.* Berkeley and Los Angeles: University of California Press.

Johnston, David Cay. 1997. "Giving at the Home Office: Municipalities Set New Charges for In-House Businesses." *New York Times,* 19 December, p. C1.

Johnston, Robert A., and Mary E. Madison. 1991. *Planning for Habitat Protection in California: State Policies and County Actions to Implement CEQA through Improved General Plans.* Contract 8CA85456. Sacramento: Forest and Rangeland Resources Assessment Program, California Department of Forestry and Fire Protection.

Jones, Lisa. 1996a. "Howdy, Neighbor! As a Last Resort, Westerners Start Talking to Each Other." *High Country News* 28, no. 9 (May 13).

———. 1996b. "El Nueva West: The Region's New Pioneers Buoy the Economy and Live on the Edge." *High Country News* 28, no. 24 (23 December).

Joseph, A., and B. Smit. 1981. "Implications of Exurban Residential Development." *Canadian Journal of Regional Science* 4 (2): 207–24.

Juvinall, Todd. 1995a. "Proponents of Strict Zoning Dishonor Constitution." *Grass Valley–Nevada City Union,* 15 September, p. A4.

———. 1995b. Personal communication, 11 April.

———. 1996a. Letter to the Nevada County Board of Supervisors regarding build-out projections on behalf of the California Association of Business, Property and Resource Owners (CABPRO). October 17.

———. 1996b. "Editorial Right-On On Plan" (letter to the editor). *Grass Valley–Nevada City Union,* 1 May, p. A6.

Kagan, Robert A. 1996. "American Lawyers, Legal Cultures and Adversarial Legalism." In Friedman and Scheiber 1996, pp. 7–51.

Kahrl, William L. 1982. *Water and Power: The Conflict over Los Angeles' Water Supply in the Owens Valley.* Berkeley and Los Angeles: University of California Press.

Kanigel, Robert. 1996. Review of *The Song of the Dodo: Island Biogeography in an Age of Extinctions,* by David Quammen. *New York Times Book Review* 21 April, p. 11

Kattelmann, Richard. 1996. "Hydrology and Water Resources." In *Sierra Nevada Ecosystem Project Final Report to Congress: Status of the Sierra Nevada,* 2:855–920. Davis: Center for Water and Wildland Resources, University of California.

Katz, Peter. 1994. *The New Urbanism: Toward an Architecture of Community.* New York: McGraw-Hill.

Keely, J. E., ed. 1993. *Interface between Ecology and Land Development in California.* Los Angeles: Southern California Academy of Sciences.

Keeney, Ralph L., and Howard Raiffa. 1993. *Decisions with Multiple Objectives: Preferences and Value Tradeoffs.* New York: Cambridge University Press.

Keiter, Robert B., and Mark S. Boyce, eds. 1991. *The Greater Yellowstone Ecosystem: Redefining America's Wilderness Heritage.* New Haven, Conn.: Yale University Press.

Kellert, Stephen R. 1995. *The Value of Life: Biological Diversity and Human Society.* Washington, D.C.: Island Press.

Kelley, Robert. 1959. *Gold vs. Grain: The Hydraulic Mining Controversy in California's Sacramento Valley.* Glendale, Calif.: A. H. Clark.

Kelly, Nik. 1997. "Advance Planning." *Rural Quality News* (Rural Quality Coalition of Nevada County, Nevada City, Calif.) (November): 2.

Kemmis, Daniel. 1990. *Community and the Politics of Place.* Norman: University of Oklahoma Press.

Kempton, Willett, James S. Boster, and Jennifer A. Hartley. 1995. *Environmental Values in American Culture*. Cambridge: MIT Press.

Kenidy, Ron. 1994. North San Juan–Nevada City, Calif. Personal communication, May.

Kent, T. J. 1964. *The Urban General Plan*. 2^d ed. Chicago: Planners Press, American Planning Association.

Kenworthy, Tom. 1991. "Park, Forest Officials Allege GOP Pressure." *Washington Post* 25 September, p. A23.

Keohane, Robert O. 1984. *After Hegemony: Cooperation and Discord in the World Political Economy*. Princeton, N.J.: Princeton University Press.

Keystone Policy Dialogue. 1991. *Final Consensus Report of the Keystone Policy Dialogue on Biological Diversity on Federal Lands*. Keystone, Colo.: Keystone Center.

King, Gary, Robert Keohane, and Sidney Verba. 1994. *Designing Social Inquiry: Scientific Inference in Qualitative Research*. Princeton, N.J.: Princeton University Press.

Kirp, David L., John P. Dwyer, and Larry A. Rosenthal. 1995. *Our Town: Race, Housing, and the Soul of Suburbia*. New Brunswick, N.J.: Rutgers University Press.

Knaap, Gerrit. 1991. "Comment: Measuring the Effects of Growth Controls." *Journal of Policy Analysis and Management* 10 (3). Cited in Knaap and Nelson 1992.

Knaap, Gerrit, and Arthur C. Nelson. 1992. *The Regulated Landscape: Lessons on State Land Use Planning from Oregon*. Cambridge, Mass.: Lincoln Institute of Land Policy.

Knudson, Tom. 1991. "Majesty and Tragedy: The Sierra in Peril." *Sacramento Bee*, 9–13 June, p. A1.

———. 1996. "Sierra's Problem: Too Many People," *Sacramento Bee*, 11 June, p. B1.

Koda, Carole. 1995. "Dancing in the Borderland: Finding Our Common Ground in North America." Manuscript, Nevada City, Calif.

Kohler, Judith. 1998. "Western Resort Areas Far Too Expensive for Live-In Workers: Money Wags the Dog as Millionaires Sell to Billionaires." *San Francisco Examiner*, 4 January, p. E1.

Kohm, Kathryn A., and Jerry F. Franklin, eds. 1997. *Creating a Forestry for the 21st Century: The Science of Ecosystem Management*. Washington, D.C.: Island Press.

Kondolf, G. Mathias, Richard Kattelmann, Michael Embury, and Don C. Erman. 1996. "Status of Riparian Habitat." In *Sierra Nevada Ecosystem Project Final Report to Congress: Status of the Sierra Nevada*, 2:1009–32. Davis: Center for Water and Wildland Resources, University of California.

Kostof, Spiro. 1991. *The City Shaped: Urban Patterns and Meanings through History*. Boston: Little, Brown and Co.

Krebs, Charles J. 1978. *Ecology: The Experimental Analysis of Distribution and Abundance*. 2^d ed. New York: Harper and Row.

Krikelas, A. C. 1992. "Why Regions Grow: A Review of Research on the Economic Base Model." *Economic Review* 77 (4): 16–29. Cited in Wilderness Society 1997.

Kroeber, Theodora. 1961. *Ishi in Two Worlds: A Biography of the Last Wild Indian in North America*. Berkeley and Los Angeles: University of California Press.

Krutilla, John V. 1967. *Conservation Reconsidered*. Washington, D.C.: Resources for the Future.

———, ed. 1972. *Natural Environments: Studies in Theoretical and Applied Analysis*. Baltimore, Md.: Johns Hopkins University Press for Resources for the Future.

Kuhn, Thomas. 1962. *The Structure of Scientific Revolutions*. Chicago: University of Chicago Press.

Kunstler, James Howard. 1993. *The Geography of Nowhere: The Rise and Decline of America's Man-Made Landscape*. New York: Simon and Schuster.

Kusel, Jonathan. 1994. Memorandum to the Sierra Nevada Ecosystem Project Team. November 14.

———. 1996. "Well-Being in Forest-Dependent Communities, Part I: A New Approach." In *Sierra Nevada Ecosystem Final Report to Congress: Status of the Sierra Nevada*, 2:361–73. Davis: Center for Water and Wildland Resources, University of California.

Kusel, Jonathan, and Louise Fortman. 1991a. *Well-Being in Forest-Dependent Communities*. Vol. 1. Forest and Rangeland Resources Assessment Program. Sacramento: California Department of Forestry and Fire Protection.

———. 1991b. *Well-Being in Forest-Dependent Communities*. Vol. 2. Forest and Rangeland Resources Assessment Program. Sacramento: California Department of Forestry and Fire Protection.

Lake Vera/Round Mountain Neighborhood Association (LVRMNA). 1995. *Neighborhood Plan*, p. 7. Nevada City, Calif.: Lake Vera/Round Mountain Neighborhood Association.

Laidlaw, Robert. 1992. Recreation Planning Staff, U.S. Bureau of Land Management, Sacramento. Personal communication.

Lamar, Howard R., ed. 1997. *The Reader's Encyclopedia of the American West*. New York: Harper and Row.

Landis, John D. 1988. *Estimating the Housing Price Effects of Alternative Growth Management Strategies in the City of San Diego*. Working Paper No. 88–148. Berkeley: Institute of Urban and Regional Development, University of California at Berkeley.

———. 1992. *Do Growth Controls Work? An Evaluation of Local Growth Control Programs in Seven California Cities*. Berkeley: California Policy Seminar.

———. 1993a. "Regional Growth Management." *California Policy Choices* 8:83–126.

———. 1993b. *How Shall We Grow? Alternative Futures for the Greater San Francisco Bay Region*. Berkeley: California Policy Seminar.

Landis, John D., William Huang, Robert Olshansky, and Rolf Pendall. 1995. *Fixing CEQA: Options and Opportunities for Reforming the California Environmental Quality Act*. Berkeley: California Policy Seminar.

Landon, Dan. 1994–95. Executive Director, Nevada County Transportation Commission. Personal communication.

Landowski, Lowell. 1994–96. Executive Director, Sierra Communities Council. Personal communication.

Lang, Marvel. 1986. "Redefining Urban and Rural for the U.S. Census of Population: Assessing the Need and Alternative Approaches." *Urban Geography* 2:118–134.

Langston, Nancy. 1995. *Forest Dreams, Forest Nightmares: The Paradox of Old Growth in the Inland West*. Seattle: University of Washington Press.

Lapping, Mark B., Thomas L. Daniels, and John W. Keller. 1989. *Rural Planning and Development in the United States*. New York: Guilford Press.

Larmer, Paul. 1993. "Areas Fear Glitzification." *High Country News* 25, no. 6 (5 April): 20.

———. 1996. Can a Colorado Ski County Say Enough Is Enough: Eagle County Balks at Fourth Mega-Resort." *High Country News* 28, no. 3 (19 February): 1.

———. 1997. "Habitat Conservation Plans: Who Wins and Who Loses When Uncle Sam Cuts Deals with Landowners to Protect Endangered Species?" *High Country News* 29, no. 14 (4 August): 1.

Larson, Erik. 1995. "Unrest in the West." *Time* (23 October): 52–66.

Lashbrook, Tony. 1994–97. Director, Community Development Department, Town of Truckee, Calif. Personal communication.

Lauer, Susan. 1994a. "Glenwood Reduction Proposed." *Grass Valley–Nevada City Union,* 3 October, p. A1.

———. 1994b. "Glenwood Appeal Rejected." *Grass Valley–Nevada City Union,* 5 October, p. A1.

———. 1994c. "Public Hearings on Project Start." *Grass Valley–Nevada City Union,* 5 October, p. A1.

———. 1994d. "Weir: No Conflict on Glenwood Vote." *Grass Valley–Nevada City Union,* 5 October, p. A1.

———. 1994e. "Glenwood Road Topic of Debate." *Grass Valley–Nevada City Union,* 6 October, p. A1.

———. 1994f. "Glenwood Pines Cut to 20 Homes." *Grass Valley–Nevada City Union,* 7 October, p. A1.

———. 1994g. "Glenwood Neighbors Set to Sue." *Grass Valley–Nevada City Union,* 8 October, p. A1.

———. 1994h. "Glenwood Deal Negotiated as Decision Nears." *Grass Valley–Nevada City Union,* 11 October, p. A1.

———. 1994i. "Resolution Panel Tackles Population Cap." *Grass Valley–Nevada City Union,* 20 October, p. B1.

———. 1994j. "Glenwood Negotiations Fail." *Grass Valley–Nevada City Union,* 21 October, p. A1.

———. 1994k. "Advisory Panel Draws Protest." *Grass Valley–Nevada City Union,* 25 October, p. A1.

———. 1994l. "Panel Addresses Issues of Land Use." *Grass Valley–Nevada City Union,* 25 October, p. A1.

———. 1994m. "Juvinall Pulls the Plug on Glenwood." *Grass Valley–Nevada City Union,* 27 October, p. A1.

———. 1994n. "Threats to Clean Water Debated." *Grass Valley–Nevada City Union,* 3 December, p. A1.

———. 1994o. "General Plan's EIR Reveals Impacts." *Grass Valley–Nevada City Union,* 10 December, p. A1.

———. 1994p. "Furor Erupts on EIR Results." *Grass Valley–Nevada City Union,* 15 December, p. A1.

———. 1994q. "Sierra Communities Council Seeks County's Backing." *Grass Valley–Nevada City Union,* 5 September, p. A3.

———. 1995a. "County Says It Will Repay State Loan: Cascade Shores Sewage Woes Could Threaten Properties." *Grass Valley–Nevada City Union,* 8 March, p. A1.

———. 1995b. "Frustration to Mark General Plan Birthday." *Grass Valley–Nevada City Union,* 4 February, B1.

———. 1995c. "Rural Quality Has Different Meaning." *Grass Valley–Nevada City Union,* 4 February, p. B1.

———. 1995d. "Public Unworried about Length of Plan Process." *Grass Valley–Nevada City Union,* 4 February, p. B1.

———. 1995e. "State Wants County's Financial Guarantee on Sewer Project." *Grass Valley–Nevada City Union,* 6 March, p. B1.

———. 1995f. "Subdivision to Get New Sewer." *Grass Valley–Nevada City Union,* 22 April, p. A1.

———. 1995g. "Residents Address General Plan Draft EIR." *Grass Valley–Nevada City Union*, 13 January, p. B1.

———. 1995h. "Panel's Ideas Part of EIR Work." *Grass Valley–Nevada City Union*, 20 January, p. A1.

———. 1995i. "General Plan Environmental Report to Be Reviewed." *Grass Valley–Nevada City Union*, 21 January, p. A1.

———. 1995j. "Grattan Received Financial Edge at Race's End." *Grass Valley–Nevada City Union*, 4 February, p. A1.

———. 1995k. "Grattan Taps White for Planning Commission Post." *Grass Valley–Nevada City Union*, 8 February, p. A1.

———. 1995l. "Stalled Plan Angers Board." *Grass Valley–Nevada City Union*, 15 March, p. A1.

———. 1995m. "EIR Spurs Debate on Area Future." *Grass Valley–Nevada City Union*, 13 April, p. A1.

———. 1995n. "Residents Air Views at Plan Hearing." *Grass Valley–Nevada City Union*, 12 May, p. A1.

———. 1995o. "General Plan Hearing Draws 150." *Grass Valley–Nevada City Union*, 13 May, p. A1.

———. 1995p. "Residents Threaten General Plan Appeal." *Grass Valley–Nevada City Union*, 18 May, p. A1.

———. 1995q. "Progress Made on Growth Plan: Resolution Committee Recommendations Approved." *Grass Valley–Nevada City Union*, 19 May, p. A1.

———. 1995r. "Residents to Appeal Plan Decisions." *Grass Valley–Nevada City Union*, 22 May, p. A1.

———. 1995s. "Group Files Appeal of EIR." *Grass Valley–Nevada City Union*, 23 May, p. A1.

———. 1995t. "Plan EIR Hearings to Begin." *Grass Valley–Nevada City Union*, 19 July, p. A1.

———. 1995u. "Appellants Challenge EIR's Value." *Grass Valley–Nevada City Union*, 21 July, p. A1.

———. 1995v. "EIR Appellants Take Case to Board." *Grass Valley–Nevada City Union*, 22 July, p. A1.

———. 1995w. "Appeals Opposition Speaks for EIR." *Grass Valley–Nevada City Union*, 24 July, p. A1.

———. 1995x. "Plan Adoption Next Step." *Grass Valley–Nevada City Union*, 28 July, p. A1.

———. 1995y. "Tobiassen Dead at 66." *Grass Valley–Nevada City Union*, 28 July, p. A1.

———. 1995z. "Board Rejects Appeal of EIR." *Grass Valley–Nevada City Union*, 29 July, p. A1.

———. 1996a. "Woodcutter Tries to Settle Dispute with Chainsaw." *Grass Valley–Nevada City Union*, 18 January, p. A1.

———. 1996b. "Boy Arrested for Handgun at School." *Grass Valley–Nevada City Union*, 18 January, p. A3.

———. 1997. "Shopping for Your School." *Grass Valley–Nevada City Union*, 12 April, p. A1.

Laurie, Michael. 1992. Chair, Department of Landscape Architecture, University of California at Berkeley. Personal communication.

Lauter, David. 1992. "Environmentalists Flex Muscle Over Key Appointment." *Los Angeles Times*, 10 December, p. A27.

Lawler, Mark. 1993. *Ancient Forest and the Future of the Pacific Northwest: An Overview of the Oregon and Washington Timber Economy and the Effects of Preserving Ancient Forests*. Seattle: Sierra Club Northwest Office.

Lawrence, Andrea. 1991–96. Supervisor, Mono County, Calif., and President of Sierra Nevada Alliance. Personal communication.

Leaf, Clifton. 1997. "When Nature Calls." *Continental Magazine* (June): 42–47.

Lee, Kai. 1993. *Compass and Gyroscope.* Washington D.C.: Island Press.

Lehr, Stafford. 1995. Fishery Biologist, California Department of Fish and Game. Personal communication.

Lenahan, Antoinette. 1995. "Cascade Shores Sewer Renovation Under Way." *Grass Valley–Nevada City Union,* 4 October, A3.

Leontief, Wassily W. 1986. *Input-Output Economics.* 2^d ed. San Francisco: W. H. Freeman and Company, 1951. Reprint, New York: Oxford University Press.

Leopold, Aldo. 1970. *A Sand County Almanac, with Essays on Conservation from Round River.* Oxford: Oxford University Press, 1949. Reprint, New York: Ballantine Books.

Lester, James P., ed. 1989. *Environmental Politics and Policy: Theories and Evidence.* Durham, N.C.: Duke University Press.

Lillard, Richard. 1966. *Eden in Jeopardy: Man's Prodigal Meddling with the Environment (the Southern California Experience).* New York: Knopf. Cited in Mike Davis 1990.

Limerick, Patricia Nelson. 1988. *The Legacy of Conquest: The Unbroken Past of the American West.* New York: W. W. Norton and Company.

———. 1997. "The Shadows of Heaven Itself." In Riebsame and Robb 1997, 151–78.

Lin, Annie. 1996. Untitled paper analyzing two community-based environmental management projects in California. Prepared for Prof. Timothy P. Duane, University of California at Berkeley.

Linton, Michael, and Thomas Greco. 1990. "LETS: The Local Exchange Trading System." In Andruss et al. 1990, pp. 155–58.

Lipset, Seymour Martin. 1997. "American Exceptionalism." Speech to the World Affairs Council, San Francisco, broadcast on KQED-FM on July 14, 1997.

Litton, R. B., Jr. 1972. "Aesthetic Dimensions of the Landscape," in Krutilla 1972, pp. 262–91.

Livingston County Planning Department. 1991. *PEARL: Protect Environment Agriculture and Rural Landscape: An Open Space Zoning Technique.* Livingston County, Mo.: Livingston County Planning Department.

Local Government Commission. 1992. *Land Use Strategies for More Livable Places.* Sacramento: Local Government Commission.

Logan, John R., and Harvey L. Molotch. 1987. *Urban Fortunes: The Political Economy of Place.* Berkeley and Los Angeles: University of California Press.

Loma Prieta Chapter of the Sierra Club. 1978–90. Newspaper clippings files. Peninsula Conservation Center, Palo Alto, Calif.

Loomis, John B. 1993. *Integrated Public Lands Management: Principles and Applications to National Forests, Parks, Wildlife Refuges, and BLM Lands.* New York: Columbia University Press.

Lopez, Barry. 1992. "The American Geographies." In Sauer 1992, pp. 116–33.

Loury, Glenn. 1977. "A Dynamic Theory of Racial Income Differences." In *Women, Minorities, and Employment Discrimination,* ed. by P. A. Wallace and A. Le Mund. Lexington, Mass.: Lexington Books. Cited in Putnam et al. 1993.

———. 1987. "Why Should We Care about Group Inequality?" *Social Philosophy and Policy* 5:249–71. Cited in Putnam et al. 1993.

Lovejoy, T. E., R. O. Bierregaard, Jr., A. B. Rylands, J. R. Malcom, C. E. Quintela, L. H. Harper, K. S. Brown, Jr., A. H. Powell, G. V. N. Powell, H. O. R. Shubart, and M. B. Hays.

1986. "Edge and Other Effects of Isolation on Amazon Forest Fragments." In Soule 1986, pp. 257–85.

Lovins, Amory B. 1990. Testimony before the Nevada Public Service Commission, in Docket 89–752, 8 August, Carson City, Nevada.

Lovins, Amory B., and L. Hunter Lovins. 1982. *Brittle Power: Energy Strategy for National Security.* Andover, Mass.: Brickhouse Publishing.

Luccarelli, Mark. 1995. *Lewis Mumford and the Ecological Region: The Politics of Planning.* New York: Guilford Press.

Lufkin, Alan, ed. 1991. *California's Salmon and Steelhead: The Struggle to Restore an Imperiled Resource.* Berkeley and Los Angeles: University of California Press.

Lukas, David. 1993. *Birds of the San Juan Ridge.* Nevada City, Calif.: Yuba Watershed Institute.

Lyons, James R. 1996. Memorandum to Jack Ward Thomas, Chief of the Forest Service (Subject: California Owl Revised Draft Environmental Impact Statement), September 4.

MacArthur, Robert H., and Edward O. Wilson. 1967. *The Theory of Island Biogeography.* Princeton, N.J.: Princeton University Press.

Macdonald, Heather. 1995. "Chinatowns Were Immigrant Havens" *Grass Valley–Nevada City Union,* 15 July, p. C1.

MacFarquhar, Neil. 1996. "One Focus of Inquiry: The Selection of Targets." *New York Times,* 8 April, p. A12.

Machida, Dennis. 1994–96. Executive Officer, California Tahoe Conservancy, South Lake Tahoe, Calif. Personal communication.

———. 1995. Presentation to the Environmental Law and Resource Management class (IDS 233), November, University of California at Berkeley.

Malley, Dean. 1992–93. Tuolumne County 2000, Sonora, Calif. Personal communication.

Mallgren, Robin. 1994–95. Programmer, XEROX Palo Alto, Nevada City, Calif. Personal communication.

Manley, P. N. 1994. Presentation to the Sierra Nevada Ecosystem Project Science Team, March, Sacramento.

Manley, P. N., G. E. Brogan, C. Cook, M. E. Flores, D. G. Fullmer, S. Husari, T. M. Jimerson, L. M. Lux, M. E. McCain, J. A. Rose, G. Schmitt, J. C. Schuyler, and M. J. Skinner. 1995. *Sustaining Ecosystems: A Conceptual Framework.* San Francisco: Pacific Southwest Region, U.S. Forest Service. Cited in Millar 1996.

Mann, Charles C., and Mark L. Plummer. 1995. "California vs. Gnatcatcher." *Audubon* 97 (1): 38.

Mann, Ralph. 1982. *After the Gold Rush: Society in Grass Valley and Nevada City, California, 1849–1870.* Stanford, Calif.: Stanford University Press.

Manning, Elizabeth. 1996. "Santa Fe Ski-Area Growth Enrages Locals." *High Country News* 28, no. 3 (19 February): 12.

Marcus, Clare Cooper, and Wendy Sarkissian. 1986. *Housing as if People Mattered: Site Design Guidelines for Medium-Density Family Housing.* Berkeley and Los Angeles: University of California Press.

Margolis, Jon. 1997. "Critics Say 'No Surprises' Means No Protection." *High Country News* 29, no. 14 (4 August): 10–13.

Marietta, Don E., Jr., 1988. "Environmental Holism and Individuals." *Environmental Ethics* 10 (fall): 251–58. Cited in Des Jardins 1997.

Marin Independent Journal. 1997. "Residents Flee 'Craziness' of Silicon Valley: Traffic, Stress, Crowding Cited." October 7. p. B6.

Marois, Michael B. 1994. "Antonson: Smaller Government Better." *Grass Valley–Nevada City Union,* December 3. p. B1.

———. 1995a. "Home Market Flat: Real-Estate Personnel Report 'Negative Equity' in County." *Grass Valley–Nevada City Union,* 8 July, p. A1.

———. 1995b. "Todd Juvinall: Star or Villain." *Grass Valley–Nevada City Union,* 6 May, p. A1.

———. 1995c. "Tourism Brings County Big Bucks: Visitors Spend Over Half-Million Dollars a Day in '93; Investing in Promotion Pays Off." *Grass Valley–Nevada City Union,* 15 February, p. A1.

———. 1995d. "Tourism Figures Disputed: Tabulations Could Affect General Plan." *Grass Valley–Nevada City Union,* 16 February, p. A1.

———. 1995e. "Lowell Robinson: Timber Baron." *Grass Valley–Nevada City Union,* 19 August, p. A1.

———. 1996a. "County Man Brings Area Transportation before State Group." *Grass Valley–Nevada City Union,* 9 March, p. A1.

———. 1996b. "Environment Influences Economy: Study Notes Interaction." *Grass Valley–Nevada City Union,* 10 May, p. A1.

———. 1996c. "Placer Approves Wal-Mart Plan." *Grass Valley–Nevada City Union,* 20 March, p. A1.

———. 1996d. "High-Tech Engineers to Be Hired." *Grass Valley–Nevada City Union,* 20 March, p. A1.

———. 1996e. "Subdivision Map Gets OK by Planners." *Grass Valley–Nevada City Union,* 18 August, p. B1.

———. 1996f. "Tektronix Lays Off GVG Workers: Parent Company Absorbs Group, Cuts 125–150 Positions." *Grass Valley–Nevada City Union,* 18 January, p. A1.

———. 1996g. "Diversification of Economy Called a Need." *Grass Valley–Nevada City Union,* 18 January, p. A1.

Marples, Paul, and C. S. Holling. 1995. "A Statistical Measure of Discontinuous Spatial and Temporal Landscape Pattern." Paper presented to the International Association of Landscape Architecture, April, Minneapolis, Minn.

Marsh, William M. 1991. *Landscape Planning: Environmental Applications.* 2nd ed. New York: John Wiley and Sons.

Marston, Ed. 1993a. "How Boulder Preserves Its Vision." *High Country News* 25, no. 6 (5 April): 19–20.

———. 1993b. "It's Time to Clearcut the Forest Service." *High Country News* 25, no. 17 (23 September): 13.

———. 1996a. Review of *Belonging to the West,* by Eric Paddock. *High Country News* 28, no. 23 (9 December): 8.

———. 1996b. "Election Analysis: If Politics Is a Baseball Game, I Don't Even Own a Bat." *High Country News* 28, no. 22 (25 November): 16.

———. 1996c. "Denying the Warts on the West's Service Economy." *High Country News* 28, no. 24 (23 December): 14.

———. 1997. "The Timber Wars Evolve into a Divisive Attempt at Peace." *High Country News* 29, no. 18 (29 September): 1.

———, ed. 1989. *Reopening the Western Frontier.* Washington, D.C.: Island Press.

Martin, Glen. 1997. "Unlikely Group Asks Sierra Regulation," *San Francisco Chronicle,* 12 July, p. A17.

Marty, Martin E. 1996. "Were You There on Sunday? (Self-Reported Church Attendance Rates vs. Actual Attendance Rates)." *Christian Century* 113 (26): 879.

Maser, Chris. 1994. *Sustainable Forestry: Philosophy, Science, and Economics.* Delray Beach, Fla.: St. Lucie Press.

Masters, Gilbert M. 1974. *Introduction to Environmental Science and Technology.* New York: John Wiley and Sons.

Mattern, Douglas. 1998. "The Poverty Amid Riches." *San Francisco Chronicle,* 5 January, p. A23.

Mayer, K. E., and W. F. Laudenslayer, Jr., eds. 1988. *A Guide to Wildlife Habitats in California.* Sacramento: California Department of Forestry and Fire Protection.

McAdams, Deborah. 1997a. "Area's Growth 50% Less Than State Average: County Added 500 in 12 Months." *Grass Valley–Nevada City Union,* April 18. p. A1.

———. 1997b. "Area Code Changes by End of Year." *Grass Valley–Nevada City Union,* 27 June, p. A1.

McBeth, Mark K. 1995. "Rural Environmental and Economic Development Attitudes: An Empirical Analysis." *Economic Development Quarterly* 9, no. 1 (February): 39–49.

McBride, Joe. 1991–97. Professor, Department of Landscape Architecture and Environmental Planning, University of California at Berkeley. Personal communication.

———. 1993. Presentation to the Environmental Planning Studio class (LA 205), March, at University of California at Berkeley.

McBride, Joe R., and D. F. Jacobs. 1979. "Urban Forest Structure: A Key to Urban Forest Planning." *California Agriculture* 33:24.

———. 1986. "Resettlement Forest Structure as a Factor in Urban Forest Development." *Urban Ecology* 9:245–66.

McBride, Joe R., William Russell, and Sue Kloss. 1996. "Impact of Human Settlement on Forest Composition and Structure." In *Sierra Nevada Ecosystem Project Final Report to Congress: Status of the Sierra Nevada,* 2:1193–1202. Davis: Center for Water and Wildland Resources, University of California.

McBride, Joe, and Ellen Woodard. 1990. *Analysis of the Condition of Vegetation and Wildlife Habitats on Tahoe Conservancy Lands.* Berkeley: Department of Forestry and Resource Management, University of California.

McCloskey, Michael. 1996a. "The Skeptic: Collaboration Has Its Limits." *High Country News* 28, no. 9 (13 May): 7.

———. 1996b. "The Limits of Collaboration." *Harper's Magazine* (November): 34–36.

McCullough, Dale R., ed. 1996. *Metapopulations and Wildlife Conservation.* Washington, D.C.: Island Press.

McDaniel, Malcolm. 1997. Graduate student, University of California at Berkeley. Personal communication.

McEvoy, Arthur F. 1986. *The Fisherman's Problem.* New York: Cambridge University Press.

McGlashan, M. Nona. 1977. *Give Me a Mountain Meadow: The Life of Charles Fayette McGlashan.* Fresno, Calif.: Valley Publishers.

———, ed. 1986. *From the Desk of Truckee's C. F. McGlashan.* Truckee, Calif.: Truckee-Donner Historical Society.

McHarg, Ian. 1992. *Design with Nature.* Garden City, N.Y.: Natural History Press, 1969. Reprint, New York: John Wiley and Sons.

———. 1996a. *A Quest for Life: An Autobiography.* New York: John Wiley and Sons.

———. 1996b. "In His Own Image." *Pennsylvania Gazette* (March): 38–43.

McHugh, Paul. 1992a. "A Poet on the Land." *San Francisco Examiner* 13 September, "This World" section, p. 8.

———. 1992b. "Bioregionalism: Reinventing the Map." *San Francisco Examiner* 13 September, "This World" section, p. 7.

———. 1996. "Forest Recreation's Growing Impact." *San Francisco Chronicle,* 19 September, p. D8.

McKelvey, Kevin S., and James D. Johnston. 1992. "Historical Perspectives on Forests of the Sierra Nevada and the Transverse Ranges of Southern California: Forest Conditions at the Turn of the Century." In Verner et al. 1992, pp. 225–46.

McKibben, Bill. 1989. *The End of Nature.* New York: Anchor, Doubleday.

———. 1992. *The Age of Missing Information.* New York: Random House.

McKuen, Peter. 1994. Managing Partner, Cook Ranch Partners (Developers of Cinabarr Project in El Dorado County, Calif.). Personal communication.

McMullen, Ralph. 1992–95. Director of Tourism, Town of Mammoth Lakes, Calif. Personal communication.

McNulty, Robert H., Dorothy R. Jacobsen, and R. Leo Penne. 1985. *The Economics of Amenity: A Policy Guide to Urban Economic Development.* Washington, D.C.: Partners for Livable Places.

McPhee, John. 1971. *Encounters with the Archdruid (Narratives about a Conservationist and Three of His Natural Enemies).* New York: Farrar, Straus, Giroux.

———. 1989. *The Control of Nature.* New York: Farrar, Straus, Giroux.

———. 1993. *Assembling California.* New York: Farrar, Straus, Giroux; Noonday Press.

McWilliams, Carey. [1949] 1976. *California: The Great Exception.* Santa Barbara, Calif.: Peregrine Smith

Meadows, Donella H., Dennis L. Meadows, and Jorgen Randers. 1972. *The Limits to Growth.* New York: Universe Books.

———. 1992. *Beyond the Limits: Confronting Global Collapse, Envisioning a Sustainable Future.* Post Mills, Vt.: Chelsea Green.

Medbury, Scot. 1993. "Biological Invasions in the Cismontane Sierra Nevada: Prediction and Regulation." Paper prepared for Prof. Timothy P. Duane, University of California at Berkeley.

Meine, Curt. 1988. *Aldo Leopold: His Life and Work.* Madison: University of Wisconsin Press.

———. 1997. Comments at panel discussion on "Stewardship across Boundaries," at the Society for Conservation Biology conference, June 9, Victoria, B.C.

Menzel, Peter. 1994. *Material World: A Global Family Portrait.* San Francisco: Sierra Club Books.

Merchant, Carolyn. 1980. *The Death of Nature: Women, Ecology, and the Scientific Revolution.* San Francisco: Harper and Row.

———. 1992. *Radical Ecology: The Search for a Livable World.* New York: Routledge.

Messerli, B., and J. D. Ives, eds. 1997. *Mountains of the World: A Global Priority.* New York: Parthenon Publishing.

Meyer, Stephen M. 1992. *Environmentalism and Economic Prosperity: Testing the Environmental Impact Hypothesis.* Cambridge: Massachusetts Institute of Technology, Project on Environmental Politics and Policy.

———. 1993. *Environmentalism and Economic Prosperity: An Update.* Cambridge: Massachusetts Institute of Technology, Project on Environmental Politics and Policy.

Michael, Donald N. 1995. "Barriers and Bridges to Learning in a Turbulent Human Ecology." In Gunderson et al. 1995a, pp. 461–88.

Millar, Constance I. 1996. "The Mammoth-June Ecosystem Management Project, Inyo National Forest." In *Sierra Nevada Ecosystem Project Final Report to Congress: Status of the*

Sierra Nevada, 2:1273–1346. Davis: Center for Water and Wildland Resources, University of California.

Millar, Constance, Michael Barbour, Deborah L. Elliott-Fisk, James R. Shevock, and Wallace B. Woolfenden. 1996. "Significant Natural Areas." In *Sierra Nevada Ecosystem Project Final Report to Congress: Status of the Sierra Nevada,* 2:839–53. Davis: Center for Water and Wildland Resources, University of California.

Miller, Dorothy. 1996. Board Secretary, Nevada Irrigation District. Personal communication, 11 September.

Miller, Sally. 1992–95. Friends of the Inyo, Lee Vining, Calif. Personal communication.

Miller, Thomas. 1994. "Recommended Changes by the Resolution Committee to the Final Draft Nevada County General Plan." Letter to the Board of Supervisors, 15 November.

———. 1994–95. Acting Planning Director, Nevada County Planning Department. Personal communication.

Moline, Jon. 1986. "Aldo Leopold and the Moral Community." *Environmental Ethics* 8 (summer): 99–120. Cited in Des Jardins 1997.

Mollison, Bill. 1988. "Strategies for an Alternative Nation, from *Permaculture: A Designer's Manual.*" In Andruss et al. 1990, pp. 149–54.

Montgomery County. 1992a. *Land Preservation District: Land Development Standards.* Montgomery County, Penn.: Montgomery County Planning Commission.

———. 1992b. *Land Preservation: Old Challenge . . . New Ideas.* Montgomery County, Penn.: Montgomery County Planning Commission.

Montgomery County Planning Commission. 1991. *Land Preservation District: Model Zoning Provisions.* Montgomery County, Penn.: Montgomery County Planning Commission.

Mooers, Judith S. 1978. "Workshops Underway on New General Plan." *Grass Valley–Nevada City Union,* 2 November, p. 1.

———. 1980. "Brooks Seeks to Void General Plan's Effect." *Grass Valley–Nevada City Union,* 7 March, p. 1.

———. 1995a. "At Last, a General Plan." *Grass Valley–Nevada City Union,* 14 July, p. B1.

———. 1995b. "Denney to Enter Supervisor Race." *Grass Valley–Nevada City Union,* 14 October, p. A1.

———. 1995c. "GOP Backs Foster for Supervisor." *Grass Valley–Nevada City Union,* 18 August, p. 1.

———. 1995d. "Residents Make Final General Plan Requests." *Grass Valley–Nevada City Union,* 13 October, p. A1.

———. 1995e. "Foster Seated as Supervisor." *Grass Valley–Nevada City Union,* 17 October, p. A1.

———. 1995f. "Plan EIR Hearings Scheduled." *Grass Valley–Nevada City Union,* 6 July, p. A1.

———. 1995g. "Supervisors Reject Appeal of EIR." *Grass Valley–Nevada City Union,* 16 August, p. A1.

———. 1996. "Richter Chooses Foster as District 'Woman of Year.'" *Grass Valley–Nevada City Union,* 15 March, p. A3.

Moore, Ian. 1997. "The San Joaquin River Conservancy: An Application of the California Conservancy Model to River Corridor Planning." Master's thesis, Department of Landscape Architecture, University of California at Berkeley.

Moss, Elaine, ed. [Natural Resources Defense Council, Inc.]. 1977. *Land Use Controls in the United States: A Handbook on the Legal Rights of Citizens.* New York: Dial Press, James Wade.

Moss, Laurence A. G. 1987. *Santa Fe, New Mexico, Post-industrial Culture Based Town: Myth or Model?* Report prepared for the Department of Economic Development and Trade, Government of Alberta, Edmonton. Santa Fe, N.M.: International Cultural Resources Institute.

Moyle, Peter B. 1996a. "Status of Aquatic Habitat Types." In *Sierra Nevada Ecosystem Project Final Report to Congress: Status of the Sierra Nevada*, 2:945–52. Davis: Center for Water and Wildland Resources, University of California.

———. 1996b. "Potential Aquatic Diversity Management Areas." In *Sierra Nevada Ecosystem Project Final Report to Congress: Status of the Sierra Nevada*, 2:1493–1501. Davis: Center for Water and Wildland Resources, University of California.

Moyle, Peter B., and Joseph J. Cech Jr. 1996. *Fishes: An Introduction to Ichthyology*. Upper Saddle River, N.J.: Prentice Hall.

Moyle, Peter B., Ronald M. Yoshiyama, and Roland A. Knapp. 1996. "Status of Fish and Fisheries." In *Sierra Nevada Ecosystem Project Final Report to Congress: Status of the Sierra Nevada*, 2:953–74. Davis: Center for Water and Wildland Resources, University of California.

Mozingo, Louise. 1997. "The Aesthetics of Ecological Design: Seeing Science as Culture." *Landscape Journal* 16 (1): 46–59.

Mueller, Tara L. 1994. *Guide to the Federal and California Endangered Species Laws*. Sacramento: Planning and Conservation League Foundation.

———. 1995. *January, 1995 Supplement. Guide to the Federal and California Endangered Species Laws*. Sacramento: Planning and Conservation League Foundation.

Muir, John. 1988. *The Yosemite*. San Francisco: Sierra Club Books.

Muller, Brian. 1994–97. Graduate student, University of California at Berkeley. Personal communication.

Mumford, Lewis. 1938. *The Culture of Cities*. New York: Harcourt, Brace, and Co.

Nabhan, Gary Paul, and Stephen Trimble. 1994. *The Geography of Childhood: Why Children Need Wild Places*. Boston: Beacon Press.

Nadeau, Remi A. 1970. *Ghost Towns and Mining Camps of California*. Los Angeles: Ward Ritchie Press.

Naden, Corinne J., and Rose Blue. 1992. *John Muir, Saving the Wilderness*. Brookfield, Conn.: Millbrook Press.

Naess, Arne. 1989. *Ecology, Community and Lifestyle*. Trans. and ed. by David Rothenberg. Cambridge: Cambridge University Press.

———. 1995a. "The Deep Ecological Movement." In Sessions 1995, pp. 64–84.

———. 1995b. "The Deep Ecology Eight Points Revisited." In Sessions 1995, pp. 213–21.

———. 1995c. "The Shallow and the Deep, Long-Range Ecology Movements: A Summary." In Sessions 1995, pp. 141–50.

Nash, James. 1997a. "Survival Means Adapt: What Hasn't Killed Downtown Business Has Made It Stronger." *Grass Valley–Nevada City Union*, 25 April, p. A1.

———. 1997b. "Nevada City Praised for Saving Its History." *Grass Valley–Nevada City Union*, 10 July, p. A1.

———. 1997c. "Report Raps Growth Planning." *Grass Valley–Nevada City Union*, 10 July, p. A1.

———. 1997d. "Group Aims to Preserve Hell's Half Acre Wildland." *Grass Valley–Nevada City Union*, 18 March, p. A1.

———. 1997e. "Numbers Show Business Slump: Poor County Image Blamed." *Grass Valley–Nevada City Union*, 3 February, p. A1.

———. 1997f. "December Unemployment Rate Lowest Since '90." *Grass Valley–Nevada City Union*, 4 February, p. A1.

————. 1997g. "County's Population Increases to 89,016." *Grass Valley–Nevada City Union,* 21 March, p. A1.

Nash, Roderick Frazier. 1967. *Wilderness and the American Mind.* New Haven, Conn.: Yale University Press.

————. 1989. *The Rights of Nature: A History of Environmental Ethics.* Madison: University of Wisconsin Press.

————, ed. 1990. *American Environmentalism: Readings in Conservation History.* 3rd ed. New York: McGraw-Hill.

National Public Radio. 1995. "Pulse of the Planet," January 7.

————. 1996. "California Voters Consider Mountain Lion Initiative." Reported by David Baron and broadcast on "All Things Considered" on 25 March.

Natural Resources Defense Council. 1991. *Appeal of the Tahoe National Forest Land Management Plan.* San Francisco: Natural Resources Defense Council.

———— (on behalf of 111 groups and individuals). 1994. *Petition with Request for Stay to the Chief of the USDA Forest Service and the Regional Forester of the Pacific Southwest Region for Amendments to the Regional Guide and Forest Plans for Sensitive Furbearers and Other Old Growth Associated Wildlife in the Sierra Nevada National Forests.* February 10.

Nelson, Arthur C. 1992. "Characterizing Exurbia." *Journal of Planning Literature* 6, no. 4 (May): 350–68.

————. 1998. "Components of Housing Price Increases Attributable to Urban Containment." Presentation to the Lincoln Institute for Land Policy seminar series, 15 April, Institute of Urban and Regional Development, University of California at Berkeley.

Nelson, Arthur C., and Kenneth J. Dueker. 1990. "The Exurbanization of America and Its Planning Policy Implications." *Journal of Planning Education and Research* 9 (2): 91–100.

Nelson, Gaylord. 1996. Foreword. In Yaffee et al. 1996.

Nevada City, City of. 1985. *Nevada City General Plan.* Prepared by Hall, Goodhue, Haisley, and Barker (urban planning consultants) and Lord and Associates (real estate economics consultants). Nevada City, Calif.: City of Nevada City.

Nevada County Business Association and California Forestry Association. 1993. "The Sierra Economy: Sustainable Development in Harmony with Nature." Program at Sierra Economic Summit, 16–17 June, Sacramento.

Nevada County Planning Commission. 1993. *Nevada County Planning Commission Draft Nevada County General Plan.* Housing element, p. II-127. Nevada City, Calif.: Nevada County Planning Commission.

Nevada County Planning Department. 1967. *Nevada County General Plan 1990.* Nevada City, Calif.: Nevada County Planning Department.

————. 1980. *Nevada County General Plan.* Nevada City, Calif.: Nevada County Planning Department.

————. 1994a. *Final Draft General Plan—Additional Population and Parcels.* Handout at October 11 Resolution Committee meeting. Nevada City, Calif.: Nevada County Planning Department.

————. 1994b. *Resolution Committee Notes for October 11* (staff report). Nevada City, Calif.: Nevada County Planning Department.

————. 1994c. *Final Draft Nevada County General Plan.* Nevada City, Calif.: Nevada County Planning Department.

————. 1996. *Nevada County General Plan Population Buildout* (staff report). Nevada City, Calif.: Nevada County Planning Department.

Nevada County Transportation Commission. 1995. *Regional Transportation Plan.* Nevada City, Calif.: Nevada County Transportation Commission.

Nevada Irrigation District. 1994–95. Staff, Water Resources Supply Planning, Nevada Irrigation District, Grass Valley, Calif. Personal communication.

Newmark, William Dubois. 1986. "Mammalian Richness, Colonization, and Extinction in Western North American National Parks." Ph.D. diss., University of Michigan. Cited in Quammen 1996.

———. 1987. "A Land-Bridge Island Perspective on Mammalian Extinctions in Western North American Parks," *Nature* 325, no. 6103 (29 January): 430–32.

———. 1995. "Extinction of Mammal Populations in Western North American National Parks," *Conservation Biology* 9 (3): 512–26.

New York Times. 1993. "Eastward, Ho! The Great Move Reverses," 30 May, p. A1.

———. 1996. "The Environmental Counterattack," 5 February, p. A10.

———. 1997. "Extinct Species in America: An Update" (Map and tables), 25 February, p. B11.

Nicholson, Les. 1995. Operations and Planning Manager, Nevada Irrigation District, Grass Valley, Calif. Personal communication.

Niebanck, Paul L. 1984. "Dilemmas in Growth Management." *Journal of the American Planning Association* 50 (4): 403–5.

Niedorf, Shawn. 1995. "Van Zant In; Denney Out." *Grass Valley–Nevada City Union,* 27 October, p. A1.

———. 1996a. "Council in Nevada City Won't Reverse Stand on South Yuba." *Grass Valley–Nevada City Union,* 13 August, p. A1.

———. 1996b. "NC May Streamline Rules." *Grass Valley–Nevada City Union,* 13 August, p. A1.

———. 1996c. "Planners in NC Quit Posts" *Grass Valley–Nevada City Union,* 13 August, p. A1.

———. 1996d. "GV Building Fees May Jump" *Grass Valley–Nevada City Union,* 2 April, p. A1.

———. 1996e. "King Holiday Largely Ignored in County: Locals Express Ambivalence." *Grass Valley–Nevada City Union,* 16 January, p. A3.

Nolte, Carl. 1996. "Big Decline in Yosemite Bighorn Sheep: Rare Animals Vanishing from Sierra." *San Francisco Chronicle,* 28 May, p. A11.

Norgaard, Richard B. 1994. *Development Betrayed: The End of Progress and a Coevolutionary Revisioning of the Future.* New York: Routledge.

———. 1995. "Intergenerational Commons, Globalization, Economism, and Unsustainable Development," *Advances in Human Ecology* 4:141–71.

Norman, Pat. 1982. Planner, Nevada County Planning Department. Personal communication.

———. 1994–95. Senior Planner, Nevada County Planning Department. Personal communication.

Norris, Frank. 1901. *The Octopus, a Story of California.* London: Grant Richards.

North, Douglas C. 1990. *Institutions, Institutional Change, and Economic Performance.* New York: Cambridge University Press.

Norton, Bryan G. 1991. *Toward Unity among Environmentalists.* New York: Oxford University Press.

———. 1992. "A New Paradigm for Ecosystem Management." In Costanza et al. 1992.

———. 1995. "Why I Am Not a Nonanthropocentrist: Callicott and the Failure of Monistic Inherentism." *Environmental Ethics* 17 (4): 341–58.

Noss, Reed F. 1991. "Landscape Connectivity: Different Functions at Different Scales." In Hudson 1991.

———. 1992. *A Preliminary Biodiversity Conservation Plan for the Oregon Coast Range: A Report to the Coast Range Association.* Newport, Ore: Coast Range Association.

Oberholtzer, Laurie. 1993–96. City Council Member, Nevada City, Calif. Personal communication.

———. 1997–98. Planning Commissioner, Nevada City, Calif. Personal communication.

Oelschlaeger, Max. 1991. *The Idea of Wilderness.* New Haven, Conn.: Yale University Press.

Office of Planning and Research. 1987. *General Plan Guidelines.* Sacramento: Governor's Office of Planning and Research.

Office of Technology Assessment. 1991. *Rural America at the Crossroads: Networking for the Future.* OTA-TCT-471. Washington, D.C.: Congressional Office of Technology Assessment.

O'Leary Morgan, Kathleen, Scott Morgan, and Neal Quitno, eds. 1994. *State Rankings 1994.* Lawrence, Kans.: Morgan Quitno Corporation.

Olmsted Brothers and Bartholomew and Associates. 1930. "Parks, Playgrounds, and Beaches for the Los Angeles Region." Cited in Mike Davis 1996.

Olshansky, Robert B. 1996. "The California Environmental Quality Act and Local Planning." *Journal of the American Planning Association* 62 (3): 313–30.

Olson, Mancur, Jr. 1965. *The Logic of Collective Action: Public Goods and the Theory of the Group.* Cambridge: Harvard University Press.

O'Neill, R. V., D. L. DeAngelis, J. B. Waide, and T. F. H. Allen. 1986. *A Hierarchical Concept of the Ecosystem.* Princeton, N.J.: Princeton University Press.

Orr, David. 1992. *Ecological Literacy: Education and the Transition to a Post-Modern World.* Albany: State University of New York Press.

———. 1994. *Earth in Mind: On Education, Environment, and the Human Prospect.* Washington, D.C.: Island Press.

Ortolano, Leonard. 1984. *Environmental Planning and Decision Making.* New York: John Wiley and Sons.

———. 1997. *Environmental Regulation and Impact Assessment.* New York: John Wiley and Sons.

Ostrom, Elinor. 1990. *Governing the Commons: The Evolution of Institutions for Collective Action.* New York: Cambridge University Press.

O'Toole, Randal. 1988. *Reforming the Forest Service.* Washington, D.C.: Island Press.

———. 1997. "The Forest Service Chief and the End of the U.S.D.A. Forest Service." *Subsidies Anonymous,* no. 17. Distributed via electronic mail.

Owens, Peter. 1991–95. Graduate student, University of California at Berkeley. Personal communication.

Pace, Felice. 1997. Letter from the Klamath Forest Alliance (Etna, Calif.) to Jonathan Kusel of Forest Community Research (Taylorsville, Calif.), 13 May. In Blumberg 1997b.

Pacific Gas and Electric Company. 1994. Staff in Auburn, Jackson, and San Francisco. Personal communication.

Paddock, Richard. 1991. "Attacks on Oakland Fire Department Mount." *Los Angeles Times,* 1 November, p. A3.

Page, R. W., P. W. Anttila, K. L. Johnson, and M. J. Pierce. 1984. *Ground-Water Conditions and Well Yields in Fractured Rocks, Southwestern Nevada County, California.* Water Resources Investigations Report 83–4262. Prepared in cooperation with Nevada County and Nevada Irrigation District. Sacramento: U.S. Geological Survey.

Palmer, Tim. 1988. *The Sierra Nevada: A Mountain Journey.* Washington, D.C.: Island Press.

———. 1993. *California's Threatened Environment: Restoring the Dream.* Washington, D.C.: Island Press.

Parson, Edward A., and William C. Clarke. 1995. "Sustainable Development as Social Learning: Theoretical Perspectives and Practical Challenges for the Design of a Research Program." In Gunderson et al. 1995a, pp. 428–60.

Parsons, James J. 1985. "On 'Bioregionalism' and 'Watershed Consciousness.'" *The Professional Geographer* 37, no. 1 (February): 1–6.

Partos, Andrew. 1993. "The Donner Trail Village Farm: An Alternative Development Proposal for the Ernie Bierwagen Property, Chicago Park, Nevada County, California." Paper prepared for Prof. Timothy P. Duane, University of California at Berkeley.

Paul, Rodman. 1947. *California Gold: The Beginning of Mines in the Far West.* Lincoln: University of Nebraska Press.

Pearce, David W., and R. Kerry Turner. 1990. *Economics of Natural Resources and the Environment.* New York: Harvester Wheatsheaf.

Peck, Sheila. 1993. *Landscape Conservation Planning: Preserving Ecosystems in Open Space Networks.* Berkeley: Integrated Hardwood Range Management Program, Division of Agriculture and Natural Resources, University of California.

———. 1998. *Planning for Biodiversity: Issues and Examples.* Washington, D.C.: Island Press.

Peiper, Susan. 1978. "Election Day Draws Near—Over \$103,000 Spent." *Grass Valley–Nevada City Union,* 1 November, p. 1.

Pendall, Rolf. 1997. "Property Rights and Property Culture: State Property-Rights Bills and the Districts Whose Legislators Support Them." Paper presented to the Association of Collegiate Schools of Planning, 6–9 November, Ft. Lauderdale, Fla.

———. 1998. "Problems and Prospects in Local Environmental Assessment: Lessons from the United States." *Journal of Environmental Planning and Management* 41 (1): 5–23.

Peninsula Conservation Center. 1978–90. Newspaper clippings files. Palo Alto, Calif.

Pimm, Stuart L. 1986. "Community Structure and Stability." In Soule 1986, pp. 309–29.

Pinchot, Gifford. 1967. *The Fight for Conservation.* Seattle: University of Washington Press. Cited in Evernden 1992.

Pister, Edwin P. 1987. "A Pilgrim's Progress from Group A to Group B." In Callicott 1987, pp. 221–32.

———. 1993. "Species in a Bucket." *Natural History* 102 (1): 14.

Pivo, Gary. 1988. *Preserving Ruralness through Cluster Housing: Problem or Opportunity?* Seattle: Washington State Department of Natural Resources and Department of Urban Design and Planning, College of Architecture and Planning, University of Washington.

———. 1992. Associate Professor, University of Washington. Personal communication, May.

Pivo, Gary, Robert Small, and Charles R. Wolfe. 1990. "Rural Cluster Zoning: Survey and Guidelines." *Land Use Law* (September): 3–10.

Platt, Rutherford H. 1996. *Land Use and Society: Geography, Law, and Public Policy.* New York: McGraw-Hill, 1991. Reprint, Washington, D.C.: Island Press.

Platt, Rutherford H., Rowan A. Rowntree, and Pamela C. Muick, eds. 1994. *The Ecological City: Preserving and Restoring Urban Biodiversity.* Amherst: University of Massachusetts Press.

Policy Implementation Planning Team (PIP) to the Steering Committee for the California Spotted Owl Assessment. 1994. *Conserving the California Spotted Owl: Impacts of Interim Policies and Implications for the Long Term.* Report 33. Davis: Wildland Resources Center, Division of Agriculture and Natural Resources, University of California at Davis.

Pollan, Michael. 1991. *Second Nature: A Gardener's Education.* New York: Dell.

Popper, Frank J. 1984. "Rural Land Use Policies and Rural Poverty." *Journal of the American Planning Association* 50 (3): 326–34.

———. 1988. "Understanding American Land Use Regulation since 1970: A Revisionist Interpretation." *Journal of the American Planning Association* 54 (2): 291–301.

———. 1992. "Thinking Globally, Acting Regionally." *Technology Review* 95 (3): 47–53.

———. 1993. "Rethinking Regional Planning." *Society* 30 (6): 46–54.

Porter, Douglas R. 1997. *Managing Growth in America's Communities.* Washington, D.C.: Island Press.

Powell, John Wesley. 1878. *Report on the Lands of the Arid Regions.* Washington, D.C.: U.S. Government.

Power, Thomas Michael. 1988. *The Economic Pursuit of Quality.* Armonk, N.Y.: M. E. Sharpe.

———. 1994. "Extraction and the Environment: The Economic Battle to Control Our Natural Landscapes." Draft manuscript, November, Missoula, Mont.

———. 1996a. *Lost Landscapes and Failed Economies: The Search for a Value of Place.* Washington, D.C.: Island Press.

———, ed. 1996b. *Economic Well-Being and Environmental Protection in the Pacific Northwest.* Missoula, Mont.: Economics Department, University of Montana.

———. 1996c. "The Wealth of Nature: Environmental Quality, Not Mining, Logging, or Ranching, Is Driving Local Economic Development in the West." *Issues in Science and Technology* 12 (3): 48.

Press, Daniel. 1994. *Democratic Dilemmas: Trees and Toxics in the American West.* Durham, N.C.: Duke University Press.

Price, Martin F., Laurence A. G. Moss, and Peter W. Williams. 1997. "Tourism and Amenity Migration." In Messerli and Ives 1997, 249–80.

Prudential/Mammoth Sierra Properties Collection. 1991. *Fine Properties for Sale in the Mammoth Lakes Area.* Summer issue, p. 18. Mammoth Lakes, Calif.: Prudential/Mammoth Sierra Properties Collection.

Pryne, Eric. 1995. "Figuring Price for Priceless Assets Is No Idle Exercise." *Seattle Times,* 9 April, p. B1.

Public Employees for Environmental Responsibility. 1996. *Business as Usual: A Case Study of Environmental and Fiscal Malpractice on the Eldorado National Forest.* PEER White Paper No. 5. Washington, D.C.: Public Employees for Environmental Responsibility.

Purdum, Todd S. 1997. "Lake Tahoe's Legendary Clarity Is Threatened." *New York Times,* 25 July, p. A12.

Putnam, Robert D., with Robert Leonardi, and Raffaella Y. Nanetti. 1993. *Making Democracy Work: Civic Traditions in Modern Italy.* Princeton, N.J.: Princeton University Press.

Quammen, David, 1996. *The Song of the Dodo: Island Biogeography in an Age of Extinctions.* London: Hutchinson.

Quillen, Ed. 1993. "Now That Denver Has Abdicated . . . Who Will Coordinate and Inspire the West?" *High Country News* 25, no. 9 (3 May): 1.

Quincy Library Group. 1993. *Community Stability Proposal.* Quincy, Calif.: Quincy Library Group.

Quinlan, Vess. 1993. "What Ranchers Need to Do Now That the World Has Come Calling." *High Country News* 25, no. 6 (5 April): 18.

Rasker, Ray. 1993. "Rural Development, Conservation, and Public Policy in the Greater Yellowstone Ecosystem." *Society and Natural Resources* (6): 109–126.

————. 1994. "A New Look at Old Vistas: The Economic Role of Environmental Quality in Western Public Lands." *University of Colorado Law Review* 65 (2): 369–99.

Rasker, Ray, and Dennis Glick. 1994. "Footloose Entrepreneurs: Pioneers of the New West?" *Illahee* 10 (1): 34–43.

Rasker, Ray, J. Johnson, and V. York. 1994. *Measuring Change in Rural Communities: A Workbook for Determining Demographic, Economic and Fiscal Trends*. Washington, D.C.: Wilderness Society. Cited in Wilderness Society 1997.

Rasker, Ray, Norma Tirrell, and Deanne Kloepfer. 1992. *The Wealth of Nature: New Economic Realities in the Yellowstone Region*. Washington, D.C.: Wilderness Society.

Ratcliffe, John, and Judith. 1996. Brokers-Realtors, Red Oak Realty, Berkeley, Calif. Personal communication.

Ray, Mike. 1978. "NUHS Miners Top Placer, Win SFL Crown." *Grass Valley–Nevada City Union,* 4 November.

Raymond, Israel Ward. 1948. "If We Can Obtain This Grant. . . ." In Reid 1983, pp. 314–16.

Raymond, Leigh. 1996. "The Ethics of Compensation: Takings, Utility, and Justice." *Ecology Law Quarterly* 23 (3): 577–622.

Read, Ben. 1993. "Will Jackson Save Itself?" *High Country News* 25, no. 6 (5 April): 17.

Reaka-Kudla, Marjorie L., Don E. Wilson, and Edward O. Wilson., eds. 1997. *Biodiversity II: Understanding and Protecting Our Biological Resources*. Washington, D.C.: Joseph Henry Press.

Redman, Anthony D. 1992. "Making Rural Clustering Work." Paper presented to the American Planning Association, 11–14 May, Washington, D.C.

Reeves, Michael. 1995. *Nevada County Economic Base Analysis: 1995 Edition*. Auburn, Calif.: Sierra Economic Development District.

Regan, Tom, and Peter Singer, eds. 1976. *Animal Rights and Human Obligation*. Englewood Cliffs, N.J.: Prentice-Hall.

Register, Richard. 1987. *Ecocity Berkeley: Building Cities for a Healthy Future*. Berkeley, Calif.: North Atlantic Books.

Reid, Robert Leonard, ed. 1983. *A Treasury of the Sierra Nevada*. Berkeley, Calif.: Wilderness Press.

Reid, W. J. 1992. *The United States Needs a National Biodiversity Policy*. Issues and Ideas series. Washington, D.C.: World Resources Institute. Cited in Shaffer 1992b.

Reinhold, Robert. 1991. "Questions Rise with Fire Toll in Oakland Hills: Officials' Response and Urban Sprawl Cited." *New York Times,* 23 October, p. A9.

Reisner, Marc. 1986. *Cadillac Desert: The American West and Its Disappearing Water*. New York: Viking.

Repetto, Robert. 1992. "Earth in Balance Sheet: Incorporating Natural Resources in National Income Accounts." *Environment* 34 (7): 12–20.

Richardson, David. 1992–94. Water Resources Manager, CH2MHILL, Emeryville, Calif. Personal communication.

Richardson, H. W. 1985. "Input-Output and Economic Base Multipliers: Looking Backward and Forward." *Journal of Regional Science* 35 (4): 607–71. Cited in Wilderness Society 1997.

Richardson, Harry Ward, and Peter Gordon. 1989. "Counting Nonwork Trips: The Missing Link in Transportation, Land Use, and Urban Policy." *Urban Land* 48 (9).

Riddle, Lyn. 1996. "The Visionary Hilton Head Pioneer: His Sea Pines Used Covenants to Dictate Neighborhood Rules." *New York Times,* 5 May, p. 27.

Riebsame, William E., and James J. Robb. eds. 1997. *Atlas of the New West: Portrait of a Changing Region.* Prepared by the Center of the American West, University of Colorado, Boulder. New York: W. W. Norton and Company.

Riley, Michael. 1993. "Byte by Byte and Fax by Fax, the West Is Being Transformed." *High Country News* 25, no. 6 (5 April): 12.

Ring, Ray. 1995. "The New West's Servant Economy." *High Country News* 27, no. 7 (17 April): 1.

Ringholz, Raye C. 1992. *Little Town Blues: Voices from the Changing West.* Salt Lake City: Peregrine Smith Books.

———. 1996. *Paradise Paved: The Challenge of Growth in the New West.* Salt Lake City: University of Utah Press.

Rivas, Pierre. 1993–95. Senior Planner, Community Development Department, El Dorado County, Calif. Personal communication.

Roberts, William. 1997. Planning Director, City of Grass Valley, Calif. Personal communication, January.

Robertson, David. 1984. *West of Eden: A History of the Art and Literature of Yosemite.* Berkeley, Calif.: Wilderness Press; Yosemite National Park, Calif.: Yosemite Natural History Association.

Roddewig, Richard J., and Cheryl A. Inghram. 1987. *Transferable Development Rights Programs: TDRs and the Real Estate Marketplace.* Chicago: American Planning Association.

Rodriguez, Matt. 1995. California Attorney General's Office. Presentation to the Environmental Law and Resource Management class (IDS 233), October, University of California at Berkeley.

Rohlf, Daniel J. 1991. "Six Biological Reasons Why the Endangered Species Act Doesn't Work—And What to Do About It." *Conservation Biology* 5, no. 3 (September): 273–82.

Rose, Carol M. 1994. *Property and Persuasion: Essays on the History, Theory, and Rhetoric of Ownership.* Boulder, Colo.: Westview Press.

Rose, Gene. 1987. *High Odyssey.* Fresno, Calif.: Panorama West Publishing.

Rosen, Martin J. 1994. "Election Was Not a Vote against Environmental Protection." *Christian Science Monitor* (21 December): 19.

Rudel, Thomas K. 1989. *Situations and Strategies in American Land-Use Planning.* New York: Cambridge University Press.

Rural Quality Coalition of Nevada County. n.d. *County at a Crossroads: Suburban vs. Rural?* Nevada City, Calif.: Rural Quality Coalition of Nevada County.

Ruth, Larry. 1993–97. Lecturer, Department of Environmental Science, Policy and Management, University of California at Berkeley. Personal communication.

Rymber, Russ. 1996. "Back to the Future: Disney Reinvents the Company Town." *Harper's* (October): 65–78.

Sabatier, P. A., J. Loomis, and C. McCarthy. 1995. "Hierarchical Controls, Professional Norms, Local Constituencies, and Budget Maximization—An Analysis of United States Forest Service Planning Decisions." *American Journal of Political Science* 39 (1): 204–42.

———. 1996. "Policy Attitudes and Decisions within the Forest Service—Is There a Connection?" *Journal of Forestry* 94 (1): 42–46.

Sage, Larry. 1995. Sanitarian, Nevada County Environmental Health Department. Personal communication.

Sager, Tore. 1994. *Communicative Planning Theory.* Aldershot, England: Avebury. Cited in Innes 1996.

Sagoff, Mark. 1988. *The Economy of the Earth: Philosophy, Law, and the Environment.* New York: Cambridge University Press.

Sale, Kirkpatrick. 1980. *Human Scale.* New York: Coward, McCann, and Geoghegan.

———. 1991. *Dwellers in the Land: The Bioregional Vision.* San Francisco: Sierra Club Books, 1985. Reprint, Santa Cruz, Calif.: New Society Publishers.

———. 1995. *Rebels against the Future: The Luddites and Their War on the Industrial Revolution.* London: Quartet Books.

Salvesen, David, and Douglas Porter. 1996. "The Ungrateful Dead." *Planning* (May): 8–11.

Salwasser, Hal. 1997. Presentation to the Main Forestry Lecture Seminar, 4 February, at University of California at Berkeley.

Sanchez, Thomas W., and Arthur C. Nelson. 1994. *Exurban and Suburban Residents: A Departure from Traditional Location Theory?* Washington, D. C: Fannie Mae.

Sandel, Michael. 1984. "The Procedural Republic and the Unencumbered Self." *Political Theory* 12 (February): 81–96. Cited in Kemmis 1990.

Sanders, Dale, and Michael Baefsky. 1996. *Improved Methods to Evaluate the Impact of Subdivisions on Wildlife in Oak-Dominated Woodlands in California* (draft). Berkeley, California: Integrated Hardwood Range Management Program, University of California.

San Francisco Chronicle. 1996. "U.S. Forest Service Chief to Resign from Post," 11 October, p. A8.

———. 1997a. "Forest Service Vision Planted by New Chief," 7 January, p. A2.

———. 1997b. "Forest Service Lost Money on Logging, Report Says," 19 February, p. A5.

———. 1997c. "House Oks Plan to Increase Logging in Sierra," 10 July, p. A11

———. 1997d. "Who Should Determine the Fate of a Forest?" 15 June, p. 8.

———. 1997e. "Disease, Weather Claim Half of Yellowstone Bison," 15 March, p. A4.

———. 1998. "Growth Battles Prompt Lawsuits: Neither Side in El Dorado County Will Compromise." 15 May, p. D8.

San Francisco Examiner. 1997. "Serrano Wins Award," 16 February, p. E5.

Sapsis, David, Berni Bahro, James Spero, John Gabriel, Russell Jones, and Gregory Greenwood. 1996. "An Assessment of Current Risks, Fuels, and Potential Fire Behavior in the Sierra Nevada." In *Sierra Nevada Ecosystem Project Final Report to Congress: Status of the Sierra Nevada,* 3:759–86. Davis: Center for Water and Wildland Resources, University of California.

Sargent, Frederic O., Paul Lusk, Jose A. Rivera, and Maria Varela. 1991. *Rural Environmental Planning for Sustainable Communities.* Washington, D.C.: Island Press.

Sauer, Peter. 1992. *Finding Home: Writing on Nature and Culture from Orion Magazine.* Boston: Beacon Press.

Sax, Joseph L. 1971. "Takings, Private Property, and Public Rights." *Yale Law Journal* 81 (2): 149–86.

———. 1980a. *Mountains without Handrails: Reflections on the National Parks.* Ann Arbor: University of Michigan Press.

———. 1980b. "Liberating the Public Trust Doctrine from Its Historical Shackles." *U.C. Davis Law Review* 14:185.

———. 1991. "Ecosystems and Property Rights in Greater Yellowstone: The Legal System in Transition." In Keiter and Boyce 1991, pp. 77–86.

———. 1996a. "Takings Legislation: Where It Stands and What Is Next." *Ecology Law Quarterly* 23, no. 3 (autumn): 509–20.

———. 1996b. Presentation on Endangered Species Act reform proposals, 26 April, at University of California at Berkeley.

Saxenian, Annalee. 1994. *Regional Advantage: Culture and Competition in Silicon Valley and Route 128.* Cambridge: Harvard University Press.

Schiffman, Irving. 1989. *Alternative Techniques for Managing Growth.* Berkeley: Institute for Governmental Studies, University of California.

Schlesinger, Arthur Meier. 1978. *Robert Kennedy and His Times.* New York: Ballantine Books.

Schoch, Deborah. 1998. "Future Debated for Vast Piece of Open Space." *Los Angeles Times,* 12 May, p. A3.

Schoenherr, Allan A. 1992. *A Natural History of California.* Berkeley and Los Angeles: University of California Press.

Schrag, Peter. 1998. *Paradise Lost: California's Experience, America's Future.* New York: New Press.

Schuyler, John. 1993–95. Forest Planner, Inyo National Forest, Bishop, Calif. Personal communication.

Schwartz, Peter. 1991. *The Art of the Long View: Planning for the Future in an Uncertain World.* New York: Doubleday.

Scott, Allen J., and Edward W. Soja. 1996. *The City: Los Angeles and Urban Theory at the End of the Twentieth Century.* Berkeley and Los Angeles: University of California Press.

Scott, Edward B. 1957. *The Saga of Lake Tahoe.* Vol. 1. 14th ed. Pebble Beach, Calif.: Sierra-Tahoe Publishing.

Scott, J. Michael, Blair Csuti, and Steven Caicco. 1991. "Gap Analysis: Assessing Protection Needs." In Hudson 1991, pp. 3–14.

Searle, John. 1995. *The Construction of Social Reality.* New York: Free Press.

Secor, R. J. 1992. *The High Sierra: Peaks, Passes, and Trails.* Seattle: Mountaineers.

Seelye, Katherine Q. 1997. "Future U.S.: Grayer and More Hispanic," *New York Times,* 27 March, p. A18.

Sendzimir, Jan, and C. S. Holling. 1995. "Animal Eco-Assays of Landscape Structure: Cross-Biome Comparisons of Boreal Forest, Temperate Forest, Wet Savanna, and Tropical Forests." Paper presented to the International Association of Landscape Architecture, April, Minneapolis, Minn.

Serrano El Dorado. 1996. "Serrano El Dorado: The Most Eagerly Awaited New Community in California!" (advertisement). *San Francisco Focus* (May): 9.

Sessions, George. 1996. Comments at a public forum on the Auburn Dam, 21 April, Grass Valley, Calif. Also broadcast on KVMR-FM.

———, ed. 1995. *Deep Ecology for the 21st Century.* Boston: Shambala.

Sexton, Richard. 1995. *Parallel Utopias: The Quest for Community: Sea Ranch, California, Seaside, Florida.* San Francisco: Chronicle Books.

Shaffer, Mark L. 1978. "Determining Minimum Viable Population Sizes: A Case Study of the Grizzly Bear." Ph.D. diss., Duke University, Durham, N.C.

———. 1992a. *Keeping the Grizzly Bear in the American West: A Strategy for Real Recovery.* Washington D.C.: Wilderness Society.

———. 1992b. *Beyond the Endangered Species Act: Conservation in the 21st Century.* Washington, D.C.: Wilderness Society.

———. 1994. *Lifelands.* Washington, D.C.: Wilderness Society.

Shannon, Margaret, and K. Norman Johnson. 1994. "Lessons from FEMAT." *Journal of Forestry* 92 (4): 6.

Shevock, James R. 1996. "Status of Rare and Endemic Plants." In *Sierra Nevada Ecosystem Project Final Report to Congress: Status of the Sierra Nevada,* 2:691–707. Davis: Center for Water and Wildland Resources, University of California.

Shigley, Paul. 1995a. "GV Settles Dispute with Sewer Plan Contractor: Unforeseen Problems Ran Up Expenses." *Grass Valley–Nevada City Union,* 2 March, p. B1.

———. 1995b. "GV Sewer Expansion Sought." *Grass Valley–Nevada City Union,* 6 June, p. A1.

Shoup, Donald C. 1997. "The Pedigree of a Statistic." *Access* no. 11 (fall): 41.

Sibley, George. 1996. "Glen Canyon: Using a Dam to Heal a River," *High Country News* 28, no. 13 (22 July): 1.

Sichel, Werner, and Peter Eckstein. 1977. *Basic Economic Concepts: Microeconomics and Macroeconomics.* 2^{d} ed. Chicago: Rand McNally Publishing.

Sierra Business Council. 1996. *Sierra Wealth Index: Understanding and Tracking Our Region's Wealth.* Truckee, Calif.: Sierra Business Council.

———. 1997. *Planning for Prosperity: Building Successful Communities in the Sierra Nevada.* Truckee, Calif.: Sierra Business Council.

Sierra Communities Council. 1993. Materials distributed at Sierra Economic Summit, June, Sacramento.

Sierra Nevada Alliance. 1997. "The Future of the Sierra Foothills." *Sierra News* 1, no. 1 (March): 1.

———. 1998. "El Dorado Activists Send a Wake-Up Call." *Sierra News* 2, no. 2 (May): 1.

Sierra Nevada Ecosystem Project. 1994. *Progress Report.* Davis: Center for Water and Wildland Resources, University of California.

———. 1996. *Sierra Nevada Ecosystem Project Final Report to Congress: Status of the Sierra Nevada.* 3 vols. Davis: Center for Water and Wildland Resources, University of California.

Simon, Julian L. 1981. *The Ultimate Resource.* Princeton, N.J.: Princeton University Press.

Skinner, Mike. 1997. Ecosystem Management Staff, Region 5, U.S. Forest Service, San Francisco. Personal communication, March.

Slack, Gordy. 1994. "Emerald Cities: Visions or Hallucinations?" *Pacific Discovery* (spring): 27–33.

Slovic, Paul. 1987. "Perception of Risk." *Science* 236 (17 April): 280–85.

Slovic, Paul, J. H. Flynn, M. Layman. 1991. "Perceived Risk, Trust, and the Politics of Nuclear Waste." *Science* 254 (5038): 1603–7.

Small, Mary. 1996. "The Coordinated Resource Management and Planning Process: Implementation in the San Francisquito Creek Watershed." Paper prepared for Prof. Timothy P. Duane, University of California at Berkeley.

Smith, David L. 1974. *Amenity and Urban Planning.* London: Crosby Lockwood Staples.

Smith, Eleanor, and Michael Di Leo. 1983. *Two Californias: The Myths and the Realities of a State Divided against Itself.* Covelo, Calif.: Island Press.

Smith, Eleanor, Philip Griffiths, and Jumbi Edulbehram. 1992. "Planning in a Transitional Rural Economy: The Case of Plumas County, California." Paper prepared for Professors Tim Duane, Anno Saxenian, and Mike Teitz, Department of City and Regional Planning, University of California at Berkeley.

Smith, Jeffrey. 1997. "Evangelical Christians Preach a Green Gospel," *High Country News* 29, no. 8 (28 April): 1.

Smith, Michael L. 1987. *Pacific Visions: California Scientists and the Environment.* New Haven, Conn.: Yale University Press.

Sneed, David. 1994a. "Grattan, Weir Go on Offensive during Debate." *Grass Valley–Nevada City Union,* 14 October, p. B1.

———. 1994b. "Environmental Backlash: Wise-Use Movement Challenging Environmentalist Programs, Ideas." *Grass Valley–Nevada City Union,* 26 December, p. A1.

————. 1994c. "Inevitable Predicament: Wise-Use Movement Fueled by Lack of Consideration of People." *Grass Valley–Nevada City Union,* 27 December, p. A1.

————. 1995a. "'Inimim Forest Plan Released in Joint Effort." *Grass Valley–Nevada City Union,* 30 March, p. A4.

————. 1995b. "Mountain Lions Gain Attention." *Grass Valley–Nevada City Union,* 5 January, p. D4.

————. 1995c. "Gold Comes Back: The San Juan Ridge Mine Opens, Signaling a Possible Resurgence in the Region's Oldest Industry." *Grass Valley–Nevada City Union,* 21 January, p. B1.

————. 1995d. "Resource Managers Devise Fire Plan." *Grass Valley–Nevada City Union,* 8 July, p. B1.

————. 1995e. "White Resigns Third District Planner's Post." *Grass Valley–Nevada City Union,* 15 September, p. B1.

————. 1995f. "Area Conservation Easement Listed." *Grass Valley–Nevada City Union,* 19 January, p. B1.

————. 1995g. "NC's Pioneer Park Creek Sewage Spill Prompts Warning." *Grass Valley–Nevada City Union,* 17 February, p. A1.

————. 1995h. "Peter Van Zant: Activist Evokes Strong Feelings." *Grass Valley–Nevada City Union,* 20 May, p. A1.

————. 1996a. "US Protects Jumpin' Frog." *Grass Valley–Nevada City Union,* 21 May, p. A1.

————. 1996b. "Ethics: Dominion over the Earth?" *Grass Valley–Nevada City Union,* 25 September, p. B6.

————. 1996c. "Growth Plan Remains under Scrutiny: Critics Fear New Zoning," *Grass Valley–Nevada City Union,* 10 May, p. A1.

————. 1996d. "Mine Neighbors Well Levels Rise," *Grass Valley–Nevada City Union,* 15 March, p. A3.

————. 1996e. "NC's General Plan Rapped as Flawed." *Grass Valley–Nevada City Union,* 3 August, p. A1.

————. 1996f. "River Study Draws 800 Letters." *Grass Valley–Nevada City Union,* 13 August, p. A1.

————. 1996g. "SJR Mine Firm Fined for Violations." *Grass Valley–Nevada City Union,* 4 April, p. A1.

————. 1996h. "Easements Preserve Forest." *Grass Valley–Nevada City Union,* 22 January, p. A3.

Snyder, Gary. 1974. *Turtle Island.* New York: New Directions.

————. 1987. *Upriver/Downriver* (Planet Drum Foundation, Petrolia, Calif.) no. 10.

————. 1990. *The Practice of the Wild.* San Francisco: North Point Press.

————. 1992a. "Colors of the Land, Colors of the Skin." *San Francisco Examiner,* 2 March, p. A-15.

————. 1992b. "Coming into the Watershed: Diversity in the Habitat." *San Francisco Examiner,* 13 March, p. A-13.

————. 1992c. *No Nature: New and Selected Poems.* New York: Pantheon.

————. 1992d. "Crawling," *Tree Rings* (Yuba Watershed Institute, Nevada City, Calif.) 2, no. 3 (summer).

————. 1994–98. Nevada City, Calif. Personal communication.

————. 1995. *A Place in Space: Watersheds, Aesthetics, and Ethics.* Washington, D.C.: Counterpoint.

Soule, Michael E. 1991a. "Land Use Planning and Wildlife Maintenance—Guidelines for

Conserving Wildlife in an Urban Landscape." *Journal of the American Planning Association* 57 (3): 313–23.

————. 1991b. "Theory and Strategy." In Hudson 1991, pp. 91–104.

————, ed. 1986. *Conservation Biology: The Science of Scarcity and Diversity.* Sutherland, Mass.: Sinauer Associates.

Southworth, Michael. 1997. "Walkable Suburbs? An Evaluation of Neotraditional Communities at the Urban Edge." *Journal of the American Planning Association* 63, no. 1 (winter): 28–44.

Southworth, Michael, and Eran Ben-Joseph. 1993. *Regulated Streets: The Evolution of Standards for Suburban Residential Streets.* Working Paper No. 593. Berkeley: Institute for Urban and Regional Development, University of California at Berkeley.

————. 1997. *Streets and the Shaping of Towns and Cities.* New York: McGraw-Hill.

Southworth, Michael, and Peter M. Owens. 1992. *The Evolving Metropolis: Studies of Community, Neighborhood, and Street Form at the Urban Edge.* Working Paper No. 579. Berkeley: Institute for Urban and Regional Development, University of California at Berkeley.

————. 1993. "The Evolving Metropolis—Studies of Community, Neighborhood, and Street Form at the Urban Edge." *Journal of the American Planning Association* 59 (3): 271–87.

South Yuba River Citizens League. 1993. *The South Yuba: A Wild and Scenic Report.* Nevada City, Calif.: South Yuba River Citizens League.

Spectorsky, August C. 1995. *The Exurbanites.* Philadelphia: Lippincott.

Spencer, Rob. 1994. "Antonson Ponders Challenges Ahead as Supervisor." *Grass Valley–Nevada City Union,* 31 December, p. A1.

Spirn, Ann Whiston. 1984. *The Granite Garden: Urban Nature and Human Design.* New York: Basic Books.

Staneart, Mark. 1995. "Rehearsing Lines for the Plan Debate." *Grass Valley–Nevada City Union,* 22 April, p. A4.

Stanford Ranch Information Center. 1994–95. *Stanford Ranch: A Master Planned Community.* Rocklin, Calif.: Stanford Ranch.

Starr, Kevin. 1996. *Endangered Dreams: The Great Depression in California.* New York: Oxford University Press.

Starrs, Paul F. 1989. "Home Ranch: Ranchers, the Federal Government, and the Partitioning of Western North American Rangeland." Ph.D. diss., University of California at Berkeley.

————. 1994. "The Importance of Places, or, a Sense of Where You Are." *Spectrum* (summer).

Starrs, Paul F., and John B. Wright. 1994. "California, Out—Great Basin Growth and the Withering of the Pacific Idyll" (review draft). *Geographical Review.*

Steen, Harold K. 1976. *The US Forest Service: A History.* Seattle: University of Washington Press.

Stegner, Wallace. 1954. *Beyond the Hundredth Meridian: John Wesley Powell and the Second Opening of the West.* New York: Penguin Books.

————. 1969. *The Sound of Mountain Water.* New York: Doubleday.

————. 1971. *Angle of Repose.* London: Heinemann.

————. 1987. *The American West as Living Space.* Ann Arbor: University of Michigan Press.

Stein, Jay M., ed. 1993. *Growth Management: The Planning Challenge of the 1990's.* Newbury Park, Calif.: Sage.

————. 1997, "Florida's Dark Secret Is Its Schools—No Space and No Money." Paper presented to the Association of Collegiate Schools of Planning conference, 8 November, Ft. Lauderdale, Fla.

Steiner, Frederick R. 1991. *The Living Landscape: An Ecological Approach to Landscape Planning.* New York: McGraw-Hill.

Steiner, Frederick, Gerald Young, and Ervin Zube. 1988. "Ecological Planning: Retrospect and Prospect." *Landscape Journal* 7 (1): 31–39.

Steinitz, Carl. 1990. "A Framework for Theory Applicable to the Education of Landscape Architects (and Other Environmental Design Professionals)." *Landscape Journal* (October): 136–43.

Steinitz, Carl, et al. 1996. *Biodiversity and Landscape Planning: Alternative Futures for the Region of Camp Pendleton, California.* Cambridge, Mass.; Logan, Utah; Corvallis, Ore; Temecula, Calif.: n.p. (also at http://www.gsd.harvard.edu/brc/brc.html).

Steiss, A. W., and G. A. Deneke. 1980. *Performance Administration.* Lexington, Mass.: Lexington Books. Cited in Clark and Minta 1994.

Stevens, Jan. 1980. "The Public Trust: A Sovereign's Ancient Prerogative Becomes the People's Environmental Right." *U.C. Davis Law Review* 14:195.

Stevens, William K. 1996. "Salvation at Hand for a California Landscape." *New York Times,* 27 February, p. B7.

———. 1997a. "Conservation Plan for Southern California Could Be Model for Nation." *New York Times,* 16 February, p. 12.

———. 1997b. "Endangered Species Found in 'Hot Spots.'" *New York Times,* 24 January, p. A1.

———. 1997c. "A Dam Open, Grand Canyon Roars Again." *New York Times,* 25 February, p. B7.

Stewart, George Rippey. 1960. *Ordeal by Hunger: The Story of the Donner Party.* New York: Houghton Mifflin.

Stewart, William Calder. 1993. "Predicting Employment Impacts of Changing Forest Management in California." Ph.D. diss., Wildland Resource Science, University of California at Berkeley. Also, published by Forest and Rangeland Resources Assessment Program, California Department of Forestry and Fire Protection, Sacramento.

———. 1996. "Economic Assessment of the Ecosystem." In *Sierra Nevada Ecosystem Project Final Report to Congress: Status of the Sierra Nevada,* 3:973–1065. Davis: Center for Water and Wildland Resources, University of California.

———. 1997. Presentation to the California Spotted Owl Federal Advisory Committee, 7 August, Sacramento.

Stockton Record. 1997. "Sierra Sprawl." (Reprint of a three-part series of articles by Jim Nickles, Richard Hanner, and Francis Garland originally published in the *Stockton Record,* 19–21 October.)

Stokey, Edith, and Richard Zeckhauser. 1978. *A Primer for Policy Analysis.* New York: W. W. Norton and Company.

Storer, Tracy Irvin, and Robert L. Usinger. 1963. *Sierra Nevada Natural History: An Illustrated Handbook.* Berkeley and Los Angeles: University of California Press.

Streeten, Paul, et al. 1981. *First Things First: Meeting Basic Human Needs in the Developing Countries.* New York: Oxford University Press (for the World Bank).

Strong, Ann Louise, Daniel R. Mandelker, and Eric Damian Kelley. 1996. "Property Rights and Takings." *Journal of the American Planning Association* 62 (1): 5–16.

Strong, Douglas Hillman. 1984. *Tahoe, an Environmental History.* Lincoln: University of Nebraska Press.

Stuebner, Steve. 1997. "Columbia Basin Plan Staggers Home." *High Country News* 29, no. 2 (3 February): 7.

Stuebner, Steve, and Paul Larmer. 1997. "The Report Is Readable—and Grim." *High Country News* 29, no. 2 (3 February): 7.

Stuttard, R. W. 1959. *Town and Country: The Amenity Question*. London: Fabian Society.

Sunset Magazine. 1970. *National Parks of the West*. Menlo Park, Calif.: Lane Magazine and Book Company.

Sunstein, Cass R. 1996. *Legal Reasoning and Political Conflict*. New York: Oxford University Press.

Swain, Walter. 1994. United States Geological Survey, Sacramento. Personal communication, 29 June.

Swickard, Deane. 1997. Comments at *Ecology Law Quarterly* symposium "The Ecosystem Approach: New Departures for Land and Water," 21 February, at Boalt Hall School of Law, University of California at Berkeley.

Tainter, Joseph A. 1988. *The Collapse of Complex Societies*. New York: Cambridge University Press.

———. 1995. "Sustainability of Complex Societies," *Futures* 27 (4): 397–407.

Taylor, Brian. 1993. "Planning Professor Attacks General Plan." *Grass Valley–Nevada City Union*, 10 November, p. 3.

Taylor, Michael. 1996. "Stirring Up a Generation." *San Francisco Chronicle*, 8 December, p. 1.

Taylor, Paul W. 1986. *Respect for Nature: A Theory of Environmental Ethics*. Princeton, N.J.: Princeton University Press.

Tecklin, David. 1992. "The Local Formation of Federal Forest Policy: Case Studies of Environmental Activism from the Sierra Nevada, Calif." Senior thesis in Sociology and Anthropology, Swarthmore College, Penn.

Teitz, Michael B. 1990. "California's Growth: Hard Questions, Few Answers." *California Policy Choices* 6:35–74.

Thayer, Robert L., Jr. 1994. *Gray World, Green Heart: Technology, Nature, and the Sustainable Landscape*. New York: John Wiley and Sons.

Thomas, C. D. 1990. What Do Real Population Dynamics Tell Us about Minimum Viable Population Sizes? *Conservation Biology* 4:324–27.

Thomas, Chris. 1994. "Potential Impacts of Rural Development upon Habitat in El Dorado County." Paper prepared for Prof. Timothy P. Duane, University of California at Berkeley. May.

———. 1995. "The Once and Future El Dorado County: Transportation Planning Beyond the Edge." Paper prepared for Prof. Elizabeth Deakin, University of California at Berkeley.

Thomas, Craig W. 1997. "Public Management as Interagency Cooperation: Testing Epistemic Community Theory at the Domestic Level." *Journal of Administration Research and Theory* 7 (2): 221–46.

Thomas, Jack Ward. 1995. Video presentation to the conference "At the Crossroads of Science, Management, and Policy: A Review of Bioregional Assessments," 7 November, Portland, Ore.

Thomas, Jack Ward, Eric D. Forsman, Joseph B. Lint, E. Charles Meslow, Barry R. Noon, and Jared Verner. 1990. *A Conservation Strategy for the Northern Spotted Owl*. Prepared by the U.S.D.A. Forest Service, U.S.D.I. Bureau of Land Management, U.S.D.I. Fish and Wildlife Service, U.S.D.I. National Park Service. Portland, Ore.: U.S. Government Printing Office. Cited in Verner et al. 1997.

Thomas, John L. 1990. "Lewis Mumford, Benton MacKaye, and the Regional Vision." In Hughes and Hughes 1990. Cited in Luccarelli 1995.

Thompson and West. 1880. *History of Nevada County, California.* Oakland, Calif.: Thompson and West. Reprinted in Wells 1970.

Thompson, George F., ed. 1995. *Landscape in America.* Austin: University of Texas Press.

Thompson, George F., and Frederick R. Steiner, eds. 1997. *Ecological Design and Planning.* New York: John Wiley and Sons.

Thompson, Paul. 1989. *Poison Runoff.* New York: Natural Resources Defense Council.

Thompson, Robert. 1992–97. Graduate student, University of California at Berkeley. Personal communication.

Thoreau, Henry David. 1962. *Thoreau: Walden and Other Writings.* Ed. by Joseph Wood Krutch. New York: Bantam Books.

Thorne, E. Tom, Mary Meagher, and Robert Hillman. 1991. "Brucellosis in Free-Ranging Bison: Three Perspectives." In Keiter and Boyce 199, pp. 275–88.

Throgmorton, James A. 1994. "Learning from a Midwest City: Promoting Sustainable Neighborhoods in a Small Midwestern University Town." Paper presented to the Association of Collegiate Schools of Planning Conference, November, Tempe, Ariz.

———. 1996. *Planning as Persuasive Storytelling: The Rhetorical Construction of Chicago's Electric Future.* Chicago: University of Chicago Press.

Thurlow, George. 1989. "Going Bust." *Golden State Report* (November): 23–27.

Thurow, Lester C. 1996. "The Birth of a Revolutionary Class: Today's Elderly Are Bringing Down the Social Welfare State and Threatening the Nation's Economic Future." *New York Times Magazine* 19 May, p. 46.

Tibbs, Hardin. 1993. *Industrial Ecology: An Environmental Agenda for Industry.* Cambridge, Mass.: Arthur D. Little, 1990. Reprint, Emeryville, Calif.: Global Business Network.

Tiebout, Charles. 1962. *The Community Economic Base Study.* New York: Committee for Economic Development.

Tilman, David, Johannes Knops, David Wedin, Peter Reich, Mark Ritchie, and Evan Siemann. 1997. "The Influence of Functional Diversity and Composition on Ecosystem Processes." *Science* 277 (29 August): 1300–1302.

Timeline. 1996. "Why Children Need Wild Places: An Interview with Gary Paul Nabhan." *Timeline* (Foundation for Global Community, Palo Alto, Calif.) 27:15–17.

Toulan, Nohad. 1997. "The Portland Urban Growth Boundary: A 27-Year Journey." Paper presented to the Lincoln Institute of Land Policy Dinner Seminar Series, 23 April, at the Institute of Urban and Regional Development, University of California at Berkeley.

Trivelpiece, Margaret. 1970a. "Public Hearings Due on Zoning Ordinance." *Grass Valley–Nevada City Union,* 3 March, p. 1.

———. 1970b. "Planners Report Zoning Draft 'Good Foundation.'" *Grass Valley–Nevada City Union,* 18 February, p. 1.

———. 1970c. "Planners Favor Sewer Ordinance." *Grass Valley–Nevada City Union,* 16 June, p. 1.

Trombulate, Stephen C. 1997. "Edge Effects and Roads: A Review of the Literature." Paper presented to the Society for Conservation Biology, 8 June, Victoria, British Columbia, Canada.

Truckee, Town of. 1997. *Downtown Specific Plan: Public Hearing Draft.* 3 vols. Truckee, Calif.: Town of Truckee Planning Department.

Truckee-Donner Land Trust. 1997. "Clinton Visit Spotlights Sierra Problems." *Truckee-Donner Land Trust* 10 (late spring–early summer): 1.

Tuan, Yi-Fu. 1974. *Topophilia: A Study of Environmental Perception, Attitudes, and Values.* New York: Columbia University Press.

Turner, Frederick. 1983. *Beyond Geography: The Western Spirit against the Wilderness.* New Brunswick, N.J.: Rutgers University Press.

————. 1985. *Rediscovering America: John Muir in His Time and Ours.* San Francisco: Sierra Club Books.

————. 1989. *Spirit of Place: The Making of an American Literary Landscape.* Washington, D.C.: Island Press.

Turner, Frederick Jackson. 1962. *The American Frontier in American History.* New York: Harper and Brothers, 1906. Reprint, New York: Holt, Rinehart, and Winston.

Turner, Kenneth M. 1973. *Sierra Foothills Investigation, Central District.* Sacramento: California Department of Water Resources.

Tverskey, Amos, and Daniel Kahneman. 1974. "Judgment under Uncertainty: Heuristics and Biases." *Science* 185 (27 September): 1124–31.

Twain, Mark. 1871. *Roughing It.* New York: Harper and Row.

Twiss, Robert H. 1987. "Regional Environmental Thresholds and Impact Assessment." Paper presented to the International Symposium on Environmental Impact Assessment, 24 October, Beijing, China.

————. 1991. Presentation to the Process of Environmental Planning class (LA 237), September, at University of California at Berkeley.

————. 1995. Presentation to the Environmental Law and Resource Management class (IDS 233), October, at University of California at Berkeley.

————. 1997. Presentation to the Environmental Law and Resource Management class (IDS 233), November, at University of California at Berkeley.

Twiss, Robert H., and Ira Michael Heyman. 1976. "Nine Approaches to Environmental Planning." In Cowart 1976.

United Nations. 1993. *Agenda 21: Programme of Action for Sustainable Development; Rio Declaration on Environment and Development.* New York: United Nations Dept. of Public Information.

United States Bureau of Census. 1970, 1980, 1990. *Census Files.* U.S. Bureau of Census, U.S. Department of Commerce. Digital tapes.

————. 1990. "STF 3A, Population, and Housing, 1990 Census." Tape.

————. 1996. Population Estimates Program, 30 December (http://www.census.gov).

United States Department of Agriculture Forest Service. 1993. *California Spotted Owl Sierran Province Interim Guidelines Environmental Assessment.* San Francisco: U.S.D.A. Forest Service, Pacific Southwest Region.

————. 1994. *Draft Region 5 Ecosystem Management Guidebook.* 3 vols. San Francisco: U.S.D.A. Forest Service, Pacific Southwest Region.

————. 1995. *Draft Environmental Impact Statement (Managing California Spotted Owl Habitat in the Sierra Nevada National Forests of California: An Ecosystem Approach).* San Francisco: U.S.D.A. Forest Service, Pacific Southwest Region.

————. 1996. *Revised Draft Environmental Impact Statement (Managing California Spotted Owl Habitat in the Sierra Nevada National Forests of California: An Ecosystem Approach).* San Francisco: U.S.D.A. Forest Service, Pacific Southwest Region.

United States Department of Labor. 1975–92. *Survey of Occupational Injuries and Illnesses.* Washington D.C.: U.S. Department of Labor, Bureau of Labor Statistics.

United States Department of the Interior. 1988. *Glen Canyon Dam Environmental Studies Report.* Salt Lake City: U.S. Bureau of Reclamation, Upper Colorado Region.

———. 1990. *The Endangered Species Program, U.S. Fish and Wildlife Service: Audit Report.* Report No. 90–08. Washington, D.C.: U.S. Department of the Interior, Office of Inspector General. Cited in Shaffer 1992b.

United States Department of the Interior, Interagency Ecosystem Management Task Force. 1995. *The Ecosystem Approach: Healthy Ecosystems and Sustainable Economies.* Vol. I of the *Report of the Interagency Ecosystem Management Task Force.* Washington D.C.: U.S. Department of the Interior.

University of California at Berkeley. 1995–97. *General Catalog.* Berkeley: University of California.

Urban, D. L., R. V. O'Neill, and H. H. Shugart Jr. 1987. "Landscape Ecology," *BioScience* 37 (2): 119–27.

Van der Ryn, Sim, and Peter Calthorpe. 1986. *Sustainable Communities: A New Design Synthesis for Cities, Suburbs, and Towns.* San Francisco: Sierra Club Books.

Van der Ryn, Sim, and Stuart Cowan. 1996. *Ecological Design.* Washington, D.C.: Island Press.

Van Zant, Peter. 1996. Supervisor-Elect, Nevada County, Calif. Personal communication, March.

———. 1997. "Four Bridges Must Be Crossed to Reach Consensus," *Grass Valley–Nevada City Union,* 19 April, p. A7.

———. 1998. Supervisor, Nevada County, Calif. Personal communication, January.

Vaughn, Diane. 1996. *The Challenger Launch Decision: Risky Technology, Culture, and Deviance at NASA.* Chicago: University of Chicago Press.

Verner, Jared. 1997. Research Scientist, Pacific Southwest Research Station, USDA Forest Service, Fresno, Calif. Personal Communication.

Verner, Jared, Kevin S. McKelvey, Barry R. Noon, R. J. Guiterrez, Gordon I. Gould Jr., Thomas W. Beck. 1992. *The California Spotted Owl: A Technical Assessment of Its Current Status.* Gen. Tech. Rep. PSW-GTR-133. Albany, Calif.: Pacific Southwest Research Station, Forest Service, U.S. Department of Agriculture.

Vickerman, Sara E. 1989. "State Wildlife Protection Efforts: The Nongame Programs." In *Defenders of Wildlife, Preserving Communities and Corridors,* 67–96. Washington, D.C.: Defenders of Wildlife.

Victor, Peter A. 1991. "Indicators of Sustainable Development: Some Lessons from Capital Theory," *Ecological Economics* 4:191–213.

Vining, D. R., and A. Strauss. 1977. "A Demonstration That the Current Deconcentration of Population in the United States Is a Clean Break with the Past." *Environment and Planning A* 9:751–58.

Vitousek, Peter M., Lloyd L. Loope, Henning Anderson, eds. 1993. *Island Biological Diversity and Ecosystem Function.* New York: Springer Verlag.

Vorster, Peter. 1992. Consulting Hydrologist, Mono Lake Committee. Personal communication.

Voytek, Kenneth P., and Harold Wolman. 1991. *Local Strategic Planning: A Manual for Local Economic Analysis.* Lansing: Michigan Department of Commerce, Local Development Services Bureau, Center for Local Economic Competitiveness.

Wachs, Martin. 1984. "Autos, Transit, and the Sprawl of Los Angeles: The 1920s." *Journal of the American Planning Association* 50, no. 3 (summer): 297–325.

Wackernagel, Mathis, and William E. Rees. 1996. *Our Ecological Footprint: Reducing Human Impact on the Earth.* Philadelphia: New Society Publishers.

Wade, Connie L. 1996. "An Ecologically Based Decision-Making Methodology for Local

Government Planners Dealing with Blue Oak Woodlands Using GIS Analysis." Master's thesis, Graduate Group in Ecology, University of California at Davis.

Waggoner, Kevin. 1996. "Union's Position Disappointing," (letter to the editor). *Grass Valley–Nevada City Union,* May 1. p. A6.

Walker, B. H. 1981. "Is Succession a Viable Concept in African Savanna Ecosystems?" In *Forest Succession: Concepts and Applications,* ed. by D. C. West, H. H. Shugart, and D. B. Botkin, pp. 431–47. New York: Springer-Verlag. Cited in Holling 1995.

Walsh, Joan. 1991. "The Frontiers of White Flight." *San Francisco Examiner: Image Magazine,* 17 November, pp. 36–54.

Walters, C. J. 1986. *Adaptive Management of Renewable Resources.* New York: McGraw-Hill.

Walton, John. 1992. *Western Times and Water Wars: State, Culture, and Rebellion in California.* Berkeley and Los Angeles: University of California Press.

Ward, Edward J. 1986. "The New Rural Planning Problem." Paper presented to the Association of Collegiate Schools of Planning, April, Los Angeles.

Ward, Pat. 1994–95. Staff, Nevada County Board of Supervisors, Nevada City, Calif. Personal communication.

Wardle, David A., Olle Zackrisson, Greger Hornberg, and Christiane Gallet. 1997. "The Influence of Island Area on Ecosystem Properties." *Science* 277 (29 August): 1296–99.

Wardwall, John M. 1982. "The Reversal of Nonmetropolitan Migration Loss." In *Rural Society in the U.S.: Issues for the 1980s.* Ed. by Don A. Dillman and Daryl J. Hobbs. Boulder, Colo.: Westview.

Warren, Karen, and Jim Cheney. 1993. "Ecosystem Ecology and Metaphysical Ecology: A Case Study." *Environmental Ethics* 15 (summer): 99–116.

Webb, Loraine. 1993. Untitled statement read at the public hearing on the draft Nevada County General Plan, 7 December, Nevada City, Calif.

Webster, Paul. 1972. *The Mighty Sierra: Portrait of a Mountain World.* New York: Weathervane Books.

Weeks, David, A. E. Wieslander, H. R. Josephson, and C. L. Hill. 1943. *Land Utilization in the Northern Sierra Nevada.* Berkeley: Special Publication of the Giannini Foundation of Agricultural Economics, University of California, College of Agriculture, Agricultural Experiment Station.

Weiss, Philip. 1995. "Off the Grid." *New York Times Magazine,* 8 January, p. 24.

Weisskopf, Michael. 1992. "World Bank Official's Irony Backfires." *Washington Post,* 10 February, p. A9.

Wells, Harry Laurenz. 1970. *Reproduction of Thompson and West's History of Nevada County, California.* Berkeley, Calif.: Howell-North Books.

West, Kathleen A. 1992. Senior Researcher, Southern California Edison, Rosemead, Calif. Personal communication.

West, Neil E., ed. 1995. *Proceedings of the Symposium on Biodiversity on Rangelands, Natural Resources and Environmental Issues.* Vol. 4. Logan: College of Natural Resources, Utah State University.

Westley, Frances. 1995. "Governing Design: The Management of Social Systems and Ecosystems Management." In Gunderson et al. 1995a, pp. 391–427.

Westra, Laura. 1994. *An Environmental Proposal for Ethics: The Principle of Integrity.* Lanham, Md.: Rowman and Littlefield.

Wheeldon, George. 1994. Presentation to the Yuba Watershed Institute, 8 December, Nevada City, Calif.

Wheeler, Douglas. 1992. *Feather River Bulletin/Indian Valley Record/Chester Progressive/Portola Reporter.* 18 March, p. B6.

———. 1994–97. Secretary, California Resources Agency, Sacramento. Personal communication.

Wheeler, Stephen. 1995. *Sustainable Urban Development: A Literature Review and Analysis.* Oakland, Calif.: Urban Ecology

White, Lynn, Jr. 1967. "The Historical Roots of Our Ecological Crisis," *Science* 155 (March 10): 1203–7.

White, Richard. 1980. *Land Use, Environment, and Social Change: The Shaping of Island County, Washington.* Seattle: University of Washington Press.

———. 1991. *It's Your Misfortune and None of My Own: A History of the American West.* Norman: University of Oklahoma Press.

———. 1996. *The Organic Machine.* New York: Hill and Wang.

Whitney, Stephen. 1979. *The Sierra Nevada; A Sierra Club Naturalist's Guide.* San Francisco: Sierra Club Books.

Whyte, William. 1958. "Urban Sprawl." *Fortune* 57 (January): 302.

Wilcove, David S., Charles H. McLellan, and Andrew P. Dobson. 1986. "Habitat Fragmentation in the Temperate Zone." In Soule 1986, pp. 237–56.

Wilderness Society. 1992. *The Endangered Species Act—A Commitment Worth Keeping.* Washington, D.C.: Wilderness Society.

———. 1997. *The Federal Forest Lands of the Sierra Nevada: Citizens' Guide to the Sierra Nevada Ecosystem Project (SNEP) Report.* Preview ed. San Francisco: California-Nevada Region, Wilderness Society.

Wildland Resources Center. 1994. *Conserving the California Spotted Owl: Impacts of Interim Policies and Implications for the Long-Term.* Report 33. Davis: Wildland Resources Center, University of California.

Wiley, Peter, and Robert Gottlieb. 1982. *Empires in the Sun: The Rise of the New American West.* Tucson: University of Arizona Press.

Wilkinson, Charles F. 1989. *The American West: A Narrative Bibliography and a Study in Regionalism.* Niwot: University Press of Colorado.

———. 1992a. *Crossing the Next Meridian: Land, Water, and the Future of the West.* Washington, D.C.: Island Press.

———. 1992b. *The Eagle Bird: Mapping a New West.* New York: Pantheon Books.

———. 1997. "Paradise Revised." In Riebsame and Robb 1997, 15–44.

Wilkinson, Todd. 1997. "No Home on the Range." *High Country News* 29, no. 3 (17 February): 1.

Williams, Edward A. 1969. *Open Space, the Choices Before California: The Urban Metropolitan Open Space Study.* San Francisco: EDAW.

Williams, Florence. 1993a. "Future Shock Hits Livingston." *High Country News* 25, no. 6 (5 April): 14.

———. 1993b. "Propost Says Small Towns Make or Break Ecosystems." *High Country News* 25, no. 6 (5 April): 15.

Williams, Kelly. 1988. "Judge Orders Trial for Fire Suspect." *Grass Valley–Nevada City Union,* 2 November, p. A1.

Willis, K. G. 1994. "Preserving Traditional Farming Practices and Landscapes in the United Kingdom: An Economic Appraisal." Paper presented to the Association of Collegiate Schools of Planning, 3–6 Nov., Tempe, Ariz.

Willis, Tim. 1996a. "Predicted County Population Disputed." *Grass Valley–Nevada City Union*, 13 September, p. A1.

———. 1996b. "Population Estimates Boosted by County." *Grass Valley–Nevada City Union*, 18 October, p. A1.

———. 1997a. "County's Building Costs Found Lower Than Average." *Grass Valley–Nevada City Union*, 15 January, p. A1.

———. 1997b. "Construction Rate Declines." *Grass Valley–Nevada City Union*, 15 April, p. A1.

———. 1997c. "Residents Join to Get Post Office for South County." *Grass Valley–Nevada City Union*, 20 March, p. A3.

———. 1997d. "Antonson to Effect Changes with Chairmanship." *Grass Valley–Nevada City Union*, 4 January, p. A1.

———. 1997e. "Commission's Costs Questioned." *Grass Valley–Nevada City Union*, 30 January, p. A1.

———. 1997f. "Bypass Gets a Cold Shoulder." *Grass Valley–Nevada City Union*, 20 February, p. A1.

———. 1997g. "Supervisors Give Wetlands Their Vote of Support." *Grass Valley–Nevada City Union*, 19 February, p. A1.

———. 1997h. "Housing Project Sees Good, Bad Times." *Grass Valley–Nevada City Union*, 21 March, p. A1.

Wills, Leah. 1992. Plumas Corporation, Quincy, Calif. Personal communication, November.

Wilman, Elizabeth A. 1984. *External Costs of Coastal Beach Pollution: An Hedonic Approach.* Washington, D.C.: Resources for the Future.

Wilson, Edward O. 1984. *Biophilia: The Human Bond with Other Species.* Cambridge: Harvard University Press.

———. 1989. "Threats to Biodiversity." *Scientific American* 261 (3): 108.

———. 1994. *Naturalist.* Washington, D.C.: Island Press, Shearwater Books.

———, ed. 1988. *Biodiversity.* Washington D.C.: National Academy Press.

Wingo, P. A., T. Tong, S. Bolden. 1995. "Cancer Statistics, 1995," *CA: A Cancer Journal for Clinicians* 45 (1): 8–30.

Winks, Robin. 1996. "Dispelling the Myth: Many Believe the Park Service Must Balance Two Incompatible Missions: To Protect Resources and to Provide Public Access." *National Parks* (July-August): 52–53.

Wolfe, Charles R. 1990. "The Cluster Alternative: A Basis for Private Development in the Public Interest." *Connecticut Planner's Journal* 3 (4): 1–2.

Wood, Christopher A. 1995. "Counties Have No Claim on Federal Lands in West." *Sacramento Bee*, 22 May (on-line edition).

World Bank. 1992. *World Development Report 1992: Development and the Environment.* Washington, D.C.: World Bank.

World Commission on Environment and Development. 1987. *Our Common Future.* Oxford: Oxford University Press.

Worster, Donald. 1985a. *Nature's Economy: A History of Ecological Ideas.* New York: Cambridge University Press.

———. 1985b. *Rivers of Empire: Water, Aridity, and the Growth of the American West.* New York: Oxford University Press.

———. 1992. *Under Western Skies: Nature and History in the American West.* New York: Oxford University Press.

Wright, John B. 1993. *Rocky Mountain Divide: Selling and Saving the West.* Austin: University of Texas Press.

Yaffee, Steven L. 1994. *The Wisdom of the Spotted Owl.* Washington, D.C.: Island Press.

——. 1997. "Cooperation: A Strategy for Achieving Stewardship across Boundaries." Paper presented to the Society for Conservation Biology conference, 9 June, Victoria, B.C.

Yaffee, Steven L., Ali F. Phillips, Irene C. Frentz, Paul W. Hardy, Sussanne M. Maleki, and Barbara E. Thorpe. 1996. *Ecosystem Management in the United States: An Assessment of Current Experience.* Washington, D.C.: Island Press.

Yaro, Robert D., Randall G. Arendt, Harry L. Dodson, and Elizabeth A. Brabec. 1988. *Dealing with Change in the Connecticut River Valley: A Design Manual for Conservation and Development.* Boston: Massachusetts Department of Environmental Management; Amherst: Center for Rural Massachusetts; Cambridge, Mass.: Lincoln Institute of Land Policy; and the Environmental Law Foundation.

Yassa, Sami, and Adam Diamant. 1995. *Felling the Myth: The Role of Timber in the Economy of California's Sierra Nevada.* San Francisco: Natural Resources Defense Council.

Ybarra, Michael J. 1996. "Ideas and Trends: Putting City Sprawl on a Zoning Diet." *New York Times,* 16 June, p. E4.

Yollin, Patricia. 1997. "In-N-Out: Bonkers for Burgers." *San Francisco Examiner,* 23 March, p. A1.

Yoon, Carol Kaesuk. 1997. "Many Habitat Conservation Plans Found to Lack Key Data." *New York Times,* 23 December, p. B13.

Yuba County Community Services Department. 1985. *Final Environmental Impact Report on the Cumulative Impacts of Rural Residential Development on Migratory Deer in Yuba County.* Marysville, Calif.: Yuba County Community Services Department.

Yuba Watershed Institute, Timber Farmer's Guild, and Bureau of Land Management. 1991–97. Board Members and Staff, Yuba Watershed Institute, Nevada City, Calif. Personal communication.

——. 1991–97. *Tree Rings* (Nevada City, Calif.)

——. 1994. *The 'Inimim Forest Draft Management Plan.* Folsom, Calif.: Yuba Watershed Institute, Timber Farmer's Guild, and Bureau of Land Management.

Zackman, Odin. 1993. *Transitions: An Analysis of Environmental Protection and the California Timber Economy.* Oakland, Calif.: Sierra Club Northern California–Nevada-Hawaii Office.

Zube, E. H., R. O. Brush, and J. G. Fabos, eds. 1975. *Landscape Assessment: Values, Perceptions and Resources.* Stroudsburg, Penn.: Dowden, Hutchinson, and Ross.

Zuckerman, Seth. 1992. "Four Reasons You've Never Seen a Map of the Northern California Bioregion." *Upstream/Downstream* (Planet Drum Foundation, Petrolia, Calif.) no. 14.

Zukin, Sharon. 1991. *Landscapes of Power: From Detroit to Disney World.* Berkeley and Los Angeles: University of California Press.

——. 1993. Comments at the Western Humanities Conference, October, at Stanford University, Stanford, Calif.

INDEX

Compositor:	BookMatters
Text:	10/14 New Baskerville
Display:	New Baskerville
Printer and Binder:	Thomson-Shore, Inc.